CHILDREN OF RUS'

CHILDREN OF RUS'

**Right-Bank Ukraine
and the Invention
of a Russian Nation**

FAITH HILLIS

CORNELL UNIVERSITY PRESS
Ithaca and London

Copyright © 2013 by Cornell University

All rights reserved. Except for brief quotations in a review, this book, or parts thereof, must not be reproduced in any form without permission in writing from the publisher. For information, address Cornell University Press, Sage House, 512 East State Street, Ithaca, New York 14850.

First published 2013 by Cornell University Press
First paperback printing 2017
Printed in the United States of America

Library of Congress Cataloging-in-Publication Data

Hillis, Faith, author
  Children of Rus' : right-bank Ukraine and the invention of a Russian nation / Faith Hillis.
    pages cm
  Includes bibliographical references and index.
  ISBN 978-0-8014-5219-2 (cloth : alk. paper)
  ISBN 978-1-5017-1066-7 (pbk. : alk. paper)
   1. Nationalism—Ukraine—History—19th century. 2. Nationalism—Russia—History—19th century. 3. Ukraine—Politics and government—19th century. 4. Russia—Politics and government—1801–1917. 5. Ukraine—Relations—Russia. 6. Russia—Relations—Ukraine. I. Title.
  DK508.772.H55   2013
  320.540947—dc23   2013008819

Cornell University Press strives to use environmentally responsible suppliers and materials to the fullest extent possible in the publishing of its books. Such materials include vegetable-based, low-VOC inks and acid-free papers that are recycled, totally chlorine-free, or partly composed of nonwood fibers. For further information, visit our website at cornellpress.cornell.edu.

For Reese

CONTENTS

List of Maps ix
Acknowledgments xi
Note to the Reader xiii
Abbreviations xv

Introduction 1

Part One | The Little Russian Idea and the Russian Empire

1 The Little Russian Idea and the Invention of a Rus' Nation 21
2 The Little Russian Idea in the 1860s 58
3 The Little Russian Idea and the Imagination of Russian and Ukrainian Nations 87

Part Two | The Urban Crucible

4 Nationalizing Urban Politics 117
5 Concepts of Liberation 150

Part Three | Forging a Russian Nation

6 Electoral Politics and Regional Governance 181
7 Nationalizing the Empire 211
8 The Limits of the Russian Nationalist Vision 244

Epilogue 274

Selected Bibliography 285
Index 315

LIST OF MAPS

MAP 1.1
Rus' principalities, eleventh century 23

MAP 1.2
The Cossack Hetmanate and the Russian empire, eighteenth century 28

MAP 1.3
Russia's southwestern borderlands 33

MAP 4.1
Kiev, circa 1900 126

ACKNOWLEDGMENTS

It is a great pleasure to thank the institutions and individuals whose support has made this project possible. The Yale University Graduate School, Andrew Mellon Foundation, Jacob K. Javits Fellowship, International Research and Exchanges Board, Fulbright-Hays Doctoral Dissertation Research Abroad Program, and Mrs. Giles R. Whiting Foundation funded my graduate education and the researching and writing of this book. Funding from Columbia University's Harriman Institute, the American Council of Learned Societies, and the National Council for Eurasian and East European Research enabled me to expand the scope of my original project and to conduct new archival research. I am extremely grateful to the Department of History and the Social Sciences Division at the University of Chicago for permitting me to defer my arrival on campus by a year, which provided the precious time that I needed to complete the first draft of the manuscript. The views expressed in this book are my own and do not reflect the opinions of any of the institutions that have so generously supported me.

I owe my greatest intellectual and professional debt to Laura Engelstein, who convinced me as a shy and hesitant college junior that I had a future as an historian; appropriately enough, in the years that ensued she helped me to realize that goal. I will always be grateful for the generosity that she has shown me over the years and for the support that she has offered at critical junctures. Paul Bushkovitch is the patron saint of this project: he encouraged me to undertake it in the first place, understood the contribution that I could make long before I did, and provided the unstinting encouragement that I needed to make it to the finish line. I also thank Timothy Snyder, Ute Frevert, and Keith Darden for the help and constructive critiques that they provided along the way. I am grateful to Yuri Slezkine, Nancy Shields Kollmann, and Robert Wessling for making it possible for me to spend two and a half years of my graduate career in the Bay Area—time that turned out to be as productive as it was happy. My experience in California was greatly enriched by Irina Paperno, who was always willing to talk through complicated ideas, and John Connelly, who has generously offered me wise counsel and encouragement over the years.

Many colleagues offered logistical help and valuable feedback as I conceptualized my project, carried out my research, and drafted the manuscript. Olena Betliy, Heather Coleman, Robert Crews, Mikhail Dolbilov, Mayhill Fowler, Francine Hirsch,

Rebecca Kobrin, Boris Kolonitskii, Stephen Kotkin, Eric Lohr, Olga Matich, Serhii Plokhy, Kristin Roth-Ey, Ron Suny, and Mark von Hagen deserve special thanks. I am also very grateful to the hard-working librarians and archivists from California to Ukraine who assisted me as I conducted my research; I am particularly appreciative to Irina Lukka and the rest of the remarkable staff at the National Library of Finland's Slavonic Library. I feel fortunate to have landed at the University of Chicago, where my colleagues have created a friendly, supportive, and intellectually stimulating environment. I am especially grateful to Leora Auslander, Sheila Fitzpatrick, Michael Geyer, and Tara Zahra for their generous feedback and encouragement. Peter Holquist and Theodore Weeks were exemplary "anonymous" reviewers, and their suggestions improved this work immeasurably.

Many thanks to Anna Sukhorova, Yegor Stadny, Natalie Belsky, Rachel Koroloff, and Patryk Reid for helping me tie up loose ends in the final stages of researching this project; to Nicholas Levy for painstakingly checking the citations and assisting with the editing; to Kelsey Norris for preparing the bibliography; and to Chieko Maene for designing the maps. It has been a pleasure to work with the entire staff at Cornell University Press. I am especially grateful to my editor, John G. Ackerman, for his enthusiastic support for this project and his expert guidance as it came to fruition. Thanks as well to Karen Hwa and Susan Barnett, who shepherded this project through the editing and production processes.

Last but certainly not least, I express my appreciation to the friends near and far who sustained and supported me during the years I spent working on this project. Jennifer Boittin, Sarah Cameron, Megan Dean Farah, Catherine Dunlop, Nicole Eaton, Monica Eppinger, Christine Evans, Jens-Uwe Güttel, Bethany Lacina, and Victoria Smolkin-Rothrock deserve special mention. I will always be grateful to the late A. A. Strutinskii and his family for making me feel at home in Ukraine and to Toni and Santiago Casal for the warm welcome they've always offered me in Berkeley. The Reese and Cole families have overwhelmed me with their warmth, love, and hospitality. Reese Minshew has lived with this book for almost as long as I have and has supported it (and its author) in every way possible. Thank you for asking about the Shul'gins in the first place—and for sticking around through the myriad ups, downs, and uncertainties that ensued. This is for you.

With the permission of the original publishers, this work incorporates material that has appeared in "Ukrainophile Activism and Imperial Governance in Russia's Southwestern Borderlands," *Kritika* 13, no. 2 (2012): 303–28; and "Migration, Mobility, and Political Conflict in Late Imperial Kiev," in *Russia on the Move: Essays on the Politics, Society and Culture of Human Mobility, 1850–Present*, ed. John Randolph and Eugene Avrutin (Urbana: University of Illinois Press, 2012), 25–42.

NOTE TO THE READER

To make the text as readable as possible, I have used common English-language renderings of personal and place names wherever possible: for example, Kiev, Moscow, Cracow, Khmelnytsky, Alexander II. I render personal and place names less familiar to the American reader in the language of the state that ruled them at the time: thus, Lemberg instead of L'viv or Lwów; Antonovich instead of Antonovych or Antonowicz. I have made exceptions to this rule for certain individuals who unambiguously rejected the legitimacy of the empires that ruled them and declared their allegiance to national communities (thus, Mykhailo Hrushevs'kyi, not Mikhail Grushevskii or Michael Hruschewskyj). In citations, I have left personal names in the language in which they appear in the original text.

In my own characterizations of the region under study, I rely primarily on territorial ("right bank") and administrative ("southwestern borderlands") terms. Following late-nineteenth-century conventions, I use the words "Ukraine" and "Ukrainian" to refer to activists who questioned the unity of the East Slavs and the authority of the imperial state. I use "Little Russia" and "Little Russian" when discussing the views of activists who saw local traditions as compatible with imperial rule. Both ways of describing the borderlands and their inhabitants made a strong political statement, and neither should be seen as a neutral description of realities on the ground. My transliteration and terminology decisions should by no means be read as a commentary on contemporary politics or on the legitimacy of present-day states.

The footnotes do not include the subtitles or publishers of the works that I cite. Full citations can be found in the bibliography included at the end of this book.

All dates follow the Julian calendar.

ABBREVIATIONS

BA—Bakhmeteff Archive, Columbia University
ch.—chast' (part)
d.—delo (folder within archival collection)
DAK—Derzhavnyi arkhiv mista Kyeva (State Archive of the City of Kyiv)
DAKO—Derzhavnyi arkhiv Kyivskoi oblasti (State Archive of Kyiv Oblast')
DK—Dziennik Kijowski
f.—fond (archival collection)
GARF—Gosudarstvennyi arkhiv Rossiiskoi Federatsii (State Archive of the Russian Federation)
HA—Hoover Archive, Stanford University
HD—Hromads'ka dumka
IRNBUV—Instytut rukopysu Natsional'noi biblioteky Ukraini imeni V. I. Vernads'koho (Manuscript Division of the National Library of Ukraine in the Name of V. I. Vernads'kyi)
KEV—Kievskie eparkhial'nye vedomosti
KG—Kievskii golos
KM—Kievskaia mysl'
KS—Kievskaia starina
KV—Kievskii vestnik
KZ—Kievskaia zaria
l.—list (page number)
LRI—Listok russkogo izbiratelia
NV—Novyi vek
op.—opis' (subdivision within archival collection)
RGIA—Rossiiskii Gosudarstvennyi Istoricheskii Arkhiv (Russian State Historical Archive)
RS—Ridna sprava
TsDIAUK—Tsentral'nyi derzhavnyi istorychnyi arkhiv Ukrainy, m. Kyiv (Central State Historical Archive of Ukraine in the city of Kyiv)

TsDKFFAU—Tsentral'nyi derzhavnyi kinofotofono arkhiv Ukrainy imeni H. S. Pshenychnoho (Central State Film, Photo, and Sound Archive of Ukraine)

ZUNTvK—Zapysky Ukrains'koho Naukovoho Tovarystva v Kyivi

CHILDREN OF RUS'

Introduction

OVER THE COURSE of the long nineteenth century the Russian empire confronted one of the most powerful legacies of the French Revolution: modern nationalism. The Revolution had given birth to the ideal of the civic nation, proclaiming popular sovereignty the universal basis of state power. Exported across Europe in the course of the Napoleonic wars, national ideas galvanized and divided populations. From west to east, scholars, artists, and intellectuals demanded popular sovereignty for people who shared a common language, common physical traits, and a common cultural heritage. Proponents of this ethnic reinterpretation of the civic nationalist ideal looked to revise the continent's map, transforming it into a patchwork of organically unified, autonomous nation-states.[1] In both its civic and ethnic manifestations, nationalism posed a serious challenge to the Russian empire, a multiethnic state ruled by an autocratic dynasty. The dream of popular sovereignty undermined the foundations of the estate system through which the Romanovs governed their vast domains, assigning collective privileges and obligations to social groups from above. Meanwhile, ethnonational particularism threatened to divide the empire's subjects, who spoke hundreds of languages and practiced a dozen faiths.[2]

Intense debates about how to respond to the challenge of nationalism consumed imperial officials and intellectuals for the rest of the century. Some insisted that Russia could not simply ignore—or seek to contain—nationalism; if it wished to flourish in the modern world, they argued, it would need to adapt certain elements of national ideas to the imperial context. One camp favored the creation of civic mechanisms that integrated tsarist subjects from different walks of life; another sought to align the government more closely with the empire's Orthodox believers and Russian speakers.

---

1. For an overview of nineteenth-century nationalism and its varied manifestations, see Timothy Baycroft and Mark Hewitson, eds., *What Is a Nation?* (New York, 2006).
2. On the estate system, consult Gregory L. Freeze, "The Soslovie (Estate) Paradigm and Russian Social History," *American Historical Review* 91, no. 1 (1986): 11–36; Elise Kimerling Wirtschafter, *Social Identity in Imperial Russia* (DeKalb, 1997). For an overview of official efforts to cope with the empire's diversity, see Andreas Kappeler, *The Russian Empire* (Harlow, UK, 2001), 168–369; Dominic Lieven, *Empire* (New Haven, 2002), 201–87.

Other officials and intellectuals, however, opposed these schemes, arguing that it was senseless—if not dangerous—for a supranational, autocratic state to acknowledge the legitimacy of national ideas in any way. These debates continued to rage on the eve of the Old Regime's collapse in 1917, leaving the empire's national dilemma unresolved. Neither state nor society had reached a consensus about how growing demands for popular sovereignty could be reconciled with the autocratic system, or about how to understand and manage ethnonational variation within the empire.

This book is about a curious but consequential regional response to the challenge of nationalism—an ambitious effort to mobilize a nation in defense of the Russian empire. This experiment unfolded in the empire's southwestern borderlands, which stretched from the right bank (west side) of the Dnieper River to the border with the Habsburg empire. Led by local Orthodox notables and intellectuals, this nationalizing project encompassed three interlinking efforts. First, it reimagined imperial history in ethnonational terms, declaring the "Russians" (a frequently used shorthand for "Orthodox East Slavs") as the empire's titular nationality and chronicling their struggle to protect their culture from supposedly hostile and monolithic minority groups. Second, it urged officials to expand the engagement of Russians in imperial economic and political life and to minimize the influence of their non-Russian adversaries. Finally, it advocated for strong state oversight of culture, industry, and politics, which southwestern nationalists insisted was necessary to assure the preeminence of the Orthodox East Slavs in the empire that they had built.

From the beginning, right-bank activists insisted that their program would strengthen the Russian state by preserving the values on which it was founded, aligning it with the desires of the people it ruled, and enhancing its ability to compete with its rivals. Although imperial officials occasionally intervened to manage and direct the nationalizing experiment emerging on the empire's southwestern frontier, many celebrated its potential to harness the force of nationalism in the service of empire. By the early twentieth century, official tolerance for nationalist agitation on the right bank permitted activists to create a socially variegated and mass-oriented Russian nationalist movement, which soon became the preeminent political force in the region. And by 1910, with the support of Prime Minister P. A. Stolypin, southwestern nationalists expanded their activities beyond the borderlands, assuming a prominent role in all-imperial politics.

On many counts, the southwestern borderlands would seem an unlikely locale to give rise to a Russian nationalist imagination. They were one of the Russian empire's last territorial acquisitions, claimed during the late-eighteenth-century partitions of the Polish-Lithuanian Commonwealth, a Catholic state. They were also one of Russia's poorest and least developed corners—a place where the horizons of most residents remained purely local. They could scarcely be considered Russian in demographic or cultural terms: even in the last years of the nineteenth century, after one hundred years of imperial rule, only 4 percent of their inhabitants spoke Russian as a first language. About three-quarters of local residents were Ukrainian speakers (called "Little Russians" in official parlance); most, but not all, were Orthodox believers of peasant stock. About 12 percent of local residents practiced the Jewish faith: some were Russian speakers who populated urban centers, but most were Yiddish speakers who lived in shtetls or district cities. About 4 percent were Polish-speaking Catholics; Polish nobles controlled much of the right bank's land and played an important role in culture and industry, though some déclassé Polish families also toiled in the fields alongside Orthodox peasants.³ Although the borderlands sometimes witnessed social and confessional conflict, their economic and cultural life served as powerful forces of integration. Peasants, nobles, and urban merchants relied on each other for survival, and the region's elites created a unique, multilingual hybrid culture of their own.⁴

How did national ideas take root in a culturally complex and socially stratified local society? Why did a diverse, peripheral region nearly one thousand miles from Moscow and St. Petersburg lead the empire on a search for a Russian nation? What did nationalist activists mean when they called themselves Russian, and how did they manage to convince local residents to join their cause? Why did they believe that a nationalist mass movement could strengthen the integrity of an autocratic empire, and why did so many imperial officials accept this claim? These are the questions at the heart of this book. It chronicles how the nationalist vision that emerged from the right bank reshaped local society and politics, and it shows how developments in the region transformed governance practices, everyday life, and identities beyond its borders.

The Russian Empire and the National Challenge

Russia first encountered the challenge of modern nationalism on its western frontier. When Catherine the Great colluded with Austria and Prussia to destroy the Polish-Lithuanian Commonwealth in the late eighteenth century, she acquired millions of subjects who spoke Polish and practiced the Roman Catholic faith—many of whom longed to restore their state. After a failed revolt against the partitioning powers, Polish patriots appealed to revolutionary France for help. In 1807, Napoleon created the Duchy of Warsaw, a Polish state under his protection; in 1812, Polish patriots flocked to join the Grand Armée's invasion of Russia, hopeful that a French victory would allow them to reclaim the lands between the Baltic and the Black Seas. In the aftermath of Napoleon's defeat, the Russian empire claimed most of the territory that had comprised the Duchy of Warsaw. In an effort to appease local notables, Tsar Alexander I granted the residents of this territory substantial autonomy, an elected parliament, and basic civil rights—privileges that other imperial subjects did not enjoy. But these concessions did not satisfy the ambitions of the Polish patriots determined to restore their state. In 1830–31 and again in 1863, Polish Catholic nobles (or *szlachta*),

---

3. Demographic data culled from *Pervaia vseobshchaia perepis' naseleniia Rossiiskoi imperii 1897 g.,* vyp. 7 (St. Petersburg, 1905), 12, 15, 20–21.
4. For example, Renata Król-Mazur, *Miasto trzech nacji* (Cracow, 2008); Mayhill C. Fowler, "Beau Monde: State and Stage on Empire's Edge" (PhD diss, Princeton University, 2011), 41–107; Amelia M. Glaser, *Jews and Ukrainians in Russia's Literary Borderlands* (Chicago, 2012).

who were the dominant social force across the western borderlands that had once comprised the Commonwealth, participated in armed insurrections against the Russian state.[5]

Russia's troubling "Polish question" posed a dual challenge to the men who ruled the empire. On the one hand, it convinced them of the need to stamp out nationalist separatist movements; on the other, it challenged them to locate new ideas and institutions capable of unifying loyal imperial subjects behind the tsar.[6] During the Napoleonic wars, conservative journalists and imperial officials called on tsarist subjects to join a "people's war" against the foreign invaders—and denounced the Polish patriots who supported French forces as parties to an international, revolutionary conspiracy against Russia.[7] In the aftermath of the 1830–31 revolt, Tsar Nicholas I aggressively promoted the Orthodox faith and attempted to enhance the authority of the central state across the empire; in the western borderlands, he oversaw a campaign to diminish the influence of the szlachta, stripping thousands of Polish families of their noble ranks and closing Polish-operated banks and schools.[8]

In the wake of the 1863 revolt, more officials began to see the ethnoconfessional status of individuals as an indicator of their loyalty to the state—and therefore as a legitimate consideration in imperial governance. In a set of policies that some referred to as "Russification," bureaucrats struggled to enhance the status of the Orthodox Church and the Russian language across the empire and to reduce the influence of Polish-speaking Catholics as well as other non-Russian minorities in its western borderlands.[9] These policies were replete with internal contradictions and unevenly applied; they also garnered substantial opposition from prominent figures in the government, including Minister of the Interior P. A. Valuev, who insisted that identifying any one culture as normative (or another as potentially subversive) undermined the integrity of the entire imperial system.[10] Nevertheless, the political crisis connected to the second Polish revolt stimulated a conversation about how to manage ethnic and national difference within the empire—one that ultimately transcended the confines

---

5. The best overview of these developments is Piotr Wandycz, *The Lands of Partitioned Poland, 1795–1918* (Seattle, 1974), 3–192.
6. For a consideration of how European empires endeavored to use national ideas to serve their own interests, see Jane Burbank and Frederick Cooper, *Empires in World History* (Princeton, 2010), 331–68.
7. Andrei Zorin, *Kormia dvuglavogo orla* (Moscow, 2001), 159–266.
8. On Nicholaevan efforts to promote Orthodoxy, see Paul W. Werth, *At the Margins of Orthodoxy* (Ithaca, 2002), 44–123; M. D. Dolbilov, *Russkii krai, chuzhaia vera* (Moscow, 2010), 68–108. On imperial policies in the western borderlands, consult M. Dolbilov and A. Miller, *Zapadnye okrainy rossiiskoi imperii* (Moscow, 2006), 96–122.
9. Theodore R. Weeks, *Nation and State in Late Imperial Russia* (DeKalb, 1996); Witold Rodkiewicz, *Russian Nationality Policy in the Western Provinces of the Empire, 1863–1905* (Lublin, 1998); Dolbilov and Miller, *Zapadnye okrainy*, 179–300; Darius Staliunas, *Making Russians* (New York, 2007); Robert P. Geraci, *Window on the East* (Ithaca, 2001).
10. Mikhail Dolbilov, "Russification and the Bureaucratic Mind in Russia's Northwestern Region in the 1860s," *Kritika* 5, no. 2 (Spring 2004): 245–71; A. A. Komzolova, *Politika samoderzhaviia v Severo-Zapadnom krae v epokhu Velikikh reform* (Moscow, 2005).

of government offices and engaged the imperial educated public.[11] Perhaps the most influential nonbureaucratic interlocutor in this dialogue, the journalist M. N. Katkov, professed his devotion to the "Russian cause" and his determination to save the empire from dangerous external threats as well as its internal enemies.[12]

An alternative nation-building process also coalesced in the 1860s—one that sought to unify imperial residents in common civic and political endeavors. Tsar Alexander II's "Great Reforms"—which emancipated the serfs, created organs of local self-governance in cities and rural areas, implemented universal conscription, and established a new judicial system—aspired to cultivate and empower local communities so that they might better serve the modernizing and rationalizing imperial state.[13] In the more fluid and mobile society that emerged from the reforms, subjects from very different walks of life established contacts with one another. Peasants and professionals worked together to improve sanitation and education in the countryside. A new class of upwardly mobile professionals coalesced in Russia's rapidly growing cities, founding dense networks of newspapers, journals, and voluntary societies. Cooperating with scholars and activists, officials founded new institutions of higher education and conducted scientific, statistical, and ethnographic research.[14]

However, all these efforts to adapt national ideas borrowed from Europe to the imperial context were fraught with complications and internal contradictions. Those participating in the discussions about ethnicity and national interest debated how to understand and describe the empire's diversity in the first place: some thought of confession or language as the most significant markers of difference; others discerned different tribes (*plemeni*), people (*narody*), ethnicities (*narodnosti*), or nations (*natsii*) within Russia's boundaries.[15] This epistemological and terminological uncertainty created practical problems for the official advocates of Russification; lacking comprehensive census data and standardized systems of taxonomy, they were left to debate what distinguished a Pole from a Russian.[16] Additionally, the logic of the autocratic system demanded that the purveyors of nationalist language distort its meaning to deny the

---

11. Henryk Głębocki, *Fatalna sprawa* (Cracow, 1997); Charles Steinwedel, "To Make a Difference: The Category of Ethnicity in Late Imperial Russian Politics, 1861–1917," in *Russian Modernity*, ed. David L. Hoffmann and Yanni Kotsonis (New York, 2000), 67–86; Olga Maiorova, *From the Shadow of Empire* (Madison, 2010).
12. On Katkov and other self-professed Russian nationalists of the era, see Andreas Renner, *Russischer Nationalismus und Öffentlichkeit im Zarenreich 1855–1875* (Cologne, 2000).
13. Ben Eklof, John Bushnell, and Larissa Zakharova, eds., *Russia's Great Reforms, 1855–1881* (Bloomington, IN, 1994).
14. See Edith W. Clowes, Samuel D. Kassow, and James L. West, eds., *Between Tsar and People* (Princeton, 1991), 343–66; Harley D. Balzer, ed., *Russia's Missing Middle Class* (Armonk, NY, 1996); Joseph Bradley, *Voluntary Associations in Tsarist Russia* (Cambridge, MA, 2009).
15. Nathaniel Knight, "Ethnicity, Nationality and the Masses: Narodnost' and Modernity in Imperial Russia," in Hoffmann and Kotsonis, *Russian Modernity*, 41–64; Alexei Miller, "Natsiia, Narod, Narodnost' in Russia in the Nineteenth Century: Some Introductory Remarks to the History of Concepts," *Jahrbücher für Geschichte Osteuropas* 56, no. 3 (2008): 379–90.
16. L. E. Gorizontov, *Paradoksy imperskoi politiki* (Moscow, 1999), especially 100–118; Dolbilov, "Russification." The first imperial census was conducted in 1897, and even then it did not inquire about the

legitimacy of popular sovereignty. Ardent bureaucratic supporters of Russification thus intervened to limit the activities of Orthodox activists whose nationalist fervor they deemed too extreme.[17] Katkov himself presented the Russian nation as a reflection of the bureaucratic interests of the state, treating it as a force that fortified rather than challenged autocratic power.[18] Civic activization posed its own challenges to the autocratic system. Officials vigorously policed the new order that the Great Reforms had created, censoring the periodicals and monitoring the associations that the state itself had sanctioned. In the 1880s and '90s, Tsar Alexander III instituted a series of counterreforms that limited the power of many of the institutions that his father had introduced.

By the beginning of the twentieth century, the Russian state's difficulty formulating a coherent response to the challenge of nationalism intensified an emergent political crisis. While Polish patriots in the western borderlands continued the struggle to restore their state, Ukrainian, Lithuanian, Jewish, Georgian, Armenian, and pan-Turkic nationalist movements emerged on the empire's peripheries.[19] Meanwhile, socialist and liberal activists decried the abuses of the autocratic state. Gradually, national and ideological grievances became intertwined. Many non-Russian nationalist activists joined forces with political movements pressing for reform.[20] And many Russian critics of the regime came to see the struggle of national minorities as representative of the plight of all imperial residents, who remained subjects rather than citizens, deprived of inalienable civil or political rights.[21]

By 1905, ethnic minorities, peasants, workers, and professionals of many political persuasions had taken to streets across the empire demanding political reform. They ultimately wrested key concessions from the government, which agreed to convoke an all-imperial elected parliament (Duma) and to liberalize statutes that limited public association and free expression. In the years that followed, the Russian empire developed a boisterous mass political system, which many hoped could serve as a foundation for a regime based on the rule of law. By 1907, however, political radicalization, violence, and counterreforms from above had destroyed the revolutionary coalition—and

---

respondents' ethnicity or nationality. Rather, it treated native language (and in some cases, confession) as a proxy for ethnicity. On the census, see Juliette Cadiot, *Le laboratoire impérial* (Paris, 2007), 37–61.

17. S. V. Rimskii, *Rossiiskaia tserkov' v epokhu Velikikh reform* (Moscow, 1999), 333–34; 362–69.
18. Andreas Renner, "Defining a Russian Nation: Mikhail Katkov and the Invention of National Politics," *Slavonic and East European Review* 81, no. 4 (2003): 659–82.
19. Timothy Snyder, *The Reconstruction of Nations* (New Haven, 2003), 31–51, 119–22; Jacob M. Landau, *Pan-Turkism* (Bloomington, IN, 1995), 7–28; Ronald Grigor Suny, *The Making of the Georgian Nation* (Bloomington, IN, 1988), 63–182; Ronald Grigor Suny, *Looking toward Ararat* (Bloomington, IN, 1993), 15–116.
20. Jonathan Frankel, *Prophecy and Politics* (New York, 1981); Stephen F. Jones, *Socialism in Georgian Colors* (Cambridge, 1995); Olga Andriewsky, "The Politics of National Identity: The Ukrainian Question in Russia, 1904–12" (PhD diss., Harvard University, 1991); Joshua D. Zimmerman, *Poles, Jews, and the Politics of Nationality* (Madison, 2004).
21. Vera Tolz, *Russia's Own Orient* (New York, 2011), 23–46; Juliette Cadiot, "Russia Learns to Write: Slavistics, Politics, and the Struggle to Redefine Empire in the Early 20th Century," *Kritika* 9, no. 1 (2008): 135–67.

frustrated reformers' hopes that they could topple the autocracy and create an inclusive, civic nation in its place.[22] Many non-Russian nationalist leaders who had joined the struggle for civil and political rights now turned their attention to the elaboration of their own national projects.[23] Meanwhile, some of the most prominent Russian socialists and liberals who had spearheaded the campaign for political reform castigated the national liberation struggles of ethnic minorities as chauvinist and divisive.[24]

In response to the latest political crisis, Tsar Nicholas II pledged to defend "Russian" traditions (which he never clearly defined) from the threats that "alien" populations (*inorodtsy*) within the empire posed to them. (The term *inorodtsy* originally referred to the nomadic and semi-nomadic indigenous populations of Siberia, but assumed a broader meaning after 1905, when it was commonly applied to Jews, Poles, Caucasians, and other populations that supposedly had turned against the state during the revolution.)[25] Right-wing "truly Russian" (*istinno russkie*) political activists mobilized across the empire; though few in number, they garnered substantial attention for their violent verbal—and sometimes physical—attacks on Jews, students, and others they suspected of liberal and socialist sympathies.[26] Yet those who invoked national ideas in defense of the Old Regime continued to acknowledge the paradoxical nature of their ventures. Nicholas II recognized that he could not definitively align the empire with Russian interests or exclude supposedly dangerous minority groups from intellectual and political life without undermining the integrity of the imperial system. And right-wing activists readily admitted that political mobilization in defense of the autocracy created a contradiction in terms.[27]

Russian tsars, bureaucrats, and intellectuals thus proved unable to reach a consensus about how the empire should respond to the national challenges that it faced. They could neither grant ethnonational considerations a leading role in imperial governance nor guide the empire toward civic nationhood without undermining the foundations of the entire autocratic system. Russian leaders' failure to locate ideas and institutions that could unify tsarist subjects in a nationalizing world weakened the internal stability of the empire.[28] In spite of its vibrant political and intellectual life

---

22. Abraham Ascher, *The Revolution of 1905*, 2 vols. (Stanford, 1988–92).
23. For example, Edward Chmielewski, *The Polish Question in the Russian State Duma* (Knoxville, 1970); Andriewsky, "Politics."
24. Paul Miliukov, *Political Memoirs, 1905–1917*, ed. Arthur P. Mendel (Ann Arbor, 1967), 101; P. B. Struve, "Velikaia Rossiia," *Russkaia mysl'* 29, no. 1 (1908): 143–57.
25. On the evolution and application of the term *inorodtsy*, see John W. Slocum, "Who, and When, Were the Inorodtsy? The Evolution of the Category of 'Aliens' in Imperial Russia," *Russian Review* 57, no. 2 (1998): 173–90; on the intensifying bureaucratic campaigns against "others" after 1905, see Hans Rogger, *Jewish Policies and Right-Wing Politics in Imperial Russia* (Berkeley, 1986).
26. Don C. Rawson, *Russian Rightists and the Revolution of 1905* (New York, 1995).
27. Richard S. Wortman, *Scenarios of Power* (Princeton, 2000), 2:309–523; Rogger, *Jewish Policies*, 188–211.
28. For analysis of this failure from various angles, see Geoffrey Hosking, *Russia and the Russians* (Cambridge, MA, 2003); Vera Tolz, *Russia* (New York, 2001); Ronald Grigor Suny, "The Empire Strikes Out: Imperial Russia, 'National' Identity, and Theories of Empire," in *A State of Nations*, ed. Ronald Grigor

and economic dynamism, Russia, in the words of historian Alfred J. Rieber, remained a "sedimentary society" transected by deep social and ideological divides.[29]

Russia's difficulty responding to the challenge of nationalism also placed it at a geopolitical disadvantage. Over the nineteenth century, its imperial rivals, the Habsburg and Ottoman empires, had worked to harness national ideas to serve their own interests. Attempting to benefit from the integrative force of civic nationalism, the leaders of both states equalized the legal rights of their male subjects and endeavored to unify the peoples they ruled in common political and cultural endeavors.[30] In different ways, both regimes also encouraged nation-building processes based on ethnicity. In an effort to maintain the loyalty of its non-German speakers, the Habsburg state offered special "bargains" to nationalist activists: Hungarian nobles received an autonomous government within the empire, while minority groups that constituted local majorities won the right to use their native tongue as an official language of administration and education.[31] In the last years of the nineteenth century, the Ottoman sultan, Abdülhamid II, aligned the empire more closely with the interests of its Muslims and marginalized certain minority populations—especially the Christian Armenians of Eastern Anatolia. The Young Turks who rose to power in the early twentieth century embraced an even clearer nationalist agenda, declaring their intent to promote the putative collective interests of the empire's Turks and to "resolve" the Armenian question once and for all through mass conversions and violence.[32] Noting Russia's vulnerability on national issues, the Habsburg and Ottoman regimes funded Ukrainian and pan-Turkic irredentist movements in the Romanov empire in an effort to undermine their common rival.[33] With the outbreak of the First World War in 1914, Russia's leaders would struggle not only to contain the intensified separatist movements that

---

Suny and Terry Martin (New York, 2001), 23–66; Astrid S. Tuminez, *Russian Nationalism since 1856* (New York, 2000).
29. Alfred J. Rieber, "The Sedimentary Society," in Clowes, Kassow, and West, *Between Tsar and People*, 343–366. For a similar argument, see Leopold Haimson, "The Problem of Political and Social Stability in Urban Russia, 1905–1914 (Part One)" *Slavic Review* 23, no. 4 (1964): 619–42; Leopold Haimson, "The Problem of Political and Social Stability in Urban Russia, 1905–1914 (Part Two)" *Slavic Review* 24, no. 1 (1965): 1–22.
30. On imperial integration attempts, see Daniel L. Unowsky, *The Pomp and Politics of Patriotism* (West Lafayette, IN, 2005); John D. Deak, "The Austrian Civil Service in an Age of Crisis" (PhD diss., University of Chicago, 2009); M. Şükrü Hanioğlu, *A Brief History of the Late Ottoman Empire* (Princeton, 2008), 72–108.
31. On the local results of these policies, see Jeremy King, *Budweisers into Czechs and Germans* (Princeton, 2005); Pieter M. Judson, *Guardians of the Nation* (Cambridge, MA, 2006).
32. On late Ottoman nationality policy, see Hanioğlu, *Brief History*, 138–202; Michael A. Reynolds, *Shattering Empires* (New York, 2011), 22–106.
33. See Aviel Roshwald, *Ethnic Nationalism and the Fall of Empires* (New York, 2002), 7–67. Recent studies have demonstrated that in spite of Russia's difficulty resolving its "national questions," it too engaged in irredentist adventures. See Anna Veronika Wendland, *Die Russophilen in Galizien* (Vienna, 2001); A. Iu. Bakhturina, *Politika Rossiiskoi Imperii v Vostochnoi Galitsii v gody Pervoi mirovoi voiny* (Moscow, 2000); Reynolds, *Shattering Empires*.

INTRODUCTION

its opponents supported on the empire's peripheries but also to compete against the citizen armies that had mobilized behind a total war.[34]

Nation and Empire in the Southwestern Borderlands

How, then, do we explain the successes of the southwest's Russian nationalists, who simultaneously reimagined the empire as the creation of the East Slavs and sought to expand the access of this titular nationality to political and economic power? Although several studies have remarked on the influence that nationalist parties enjoyed in the region after 1905, scholars have devoted little attention to the Russian nationalist imagination that emerged from the right bank.[35] Rather, generations of historians specializing on the region have echoed the narrative of disintegration outlined above, focusing on the conflicts between its non-Russian residents and the imperial state. In the late nineteenth and early twentieth centuries, Polish, Jewish, and Ukrainian intellectuals lamented the suffering of their people under tsarist rule.[36] In the aftermath of the Russian Revolution, the right bank became part of a short-lived Ukrainian nation-state and eventually part of the USSR. Initially, the new Soviet state encouraged the consolidation of Ukrainian culture, as well as the activities of the men who had led the Ukrainian national movement under the tsarist regime. By the 1930s, however, apparatchiks reversed course, denouncing Ukrainian nationalism as a "bourgeois" and retrograde force.[37] For nearly half a century, it remained taboo to discuss the "Ukrainian question" within the Soviet Union. Unable to gain access to relevant archival sources, the few Western and émigré scholars who wrote on national themes largely relied on sources compiled by the very nationalist activists whom they studied.[38]

In the immediate aftermath of the Soviet collapse, scholars hastened to create a "coherent narrative of national history" for the independent Ukrainian state that had emerged from the rubble of the USSR.[39] Multiple studies chronicled the

---

34. Hubertus Jahn, *Patriotic Culture in Russia during World War I* (Ithaca, 1995).
35. For example, Michael F. Hamm, *Kiev* (Princeton, 1993), 80–81; Rawson, *Russian Rightists*, 98–103; Natan M. Meir, *Kiev, Jewish Metropolis* (Bloomington, IN, 2010), 204–6; D. A. Kotsiubinskii, *Russkii natsionalizm v nachale XX stoletiia* (Moscow, 2001), 36. The one monograph to analyze the southwest's Russian nationalists in detail focuses primarily on their party structures and platforms in the post-1905 period. See Robert Edelman, *Gentry Politics on the Eve of the Russian Revolution* (New Brunswick, NJ, 1980).
36. For example, S. M. Dubnow, *History of the Jews in Russia and Poland*, trans. I. Friedlaender, 3 vols. (Philadelphia, 1916–20); Fr. Rawita-Gawroński, *Rok 1863 na Rusi* (Lviv, 1909); M. Grushevskii, *Osvobozhdenie Rossii i ukrainskii vopros* (St. Petersburg, 1907).
37. For examples of Ukrainian nationalist scholarship conducted under the early Soviet regime, see Fedir Savchenko, *Zaborona ukrainstva 1876 r.* (1930; repr., Munich, 1970); and the journal *Ukraina*. On the shift in official attitudes toward the Ukrainian national project, see Serhii Plokhy, *Unmaking Imperial Russia* (Toronto, 2005), 264–77; Terry Martin, *The Affirmative Action Empire* (Ithaca, 2001), 309–93.
38. For example, D. Doroshenko, *History of the Ukraine*, trans. Hanna Keller (Edmonton, 1939); Ivan L. Rudnytsky, *Essays in Modern Ukrainian History* (Cambridge, MA, 1987); Thomas M. Prymak, *Mykhailo Hrushevsky* (Toronto, 1987).
39. The quote is from Mark Von Hagen, "Does Ukraine Have a History?" *Slavic Review* 54, no. 3 (1995): 666–67.

nineteenth-century Ukrainian "national awakening" that occurred on both sides of the Russo-Austrian border and followed the efforts of Ukrainian nationalists to establish a state of their own.[40] Several works have placed Ukrainian "national awakeners" in dialogue with the Polish patriots and Russian officials who claimed Ukrainian-speaking territories as an integral part of their domains. These studies have added valuable nuance to the national awakening paradigm, revealing that Ukrainian activists learned much from Polish nationalists and that tsarist officials permitted limited discussion of Little Russian peculiarities, provided these conversations did not challenge the myth of East Slavic unity.[41]

The original works on the Ukrainian national awakening as well as recent studies that reframe this literature in a multinational context draw heavily on constructivist theories of nationalism, which present national communities as creations of social, economic, and cultural modernization processes.[42] Yet there is also a strong tendency in the existing literature to deproblematize the Ukrainian national project. Underestimating the complications that accompanied efforts to adapt national ideas to the Russian imperial context, scholars of the lands that ultimately came to constitute Ukraine have tended to take it for granted that nationalism would emerge as a driving force of politics; they have also presented Ukrainian national identity as the natural and expected by-product of discussions about local folk traditions and culture.[43]

This book takes a different approach. Rather than chronicling the Ukrainian national awakening—or the competition between Ukrainian nationalists and their rivals—it asks how residents of the right bank came to conceive of local society in national terms in the first place. Rather than assuming that these residents would automatically identify the traditions that they held so dear as Ukrainian, it embarks on an open-ended exploration of how they thought and what they said about local culture. Informed by a new literature that treats the rise of nationalist sentiment as a product of protracted agitation (and often, sleights of hand) by committed activists—not as

---

40. For example, H. V. Kas"ianov, *Ukrains'ka intelihentsiia na rubezhi XIX–XX stolit* (Kiev, 1993); Iaroslav Hrytsak, *Narys istorii Ukrainy* (Kiev, 2000); Mykola Riabchuk, *Vid Malorosii do Ukrainy* (Kiev, 2000); Paul R. Magocsi, *The Roots of Ukrainian Nationalism* (Toronto, 2002); Serhy Yekelchyk, *Ukrainofily* (Kiev, 2010).
41. For example, Alexei Miller, *The Ukrainian Question* (New York, 2003); Ricarda Vulpius, *Nationalisierung der Religion* (Wiesbaden, 2005); Serhiy Bilenky, *Romantic Nationalism in Eastern Europe* (Stanford, 2012). For more on Little Russian culture in the Russian empire, see Andreas Kappeler, "'Great Russians' and 'Little Russians': Russian-Ukrainian Relations and Perceptions in Historical Perspective," Donald W. Treadgold Papers, University of Washington, 2003; Olga Andriewsky, "The Russian-Ukrainian Discourse and the Failure of the 'Little Russian Solution,' 1782–1917," in *Culture, Nation, and Identity*, ed. Andreas Kappeler, Zenon E. Kohut, Frank E. Sysyn, and Mark von Hagen (Edmonton, 2003), 182–214.
42. For example, Benedict Anderson, *Imagined Communities* (London, 1983); Ernest Gellner, *Nations and Nationalism* (Ithaca, 1983); Eric Hobsbawm and Terence Ranger, *The Invention of Tradition* (New York, 1983); Miroslav Hroch, *Social Preconditions of National Revival in Europe*, trans. Ben Fowkes (New York, 1985).
43. Even authors who describe their primary goal as reframing Ukrainian history in cross-cultural context have taken it for granted that local residents would come to identify as Ukrainian. For example, Yohanan Petrovsky-Shtern's study of Jews who aligned themselves with the Ukrainian national cause speaks of "the repressed nationhood of Ukrainians" under the tsarist regime. See Yohanan Petrovsky-Shtern, *The Anti-Imperial Choice* (New Haven, 2009), 1.

an ineluctable feature of modernity or a reflection of the interests of stable and self-evident communities—this book reconstructs the dynamic and contingent process through which national ideas took root in the borderlands.[44]

This focus on process provides a new perspective on right-bank culture, society, and politics—and on the Russian empire's encounter with nationalism. It reveals that men who expressed great pride in the cultural and historical peculiarities of the southwestern borderlands were among the first to imagine imperial society as a conglomeration of distinct and mutually exclusive national collectives. It allows us to see how local patriots (among them, men typically seen as key players in the Ukrainian national awakening) helped to invent a Russian nation that reinforced rather than challenged the integrity of the empire. Finally, it shows the role that imperial officials played in creating an environment in which national ideas could take root and flourish—and in promoting these ideas once they began to coalesce.

Although the emergence of a Russian nation-building project on the right bank is very much a local story, this book intervenes in a broader debate about the role that nationalism played in shaping modern societies. Scholars of national awakenings have generally taken for granted the transformative power of nationalism—a tendency recently challenged by historians who argue that the traditional focus on nation-building has obscured the fact that popular indifference and even hostility toward national ideas persisted well into the modern period.[45] Rather than focusing on expressions of consciousness or indifference, this book analyzes how nationalist agendas evolved through time and across space, often in convoluted and nonlinear ways. Bureaucratic imperatives, the activity of intellectuals, social and economic concerns, as well as urban and rural politics all played a role in shaping the nationalizing impulses that emerged from the southwestern borderlands. Depending on the venue in which they were aired, national ideas assumed different forms and attracted different audiences; a constituency that might greet national ideas articulated in an ethnic or religious key with indifference might respond more positively to the same ideas repackaged as a crusade for social equity. Even once an individual declared his devotion to the national community—an act that would qualify him as nationally conscious according to any litmus test—the nationalizing agenda that he carried could experience rapid mutations that dramatically altered its form, function, and ideological orientation.[46] As we shall see, Russian nationalist agitation spawned accidental by-products

---

44. For example, Rogers Brubaker, *Ethnicity without Groups* (Cambridge, MA, 2004); King, *Budweisers*; Judson, *Guardians*; Chad Bryant, *Prague in Black* (Cambridge, MA, 2007); Tara Zahra, *Kidnapped Souls* (Ithaca, 2008).
45. The most eloquent statement of this position is Tara Zahra, "Imagined Noncommunities: National Indifference as a Category of Analysis," *Slavic Review* 69, no. 1 (2010): 93–119.
46. Chad Bryant explores the phenomenon of "national amphibianism"—in which ordinary residents of Prague and its environs chose to identify with different nationalities at different times—in his *Prague in Black*. Here, I explore how dedicated nationalists themselves could shift their national allegiances, sometimes despite themselves.

that would ultimately undermine the coherence of the nationalist movement as well as the stability of the empire that its proponents claimed to support.

The Little Russian Idea and the Invention of a Russian Nation

The first efforts to imagine the population of the Dnieper region as consisting of coherent and mutually exclusive groups defined by their cultural values and historical experiences pre-dated the rise of modern nationalism. In the seventeenth century, when the region was still under Polish rule, Orthodox clerics and the leaders of the Cossacks, a free military caste, began to present local Orthodox believers—regardless of their social station—as members of a unified community that shared common interests. They traced the origins of this confessional community to the ancient Rus' state, which Orthodox princes had ruled from Kiev. Declaring the Orthodox people descended from Rus' to be the native inhabitants of the Dnieper region—and therefore the rightful owners of its resources—clerics and Cossacks challenged the authority of the Catholic state that ruled them in an age of growing confessional conflict. By identifying the territory that they interchangeably called Little Russia and Ukraine as the birthplace of the Rus' faith, they also situated themselves at the center of a larger Orthodox world, for the rapidly growing state of Muscovy traced its origins to Rus' as well. In the centuries to come, Orthodox notables would continue to present local traditions as authentic and essential manifestations of Rus' culture; as we shall see, discussions about the cultural peculiarities of the Dnieper region did not necessarily challenge the myth of East Slavic unity—and often could reinforce it.[47]

By the eighteenth century, the Russian empire had claimed the left bank (east side) of the Dnieper and had absorbed the descendants of the Cossack generals who lived there into the imperial nobility. In the hands of the so-called Little Russian gentry, the Rus' confessional community that early modern clerics and Cossacks had envisioned acquired ethnonational characteristics. Left-bank nobles compiled chronicles and wrote histories that portrayed their Cossack ancestors as the saviors of the Orthodox East Slavic people descended from Rus'; these same accounts highlighted the Cossacks' role in protecting Orthodox believers from the supposedly coherent Polish and Jewish nations that the chroniclers claimed had sought to destroy Rus' traditions. Continuing to depict Little Russia as a repository of authentic Orthodox practices, these accounts also portrayed the region as a citadel that defended all of East Slavic civilization from dangerous "foreign" threats. This constellation of beliefs—which I will henceforth refer to as the Little Russian idea—simultaneously highlighted the

---

47. In this text I will frequently refer to the "Rus' people" or "children of Rus'" to emphasize the importance of the Rus' heritage in the invention of an East Slavic nation, as well as the common origins of the Russian and Ukrainian national narratives. This terminology is my own. For considerations of how peripheral zones have helped to constitute broader identities in other early modern European contexts, see Peter Sahlins, *Boundaries* (Berkeley, 1989); Tamar Herzog, *Defining Nations* (New Haven, 2003).

cultural and historical peculiarities of the Dnieper region and presented it as the true homeland of all the East Slavs.

Through the first third of the nineteenth century, officials expressed little interest in the left-bank gentry's efforts to reimagine the empire in ethnonational terms and to define the Dnieper region as the spiritual center of East Slavic civilization. Indeed, when Russia acquired the right bank—which had been one of the core Rus' territories—the authorities left intact the local society and culture that they had inherited from the Commonwealth. They absorbed the gentry, virtually all Polish-speaking Catholics, in the all-imperial noble rolls; they permitted cities with substantial Jewish populations to retain the self-governance rights that they had enjoyed under the Commonwealth; and they obligated Orthodox peasants to serve as the serfs of Catholic lords.

In the aftermath of the 1830–31 revolt, however, officials began to warm to the Little Russian idea, whose capacity to counteract Polish nationalism and to claim the borderlands as a primordially Orthodox locale they recognized. In the aftermath of the insurrection, the left bank's Little Russian patriots poured into Kiev, the administrative capital of the southwestern borderlands, where they assumed high-ranking positions in local government and in official historical, archeological, and ethnographic commissions. Working within these institutions, they unearthed traces of the native East Slavic culture that had supposedly flourished in the region prior to the imposition of Polish rule, and they continued to portray the Poles and the Jews of the borderlands as monolithic groups that had exploited the children of Rus' for centuries. The Little Russian idea had begun to acquire the imprimatur of the imperial state.

By the 1840s, '50s, and '60s, the small circle of Little Russian patriots active in Kiev expanded to include an emergent urban intelligentsia composed of many men of modest means. As it grew more socially variegated, the Little Russian lobby, which had once presented Cossack generals and Orthodox clerics as the representatives of the Rus' people, now incorporated the right-bank peasantry (*narod*) into its historical narratives.[48] Activists presented Little Russian peasants as the guardians of authentic Rus' traditions and celebrated their struggle against the Poles and Jews who allegedly had endeavored to destroy their culture; some went so far as to celebrate violent jacqueries against the szlachta as laudable expressions of popular resistance. This new interpretation of the Little Russian idea infused it with a social agenda, presenting the Rus' nation's struggle to liberate itself from poverty and oppression as part and parcel of its effort to protect its cultural traditions.

Other currents in mid-nineteenth-century Russian intellectual life shared certain commonalities with the Little Russian idea. Radical publicists and Slavophile intellectuals sharply criticized the oppression of the peasantry; Siberian regionalists claimed that their native region, which remained untouched by serfdom, had preserved true

---

48. The Russian word narod has several connotations: it can mean "people," "nation," or "simple folk." In the nineteenth century, it was often used to refer to the Orthodox peasantry, but even when employed to describe a social class it frequently carried national connotations. I will use this term in the original Russian in order to capture its multiple meanings, which are difficult to render in English.

Russian values.[49] But only the Little Russian activists of the right bank could claim to mobilize the ancient heritage of the East Slavs against Polish nationalism, which officials regarded as the most troubling threat to imperial stability by far. Thus, although many within the bureaucracy expressed unease about the organic nationalist and radically populist ideas that Little Russian activists promoted, few were willing to argue that the Little Russian idea posed a serious danger to the empire.

In the aftermath of the 1863 revolt, officials in the northwestern borderlands (contemporary Belarus, eastern Poland, and the Baltic states) took decisive action to enhance imperial authority and to police the political and cultural expression of local, non-Russian populations. Although the state placed some new limits on southwestern activists in the immediate aftermath of the revolt, issuing edicts in 1863 and 1876 that limited the use of the Ukrainian language, the Little Russian idea survived the political crisis intact. Indeed, in the ensuing decades, Little Russian activists dramatically expanded their influence on the right bank. They launched new periodicals and created dense networks of voluntary associations, many of which enjoyed considerable support from the state. They organized outreach campaigns that aimed to familiarize urban dwellers as well as peasants with their views. They played an active role in Kiev city politics, where they created political coalitions and mobilized local residents behind them. Struggling to raise popular awareness of the value of Little Russian culture—and the role that it played in forging East Slavic civilization—they also launched a campaign to nationalize governance structures, lobbying imperial officials to enhance the access of the East Slavs to wealth and political power and to limit the influence of Poles and Jews.[50]

In the revolutionary upheaval of 1905 and the years of crisis that followed, men who had been involved in the Little Russian lobby for decades insisted that their ideas could serve as the centerpiece of an empire-wide effort to mobilize a Russian nation and to defend it from dangerous foreign threats. Presenting themselves as a loyalist opposition, they pressured the authorities to do more to uplift and enfranchise the Orthodox masses—and to protect them from exploitation at the hands of Poles and Jews. Benefiting from the mass political system that emerged from the revolution, they consolidated their control of Kiev city politics and then expanded their influence across the countryside, enlisting nobles, urban professionals, workers, and peasants in their cause. Ultimately, the southwest's Russian nationalists established themselves as a leading force in imperial politics. They helped to organize the All-Russian National Union, which became the second-largest political party in the empire; they operated clubs and newspapers as far away as Siberia. They scored their greatest victory in 1911,

---

49. On the intelligentsia's campaign against serfdom, see Martin E. Malia, *Alexander Herzen and the Birth of Russian Socialism* (Cambridge, MA, 1961); Andrzej Walicki, *The Slavophile Controversy* (Oxford, 1975). On Siberian regionalism: S. G. Svatikov, *Rossiia i sibir'* (Prague, 1929).
50. On local patriotism as a component of nation-building projects in other locales, consult Celia Applegate, *A Nation of Provincials* (Berkeley, 1990); Caroline Ford, *Creating the Nation in Provincial France* (Princeton, 1993); Alon Confino, *The Nation as a Local Metaphor* (Chapel Hill, 1997).

when they convinced Prime Minister P. A. Stolypin to reorganize elections in the western borderlands on a national basis, expanding the electoral power of Orthodox East Slavs. Although growing numbers of officials complained that these developments threatened to corrode the stability of the empire, Stolypin and other prominent bureaucrats insisted that southwestern nationalists were invaluable allies who defended state interests on the embattled western frontier.

Southwestern Nationalism and the Fate of the Empire

The story of the Little Russian idea and the role that it played in the invention of a Russian nation provides a new perspective in the ongoing debate about the stability of the imperial system. Like other recent studies that have challenged the once-dominant view of tsarist society as atomized and shackled by a heavy-handed state, this book argues for the dynamism and resilience of late imperial society. It shows how local communities with their own historical memories and cultural traditions integrated themselves into the empire (and even an incipient Russian nation) without renouncing the values that they held dear.[51] It chronicles the accomplishments of civic society, revealing how associations, political parties, lobbying groups, and the mass media managed to unite tsarist subjects from very different walks of life—and even to shape the policies of the autocracy.[52] It argues that the periphery could make important contributions to the intellectual and political life of the Russian heartland, reconstructing the efforts of provincial intellectuals to reconcile the interests of state and society and to strengthen the imperial system.[53]

This book also treats the nationalizing experiment that unfolded in the southwest as an ambitious attempt to modernize the empire. In spite of their romantic belief in an organic Rus' nation, right-bank activists were consummately modern men who hoped to see Russia catch and overtake its rivals. Leveraging the substantial autonomy that trusting officials offered them, they imported cutting-edge social science techniques and new ideas about politics and governance into the empire. At points, our narrative will pause to consider junctures at which local activists found themselves at the very vanguard of intellectual, cultural, and ideological developments in Europe, in spite of their distance from the centers of imperial power and the liminal position that they occupied on the continent.[54]

---

51. For similar arguments, see Benjamin Nathans, *Beyond the Pale* (Berkeley, 2002); Robert D. Crews, *For Prophet and Tsar* (Cambridge, MA, 2006).
52. See Bradley, *Voluntary Associations*; Boris B. Gorshkov, *Russia's Factory Children* (Pittsburgh, 2009); Wayne Dowler, *Russia in 1913* (DeKalb, 2010); Anton A. Fedyashin, *Liberals under Autocracy* (Madison, 2012).
53. See Catherine Evtuhov, *Portrait of a Russian Province* (Pittsburgh, 2011).
54. Several studies have argued that modern practices of nation building and mass political mobilization began to emerge in the last years of the empire, particularly during the First World War. See Peter Holquist, *Making War, Forging Revolution* (Cambridge, MA, 2002); Eric Lohr, *Nationalizing the Russian Empire* (Cambridge, MA, 2003); Joshua Sanborn, *Drafting the Russian Nation* (DeKalb, 2003). This book

However, unlike many other studies that have argued that imperial Russia was developing a robust civil society capable of responding to the challenges of modernity, this book does not treat the consolidation of a liberal-democratic opposition to the autocracy as the natural outcome of social and political mobilization.[55] Rather, it shows how civic activity in the southwest generated uncivil ideas and illiberal ideologies.[56] Denouncing Poles and Jews as irredeemable, even racial, enemies of the children of Rus', Little Russian patriots and Russian nationalists attacked long-standing practices of intercultural accommodation and produced debilitating social conflicts. The clubs, journals, and rallies that they used to denounce the putative adversaries of the East Slavs celebrated and even organized physical violence. Nationalist activization thus destabilized local society, presenting serious challenges to the officials who struggled to maintain order. Paradoxically, it also undermined the independence and viability of the public sphere that the nationalist movement had helped to constitute. Denouncing the very notion of civic equality as an existential threat to Rus' traditions, right-bank nationalists demanded a strong, interventionist, and illiberal state that would promote the welfare of some of its subjects and marginalize others. The achievements of civic society in the southwest cannot be considered in isolation from their self-destructive potential.

The search for a Rus' nation in the right bank challenged the stability of the imperial system in another sense as well, playing an unwitting role in the creation of the Ukrainian nationalist project on which so many other studies of the region have focused. Many of the first intellectuals to imagine a separate Ukrainian nation were in fact alumni of the Little Russian lobby. Following a series of internecine disputes, they broke with their former comrades and used the ideas and tools that they had first acquired in state-sponsored institutions to formulate a rival national project. Ukrainian nationalists created a new historiography that excised the Little Russian idea from the intellectual history of the southwestern borderlands; the Russian nationalists who remained loyal to the Little Russian idea denounced their onetime collaborators as traitors.[57] The dispute between the two camps not only created additional divisions in southwestern society but also obscured the common origins of the Russian and Ukrainian national projects; this fact explains why it has been so difficult

---

argues that these projects coalesced even earlier in the southwestern borderlands—where, of course, much of the war on the eastern front was waged.

55. A notable exception that explores how processes of civic mobilization and social integration led to new forms of exclusion is Nathans, *Beyond the Pale*.

56. Treatments of similar processes in modern Europe include John W. Boyer, *Political Radicalism in Late Imperial Vienna* (Chicago, 1981); Roger Chickering, *We Men Who Feel Most German* (Boston, 1984); Maria M. Kovacs, *Liberal Professions and Illiberal Politics* (New York, 1994). I refer to "civic society" rather than "civil society" to emphasize the uncivil potential of southwestern politics, and their tendency to invite greater state intervention in local politics and society.

57. For example, Grushevskii, *Osvobozhdenie*; A. V. Storozhenko, *Proiskhozhdenie i sushchnost' ukrainofil'stva* (Kiev, 1912); S. N. Shchegolev, *Ukrainskoe dvizhenie kak sovremennyi etap iuzhnorusskago separatizma* (Kiev, 1912).

for subsequent historians to notice the role that Little Russian patriots played in the invention of a Russian nation.

In the last years of the empire, tensions between self-professed Russian nationalists and the Poles, Jews, and Ukrainians whom they so vehemently denounced continued to grow, at times threatening the authorities' ability to maintain law and order. Meanwhile, nationalist rhetoric demanding popular liberation had created expectations for political democratization that the autocracy could not easily meet. As concerned imperial officials and nationalist leaders themselves debated how to move forward, radical voices within the nationalist lobby refused to compromise. Insisting that devoted nationalists must see to fruition their mission to deliver the children of Rus' from their enemies, Kiev-based activists incited the notorious Beilis case, accusing a local Jew of murdering an Orthodox boy as part of a blood ritual. The case further discredited the imperial state, which agreed to prosecute Beilis, and deepened the rifts within the nationalist lobby. Rather than reinforce the unity of local society and the integrity of the imperial system, nationalist activity in the southwest had in fact created new sources of instability.

Framework

This book is divided into three sections. Part 1, "The Little Russian Idea and the Russian Empire," explores how officials and intellectuals came to see the right bank as a battleground between competing national collectives and traces their first efforts to ensure that the children of Rus' triumphed in this struggle. Covering the early modern period through the 1870s, it explores the role that Little Russian patriots played in the imagination of a Russian nation that unified the East Slavs; it also documents how their efforts unwittingly facilitated the emergence of a rival Ukrainian national project.

Part 2, "The Urban Crucible," chronicles how activists in the city of Kiev reframed the Little Russian idea in an urban setting between 1870 and 1905, allowing them to undermine long-standing traditions of inter-cultural accommodation and to consolidate a real political following for the first time. Presenting Kiev's social problems, corruption, and public health challenges as by-products of the engagement of non-East Slavs in local politics and industry, they folded urban concerns into the narrative of national suffering and defiance that Little Russian patriots had created. During the 1905 revolution, the attack against the city's non-East Slavs developed into an organized and mass-oriented campaign for popular liberation through illiberal means. Denouncing the all-imperial crusade for equal rights as a ploy by Poles and especially Jews to consolidate their power, Kiev's Russian nationalists called on the children of Rus' to emancipate themselves from foreign domination, through violent means if necessary. At the same time, they demanded that imperial officials create a stronger and more effective state capable of guaranteeing the Orthodox East Slavs a preeminent role in politics and society.

Part Three, "Forging a Russian Nation," explores how southwestern nationalists expanded their influence beyond the borderlands in the aftermath of the 1905 revolution—and how they unwittingly undermined the unity of their movement and of the empire that they claimed to support in the process. It was between 1908 and 1911 that right-bank nationalists reached the pinnacle of their success, creating a cross-class political coalition and effective lobbying organizations that managed to shape imperial policies. But the radicalization of the movement in these years—driven in part by the mass following that it had achieved—also challenged its coherence. Successive attempts by imperial officials and nationalist leaders to restrain the most extreme segments of the movement further radicalized the hardliners, who now accused moderate nationalists of having betrayed the children of Rus'. By the eve of the First World War, the nationalist lobby had shattered into rival camps; although onetime nationalists disagreed about much, almost all expressed disgust toward the tsarist state. The ambitious attempt to reconcile the interests of society and state in a symbolically crucial locale had unleashed forces that the empire proved unable to bear—and internecine conflicts that tore right-bank society apart.

Although the Russian nationalist imagination that emerged from the southwest ultimately helped to bring about the empire's demise, a brief epilogue shows that its ideological byproducts proved remarkably resilient. The organic nationalism and illiberal mass politics that the southwest's nationalists had spawned would continue to flourish in the borderlands for decades, frustrating as well as inspiring the regimes that clamed control of the right bank after the collapse of the autocracy. And onetime Russian nationalists, who followed divergent paths after 1917, would repurpose the agenda that they had developed under tsarism in the service of independent Ukrainian states, the Bolshevik regime, and emerging fascist movements. Having laid bare the strengths as well as the vulnerabilities of the Russian Old Regime, the Little Russian idea and the Russian national project to which it gave rise survived long enough to help shape a new era of ideological extremism and total war.

PART ONE

The Little Russian Idea and the Russian Empire

1
The Little Russian Idea and the Invention of a Rus' Nation

FROM THE BEGINNING of their recorded history, the fertile lands surrounding the Dnieper River played host to a diverse array of peoples speaking different languages and professing different faiths. For most of the early modern and modern periods, the region found itself on the periphery of two sprawling multiethnic states: the Polish-Lithuanian Commonwealth and the Russian empire. Both states instituted socially stratified estate systems to cope with their heterogeneity, enlisting a diverse cast of local elites as partners in governance. The Polish kings guaranteed citizenship and self-governance rights to the Polish Catholic szlachta, Orthodox notables, and Jewish, Armenian, and Lutheran burghers and mercantile elites; they obligated peasants of many faiths to serve local gentry as serfs. Although the Russian empire, which claimed the left bank of the Dnieper in the seventeenth century and its right bank in the eighteenth, revoked the citizenship rights that Commonwealth elites had enjoyed, it left the basic social structure of the Polish-Lithuanian state in place. Tsarist officials affirmed the estate privileges of local notables—regardless of their confession, mother tongue, or cultural traditions—and obligated millions of Orthodox believers to serve as the serfs of non-Orthodox lords.

This chapter examines how residents of the Dnieper region came to envision alternatives to the estate system. The first challenges to estate society arose in the seventeenth century, when Orthodox clerics and Cossack leaders reimagined the region as the center of an epic struggle for survival among coherent and hostile confessional communities. By the eighteenth and early nineteenth centuries, Little Russian nobles descended from the early modern Cossack generals came to see the confessional communities that their ancestors had imagined in ethnonational terms. They described the Orthodox East Slavs as the "native" inhabitants of the lands surrounding the Dnieper and chronicled their efforts to protect the traditions that they had inherited from Rus'; they portrayed Poles and Jews as members of coherent nations that had long subjugated the Rus' people and their culture. Presenting their native region as a citadel that had preserved authentic East Slavic values as well as a battlefield on which local residents struggled to defend their traditions, the Little Russian gentry thus insisted that the future of the East Slavs and the Russian empire would be decided on the banks of the Dnieper.

Although this Little Russian idea enjoyed great influence among local notables, through the first third of the nineteenth century it remained a purely regional phenomenon, exercising little influence on imperial policy or intellectual life. Beyond the borderlands, Russian intellectuals and officials tended to view the empire as the creation of an autocratic dynasty, not as a conglomeration of national groups engaged in a zero-sum battle. This rapidly changed in the aftermath of the 1830–31 revolt, however. Focusing on the interactions between imperial bureaucrats and Little Russian patriots between 1830 and 1860, this chapter traces the emergence of an informal alliance between the two camps. Recognizing the potential of the Little Russian idea to contest Polish claims on the southwestern borderlands, officials enabled its proponents to use the cultural institutions of the imperial state to their benefit—and even to present their agenda on an all-imperial stage. Little Russian activists, for their part, pressed officials to acknowledge and rectify the injustices of the estate system. The engagement of Little Russian patriots in the official campaign to marginalize Polish nationalism in the southwest was a creative attempt to reconcile the interests of state and society at a moment of crisis. But as we shall see, it also created new national dilemmas, challenging imperial officials to maintain control of the nationalizing project that they allowed to unfold in the southwest.

The Rus' Lands in Antiquity and Early Modernity

According to chronicles, in the ninth century warring Slavic tribes inhabiting the forests of what is today western Russia invited the Varangians of Scandinavia to bring peace to the region. The Varangians soon established a state ruled from Kiev, which they built on bluffs overlooking the Dnieper River, then a major trade route connecting the Baltic Sea to the Byzantine world. Before long, the Rus' state developed into a complex and diverse polity: it swallowed up lands stretching from the Baltic to the Black Sea, from the Carpathians to the Volga, and acquired Jewish, Muslim, Greek, Slavic, and Lithuanian subjects along the way. The Greek missionaries Cyril and Methodius provided the Rus' people with an alphabet and literary Slavic language, and in the tenth century, the Kievan prince Vladimir adopted the Eastern Christian faith of Byzantium and spread it throughout his realm.[1] Although the Rus' polity remained heterogeneous, its leaders forged an "ethnocultural and territorial" identity based on the dynastic state and the literary language used by its Eastern Christian clerics. Indeed, the Rus' identity would prove remarkably resilient, outlasting the Kievan state itself (see map 1.1).[2]

In the thirteenth century, Tatar armies swept across the Eurasian plain, sacking Kiev in 1240 and subordinating the former Rus' lands to the Golden Horde. By the early fourteenth century, the southwestern portion of Rus'—stretching roughly from Galicia (contemporary western Ukraine/southeastern Poland) to the Dnieper's left

---

1. For an overview, see Simon Franklin and Jonathon Shepard, *The Emergence of Rus'* (London, 1996).
2. On Rus' identity and its legacy, see Serhii Plokhy, *The Origins of the Slavic Nations* (New York, 2006), 10–48. The quote is from 33.

Map 1.1
Rus' principalities, eleventh century

bank—had managed to cast off Mongol rule, and by midcentury, these areas had been incorporated into Grand Duchy of Lithuania. The northeastern portion of the former Rus' lands (today located in western and northern Russia), remained subordinated to the Golden Horde until the fifteenth century. Although the former Rus' lands were now divided, the rulers of both segments cast themselves as the rightful successors of the Kievan princes. The Lithuanian princes, who ultimately embraced Catholicism, which they spread across their domains, enjoyed territorial control over the former Rus' heartland. The leaders of the northeastern principalities boasted that they had preserved the Orthodox faith of Rus' (the Orthodox metropolitan of Kiev fled north in 1299 and ultimately installed himself in the rapidly growing polity of Muscovy). On this basis, they claimed to be the true heirs of the Kievan princes.[3]

Threatened by the continued expansion of Muscovy, the Grand Duchy of Lithuania sought an alliance with its larger neighbor, Poland. The rapprochement between the two powers ultimately resulted in the creation of the Polish-Lithuanian Commonwealth in 1569. Catholic nobles from central Poland migrated en masse to the former Rus' lands, where they established huge agricultural estates. Although the movement of the szlachta east made Polish culture and the Catholic Church the dominant forces in the region, the Commonwealth's leaders affirmed the rights of the region's diverse inhabitants to maintain their own cultural traditions. The Polish kings ennobled Orthodox families who traced their origins to the Rus' state, although they encouraged these elites to convert to Catholicism and to embrace Polish culture. Armenians, Lutherans, and Jews settled in cities, where they established a bustling grain trade and enjoyed self-governance rights under Magdeburg law (Germanic city code). Proud citizens of the Commonwealth, these notables prided themselves on having brought European civilization to a region that had been depopulated and isolated since the Tatar invasion.[4]

Although the Commonwealth treated elites of many faiths as valued members of society, it also enslaved millions of peasants. The Commonwealth's serfs represented a variety of confessional and linguistic groups, but the majority on its eastern fringes were Orthodox believers who spoke regional East Slavic dialects. As the szlachta's demands on peasants gradually grew more onerous, thousands of serfs fled to the eastern and southern borders of the Commonwealth. There, on the steppe east of the Dnieper and on the islands amid the river's southern rapids, they mixed with Tatars and refugees from Muscovy, creating a new society of Cossacks—a free martial caste that elected its own leaders and offered its services to Commonwealth, Muscovite, and Ottoman armies.[5]

---

3. Ibid., 49–160.
4. On the Polish-Lithuanian elite and concepts of civic belonging in the Commonwealth, see N. M. Iakovenko, *Ukrains'ka shliakhta z kintsia XIV do seredyny XVII st.* (Kiev, 1993); Daniel Stone, *The Polish-Lithuanian State* (Seattle, 2001); Snyder, *Reconstruction*, 15–25, 105–17. On the Commonwealth and its "civilizing mission," see Joachim Bartoszewicz, *Na Rusi* (Kiev, 1912).
5. On the origins of the Cossacks, see Serhii Plokhy, *The Cossacks and Religion in Early Modern Ukraine* (New York, 2002), 16–26.

By the early seventeenth century, however, the relationship between the Cossacks and the leaders of the Commonwealth had become strained. The Polish kings struggled to expand their political control over Cossack regiments, which frequently engaged in brigandage and unauthorized raids into foreign territory. Cossack generals pressed back, demanding lower tax burdens, more autonomy in their private affairs, and land grants to honor their service to the state.[6] In spite of the diverse origins of the Cossacks, their leaders soon began to think of themselves as defenders of the Orthodox faith that had been forged in the Dnieper region—an area they referred to interchangeably as Rus', Little Russia, and Ukraine. Meanwhile, the confessionalization of Cossack identity heightened the tensions between Cossack leaders and the Commonwealth's non-Orthodox elites.[7]

As the Reformation and Counter-Reformation swept Europe, religious strife spread across the Polish-Lithuanian state. By the late sixteenth century, the Commonwealth's religious policy had grown distinctly less tolerant: the Polish kings limited the political rights of Orthodox believers and dispatched Jesuits to convert them to Catholicism. After protests from Orthodox clergy, in 1596 the Commonwealth's leaders offered Orthodox believers a compromise, reaffirming the rights of local parishioners to retain Orthodox traditions and sacraments provided they recognized the authority of the Roman pope. The ensuing agreement, which created the new Uniate (or Greek Catholic) Church, only heightened religious tensions, however. Clerics and laymen who remained loyal to the Orthodox Church denounced the Union as an abomination and turned to the Muscovite tsar for support, begging him to protect the Eastern rite that had been forged in Rus'.[8] Polish kings and Catholic clergy tended to support the Greek Catholic Church, whose potential to undermine Orthodox claims on the region they recognized.[9]

In the aftermath of the Union, educated residents of the Commonwealth who remained loyal to the Orthodox Church intensified their struggle to protect the rights of their co-confessionalists. In the 1630s, Petr Mogila (1596–1646), the Orthodox bishop of Kiev, launched an ambitious campaign to revive the Orthodox Church and Rus' cultural traditions on the Commonwealth's eastern fringes. He founded a network of schools to educate Orthodox clergy (its flagship institution was the Mogila Collegium, located in Kiev), spearheaded the publication of materials in Church Slavonic and other East Slavic tongues, and used a combination of suasion and force to wrest churches and monasteries—including Kiev's symbolically important St. Sophia Cathedral, which had been built by the Rus' princes—from Greek Catholic

---

6. Mykhailo Hrushevsky, *History of Ukraine-Rus'*, ed. Serhii Plokhy and Frank Sysyn, vols. 7–8 (Edmonton, 1999–2002); Plokhy, *Cossacks*, 26–48.
7. Plokhy, *Cossacks*, 100–144.
8. Plokhy, *Origins*, 230.
9. On confessional struggles in this period, see Kazimierz Chodynicki, *Kościół prawosławny a Rzeczpospolita Polska* (Warsaw, 1934); M. V. Dmitriev, B. N. Floria, and S. G. Iakovenko, eds., *Brestkaia uniia 1596 g. i obshchestvenno-politicheskaia bor'ba na Ukraine i v Belorusii v kontse XVI–nachale XVII v.* (Moscow, 1996).

control.[10] Although Cossack leaders generally approved of the hard line that Mogila had adopted against the Uniates, they accused Orthodox hierarchs of establishing too friendly a relationship with Catholic notables. In the 1620s and '30s, Cossack regiments organized a series of attacks on the szlachta, which they explained as efforts to defend the "ancient Greek faith" against its "enemies."[11]

In the mid-seventeenth century, the ongoing efforts of Cossacks to protect their corporate rights collided with intensifying confessional conflicts, producing an explosion of epic proportions. In 1648, Bohdan Khmelnytsky (1595–1657), the commander of the Zaporozhian Cossacks, declared war on the Polish-Lithuanian state. Khmelnytsky was determined to curb infringements on Cossack freedoms, from which he personally had suffered. (Shortly before the revolt, Khmelnytsky had become embroiled in a bitter dispute with a Polish provincial official, who had harassed him for failing to pay an ox tax; when the Cossack denounced the official to his superiors, the official kidnapped Khmelnytsky's young son and beat him to death.)[12] Whatever their personal motivations, however, Khmelnytsky and his fellow Cossacks explained their struggle as a religious war to defend the Orthodox world from dangerous external threats.[13] As Cossack forces advanced deep into the Commonwealth's territory, Orthodox serfs joined them, attacking Uniates, the szlachta, and Jews along the way. Orthodox clerics, whose relationship with Cossack leaders had traditionally been troubled, now hailed Khmelnytsky as the "prince of Rus'"; some even lauded his desire to see the Rus' lands "cleansed of all those professing other faiths, Armenians, Jews, and Catholics."[14]

By 1649, Khmelnytsky had pushed the Commonwealth's armies hundreds of miles west of the Dnieper. He founded a Cossack polity known as the Hetmanate that stretched across the newly captured lands on both banks of the Dnieper and was chosen as its first leader by a Cossack council. In 1654, Khmelnytsky forged an alliance with the Muscovite tsar, who pledged to protect the Cossack polity and to support its Orthodox believers in the ongoing struggle against the Commonwealth. War and unrest continued to plague the region for another twenty years, and the Commonwealth eventually recaptured some of the right-bank lands that it had lost in Khmelnytsky's initial campaign. In 1667, the Commonwealth and Muscovy finally signed a

---

10. On Mogila's campaigns and influence, see Hrushevsky, *History*, 8:140–46; Ihor Ševčenko, *Ukraine between East and West* (Edmonton, 1996), 164–86.
11. Plokhy, *Cossacks*, 133–44. The quotes are from 141–42.
12. Hrushevsky, *History*, 8:382–83.
13. Plokhy, *Cossacks*, 176–206; Hrushevsky, *History*, 8:655–718. The origins and aims of the Khmelnytsky revolt remain a subject of substantial controversy. Hrushevsky saw the social concerns of the peasant masses as its driving force. The interwar historian Viacheslav Lypyns'kyi, by contrast, interpreted it as an attempt by Cossack elites to build their own state. See Viacheslav Lypyns'kyi, *Ukraina na perelomi* (Vienna, 1920). Serhii Plokhy portrays the revolt as a religious war; some Ukrainian historians and politicians hail Khmelnytsky as the founder of a Ukrainian nation. For a short overview of efforts to make sense of Khmelnytsky's legacy over the centuries, see Frank Sysyn, "The Changing Image of the Hetman," *Jahrbücher für Geschichte Osteuropas* 46, no. 4 (1998): 531–45.
14. Hrushevsky, *History*, 8:518–19.

treaty ending the conflict. The agreement returned the right bank (with the exception of the city of Kiev) to the Commonwealth and officially incorporated the eastern half of the Hetmanate into Muscovy. The agreement forced the Cossacks to renounce their claims to the right bank, but it offered them substantial autonomy within their left-bank domains, which encompassed much of contemporary central Ukraine (see map 1.2).[15]

The Cossack Hetmans destroyed the Commonwealth's estate system in their new domains, expelling the great Polish magnates and redistributing their land among themselves. They reclassified local Orthodox serfs as free Cossack peasants, relieving them of their former obligations. Continuing to present themselves as the defenders of the region's Orthodox believers, Cossack leaders banned the Uniate Church, offered tax exemptions to Orthodox churches and monasteries, and established a dense network of schools and publishing houses that churned out materials in Church Slavonic as well as East Slavic vernaculars. These policies—coupled with the flight of Catholics and Jews out of the Hetmanate—permitted the Orthodox Church to become the dominant political and intellectual force in the Cossack polity. The Mogila Academy became the largest and most prestigious institution of higher education in the lands controlled by Muscovy, producing clergy, statesmen, and intellectuals who shaped politics and culture across the Orthodox world.[16] In the eighteenth century, clerics from the Hetmanate and the nearby western reaches of the former Rus' state dominated the leadership of the Orthodox Church.[17]

The clerical elites of the Hetmanate who worked to improve the future of the region's Orthodox believers also expressed interest in the distant past. In the 1670s, a Kiev monk published the Kievan Synopsis, the first synthetic history of East Slavic civilization. The Synopsis, which would become the most widely read text in Muscovy, identified the Rus' state as the birthplace of the cultures and religious traditions that now dominated the territory stretching from the Dnieper to the Pacific Ocean. In the eyes of its author, Kiev was far from an outpost on the western fringe of the Orthodox world; rather, it was the spiritual center of the East Slavic homeland that he now referred to simply as "Russia" (*Rossiia*).[18]

---

15. Historians (and post-Soviet politicians) continue to debate the precise nature of the relationship between Muscovy and the Hetmanate in these years. See Hans-Joachim Torke, "The Unloved Alliance: Political Relations between Muscovy and Ukraine in the Seventeenth Century," in *Ukraine and Russia in Their Historical Encounter*, ed. Peter J. Potichnyj, Marc Raeff, Jaroslaw Pelenski, and Gleb N. Žekulin (Edmonton, AB, 1992), 39–66; Serhii Plokhy, "The Ghosts of Pereyaslav," *Europe-Asia Studies* 53, no. 3 (May 2001): 489–505.
16. On the social structure and policies of the Hetmanate, consult Hrushevsky, *History*, vol. 9, bk. 1 (2005) and vol. 9, bk. 2 (2008); Plokhy, *Cossacks*. On its religious policies: Barbara Skinner, *The Western Front of the Eastern Church* (DeKalb, 2009), 88–143. On the Mogila Academy and Hetmanate intellectual life, Max J. Okenfuss, *The Rise and Fall of Latin Humanism in Early Modern Russia* (Leiden, 1995), 45–63.
17. Skinner, *Western Front*, 92.
18. On the Synopsis and its meaning, Zenon E. Kohut, "A Dynastic or Ethno-Dynastic Tsardom? Two Early Modern Concepts of Russia," in *Extending the Borders of Russian History: Essays in Honor of Alfred J. Rieber*, ed. Marsha Siefert (New York, 2003), 17–30; Stephen Velychenko, *National History as Cultural Process* (Edmonton, 1992), 145–46.

Map 1.2
The Cossack Hetmanate and the Russian empire, eighteenth century

The Hetmans and Orthodox clerics thus situated themselves at the very center of the Orthodox world and claimed to defend all Orthodox believers. However, Cossack notables continued to display a deep concern for preserving their corporate status and special privileges—one of the primary concerns that had instigated Khmelnytsky's revolt in the first place. By the late seventeenth century, the Cossack officer class had begun to evolve into a closed hereditary nobility. As this elite grew more powerful in the eighteenth century, it demanded more from the Cossack peasants whom it had emancipated, imposing high tax burdens and corvée duties on villages and rural settlements. By the mid-eighteenth century, most Cossack peasants toiled on land owned by the descendants of Cossack generals or the church, struggling to maintain a meager existence.[19]

Cossack leaders and Orthodox clerics imagined the Hetmanate as a brotherly community of Orthodox believers connected by common linguistic, spiritual, and cultural traditions; their policies had homogenized the population of the left bank substantially. But obvious tensions undergirded the efforts of Hetmanate elites to present the Dnieper region as the center of the Orthodox world and themselves as the defenders of the Rus' people. Deep geopolitical, linguistic, and confessional fault lines continued to transect the region; the Commonwealth remained in control of the lands just to the west of the river, where estate society, the Catholic Church, and the Uniate rite continued to flourish. And in spite of their efforts to style themselves as the defenders of the Orthodox masses, the Cossack generals and their descendants had reconstructed an estate society no less stratified than that which the Khmelnytsky revolt had destroyed.

The Rus' Lands under Russian Rule

In the eighteenth century, the ambiguous political status of the Cossack polity produced growing tensions between local elites and the men who governed the empire. On the one hand, Hetmanate elites played an integral role in Muscovy's evolution into a vast empire. Cossacks served at the front lines in Russia's wars of imperial expansion; the Hetmanate's clerics provided powerful spiritual justifications for the autocracy. The author of the Kievan Synopsis, for all his pride in the role of Little Russia in creating and defending East Slavic civilization, clearly identified the Muscovite tsar as the rightful successor to the Rus' princes. Feofan Prokopovich (1681–1736), a graduate of the Mogila Academy, served as one of Peter the Great's closest advisers and most brilliant ideologists.[20] On the other hand, Cossack elites since Khmelnytsky had struggled to defend their political autonomy and unique traditions against administrative centralization. In the early eighteenth century, Hetman Ivan Mazepa (1639–1709),

---

19. See Lev Okinshevych, *Znachne viis'kove tovarystvo v Ukraini-Het'manshchyni XVII–XVIII st.* (Munich, 1948); V. V. Panashenko, *Sotsial'na elita het'manshchyny* (Kiev, 1995).
20. Okenfuss, *Rise and Fall*.

whose troops were serving Peter the Great in his campaigns against Sweden, became alarmed that the tsar planned to further undermine the historical privileges of the Cossack elite. By 1709, having concluded that an alliance with Sweden would better serve Cossack interests, the Hetman stunned Peter by joining the Swedish army to fight against Russian troops at the Battle of Poltava.[21]

Mazepa's defection marked a decisive turning point in the imperial authorities' relationship with the Hetmanate, initiating a concerted attack on the polity's autonomy. In the immediate aftermath of Poltava, Russian troops razed the Cossack capital and massacred its inhabitants; Orthodox clerics excommunicated Mazepa and burned him in effigy. In the ensuing decades, Peter the Great would continue to enhance imperial oversight of the Hetmanate, appointing a governor to oversee Cossack affairs and constructing a huge fortress in Kiev—a physical reminder that the Russian state would be watching the Cossacks more closely. Peter's successors continued to retrench the Hetmanate's freedoms. In the late eighteenth century, Catherine II presided over the administrative abolition of the office of Hetman and divided the polity's former domains into three separate provinces ruled by an imperial military governor.[22]

Although the descendants of Cossack generals bemoaned having lost the autonomy that their ancestors had enjoyed, they retained their cultural and political influence even after the demise of the Hetmanate. Imperial bureaucrats officially ennobled the Cossack officer class and affirmed its rights over local peasants. Scions of the left-bank gentry assumed key positions at the imperial court: A. A. Bezborodko, Catherine II's grand chancellor, and V. P. Kochubei, a close aide of Alexander I, are just two of many examples.[23] Meanwhile, left-bank nobles continued to nourish the unique historical consciousness that had emerged under the Hetmanate. In historical chronicles, they celebrated the exploits of their Cossack ancestors and their struggle to protect the Orthodox faith on its embattled western frontier.[24]

---

21. On Mazepa and his motivations, see N. I. Kostomarov, *Mazepa* (Moscow, 1882); Orest Subtelny, *The Mazepists* (Boulder, 1981).
22. On growing state presence in the region in the eighteenth century, see V. S. Ikonnikov, *Kiev v 1654–1855 gg.* (Kiev, 1904), 14–22; Zenon E. Kohut, *Russian Centralism and Ukrainian Autonomy* (Cambridge, MA, 1988).
23. Little research has been done on the administrative structure and cultural life of the Hetmanate leading up to and immediately following its absorption into the empire. For general overviews, see Kohut, *Russian Centralism*, 237–98; Serhii Plokhy, *The Cossack Myth* (New York, 2012), 131–350.
24. Frank E. Sysyn, "The Cossack Chronicles and the Development of Modern Ukrainian Culture and National Identity," *Harvard Ukrainian Studies*, 14, no. 3–4 (1990): 593–607; Zenon E. Kohut, "Origins of the Unity Paradigm: Ukraine and the Construction of Russian National History (1620–1860)," *Eighteenth-Century Studies* 35, no. 1 (2001): 70–76. As the title of Sysyn's piece suggests, historians have tended to interpret the local patriotism and nostalgia for the Hetmanate that these chronicles express as evidence of a developing Ukrainian national project. I argue, by contrast, that the Cossack chroniclers expressed such pride in the feats of their ancestors primarily because they believed that they had defended the entire Orthodox world from exogenous onslaughts. Conflicts between the Hetmanate and Muscovy about the status of the Cossack polity are of far less interest to their authors than the struggle between the Orthodox East Slavs on the one hand and Poles, Jews, and Uniates on the other.

While left-bank nobles preserved their cultural traditions and political influence even after the imperial absorption of the Hetmanate, the Polish-controlled right bank experienced rapid transformations in the eighteenth century. Since the establishment of the Hetmanate, a steady stream of szlachta and Jews had fled the Cossack polity and its strongly pro-Orthodox policies for the eastern reaches of the Commonwealth. There the szlachta expanded its land holdings; Jews congregated in cities, shtetls, and on szlachta estates, where they worked as estate managers and held long-term leases on rural land.[25] As the non-Orthodox assumed an ever-more prominent role in local society, the right bank's Orthodox communities (composed mostly of serfs in isolated rural locales) found themselves under increasing pressure to join the Uniate rite. And as confessional and social conflicts became more intertwined, the Commonwealth's society grew less stable. At three points over the eighteenth century, Orthodox believers decrying the suppression of their faith and their "exploitation" by the non-Orthodox attacked Uniate villages, szlachta, and Jews in massive jacqueries collectively known as the Haidamak revolts.[26]

Over the eighteenth century, the entrenched Orthodox elite in the left bank expressed growing concern about the welfare of the right bank's Orthodox believers. Cossack units and Orthodox clerics routinely crossed the Dnieper to offer moral and material support to their co-confessionalists; some even joined the Haidamak revolts.[27] Perhaps in reaction to the intense and intertwined social and confessional strife unfolding on the right bank, left-bank gentry chroniclers again reinterpreted the seventeenth-century Cossack revolts, which they now portrayed as struggles between distinct ethnonational communities. Presenting "Poles" (*liakhy*) and Jews as monolithic groups that historically had exploited Orthodox believers, they perceived an equally coherent Rus' or Little Russian *narod* stretching across both banks of the Dnieper.[28]

Ultimately, however, it would not be Little Russian notables who determined the fate of the right bank but the great powers. Beginning in 1772, Prussia, Austria, and Russia colluded to destroy the Commonwealth and to partition its lands. In the second of three partitions, in 1793, Russia claimed the land west of the Dnieper and east of the Zbruch River, dividing the new territorial acquisitions into the provinces of Kiev, Volynia, and Podolia, which collectively became known as the southwestern region. Catherine II boasted that she had united under Russian rule the former domains of Rus' (with the exception of Galicia, which lay beyond the newly formed Austrian border), and she soon launched an ambitious campaign to strengthen the Orthodox

---

25. On the economy and society of the eighteenth-century Commonwealth, see Stone, *Polish-Lithuanian State*, 289–335; Gershon David Hundert, *Jews in Poland-Lithuania in the Eighteenth Century* (Berkeley, 2004), especially 32–56.
26. Skinner, *Western Front*, 112–95.
27. Ibid., 105–111, 131–33.
28. See, for example, Samiilo Velychko, *Litopys* (Kiev, 1991), and Hryhorij Hrabjanka's *The Great War of Bohdan Xmel'nyc'kyj* (Cambridge, MA, 1991). On the evolving portrayal of Jews in Cossack chronicles, see Zenon E. Kohut, "The Khmelnytsky Uprising, the Image of Jews, and the Shaping of Ukrainian Historical Memory," *Jewish History* 17, no. 2 (2003): 141–63.

Church in the southwest and to convert local Uniates.[29] But though the empress and her inner circle claimed that the right bank was an integral part of the Orthodox world, they did not share the left-bank gentry's view of the Dnieper region as the center of East Slavic civilization. The imperial court's official historians traced the origins of the Orthodox Church and Russian state to Rus', but they devoted little attention to the region after the demise of the Kievan state. They emphasized the role of the Muscovite princes and Russian tsars rather than local residents or clerics in defending Orthodoxy and "gathering" the Rus' lands (see map 1.3).[30]

The bureaucrats who administered Russia's southwestern borderlands showed no more interest than their St. Petersburg superiors in the ethnonational conceptions of community that Hetmanate elites had presented as an alternative to estate society. Indeed, they forcefully affirmed the estate structures that the Commonwealth had created in the right bank, leaving the unique socioeconomic order that they found there virtually unchanged. They absorbed the szlachta, which by the early nineteenth century was 97 percent Catholic and Polish-speaking, into the empire's noble ranks, affirming its corporate rights over local peasants (even the Orthodox believers among them).[31] Jewish mercantile elites and professionals maintained their close ties to the szlachta and their privileged position in society, joining the region's greatest magnates at the lavish dinners and balls that accompanied the colossal trade fair held in Kiev every winter.[32] Tsar Alexander I reconfirmed the right of the southwest's cities—many of which boasted majority non-Orthodox populations—to govern themselves under Magdeburg law.[33] Polish remained the dominant language of high culture and education, and imperial administrators even staffed their offices with the same Polish-speaking bureaucrats who had served the Commonwealth.[34]

In the wake of the Napoleonic wars, modern nationalism began to penetrate the Russian empire. On the right bank, the szlachta expressed particular interest in the romantic, völkisch ideas emerging from the German states, producing documentary histories and sentimental sketches of folk customs in a region that Polish patriots considered an integral part of their partitioned nation. By the 1820s and '30s, these efforts had begun to support a clear Polish nationalist agenda. Cataloging the distinct culture and language of right-bank peasants, Polish-speaking Catholics who dreamed of the

---

29. Skinner, *Western Front*, 196–225.
30. David B. Saunders, "Historians and Concepts of Nationality in Early Nineteenth-Century Russia," *Slavonic and East European Review* 60, no. 1 (January 1982): 44–47; Cynthia Hyla Whittaker, "The Idea of Autocracy among Eighteenth-Century Russian Historians," in *Historiography of Imperial Russia*, ed. Thomas Sanders (Armonk, NY, 1999), 17–44.
31. Ikonnikov, *Kiev*, 97–98.
32. On the contract fair and its associations with Jewish and Polish elites, see Henryk Ułaczyn, *Kontrakty kijowskie* (St. Petersburg, 1900); F. Ernst, *Kontrakty i kontraktovyi budynok u Kyivi* (Kiev, 1924).
33. I. Kamanin, *Poslednie gody Samoupravleniia Kieva po Magdeburgskomu Pravu* (Kiev, 1888); Volodymyr Shcherbyna, "Kyiv v 20-r rokakh XIX stolittia," *Ukraina* 3 (1925): 112–18.
34. For overviews of the administration and high culture of the southwest, see Daniel Beauvois, *Pourvoir russe et noblesse polonaise en Ukraine* (Paris, 2003); Wandycz, *Lands*, 3–102.

The Little Russian Idea and the Invention of a Rus' Nation

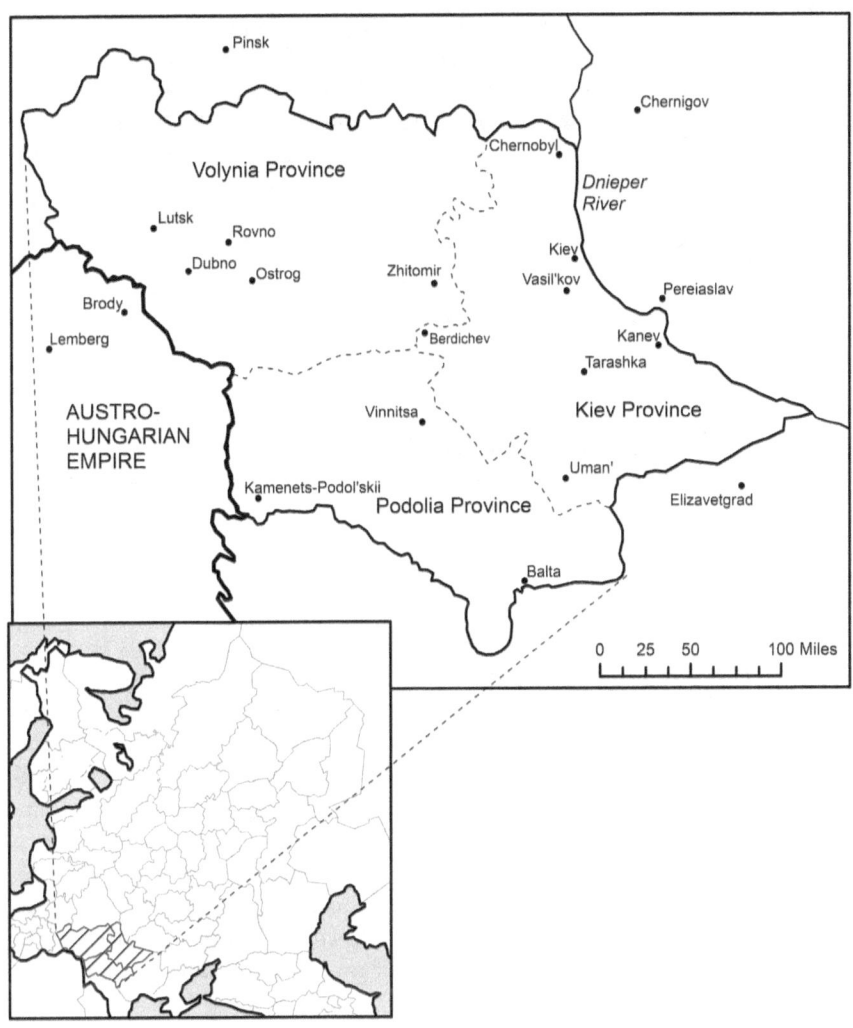

Map 1.3
Russia's southwestern borderlands

resurrection of the Commonwealth argued that the right bank was not and never had been part of Russian civilization.[35]

Although the left-bank gentry decried the agenda of the right-bank's Polish patriots, it also emulated their tactics. Ivan Kotliarevskii (1769–1838), a decorated military

---

35. On the role of Polish historians in introducing national ideas to imperial historiography, see Saunders, "Historians," 44–62; Velychenko, *National History*, 16–26.

veteran of Poltava Cossack stock, began to write plays and poetry in the Ukrainian tongue of the local peasantry; meanwhile, scholars at Khar'kov University compiled folk songs and proverbs. Each of these genres portrayed the local narod as deeply devoted to the Orthodox faith and the cultural traditions that it had inherited from Rus'.[36] The "Istoriia Rusov" ("History of the People of Rus'"), an anonymous tract circulated among the Poltava and Chernigov gentry in the early nineteenth century, reflected the growing influence of national ideas as well, presenting the Dnieper region as the site of an epic battle between bounded and mutually opposed ethnonational groups. Charging that Jews and Poles had intentionally conspired to oppress the children of Rus' and to degrade the traditions that they had inherited from their ancestors, the chronicle celebrated the exploits of the Cossack generals who had struggled "to cleanse Little Russian cities and villages of the Polish administration, the Uniate rite, and Jewry [Zhidovstvo] and to resurrect in them older customs and freedoms based on the law and the customs of the Rus' people [Ruskie]."[37]

A handful of officials recognized the potential of the nationalizing vision developing in the left bank to serve the imperial state. Prince N. G. Repnin (1778–1845), the military governor of the left bank, noted that the Little Russian idea aggressively promoted the Orthodox Church and East Slavic culture in a contested frontier zone that growing numbers of Polish patriots claimed as an integral part of the Catholic world. Defending the cultural activities of the left-bank gentry before his St. Petersburg superiors, Repnin even lobbied for the restoration of Cossack autonomy.[38] D. N. Bantysh-Kamenskii (1788–1850), who had directed Repnin's chancery and later went on to serve as the governor of several provinces, concurred with Repnin. The widely read history of Little Russia that he penned in the 1820s—and dedicated to Tsar Nicholas I—echoed the central themes of "Istoriia Rusov." It assigned the Dnieper region a leading role in East Slavic history and traced the efforts of local residents to defend themselves from the "Yids" (zhidy) and Poles who supposedly had attempted to destroy their values. Embellishing earlier allegations that Jews and Poles had conspired to torment the children of Rus', Bantysh-Kamenskii charged that Jews with whom the szlachta had entrusted keys to Orthodox churches had stolen ritual objects and sold them for their own profit.[39]

---

36. On early Little Russian responses to romantic nationalism, see Miller, *Ukrainian Question*, 50–52; Bilenky, *Romantic Nationalism*. Both works make the point that the rival national projects emerging in the Ukrainian lands were very much in dialogue with each other.
37. Quote from *Istoriia rusov ili Maloi Rossii* (Moscow: Universitetskaia tipografiia, 1846), 80. For an investigation of the cultural milieu from which this text arose, see Plokhy, *Cossack Myth*. On the text's continuities with and divergences from earlier Cossack chronicles, consult Zenon E. Kohut, "The Image of Jews in Ukraine's Intellectual Tradition," *Harvard Ukrainian Studies* 22 (1998): 343–58. Many authors—including the two cited above—emphasize the text's importance in the creation of a Ukrainian historical narrative. As Plokhy notes, however, its author referred to the Cossacks as the defenders of the Rus' (or sometimes, "Russkii") people and presented Little Russia as an integral part of the Orthodox, East Slavic world. See Plokhy, *Cossack Myth*, 59, 166–69.
38. Valentyna Shandra, *Malorosiis'ke heneral-hubernatorstvo* (Kiev, 2001), 108–73.
39. D. N. Bantysh-Kamenskii, *Istoriia Maloi Rossii* (Moscow, 1830). This allegation appears on 217.

However, other officials—and most important, Nicholas I—remained suspicious of the Little Russian idea.[40] And for good reason: efforts to identify the Dnieper region as the spiritual center of East Slavic civilization and to reimagine the empire as a conglomeration of competing ethnonational groups posed obvious risks to the tsarist regime. The left-bank gentry's conception of a Rus' nation was founded on local particularism and a nostalgic longing for the freedoms and pure Orthodox traditions that their Cossack ancestors had supposedly enjoyed. It highlighted moments of discord and violence in a state that valued order and stability. And it implicitly challenged the validity of the estate system on which the imperial state continued to rely, perceiving cohesive and bounded national communities where tsarist bureaucrats saw only stratified social castes.

In spite of the extent to which it had energized the left-bank gentry, the Little Russian idea remained a fantasy. The notion that the Orthodox children of Rus' had been at war for centuries against Polish and Jewish adversaries seriously distorted the history of both the Rus' polity and the Commonwealth. Furthermore, the realities of everyday life in the early nineteenth century militated against the claims made by Little Russian patriots. For all the confessional strife that continued to grip the empire's southwestern borderlands, diverse local communities remained mutually interdependent: szlachta clans that had fallen into poverty toiled alongside Orthodox and Uniate serfs; Gentile peasants relied on Jewish middlemen and merchants and lived in close proximity to the residents of rural shtetls. Only decisive intervention from above would transform the Little Russian idea into something more than a reflection of the long-standing social and political interests of a minuscule gentry class.

"Orthodoxy, Autocracy, and Nationality" and the Right Bank

In November 1830, a band of Polish patriots attacked Russian imperial troops as they slept in their Warsaw garrison. The surprise assault soon evolved into a regional insurrection, which united Polish gentry across the western borderlands in an effort to resurrect an independent Polish state.[41] Although imperial troops managed to defeat the insurgency by the fall of 1831, the revolt instituted a deep crisis among officials, who were now forced to acknowledge that the imperial estate system could no longer guarantee the loyalty of the szlachta who had heeded the siren call of nationalism. In the years to come, Nicholas I and his inner circle would embark on a search for new principles and institutions capable of unifying loyal imperial subjects and defeating the threat of Polish nationalism.

Nicholas I's minister of education, Count S. S. Uvarov, was among the first to formulate a response to this challenge. Having spent much of the Napoleonic era living in Europe, he admired the mobilizational power of national ideas even as he recognized

---

40. Indeed, Repnin was accused of harboring "separatist" sympathies. Shandra, *Malorosiis'ke heneral-hubernatorstvo*, 19.
41. On 1830–31 in the southwest provinces, see *Pamiętnik Kijowski* (London, 1959), 1:74–77.

the challenge that they posed to the empire's stability.[42] By 1833, Uvarov had identified "Autocracy, Orthodoxy, and Nationality" as the "principles which form the distinctive character of Russia, and which belong only to Russia... [and] gather into one whole the sacred remnants of Russian nationality."[43] Convinced that these concepts could rally the tsar's subjects against the threat posed by Polish patriots without challenging the fundamental integrity of the government or the estate system, he commanded his subordinates to craft policies inspired by this sacred trinity.

Guided by Uvarov's concept of "Official Nationality," imperial officials aggressively struggled to enhance the power of the autocracy and the Orthodox Church in the southwestern borderlands. In 1832, Nicholas appointed the first governor-general of Kiev, Podolia, and Volynia, whom he directed to "merge" (*sliiat'*) the right bank with the Russian interior. The governor-general's office identified and punished Polish nobles who had joined the insurrection, stripped of their noble ranks szlachta families who could not produce documentary proof of their social status, replaced Polish banks and schools with state institutions, and revoked Magdeburg law.[44] Nowhere was the imperial state's effort to consolidate its control over the borderlands more apparent than in the city of Kiev, the seat of the southwestern governor-general. Between the 1830s and '50s, an ambitious urban planning campaign transformed the ramshackle and underpopulated city—whose population of 35,000 inhabitants was less than half the size it had been at the pinnacle of Rus' power[45]—into a model imperial city. Engineers widened Kiev's narrow alleys into grand boulevards, built bridges over the deep ravines that divided its hilltop neighborhoods, and gave the city's new landmarks names that invoked autocratic power (Tsar's and Elizabeth's Boulevards), the might of the tsarist state's military and police apparatus (Gendarme and Cadet Ways), and the memory of Rus' (Iaroslav's Embankment).[46]

As they worked to consolidate autocratic power in the borderlands, officials struggled to claim the confessionally heterogeneous borderlands as a primordially Orthodox locale. The Kiev governor-general's office convened special archeological committees that excavated ancient churches and other remnants of Orthodox Rus'; in the 1850s it erected a statue of St. Vladimir, the Kievan prince who had embraced Eastern Christianity, towering over the Dnieper's cliffs with a cross in hand.[47] Meanwhile, imperial bureaucrats struggled to reduce the influence of other confessional

---

42. On Uvarov's background and the European provenance of his ideas, see Cynthia H. Whittaker, *The Origins of Modern Russian Education* (DeKalb, 1984); A. L. Zorin, "Ideologiia 'Pravoslaviia—samoderzhaviia-narodnosti' i ee nemetskie istochniki," in *V razdum'iakh o Rossii* (Moscow, 1996), 105–28. On other official efforts to accommodate the tsarist system to the challenge of nationalism in the wake of Napoleon, see Alexander M. Martin, *Romantics, Reformers, Reactionaries* (DeKalb, 1997).
43. Quote from Nicholas V. Riasanovsky, *Russian Identities* (New York, 2005), 133.
44. Daniel Beauvois, *La Bataille de la Terre en Ukraine, 1863–1914* (Lille, 1993), 19–20; Valentyna Shandra, *Kyivs'ke heneral-hubernatorstvo* (Kiev, 1999), 13–30.
45. Ikonnikov, *Kiev,* 198.
46. M. O. Rybakov, *Nevidomi ta malovidomi storinki istorii Kyeva* (Kiev, 1997), 185–90.
47. A description of these early efforts is included in "Delo o provedenii rabot po predokhraneniiu ot razrusheniia pamiatnika 'Zolotye vorota,'" 1868–69, DAK, f. 17, op. 4, d. 949.

Monument to St. Vladimir, erected in the 1850s. Source: *Vidy Kieva* (Kiev, 1917). Courtesy of Slavonic Library, National Library of Finland.

communities. They intensified their efforts to convert Uniates, whom officials claimed had been led astray from true Orthodox traditions by Polish notables and Jesuits. In 1839, the imperial authorities dissolved the Greek Catholic church in the borderlands, "reuniting" its members with the Orthodox rite.[48] Deeming the presence of Jews unseemly in a place they were reinventing as the "cradle of Russian Orthodoxy," local bureaucrats excluded Kiev from the Pale of Settlement and expelled its Jewish population en masse.[49]

Concomitant with imperial officials' efforts to promote the Orthodox Church as the native faith of the right bank came a drive to create a new Orthodox elite. Bureaucrats founded a university in Kiev, intended to replace the University of Vil'na, which was closed after it became a major organizational center for Polish rebels.

---

48. M. L. Moroshkin, "Vozsoedinenie Unii," *Vestnik Evropy* 35 (1872): 588–648; 36 (1872): 60–111; 37 (1872): 524–93. The effort to promote the Orthodox faith was not limited to the southwest. On post-1830 religious policy in the northwest, see Daniel C. Ryan, "The Tsar's Faith: Conversion, Religious Politics, and Peasant Protest in Imperial Russia's Baltic Periphery, 1845–1870s" (PhD diss., UCLA, 2008); Dolbilov, *Russkii krai*, 68–108.
49. Hamm, *Kiev*, 119–20.

As the institution's name—St. Vladimir's—indicates, officials hoped that it would create an Orthodox cultural elite that would support imperial rule and gradually supplant the influence of local Polish Catholic notables.⁵⁰ Following a brief closure in the early nineteenth century, the former Mogila Collegium reopened as the Kiev Theological Academy; it would soon join the ranks of imperial Russia's most elite clerical institutions.⁵¹ The governor-general's office instituted new tax incentives that encouraged entrepreneurs in the Russian interior to resettle in the southwest; the St. Petersburg ministries banned new appointments of non-Orthodox believers to posts in the southwest and reassigned Orthodox officials posted in interior provinces to the borderlands.⁵²

By the midthirties, officials had made great strides in promoting autocracy and orthodoxy in the newly claimed right bank. But what would it mean for bureaucrats to develop awareness of nationality in the southwest? Uvarov himself had struggled to adapt the term to suit the ideological needs of the Russian imperial state. Having composed his original notes on the Official Nationality doctrine in French, Uvarov was well aware of the term's etymological connection to the French Revolution and eager to strip it of its inherent ideological dangers. When it came time to translate his doctrine into Russian, he avoided rendering the original *nationalité* with the Latin calque *natsional'nost'*. Instead, he opted for *narodnost'*, which like the German *Volkstum* referred more to the traditions and everyday life of the peasantry than to dreams of popular sovereignty.⁵³ Over the course of the 1830s, Nicholas I and a coterie of conservative ideologists who surrounded him imagined the narod as loyal devotees of the Orthodox Church and their beneficent "little father," the tsar; thus the defenders of the regime invoked the concept of nationality to buttress the power of the autocracy and the Orthodox Church.⁵⁴

In the Dnieper region, however, the Little Russian idea—a creation of local elites rather than tsarist bureaucrats—became the centerpiece of efforts to identify the area's native essence. In writings such as *Evenings on a Farm Near Dikanka* (1831–32), the Poltava noble Nikolai Gogol (1809–1852) presented the Little Russian narod as the true embodiment of the values and culture of the East Slavs and a potential source of spiritual renewal for the entire Orthodox world; *Taras Bul'ba* (1835) chronicled the seventeenth-century struggle of the Zaporozhian Cossacks to destroy the Commonwealth's feudal system and to defend Orthodox traditions and Rus' unity

---

50. Johannes Remy, *Higher Education and National Identity* (Helsinki, 2000), Ol'ha Tarasenko, *Stanovlennia ta rozvytok istorychnoi osvity i nauky u Kyivs'komu Universyteti u 1834–1884 rr.* (Kiev, 1995).
51. See F. Titov, "Preobrazovaniia dukhovnykh akademii v Rossii v XIX v.," *Trudy Kievskoi Dukhovnoi Akademii* 4 (1906): 622–66.
52. Minister of Internal Affairs D. G. Bibikov to Kiev Governor-General I. I. Vasil'chikov, 6 February 1855, TsDIAUK, f. 442, op. 805, d. 474, ll. 1–2.
53. Andrei Zorin, "Ideologiia 'Pravoslaviia-samoderzhaviia-narodnosti': Opyt rekonstruktsii," *Novoe literaturnoe obozrenie* 26 (1997): 71–104. For more on the term *narodnost'*, see Knight, "Ethnicity, Nationality and the Masses," 41–64.
54. Nicholas V. Riasanovsky, *Nicholas I and Official Nationality in Russia* (Berkeley, 1959).

against foreign incursions.⁵⁵ The magisterial history of Little Russia written in 1840 by the Chernigov noble and military official N. A. Markevich (1804–1860) echoed Gogol's central themes. Following the struggles of Cossack generals and Orthodox clerics against Poles, Uniates, and Jews, it claimed that the fierce battles on the western boundary of the Orthodox world had saved "Ukraine"—and all the East Slavic children of Rus'—from dangerous internal enemies.⁵⁶

Indeed, in the decade after 1830, defenders of the tsarist regime with no personal connections to the southwest began to express interest in the role that the Dnieper region had played in crafting the cultures that would ultimately become associated with East Slavic civilization as a whole. In sharp contrast to eighteenth- and early-nineteenth-century official histories of the empire, which had all but ignored the southwest after the collapse of Rus', N. G. Ustrialov's 1837 history of Russia—praised by both Nicholas I and Uvarov and designated as the official history text used in the empire's schools—assigned the region a leading role in the history of the empire. Echoing the claims of the Kievan Synopsis, it presented the borderlands as the very center of the Slavic world—the place where the Orthodox Church had been born, where the foundations of the Russian state had been laid, and where the struggle to maintain the political unity of the Rus' lands continued to unfold.⁵⁷ Imperial interest in Little Russian history and culture only continued to grow in the 1840s, sparked by the establishment of the Imperial Geographic Society, which engaged in ethnographic research, and the 1846 publication of "Istoriia Rusov" by the Society for Russian History and Antiquities.⁵⁸

The Left-Bank Gentry and the De-Polonizing State

It was not happenstance that the evolving discussions about the "native" essence of the East Slavs within the imperial bureaucracy and educated society so often echoed the Little Russian idea. Perceiving an opportunity to advance their historical and political agenda in the post-1830 political climate, dozens of left-bank gentry relocated to Kiev. Once there, they provided much of the ideological power behind the campaign to claim the southwestern borderlands for the empire. The Poltava noble M. V. Iuzefovich (1802–89) accepted a job in the new regional school administration

---

55. Indeed, Uvarov supported Gogol's nomination for a history chair at St. Vladimir's; although the appointment was blocked by bureaucrats who pointed out that the author did not hold a history degree, Gogol eventually secured a position at St. Petersburg University. For one attempt to reconcile Gogol's ardent Little Russian patriotism with his professions of all-Russian national pride, see Edyta M. Bojanowska, *Nikolai Gogol* (Cambridge, MA, 2007).
56. See N. A. Markevich, *Istoriia Malorossii* (Moscow, 1842–43). For biographical information, see "N.A. Markevich," in *Russkie pisateli, 1800–1917: Biograficheskii slovar'* (Moscow, 1994), 3:521–23.
57. On the work's significance, see Kohut, "A Dynastic or Ethno-Dynastic Tsardom?" 26–27; Saunders, "Historians," 60–61.
58. See Paul Bushkovitch, "The Ukraine in Russian Culture, 1790–1860: The Evidence of the Journals," *Jahrbücher für Geschichte Osteuropas* 39, no. 3 (1991): 339–63.

and would soon be promoted to its head. M. A. Maksimovich (1804–73), a Poltava noble and Moscow University professor who had recently compiled a collection of Little Russian folk songs, was appointed the first rector of St. Vladimir's University. Orthodox clerics flooded into the right bank, where they worked to revive local parishes and continued the struggle against the Roman and Greek Catholic rites.[59]

In their official positions and in the imperial press, Kiev's Little Russian activists continued to develop the myth that the Dnieper region was a citadel of East Slavic culture and that its native inhabitants were the true Rus' people, who had fought to defend their traditions from foreign incursions. In his first major publication following his appointment at St. Vladimir's, Maksimovich challenged the historical consensus that Scandinavian Vikings had founded the Rus' state—the so-called Normanist theory—claiming instead that the Rus' government was the product of purely East Slav initiative.[60] In 1840, the scholar launched *Kievlianin (The Kievan)*, a historical almanac dedicated to the "daily life and native cultures" of "southern Rus'"—which, in Maksimovich's view, stretched from the Don River into Austrian Galicia. Compiling documentary evidence that pointed to Kiev as the cradle of the Russian state and people, the journal chronicled the efforts of local Orthodox leaders and Cossacks to preserve the values of the Kievan princes and to maintain the cultural traditions and territorial integrity of the Rus' lands over the centuries.[61]

Eager to coordinate the literary and historical efforts to claim the southwest as a primordially Orthodox locale, in 1843 Kiev's governor-general, D. G. Bibikov, convened the Commission for the Analysis of Historical Documents. Bibikov directed its founding members—Maksimovich, Iuzefovich, local bureaucrats, and elite Orthodox clergy—to consolidate early modern church registers and court documents in order to prevent Poles from forging proof of their noble status or claiming other historical privileges. Commission members fanned out across the countryside, collecting records and organizing an archive to hold them. Along the way, they also assembled a variety of materials related to local history and culture. Soon, the Commission embraced a more ambitious aim—in the words of one member of the group, to "show on the basis of documents that the southwest region truly belonged to the Russian narod; that its polonization began relatively recently; that it was always resisted by the people, who have never completely liberated themselves from Polish power; and that the freedom of religion and popular prosperity will be assured only once the southwest region is definitively subjected to Russian domination."[62] Previously the Little

---

59. O. I. Levitskii, *Piatidesiatiletie Kievskoi Kommissii dlia razbora drevnikh aktov, 1843–1893* (Kiev, 1893), 4–7. On local Orthodox activists as the driving force in the struggle against the Uniate Church, see Barbara Skinner, "Orthodoxy Triumphant? Reassessing the 1839 'Reunification' of Greek Catholics" (unpublished paper, 2011).
60. M. A. Maksimovich, *Otkuda idet russkaia zemlia, po skazaniiu Nestorovoi povesti i po drugim starinnym pisaniiam russkim* (Kiev, 1837).
61. For example, M.A. Maksimovich, *Kievlianin* (Kiev, 1840).
62. Z. [N.A. Rigel'man], "Sovremennoe ukrainofil'stvo," *Russkii vestnik* 2 (1875): 838. For an overview of the Commission's activities, see Patricia Kennedy Grimsted, "Archeography in the Service of Imperial Policy," *Harvard Ukrainian Studies* 17, no. 1–2 (1993): 27–44.

Russian idea had focused on the role that Orthodox clergy and especially Cossack generals had played in defending the native cultures of Rus'. Now the Commission accorded the Orthodox residents of the borderlands a vital role in the struggle for the control of the borderlands.

The documents that Commission members collected presented the narod as victims of foreign domination as well as foot soldiers in the struggle to defend Orthodox traditions. They illuminated the difficult plight of "privately enserfed [*vladel'cheskikh*] peasants of the Russian ethnicity [*russkoi narodnosti*]" under the Commonwealth, revealing that Polish Catholic nobles had subjected their serfs to mass conversions, onerous obligations, and cruel punishments.[63] However, the Commission also celebrated the struggle of peasants and parish priests to protect their Orthodox faith—"the primary basis of narodnost'"—as a form of passive resistance.[64]

In the midforties, a group of young men of mixed social origins joined the Commission. One, G. P. Galagan (1819–88), was the scion of a fabulously wealthy Little Russian clan, which owned vast tracts of land in Chernigov and Poltava provinces and elegant properties in Kiev. Others, such as N. I. Kostomarov (1817–85), a novice St. Vladimir's historian, and P. A. Kulish (1819–97), a gymnasium teacher, came from impoverished left-bank noble families. T. G. Shevchenko (1814–61), who had already gained acclaim for his Ukrainian-language poems highlighting the struggle of local peasants, came from the most modest origins of all: he had been born a serf in Kiev province. Intensely interested in the plight of the narod, they pressed the Commission to further develop its emergent social agenda. As he roamed the countryside assembling documents for the Commission, Kulish collected folk songs and oral histories that chronicled ordinary people's struggle against Polish rule; Shevchenko illustrated Commission pamphlets on Little Russian folk traditions with scenes of "ancient everyday life."[65]

Commission members, who had begun to create a narrative of national struggle in which the local peasantry played an important role, gradually expanded the geographical focus of their activities. Insisting, like Maksimovich, that the region to which they interchangeably referred as "southern Rus'," "southwestern Rus'," "Little Russia," and "western Russia" extended into Austrian Galicia, the Commission recruited members in the Habsburg empire. D. I. Zubritskii (1777–1862), a distinguished Lemberg-based scholar of Galician history and folklore who joined the group, argued that the Little Russian people on both sides of the Russo-Austrian border constituted an unbreakable whole.[66] Leading Commission members traveled to Vienna, where they acquainted themselves with the plight of the "Russians" living in that empire (that is, Ukrainian-speaking East Slavs of the Orthodox or Greek Catholic

---

63. Levitskii, *Piatidesiatiletie*, 26.
64. *Pamiatniki, izdannye Vremennoiu kommissieiu dlia razbora drevnikh aktov, Vysochaishe uchrezhdennoiu pri Kievskom voennom, Podol'skom i Volynskom General-Gubernatore* (Kiev, 1848), 1:vi.
65. "Pis'ma P.A. Kulisha k M.V. Iuzefovichu (1843–1861 g.g.)," *KS* 64, no. 2 (1899): 191; Levitskii, *Piatidesiatiletie*, 57.
66. On Zubritskii's membership, see Levitskii, *Piatidesiatiletie*, 139. On his activities, Wendland, *Die Russophilen*, 49–56.

confession—a group the Habsburg authorities called "Ruthenians"). When these emissaries returned home, they established scholarship programs to support Austrian subjects who wished to study in the Russian empire.[67]

The activities of the state-sponsored Commission—which presented Orthodox believers of all social stations and even the Ruthenians of the Habsburg empire as valued members of an indivisible nation whose origins could be traced to Rus'—posed obvious challenges to the institutions and ideology of the autocracy. Assigning the Cossacks, clergy, and peasants who populated the fringes of the Orthodox world a leading role in the struggle to defend the children of Rus' from their putative enemies, the group implicitly challenged the notion that the tsar and his state were the motive forces of Russian history. Its sharp condemnations of the Commonwealth's landed elite also raised serious questions about the validity of the estate system on which the imperial state continued to rely. Furthermore, Commission members themselves wondered how the strong local patriotism implicit in the Little Russian idea could be reconciled with the centralizing and standardizing impulses of the post-1830 imperial state. In an 1844 letter to Iuzefovich, Kulish rejoiced that the administrative and political "merging" of Little Russia with the central Russian interior would create a powerful and unified nation that could protect all the children of Rus' from the threats that lurked on the empire's western frontier. At the same time, however, he lamented that the absorption of Little Russia's "magnificent folk life" into all-imperial culture threatened to deprive this elemental force, which had defended Rus' traditions so valiantly, of its power.[68]

Nevertheless, both local and imperial authorities tended to overlook the dangerous potential of the Little Russian idea. Its proponents played a key role in official efforts to defeat the threat of Polish nationalism and in the concomitant campaign to claim the southwestern borderlands as a primordially Orthodox locale. And although the Little Russian lobby had become more socially variegated (and its interest in the peasant masses more pronounced), it remained dominated by loyalist gentry.[69] The Ministry of Education firmly supported the mission of the Kiev Commission, providing funds in the 1850s for the creation of an archive at St. Vladimir's to house the nearly half-million documents that the group had by then collected.[70] Bibikov ignored complaints from szlachta magnates that the Commission's scholarly activities encouraged national and confessional animus in the borderlands; meanwhile, he continued to undercut Polish notables' economic power, imposing new limitations on the obligations

---

67. *Ocherk deiatel'nosti Kievskogo slavianskogo blagotvoritel'nogo obshchestva za 25 let ego sushchestvovaniia* (Kiev, 1894), 58–60, 62.
68. "Pis'ma P.A. Kulisha," 199–200.
69. Indeed, B. N. Repnina (1808–91), the daughter of the military governor of Little Russia who had expressed great interest in the Little Russian idea in the early nineteenth century, was a close friend of Shevchenko: see N. S., "Pamiati kn. V.N. Repninoi," *KS* 36, no. 2 (1892): 312–13.
70. "Tsentral'nye arkhivy drevnikh aktovykh knig: Vilenskii i Kievskii," *Zhurnal ministerstva narodnogo prosveshcheniia* (1883): 37.

that right-bank nobles could demand from their serfs.[71] In his clearest attempt of all to align himself with the Little Russian idea, the governor-general even petitioned the Ministry of the Interior to punish the censors who had permitted Polish patriots to publish negative reviews of Markevich's history of Little Russia; the reviewers, Bibikov complained, had made "insulting" remarks about the Little Russian nationality and displayed "the most pernicious anti-national tendencies."[72]

In the dispute over Markevich's text, Nicholas I expressed more ambivalence about the Little Russian idea than Bibikov had. He opted not to punish the censors who had approved the Poles' response to Markevich, who had defended their actions by arguing that "Little Russia was never a separate political community." Nicholas did, however, encourage Bibikov to continue his attempts to refute the "lies" of Polish patriots through "literary means."[73] Yet in other instances, the tsar himself echoed the rhetoric of the Commission and its Little Russian patriots, presenting southwestern peasants as long-suffering victims of foreign exploitation and faithful defenders of East Slavic traditions. In an 1843 memorandum, Nicholas I argued that the imperial state bore an obligation to improve the plight of "southern Russian" peasants, who had "managed for several centuries to protect their Orthodox faith in all its purity, their ties to Russia, and their ability to faithfully serve their Sovereign, despite the oppression of the Polish szlachta, the Catholic clergy, and the Yids [zhidy]."[74] He promoted Bibikov to the post of minister of internal affairs in 1853, appointing I. I. Vasil'chikov as the new governor-general of the southwest. Vasil'chikov, like his predecessor, presented himself to the St. Petersburg authorities not as the representative of the region's Polish notables but as the defender of its Little Russian peasants.[75]

The Little Russian Idea and the Narod

By the 1840s, an intellectual class of varied origins had begun to emerge from the empire's thick journals and urban salons, staking out space independent of the state and

---

71. On the complaints of the szlachta, see Levitskii, *Piatidesiatiletie*, 37–38, 72. On the limits on peasant obligations, David Moon, "The Inventory Reform and Peasant Unrest in Right-Bank Ukraine in 1847–48," *Slavonic and East European Review* 79, no. 4 (2001): 653–97. The reform followed on the heels of the massive peasant revolts that rocked Galicia in 1846 and was certainly an attempt to forestall similar unrest in the Russian empire.
72. This episode is discussed in Aleksandr Nikitenko, *The Diary of a Russian Censor*, ed. and trans. Helen Saltz Jacobson (Amherst, 1975), 99.
73. Ibid.
74. "Doklad Nikolaia I o deiatel'nosti general-guberatora za 1843 g.," TsDIAUK, f. 442, op. 1, d. 4823, l. 10. Although this quote testifies to Nicholas's special concerns about the threats that he perceived in the borderlands, it also reflects the imperial government's growing suspicion toward great noble magnates, encouraged by the rise of a new class of "enlightened bureaucrats" who were drawn from the low and middling nobility and claimed to serve the interests of the people at large. See W. Bruce Lincoln, *In the Vanguard of Reform* (DeKalb, 1982).
75. For example, "O bedstvennom sostoianii kazenykh krest'ian Volynskoi gubernii," 1855, TsDIAUK, f. 442, op. 805, d. 477. Indeed, in the 1850s, the governor-general considered banning Poles from studying at St. Vladimir's: see Staliunas, *Making Russians*, 101.

officialdom. This group, which by the 1860s would be referred to as the intelligentsia, played an active role in the ongoing effort to define the essence of the Russian people and their proper relationship with the state. One camp of intellectuals, known as Westernizers, saw the empire's autocratic government, estate society, and the collectivist traditions of its peasantry as impediments to its political, economic, and moral development. While a liberal wing of the Westernizers hoped to see the empire evolve into a bourgeois-democratic state founded on the rule of law, a radical wing dreamed of the demise of the tsarist state and its replacement by a democratic, socialist society. Another camp, the Slavophiles, celebrated the peasant commune and Orthodox traditions as the foundations of East Slavic civilization, which they sought to distance from the capitalism and individualism that they believed had corrupted European society. In spite of their support for the Orthodox Church and their insistence on Russia's cultural distinctiveness, many early Slavophile thinkers were rather critical of the autocracy, criticizing the inhumanity of its bureaucratic institutions and the institution of serfdom.[76]

The Little Russian idea occupied a peculiar space in imperial intellectual life, combining socially emancipatory ideas, traditional defenses of Cossack corporate privileges, and a fierce loyalty to Orthodox traditions. Its internal contradictions ultimately served it well, allowing liberal Westernizers, radical intellectuals, and Slavophiles alike to find something to admire in its positions. Westernizers shared Kiev intellectuals' distaste for estate society and their admiration for administrative decentralization; the radical critic A. I. Herzen even envisioned the Cossack Hetmanate as the model for the consensual society of equals he hoped one day would take hold in Russia.[77] Slavophiles cooperated with Little Russian activists interested in folk culture and Orthodox traditions. The Slavophile historian M. P. Pogodin spent much of the 1830s and '40s in Lemberg, cultivating a generation of Ruthenian scholars who sought to pull Galicia out of the orbit of Polish culture and into East Slavic civilization.[78] Ivan Aksakov, who spent substantial time in the southwest conducting research for the Imperial Geographic Society in the 1850s, wrote frequently (and admiringly) about the everyday life and folk traditions of the Little Russian narod.[79]

Meanwhile, Kiev-based proponents of the Little Russian idea, who since 1830–31 had worked within official institutions to define the essential qualities of the Rus' nation, began to organize in venues free from state patronage. In 1845, Kostomarov, Kulish, and Shevchenko, along with several young bureaucrats and St. Vladimir's students, formed the Cyril and Methodius Brotherhood. The group, whose name

---

76. Classic histories of the emergence of the intelligentsia include Malia, *Alexander Herzen*; Walicki, *The Slavophile Controversy*.
77. Maiorova, *From the Shadow of Empire*, 49. A notable exception to this rule was the critic V. G. Belinskii, who heaped scorn on the Ukrainian language and culture. See Andrea Rutherford, "Vissarion Belinskii and the Ukrainian National Question," *Russian Review* 54, no. 4 (1995): 500–515.
78. Wendland, *Die Russophilen*, 53–55.
79. See I. Aksakov, *Issledovanie o torgovle na Ukrainskikh iarmarkakh* (St. Petersburg, 1858). Aksakov also wrote on Little Russian themes regularly in his journal *Den'*.

invoked the Greek missionaries who had given the Slavs their alphabet, aspired to reclaim the "authentic" traditions that its members traced to Rus'. Kostomarov, the author of the group's manifesto, argued that the consensual political culture and federalist traditions that he believed had existed in Rus' were an expression of the true "Slavic spirit." Juxtaposing these traditions—which he argued that the place he interchangeably called Ukraine and Little Russia had preserved faithfully over the centuries—to the autocratic practices that he claimed the Muscovite tsars had learned from "German and Tatar" interlopers, Kostomarov called for a unified federation of Slavic "people's governments" ruled from Kiev—which he declared the "capital of the Slavic race."[80] Founded on the principles of Orthodox brotherhood and social justice, this state would outlaw serfdom and capital punishment, guarantee the cultural autonomy of its members, and disavow "the influence of foreign [*chuzhezemnye*] ideas that are saturated by cosmopolitanism and alien to the Slavic sensibility."[81]

In 1847, a student denounced the Brotherhood to the tsarist authorities. Officials fiercely debated how to respond to the group, which had excoriated the autocracy as an institution even as it claimed to promote Slavic unity and to demonstrate the primordially Orthodox character of the southwest. Noting that Kostomarov had plagiarized parts of its manifesto from a work by the Polish nationalist poet Adam Mickiewicz, some officials expressed concern that the Brotherhood was a separatist conspiracy organized by Poles. Others perceived the group as an outgrowth of the semiofficial Little Russian milieu, noting that the Brotherhood simply echoed themes and ideas that appeared in the works of the Kiev Commission and other texts that had passed through censors.[82] Prominent Kiev Commission members and local notables begged police officials to show mercy to the young men, reminding them of the valuable role that Little Russian patriots had played in the struggle to claim the southwest for the Russian empire.[83]

In a report to Nicholas I summarizing the results of the comprehensive government investigation that ensued, Count A. F. Orlov, the head of the Third Section

---

80. "Zakon Bozhii," in P. S. Sokhan', ed., *Kyrylo-Mefodiievs'ke tovarystvo* (Kiev, 1990), 1:168–69; Thomas M. Prymak, *Mykola Kostomarov* (Toronto, 1996), 44; "Kievskie slavianisty sorokovykh godov," *KS* 56, no. 2 (February 1897): 178. Serhii Plokhy notes that in the late eighteenth and early nineteenth centuries, some authors referred to the left bank of the Dnieper—the old Cossack Hetmanate—as Little Russia and the right bank as Ukraine. See Plokhy, *Cossack Myth*, 144. The Cyrillo-Methodians, by contrast, did not make this distinction, referring to both sides of the Dnieper as both Little Russia and Ukraine. See Brian J. Boeck, "What's in a Name? Semantic Separation and the Rise of the Ukrainian National Name," *Harvard Ukrainian Studies* 27, no. 1–4 (2004–2005): 33–65.
81. "Kievskie slavianisty sorokovykh godov," *KS* 56, no. 2 (1897): 178.
82. See the government and police documents republished in Sokhan, *Kyrylo-Mefodiivs'ke tovarystvo*; for detailed analysis of these debates, see P. A. Zaionchkovskii, *Kirillo-Mefodievskoe obshchestva* (Moscow, 1959).
83. "Opovidanyia A.A. Soltanovs'koho pro kyivs'ke zhyttia 1840-kh rr.," *Ukraina* 3 (1924): 77–98; Sokhan, *Kyrylo-Mefodiivs'ke tovarystvo*, 2:338. Most existing treatments of the Cyrillo-Methodian affair downplay officials' difficulty in ascertaining the true aims of the group; portraying it as an early manifestation of Ukrainian nationalist-separatist tendencies, they miss the group's repeated claims that the East Slavs (and sometimes even the Slavs in general) constitute an indivisible cultural and historical community.

(the tsar's secret political police), argued that the Cyrillo-Methodians' efforts to "locate and protect antiquities, to restore narodnost' in mores and literature" had aimed only to express their "love toward their motherland" and to "strengthen the self-sufficiency and power of the narod" of the right bank. Nevertheless, he expressed concern that similar activities in the future might estrange the empire's "subjugated tribes" (*plemena podvlastnye*) from the imperial center, which could only embolden the Polish nationalists determined to destroy the Russian state.[84] As the authorities enhanced their surveillance of Slavophile activities across the empire, Uvarov sternly warned intellectuals that when discussing the "nationality [narodnost'] or language of Little Russia and the other lands that comprise Russia," they must not allow "love for the motherland to overshadow their love for the fatherland"; they should also avoid discussing "the imagined current suffering or the supposedly fortunate situation of subjugated tribes in the past, so that the works of scholars and writers will reinforce the Russian empire, not Little Russia, Poland, or other separate countries (*strany*)."[85] The Third Section concluded that the Cyrillo-Methodians must be punished for their actions, but it also intervened to mitigate several of their sentences. Officials ordered Kostomarov to serve in the chancery of the Saratov governor and assigned Kulish a similar position in Tula. Shevchenko, who had cursed the tsars for subjugating the narod to Poles and Jews in poems found by the Third Section, received the harshest sentence of all the conspirators—a ban on the publication of his work and one year's imprisonment, followed by a bureaucratic post in Saratov and state service in ethnographic expeditions.[86]

The infiltration of the Cyrillo-Methodian Society coincided with massive peasant revolts that rocked Austrian Galicia and the European revolutions of 1848–49. In the wake of these disturbing developments, Nicholas exhibited a new determination to combat the destabilizing potential of national ideas. He removed Uvarov from office in 1849, and the term *narodnost'* virtually disappeared from official discourse. But because the Little Russian idea had been a key component of the official campaign to defeat Polish nationalism and to enhance imperial authority in the southwestern borderlands, many officials continued to support its proponents. While in exile, Kostomarov, with the full knowledge of the governor he served, continued his ethnographic research, which aspired to unearth the "authentic" traditions of the Little Russian peasantry. (However, when the scholar claimed that two young boys murdered in Saratov had been killed as part of a Jewish blood ritual and launched a historical study of alleged Jewish crimes against Christians, the governor intervened

---

84. Sokhan, *Kyrylo-Mefodiivs'ke tovarystvo*, 3:306–7.
85. Ibid., 3:323.
86. My interpretation of the Cyrillo-Methodian affair is indebted to Zaionchkovskii, *Kirillo-Mefodievskoe obshchestvo* and Miller, *Ukrainian Question*. For Shevchenko's poem and official interpretations of them, see Sokhan, *Kyrylo-Mefodiivs'ke tovarystvo*, 2:225–37, 308–9. V. N. Repnina appealed to Orlov to request that the injunction preventing her friend from drawing be lifted. Although Orlov expressed sympathy for her position, Nicholas apparently refused to grant the request. Ibid., 2:338–44.

to halt Kostomarov's research on this issue.)[87] Back in Kiev, the authorities authorized Iuzefovich and Galagan to organize an ethnographic division under the Kiev school district. Overseeing efforts to document the physical traits of the Little Russian narod and their struggle against foreign incursions, the group would claim more than two hundred members within five years.[88]

Kulish, Kostomarov, and Shevchenko completed their sentences in 1850, 1855, and 1857, respectively, reconvening in St. Petersburg. Although the Third Section intermittently continued to express concern about their activities, the onetime exiles soon became fixtures of the capital's elite bureaucratic and intellectual circles. Kostomarov, appointed to a history chair at St. Petersburg University, published widely on Cossack history and Little Russian folk culture. Kulish, who maintained close ties with Kiev Commission members as well as Moscow Slavophiles in these years, received permission from imperial censors to publish a groundbreaking collection of Ukrainian folklore and literature, a Ukrainian-language primer (using a new, standardized orthography he had developed), and a historical novel about the Hetmanate in both Russian and Ukrainian. Grand Duchess Mariia Nikolaevna, a daughter of Nicholas I and the president of the Imperial Academy of Arts, intervened to ensure that Shevchenko was permitted to enroll in the academy; following his return to the capital, he composed dozens of new poems and secured permission to reprint older collections.[89] By the late 1850s, the returned exiles convened a regular discussion group, which they called the *hromada* (Ukrainian for "community"), in which they discussed their research in progress and coordinated their efforts to publish Ukrainian-language literature in both the Russian and Habsburg empires.[90]

As the Cyrillo-Methodians claimed a leading role in imperial intellectual life, Little Russian intellectuals promoted ever more radically nationalist ideas. In an 1857 polemic with a Polish journalist, Maksimovich claimed that as early as the seventeenth century, the Little Russian narod had come to see its interests as mutually incompatible with those of its putative Polish oppressors.[91] In that same year, on the two hundredth anniversary of Khmelnytsky's death, he called for a monument to be erected to the Hetman, whom he hailed as the "glorious liberator of Kiev and all Little Russia from the Poles" and the savior of the entire Orthodox world.[92] Kostomarov went further still, penning a history of the Khmelnytsky revolt that presented the "southern Russian people" themselves as its motive force. Sparing none of the revolt's

---

87. N. I. Kostomarov, *Istoricheskie proizvedeniia. Avtobiografiia* (Kiev, 1989), 494–95.
88. Savchenko, *Zaborona*, 7–8.
89. On Kulish's activities in these years, see Sokhan, *Kyrylo-Mefodiivs'ke tovarystvo* 2:168–90; on Kostomarov, ibid., 1:350–57; on Shevchenko, ibid., 2:353–69.
90. The point that the returned exiles were welcomed by the imperial capital's educated elites is made strongly in E. Bobrov, "Epizod iz zhizni N.I. Kostomarova," *Russkaia starina* 1 (1904): 603–14; Ol'ha Hrushevs'ka, "Z diial'nosty Kulisha v 1850-x rokakh," *Naukovyi Zbirnyk za rik 1924*, 19:165–75.
91. M. A. Maksimovich, "O prichinakh vzaimnogo ozhestocheniia Poliakov i Malorossiian, byvshego v XVII vek," in *Sobranie Sochinenii M.A. Maksimovicha* (Kiev, 1876), 1:248–76.
92. M. A. Maksimovich, "Vospominanie o Bogdane Khmel'nitskom," in ibid., 476.

gory details, his account celebrated the violence that it unleashed as a justified, even laudable, effort to deliver the Rus' people from their enemies.[93] A journal launched by the Kiev Commission for the Analysis of Historical Documents in 1859, *Arkhiv Iugo-Zapadnoi Rossii* (*Archive of Southwestern Russia*), frequently expressed similar views. Featuring original documents alongside commentary from the group's experts that highlighted the efforts of "the southwestern Russian" people to maintain their "internal moral bond" with their Orthodox brothers near and far, the journal presented the Khmelnytsky revolt and the Haidamak insurrections as national liberation movements that endeavored to destroy Polish and Jewish influence and to "reunite" the children of Rus'.[94]

Some bureaucrats and intellectuals raised concerns about the organic nationalism and radical social agenda that Little Russian activists endorsed. Polish patriots argued that Cossacks were not heroes but mere brigands, expressing astonishment that Little Russian patriots had not been punished for praising peasant revolts and communal violence.[95] Perceptive censors raised alarms about Commission publications that expressed "excessively overt passion for the Little Russian nationality [*natsional'nost'*]," leading the St. Petersburg ministries to repeat Uvarov's earlier warning that Little Russian patriots should not permit their pride in their local traditions to detract from their loyalty to their imperial fatherland.[96]

Pogodin, a close associate of the Little Russian lobby since the 1830s, continued to insist that the survival of the Russian empire depended on its ability to harness national ideas. But by the 1850s, he was expressing concern that the Little Russian patriotism that had guided so many of the self-professed defenders of East Slavic civilization might divide rather than unify the Rus' people. Marginalizing the role of the southwestern borderlands in creating the foundations of East Slavic culture and the Russian state, he focused instead on the contributions of the Great Russians of the imperial center. It was Great Russians, not Little Russians, he argued, who had created the Rus' state and carried its traditions with them when they migrated north following the Mongol invasion; Russian, not Ukrainian, was the most direct descendant of the Rus' literary language.[97]

The Cyrillo-Methodian affair and the new critiques of the Little Russian idea that emerged in its aftermath focused attention on the potential dangers that the

---

93. The first of three volumes was published in 1859, the last in 1884. For a reprint of the entire work, see N. I. Kostomarov, *Bogdan Khmel'nitskii* (Moscow, 1994).
94. The quotes are from *Arkhiv iugozapadnoi Rossii* 1, no. 1 (1859): lxxxvi.
95. On the polemics between Commission members and Polish patriots, see Levitskii, *Piatidesiatiletie*, 95–97; "Pamiatnik Bogdanu Khmel'nitskomu v Kieve," *KS* 22, no. 7 (1888): 146. On the attitudes and political activities of the mid-nineteenth-century szlachta more generally, consult Tadeusz Bobrowski, *Pamiętnik mojego życia* (Warsaw, 1979); Józef Olechnowicz, "Polska myśl patriotyczna i postępowa na ziemiach ukrainnych w latach 1835–1863," in *Pamiętnik Kijowski*, 2:1–48.
96. "Tsenzura v tsarstvovanie Imperatora Nikolaia I," *Russkaia starina* 2 (1904): 441.
97. See Plokhy, *Unmaking Imperial Russia*, 135; Maiorova, *From the Shadow*, 53–93; on the growing tensions between Great Russian and Little Russian intellectuals in this period, consult Andriewsky, "The Russian-Ukrainian Discourse," 182–214.

nationalist vision coalescing in the southwestern borderlands posed to the imperial state. However, the Little Russian idea continued to serve as a key weapon in the imperial struggle against Polish separatism. It remained an open question in the late fifties how imperial officials would balance the threats that Little Russian activists posed to the tsarist order with their potential to rally the empire behind the Orthodox Church and East Slavic traditions.

The "New Men" and the Masses

By the late 1850s and early 1860s, a new generation of Russian intellectuals was coming of age. Steeped in positivist philosophy and radical social thought, these "new men" emphasized the value of practical political action and scoffed at the genteel idealism of their fathers. The first organized populist groups appeared across the empire, reaching out to the peasant masses in an effort to engage them in a democratic revolution. Young radicals who rallied around Herzen's *Kolokol* and N. G. Chernyshevskii's *Sovremennik* expressed outrage not only at the suffering of the peasantry but also at the plight of the empire's national minorities—including Poles—whom they saw as victims of tsarist oppression.[98]

The growing sympathy for the Polish cause in the Russian radical press emboldened the Poles of the right bank. Students at St. Vladimir's, insistent that their fathers' polemics with Kiev Commission members would not by themselves resurrect the Polish state, now took their cause directly to the peasant masses, organizing underground cells that canvassed right-bank hinterlands. Working to enlist peasants in the struggle for a free Poland, these young radicals promised that the future state would restore the freedoms of the Hetmanate and liberate the simple folk from their heavy economic burdens.[99] Although the organization of these cells remained primitive, the fact that Polish patriots had established unmediated contact with peasant communities deeply alarmed southwestern officials.[100]

Kiev's Orthodox young men, too, had begun to appeal to the peasant masses, although their varied backgrounds and political orientations complicated their outreach efforts. Student leaders from the right bank—such as V. M. Iuzefovich (1841–1895), the son of the Kiev Commission member—had come of age amid the campaign against the szlachta; as outspoken critics of Polish culture and self-professed defenders of the narod, they tended to regard the imperial state as the protector of the Little Russian people and their customs. Students from the left bank, where pride in the Cossack past had continued to develop free of the sharp ethnocultural conflicts that dominated right-bank politics, tended to sympathize with radical critics such as

---

98. Franco Venturi, *The Roots of Revolution* (London, 1960), 232–52.
99. See G. I. Marakhov, *Sotsial'no-Politicheskaia bor'ba na Ukraine v 50–60-e gody XIX veka* (Kiev, 1981); O. Levits'kyi, "Storinka z zhyttia Volodymyra Antonovycha," IRNBUV, I.8076, ll. 4–5.
100. See the correspondence, for example, in "Ob obrazovanii mezhdu studentami Universteta Sv. Vladimira tainom obshchestve pod nazvaniem PURISTOV," TsDIAUK, f. 707, op. 261, d. 4.

Herzen and Chernyshevskii rather than the state. When the left-bank native M. P. Dragomanov (1841–95) arrived at St. Vladimir's to study history in the late 1850s, he was a committed atheist and materialist opposed to the autocracy, which he believed was rapidly destroying the traditions of his Cossack ancestors. Viewing both Poles and Little Russians as victims of tsarist despotism, the young man was appalled at his right-bank peers' violent denunciations of the szlachta and their rather positive view of the imperial state, which he considered "reactionary."[101]

In October 1859, Dragomanov, along with a handful of other students from the left bank, established a Sunday school in a commercial district of Kiev to educate the peasants streaming into the city to work in factories and as artisans. The school soon became renowned for its "cosmopolitan" interpretation of the region's history, emphasizing the freedoms that Little Russians had enjoyed under the Hetmanate and the value of Little Russian culture and language in the multinational empire. Shortly thereafter, V. M. Iuzefovich and his friend P. I. Zhitetskii (1837–1911) opened their own school. Known for its Slavophile inclinations, this school emphasized the narod's devotion to the Orthodox Church and the tsar, but it also celebrated the peculiarities of Little Russian culture and became renowned for its strong Ukrainian-language curriculum.[102]

While self-identified Little Russians from both sides of the Dnieper reached out to the masses, the ideas of a St. Vladimir's student named Vladimir Antonovich (1834–1908) created fissures in the Polish patriotic movement. Born into an impoverished szlachta clan in Kiev province, Antonovich grew up hearing tales of how his ancestors had fought for Polish independence and supported national liberation movements across Europe. While still a schoolboy, he discovered the works of Montesquieu, Rousseau, and Voltaire and came to identify as a populist and democrat.[103] Yet as he matured, Antonovich perceived a contradiction between the retrograde tendencies he observed in the social and political attitudes of the szlachta and its purported devotion to the principle of national self-determination. He despised the "caste principle" of Polish notables, who heaped scorn on fellow nobles who entered the free professions or joined the ranks of the intelligentsia. Antonovich was even more appalled by the szlachta's lack of concern for the well-being of the serfs, whom he perceived as doubly victimized—by their Polish overlords and by the Jewish merchants and middlemen on whom they depended for necessary commodities.[104]

By the time he entered St. Vladimir's, Antonovich had become convinced that he was witnessing the dawn of a new society—one that would be defined not by estates

---

101. M. P. Dragomanov, "Avtobiograficheskaia zametka," in *Literaturno-publitsystychni pratsi* (Kiev, 1970), 1:43–44.
102. Gnat Pavlovych Zhytets'kyi, "Kyivs'ka hromada za 60-ti roki," IRNBUV, I.46884, ll. 4–5; B. M. Iuzefovich, "Tridtsat' let tomu nazad: Ocherk iz studencheskoi zhizni,"*Russkaia starina* 84 (1895): 167–200; Dragomanov, "Avtobiograficheskie zametki," 42.
103. "Avtobiografichni zapysky Volodymyra Antonoycha," 1897, TsDIAUK, f. 832, op. 1, d. 108, ll. 4–5, 38.
104. Ibid., l. 16, 18, 26, 32–33.

but by nations founded on the values of the simple folk themselves.¹⁰⁵ Antonovich and a small coterie of fellow Polish nobles converted to Orthodoxy, learned Ukrainian, memorized the poems of Shevchenko, and traveled the countryside dressed in peasant garb, declaring themselves servants of the Little Russian people.¹⁰⁶ The young man and his followers recorded folk customs and familiarized themselves with peasant mores as they denounced "any form of coercion [*nasyl'stvo*], the domination of one ethnicity [*narodnost'*] over another, the exploitation [*vykorystovuvannia*] of one social stratum by another."¹⁰⁷

Antonovich's attacks on estate society and his radically nationalist and populist ideas provoked great consternation among the szlachta. Local Polish society derisively dubbed his followers *khlopomany* (or alternatively, *khokhlomany*—both terms translate roughly as "peasant fans"), and claimed that they were encouraging serfs to "slaughter" their lords.¹⁰⁸ In 1860, Kiev's Polish notables convened a community meeting, in which they warned Antonovich that they would denounce him to the authorities if he did not stop his activities. Antonovich refused—and in fact, only intensified his attacks on the szlachta thereafter. From that point on, the Kiev authorities routinely received anonymous denunciations informing them that Antonovich was a revolutionary and a "communist."¹⁰⁹

In February 1861, Tsar Alexander II emancipated Russia's serfs, offering the right-bank peasantry a substantially more generous settlement than peasants in central Russia received.¹¹⁰ (Galagan and other Kiev Commission members who sat on local emancipation committees advocated for the interests of peasants and continued to lobby the local authorities to reduce their obligations even after the emancipation.)¹¹¹ The terms of the emancipation outraged the szlachta: in some parts of the borderlands, Polish-speaking Catholics and Orthodox believers came to blows as local officials read the emancipation manifesto aloud.¹¹² The disputes caused by the emancipation—and the ongoing conflict between Antonovich and the local spokesmen for the szlachta—transformed the political landscape of the southwest. Dragomanov, who

---

105. Ibid., ll. 32–34, 46.
106. Ibid., ll. 38–39, 56.
107. The quote is from: Mik. Hrushevs'kyi, "Volodymyr Antonovych, osnovni idei ioho tvorchosty i diial'nosty," *Zapysky Ukrains'koho Naukovoho Tovarystva v Kyivi* 3 (1908): 13.
108. "Avtobiografichni zapysky Volodymyra Antonoycha," l. 39.
109. Mykhailo Drahomanov, "Do istorii ukrainskoi khlopomanii v 1860-ti- rr.," IRNBUV, f. 172, no. 23, l. 6; Undated report on Antonovich's political activities in the files of the Ministry of Internal Affairs, RGIA, f. 1282, op. 1, d. 352, ll. 134–340b.
110. Takeshi Matsumura, "To What Extent Could the Empire Be Constructed?" in *Imperiology*, ed. Kimitaka Matsuzato (Sapporo, 2007), 174. In 1864, officials used a similar tactic in the Kingdom of Poland, offering a generous settlement to Polish peasants in an effort to win their loyalty and turn them against the Polish gentry.
111. "Ob otnoshenii mezhdu pomeshchikami i vremenno-obiazannymi krest'ianami," IRNBUV, f. 57, d. 75; correspondence of Galgan and Governor-General Annenkov in IRNBUV, I.6998–7017.
112. N. K. Rennenkampf, "Kievskaia universitetskaia starina,"*Russkaia starina* 30, no. 7 (1899): 37. On the political views and organization of the szlachta in the wake of the emancipation, see Zygmunt Chojecki, *Społeczeństwo polskie na Rusi* (Warsaw, 1937), 5–6.

had once been disturbed by the anti-Polish rhetoric and pro-tsarist views of right-bank activists, now began to see Poles as exploiters of the narod rather than as victims of the tsarist regime.[113] By the spring of 1861, Dragomanov had joined V. M. Iuzefovich and other Little Russian activists at meetings at St. Vladimir's, criticizing the attempts of Poles to "subordinate" the Orthodox believers of the borderlands.[114]

United by their common desire to defend local culture and peasants from Polish oppression, the khlopomany and student activists from both sides of the Dnieper formed the Kiev Hromada. Quickly expanding beyond its core base of student activists, the group claimed two hundred members by 1862, including prominent clergymen, St. Vladimir's professors, and even bureaucrats.[115] Bankrolled by Galagan, the group organized a wide variety of activities to raise awareness of Little Russia's cultural and historical traditions and to discredit the Polish patriots who continued to portray the southwest as a Polish province.[116] Although Hromada members were united by their claims to represent the interests of the narod against the Polish aristocracy, they used a wide variety of tactics to pursue divergent goals. Some limited their interest to cultural endeavors, organizing public events to celebrate Shevchenko's legacy after his death in 1861 and expanding the local Sunday school network to one hundred rural locales. Others dreamed of resurrecting the Cossack Hetmanate or inciting massive peasant uprisings to destroy the szlachta. Still others worked with local clergy to convert Roman Catholic and Uniate peasants to Orthodoxy.[117] Despite the varied agendas of Hromada affiliates, most seem not to have challenged the legitimacy or authority of the tsarist system—a fact that irritated the smaller but more radical hromady proliferating across the left bank, which called for greater autonomy from St. Petersburg.[118]

In early 1861, Kiev- and St. Petersburg-based Little Russian activists pooled their resources to launch a Russian- and Ukrainian-language journal called *Osnova (The Foundation)*. The journal's founders and frequent contributors included onetime Cyrillo-Methodians (Kulish and Kostomarov), Kiev Commission members (Galagan and Iuzefovich), and Hromada activists (Antonovich). Iuzefovich and others used *Osnova* to lament that Polish-speaking Catholics, who constituted a mere one-eleventh of the southwest's population, continued to dominate it culturally, economically, and

---

113. Dragomanov, "Avtobiograficheskaia zametka," 43.
114. Rennenkampf, "Kievskaia universitetskaia starina," 38.
115. For a partial list of Kiev Hromada members, consult Ihnat Zhytets'kyi, "Kyivs'ka Hromada za 60-tykh rokiv," *Ukraina* 1 (1928): 91–125.
116. On Galagan's financial support, see Efraim Vol'f, *K istorii ukrainskogo i evreiskogo natsional'nykh dvizhenii do 1917* (Jerusalem, 2000), 33. For more on the group's activities, see Zhytets'kyi, "Kyivs'ka Hromada"; A. A. Rusov, "Kak ia stal chlenom 'hromady,'" *Ukrainskaia zhizn'* 10 (1913): 40–49; V. Miiakovskii, "Kievskaia gromada," *Litopys'revoliutsii* 4 (1924): 127–50.
117. Dragomanov, "Avtobiograficheskaia zametka," 1:40–45; Boris P-skii, "Vospominanie iz nedalekogo proshlogo," *KS* 11, no. 2 (1885): 235–67; Savchenko, *Zaborona*, 350–51; "Hovors'kyi ta Kalistriv (Z kyivs'koho zhittia 60-kh rr. XIX st.)," *Ukraina* 5 (1927): 57; David Saunders, "Russia and Ukraine under Alexander II: The Valuev Edict of 1863," *International History Review* 17, no. 1 (1995): 34, 38–39.
118. Miiakovskii, "Kievskaia gromada," 139. A notable exception is the one-time Hromada member Vladimir Sinegub, who with a handful of followers split from the group in 1862 and called for a full-fledged revolution—an act that led to his arrest and exile. See "O Sinegube V.," 1863–65, TsDIAUK, f. 473, op. 1, d. 20.

politically.[119] Antonovich denounced the szlachta's "religious fanaticism, estate egoism, disrespect for personal rights [*prava lichnosti*], enslavement of the peasantry, and arbitrariness [*samoupravstvo*] in all arenas of social life"; other contributors complained that Jews, whom they portrayed as the szlachta's partners in exploitation, had brought spiritual ruin to a region in which Orthodox values had flourished before their arrival.[120] Journal contributors also hoped that their endeavor—which showcased local ethnographic research and coordinated efforts to compile the first Ukrainian-language dictionary—would establish the value of Little Russian culture and demonstrate the role that the people of "southern Russia" had played in forging and defending East Slavic civilization. This in turn, they hoped, would give the narod of the southwest the courage they needed once and for all to cast off foreign oppression.[121]

In response to skeptics such as Pogodin, *Osnova* contributors insisted that recognizing the unique history and culture of Little Russia did not undermine the unity of the children of Rus'. In writings of the early 1860s, Kostomarov juxtaposed the political cultures of the "two Russian nationalities [*narodnosti*]," contrasting the predilection for personal freedoms and federalist structures that "southern Russians" had inherited from the Rus' state with the autocratic tendencies that "northern Rus'" had developed under the Mongol yoke. He sharply criticized centuries of tsarist policies that had undermined the emancipationist dreams and degraded the native traditions of southern Rus'; he expressed great dismay about the dismissive attitude with which Great Russian intellectuals such as Pogodin had treated Little Russia's historical contributions as of late.[122] Although many scholars have interpreted these writings as clarion calls of Ukrainian national separatism, Kostomarov repeatedly stated in these same pieces that he saw northern and southern Russians as "internally linked" tribes that together formed a unitary Rus' nation and expressed his desire to see all the Slavic people united under a benevolent tsar who could serve as the "sovereign of free peoples [*narody*]."[123] Rather than viewing Little Russian patriotism as a force that would challenge the unity of the East Slavs and the state that ruled them, Kostomarov championed the Little Russian idea precisely because he connected it to authentic Rus' traditions and believed that it could revive the organic links connecting all the children of Rus' and their rulers.

Continuing a tradition begun by Maksimovich and the Kiev Commission, *Osnova* contributors also reached out to their compatriots on the other side of the

---

119. M. V. Iuzefovich, "Ob"iasnenie ot predsedatel'ia Kievskoi kommissii dlia razbora drevnikh aktov," *Osnova* 3 (1861): 8.
120. The quote is from V. B. Antonovich, "Moia ispoved'," *Osnova* 1 (1862): 86. On Jews, Anna Barvinok, "S volyny," *Osnova* 1 (1861): 282–92; P. A. Kulish, "Peredovye zhidy," *Osnova* 9 (1861): 135–38.
121. For example, *Osnova* 1 (1861): 2–7.
122. N. I. Kostomarov, "Dve russkie narodnosti," *Osnova* 3 (1861): 33–80; letter to the editor of *Kolokol*, 15 January 1860, republished in M. V. Nechkina, ed., *Kolokol* (Moscow, 1962), 2:499–503.
123. Quotes from N. I. Kostomarov, "Dve russkie narodnosti," *Osnova* 3 (1861): 33 (see also 79–80 for a similar elaboration); Nechkina, *Kolokol*, 2:502–3. It is interesting to note that the arguments Kostomarov presented in *Kolokol*, which was published in London, were virtually the same as those that he advanced in *Osnova*, which was subject to imperial censors.

Austrian border. In 1861, Lemberg-based intellectuals who had established ties with Little Russian activists launched a Ukrainian-language newspaper called *Slovo (The Word)*. The paper insisted on the fundamental unity of the Ruthenians (*rusyny*) who stretched from Lemberg to the left bank and denounced Polish oppression of East Slavs in the Habsburg and Russian empires.[124] *Osnova* republished excerpts from the paper, praising its mission to unite the southern Russian branch of East Slavic people and to defend the "holy cause of the people of Rus' [*Rus'kyi narod*]."[125]

As *Osnova* and its allies conjured up a Rus' nation that stretched across international borders—and affirmed the role that the Little Russian narod had played in forging it—Kostomarov, who remained an influential figure in St. Petersburg intellectual life, struggled to introduce the Little Russian idea to a broader audience. In 1860 he published a new account of the founding of Rus' in Chernyshevskii's *Sovremennik*, which infused Maksimovich's earlier anti-Normanist theories with more radically nationalist ideas. The historian charged that the Normanist theory was a conspiracy by Germanic scholars to demonstrate that the East Slavs were incapable building a "state and a civic life" on their own. Charging that the Varangians had played a purely "negative role" in Rus' history, he traced the foundation of the Rus' state not to their arrival but rather to their expulsion from East Slavic territory.[126] Kostomarov's reimagination of Rus' history scandalized the academic establishment—including Pogodin, who challenged him to a public debate in the spring of 1860.[127] But in spite of the opposition generated by his work, Kostomarov continued to elaborate on these ideas in his ethnographic and historical writing over the next decade and a half, chronicling the role of the "southern Russian" masses in creating authentic Slavic traditions—and defending them from inimical foreign forces. In the words of literary historian Olga Maiorova, he thus portrayed the residents of the Ukrainian lands "as guardians of a pure national identity for all East Slavs."[128]

Kostomarov's interpretation of Rus' history informed his thinking on contemporary politics as well. In an 1862 essay in *Sankt-Peterburgskie Vedomosti* on the occasion of the millennium of the founding of Rus', the scholar celebrated the East Slavs' success over the last thousand years in consolidating the lands "from the Carpathian mountains to the unknown limits of North America's icy wilderness, from the North Pole to the parched steppes of Central Asia." Hailing the recent emancipation of the serfs as a key step toward the realization of the historical destiny of the Rus' people, he expressed his hope that the next millennium would see Russia preside over the creation of a new international order. The "utopia" that the East Slavs would create would bear no resemblance to the "feudal system," "papism," and "liberal" regimes that the "Germano-Latin tribes" had constructed in western Europe over the centuries.

124. See, for example, *Slovo*, 16/28 December 1861.
125. "Galitsko-russkaia gazeta 'Slovo,'" *Osnova* 3 (1861): 81.
126. Quotes from Kostomarov, "Nachalo Rusi," *Sovremennik*, 79 (1860): 28, 20.
127. The conflict is described in detail in Maiorova, *From the Shadow*, 75–81.
128. Ibid., 80; for more on Kostomarov's work in these years, see Prymak, *Mykola Kostomarov*, 147.

Rather, the children of Rus' would create a strong and unified nation-state guided by the "vital strength of the narod."[129]

By 1860, proponents of the Little Russian idea had rewritten the history of their native region—and the empire as a whole—in a radically populist and organic nationalist key. Presenting the Orthodox East Slavs as the "native" residents of the Dnieper region and the creators of the Russian empire, they celebrated popular resistance and even peasant revolts against Polish and Jewish notables. Envisioning a "southern Russian" tribe that stretched into Austrian Galicia, they challenged the existing geopolitical order.

In spite of the fact that the Little Russian idea challenged the stability of the empire and the estate system on all these counts, it continued to enjoy the support of influential bureaucrats, who relied on it to discredit Polish claims on the southwest and to mobilize the region's Orthodox believers behind the tsarist state. The curator of the Kiev school district, N. I. Pirogov, praised Hromada Sunday schools as valuable forms of "Russo-Little Russian propaganda"; Governor-General I. I. Vasil'chikov and Tsar Alexander II personally assisted Sunday school activists in their effort to raise funds.[130] The authorities did express concern that the Ukrainian orthography that was common in Austrian Galicia used "Polish"—that is, Latin—letters, which they feared might draw Little Russians into the orbit of Polish culture.[131] Although officials ordered that all Ukrainian-language materials aimed at the "simple people" of the Russian empire use "Russian letters," they implemented no other restrictions on Ukrainian publishing efforts.[132] In fact, in the early 1860s, St. Petersburg officials not only tolerated *Osnova* but also commissioned Kulish to translate the Emancipation Manifesto into Ukrainian; permitted Kostomarov, Shevchenko, and Kiev Hromada activists to publish and distribute Ukrainian-language primers; and authorized the translation of the Bible into Ukrainian.[133]

---

129. N. I. Kostomarov, "862–1862," *Sankt-Peterburgskie Vedomosti*, 3 January 1862, 1–2. Kostomarov signed the article "-d," but it was widely recognized as his work by contemporaries.
130. The quote is from N. I. Pirogov, "O voskresnykh shkolakh," in *Sochineniia* (St. Petersburg, 1887), 2:220; see also I. A. Stepovich, "Nedel'ni shkoly u Kyevi," IRNBUV, f. 179, no. 897, ll. 1–3; Mykhailo Drahomanov, "Literatura Rosiis'ka, Velykorus'ka, ukrains'ka i halyts'ka," in *Literaturno-publitsystychni pratsi*, 1:163; M. P. Drahomanov, "Antrakt z istorii Ukrainofil'stva (1863–1872)," in *M. P. Drahomanov. Vybrane* (Kiev, 1991), 210. Pirogov was a famed surgeon, one of the founders of military medicine. A native of Moscow, he did not identify as a Little Russian.
131. O. M. Novitskii to N. I. Pirogov, 14 March 1859, TsDIAUK, f. 707, op. 261, d. 7, ll. 1–2. The Russian authorities' fears were not unfounded; in 1859, the Polish viceroy of Galicia had banned the use of Cyrillic characters in Ukrainian-language publications to promote the use of the Latin alphabet. See Alexei Miller, *The Romanov Empire and Nationalism* (New York, 2008), 75. In 1864, officials enacted a similar policy in the northwest, banning the use of Latin letters in the Lithuanian alphabet. See Mikhail Dolbilov, "Prevratnosti kirillizatsii: Zapret latinitsy i biurokraticheskaia rusifikatsiia litovtsev v vilenskom general-gubernatorstve v 1864–1882 gg.," *Ab Imperio* 2 (2005): 255–96; Staliunas, *Making Russians*, 233–82.
132. Ministry of Education to N. I. Pirogov, 30 May 1859, TsDIAUK, f. 707, op. 261, d. 7, l. 7.
133. Dolbilov and Miller, *Zapadnye okrainy*, 157–58; Andrii Danylenko, "The Ukrainian Bible and the Valuev Circular of July 18, 1863," *Acta Slavica Japonica* 28 (2010), 13; Saunders, "Russia and Ukraine," 34, 38.

Kiev officials even protected the most radical Little Russian activists from their opponents. The governor-general's office rejected anonymous allegations that the khlopomany aimed to tear Little Russian peasants away from the imperial state and resurrect an independent Poland as efforts by Polish provocateurs to discredit the movement in the eyes of the government.[134] Far from presenting a threat to imperial unity, bureaucrats insisted, the khlopomany had done a great service to the state by demonstrating that "the majority of the population of this region is southern Russian" and contesting the popular notion that the southwest was a "Polish province."[135] Officials dismissed the denunciations of Antonovich that continued to pour in to local authorities. As one police official noted, "Not only do I find no data that would justify the accusations of Antonovich's unreliability, but on the contrary, I see that he is well acquainted with the history of this region and the character and life of its population..., understands its current political situation, and rightly and logically demonstrates the absurdity of the Poles' tendency to imagine this region as belonging to the Polish nationality and to dream of the possibility of unifying it with Poland, etc."[136] Frustrated by officials' tolerance for the radically populist and nationalist ideas emanating from Kiev, Polish patriots bitterly complained that the Hromada and other Little Russian organizations practiced a "legal Ukrainophilia" that aided "the harsh Russification of the Ukrainian lands."[137]

::

In the early nineteenth century, a small but influential group of Little Russian gentry and intellectuals reimagined the southwestern borderlands, which remained a complex patchwork of people and cultures, as a battlefield on which coherent national groups struggled with each other for survival. Noting that the right bank had given rise to the Rus' state and the Orthodox faith, they saw the region as the spiritual center of East Slavic civilization rather than a distant periphery to the political center of St. Petersburg; claiming that the narod of Little Russia was engaged in a centuries-long struggle to defend ancient Rus' traditions, they insisted that the outcome of this contest would determine the fate of all Orthodox believers. In the aftermath of the 1830–31 revolt, as imperial officials simultaneously struggled to repress the dangerous potential of national separatism and to mobilize and unify the borderlands' Orthodox residents behind the tsar, many came to see Little Russian patriots as indispensable allies in these tasks. Although some officials pointed out that the Little Russian idea's

---

134. Drahomanov, "Do Istorii ukrainskoi khlopomanii," IRNBUV, f. 172, no. 23, l. 2.
135. Ibid., ll. 3–4.
136. Unsigned memorandum to chief of the Kiev police, 17 January 1862, TsDIAUK, f. 442, op. 812, d. 4, ll. 6–60b.
137. The quote is from Witold Kazimierz Wierzejski, *Fragmenty z dziejów polskiej młodzieży akademickiej w Kijowie* (Warsaw, 1939), 45. See also Fr. Rawita Gawroński, *Włodzimierz Antonowicz* (Lviv, 1912), 6, 31; Roman Serbyn, "Kyiv—ne Varshava. Pohliad ukrainofiliv na students'ke sluzhinnia narodovi u 1861–62 rokakh," in *Viiny i myr*, ed. Larysa Ivshyna (Kiev, 2004), 393.

radical populism, local patriotism, and aspirations to dismantle estate society in favor of an order based on ethnonational identifications posed serious threats to the tsarist regime, others depended on it to claim the southwest for the empire. In the years to come, right-bank bureaucrats and Little Russian activists would grow more interdependent—even as their relationship became more complicated. A second revolt by the szlachta in the 1860s would remind officials of the corrosive potential of nationalism in imperial governance and society. But it would also compel them to promote with more gusto than ever the nationalizing vision of Little Russian patriots.

2 The Little Russian Idea in the 1860s

IN THE EARLY 1860s, imperial bureaucrats faced their most daunting challenge yet in the western borderlands. By late 1861, it had become clear that the szlachta across the region was conspiring to launch a new assault on the imperial state. In the southwest, Polish Catholic nobles organized open demonstrations in district cities and rural areas; police confiscated countless French, Polish, and Ukrainian-language pamphlets that called on both the educated classes and the narod to rise up against the tsar.[1] The intensified agitation in the borderlands unfolded amid a series of crises—peasant revolts, student strikes, attempted assassinations, and mysterious fires in St. Petersburg—that bred an atmosphere of fear and paranoia across the empire. In January 1863, the long-expected Polish revolt finally broke out in Warsaw. Within a month, the unrest had spread across the lands of the former Commonwealth as organized bands of patriots attacked arsenals and Russian officials and declared a provisional government in the lands that had been taken by Russia in the Polish partitions. Significant portions of the szlachta from the Baltic to the Black Sea joined the revolt, engaging tsarist troops in a series of battles that lasted into 1864.[2]

A substantial body of research, much of which focuses on the northwestern borderlands, has painstakingly reconstructed the efforts of imperial officials to respond to the intensification of the Polish nationalist challenge in the 1860s. Early in the decade, two distinct camps emerged within the bureaucracy: one favored a conciliatory approach that would attempt to integrate the szlachta into all-imperial political and intellectual life; the other sought to systematically undermine the influence of the Polish Catholic gentry. In the aftermath of 1863, the latter camp gradually gained the upper hand, and imperial officials launched campaigns to enhance the influence of the faith, language,

---

1. See Marakhov, *Sotsial'no-politicheskaia bor'ba*, 101–11; "Demonstratsii Poliakov zhivushchikh na Volynii," *Vestnik Iugo-Zapadnoi i zapadnoi Rossii* 1, no. 2 (1862): 100–116 (third pagination); TsDIAUK, f. 442, op. 812, d. 4.
2. A magisterial treatment of the revolt is Stefan Kieniewicz, *Powstanie styczniowe* (Warsaw, 1972). On the southwest in particular, see G. I. Marakhov, *Pol'skoe vosstanie 1863 g. na pravoberezhnoi Ukraine* (Kiev, 1967); Otton Beiersdorf, "Kijów w powstaniu styczniowym," in *Kraków-Kijów,* ed. Antoni Podraza (Cracow, 1969), 73–130; Tadeusz Bobrowski, *Pamiętnik mojego życia* (Warsaw, 1979).

and culture of the Great Russian heartland on the western frontier. Although several studies have argued that these campaigns, which were unsystematically applied, full of internal inconsistencies, and hotly contested by officials who opposed them, should not be seen as constituting a coherent policy of Russification, scholars still view 1863 as a key turning point in imperial history.[3] In the words of historian Darius Staliunas, "The suppression of the 1863–1864 uprising marks a sea change in Russian nationality policy and a move towards clearly expressed discrimination against non-Russians not only in Lithuania and Belarus but also in other western borderlands of the empire."[4]

This chapter, which follows the continued development of the Little Russian idea in the 1860s, finds many similarities between developments in the northwestern and southwestern borderlands. It reconstructs the schisms that emerged between the officials charged with governing the borderlands' diverse populations and notes the ultimate victory in this debate of strident de-polonizers. It shows how Little Russian activists experienced new pressure from the centralizing state to explain how their activities benefited the empire—and to clarify their relationship with the Russian heartland and the imperial regime. But it also argues that state-society dynamics in the southwest, where Little Russian activists could claim that their activities undermined Polish influence *and* promoted the faith and the values that underpinned a unified East Slavic civilization, diverged from the general pattern that Staliunas describes. In the decade following the revolt, Little Russian activists further expanded their influence: they established new newspapers and voluntary associations, left lasting marks on Kiev's public space, peddled their ideas to the masses, and lobbied imperial officials to devise even more aggressive measures to reduce the influence of the non-Orthodox and to enhance that of the children of Rus'. In the process, the small but influential Little Russian lobby that had coalesced in Kiev evolved into a larger and more socially variegated urban intelligentsia. Far from being hapless victims of a centralizing state, Little Russian activists both shaped and benefited from the new policies that emerged from the 1863 revolt.

Assessing the Little Russian Idea in the Early 1860s

As we saw in chapter 1, the Little Russian lobby occupied a peculiar place in the empire's intellectual life and melded several distinct ideological agendas. A creation of a minuscule gentry class, it had embraced a social agenda by the 1850s, claiming to defend the interests of the Orthodox narod. Sharply critical of the Poles and Jews who had allegedly exploited the children of Rus' for centuries, it had benefited from the patronage of an autocratic state. The enigmatic quality of the nationalizing vision coalescing in Kiev had served the Little Russian idea well in the 1850s, attracting the

---

3. Weeks, *Nation*; Rodkiewicz, *Russian Nationality*; Gorizontov, *Paradoksy*; Miller, *Ukrainian Question*; "Forum: Reinterpreting Russification in Late Imperial Russia," *Kritika* 5, no. 2 (Spring 2004): 245–97; Dolbilov and Miller, *Zapadnye okrainy*, 125–300; Staliunas, *Making Russians*.
4. Staliunas, *Making Russians*, 297.

support of Westernizers and Slavophiles alike. By the early 1860s, however, as imperial politics grew more radical and polarized, both camps would grow less tolerant of its internal contradictions.

Several points of contention emerged between Little Russian activists and radical critics in the early sixties. The most significant centered on southwestern activists' efforts to uplift and promote the Orthodox peasantry at the expense of local Polish and Jewish populations. This conflict first took shape in an 1859–60 exchange between Kostomarov and Herzen in the latter's London-based periodical, *Kolokol*. By the late fifties, Herzen, like many radical critics, had become a strong supporter of the Polish patriotic cause, which he treated as part of a broader struggle between imperial subjects and an unjust, autocratic regime. Endorsing Poland's "full right to exist as a state [*gosudarstvennoe sushchestvovanie*] independent from Russia," he added that the inhabitants of "Ukraine" should enjoy the right to develop their own culture and language.[5] Although Kostomarov thanked Herzen for supporting "southern Russian" cultural traditions, he made it clear that he disagreed with the critic on several counts.[6] In contrast to Herzen, who regarded Poles and "Ukrainians" as common victims of the autocracy, Kostomarov held Poles and Jews accountable for the suffering of the narod; he excoriated those who held "liberal" views (including the Saratov governor who had halted Kostomarov's research on blood rituals while he was in exile) for silently assenting to the exploitation of the masses.[7]

By the early sixties, the tensions between the radicals who insisted that all tsarist subjects should join together in a common struggle against autocratic rule and the Little Russian activists who blamed the suffering of the narod on their Polish and Jewish neighbors produced open and bitter disputes. In the pages of *Sovremennik*, the radical critic N. G. Chernyshevskii condemned the Galician journal *Slovo*, which as we saw in chapter 1, was closely linked to the *Osnova* circle. Although he approved of the efforts of "Galician Little Russians" to develop their local culture and language, he harshly criticized the newspaper's contributors for their repeated attacks on Galicia's Polish-speaking Catholics. How could a population struggling to protect its culture from centralizing and assimilating empires, he wondered, begrudge another minority group the opportunity to do the same?[8] A year later, *Sovremennik* excoriated Kostomarov's reinterpretation of Rus' history—and the article he had published in *Sankt-Peterburgskie Vedomosti* on the occasion of the millennium of Rus'—as retrograde, condemning the scholar's apparent hostility toward the minority "nationalities" (*national'nosti*) that had played a constructive role in shaping Russian history and

---

5. "Rossiia i pol'sha," *Kolokol*, 15 January 1859, reprinted in Nechkina, *Kolokol*, 2:273–74.
6. "Ukraina," *Kolokol*, 15 January 1860, reprinted in Nechkina, *Kolokol*, 3:499–503.
7. Ibid., 3:502–3. In contrast to Herzen, Kostomarov also stressed that he had no desire to break the ties between "southern Rus'" and "the rest of Russia." On the contrary, he explained, he and his compatriots hoped to help all the Slavs reclaim their supposedly authentic traditions that had predated the "Tataro-Germanic" autocracy.
8. The article appeared in *Sovremennik* in July 1861. It is reprinted in its entirety as N. G. Chernyshevskii, "Natsional'naia beztaktnost'," *Polnoe sobranie sochinenii* (St. Petersburg, 1905–6), 8:279–91.

politics over the centuries.⁹ Meanwhile, both radical and liberal journalists decried *Osnova*'s negative depictions of Jews—and its repeated used of the word *zhid* (Yid), which carries pejorative connotations in Russian. One critic writing in the Russian-Jewish journal *Sion* accused *Osnova*'s editorial board of fomenting violent anti-Semitism, charging that it longed for the days of Khmelnytsky, when the "infuriated mob" had spilled "the blood of almost half a million innocent Jews...across Ukraine."¹⁰

Little Russian activists did not allow these attacks to pass unanswered. Kulish, who penned the initial responses to the critics of *Osnova*, insisted that his compatriots had meant no offense in their use of the word *zhid*, which he argued was the neutral and correct term for "Jew" in Ukrainian. (He failed to mention that he himself had used the word in Russian in one of these responses.) He insisted that Little Russians were prepared to live in peace with non-East Slavs who defended the "southern Russian" people and their culture; the problem was, he complained, that Jews in particular had repeatedly shown that they had little regard for the welfare of the Little Russian masses.¹¹ After *Sovremennik*'s attacks on Kostomarov, another *Osnova* contributor expressed umbrage at the radical journal's inference that Little Russians could not "distinguish a Yid from a dog." Little Russians, he explained, "dislike Yids not because they are Yids, but because they have not gotten on well [*ne khorosho postupali*] with the narod."¹²

Slavophile support for the Little Russian lobby also began to erode in the early sixties, amid concerns that focusing on the cultural peculiarities of the southwest would undermine the unity of the children of Rus'. For example, one contributor to Aksakov's *Den'*, which had expressed enthusiasm for the Little Russian idea in the fifties, now complained that activists' ongoing efforts to promote the Ukrainian language would sow enmity and misunderstanding between "northern" and "southern" Russians. Claiming that the emergence of two literary East Slavic languages would destroy the unity of the children of Rus', he insisted that Russian must remain the sole language of literary and intellectual endeavors in Russian Ukraine as well as Galicia.¹³

Little Russian activists struggled to craft a coherent response to this line of criticism. Some southwestern activists took the Slavophiles' concerns about the Ukrainian literary language quite seriously. A new journal launched in 1862 by a Hromada member, *Vestnik Iugo-Zapadnoi i zapadnoi Rossii* (*Messenger of Southwestern and Western Russia*), continued to present Little Russian culture as the most authentic manifestation of East Slavic civilization and to tout its capacity to "counteract Polish-Latin

---

9. "Svistok," *Sovremennik* 1 (1862): 1–61 (especially 23–26, second pagination).
10. Cited in "Nedorazumenie po povodu slova 'Zhid,'" *Osnova* 6 (1861): 135. For more on this controversy, see Roman Serbyn, "The Sion-Osnova Controversy of 1861–62," in *Ukrainian-Jewish Relations in Historical Perspective*, ed. Peter J. Potichnyj and Howard Aster (Edmonton, 1988), 85–110; Miller, *Ukrainian Question*, 83.
11. "Nedorazumenie," 142; "Peredovye zhidy," *Osnova* 9 (1861): 135–38.
12. "Vsegda li verno svistiat v 'Sovremennike,'" *Osnova* 2 (1862): 103.
13. For example, Vladimir Lamanskii, "Natsional'naia beztatknost'," *Den'*, 21 October 1861, 14–19.

propaganda."¹⁴ However, journal contributors also concurred with Slavophile critics that Little Russian patriots should be more cautious in their efforts to promote the Ukrainian language. Raising the possibility that Polish nationalists working to polonize Ukrainian orthography and lexicon might succeed in estranging Little Russians from their brothers to the north, one contributor called on activists to use the Great Russian "literary language" exclusively until a standardized Ukrainian language fully distinct from Polish could be "worked out."¹⁵

Other right-bank intellectuals assumed a more defiant tone toward their critics. In the pages of *Osnova*, Zhitetskii, the Kiev Sunday school activist and Hromada member, expressed his offense at *Den"*'s implication that Little Russian patriots had placed the interests of their native region over those of the empire. Enumerating the many junctures at which Little Russians had defended the Orthodox Church and Rus' traditions from external threats, he insisted that the Little Russian tongue expressed the "national genius" of the people who constituted "half of the unified Russian [*russkii*] tribe."¹⁶ Dismissing claims that the emergence of a Little Russian literary language would undermine the unity of the empire or the Rus' people, Zhitetskii retorted that Little Russians' desire to "think and write in their own way" demonstrated their eagerness to preserve East Slavic traditions and to resist Polish culture—not a desire to "isolate themselves from general Russian life."¹⁷

Other Kiev Hromada activists, too, defended their efforts to consolidate the "national identity" *(natsional'naia lichnost')* of the Little Russian people.¹⁸ Far from spreading revolutionary ideas, they argued, their activities affirmed the value of peasant traditions and Orthodox piety. They were wholly opposed to political separatism; their focus on "southern Russian language and southern Russian literature" reflected their interest in documenting the techniques of cultural resistance that "Russian Ruthenians" *(rusyny)* had used to survive generations of Polish oppression. Urging intellectuals not to be distracted by debates about whether the "Little Russian" tongue should be considered a literary language, the Kiev Hromada insisted, "It's enough to say that a Little Russian nationality exists, [and] that there are educated people belonging to it who are equipped to recognize and point out its individual distinguishing features, both moral and ethnographic."¹⁹

---

14. The quote is from a memorandum of Kiev governor-general N. N. Annenkov, 23 February 1863, RGIA, f. 1282, op. 2, d. 1945, l. 11; see also "Ob"iasnenie odnoi frazy v ob"iavlenii ob izdanii 'Vestnika Iugozapadnoi i zapadnoi rossii,'" *Vestnik Iugo-Zapadnoi i zapadnoi Rossii* 4 (1862): 65–84. The Hromada member in question is K. A. Govorskii. Other regular contributors to the journal included A. F. Voronin, a member of the Kiev Commission who had played an active role in his local emancipation committee; M.V. Iuzefovich; and his son Vladimir.
15. "Zametka na stat'iu Sovremennika 'Natsional'naia beztaktnost'," *Vestnik Iugo-Zapadnoi i zapadnoi Rossii* 1 (1862): 1–27 (fourth pagination). The quote is from 26.
16. P. Zhitetskii, "Russkii patriotism," *Osnova* 3 (1862): 21, 7.
17. Ibid., 17.
18. "Otzyv iz Kieva," *Sovremennaia letopis'* 46 (1862): 4.
19. Ibid., 5–6.

Proponents of the Little Russian idea soon faced a powerful new adversary within the bureaucracy as well. From his first days in office in 1861, Minister of Internal Affairs P. A. Valuev (1815-90) consistently opposed the efforts of southwestern activists to reimagine estate society in ethnonational terms; instead, he insisted that the imperial state should continue to seek out alliances with notables of many backgrounds.[20] Deeming the populist rhetoric of southwestern Sunday schools a threat to state stability, he ordered officials to close them.[21] Meanwhile, his ministry exiled the most radical Little Russian activists on the left bank and deprived Kostomarov, who had been the most outspoken promoter of the Ukrainian language, of his history chair at St. Petersburg University.[22]

Valuev's alarm at the nationalizing experiment that had been coalescing in Kiev since 1830–31 was far from universal, however. Some within the imperial bureaucracy continued to facilitate southwestern activists' efforts to demarcate ethnonational groups in the borderlands and to mobilize local Orthodox residents against Polish separatism. After Kostomarov's dismissal from his university position, St. Petersburg officials permitted the scholar to participate in the planning of an expedition sponsored by the Imperial Geographic Society that would identify and map the nationalities of the empire's western borderlands.[23] Kiev governor-general Vasil'chikov enlisted the Kiev Commission to formulate and circulate responses to the Polish patriotic pamphlets proliferating across the southwest.[24] And although Vasil'chikov reported to his superiors that the Kiev Hromada continued to be dogged by rumors that its members were "communists," he noted that its success thus far in contesting Polish claims on the region had provided a valuable service to the state.[25]

Divided about whether the Little Russian lobby was an indispensable ally of or a dangerous threat to a state facing a deepening political crisis, officials responded to it on an ad hoc basis. The Kiev governor-general's office tended to tolerate (or even

---

20. The quote is from Alexander Polunov, *Russia in the Nineteenth Century* (Armonk, NY, 2005), 112.
21. Marakhov, *Sotsial'no-politicheskaia bor'ba*, 64–65.
22. Gnat Pavlovych Zhytets'kyi, Notes for the article "Kyivs'ka hromada za 60-ti roki," IRNBUV, I.46884, l. 30b; David Saunders, "Russia and Ukraine under Alexander II: The Valuev Edict of 1863," *International History Review* 17, no. 1 (1995): 42–43.
23. Staliunas, *Making Russians*, 109–10. For more on the Geographic Society and its activities, see Nathaniel Knight, "Constructing the Science of Nationality" (PhD diss., Columbia University, 1995). In the early sixties, imperial officials and loyalist intellectuals in the northwestern borderlands contemplated mobilizing Belarusian, Estonian, and Latvian culture (and peasant populations) against the szlachta. However, these efforts were never pursued wholeheartedly, and they ceased entirely by about 1864. See Staliunas, *Making Russians* 43–56; Dolbilov, *Russkii krai*, 202–26. This chapter argues that in the southwest, by contrast, official efforts to marshal local peculiarities in pursuit of the imperial state's centralizing goals were quite systematic and lasted long beyond 1863.
24. Ministry of Education to I. I. Vasil'chikov, 13 January 1862, TsDIAUK, f. 442, op. 812, d. 4. 1862, ll. 10–100b; I. I. Vasil'chikov to M. V. Iuzefovich, 3 February 1862, in ibid., ll. 13–130b.
25. I. I. Vasil'chikov to Ministry of Education, 23 October 1862, TsDIAUK, f. 442, op. 812, d. 85, ll. 25–300b; Drahomanov, "Do Istorii ukrainskoi khlopomanii v 1860-ti- rr," l. 5; Zhytets'kyi, "Kyivs'ka hromada za 60-ti roki," ll. 10–11. After receiving Vasil'chikov's report, censors cleared the Kiev Hromada's response to its critics for publication in Katkov's *Sovremennaia letopis'*.

promote) it, while Valuev struggled to limit its influence. As officials rather candidly admitted, however, it was not always easy to distinguish the subversive from the salutary elements of the Little Russian idea. When a special committee investigating political crimes in the southwest met to consider the case of P. P. Chubinskii (1839–84)—a khlopoman, *Osnova* contributor, and Kiev Hromada member who in 1862 had visited right-bank peasant settlements and encouraged the residents to rise up against Polish nobles—the group concluded that it could not find Chubinskii guilty of inciting an "antigovernment movement," since his agitation against the szlachta in fact aided the official de-polonization campaign. Nevertheless, the committee members agreed that "allowing similar attempts to continue...could have a dangerous influence on the minds of the simple folk."[26] Like the Cyrillo-Methodians a decade and a half before him, Chubinskii was spared hard labor or Siberian exile and ordered instead to serve in the governor's chancery in Arkhangel'sk; there officials used his skills in the service of the state, appointing him editor of the local government paper and a member of the statistical commission.[27] In correspondence to a friend back home, however, Chubinskii expressed dismay and astonishment that he had been punished at all: how, he wondered, could anyone mistake him for an "enemy of the government" that, with the emancipation decree of 1861, "liberated 22 million slaves and gave them rights as human beings [*chelovecheskie prava*]?"[28]

Little Russian Activists and the Polish Insurrection

If differences of opinion had emerged within the Little Russian lobby about the direction in which its program should evolve, once the insurrection began in 1863, southwestern activists overlooked their differences and mobilized against the threat. Antonovich and fellow khlopomany rallied St. Vladimir's students opposed to the revolt, denouncing Poles as mere "guests" in the southwest and calling on local residents and officials to put down the Polish demonstrations with force.[29] Dragomanov and Kostomarov continued their efforts to instill peasants with pride in their native traditions, soliciting funds in the newspapers of the imperial capitals to support Ukrainian-language primary schools and the publication of religious materials in the local vernacular.[30] *Vestnik Iugo-Zapadnoi i zapadnoi Rossii* presented the struggle unfolding in the southwestern borderlands as a clash of civilizations that would

---

26. Memorandum on P. P. Chubinskii's record, 15 April 1876, RGIA, f. 1282, op. 1, d. 352, ll. 540b–55.
27. P. P. Chubinskii, P. A. Gil'tebrandt, N. I. Kostomarov, and S. V. Mishanich, eds., *Pavlo Chubyns'kyi, Pratsi etnohrafichno-statystychnoi ekspeditsii v zakhidno-Rus'kyi krai* (Donetsk, 2008), 20.
28. P. P. Chubinskii to Ia. P. Polonskii, 11 June 1863, collected by Lev Peretts for the article "P. P. Chubinskii v ssylke i ego perepiska (1862–1869 gg.)," IRNBUV, I.17930, l. 19. A patriotic poem that Chubinskii wrote in 1863, "Ukraine Has Not Yet Perished," has been set to music and is today the national anthem of Ukraine.
29. See the undated perlustrated letter included in TsDIAUK, f. 442, op. 813. d. 3, l. 165.
30. Gnat Pavlovych Zhytets'kyi, "Kyivs'ka hromada za 60-ti roki," IRNBUV, I.46884, l. 24.

determine the future of all the children of Rus'.[31] Aiming to win over European public opinion, which tended to be sympathetic toward the Polish cause, Iuzefovich advanced the same argument in a pamphlet he published in Leipzig.[32]

Yet even as Little Russian intellectuals sought to discredit the Polish nationalist cause, officials expressed growing concern about their intentions. Local censors warned that the Hromada's popular education efforts might ultimately benefit the rebels, noting that Polish patriotic gatherings had openly discussed opportunities to promote the Ukrainian language as a means of estranging right-bank peasants from imperial intellectual life.[33] An anonymous denunciation sent to the Third Section in early 1863 described this threat in more vivid terms, denouncing Little Russian activists as "the most zealous separatists and enemies of Russia." Condemning activists' ongoing efforts to introduce Ukrainian into schools and to translate the Bible into the local vernacular, the writer complained that these endeavors aimed to replace the imperial lingua franca with a local "dialect"—which he saw as the first step toward the "separation of Little Russia from Great Russia and a federation with Poland."[34] The chief of the Third Section, Prince V. A. Dolgorukov, apparently found the writer's claims convincing. Noting the Polish origins of Antonovich and other khlopomany active in the Hromada, he expressed concern that the organization served the aims of Polish patriots and directed the new governor-general of Kiev, N. N. Annenkov, (Vasil'chikov had died in the first days of the revolt), to disband it.[35]

Other officials, especially in the Kiev governor-general's office, brushed off these concerns. Annenkov agreed that it was inappropriate to translate the Bible into "a plebeian language that has no grammar and no literature" and pledged to subject local activists to "vigilant supervision." Nevertheless, he vehemently denied that the Little Russian idea could ever serve Polish interests, insisting that the "Little Russian party's" interest in the "independent development of folk life [*narodnaia zhizn'*] in Little Russia" had consistently served "to counteract Polish Catholic [*latino-pol'skaia*] propaganda."[36] Indeed, Annenkov seems to have defied Dolgorukov's instructions to

---

31. For example, "O soedinenii Pol'shi s Rossieiu. Istoricheskii ocherk," *Vestnik Iugo-Zapadnoi i zapadnoi Rossii* 3 (1863): 24–58; "Pol'skii vopros," *Vestnik Iugo-Zapadnoi i zapadnoi Rossii* 4 (1863): 54–76; "Pol'skii katikhizis. Russkii katikhizis," *Vestnik Iugo-Zapadnoi i zapadnoi Rossii* 4 (1863): 22–36.
32. M. Jouzéfovitch, *La question russo-polonaise jugée par un petit-russien* (Leipzig, 1863).
33. Saunders, "Russia and Ukraine," 28–29.
34. Unsigned letter, 1863, RGIA, f. 1282, op. 1, d. 166, ll. 7–9. For differing views on the letter's influence on later policies toward the Ukrainian language, see Ricarda Vulpius, "Iazykovaia politika v Rossiiskoi imperii i ukrainskii perevod Biblii (1860–1906)," *Ab Imperio* 2 (2005): 191–224; Andrii Danylenko, "The Ukrainian Bible and the Valuev Circular of July 18, 1863," *Acta Slavica Japonica* 28 (2010): 1–21.The Bible was not translated from Church Slavonic into the Russian vernacular until 1858.
35. Zhytets'kyi, "Kyivs'ka hromada," ll. 180b-19.
36. Governor-General Annenkov to Prince Dolgorukov, 17 March 1863, RGIA, f. 1282, op. 1, d. 166, ll. 30b–4. In debates over whether to offer an official subsidy to *Vestnik Zapadnoi and Iugo-Zapadnoi Rossii* one month earlier, Annenkov had advanced a similar argument. Although he acknowledged the immoderate rhetoric and radical views of Little Russian patriots, he insisted that they had played and could continue to play a key role in counteracting Polish threats and advancing Orthodox interests in the region. Memorandum of the Kiev governor-general's chancery, 23 February 1863, RGIA, f. 1282, op. 2, d. 1945, l. 11.

disband the Kiev Hromada, which continued to organize public protests against the Polish revolt—and even to solicit funding for its translation projects in St. Petersburg newspapers.[37]

As officials struggled to clarify their stance on the Little Russian idea, an influential figure who had previously maintained cordial relations with Kiev-based activists reconsidered his support for them. In the summer of 1863, the publicist M. N. Katkov—a close associate of Maksimovich and the publisher of the Kiev Hromada's 1862 response to its critics[38]—now denounced Kostomarov and his colleagues for their efforts in the field of popular education. Arguing that the Russian literary language exerted a powerful unifying force on the diverse peoples of the empire, he claimed that the recognition of the Ukrainian vernacular as an alternative mode of communication would break this important bond, thereby providing comfort to the Polish patriots attempting to tear the southwest from the rest of East Slavic civilization. Claiming that the activities of Little Russian intellectuals unwittingly served "the sworn enemies of their own Ukraine," Katkov argued that their efforts departed from a fundamentally flawed supposition.[39] "Ukraine has never had its own history, its own government, and the Ukrainian people are purely Russian people.... The Little Russian language never existed, and despite all the efforts of the Ukrainophiles, still does not exist."[40] Having only a few years earlier wished Little Russian activists well in their efforts to introduce a vital new national spirit into the empire, Katkov had now come to see the very discussion of the Dnieper region's unique traditions as subversive.

In the aftermath of Katkov's intervention, Valuev grew ever more determined to quash the nationalist ideas that had emerged from the southwest. In July 1863, he circulated a document among his censors branding the Ukrainian language a mere "dialect" of Russian that had been "corrupted by Polish influence." Paraphrasing Katkov in the formulation that became the circular's most infamous line—"there was not, is not, and cannot be any special Little Russian language"—Valuev ordered a thorough review of the implications of the Little Russian idea in the context of the Polish revolt. He demanded that censors refuse to approve Ukrainian-language religious texts and primers aimed at the masses until this review had been completed.[41]

Valuev's circular shocked Little Russian activists, and it alarmed officials who had supported their activities. Kostomarov and Minister of Education A. V. Golovnin protested the circular, arguing that Little Russian activists had consistently insisted on the

---

37. On Hromada activities in this period, see Zhytets'kyi, "Kyivs'ka hromada," ll. 16–160b; O. I. Stoianov to unidentified acquaintance, 18 February 1863, IRNBUV, III.4085. Having situated Annenkov in his local as well as his imperial context, my interpretation of these events is quite different from Alexei Miller's, who sees Annenkov's apparent tolerance toward the Hromada as a "provocation" designed to elucidate the group's true (and presumably dangerous) aims. Miller, *Ukrainian Question*, 99.
38. Indeed, Maksimovich had offered the publicist a chair at St. Vladimir's in the 1840s. See Martin Katz, *Mikhail N. Katkov* (Paris, 1966), 35.
39. M. N. Katkov, *1863 god* (Moscow, 1887), 1:277.
40. Ibid., 1:278.
41. See the version of Valuev's circular reprinted in Miller, *Ukrainian Question*, 265–66.

fundamental unity of the children of Rus' and had never questioned the legitimacy of the imperial state.⁴² But Valuev refused to reconsider the injunctions against what he referred to disparagingly as the "southwestern yokel dialect" (*khokholskoe narechie*), rigorously enforcing the circular for as long as he remained in his post. (The report that he had commissioned apparently was never completed.)⁴³ The Valuev decree had a disastrous effect on Ukrainian publishing ventures: in 1862, thirty-three Ukrainian-language books had been published in the Russian empire; by 1868—the year Valuev left office—that number had dropped to one.⁴⁴

The Valuev circular was an important intervention in the evolving debate about the appropriate role of the Little Russian idea within the imperial struggle to claim the southwest and to defeat Polish separatism. But it was far from the last word. As early as November 1863, the Third Section—which had helped raise alarms about the activities of Little Russian activists in the first place—released a report that warned of the potentially negative consequences of officials' efforts to rein in Little Russian intellectuals. Although the report ordered officials to show no tolerance for any effort to encourage "the political separation of Little Russia from the other parts of the Russian empire," it also cautioned that new restrictions on the activities of southwestern activists might well alienate the many who had remained loyal to the imperial state and thus "destroy for good the existing ties between the two Russian nationalities [*narodnosti*]."⁴⁵

Governing the Southwest, Remaking the Borderlands

By 1864, imperial officials had reclaimed control of the western borderlands. As special commissions met to identify and punish the rebels, bureaucrats reached a consensus that they needed to create a long-term strategy to halt the rise of national separatism and to better integrate the residents of the southwest into the empire's political and intellectual life. Officials sharply disagreed about how best to accomplish this aim, however, deepening the schisms that had emerged between those who highlighted the value of the Little Russian idea and those who drew attention to its dangers.

In the aftermath of the 1863 revolt, the southwestern governors-general often echoed the arguments that Little Russian activists had already been making for several decades. Questioning the ability of Poles and Jews to be loyal imperial subjects, they argued that the state should strive to enhance the political and economic influence of

---

42. These efforts are described in Miller, *Ukrainian Question*, 118–20.
43. *Dnevnik P.A. Valueva* (Moscow, 1961), 1:239. The term *khokholskii* is difficult to translate into English. It is clearly pejorative, marking explicitly southwestern traditions as benighted and deserving of condescension if not mockery.
44. Johannes Remy, "The Valuev Circular and Censorship of Ukrainian Publications in the Russian Empire," *Canadian Slavonic Papers*, 49, no. 1–2 (2007): 97.
45. Memorandum of N. V. Mezentsov, 7 November 1863, RGIA, f. 1282, op. 1, d. 166, l. 280b; 35. Note the invocation of Kostomarov's concept of two distinct yet internally linked "Russian nations" in the latter citation.

"Russians" of all social stations—identified primarily by their Orthodox faith—in the borderlands. An opposing camp, headed by Valuev, the most outspoken bureaucratic opponent of the Little Russian idea, insisted that marginalizing the non-Orthodox populations of the borderlands would only alienate them. Instead, he argued that the state should engage the empire's "best people"—that is, nobles and wealthy elites of all ethnoconfessional backgrounds—more fully in civic affairs.[46] The minister of internal affairs insisted that local gentry should dominate *zemstva*—new organs of local-self governance introduced in rural areas across central Russia in 1864. And his blueprints for the elective city councils implemented in the major cities of European Russia in 1870 set the economic thresholds for voting high but permitted broad Polish and Jewish involvement in city councils.[47]

In the bureaucratic tug-of-war that followed the 1863 revolt, both camps left a mark on the social, economic, and political life of the southwest. Valuev's elitist but cosmopolitan worldview—which officials in the Ministry of Finance tended to share—played an important role in structuring local economic affairs. By midcentury, the southwestern borderlands had become the empire's chief producer of raw sugar beets as well as refined sugar. The szlachta, which possessed the large tracts of land necessary to turn a profit on an extremely labor-intensive crop and the capital to build refineries, had played a key role in the industry since its early-nineteenth-century origins; in the 1850s, Jewish mercantile elites had also begun to invest in the cash crop.[48]

The influence of the non-Orthodox only grew after 1863, as Jewish merchants and szlachta clans that had remained loyal to the government acquired new rural and industrial properties that had been requisitioned from rebels.[49] The continued growth of the sugar industry after 1863 spurred further development, necessitating new rail lines to supply southwestern factories and to transport the sugar they produced. Again, non-Orthodox entrepreneurs played key roles in these efforts. In the 1860s and '70s, private joint stock companies operated by Jews, Poles, and foreign capitalists secured government guarantees on their investments and built rail lines that connected the southwest with the Black Sea region, the Kingdom of Poland, and central Russia.[50]

Impressed by the leadership of the southwest's diverse capitalist elites, officials in the Ministry of Internal Affairs (MVD) and Ministry of Finance convinced Tsar

---

46. For further details on conflicts within the bureaucracy, see Komzolova, *Politika*; Rodkiewicz, *Russian Nationality*; Alfred Rieber, "Interest-Group Politics in the Era of the Great Reforms," in *Russia's Great Reforms, 1855–1881*, ed. Ben Eklof, John Bushnell, and Larissa Zakharova (Bloomington, IN, 1994), 58–83; Thomas S. Pearson, *Russian Officialdom in Crisis* (New York, 1989), 21–59.
47. Polunov, *Russia*, 112–13; Daniel R. Brower, *The Russian City between Tradition and Modernity* (Berkeley, 1990), 103.
48. See Oleksander Ohloblyn, *Narysy z istorii ukrains'koi fabryky* (Kiev, 1931).
49. Witold Walewski, "Cukrownictwo na Ukrainie," *Pamiętnik Kijowski*, 2:179–81.
50. Major investors in southwestern railroad lines included the self-made S. S. Poliakov, the product of a left-bank shtetl; I. S. Bliokh, born into a poor Jewish family in the Kingdom of Poland; and a joint stock company controlled by Count Vladislav Branicki, a major Polish landowner who had remained loyal to the imperial state in 1863. Valentine Tschebotarioff Bill, "The Early Days of Russian Railroads," *Russian Review*, 15, no. 1 (1956): 14–28; Daniel Beauvois, *La bataille de la terre en Ukraine* (Lille, 1993), 247.

Alexander II to overturn the laws that had banned Jewish settlement in Kiev since the 1830s. They invited "useful" Jews—that is, merchants of the first and second guilds—to return to the city, although the continued exclusion of Kiev from the Pale initially obligated Jewish merchants to settle in less desirable, outlying neighborhoods and forbade them from acquiring immovable property.[51] This reform attracted new Jewish entrepreneurs to the city and further encouraged Jewish engagement in the local economy. The Brodskii family, which arrived in Kiev shortly after the lifting of the ban on Jewish settlement, invested heavily in the sugar industry, eventually assuming control of dozens of sugar factories.[52] The Gintsburgs, natives of the southwest who made millions investing in government-guaranteed land bank and railroad obligations, established a commercial bank with their earnings and acquired ownership of half a dozen sugar refineries.[53]

As we will see in chapter 4, the first Jewish families to reenter the Kiev market economy would play a key role in shaping the city's urban politics and the political culture of the southwest more broadly. Although few Jewish migrants to Kiev would ever attain the wealth and influence of the Brodskiis and Gintsburgs, the families set an example of success and assimilation that many would try to emulate. Both families lived like landed gentry, acquiring massive estates with lavish manor homes and gardens; in the 1870s, the Gintsburgs, who welcomed foreign dignitaries and tsarist ministers alike to their table on a regular basis, even acquired baronial titles. Both families benefited from close personal relationships with Valuev, who invited them to serve on official committees on Jewish affairs.[54] The diverse leaders of industry in the southwest had already begun to formulate a cosmopolitan (yet elitist) point of view that conflicted with the nationalizing and populist vision of the Little Russian lobby.

However, Valuev's opponents also played a vocal role in southwestern politics in the years immediately following the revolt. Annenkov, the region's governor-general from 1862 to 1865, and his successor A. P. Bezak, who served from 1865 to 1868, oversaw aggressive attacks on the political and economic prerogatives of Poles and Jews. They convinced their St. Petersburg superiors to ban the acquisition of new land by Poles and to assess a flat tax on properties that they had already acquired, to close Polish clubs, to purge Poles from the local bureaucracy, and to institute quotas on Polish students at local educational establishments.[55] Ignoring the social and ideological

---

51. See B. V. Anan'ich, *Bankirskie doma v Rossii, 1860–1914 gg.* (Leningrad, 1991) 39; Meir, *Kiev*, 24–25. On the "selective integration" of "useful Jews," see Nathans, *Beyond the Pale,* 23–82.
52. Alexandra Fanny Brodsky, *Smoke Signals* (London, 1997); Victoria Khiterer, "Jewish Life in Kyiv at the Turn of the Twentieth Century," *Ukraina moderna* 10 (2006): 78.
53. See Anan'ich, *Bankirskie doma,* 40; Henri Sliosberg, *Baron Horace-O. de Gunzbourg: Sa vie, son oeuvre* (Paris, 1933); Walewski, "Cukrownictwo na Ukrainie," 2:181.
54. See "Mémoire du Baron Alexandre de Gunzburg" (unpublished manuscript c. 1939), 23, 26, 35, 38; Nathans, *Beyond the Pale,* 38–79, 173–74; Klier, *Imperial Russia's Jewish Question,* 245–62; Brodsky, *Smoke Signals,* 6–7. I am grateful to Benjamin Nathans for providing me with a copy of the unpublished Gintsburg manuscript.
55. See Rodkiewicz, *Russian Nationality Policy,* 21–26; TsDIUAK, f. 442, op. 814, d. 381.

cleavages within the szlachta, they portrayed Poles as irredeemable opponents of the empire and the children of Rus'; in the fierce debates among officials about how to distinguish Poles from other imperial populations, they pressed for the broadest possible definition.[56] By the mid-1860s, Bezak (who had married into the Storozhenko family, an old Cossack clan) convinced the ministries to implement new laws preventing the acquisition of land by Jews, who he claimed were acquiring land from ruined Polish families through long-term leases and joint stock companies and in some cases were assuming the seigniorial privileges that the szlachta had once enjoyed.[57]

As it worked to undermine the influence of the non-Orthodox in the borderlands, the Kiev governor-general's office sought to promote "Russians" in their place. Officials replaced the Poles purged from state service with five thousand bureaucrats previously posted in the Russian interior.[58] Aiming to consolidate property in the hands of the Orthodox majority, which owned less than one-fifth of the land in the southwest in the 1860s, officials rewarded those who had served the state with estates confiscated from Poles and offered low-interest loans to Orthodox believers who purchased land.[59]

The governors-general not only endeavored to consolidate an East Slavic elite in the southwest; they also expressed their desire to protect and promote the Orthodox peasantry. Annenkov lobbied Valuev further to reduce peasants' obligations to landlords, to expand the network of church and state schools in the region, and to use the millions of rubles raised by the flat tax on the szlachta to support Orthodox parish communities.[60] He urged the authorities to implement zemstva—introduced in European Russia in 1864—in the southwest, arguing that they would enhance peasant self-reliance and rectify the region's underdevelopment and public health challenges. He added, however, that the hostility of the "Polish element" toward the imperial state and local peasantry would demand special measures to protect the interests of the "native population" in these organs. He encouraged officials to set quotas that limited Polish participation in the bodies; to lower the economic thresholds that qualified voters for the franchise, which would expand the Orthodox electorate; and to create local exceptions to all-imperial statutes that banned the participation of Orthodox priests in elections.[61]

---

56. Rodkiewicz, *Russian Nationality Policy*, 58–63; Staliunas, *Making Russians*, 73–84.
57. Beauvois, *La Bataille*, 48, 314; L. E. Gorizontov, "Pol'sko-evreiskie otnosheniia vo vnutrennei politike i obshchestvennoi mysli rossiiskoi imperii (1831–1917)," in *Istoriia i kul'tura rossiiskogo i vostochnoevropeiskogo evreistva*, ed. Oleg Budnitskii et al. (Moscow, 2004), 262–63.
58. Rodkiewicz, *Russian Nationality Policy*, 137.
59. Ibid., 64–68.
60. See Annenkov to Valuev, 6 November 1863, TsDIAUK, f. 442, op. 812, d. 654, l. 54, 56ob.; *Dnevnik P.A. Valueva*, 1:66.
61. Memorandum of Annenkov, 26 November 1863, TsDIAUK, f. 442, op. 812, d. 654, ll.61–69; the quote is from 62. Olga Maiorova has noted that many officials and intellectuals in mid-nineteenth-century Russia expressed suspicion about the loyalty of the empire's nobles (not only the szlachta) and aligned themselves with its peasants (including the non-Russians among them). See Maiorova, *From the Shadow*, 94–127.

In short, Annenkov argued that political participation in the zemstva—which was determined by estate status in other corners of the empire—should be determined by ethnonational status in the southwest. Indeed, later in the same memorandum, he suggested that national ideas could serve as a new guiding principle of governance in the region more generally. Local peasants, he complained, faced an "uneven battle with the Poles for land and... with Yids in industry" that they could not expect to win on their own. He continued, "In order to neutralize, at least to a certain extent, the strength of their enemies, it is necessary to endow Russian people in the region with certain privileges vis-à-vis Poles and Jews; otherwise, they will not survive this battle and we will have to cede both our nationality [*narodnost'*] and our government to our enemies."[62]

Valuev resisted the attempts of the southwestern governor-general's office to introduce ethnonational considerations into the governance process, charging that the policies proposed by right-bank officials would promote "devastation as a principle of administration."[63] He vetoed Bezak's radical blueprints for new laws governing land ownership, which would have prevented all Catholics and even Germans from acquiring land in the southwest.[64] He failed to eliminate loopholes in the new land laws, which permitted Poles to retain land in lien or to acquire new property through joint stock companies.[65] Valuev also refused to implement the nationalized zemstva proposed by Annenkov, opting instead to forgo the implementation of the reform in the western borderlands altogether.[66] By the late 1860s, however, the nationalizing agenda of the governors-general had begun to triumph over Valuev's vision of a multiethnic polity built on the loyalty of elites.[67] Over the next several decades, the southwestern governors-general, who were inclined to see local society as a conglomeration of coherent and well-defined national groups pursuing conflicting agendas, would implement ambitious policies designed to enhance the economic and political power of the East Slavic children of Rus'—and to reduce that of Poles and Jews. By the early 1870s, the number of Orthodox landowners in Kiev province would surpass the number

---

62. Memorandum of Annenkov, 26 November 1863, TsDIAUK, f. 442, op. 812, d. 654, l. 64. See also "Kimitaka Matsuzato, The Issue of Zemstvos in Right Bank Ukraine, 1864–1906," *Jahrbücher für Geschichte Osteuropas* 51, no. 2 (2003): 218–35. This expression of nationalist fervor is substantially more radical than the ideas of Katkov, who is often thought of as a rabid Russian nationalist. Although Katkov considered East Slavs the titular nationality of the empire, like Valuev he argued that Poles and Jews who accepted the language and culture of the imperial center could be loyal imperial subjects. Insistent that the Russian nation must be built on the foundation of landowning elites, not the peasant masses, the journalist also advocated for plutocratic zemstva. See Renner, "Defining a Russian Nation," 670; Maiorova, *From the Shadow,* 89; Miller, *Romanov Empire,* 114–15; Katz, *Mikhail N. Katkov,* 78–103.
63. Cited in Rodkiewicz, *Russian Nationality Policy,* 63.
64. *Dnevnik P.A. Valueva,* 2:78. Nevertheless, the proponents of maximalist de-polonization measures scored other victories, managing to disqualify from state service even Russians who had married Polish women. Rodkiewicz, *Russian Nationality Policy,* 133.
65. Rodkiewicz, *Russian Nationality Policy,* 68–71.
66. For an overview of the western zemstvo issue, see the Memorandum of the MVD's Main Directorate on Local Governance Affairs, 2 April 1903, TsDIAUK, f. 442, op. 656, d. 132, ch. 1, l. 176.
67. Rodkiewicz, *Russian Nationality Policy,* 26.

of Polish-speaking Catholics. (The large size of the average estate held by the latter, however, meant that those classified as Poles still controlled nearly 70 percent of the province's private property).[68]

The Little Russian Idea after the Revolt

The policies endorsed by the southwestern governors-general echoed the central premises of the Little Russian idea. They rested on the belief that East Slavs from all walks of life belonged to a single nation defined by its historical, cultural, and religious traditions; that the children of Rus' needed help to defend their culture from external onslaughts; and that the struggle unfolding in the southwest between Orthodox believers and their putative enemies would determine the future of the East Slavs and the Russian empire. Now enlisted in the service of the centralizing and standardizing imperial state, however, these ideas lost the pronounced Little Russian patriotism that had accompanied their original articulation.

Some southwestern activists insisted that the concept of an East Slavic nation defined from above and denuded of its Little Russian patriotism was nonsensical. Kulish denounced the efforts of officials to monitor and control the activities of local activists. He also excoriated contributors to *Vestnik Zapadnoi i Iugo-Zapadnoi Rossii*, arguing that by warning of the potential dangers associated with the advancement of the Ukrainian literary language, they had capitulated to the critics of the Little Russian idea.[69] (Kulish's critique of fellow members of the Little Russian lobby provoked substantial controversy within the Kiev Hromada, which fell into disarray in 1864.)[70]

The Valuev circular (and the demise of *Osnova*, which had gone bankrupt in late 1862) also encouraged Little Russian activists to search for new outlets for their activities. Some looked to Austrian Galicia, where the Habsburg authorities had begun to experiment with policies that encouraged Ukrainian-language publications and Ruthenian cultural organizations as a means of neutralizing the power of the szlachta and counteracting Russian influence. Right-bank activists sent their Ukrainian-language printing presses to Lemberg, and Kulish, Kostomarov, Dragomanov, Antonovich, and khlopoman activists all contributed to the region's lively press.[71]

Yet despite the frustration that some felt at the growing interest of the imperial state in managing and directing the evolution of the Little Russian lobby, the agenda that southwestern activists promoted in the Galician press was remarkably consistent with the ideas that they had articulated in the Russian public sphere prior to 1863.

---

68. A. M. Dondukov-Korsakov, "Zapiska o bolee vazhnykh voprosakh po upravleniiu Iugo-Zapadnym kraem," 1872, RGIA, f. 932, op. 1, d. 160, ll. 80b–10.
69. For example, P. A. Kulish to A. K. Alchevskii, 28 February 1863, IRNBUV, III.4086, ll. 1–2.
70. See Zhytets'kyi, "Kyivs'ka hromada," ll. 19–22.
71. Ibid., l. 22. On the Austrian cultural laws and their effects, see Magocsi, *Roots*; John-Paul Himka, *Galician Villagers and the Ukrainian National Movement in the Nineteenth Century* (Edmonton, 1988); Keely Stauter-Halsted, *The Nation in the Village* (Ithaca, 2001).

Portraying the Cossacks as the carriers of the true Orthodox spirit forged in Rus', Kulish continued to implicitly argue for the fundamental unity of the East Slavs; it was Poles and other local minority groups, not imperial bureaucrats, whom he presented as the greatest threat to Rus' traditions.[72] However, a new generation of Galician activists with rather different views would soon use for their own ends the cultural institutions that the Russian empire's Little Russian activists had established in the Habsburg empire. In the years to come, Galician intellectuals would articulate growing hostility toward the "Muscovite" government, charging that measures such as the Valuev decree were no less oppressive and damaging to the Little Russian simple folk than the oppression of the szlachta.[73] This development, which we will discuss further in the next chapter, would have a critical influence on Russian officials' attitudes toward Little Russian activism.

Whereas some southwestern activists resented official efforts to control the evolution of Little Russian patriotism on the one hand and to instrumentalize it on the other, others celebrated the potential of the Little Russian idea to serve the post-1863 imperial state. Iuzefovich argued that the struggle to protect the "Russian national body" (*le corps national russe*) from foreign attempts to "mutilate" it had been under way for centuries in the southwest; Little Russian intellectuals such as Kostomarov had anticipated by several decades the post-1863 campaign to achieve "the tribal organic union of the Russian people."[74] Iuzefovich shared the concerns of those who feared that Polish patriots were engaged in a conspiracy to use discussions of the region's cultural and linguistic peculiarities for their own ends, and he excoriated the new Galician journals, which he charged promoted "hatred toward Moscow."[75] But even as he argued that the Little Russian idea must be protected from these dangerous attempts to pervert its true meaning, he insisted that it had a vital role to play in the official effort to de-polonize the western borderlands and to rally the East Slavs behind the tsarist regime.

Iuzefovich did not show blind obeisance to the imperial state, however; rather, he pressed local officials to adopt the most aggressive de-polonization measures possible. In a series of sharply worded letters to Annenkov, he warned the governor-general to be on guard against the treacherous intent of local Polish nobles—even those who had remained loyal to the state during the revolt. Centuries of bitter experience, he argued, had already established that the Polish nation as a whole was preternaturally hostile to

---

72. For example, P. Kulish, "Ruina," *Meta* 2 (1863): 134–48.
73. On Galician radicals, see K. Klymkovych, "Stanovyshche rusi suprotyv liads'ko-moskovs'koi borby," *Meta* 1 (1863): 61–83; "Bor'ba maloi-rusi s tsentralizmom moskovskim," *Slovo*, 14/26 August 1863, 253; "Byti ly nam obshcherusskimi chy Malo-Rusynami?" *Slovo*, 18 March/9 April 1864, 101–2. For more background on the Galician press in the sixties, see Ostap Sereda, "'Whom Shall We Be?' Public Debates over the National Identity of Galician Ruthenians in the 1860s," *Jahrbücher für Geschichte Osteuropas*, 49, no. 2 (2001): 200–212; Wendland, *Die Russophilen*, 153–72.
74. The quotes are from Jouzéfovitch, *La question*, 4; M. V. Iuzefovich, *17-e aprelia v Kieve* (Kiev, 1863), 3–4.
75. M. V. Iuzefovich, *Vozmozhen li mir s nami pol'skoi shliakhty?* (Vil'na, 1864), 6–8. Quote from 7.

the children of Rus' and to the empire that they had created.[76] Other prominent Little Russian activists soon joined Iuzefovich's lobbying campaign—and the ranks of the bureaucratic organs executing the de-polonization crusade. G. P. Galagan, appointed chair of the southwestern committee on peasant affairs, informed Annenkov that he found the governor-general's efforts to limit the power of the szlachta and to improve the lives of local peasants inadequate; Galagan advocated new measures to restrict the obligations that landlords could impose on peasants.[77] A. P. Storozhenko (1805–74), an *Osnova* contributor and the author of many works that celebrated the virtues of Little Russian folk culture, led the effort under the governor-general of Vil'na to convert Catholics to Orthodoxy.[78] Indeed, even Kulish, who had been critical of the centralization of governance after 1863, accepted an elite bureaucratic position in the Kingdom of Poland, where he oversaw Russification measures.[79]

Meanwhile, the Kiev Commission for the Analysis of Historical Documents intensified its efforts to create a national history for the borderlands and to highlight the ways in which the Little Russian idea could serve the imperial de-polonization campaign. Iuzefovich, elected president of the group in the late 1850s, touted its potential to "expose the true history of the Western region, establish its true [*istinnoe*] relationship to Poland and Russia, dispel false notions intentionally spread by Polish historians and publicists, and by this means create a firm scholarly base for the correct resolution of the Polish question in this region."[80] Antonovich, appointed editor of the group's periodical, *Arkhiv Iugozapadnoi Rossii*, in 1863, used that publication to present the southwest as a battleground where the future of East Slavic civilization would be decided. Bemoaning the exploitation of peasants and townspeople by inimical foreign forces, he lauded the region's frequent jacqueries as national liberation movements.[81] Impressed by its work, Governor-General Bezak quadrupled the group's funding in the midsixties, using the revenue collected from the new taxes on Polish estates to underwrite its activities.[82]

From Little Russian Lobby to Orthodox Intelligentsia

Although Little Russian patriots continued to debate the direction in which their ideas should evolve—and their proper relationship with the imperial state—their internal

---

76. "Pis'mo Kievskogo General-Guberatora N. N. Annenkova k M. V. Iuzefovichu," *Russkii arkhiv* 3 (1883): 204.
77. See the correspondence between Annenkov and Galagan in IRNBUV, I.6998–7018; *Dnevnik P.A. Valueva*, 1:286.
78. See Dolbilov and Miller, *Zapadnye okrainy,* 227. This is the same Storozhenko family into which Governor-General Bezak married.
79. George S. N. Luckyj, *Young Ukraine* (Ottawa, 1991), 76.
80. *Sbornik statei i materialov po istorii iugo-zapadnoi Rossii, izdavaemyi Kommissiei dlia razbora drevnikh aktov, sostiashchei pri Kievskom, Podol'skom i Volynskom General-Gubernator* (Kiev, 1911), 14.
81. See V. B. Antonovich, *Izsledovanie o gaidamachestve: Po aktam 1700–1768 g.* (Kiev, 1876); *Arkhiv Iugo-zapadnoi Rossii* 5, no. 1 (1869): 1–94; *Arkhiv Iugozapadnoi Rossii* 3, no. 3 (1876): 1–128. The latter two pieces were penned by Antonovich as well.
82. *Sbornik statei,* 14–15.

divisions did not prevent the continued expansion of their influence in local society and politics. By the 1860s the ongoing campaign against the Polish gentry (in which leading Little Russian intellectuals had played an active role) had cleared the way for the emergence of a new Orthodox intelligentsia in Kiev, where only a decade before Polish language and culture had dominated institutions of higher education and the beau monde. In contrast to the Little Russian lobby that emerged in the aftermath of the first Polish revolt, which consisted primarily of left-bank gentry who traced their origins to the Cossack Hetmanate, the Little Russian intelligentsia that coalesced after the second was larger in numerical terms and more socially variegated. Indeed, many who joined this new intellectual elite were men of very modest origins whose bureaucratic service or participation in cultural institutions such as the Kiev Commission had enabled their upward social mobility. Determined to defeat their putative adversaries and to protect their cultural patrimony, they were equally committed to improving the plight of the Little Russian narod from which they had come.[83]

The Lebedintsev brothers, born into a poor priestly family of Cossack origins, are prime examples of this new class of elites who were both beneficiaries of and participants in the imperial state's post-1863 efforts to de-polonize the borderlands.[84] The eldest, P. G. Lebedintsev (1819–96), spent most of the 1850s serving as a priest and a teacher in a district town of Kiev province, where he befriended Shevchenko. Although his efforts to educate and uplift his peasant parishioners attracted scorn from local notables, who insisted that "stupid country yokels" were not capable of joining the ranks of respectable society, they also earned accolades from church hierarchs.[85] By the 1860s, he had been appointed the first editor of *Kievskie eparkhial'nye vedomosti (News of Kiev Diocese)*, a member of the Kiev Commission, and the rector of St. Sophia's cathedral. In the latter role, he would oversee a continuing project launched by antiquarians close to Nicholas I in the 1840s to restore Rus'-era frescos and mosaics inside the cathedral, which had been painted over when the church was under Uniate control.[86]

---

83. Although the ideological orientation of Kiev's Little Russian activists contrasts sharply with the mostly liberal local intelligentsia in Nizhnii Novgorod that Catherine Evtuhov has studied, my findings support her suggestion that "provincial projects" provided a means by which socially minded intellectuals could offer "something new and original" to imperial society. Evtuhov, *Portrait*, 207, 228.

84. On the role of priests' sons, or *popovichi*, in late imperial intellectual/political culture and their commitment to popular uplift in both religious and secular settings, see Laurie Manchester, *Holy Fathers, Secular Sons* (DeKalb, 2008).

85. F. I. Titov, "Petr Gavriilovich Lebedintsev," *Trudy Kievskoi dukhovnoi akademii* 38, no. 1 (1897): 137; "Protoierei P.G. Lebedintsev," *Istoricheskii vestnik* 67 (1897): 618. Lebedintsev's commitment to uplifting the masses placed him on the extreme left of the local clergy: see Kl. Fomenko, *Iz pamiatki prikhodskogo sviashchennika o Kieve* (Kiev, 1904), 16.

86. On the cathedral restoration project, see I. Tolstoi and N. Kondakov, eds., *Russkie drevnosti v pamiatnikakh iskusstva* (St. Petersburg, 1891), 4:113–63; N. Zakrevskii, *Letopis' i opisanie goroda Kieva* (Moscow, 1858), ch. 2, 216–17; on Lebedintsev's role in the project: Kostiantyn Krainii, *Istoryky Kyevo-Pechers'koi lavry XIX–pochatku XX stolit'* (Kiev, 2000), 38.

His brother, F. G. Lebedintsev (1828–88), who began his career as a seminary teacher and an *Osnova* contributor, ultimately became a professor at the Kiev Theological Academy. He also served as secretary of the Kiev Commission and the director of schools in Kholm region (then part of the Kingdom of Poland and a remaining Uniate stronghold), where he was charged with implementing a curriculum that was "Russian" in spirit. Sharing his brother's populist inclinations, he encouraged the priests and teachers he trained to acquaint themselves with local folk culture, to compile ethnographic data about their parishioners, and to deliver liturgies in Ukrainian, the people's tongue.[87] A third brother, A. G. Lebedintsev (1826–1903), served as a priest and popular education activist in the southwest; in the 1870s, he became an important figure in the imperial campaign to suppress the Greek Catholic Church in areas of the borderlands that had escaped the "reunification" of the 1830s.[88]

Self-identified Little Russians of modest origins attained important positions in secular intellectual life as well. A. F. Kistiakovskii (1833–85), the son of a Chernigov parish priest and the grandson of a serf, began his education in local seminaries. A promising young scholar, he ultimately won a stipend to study law at St. Vladimir's and accepted a bureaucratic position in St. Petersburg in the late 1850s, where he joined the Hromada and wrote for *Osnova*. In the early sixties, Kistiakovskii left bureaucratic service to pursue graduate studies in criminal law, and in 1869, he was appointed professor of law at St. Vladimir's. Kistiakovskii went on to become one of Russia's most prominent experts on juvenile delinquency and the death penalty, but he remained devoted to the culture of the simple folk from whom he had come: between international conferences in Europe, he compiled the first collection of Little Russian customary law. In 1870, Dragomanov secured an appointment at St. Vladimir's as well. That same year, Antonovich, who was married to Kistiakovskii's sister-in-law, was appointed professor of history at the university, where he would inspire generations of students—many of whom we will meet in later chapters—interested in the unique traditions of the southwest.[89]

Of all the upwardly mobile Orthodox believers in the right bank, perhaps Vitalii Iakovlevich Shul'gin (1822–78) availed himself most effectively of the new opportunities that presented themselves to Little Russian activists after 1863. The son of a middle-ranking bureaucrat of Cossack origins, Shul'gin studied history at St. Vladimir's and worked at the Kiev school for noble girls after his graduation, first as a teacher and later

---

87. L. S. M., "Zamechatel'nye urozhentsy i deiateli Podolii proshlogo vremeni," *Pravoslavnaia Podoliia* 14–15 (1908): 244–50.
88. I. Gordievskii, "Protoierei A.G. Lebedintsev (Nekrolog)," *KEV* 5 (1904): 110–17. For more on the Lebedintsev brothers and their milieu, see Heather J. Coleman, "Pravoslavnoe dukhovenstvo, istoricheskaia pamiat' i malorossiiskaia identichnost' v Kieve XIX v.," in *Istoricheskaia pamiat' i obshchestvo v Rossiiskoi imperii i Sovetskom soiuze* (St. Petersburg, forthcoming).
89. See O. F. Kistiakivs'kyi, *Shchodennik* (Kiev, 1994), 1:9; "Avtobiograficheskaia zametka," in *Mykhailo Petrovych Drahomanov* (Kiev, 1970), 1:48.

as its inspector.⁹⁰ Involved in several local history groups working to prove the "primordially Orthodox" nature of the southwest in the fifties, he was soon invited to join the Kiev Commission and the history faculty at Kiev University.⁹¹ In the spring of 1863, in the midst of the Polish revolt, the university declined to offer Shul'gin a full-time teaching appointment, a decision that the historian attributed to the ongoing political influence of Poles at the top levels of the institution.⁹² The decision, which devastated Shul'gin, coincided with the sudden deaths of his brother, sister-in-law, and parents from an infectious disease. Left to care for his orphaned nieces and nephews—including Iakov Shul'gin, an active member of the Kiev Hromada—the historian fell into a deep depression and became incapacitated by migraine attacks that paralyzed him for days at a time.⁹³

By late 1863, Shul'gin had begun to emerge from his depression. He came to understand his own suffering as part and parcel of the misfortunes that had befallen the entire Little Russian people, and he vowed to rebuild his life—and to reclaim his native region from "the triple yoke of Catholic clergy, Poles (landlords, rentiers, and estate managers) and Jews" that he believed continued to oppress it.⁹⁴ Shul'gin enlisted the help of Dragomanov and colleagues from the Kiev Commission, procured a subsidy from the governor-general's office, and in June 1864 established Kiev's first daily newspaper, *Kievlianin*.⁹⁵ Like Maksimovich's earlier almanac of the same title, the paper worked to acquaint readers with the special features of the Little Russian people, to document their centuries-long struggle against foreign rule, and to mobilize right-bank residents in defense of East Slavic traditions. Early editions of the paper denounced the "illegal encroachments" of the szlachta on peasant communities and denounced the Brodskiis and other Jewish industrialists for subjecting their workforce to inhumane labor conditions.⁹⁶ In the ideological program he published in the paper's first issue, Shul'gin promised once and for all to disprove alien claims on the region and to reveal its true essence: "Our region isn't the Kingdom of Poland and it isn't even Lithuania," he thundered. "Our region is Russian, Russian, Russian."⁹⁷

Shul'gin agreed with Iuzefovich that efforts to promote the Little Russian idea must not detract from imperial unity. He published the paper in Russian, the imperial lingua

---

90. Passionately devoted to the cause of education for women, Shul'gin had written his master's thesis on the position of women in the reign of Peter I. On the historian's progressive views on gender, see V. Solukha, *Kratkaia istoricheskaia zapiska o sostoianii Kievo-Podol'skoi zhenskoi gimnazii* (Kiev, 1896), 3.
91. Culled from "Vitalii Iakovlevich Shul'gin," *Kievlianin* (Kiev, 1880), 1–6; Tarasenko, *Stanovlennia*, 41.
92. "Vitalii Iakovlevich Shul'gin," 8–11; Tarasenko, *Stanovlennia*, 45.
93. *Biograficheskii slovar' professor i prepodavatelei imperatorskogo universiteta Sv. Vladimira*, ed. V. S. Ikonnikov (Kiev, 1884), s.v. "Shul'gin, Vitalii Iakovlevich," 770; "Vitalii Iakovlevich Shul'gin," 8–9.
94. The quote is from V. Ia. Shul'gin, "Iugo-zapadnyi krai pod upravleniem D. G. Bibikova," *Drevniaia i novaia rossiia* 6 (1879): 89; see also *Biograficheskii slovar'*, 771.
95. "Kiev," *Kievlianin*, 1 July 1864, 1. Because Russia had relatively low literacy rates and an underdeveloped capitalist marketplace at this point, state sponsorship of Little Russian ventures proved essential to their success.
96. The quote is from "Ob"iavlenie." *Kievlianin*, 1 July 1864, 1. On Jewish "exploitation," see "Kiev," *Kievlianin*, 8 August 1864, 1.
97. "Ob"iavlenie," 1.

franca, and expressed concerns about the separatist rumblings in the Galician press.[98] Yet he remained devoted to the organic nationalist and populist values that had become the hallmark of the Little Russian idea. He demanded that the authorities requisition szlachta lands, redistribute them to Orthodox peasants, and enhance the East Slavs' access to education, culture, and political power.[99] *Kievlianin* published memoirs celebrating the role that the Sunday schools and the Kiev Hromada had played in undermining Polish claims on the region, and it praised a Ukrainian-language opera by a Hromada member as "the first successful attempt to provide an artistic rendering of the southern Russian folk motif."[100] Although later historians branded the paper and its editor as proponents of administrative centralization and Great Russian chauvinism, contemporaries (including Dragomanov) understood Shul'gin's intellectual project as a progressive and "democratic" force in local society.[101] Assuming the role that *Osnova* had played in the early sixties, *Kievlianin* became a gathering place for proponents of the Little Russian idea—but now it officially enjoyed the sanction of the imperial state.

Reaching a Broader Public

If the 1863 uprising had raised official concerns about the intentions of Little Russian intellectuals, their substantial participation in the official campaign to reduce Polish influence and promote the Orthodox East Slavs of the borderlands soon assuaged bureaucrats' fears. By the late 1860s, activists resumed many of the activities that they had interrupted earlier in the decade as they renegotiated their relationship with officials. Through ethnographic research, studies of oral traditions and Cossack chronicles, and philological work, activists continued their efforts to identify the features distinctive to the Little Russian people—which they presented as authentic manifestations of the East Slavic traditions forged in Rus'. In these years, Dragomanov published scholarly articles in *Kievlianin* and two monographs that documented both the unique qualities of Little Russian folk culture and the sacrifices that the southwestern narod had made to defend the integrity of the Orthodox Church and the unity of the former Rus' domains; this research later formed the basis of a massive ethnographic study that he coauthored with Antonovich.[102] Kostomarov, who was participating in an effort to publish a new edition of Shevchenko's work in the Habsburg empire, continued

---

98. "Kiev," *Kievlianin*, 14 July 1864, 1.
99. "Ob"iavlenie," 1; "Narod i narodnye shkoly," *Kievlianin*, 4 August 1864, 4; "Kiev," *Kievlianin*, 1 August 1864, 1.
100. "Zapiski ob universitetskoi zhizni (1860–64)," *Kievlianin*, 13 August 1864 and 25 August 1864, 1; "Novaia malorusskaia opera," *Kievlianin*, 2 February 1874, 1.
101. The citation is Dragomanov's description: see "Avtobiograficheskaia zametka," 47; also A. A. Rusov, "Kak ia stal chlenom 'hromady'" *Ukrainskaia zhizn'* 10 (1913): 45. For claims of *Kievlianin*'s "reactionary" character, see John D. Klier, "Kievlianin and the Jews," *Harvard Ukrainian Studies* 5, no. 1 (1981): 83–101; Iuliia Polovynchak, *Hazeta "Kievlianin" i Ukrainstvo* (Kiev, 2008).
102. M. P. Drahomanov, "Malorossiia v ee slovesnosti" (1869), in *Vybrane*, 5–45; Mikhail Dragomanov, *Malorusskie narodnye predanye i razskazy* (Kiev, 1867); M. Dragomanov and V. Antonovich, *Istoricheskie pesni malorusskogo naroda*, 2 vols. (Kiev, 1874–75).

to argue for the dialectical connection of "northern" and "southern" Rus'.[103] Kulish, who had been the most critical of the imperial state's centralizing tendencies after 1863, published a massive historical study of the "reunification" of the children of Rus' under Khmelnytsky.[104]

In the mid-1860s, P. P. Chubinskii, who continued to conduct ethnographic and statistical research while in Arkhangel'sk, received an invitation from the Imperial Geographic Society to move to St. Petersburg and to lead the team preparing for the long-planned ethnographic expedition to the southwestern borderlands. He was subsequently freed from police surveillance, and he launched the expedition in 1869. Kistiakovskii, Antonovich, Kostomarov, and Shul'gin all participated in the three-year undertaking, which dispatched intellectuals to remote locales across the right bank to record peasant customs, chart dialects, and collect statistical data about the social and economic condition of the region's inhabitants.[105] The results—published in six volumes between 1872 and 1876—documented the special features of the Little Russian simple folk and their efforts to defend the unity of the Orthodox Church and the children of Rus' from allegedly monolithic Jewish and Polish interests.[106] In recognition of Chubinskii's service to the empire, the MVD decorated the onetime exile with a prize; for his contributions, Antonovich received an estate.[107]

In the early stages of the ethnographic expedition, Chubinskii published a series of articles in *Kievlianin* encouraging further "Ukrainian self-organization" to counteract exogenous influence in the southwest. Shortly thereafter, Shul'gin, Iuzefovich, Galagan, Zhitetskii, and other Hromada alumni composed a petition asking the authorities to open a southwestern chapter of the Imperial Geographic Society in Kiev.[108] In 1872, the group received authorization to begin its activities. At its opening meeting, Chubinskii celebrated the fact that "the non-Russian intelligentsia that formerly dominated the region has switched places with the Russian, and the Russian element has come back to life [*ozhil*]."[109]

The new governor-general of Kiev, Prince A. M. Dondukov-Korsakov—who shared Little Russian activists' interest in consolidating political and economic power in the

---

103. N. I. Kostomarov, "Istoricheskoe znachenie iuzhno-russkogo narodnogo pesennogo tvorchestva," *Beseda* 4 (1872): 5–68; N. I. Kostomarov and M. O. Mikeshin, eds., *Kobzar* (Prague, 1876). The historian was a strong supporter of developing the "local languages" of the Slavs but also insisted that Russian should remain their lingua franca. See Prymak, *Mykola Kostomarov*, 144–45.
104. P. A. Kulish, *Istoriia vozsoedineniia Rusi*, 3 vols. (St. Petersburg, 1874).
105. See P. P. Chubinskii, "Ocherk narodnykh iuridicheskikh obychaev i poniatii v Malorossii," *Zapiski Imperatorskogo russkogo geograficheskogo obshchestva, po otdeleniiu etnografii* 2 (1869): 677–715; Chubinskii et al., *Pavlo Chubyns'kyi*, 20–23, 70–72.
106. P. P. Chubinskii, ed., *Trudy etnografichesko-statisticheskoi ekspeditsii v Zapadno-Russkii krai*, 6 vols. (St. Petersburg, 1872–76); Chubinskii et al., *Pavlo Chubyns'kyi*, 46.
107. Chubinskii to A. E. Timashev, 29 July 1876, RGIA, f. 1282, op. 1, d. 374, l. 160b; MVD internal memorandum, 1868, RGIA, f. 1282, op. 1, d. 352, l. 135.
108. Savchenko, *Zaborona ukrainstva*, 14, 17, 233.
109. F. Volkov, "P. P. Chubinskii," *Ukrainskaia zhizn'* 1 (1914): 48; Savchenko, *Zaborona ukrainstva*, 31.

hands of Orthodox East Slavs[110]—proved a reliable supporter of the southwestern branch of the Geographic Society. Thanks to his strong support and the group's loyal membership base, which built on the preexisting Little Russian lobby, it rapidly became one of the all-imperial organization's most active local chapters. Its members conducted a census in Kiev, published collections of folk songs and proverbs from the Dnieper region and Austrian Galicia, and began to compile the collected works of Maksimovich, who died in 1873. It organized an all-Russian archeological congress held in Kiev in 1874, at which its members hailed the "national consciousness" of the southwest's Orthodox inhabitants as a powerful force leading the struggle against Polish culture and regenerating the children of Rus'.[111] The foundation of the Kiev chapter of the Geographic Society—which coincided with Valuev's 1868 departure from office—also ushered in a renaissance in Ukrainian-language publishing ventures, which in 1874 rebounded to their pre-1863 levels.[112]

Meanwhile, Kiev-based activists launched a new effort to strengthen the ties between the East Slavs of the right bank and Austrian Galicia. In 1869, Shul'gin, Iuzefovich, Galagan, and Antonovich opened the Kiev Slavic Philanthropic Society. The group offered scholarships to Galician students who wished to study in Russia, worked with local Orthodox priests to convert Roman and Greek Catholic believers, and took over the Lemberg-based newspaper *Slovo*, which allowed it to reach literate Galicians directly. It published an almanac of ethnographic and historical research that aspired to document the essential traits of the "southern Russian" people.[113] Closely associated with the pan-Slavic committees springing up across the Russian empire, the committee celebrated the diversity of the Slavic peoples and praised Little Russian culture as the most authentic expression of the Slavic spirit—an elemental force that had allowed the simple folk to resist Polish rule and to defend the integrity of the Orthodox Church.[114] However, the group also insisted that Russian was "the tongue of

---

110. See, for example, the governor-general's memorandum, "Zapiska o bolee vazhnykh voprosakh po upravleniiu Iugo-Zapadnym kraem. 1872 god," RGIA, f. 932, op. 1, d. 160, ll. 1–105.
111. M. V. Iuzefovich, "Nekotorye soobrazheniia o luchshei organizatsii deiatel'nosti arkheograficheskikh kommissii," in *Trudy tret'iago arkheologicheskogo s"ezda v Rossii byvshogo v Kieve v Avguste 1874 goda* (Kiev, 1878), 1:49–51; Ignat Zhytets'kyi, "Pivdenno-Zakhidnyi Viddil Geografichnoho Tovarystva u Kyivi," *Ukraina* 5 (1927): 31–36. Kiev was not the only locale where the Geographic Society served as a semi-official forum in which nationalist intellectuals could project their ideas on the empire. See Daniel Brower, *Turkestan and the Fate of the Russian Empire* (New York, 2003), 46–54; Mark Bassin, *Imperial Visions* (New York, 2004), especially 95–101.
112. Remy, "The Valuev Circular," 97. Remy notes that thirty-two Ukrainian books were approved by censors in 1874, just one short of the number published in 1863, attributing this rebound to corruption within the Kiev censorship apparatus. As we have seen here, however, this trend is fully consistent with the rising influence of the Little Russian lobby among southwestern officials in the late sixties and early seventies.
113. On the group's activities, see *Ocherk deiatel'nosti Kievskogo slavianskogo blagotvoritel'nogo obshchestva za 25 let ego sushchestvovaniia, 1869–1894* (Kiev, 1894). On *Slovo*, see RGIA, f. 821, op. 4, d. 2132. The almanac is A. V. Storozhenko, ed., *Slavianskii ezhegodnik* (Kiev, 1877).
114. See S. A. Nikitin, *Slavianskie komitety v Rossii v 1858–1876 godakh* (Moscow, 1960). By the 1860s, the Slavophile movement had begun to give way to a pan-Slavic movement that aimed to mobilize Slavs across Europe in defense of their native cultures.

the greatest Slavic tribes, the pan-Slavic language of literature, science, and educated society..., the general language of literature and science of all the Slavic nationalities"; for this reason, it printed its newspaper and pamphlets exclusively in that language.[115]

In the sixties and early seventies, Little Russian activists also expanded their efforts to establish contact with the simple folk whom they claimed to represent. In the early 1860s, A. F. Andriiashev, a high school principal who would eventually join the Slavic Philanthropic Society, founded *Kievskii narodnyi kalendar'* (*Kiev People's Calendar*). An Orthodox alternative to the popular almanacs circulated by Catholic monasteries in the southwest, the publication was used to promote Orthodox piety and to raise awareness of Little Russian folk culture and the role that it had played in the struggle against external encroachments.[116] In 1867, Andriiashev launched a "people's newspaper for the southwest region" called *Drug naroda* (*Friend of the People*). Like *Kievlianin*, the paper lamented the historical "exploitation" of the southwest by Poles and Jews, who it complained had "squeezed all the juices from the Russian lands," and it advocated the devolution of power to local communities and the redistribution of resources to benefit the narod.[117] Exasperated that the nationalizing measures implemented by the authorities after 1863 had not yet guaranteed the preeminence of the Orthodox East Slavs in the state they had built, Andriiashev argued that the Little Russian people needed a new popular leader, a new Khmelnytsky, to "free the people from Polish and Latin slavery and...to reunite under the protection of the Orthodox Russian tsar the parts of the indivisible Russian lands torn away by enemies."[118]

Indeed, Little Russian activists frequently looked to Khmelnytsky as the embodiment of authentic East Slavic values and a carrier of the national spirit that they hoped to encourage across the empire. As early as the 1850s, Maksimovich proposed erecting a monument to the Hetman in Kiev, which he believed would remind all residents of the city of the value of Little Russian culture and the role it had played in shaping and protecting the Rus' lands.[119] In the aftermath of the 1863 revolt, Iuzefovich convened a working group under the Commission for the Analysis of Historical Documents to collect money and rally support for the project. The group, which included Antonovich, Maksimovich, and other leading Commission members, chose the St. Petersburg-based sculptor M. O. Mikeshin to execute the monument. Famed for his intricate creations and his pride in the empire—he had completed the monument to the millennium of Russia in Novgorod in 1859 and would finish his homage to Catherine the Great in St. Petersburg in 1873[120]—Mikeshin was also devoted to the radically populist, organic nationalist ideologies that underpinned the Little Russian idea.

---

115. See *Ocherk deiatel'nosti Kievskogo slavianskogo blagotvoritel'nogo obshchestva*, 55; *Otchet o deiatel'nosti Kievskogo otdela Vysochaishe utverzhdennogo Slavianskogo blagotvoritel'nogo komiteta* (Kiev, 1872), 26.
116. K. Fomenko, "Kiev vtoroi poloviny XIX veka," *KEV* 20 (1909): 471.
117. For example, *Drug naroda*, 1 July 1867, 382–83; *Drug naroda*, 15 July 1867, 415–16.
118. *Drug naroda*, 15 August 1867, 475.
119. M. A. Maksimovich, "Pis 'ma o Bogdane Khmel'nitskom k M. P. Pogodinu," *Ukrainets* 1 (1859): 151.
120. For analysis of the sculptor's millennial monument, see Maiorova, *From the Shadow of Empire*, 61–71; Wortman, *Scenarios*, 2:80–84, 125–28.

The son of Belarusian petty traders, Mikeshin had been friendly with Shevchenko, who admired the artist's "democratic worldview" (*demokratizm*).[121] Having illustrated an 1860 version of Shevchenko's *Kobzar* published by Kulish, in the 1870s, the artist joined Kostomarov and Galician activists working to publish a new edition of the poet's work in Prague.[122]

Mikeshin finished his first prototype for the Khmelnytsky statute in 1869. It depicted the hetman primed for war atop a steed; to ensure the historical accuracy of the hetman's garb and weapons, Mikeshin had borrowed artifacts from Antonovich's personal collection.[123] Below the horse's hooves, in the artist's words, lay the trampled body of "the three enemies against whom Khmelnytsky fought so gloriously in Ukraine": a Jesuit priest covered by a tattered Polish flag, a Polish noble, and a Jew holding stolen ritual objects and money in his hands.[124] On the pedestal supporting the statue, Mikeshin inscribed a traditional folk song of the seventeenth century recently collected by Dragomanov: "Oh, it will be better / oh, it will be more beautiful / When in our Ukraine / There are no Jews, no Poles / And no Union."[125]

A glorification of popular liberation through violence, the statue also demonstrated how Khmelnytsky's struggle to liberate Little Russians from their national rivals reinforced the unity of all the children of Rus'. A *kobzar* (itinerant folk poet) who bore a striking resemblance to Shevchenko sat in the center of the pedestal that supported the image of the hetman, surrounded by figures of Great, White, Little, and Galician Russian ethnographic types.[126] An inscription on the front of the monument read, "A united, indivisible Russia—to Hetman Bohdan Khmelnytsky"; scenes of the hetman's military victories over Polish forces and the names of "heroes of Little Russian Cossackdom" were emblazoned on the four corners of the pedestal.[127] In 1869, Tsar Alexander II himself expressed his approval of the prototype of the Khmelnytsky statue, which he saw in Mikeshin's studio.[128]

---

121. A. M. Umanskii, "Pamiati M.O. Mikeshina," *Istoricheskii vestnik* 67 (1897): 625, 650.
122. M. O. Mikeshin, ed., *Kobzar* (St. Petersburg, 1860); Kostomarov and Mikeshin, *Kobzar*; A.A. Rusov, "Kak ia stal chlenom 'hromady,'" *Ukrainskaia zhizn'* 10 (1913): 47.
123. "Opisanie Vysochaishe uchrezhdennogo proekta pamiatnika," c. 1873, DAK, f. 301, op. 1, d. 8, l. 32; also "Pamiatnik Bogdanu Khmel'nitskomu," *KS* 22, no. 7 (1888): 145–56.
124. The quote is from "Opisanie Vysochaishe uchrezhdennogo proekta pamiatnika," c. 1873, DAK, f. 301, op. 1, d. 8, l. 32. For descriptions of the monument, see Mikeshin to Iuzefovich, 19 February 1869, TsDIAUK, f. 873, op. 1, d. 48, l. 300b.; also, M. G., "Istoriia odnogo pamiatnika, " *Golos minuvshego* 7 (1913): 284.
125. "Istoriia odnogo pamiatnika," 284–85. "Union" refers to the 1596 Union of Brest, which established the Greek Catholic Church.
126. "Istoriia odnogo pamiatnika," 284–85; on the monument's democratic message, see TsDIAUK, f. 873, op. 1, d. 48, l. 290b.
127. Mikeshin to Iuzefovich, 2 January 1869, TsDIAUK, f. 873, op. 1, d. 48, l. 45. The quotes are from DAK, f. 301, op. 1, d. 8, l. 320b.; TsDIAUK, f. 873, op. 1, d. 48, l. 29.
128. Mikeshin to Iuzefovich, 10 February 1869, TsDIAUK, f. 873 op. 1, d. 48, ll. 48–480b. By 1869, Katkov had again revised his position on the Little Russian idea, hailing the Khmelnytsky project—and the national ideas emerging from Kiev more generally—as salutary efforts to cast off foreign influences and to unite the children of Rus'. See "Davnost' natsional'noi idei," 18 March 1869, in M. N. Katkov, *Imperiia i kramola* (Moscow, 2007), 99–101.

Проектъ памятника Богдану Хмельницкому въ Кіевѣ.

M. O. Mikeshin's original blueprint for Kiev's Khmelnytsky statue. Source: A. M. Umanskii, "Pamiati M. O. Mikeshina," *Istoricheskii vestnik* 47 (1897): 633. Courtesy of Slavonic Library, National Library of Finland.

Granted permission in 1870 to move into the next stages of the project, committee members worked to engage the largest public possible in the endeavor, cooperating closely with Governor-General Dondukov-Korsakov. Iuzefovich penned articles in local history journals explaining how "a simple person of the land, a Little Russian Cossack" had become a "southern Russian hero" and a nation builder who "reunited" the scattered children of Rus'. The monument, he wrote, not only celebrated the contributions of the "higher classes of Russian society" but also sought to rally all the children of Rus' in celebration of the man who had presided over "the defeat of our most irreconcilable enemy, who returned Kiev holy sites to the Russian people; who saved Orthodoxy... on the banks of the Dnieper and laid the foundation stone that supports the present government structure of all Russia."[129] While *Kievlianin* admiringly reviewed popular histories of Khmelnytsky's campaigns—and reprinted the folk song that appeared on the statue's pedestal—the members of the committee overseeing the statue's completion circulated appeals for funding that welcomed "donations of a few cents from simple people."[130]

The efforts of Little Russian activists to raise awareness of the southwest's special culture and to claim the borderlands for the children of Rus' were not without their limits. Kiev censors praised *Drug naroda*'s efforts to "proliferate among its semi-educated readership [an understanding of] the benefits of morality, the usefulness of labor, the practical meaning of economic thriftiness [*sberezhenii*], the dangers of drunkenness, love for the fatherland, etc." However, they complained that the publication employed "excessively harsh" rhetoric when denouncing the influence of non-Orthodox populations, leading uneducated readers to potentially "dangerous" conclusions.[131] Censors expressed similarly mixed emotions about *Kievlianin*. Although they noted that the paper had played an important role in disputing Polish claims on the region and promoting the interests of East Slavs, they worried that its colossal influence jeopardized official control over its editorial positions.[132]

The Khmelnytsky project generated similar concerns. In the early 1870s, Alexander II's brother, Grand Duke Konstantin Nikolaevich, a leading liberal voice within the government, announced his opposition to the statue's violent message, demanding that Mikeshin remove the depictions of the hetman's "enemies."[133] After the exhibition of the model of the statue in Kiev in 1872, the city's Catholic community voiced its own objections, complaining that the monument encouraged the

---

129. M. Iuzefovich, "Bogdan Khmel'nitskii v russkoi istorii," *Vestnik zapadnoi Rossii* 7, no. 3 (1870): 58–61 (fourth pagination).
130. "Po povodu odnoi knizhki," *Kievlianin*, 27 June 1868, 1–2; Iuzefovich to Dondukov-Korsakov, 10 February 1870, DAK, f. 301, op. 1, d. 3, l. 14; see also Iuzefovich's notes on the matter, ibid., l. 10.
131. Report of Kiev censor, 23 June 1868, TsDIAUK, f. 294, op. 1, d. 59, l. 1.
132. For example, Main Directorate on Press Affairs to Kiev censor, 21 November 1868, TsDIAUK, f. 293, op. 1, d. 828, l. 14; Ministry of Internal Affairs to local censor, 9 October 1882, TsDIAUK, f. 294, op. 1, d. 151, l. 103.
133. Mikeshin first mentioned intrigue against the statue in 1872: see his letter to Iuzefovich, 9 February 1872, TsDIAUK, f. 873, op. 1, d. 48, l. 23; for Mikeshin's later reflections on the grand duke's opposition, see his 24 May 1888 letter to Iuzefovich, TsDIAUK, f. 873, op. 1, d. 48, l. 3.

"incitement of national hatred" and the "kindling of anti-social passions" (*razzhiganie antisotsial'nykh strastei*).[134] One Kiev Commission member agreed that the statue would stand as a "shameful pillory" to the "Catholic Polish and Jewish" residents who encountered it, and he resigned from the committee overseeing the statue's completion.[135] Others, however, remained defiant in the face of this criticism. Denouncing the statue's critics, *Kievlianin* insisted that "neither the Polish landlord, nor the priest, nor the Jew has yet been cast off the precipice; this region is still put to the test by their tenacity."[136] Dondukov-Korsakov, still supportive of the statue's proponents, continued to argue for the monument's merits before the St. Petersburg authorities. Ultimately, however, Alexander II and the MVD sided with the project's critics, ordering that the figures of the Polish noble, Jesuit, and Jew—as well as the bas relief figures of ethnographic types—be removed. In 1888, the monument, now portraying only the hetman on his steed, was erected before St. Sophia's Cathedral.[137]

::

In the years immediately before and after the 1863 revolt, the Little Russian lobby struggled to define its proper relationship with the tsarist state and imperial society at large—a process prompted by external crises that also produced internal dissent. By the late sixties, however, southwestern activists had overcome the adversity that they faced earlier in the decade. They effectively marketed their movement as a servant of imperial interests, advocate of East Slavic unity, and enemy of national separatism, which in turn allowed them to attain unprecedented influence in intellectual and political life. Having secured the support of local bureaucrats and well-placed St. Petersburg officials, they constituted an Orthodox educated society in Kiev, formed new organizations to promote their ideas, and reached out to the simple folk from whom many of them had come. Although by the early seventies some voices in the bureaucracy were airing new concerns about the violent rhetoric and substantial influence of Little Russian activists, the powerful lobby that had emerged in the southwest remained a key ally in the official campaign to claim the southwest for the Russian empire.

But while Little Russian activists had largely succeeded in renegotiating their relationship with the imperial state in the tumultuous 1860s, the tensions that had long lurked within their program had continued to grow more pronounced. Although the Little Russian lobby had grown more socially variegated—and its rhetoric distinctly more populist—gentry such as Iuzefovich remained at the helm of the movement; the fact that activists presented an illustrious Cossack general rather than the toiling

---

134. N. V-tskii, "Vnutrennye izvestiia," *Sankt-Peterburgskie Vedomosti*, 12 November 1872, 1 (second pagination).
135. "Mnenie po protokolu zasedaniia Komiteta po sooruzhenii pamiatnika Bogdana Khmel'nitskomu ot 8 okt. 1872 goda," TsDIAUK, f. 442, op. 28, d. 232, ch. 1, l. 33–34ob.
136. "Po povodu pamiatnika Bogdanu Khmel'nitskomu," *Kievlianin*, 18 November 1872, 2.
137. For a more thorough discussion of the monument and the controversies that surrounded it, see Faith Hillis, "Ukrainophile Activism and Imperial Governance in Russia's Southwestern Borderlands," *Kritika* 13, no. 2 (2012): 301–26.

The Khmelnytsky monument, central Kiev. Source: *Vidy Kieva* (Kiev, 1917). Courtesy of Slavonic Library, National Library of Finland.

masses as the great symbol of the Rus' national spirit showed that many leaders of the lobby had not abandoned the elitist views of its founders. In spite of their contributions to an official campaign that aimed to delegitimize Polish claims on the southwest and to more fully assimilate residents into all-imperial culture, Little Russian activists continued to draw attention to the peculiarities of local culture. And the fundamental questions that radical critics and Great Russian Slavophiles had raised about the Little Russian idea in the early sixties remained unresolved. Was the movement primarily a conservative project that aimed to unify and strengthen the East Slavs by helping them rediscover their native values? Or was it a revolutionary program of social emancipation? Would its denunciations of Polish and Jewish interests reinforce imperial unity by aligning the state with the interests of its East Slavic majority? Or would they encourage discord or even violence and thus destabilize the tsarist order? Little Russian activists' inability to answer these questions themselves would soon lead to a deep schism in their ranks that would splinter their lobby into two competing factions. It is to the series of events that led to this break—which would have a momentous impact on the Little Russian idea and its proponents' relationship with the official world—that we now turn.

3

The Little Russian Idea and the Imagination of Russian and Ukrainian Nations

IN THE 1870S, developments on both sides of the Russo-Austrian border created new challenges for the Little Russian lobby. Over the course of that decade, a radical populist movement emerged in Russia, which saw educated youth fan out across the countryside to acquaint themselves with the needs and desires of peasant communities. Unlike the Little Russian activists who conducted agitation in rural areas, however, the all-Russian populist movement of the sixties and seventies strongly defined itself against the imperial state; some activists turned to terrorism and violence in an effort to topple the tsarist order.[1] Meanwhile, in Austrian Galicia, criticism of the Valuev decree gradually evolved into comprehensive critiques of the imperial state. Building on the organizational infrastructure created by Little Russian activists—who had forged contact between elites in the right bank and Galicia and insisted that the peasant masses on both sides of the border belonged to the Little Russian branch of the Rus' nation—young Galician activists reinterpreted their ideas in a new key. Claiming the Haidamaks, Shevchenko, Kulish, and Kostomarov as heroes of a Ukrainian nation distinct from the Great Russian heartland, Galician activists called on the toiling masses to free themselves not only from putative Polish and Jewish domination but also from the Russian autocracy.[2]

Little Russian activists fiercely debated how to respond to these developments. One camp, led by Iuzefovich and Shul'gin, expressed horror at efforts to turn the populist ideas and local patriotism that the Little Russian lobby had long championed against the imperial state. In the early seventies, its members redoubled their efforts to align the Little Russian idea with the autocratic state. Another camp, elaborating on a critique that had first emerged in the aftermath of the Valuev decree, expressed

---

1. Franco Venturi, *Roots of Revolution* (New York, 1960); S. I. Svitlenko, *Narodnytstvo v Ukraini 60–80-kh rokiv XIX stolittia* (Dnipropetrovsk, 1999).
2. On this new current in Galician intellectual life, which historians have often labeled "populist," see O. Terlets'kyi, *Moskvofily i narodovtsi v 70-ykh rr.* (Lviv, 1902); Magocsi, *Roots*. For examples of Galician radicals' attempts to claim Little Russian heroes for the Ukrainian national cause, see *Rus'*, 28 March 1867, 1; *Pravda* 9 (Lviv, 1876). These efforts outraged Dragomanov, who insisted that Little Russian culture had consistently aimed to strengthen and mobilize, not destroy, a fundamentally indivisible nation of East Slavs. See "Shevchenko, Ukrainofili i sotsializm" (1879), reprinted in *Vybrane*, 327–429.

dissatisfaction about the ongoing centralization of imperial governance, distancing itself from the state.

The debate between these two camps initially centered on the tactics that Little Russian activists should use and did not question the notion that "northern" and "southern" Rus' were indivisible parts of a unitary East Slavic civilization. However, by the midseventies, Shul'gin and Iuzefovich would escalate the conflicts emerging in the Little Russian lobby, denouncing their rivals to the imperial authorities and charging that they were colluding with Galician activists in "Ukrainophile" plots to undermine the integrity of the empire. Although local officials denied these allegations, the MVD and Tsar Alexander II acted decisively to restrain this perceived threat. In 1876, they issued new limitations on the use of the Ukrainian language and punished the individuals whom Iuzefovich and Shul'gin had identified as turncoats.

This chapter reconstructs the disputes that divided Little Russian activists, follows the efforts of imperial officials to manage these conflicts, and considers how internal tensions and external intervention altered the behavior of the lobby and its relationship with the state between the 1870s and '90s. Noting the intensifying efforts of imperial officials to police discussion of local culture in this period, historians have conventionally seen these years as a time of repression that witnessed the final parting of ways between right-bank activists and imperial state.[3] This chapter suggests an alternative way of understanding the evolving relationship between center and periphery, between state and society. It acknowledges that the ability of obscure provincial activists such as Shul'gin and Iuzefovich to gain the attention of the empire's most prominent bureaucrats—and to convince them to intervene in what had begun as a local dispute—reflects a growing wariness among many officials about the nationalizing experiment under way in the southwest. However, the fact that high-ranking bureaucrats proved so responsive to the concerns of Iuzefovich and Shul'gin also testifies to some officials' desire to maintain their cooperative relationship with Little Russian patriots who had demonstrated their loyalty to the imperial state. Indeed, the Little Russian idea remained a centerpiece of official efforts to claim the southwestern borderlands for the empire long after 1876; as we will see, well into the twentieth century, influential figures in the St. Petersburg ministries and the Kiev governor-general's office would hail its potential to reinforce the unity of the empire and the East Slavic descendants of Rus'.

But in spite of the continued efforts of imperial officials to harness carefully monitored expressions of Little Russian patriotism for their own purposes, they proved increasingly unable to maintain control of the national ideas emerging from the southwest. The 1876 regulations alienated some activists, who ultimately abandoned the Little Russian lobby and rejected the myth of East Slavic unity. Over the years

---

3. The classic statement of this thesis is Savchenko, *Zaborona*. Alexei Miller, who notes junctures at which imperial officials accommodated Little Russian patriotism, ends his account in the early 1880s, by which point, he argues, the official effort to assimilate Ukrainians into the "All-Russian nation" had failed. Miller, *Ukrainian Question*.

to come, these activists would play a key role in formulating the nascent Ukrainian national project, using the ideas and tools that they had acquired in the Little Russian lobby to promote liberal and radical political projects that explicitly opposed the autocratic regime. Outraged by these defections, those Little Russian activists who continued their efforts to marshal local culture in defense of the empire and East Slavic unity distanced themselves both rhetorically and ideologically from their "Ukrainophile" opponents. Declaring themselves members of a Russian nation threatened not only by Poles and Jews but also by self-professed Ukrainians, they insisted that the true liberation of the Little Russian masses could happen only under the protection of a strong and illiberal state that limited the influence of these putative enemies of the narod. Official interventions aiming to forestall the possibility that the salutary local patriotism of the Little Russian lobby could give rise to dangerous expressions of Ukrainian separatism unwittingly hastened the fracturing of the lobby into distinct and mutually hostile camps.

The Struggle for Control of the Little Russian Idea

In the early 1870s, the ongoing struggle to define the ideological contours of the Little Russian lobby and its proper relationship to the imperial state intensified. In the seventies, P. A. Kulish, who had sharply criticized the centralizing policies of the imperial government in the immediate aftermath of the Valuev decree, experienced a dramatic change of heart: now, like Shul'gin and Iuzefovich, he defined the Little Russian idea as a loyalist ideology that reinforced state power. Echoing the arguments of the Polish critics of the Little Russian idea in the 1840s and '50s, he portrayed the Cossacks as mere brigands whose violence had harmed the "Ukrainian simple folk" as well as their enemies.[4] In a multivolume history, he hailed the tsars and the autocratic state as the motive forces in the "reunification" of the children of Rus'.[5]

Kostomarov, by contrast, continued to insist that the narod—not the state—must stand at the center of any effort to define the meaning and uses of the Little Russian idea and publicly denounced Kulish—whom he called the "former patriarch of the Ukrainophiles"—for his recent "philippics against Cossackdom."[6] Meanwhile, O. I. Levitskii (1848–1922), the son of a parish priest and one of Antonovich's first students at St. Vladimir's, penned a "people's history of Ukraine" based on the archives collected by the Kiev Commission for the Analysis of Historical Documents.[7] Although Kostomarov and Levitskii sought to guide the Little Russian idea in a more populist

---

4. P. Kulish, "Kazaki po otnosheniiu k gosudarstvu i obshchestva," *Russkii arkhiv* 15, no. 1 (1877): 367. The article continues in: *Russkii arkhiv* 15, no. 2 (1877): 113–35.
5. See P. A. Kulish, *Istoriia vozsoedineniia Rusi*.
6. N. Kostomarov, "O kazakakh," *Russkaia starina* 21 (1878): 402.
7. Quote from Nikolai Vasylenko, "Akademyk Orest Ivanovych Levyts'kyi," *Zapysky Sotsiial'no-ekonomichnoho Viddilu Ukrainskoi Akademii Nauk* 1(1923): lxiv. On Levitskii's early life, see Orest Levyts'kyi, "Moia pochakova shkola (Zgadka)," *Svitlo* 2 (1912): 41–50; "Korotki biohrafichni vidomosti pro Or. Levits'koho," IRNBUV I.11809.

direction, they remained very much a part of the officially sanctioned Little Russian milieu that flourished in Kiev. In the sixties Kostomarov transferred to the Imperial Academy of Sciences the funds that he had collected to publish Ukrainian-language books for the masses, which the academy used to endow a prize for the first scholar to complete a Ukrainian dictionary.[8] Levitskii ultimately became the secretary of the Kiev Commission and a member of the committee working on the Khmelnytsky statue.

Meanwhile, Dragomanov, the one-time Hromada activist and a founding member of *Kievlianin*'s editorial board, developed a devastating critique of the internal contradictions of the Little Russian idea. Between 1870 and 1873, the activist conducted an extended research trip to central and western Europe, funded by St. Vladimir's. During his travels across the continent, he became greatly disturbed by what he perceived as Polish oppression of Galician peasants and by the massive expansion of the centralized Prussian state—both of which he saw as threats to the East Slavs and their traditions. His experiences convinced him more than ever that the Rus' people would need to channel a strong national spirit to unify them and to eradicate the influence of foreign practices in the lands where they lived. He continued to insist that the southwest, where Slavic civilization had first emerged and where ordinary people had struggled for centuries to protect their native customs, was the most likely site from whence this spirit could arise.[9]

In the early seventies, Dragomanov remained deeply committed to the idea of a unitary Rus' nation—a stance that provoked scorn from Galician radicals, who denounced him as a "Russifier."[10] However, he criticized his fellow southwestern activists for proving too willing to compromise on the very nationalizing ideas that promised to revitalize all the children of Rus' as soon as they perceived the slightest resistance from ideological critics. He complained that his compatriots—including Shul'gin, whom he mentioned by name—had failed to adequately defend the cause of Ukrainian-language education from Polish revanchists, Slavophile critics, and Katkov.[11] Dragomanov also expressed alarm about the changing tenor of the relationship between Little Russian activists and the state. Prior to the revolt, he argued, the government had relied on the "simple folk and their national spirit [*narod i narodnost'*]...to preserve the unity of the government at the time of the Polish revolutionary movement."[12]

---

8. Prymak, *Kostomarov*, 168.

9. M. T-ov, "Vostochnaia politika germanii i obrusenie," *Vestnik Evropy* 3 (1872): 184–90; see also M. P. Dragomanov, "Literatura Rosiis'ka, Velykorus'ka, ukrains'ka i halyts'ka" (1873), reprinted in *Literaturno-publitsystychni pratsi*, 1:211.

10. "Avtobiograficheskaia zametka," in *Literaturno-publitsystychni pratsi*, 1:55. This point is also made strongly in Anatolii Kruhlashov, *Drama intelektuala: polytychni idei Mykhaila Drahomanova* (Chernivtsi, 2000), 293.

11. See "Avtobiograficheskaia zametka,"1: 59; "Vostochnaia politika germanii i obrusenie," 239. Dragomanov echoes these arguments in an article published in 1876: see "Antrakt z istorii ukrainofil'stva," in *Vybrane*, 204–33.

12. M. T-ov, "Vostochnaia politika germanii i obrusenie," *Vestnik Evropy* 4 (1872): 678.

But since 1863, he charged, the authorities had been more inclined to govern the borderlands "primarily through bureaucratic and administrative means, with substantial distrust for local forces and populations." Likening this "mechanistic theory of governmental and national centralism" to the governance practices of the Prussian state, he complained that it was fundamentally opposed to Rus' traditions, which he claimed had historically centered on consensus building.[13]

Although Dragomanov's critique of the evolution of the Little Russian idea perceptively captured new trends in political and intellectual life, it was also likely an effort to enhance his own influence in a movement in the midst of generational turnover. By the early 1870s, Maksimovich had passed away, Iuzefovich had turned seventy, and Shul'gin had fallen victim to chronic illness. Upon his return to Kiev in 1873, Dragomanov became one of the most vocal members of the Little Russian lobby, having secured a professorship at St. Vladimir's and attained a leadership role in the Kiev Hromada, which resumed its activities in earnest in the early seventies. Chubinskii, who had gained acclaim for his work in the Imperial Geographic Society, also expanded his influence in these years. In 1873, members of the Kiev Geographic Society elected him to a leading position within that organization, relegating Shul'gin and Iuzefovich to purely symbolic roles; society members later excluded both Iuzefovich and Shul'gin from the committee planning the regional census and from the archeological congress that the group organized with the blessing of the local authorities.[14]

Outraged at the impertinent attempts of these younger men to claim leadership of the Little Russian lobby, Shul'gin and Iuzefovich initiated a propaganda campaign against Dragomanov, Chubinskii, and their allies. In an 1874 editorial in *Kievlianin*, Shul'gin, who had done so much to promote the Little Russian idea, now attacked some of its most prominent proponents, reviving the argument that had been articulated by Katkov a decade earlier. Claiming that the Geographic Society had rejected potential members who could not speak Ukrainian, Shul'gin alleged that the group's devotion to the study of local peculiarities had superseded its interest in maintaining imperial unity—a reversal of priorities that gave its activities a subversive edge.[15] Several months later, in the presence of Governor-General Dondukov-Korsakov, Iuzefovich repeated another allegation that opponents of the Little Russian idea had long used against the movement, claiming that Chubinskii and Dragomanov served Polish revanchist interests and hoped to see Ukraine secede from the empire and join a free Poland.[16]

Both the targets of the campaign organized by Shul'gin and Iuzefovich and local officials dismissed these allegations as absurd. Chubinskii, Dragomanov, and their

---

13. M. T-ov, "Vostochnaia politika germanii i obrusenie," *Vestnik Evropy* 5 (1872): 238.
14. F. Volkov, "P. P. Chubinskii," *Ukrainskaia zhizn'* 1 (1914): 47; 52–53. On the growing rift in Little Russian society, see Kistiakivs'kyi, *Shchodennyk*, 1:28; Savchenko, *Zaborona*, 32–60; Miller, *Ukrainian Question*, 162–63.
15. *Kievlianin*, 3 October 1874, 1.
16. Zhytets'kyi, "Pivdenno-Zakhidnyi Viddil Heohrafichnoho Tovarystva," 34–35; Kistiakivs'kyi, *Shchodennyk*, 1:64; Drahomanov, "Avtobiograficheskaia zametka," 1:55–64.

supporters assumed editorial control of the floundering daily *Kievskii telegraf* (*Kiev Telegraph*), which they used to defend themselves. They pointed out that both local and imperial authorities had approved all of the Geographic Society's activities; Dragomanov noted that he had long insisted that all the East Slavs belonged to a single and inseparable Rus' nation—a stance that had invited criticism from radical critics of the tsarist regime and Ruthenian populists alike.[17] The curator of the Kiev school district, asked to share his insights on the allegations, insisted that Dragomanov and Chubinskii were completely politically reliable.[18] Governor-General Dondukov-Korsakov himself intervened to ensure that censors would not print the angry letter of resignation from the Geographic Society that Iuzefovich had penned in the spring of 1875.[19]

Dismissed by fellow Little Russian activists and local officials, Iuzefovich forwarded his grievances to St. Petersburg. In a long manifesto describing the dangerous activities of the "so-called Ukrainian movement," Iuzefovich argued that enemies of the imperial state had been struggling to tear the southwest from the Russian empire since the 1860s. He traced these seditious activities to *Osnova*, neglecting to mention that he himself had contributed to the journal. Cooperating with Polish revanchists, he claimed, the journal's contributors had promoted the Ukrainian language in the hopes of estranging the Little Russian simple folk from the other children of Rus' and pulling them into the orbit of Polish civilization. The Valuev decree had not halted these dangerous activities, he added, for it had only deepened the contacts between Ukrainophiles in the Russian empire and Galician activists acting on Polish orders. Now, he complained, Dragomanov, Chubinskii, and other individuals who posed an immediate threat to the "integrity of the state" (*gosudarstvennaia tselost'*) had seized control of the Geographic Society and *Kievskii telegraf*. Warning that their dangerous ideas would soon spread beyond Kiev, Iuzefovich insisted that officials intervene quickly and decisively.[20]

In light of developments in Austrian Galicia, some imperial officials had already expressed concern about the influence of the Little Russian lobby and Dragomanov's denunciation of the imperial state's centralizing tendencies. Iuzefovich's allegations further raised alarm that a subversive "Ukrainophile" conspiracy was afoot in the southwest. The MVD soon convened a special commission to elucidate the aims of

---

17. *Vydumki "Kievlianina" i pol'skikh gazet o malorusskom patriotizme* (Kiev, 1874). Dragomanov's protest was not merely an effort to defend himself before the authorities: he expressed similar opinions in his correspondence of the time and in his autobiography, which he penned much later. "Avtobiograficheskaia zapiska," 61–62; *Arkhiv Mykhaila Drahomanova* (Warsaw, 1937).
18. See P. A. Antonovich to A. P. Shirinskii-Shikhmatov, 19 July 1875, TsDIAUK, f. 707, op. 261, d. 17, ll. 13–200b. O. I. Levitskii, an important figure in the Little Russian lobby in these years, noted that personal animosities also informed the ideological conflicts and rivalries that had emerged within the group. Around the time that Iuzefovich was ousted from the leadership of the Geographic Society his son Boris was arrested in a homosexual dragnet in Moscow. His local rivals taunted the elder activist by sending him tabloid coverage of the sensational trial that followed, intensifying Iuzefovich's resolve to wreak revenge on them. See Vasylenko, "Akademyk," 74.
19. The letter is reprinted in Savchenko, *Zaborona*, 368–72.
20. "O tak nazyvaemym ukrainofil'skom dvizhenii," c. 1875, TsDIAK, KMF-22, op. 1, d .21, l. 230b.

Little Russian activists and invited Iuzefovich to join.[21] Throughout the investigation, officials showed remarkable deference to Iuzefovich, soliciting his comments on ministerial memoranda about the investigation and enlisting him to pen drafts of the commission's findings.[22] Its final report, issued in May 1876, included verbatim large portions of Iuzefovich's original denunciation and subsequent writings on the topic, concluding that the Kiev branch of the Geographic Society had become a gathering place for "unreliable and dangerous individuals" working with Polish revanchists and Galician radicals to propagate "ideas about the independence of the Little Russian nationality among the simple folk."[23] The commission's reliance on Iuzefovich—and its willingness to believe his allegations in spite of the contradictory information that it received from local officials—testified both to its members' intense fear of Ukrainian national separatism and to their desire to maintain their collaborative relationship with trusted elites in the southwest.

Having reviewed the report, Alexander II issued a decree from the German spa town of Ems ordering that *Kievskii telegraf* and the Kiev branch of the Geographic Society be closed. The Ems decree also prohibited publications (with the exception of historical documents) in the "Little Russian dialect" and extended a subsidy to the Lemberg Russian-language newspaper *Slovo*, which officials hoped would combat Polish revanchist and Ukrainian separatist ideas.[24] Concurrent investigations of Chubinskii and Dragomanov by the Ministry of Internal Affairs recommended that the former should be banished from the "Little Russian" provinces and that the latter should be relieved of his position at St. Vladimir's.[25]

Conforming to the pattern we have seen earlier, Governor-General Dondukov-Korsakov intervened with St. Petersburg on behalf of Little Russian activists. He obtained a foreign passport for Dragomanov, which the scholar used to emigrate from Russia.[26] The governor-general also won Chubinskii a temporary reprieve from the order banishing him from the southwest.[27] Forced to leave his native region in early 1877, Chubinskii settled in St. Petersburg, where he again joined the imperial

---

21. "Kopiia s otnosheniia Glavnogo Nachal'nika III Otdeleniia Sobstvennoi EGO IMPERATORSKOGO VELICHESTVA Kantseliarii," 28 August 1875, RGIA, f. 1282, op. 1, d. 352, l. 2. After Dragomanov's return to the Russian empire in 1873, police began to trail him and his Hromada compatriots. "Spomyny Iryny Volod. Antonovych pro M. P. Drahomanova," *Ukraina* 4 (1926): 124.
22. See Ministry of Internal Affairs to Iuzefovich, 4 May 1876, RGIA, f. 1282, op. 1, d. 352 l. 79; undated draft report in ibid., ll. 105–118ob.
23. Report of 18 May 1876, in RGIA f. 1282, op. 1, d. 352, l. 86ob.
24. The edict is reprinted in Miller, *Ukrainian Question*, 267–69.
25. See RGIA, f. 1282, op. 1, d. 374.
26. "Avtobiograficheskaia zametka," 1:63–64.
27. For the request, see Dondukov-Korsakov to Ministry of Internal Affairs, 2 August 1876, RGIA, f. 1282, op. 1, d. 374, ll. 14–16ob. Ironically, Chubinskii, whose ethnographic work frequently complained of Jewish "domination" in southwestern economic life, worked as an accountant in a Jewish-owned sugar factory in these years. His employer also petitioned the authorities to grant him a reprieve, at least through the end of the fall refining season.

bureaucracy.[28] Two years later, in recognition of his outstanding service as a bureaucrat, he was permitted to return to the southwest; that same year, he received the Russian Academy of Science's Uvarov Prize for his contributions to ethnography.[29] In 1881, Dondukov-Korsakov lobbied officials to invalidate the Ems decree altogether, but his effort, which coincided with the assassination of Tsar Alexander II, failed amid the political crises that ensued.[30]

From exile, Dragomanov bitterly complained that once again officials had misunderstood the Little Russian idea and the intent of southwestern activists; neither the *Osnova* circle nor those targeted by the Ems decree had ever advocated separatist ideas, he insisted. The imperial authorities had quashed the nationalist and populist ideas that they had once encouraged, thus hampering the efforts of Little Russian patriots to renew the empire with a vital national spirit. And the aspersions that officials had cast on the Little Russian idea, complained Dragomanov, would only permit the Galician radicals who argued that a unified Rus' nation had never existed to use the southwest's cultural peculiarities for their own purposes; already, he noted, Ukrainophile activists in the Austrian empire were reimagining Shevchenko as an opponent of all-Russian unity and claiming him as a Ukrainian national hero.[31] In an 1881 article, Kostomarov, too, expressed dismay at recent events. Far from harboring separatist ambitions, he argued, the southwest's Little Russian activists merely sought to raise awareness of the centuries-long struggle of the local narod to drive out foreign enemies and to maintain the political and cultural traditions that had been forged in Rus'.[32]

Citing the continued threat of Ukrainian separatism within the empire and in Galicia, the imperial ministries refused to reconsider the new injunctions against the Ukrainian language, which formally remained in place until the 1905 revolution. As Dragomanov predicted, the state's ultimate intransigence on this score brought unintended consequences. In the decade that followed 1876, the rifts within the Little Russian lobby further solidified as alienated members embraced the very oppositional ideas that the Ems decree had aimed to vanquish.

From Coherent Lobby to Competing Camps

After his emigration from the Russian empire, Dragomanov settled in Geneva. In his first years in exile, the scholar maintained close relations with the Kiev Hromada.

---

28. Third Division to A. E. Timashev, 8 November 1876, RGIA, f. 1282, op. 1, d. 374, ll. 28–29; Ministry of Internal Affairs to Dondukov-Korsakov, 1 December 1876, ibid., l. 33.
29. On Chubinskii's return: Third Department to L. S. Makov, 3 March 1879, ibid., ll. 37–39. On the prize: Volodymyr Kubijovyč, ed., *Encyclopedia of Ukraine* (Toronto, 1984), 1:465.
30. Dondukov-Korsakov, "Zapiska o Malorusskom iazyke," 31 January 1881, IRNBUV, I.8004. This effort is recounted in detail in Miller, *Ukrainian Question*, 221–46.
31. See his 1879 article, "Shevchenko, Ukrainofili i sotsializm," in *Vybrane*, 327–429. The theme that officials had squandered the opportunity with which the Little Russian idea presented them appears repeatedly in Dragomanov's writings of the seventies, including "Antrakt," "Avtobiograficheskaia zapiska," and "Literatura."
32. N. I. Kostomarov, "Ukrainofil'stvo," *Russkaia starina* 2 (1881): 319–31.

Publishing a Ukrainian-language journal funded largely by Kiev activists, Dragomanov continued to raise awareness of the role that Little Russian peasants had played in forging East Slavic civilization and defending the children of Rus' from foreign exploitation.[33] Gradually, however, under the influence of socialist émigrés he met in Geneva—as well as the Marxist economist N. I. Ziber, who resigned from his post at St. Vladimir's after Dragomanov's emigration and joined him in Switzerland—the scholar began to develop a more radical critique of the imperial state. By the 1880s, Dragomanov had come to believe that the autocratic system had stifled the political, spiritual, and economic development of the narod, and he called for a constitutional regime organized on a federal basis. Seeking to reconcile socialist and nationalist ideas, he dreamed of a state that was attuned to the needs of the masses but also affirmed the rights of ethnic and religious minorities.[34]

Dragomanov's reinterpretation of the Little Russian idea alarmed Antonovich and other members of the Kiev Hromada, which formally broke off relations with him in the mideighties.[35] Following this schism, the scholar established closer contacts with more radical Hromada groups on the left bank and on the Black Sea coast that had connections to underground populist and socialist cells. Amid the growing political radicalism of 1880s, youth on both sides of the Russo-Austrian border expressed interest in his ideas.[36] Dragomanov attracted small groups of followers in the Russian empire, including Iakov Shul'gin, the nephew of the *Kievlianin* editor and a member of the radical Odessa Hromada; the younger Shul'gin would eventually disown his uncle and donate his inheritance to the émigré scholar.

Dragomanov's influence was even more profound in Austrian Galicia, where Ukrainian activists were working to distinguish their culture from Polish and Russian claims on it. Ivan Franko (1856–1916), the son of a village blacksmith and a prolific writer of Ukrainian-language plays, political tracts, and reportage, would become Dragomanov's most famous disciple in the Habsburg empire, but Austrian cultural policies that encouraged Ukrainian activism would create many others. The Shevchenko Scientific Society, founded by Lemberg activists in 1873 to promote the Ukrainian language and culture, by the 1880s became a major proponent of Dragomanov's ideas and published many of his works.[37]

Meanwhile, left-bank elites were reinterpreting the Little Russian idea on their own terms. In the late seventies, the Poltava noble I. I. Petrunkevich launched a movement within the left-bank zemstva to deepen the contacts between local professionals and

---

33. "Koly bytys', to ne myrytys'!" *Lystok hromady* 4 (1878): 1. An associate of Dragomanov in these years later reported that the publicist remained outspoken in his criticism of Jews. See Ben-Ami, "Moi snosheniia s M. Dragomanovym i rabota v 'Vol'nom slove,'" *Evreiskaia starina* 3–4 (1915): 347–64.
34. M. Dragomanov, *Liberalizm i zemstvo v Rossii* (Geneva, 1889); M. P. Dragomanov, *Velikorusskii internatsional i pols'ko-ukrainskii vopros* (Kazan', 1906).
35. "Spomyny Iryny Volod. Antonovych," 131.
36. On Dragomanov's intellectual influence more generally, see Taras Hunchak, ed., *Tysiacha rokiv ukrains'koi suspil'no-politychnoi dumki* (Kiev, 2005), vol. 5; L. P. Horkina, *Narysy z istorii politychnoi ekonomii v Ukraini* (Kiev, 1994).
37. Halyna Korbych, *Zhurnal "Literaturno-naukovyi visnyk" l'vivs'koho periodu* (Kiev, 1999), 20.

the peasants they served; these efforts gradually evolved into an organized political campaign that built on older demands by liberal gentry to devolve power to localities. Petrunkevich embraced the populist politics of the Little Russian lobby while rejecting its emphasis on liberating the children of Rus' from their putative enemies: only a rule-of-law state that transformed subjects into equal, fully enfranchised citizens, he argued, could improve the welfare of the peasants of the borderlands and imbue their lives with dignity and meaning. Although Petrunkevich won the support of many left-bank nobles and zemstvo activists, by the early 1880s, his movement had been decimated by arrests and official interference.[38] Petrunkevich's liberal reworking of the Little Russian idea, however, would live on. Coalescing at the same moment as Dragomanov's radical critique, it would create new cleavages within the Little Russian lobby.

By the early 1880s, the St. Vladimir's professor and Hromada activist A. F. Kistiakovskii had embraced Petrunkevich's ideas and begun to popularize them on the right bank. The scholar expressed disgust at Shul'gin and Iuzefovich's "artificial" campaign against alleged Ukrainophile plots; he dismissed Dragomanov's newfound radicalism as a disingenuous attempt to enhance his own standing within the local intelligentsia.[39] Complaining bitterly of Little Russian activists' attempts to cast Poles and Jews as the national enemies of the toiling masses and the cause of their suffering, he argued instead that intellectuals should be working to build a "fundamentally democratic" order "inclusive of all nationalities and peoples [*obshchenarodnaia*]."[40] Adopting the label "Ukrainophile," which Iuzefovich had used to discredit his rivals, Kistiakovskii imbued it with positive overtones: "Every inhabitant of Little Russia can be a Ukrainophile," he wrote. "Land owner and home owner, industrialist and artisan, merchant and tavern owner, priest and scholar, pedagogue and teacher, estate manager and settler—each and all should be a conscious Ukrainophile."[41]

Kistiakovskii died in 1885. However, two of his younger followers would continue to develop a liberal interpretation of the Little Russian idea. V. P. Naumenko (1852–1919), a Poltava native of Cossack descent, St. Vladimir's alumnus, gymnasium

---

38. See Fedor Rodichev, "The Veteran of Russian Liberalism: Ivan Petrunkevich," *Slavonic and East European Review* 7, no. 20 (1929): 318; Fedor A. Petrov, "Crowning the Edifice: The Zemstvos, Local Self-Government, and the Constitutional Movement," in Eklof, Bushnell, and Zakharova, *Russia's Great Reforms*, 197–213.
39. Kistiakivs'kyi, *Shchodennyk*, 1:64; 2:105. In his diary, Kistiakovskii remarked that he, Kulish, and Zhitetskii were puzzled by Dragomanov's sudden turn against the imperial state, noting that as late as 1875, Dragomanov had praised Iuzefovich in print as a "positive Little Russian character." Ibid., 1:98.
40. Ibid., 2:392. Kistiakovskii still viewed Jewish capitalists and Polish nobles as exploitative forces in society, but he charged that bureaucrats, Orthodox capitalists, and Little Russian "sycophants" who sought to expand their influence with imperial officials had placed their own personal interests before those of the narod and therefore belonged to the ranks of exploiters as well. For example, ibid., 2:167, 347 (source of quote).
41. Ibid., 2:455. This quote is often cited as indicative of the right-bank intelligentsia's views. See, for example, Maryna Palienko, *"Kievskaia starina" u hromads'komu ta naukovomu zhytti Ukrainy* (Kiev, 2005), 1:29; and the approach of Susan Heuman, *Kistiakovsky* (Cambridge, MA, 1998). As we have seen, however, Kistiakovskii's thinking was in fact quite exceptional and placed him at odds with many of the Little Russian activists with whom he had once been close.

teacher, and Hromada activist, authored dozens of articles on Little Russian literature and linguistics and served on committees working to compile a Ukrainian dictionary and to reprint the works of Shevchenko. But he rejected the notion that foreign influence was to blame for the difficult plight of the peasants, arguing that the welfare of the narod could best be served by a program of cultural enlightenment and political reform that improved the position of all tsarist subjects.[42] I. V. Luchitskii (1845–1918), the son of a seminary teacher from Podolia and a graduate of the St. Vladimir's history department who went on to become a professor at his alma mater, became another outspoken proponent of liberal ideas on the right bank. A self-professed Judeophile (Luchitskii attributed this trait to the influence of his father, who taught biblical Hebrew) and a close associate of Kistiakovskii, he was influenced by the ideas of left-bank liberals. (The professor owned land and served as a justice of the peace in Poltava province.)[43] Both men soon became leaders in the Kiev Literacy Society, which published popular reading materials, organized cultural events, and provided scholarships for students—work that Naumenko and Luchitskii hoped would uplift and empower the southwest's simple folk.[44]

Despite the differences in their aims and tactics, both the radical and the liberal movements that emerged from the Little Russian lobby in the 1870s and '80s distanced themselves from the organic nationalism classically associated with the Little Russian idea. They viewed the suffering of the southwest's peasants as a result of their political and economic disenfranchisement rather than their struggle against foreign enemies; they pointed to the imperial bureaucracy and the autocratic system rather than supposed exploitation at the hands of Poles and Jews as the chief impediments to the people's liberation. As these critiques challenged the basic premises of the Little Russian idea, however, others who had emerged from the lobby placed even more emphasis on the struggle against ethnic and national others—and insisted that the state remained the people's most valuable ally in this battle.

D. I. Pikhno (1853–1913) was the most eloquent and influential spokesman for this camp. The son of a peasant turned merchant from the right bank, Pikhno had received his primary education at one of the earliest schools run by Hromada activists. Shepherded through St. Vladimir's by Kistiakovskii, who recognized the young man's talent, Pikhno ultimately received a doctorate in political economy from the university.[45] A close associate of Shul'gin, Pikhno was named editor of *Kievlianin* following the former's death in 1879. Pikhno's new position rendered him one of the southwest's

---

42. On Naumenko's career, activities, and views, see "Formuliarnyi spisok o sluzhbe Naumenko," TsDIAUK, KMF-19, op. 1, d. 20, ll. 107–112; V. Naumenko, "K voprosu o nauchnom izdanii 'Kobzaria' T. G. Shevchenko," *KS* 36, no. 2 (1892): 314–21; Kistiakivs'kyi, *Shchodennyk* 2:390. The views of these Ukrainophile liberals are very much in line with the "small-deeds liberalism" and all-Russian populism of the 1870s.
43. On Luchitskii's life and work, see Ol. Hrushevs'kyi, "Pamiati prof. Iv.V. Luchits'koho," *Nashe mynule* 3 (1919): 100.
44. *Ustav Kievskogo Obshchestva Gramotnosti* (Kiev, 1894).
45. O Levits'kyi, "Storinka z zhyttia Volodymyra Antonovycha," IRNBUV I.8076; Ikonnikov, *Biograficheskii slovar'*, s.v. "D. I. Pikhno," 553.

most powerful opinion makers; indeed, he secured privileges that even Shul'gin had not enjoyed, including the right to read periodicals before they were sent to the censors.[46] Yet the editor never managed—or perhaps never tried—to conceal his modest origins. The urban beau monde scorned his lack of foreign travel experience and his unrefined manners. Pikhno's unconventional personal life became another fixture of high society gossip. Just weeks after Shul'gin's death, Pikhno acknowledged that he had consummated his relationship with the late editor's widow; when the widow died several years later, Pikhno eloped with Shul'gin's underage daughter (his own stepdaughter)—a union that Ober Procurator K. P. Pobedonostsev himself later intervened to annul.[47]

Despite the fact that Shul'gin's *Kievlianin* had led the attack against the Geographic Society, under Pikhno's guidance it continued to present Little Russian culture as a salutary force that imbued the local peasantry with dignity, allowed the simple folk to resist foreign incursions, and served as a possible source of national renewal for all the children of Rus'. Contributors to the paper enumerated the "unique features of the southern Russian people" and celebrated authors such as Kostomarov for raising awareness of the value of these characteristics.[48] However, the paper's affiliates vehemently opposed any effort to interpret the peculiarities of local culture in a Ukrainian separatist vein, insisting that the Little Russian idea naturally reinforced the fundamental unity between the southwest and the rest of the East Slavic lands. One contributor to the paper who wrote under the name "Little Russian" called for Ukrainian-language instruction to be introduced in local schools. However, he insisted that residents of the borderlands must master the Russian "literary language" as well. The estrangement of right-bank peasants from all-Russian culture and the imperial lingua franca, he argued, would permit "Jews and Poles to gather all the power of Russian civilization into their own hands." Citing a proverb in Ukrainian, "Little Russian" argued that the only choice that local peasants would be able to make in this situation would be "whether to guard the property of the Polish lords or to fetch water for the Jews" (*panskie budynki sterehti, abo shche krashche, zhidam vodu nosyty*).[49]

In his own writings, Pikhno praised the southwest as the birthplace of the "Russian national-state idea," which he viewed as a product of the local struggle to defend the "national character [*narodnost'*] and faith" of the simple folk against "convolutions and machinations of political and economic intrigues that are hostile to us."[50] In recognition of the contributions that Little Russian peasants had made in the struggle to defend East Slavic civilization, he insisted, imperial officials should promote their welfare. He

---

46. "MVD Otdel'nomu tsenzoru," 15 January 1883, TsDIAUK, f. 294, op. 1, d. 151, l. 126.
47. For example, Sidney Harcave, ed., *The Memoirs of Count Witte* (Armonk, NY, 1990), 82–83; Kistiakivs'kyi, *Shchodennyk*, 2:30; B. V. Anan'ich et al., eds., *Iz arkhiva S. Iu. Vitte* (St. Petersburg, 2003), 1:147–49.
48. The quote is from N. Petrov, "O stepeni samobytnosti ukrainskoi literatury," *Kievlianin*, 20 March 1881, 1.
49. "Narodnaia shkola na iuge rossii," *Kievlianin*, 14 February 1881, 1. For a similar argument, see Andrei Ivanov, "Po povodu khokhlomanii," *Kievlianin*, 20 March 1881, 2.
50. *General-gubernator ili gubernator?* (Kiev, 1889), 12, 15.

agitated for the democratization of local courts and governance, as well as new initiatives to expand peasants' access to land, cheap credit, and education. But though Pikhno shared radicals' and liberals' interest in uplifting the narod and easing its difficult plight, the scholar, unlike his rivals on the left, did not associate popular liberation with the creation of an equal rights regime or the demise of the tsarist state. Rather, he insisted that popular emancipation could be accomplished only by a strong, illiberal state that promoted the interests of East Slavs and marginalized those of Poles and Jews.[51]

In his final public interventions before his 1889 death, M. V. Iuzefovich made a similar case. He lamented that even after the Polish revolt, self-professed "liberals" and "cosmopolitans" in the government and in high society had prevented southwestern activists—who had long argued for the need to establish narodnost' as a principle of imperial governance—from attaining their vision. Instead of "moral schools for the people," officials skeptical of the nationalizing experiment had created "schools of popular depravity" and "dens of international rapaciousness." Instead of devolving self-governance to localities and pursuing economic development in an orderly manner, they had invested resources in the hands of a few and enabled "economic exploitation [gesheftmakherstvo] by the Yids." The continued stability and vitality of the empire, he argued, would depend on officials' willingness to promote the collective interests of the narod, which had consistently defended East Slavic civilization from attacks by internal enemies within the empire.[52]

Rather than resolving the disputes that had arisen within Little Russian circles in the 1870s, the Ems decree thus intensified them, creating three rival movements. A radical camp, led by Dragomanov, came to see the imperial state as a threat to, rather than the guardian of, the welfare of ordinary people; only the rapid devolution of power to local communities and the reorganization of society according to socialist principles, this camp argued, could rectify the social and political injustices that southwestern peasants faced. A liberal critique of the Little Russian idea—which originated in the zemstva of the left bank and was popularized on the right bank by Kistiakovskii and his followers—countered that a rule-of-law state that guaranteed equal rights could best protect the interests of the masses. Pikhno, Iuzefovich, and *Kievlianin* contributors, who remained loyal to the basic precepts of the Little Russian idea, worked to resolve the ideological contradictions that had long undergirded it. Merging the idea of a historical East Slavic nation with a distinctly antiliberal agenda, they argued that a strong state devoted to promoting the interests of the children of Rus' at the expense of other groups was necessary to liberate the simple folk from their heavy burdens.

---

51. For example, "Kredit i sel'skoe khoziastvo," *Kievlianin*, 24 February 1883, 1; *Kievlianin*, 18 February 1883, 1; "Eshche raz o volostnykh sudakh," *Kievlianin*, 7 April 1882, 1.
52. M. V. Iuzefovich, *Neskol'ko slov ob istoricheskoi zadache Rossii* (Kiev, 1890), 39; see also M. Iuzefovich, *Nasha liberal'naia intelligentsia* (Kiev, 1882). When this collection was republished several years later, the authorities censored this passage, which they evidently found excessively critical of official polices. See O. Elenev to B. M. Iuzefovich, 6 June 1895, RGIA, f. 776, op. 20. d. 1197, l. 135.

Although the Little Russian lobby had begun to split into distinct camps, the intensifying controversies about the meaning and uses of local culture had not yet produced a full-fledged schism. Through the 1890s, proponents of the radical, liberal, and illiberal camps emerging from the Little Russian lobby continued to work side by side in ventures that charted the peculiarities of southwestern culture and chronicled its contributions to East Slavic civilization. Even in the aftermath of Ems, these activities enjoyed substantial toleration and even support from the imperial authorities, who at many junctures continued to regard Little Russian culture as a valuable tool in the ongoing campaign to claim the southwest for the Russian empire and to unite its residents behind the tsar. It is to the ongoing efforts of southwestern activists to raise awareness of the peculiarities of local culture—and to their complex relationship with the imperial state—that we now turn.

Little Russian Culture and the Imperial State

The Ems decree had a disastrous impact on Ukrainian-language publishing ventures and provoked acrimonious debates within the Little Russian lobby about the proper relationship of the movement with the state. Yet, as in the years following the Valuev decree, southwestern activists managed to locate social space in which they could continue to carry out their activities. The Kiev Hromada functioned with the full knowledge of local officials and claimed members of many different ideological orientations. Although the group formally cut off contact with Dragomanov in the mideighties, some of its members considered themselves his disciples; affiliates of the group even hosted the Galician radical Ivan Franko for an extended stay in Kiev. Liberals such as Kistiakovskii, Naumenko, and Luchitskii also played an active role in the group.[53] Other Hromada members professed views closer to those of Pikhno and Iuzefovich. The newspaper *Trud* (*Labor*)—considered the unofficial organ of the group in the early 1880s—praised *Kievlianin* for its attention to the "needs and desires" of the southwestern peasantry, echoing the paper's calls for the expansion of local self-governance and the implementation of land, credit, and educational reforms in the southwest.[54] Like *Kievlianin,* it insisted that this liberationist agenda could be accomplished only through antiliberal policies that reduced the power of Poles and Jews and enhanced the influence of the children of Rus' on both sides of the Russo-Austrian border.[55] Antonovich, who emerged as the Hromada's leader in the early eighties, skillfully worked to reconcile the interests of these divergent camps. Encouraging

---

53. Omelian Kyrychyns'kyi, "Franko v Kyivi," *Ukraina* 6 (1926): 170–72; Ol. Riabinin-Skliarevs'kyi, "Kyivs'ka hromada 1870-x r.r." *Ukraina* 1–2 (1927): 144–62.
54. The quote is from "Zadachi provintsional'noi gazety," *Trud,* 20 February 1881, 1. On *Trud*'s affiliation with the Kiev Hromada, see Mykola Bilins'kyi, "Z mynuloho perezhytoho, 1870–1888," *Ukraina* 2 (1928): 126.
55. For example, "Pol'skaia pechat' o 'russkom voprose' v Galichine," *Trud,* 29 May 1881, 1; "Zhurnal'noe obozrenie," *Trud,* 11 March 1881, 2–3.

members to focus on their common cultural interests rather than on their political differences, he oversaw the group's efforts to publish Ukrainian-language literature outside the Russian empire, to organize performances and concerts that showcased Little Russian folk culture, and to compile a Ukrainian-language dictionary.[56]

In August 1881, F. G. Lebedintsev, O. I. Levitskii, and a handful of fellow Hromada members launched *Kievskaia starina* (*Kiev Antiquity*), a journal that aspired to document the "characteristic peculiarity" of the Dnieper region and to document the struggle of the "Southern Russian narod" against "Polish culture."[57] Like the Hromada, the journal, which remained in publication until 1906, unified diverse segments of the local intelligentsia. It featured the writings of radicals such as Dragomanov, Franko, and Iakov Shul'gin. Kistiakovskii, Luchitskii, and Naumenko used the journal to promote their liberal reinterpretation of the Little Russian idea and eventually to assume from the Hromada the task of compiling a Ukrainian-language dictionary.[58] Other regular contributors to the journal decried the oppression of the toiling masses by non-East Slavs—and praised the Little Russian peasantry's resistance against these foreign onslaughts. Antonovich described the role that Kiev and its inhabitants had played in defending Orthodoxy and all the children of Rus' from "external encroachments" through the "dark years" of Polish-Lithuanian rule.[59] Kostomarov published accounts of Cossack attacks on Jews, depicting their violent acts as justified—and even laudable—efforts to improve the plight of the Little Russian masses.[60] Iuzefovich, one of the leading proponents of the antiliberal interpretation of the Little Russian idea, was also an ardent supporter of the journal. On the eve of its launch, he expressed to Lebedintsev his approval for the project and promised to intervene on the journal's behalf with the censorship authorities.[61]

Meanwhile, men who had devoted their lives to the study of Little Russian history and culture continued to expand their influence in southwestern intellectual life, securing prominent positions at the Kiev Theological Academy and St. Vladimir's. S. T. Golubev (1848–1920), the son of a parish priest, a frequent contributor to *Kievskaia starina*, and a member of the Kiev Commission for the Analysis of Historical Documents, became one of the academy's most influential scholars in the 1880s. He published numerous books and articles on the historical struggle of "western Rus'" to preserve Orthodox traditions and a multivolume work on the life of Petr Mogila, which highlighted both the clergyman's Little Russian patriotism and his efforts to

---

56. Riabinin-Skliarevs'kyi, "Kyivs'ka hromada."
57. Quotes from "Programma istoricheskogo zhurnala pod nazvaniem *Kievskaia starina*," 1881, TsDIAUK, f. 295, op. 1, d. 16, l. 2; F. G. Lebedintsev to Main Directorate on Press Affairs, 10 August 1881, TsDIAUK, KMF-19, op. 1, d. 20, l. 40b.
58. "Slovar' knizhnoi malorusskoi rechi po rukopisi XVII v.," *KS* 23, no. 2 (1888), frontispiece. For biographies and indexes of journal contributors, see Palienko, "*Kievskaia starina.*"
59. V. B. Antonovich, "Kiev, ego sud'ba i znachenie s XIV po XVI stoletie," *KS* 1, no. 1 (1882): 1–48.
60. N. Kostomarov, "Zhidotrepanie v nachale XVIII veka," *KS* 2, no. 5 (1883): 477–492.
61. Lebedintsev refers to Iuzefovich's enthusiasm in F. G. Lebedintsev to M. V. Iuzefovich, c. 1882, TsDIAUK, f. 873, op. 1, d. 40, l. 2.

protect all of East Slavic civilization from Catholic incursions.[62] Golubev's colleague at the academy, F. I. Titov (1864–1922?), the descendent of a priestly family of mixed Great Russian-Little Russian heritage, also gained fame for his interest in the unique history and traditions of the southwestern region. In his academic work and contributions to *Kievskaia starina* and *Kievskie eparkhial'nye vedomosti* (which he edited following Lebedintsev's death), he too chronicled the efforts of Little Russians to preserve their faith and their "national character" (*narodnost'*) over the centuries.[63] Alarmed about the rise of Galician radicals who peddled "extremely dangerous, anti-Christian ideas," Titov cultivated ties with Orthodox priests in the Habsburg empire and visited the region frequently to acquaint himself with political conditions on the ground there.[64]

Meanwhile, Antonovich and Golubev, who joined the St. Vladimir's faculty in 1885, built an acclaimed program in local history at the university. Together the two men pioneered what became known as the "Kiev school," which relied on imaginative uses of documentary evidence to trace the political practices and cultures of Kievan Rus' through the early modern period and into the present. O. I. Levitskii, the son of a Ukrainian-speaking parish priest, was one of the Kiev school's first success stories.[65] A. V. Storozhenko (1857–1920s?), another Antonovich student, became the editor of the Kiev Slavic Philanthropic Society's almanac and the author of numerous articles on Little Russian history and culture, many of which appeared in *Kievskaia starina*. His brother, N. V. Storozhenko (1862–1942), a *Kievskaia starina* contributor, Hromada member, and popular education activist, was also an alumnus of the Kiev school.[66]

M. S. Hrushevs'kyi (1866–1934) would go on to become the most famous of all of Antonovich's students. Hrushevs'kyi was born in Kholm, where his father, a teacher, literary scholar, and the product of a right-bank clerical family, served in the depolonization campaign overseen by F. G. Lebedintsev. (The two families were close on personal terms as well: Lebedintsev's wife was the young man's godmother.)[67] Having discovered *Kievskaia starina* while still in his teens, Hrushevs'kyi enrolled in St. Vladimir's, where he studied local history under Antonovich and received a history degree in 1890. Thanks to Antonovich's intervention, the talented young scholar was

---

62. S. Golubev, "V zashchitu kievskogo mitropolita Petra Mogily," *KEV* 11 (1893): 282–98; S. Golubev, "Neizvestnoe polemicheskoe sochinenie protiv popskikh pritiazanii v iugo-zapadnoi Rossii," *Trudy Kievskoi Dukhovnoi Akademii* 2 (1899): 300–341. For a survey of his life and influence, see V. I. Ul'ianovs'kyi, *Dvichi profesor: Stepan Holubev v akademichnomu ta universytets'komu kontekstakh* (Kiev, 2007).
63. The quote is from "Avtobiografiia. Protoierei Feodor Ivanovich Titov," IRNBUV, f. 129, no. 1, l. 13. See also F. I. Titov, "Okonchatel'nyi perekhod Kieva ot Pol'shi k Rossii po dogovoru o vechnom mire mezhdu nimi v 1686 godu," *Trudy Kievskoi Dukhovnoi Akademii* 7 (1904): 433.
64. F. I. Titov, *Russkoe dukhovenstvo v Galitsii (iz nabliudenii puteshestvennika)* (Kiev, 1903), 83. For more on Titov's views and career, see Krainii, *Istoryky*, 176–226.
65. See Levyts'kyi, "Moia pochakova shkola," 41–50; "Korotki biohrafichni vidomosti pro Or. Levits'koho," IRNBUV, I.11809.
66. For biographical information on the Storozhenko brothers, see Mykola Storozhenko, *Z moho zhyttia* (1920s; repr., Kiev, 2005).
67. V. V. Kovalinskii, *Metsenaty Kieva* (Kiev, 1998), 408.

invited to join the Kiev Commission while still in his twenties. Using documents from its archives, he published articles in *Kievskaia starina* as well as in Galician journals that chronicled the struggle of the southwest's Orthodox inhabitants to protect their culture and to fend off external incursions.[68]

Meanwhile, another young scholar associated with Kiev's Little Russian milieu was making St. Vladimir's a center for cutting-edge research on ethnography—a discipline that had long fascinated Little Russian activists. I. A. Sikorskii (1842–1919), the son of a right-bank village priest, had studied under F. G. Lebedintsev at the Kiev Theological Academy in his youth; his classmates later remembered him as a great enthusiast of *Osnova* and the Little Russian idea in the early sixties. He went on to earn a doctorate in medicine and an appointment as professor of psychiatry at St. Vladimir's and to become a member of the Kiev Slavic Philanthropic Society.[69]

The struggle for political and cultural control of the southwest was a prominent theme in Sikorskii's academic work, which combined psychology, anthropology, and the emergent field of scientific racism. Sikorskii insisted that the descendants of Rus'—whom he considered representatives of the superior Aryan race—were locked in a struggle for survival against "degenerates" who desired nothing more than to degrade the East Slavs' racial stock and destroy their civilization.[70] Even as the official de-polonization campaign had begun to diminish the influence of Poles in the region, he cautioned, the growing power of "baptized Jews" and "the German element" in the southwest posed dangerous new threats to local traditions and Slavic racial purity.[71] (Sikorskii insisted that conversion to Christianity could not ameliorate the moral and physical deficiencies that he perceived in Jews, whom he presented as racially inferior "Russian negroes.")[72] Although Sikorskii's tendency to interpret history and politics through the lens of racial science—already evident in the 1880s—rendered him an outlier in Russian academic circles, it situated him at the very vanguard of cultural and political developments in Europe.[73] It also heightened the stakes of the ongoing

---

68. For example, M. Grushevskii, "Volynskii vopros 1097–1102 g.," *KS* 10, no. 33 (1891): 32–55. On the scholar's early career, see Plokhy, *Unmaking Imperial Russia*, 29–34.

69. L. S. M., "Zamechatel'nye urozhentsy i deiateli Podolii proshlogo vremeni," *Pravoslavnaia Podoliia* 14–15 (1908): 250; "Biografiia Sikorskogo, Ivana Alekseevicha," IRNBUV, f. 8, no. 3548.

70. The quote is from Marina Mogil'ner, *Homo imperii* (Moscow, 2008), 249. For more on Sikorskii and his ideas, see Marina Mogilner, "Russian Physical Anthropology of the Nineteenth–Early Twentieth Centuries," in *Empire Speaks Out*, ed. Ilya Gerasimov, Jan Kusber, and Alexander Semyonov (Boston, 2009), 155–89; Vadim Menzhulin, *Drugoi Sikorskii* (Kiev, 2004).

71. Menzhulin, *Drugoi Sikorskii*, 153–54.

72. Ibid., 401.

73. Wilhelm Marr, who founded the Antisemiten-Liga in 1879, is generally seen as the first intellectual to appeal to scientific racism (and racist anti-Semitism) as a political mobilization tool. As late as the turn of the century, however, racist ideas played a marginal and controversial role among the very groups that opposed Jewish influence across the continent. See William I. Brustein, *Roots of Hate* (New York: Cambridge University Press, 2003), 95–176; Chickering, *We Men*, 236–45; Carl E. Schorske, *Fin-de-Siècle Vienna:* (New York, 1981), 116–80. For a discussion of the application of European race science—and its limits—in Russia, see Eugene Avrutin, "Racial Categories and the Politics of (Jewish) Difference in Late Imperial Russia," *Kritika* 8, no. 1 (2007): 13–40.

contest for control of the borderlands, reframing it as a racial struggle that would determine the future of the children of Rus'.

How did officials receive these ongoing attempts by local intellectuals to draw attention to the historical and cultural peculiarities of the right bank and to argue for the relevance of ethnonational considerations in imperial governance? After the Ems decree, which had raised alarms about the threat posed by separatist ideas within the empire and beyond its borders, they struggled to stamp out Ukrainian nationalism in the Russian empire. Police confiscated the writings of Dragomanov and other commentators who promoted "extreme Ukrainophilism."[74] Censors viewed the Galician Ukrainian orthography, which used the Latin letter "i" in place of the Cyrillic "и," as a marker of subversive intent; indeed, when several issues of *Kievskaia starina* went to press using the banned orthography, Naumenko, who became the journal's editor in 1893, was severely reprimanded.[75]

Nevertheless, many officials maintained that the activities of right-bank activists to document the history and "native" cultures of the southwest could only aid the ongoing struggle to defeat national separatism and to unify the East Slavs. Kiev governor-general A. R. Drentel'n made exactly this argument when he lobbied his St. Petersburg superiors to exempt *Kievskaia starina* from preliminary censorship in the early eighties. Although the ministries declined this request, Minister of Internal Affairs D. A. Tolstoi concurred that the periodical "undoubtedly aids in the illumination of the historical fate and past life of the region." He would later go on to grant it a generous subsidy and to intervene on several occasions to rescue it from bankruptcy.[76] On numerous occasions, censors granted its editors special waivers to publish "scholarly" and "historical-literary" pieces in Ukrainian; they also authorized Naumenko to publish the first comprehensive "Little Russian Dictionary" under the auspices of the journal even after he had been reprimanded for his unauthorized use of the Galician orthography.[77] Sympathizing with the point of view expressed in organs such as *Kievlianin* and *Trud,* the southwestern governors-general repeatedly petitioned St. Petersburg to introduce more aggressive measures to limit the political

---

74. Report of Kiev Special Censor on Foreign Publications, 28 June 1885, TSDIAK, MF-19, op. 1, d. 20, l. 40.

75. Naumenko justified his actions by explaining that the Russian-language typesetting machine had broken down just before the issues went to print. See "K delu 'Kievskaia starina,'" 21 December 1896, TsDIAUK, MF-19, op. 1, d. 20, ll. 207–8.

76. The quote is from Tolstoi to N. Kh. Bunge, 21 December 1883, TsDIAUK MF-19, op. 1, d. 20, ll. 27–28. See also Ih. Zhytets'kyi, "Pershi roky 'Kyivs'koi Stariny' ta M.I. Kostomarov," *Ukraina* 4 (1926): 98–100. Palienko and other scholars have emphasized the importance of the journal in consolidating a Ukrainian national history and culture, downplaying the extensive support that it received from the imperial state.

77. The quotes are from two examples of such waivers: St. Petersburg Censorship Committee to Main Directorate on Press Affairs, 13 August 1897, TsDIAUK, MF-19, op. 1, d. 20, l. 2150b; St. Petersburg Censorship Committee to Main Directorate on Press Affairs, 15 October 1895, in ibid., l. 165. On Naumenko's dictionary, Main Directorate on Press Affairs to Kiev Independent Censor, 2 November 1896, TsDIAUK, f. 294, op. 1, d. 275, l. 86. Likewise, local officials approved scores of requests from local activists (many Hromada members) to organize Ukrainian-language plays and concerts. See TsDIAUK, f. 442, op. 847, d. 5.

and economic influence of non-East Slavs in the region and to implement local organs of self-governance structured on national principles. The imperial ministries resisted their pleas, however, refusing to introduce zemstva to the borderlands.[78]

While struggling to limit dangerous expressions of "Ukrainophile" sentiment even as they promoted salutary Little Russian patriotism in the public sphere, officials often found it challenging to ascertain the political loyalties of individual activists. As an employee of the Kiev Commission and a member of the Khmelnytsky statue committee, Levitskii served the governor-general, who oversaw the activities of both groups; furthermore, he presented himself as a loyal imperial subject, denouncing a colleague at the school at which he taught for his alleged political unreliability.[79] Yet the scholar's radically populist interpretation of local history and his frequent contributions to Ukrainian-language journals in Lemberg rendered him potentially suspect, leading local police to place him under clandestine surveillance.[80] I.M. Reva (1853–1915), a primary school teacher and Kiev Hromada member, was exiled in the late 1870s following his publication of a memoir that chronicled the 1768 Haidamak revolt; in this book he not only effusively praised the violence that Little Russian peasants had unleashed against their supposed national enemies but also condemned Iuzefovich's recent conduct.[81] Within a year or two, however, Reva was allowed to return to Kiev, where he joined the ranks of Little Russian activists who enjoyed cordial relations with local officials. A close associate of Pikhno, he regularly contributed essays to *Kievlianin* that urged officials to devolve power to local communities and to play a more active role in nationalizing the economy and politics of the southwest. By the turn of the century, as we shall see, he would even attain official positions in local government.[82] Imperial officials had demonstrated their determination to more closely manage the Little Russian idea, but they often found it difficult to distinguish salutary expressions of Little Russian patriotism from dangerous ideas that threatened to undermine the empire.

Little Russians, Ukrainians, or Russians?

In 1894, the Austrian government endowed a chair of Ukrainian history at Lemberg University and invited V. B. Antonovich to fill it. (This decision outraged the more radical voices in Galician society, who argued that the scholar had supported Russian

---

78. On the ongoing debate over the introduction of zemstva to the southwestern borderlands, see Matsuzato, "The Issue of Zemstvos," 218–35; "Reforma po zakonu 2 aprelia 1903 goda," TsDIAUK, f. 442, op. 656, d. 132, ch. 1, l. 1760b.
79. The colleague whom Levitskii denounced eventually sued him for slander: see *Kievlianin*, 25 January 1881, 2; *Kievlianin*, 6 June 1881, 2.
80. Police and gendarme reports on Levitskii's political activities include "Partiia tak nazyvaemykh ukrainofilov 'Staroi gromady,'" TsDIAUK, f. 274, op. 1, d. 225, ll. 46–500b; "Ob Oreste Ivanove Levitskom i Ekaterine Nikolaevoi Mel'nike," GARF, f. 102, 3-oe deloproizvodstvo, 1883, d. 1361.
81. I. M. Reva, ed., *Umanskaia rezna* (Kiev, 1879).
82. Examples of Reva's political writings include "Mestnye organy Ministerstva Zemledeliia," *Kievlianin*, 14 February 1894, 1–2; "Sakharnoe proizvodstvo i normirovka," *Kievlianin*, 21 January 1894, 1. For further biographical details, see "Reva, I. M.," *Istoricheskii vestnik* 5 (1915): 712.

claims on Austrian Galicia too enthusiastically.) Antonovich declined the job but recommended his young protégé, Hrushevs'kyi, instead. After relocating to Lemberg, Hrushevs'kyi began to meld elements of the Little Russian idea with the national liberation program that Galician radicals had articulated. In the late nineties, he initiated work on a multivolume historical study of what he now called Ukraine-Rus'—a territory that in Hrushevs'kyi's mind stretched from Galicia into the left bank. Based in part on sources that had been collected by the Kiev Commission, the work betrayed the influence of that group on several counts. Hrushevs'kyi rejected the Normanist theory, portraying the Rus' state as a purely Slavic creation. He elucidated the ethnographic and cultural features of the civilization that he believed had descended from Rus' and chronicled its struggle to preserve the Orthodox faith and its folk traditions from external threats. In sharp contrast to the Commission, however, Hrushevs'kyi did not see a unified East Slavic civilization as the descendant of Rus'; rather, he claimed that only the lands he called Ukraine could claim this honor. Hrushevs'kyi's interpretation of Rus' culture and its legacy created a new historical narrative that reinforced the arguments of those Galician activists who insisted that Ukrainians did not share a common history or culture with Russians—and who presented the struggle for Ukrainian national liberation as primarily a struggle against the Russian imperial state.[83]

Hrushevs'kyi soon attained a leading role in Galician intellectual life, thanks in part to continued Austrian encouragement of Ukrainian nationalist activities. Elected president of the Shevchenko Scientific Society's historical division, the historian compiled and reinterpreted the historical sources compiled by the Kiev Commission. Under the auspices of the society, he also launched *Literaturno-naukovyi vistnyk (Literary-Scientific Gazette)*, a Ukrainian-language journal of history, philology, and ethnography that denounced the Russian imperial authorities as hostile to Ukrainian national interests and indifferent the plight of the narod.[84] By the turn of the twentieth century, he had joined forces with Franko to launch the National Democratic Party, which called for the liberation of the land that stretched from Austrian Galicia to the left bank of the Dnieper from the empires that controlled them and for the creation of a free and self-governing Ukraine "without serf or landlord."[85]

Radical youth on the left bank who were frustrated by the moderate politics of the Hromada and other Little Russian cultural institutions were inspired by Hrushevs'kyi's political agenda.[86] Borys Hrynchenko (1863–1910)—a graduate of St. Vladimir's, a teacher in a left-bank zemstvo school, and an active contributor to the

---

83. On Hrushevs'kyi's life and work in these years, see Plokhy, *Unmaking Imperial Russia*, 38–43.
84. M. S. Hrushevs'kyi, "Nashi tovarystva," *Literaturno-naukovyi vistnyk* 3, no. 9 (1900): 184–200; Korbych, *Zhurnal*.
85. Plokhy, *Unmaking Imperial Russia*, 43.
86. Mykola Halahan (1882–1945), a relative of the Kiev Little Russian activist G. P. Galagan, describes clearly in his memoir the tensions between the radical youth who came of age in the nineties and the generation of the sixties. The former regarded the latter as dilettantes who had done little to improve the plight of the Little Russian simple folk, in spite of all their discussions of various schemes to uplift the masses. See Mykola Halahan, *Z moikh spomyniv* (Lviv, 1930), 1:33–36.

Galician press—helped organize the Brotherhood of Taras, an underground group that called for a revolution to liberate the Ukrainian lands from the imperial powers that controlled them. Evhen Chykalenko (1861–1929), a wealthy Kherson landowner who had belonged to an underground Dragomanovite cell in his student days, worked to introduce the ideas of Galician radicals to Russian subjects. Reversing the flow of people and ideas from the Russian empire into Galicia that earlier generations of Little Russian activists had encouraged, Chykalenko established a fund to support Russian subjects who wished to study in Lemberg.[87]

Although the Little Russian idea remained entrenched in the right bank in the 1890s, a handful of activists there also embraced the rival Ukrainian national project that was coalescing in Galicia and on the left bank. Kistiakovskii's son, Bogdan (1868–1920), who traveled to Galicia to work with nationalist peasant parties while still a teenager, helped to organize underground radical groups at St. Vladimir's. In 1901 V. B. Antonovych's son, Dmytro Antonovych (1877–1945), another St. Vladimir's student, founded the Revolutionary Ukrainian Party (RUP), which melded Dragomanov's socialist ideas with Ukrainian nationalist precepts, calling for a revolution that would sweep away the capitalist system and the imperial powers.[88] A Kiev group called the Committee of Young Ukraine smuggled the writings of Galician activists into the Russian empire and called for "the separation of Little Russia [from the Russian empire] ... and the formation of an autonomous Ukraine."[89]

But as a new generation envisioned a Ukrainian nation distinct from Great Russian culture and the imperial state, those who remained loyal to the Little Russian idea insisted only more vehemently that local peculiarities were the purest expression of the unitary East Slavic culture that they believed had been forged in Rus'. In 1899, Antonovich and Levitskii presided over the organization of an international archeological conference in Kiev. Liberal Ukrainophiles such as Naumenko were invited to speak at the event, as were proponents of the Little Russian idea such as Golubev and Titov. Local history enthusiasts from other Slavic countries announced their intention to attend and deliver addresses in their native tongues.[90] However, conference organizers preemptively barred Hrushevs'kyi and other members of the Shevchenko Scientific Society—who had planned deliver their speeches in Ukrainian—from the conference, denouncing them as separatist provocateurs and their language as mere "jargon."[91]

One of the conference organizers who had insisted on excluding the Galician activists, T. D. Florinskii (1854–1919), a St. Vladimir's linguist and Kiev Slavic Philanthropic

---

87. On the left bank's milieu of radical youth, see "Chernihivs'ka Ukrains'ka Hromada," IRNBUV, I.32569; Iu. Zh. Kollard, *Spohady iunats'kykh dniv* (Toronto, 1972); Evhen Chykalenko, *Spohady* (Kiev, 2003).
88. On right-bank radical circles, consult Heuman, *Kistiakovsky*; O. Hermaize, *Narysy z istorii revoliutsiinoho rukhu na Ukraini* (Kiev, 1926).
89. Department of Police to Director of the Kiev Province Gendarme Directorate, 7 March 1898, TsDIAUK, f. 274, op. 1, d. 536. l. 17. See the "Committee of Young Ukraine" pamphlets in ibid., l. 21, 24.
90. *Izvestiia XI Arkheologicheskogo s"ezda v Kieve* 1–8 (1899).
91. *Vestnik Evropy* 6, no. 11 (1899): 398.

Society member, clarified his reasoning in *Kievlianin*. He began by acknowledging the linguistic specificities of the "dialect" spoken by the Little Russian peasants of the Russian empire and his admiration for it. Tracing its origins to Kievan Rus', he praised its authenticity and immediacy; he lauded the works of Shevchenko in particular, which he characterized as "unmediated poetic creations that come from the depths of the soul of the Little Russian people."[92] But it was precisely activists' "natural love for the Little Russian people's speech," he argued, that should place them on guard against Galician activists' attempts to popularize an artificial, "bookish," and polonized "Ukrainian-Rus'" "jargon."[93] Hrushevs'kyi and the "Ukrainian fanatics" who followed him, Florinskii insisted, intentionally aimed to undermine the stability of the empire and to corrupt the ancient Little Russian tongue. In light of this challenge, it was essential that all the children of Rus' remain conversant in the Russian "literary language," which unified Orthodox East Slavs from Galicia to Siberia.[94]

In the early nineties, liberal Ukrainophiles and even some radicals had expressed concern about Hrushevs'kyi's attempts to promote the Galician dialect of the Ukrainian language, charging that it was too heavily influenced by Polish and that the Ukrainian dialects spoken in the Dnieper region were more "authentic."[95] Now, however, activists who had shown little sympathy for Galician radicalism rushed to defend Hrushevs'kyi and to denounce Florinskii. One *Kievskaia starina* contributor—a student of Antonovich's and Florinskii's onetime colleague in the Kiev Slavic Philanthropic Society—expressed dismay at the conference organizers' heavy-handed tactics and their apparent "fear of Little Russian."[96] Naumenko read their decision as an assault on the local peasantry, chiding conference organizers for implying that the native tongue of the narod was inferior to literary Russian.[97] The willingness of liberal Ukrainophiles to defend Hrushevs'kyi's radical ideas signaled a growing rapprochement between Ukrainian nationalists with different ideological orientations—a trend that would grow only more pervasive by 1905.

While some championed Little Russian particularities but denounced Galician radicals' attempts to claim them for a separate Ukrainian nation, other southwestern intellectuals increasingly avoided discussing them altogether. In the 1890s, M. V. Iuzefovich's younger son, Boris (1843–1911), spoke out against the liberal and radical ideas that he argued were destroying the foundations of East Slavic civilization.[98] Raising

---

92. T. Florinskii, *Malorusskii iazyk i "Ukrains'ko-Rus'kyi" literaturnyi separatizm* (St. Petersburg, 1900), 22. 64. This volume was serialized in *Kievlianin* in 1899 and 1900.
93. Ibid., 96, 127, 142.
94. Quote from ibid., 127. On attempts to divide the empire, see ibid., 98–118.
95. See Plokhy, *Unmaking Imperial Russia*, 451–52n167; Magocsi, *Roots*, 97–98.
96. N. Beliashevskii, "Arkheologicheskii s"ezd v Kieve," *KS* 67, no. 10 (1899): 107.
97. V. P. Naumenko, *Reshen-li prof. T.D. Florinskim vopros o knizhnoi malorusskoi rechi?* (Kiev, 1900).
98. After being embarrassed by his sodomy trial in the 1870s, Iuzefovich rehabilitated his reputation through state service, first on the front in the Russo-Turkish war and later in Pobedonostsev's Holy Synod, the Kiev censorship apparatus, and the Paris *Okhrana* office. For Iuzefovich's service record and biographical details, consult "Formuliuarnyi spisok B.M. Iuzefovicha," RGIA, f. 776, op. 20. d. 1197, ll. 152–65; A. D. Stepanov and A. A. Ivanov, eds., *Chernaia sotnia* (Moscow, 2008), 628–30.

alarms in voluntary associations as well as in the press about the need to defend authentic Slavic traditions and the Orthodox faith from inimical foreign threats, he echoed the central premises of the Little Russian idea. Yet now, rather than presenting the southwest as the venue where this clash of civilizations would be decided (and the Little Russian people as the main protagonists in this battle), he spoke of this struggle as one in which all "Russian" people had become engaged.[99]

A similar rhetorical shift is evident in Iuzefovich's efforts to establish himself as the curator of his family legacy in the 1890s, when he published posthumous editions of his father's political writings and his brother's memoirs of his experiences in the Kiev Hromada in the early sixties. Glossing over his family's role in cataloging the unique traits of Little Russian culture, he extolled their contributions to the Russian nationalist cause—a position that he defined as opposed not only to Polish and Jewish influence but also to the Ukrainian national idea.[100] Indeed, by 1898, when he republished his brother's memoirs of the 1863 revolt in *Kievlianin,* he altered them to allege that "Little Russian" students had aligned with Polish revanchists opposed to the "Russian" and "Orthodox" cause.[101] The brand of Russian nationalism that Iuzefovich now peddled, despite its obvious debts to the Little Russian idea, avoided overt invocations of Little Russian peculiarities.

Collaboration and Divergence

Although the 1890s had seen the emergence of the most profound divisions yet among the men who had once subscribed to the Little Russian lobby, the various factions that had emerged from the movement remained in dialogue with one another. After relocating to Kiev in 1900, Hrynchenko and Chykalenko joined the Hromada, which they attempted to push in a more radical direction. Meanwhile, Luchitskii and Naumenko, who by now advocated the conclusion of a federal agreement between Great Russia and Ukraine without the latter's secession from the empire, promoted liberal views within its ranks. Older activists such as Zhitetskii and Antonovich struggled to appease the group's more radical factions. Hromada leaders organized regular seminars that brought together activists of many ideological stripes from across the Ukrainian lands to share ideas and strategies; they collaborated with the editors of *Kievskaia starina* to open a bookstore specializing in local history and Ukrainian-language literature. However, the group's elder statesmen also expressed deep concern that the radicalization of its members could negatively influence its capacity to

---

99. See "Perepiska gr. S.D. Sheremeteva s redaktorom izdatelem 'S-Peterburgskikh vedomosti' kn. Ester," 22 October 1897, RGIA, f. 1088, op. 2, d. 26, ll. 4–5; B.M. Iuzefovich to the Board of the Society of Enthusiasts of Russian Historical Education," 7 November 1897, ibid., ll. 2–3; B.M. Iuzefovich, "K evreiskomu voprosu," *Russkii vestnik* 7 (1903): 79–82.
100. M. V. Iuzefovich, *Neskol'ko slov*; B. M. Iuzefovich, "Tridtsat' let tomu nazad: Ocherk iz studencheskoi zhizni," *Russkaia starina* 84 (1895): 167–200.
101. B. M. Iuzefovich, "Tridtsat' let tomu nazad," *Kievlianin,* 11 December 1898, 3.

conduct useful cultural work.¹⁰² In fact, Antonovich and Zhitetskii continued their efforts to cooperate with the state. They established a cordial relationship with the southwestern governor-general, M. I. Dragomirov; lobbying him to overturn the Ems decree, they portrayed the Hromada and other Little Russian cultural organizations as carriers of a healthy spirit of narodnost'.¹⁰³ The conciliatory attitudes of older activists outraged the younger generation of Ukrainian nationalists in the Russian empire, as well as Hrushevs'kyi, who denounced the Kiev Hromada as hopelessly passive and bourgeois.¹⁰⁴

Kievskaia starina, too, continued to serve as an intellectual home for both Ukrainian and Russian nationalists—and the many who occupied space somewhere between these two poles. It published articles that openly discussed activists' efforts to identify Ukrainian national heroes and to build a cultural and political nation, as well as those that presented the ties between "northern" and "southern" Russia as unbreakable.¹⁰⁵ Its pages featured heated debates about the status of non-Slavic minorities in the southwest. Some contributors furiously denounced Jews as the devoted enemies of the Little Russian simple folk, citing ethnographic studies by Antonovich and Chubinskii and the notorious Moscow-based anti-Semitic lawyer and journalist A. S. Shmakov.¹⁰⁶ Others rejected the trope of internal enemies so important to the Little Russian idea, highlighting Petr Mogila's efforts to foster "conscientious and benevolent" relations between Jews and Gentiles.¹⁰⁷

The continued interweaving of the camps emerging from the Little Russian lobby complicated officials' efforts to determine their proper relationship to local activists. Indeed, in the fluid environment at the turn of the century, it proved more difficult than ever to ascertain the ideological orientations of the right bank's most prominent intellectuals. Was Antonovich, for example, a loyal imperial subject or a dangerous agitator? A force of moderation who had forged a cooperative relationship between the Hromada and local officials, he had also trained Hrushevs'kyi and sent him to Lemberg, where the young historian now headed a political movement that denounced the Russian imperial state. Decades of clandestine surveillance had yielded no evidence that impugned Levitskii's political reliability, though archival documents reveal

---

102. On these disputes, see Andriewsky, "Politics," 3–13; Chykalenko, *Spohady*, 177, 251.
103. Chykalenko, *Spohady*, 166.
104. Palienko, *"Kievskaia starina"*, 1:70, 2:9.
105. For example, F. Matushevskii, "Posetiteli mogily T. G. Shevchenka," *KS* 76, no. 2 (1902): 267–94; S. Efremov, *Prazdnik ukrainskoi intelligentsia* (Kiev, 1903) (this essay was first serialized in *Kievskaia starina*); "S"ezd russkikh zhenshchin vo L'vove," *KS* 81, no. 5 (1903): 120; "Perepiska M.A. Maksimovicha s P. G. Lebidintsev," *KS* 86, no. 9 (1904): 378–413.
106. Ir. Zhitetskii, "Evrei v iuzhnoi Rossii," *KS* 74, no. 7–8 (1901): 10; 34. Likewise, in the Ukrainian-language memoir that he composed at the turn of the century, V. B. Antonovich portrayed the impoverished Orthodox simple folk of his native village as hapless victims of the Catholic gentry and Hasidic Jews. "Avtobigrafichni zapysky Volodymyra Antonovycha," 1897, TsDIAUK, f. 832, op. 1, d. 108, l. 18.
107. I. V. Galant, "Kievskii metropolit Petr Mogila i ego otnosheniia k evreiiam," *KS* 89, no. 5 (1905): 149.

that he maintained a lively Ukrainian-language correspondence with Hrushevs'kyi after the scholar's emigration.[108]

The varied interpretations of local culture presented in *Kievskaia starina* also posed a challenge to the officials attempting to understand its ideological agenda. When Naumenko approached Dragomirov in 1898 to complain that preliminary censorship of *Kievskaia starina* placed an undue burden on the journal's editors, the governor-general petitioned the MVD to exempt the journal from review by St. Petersburg censors. Assuring his superiors that the publication performed the "useful task of developing local historical and ethnographic research" and that he had no reason to doubt the political loyalty of its editors, he insisted that local censors possessed "fully sufficient resources" to monitor its activities.[109] A mere four years later, however, Dragomirov reversed his position on the journal and its editor. Noting that Naumenko's continued contacts with Galician radicals suggested that he had adopted a dangerous "Ukrainophile orientation," he recommended that the scholar be deprived of his seat on the journal's board.[110]

Nevertheless, the MVD and the Kiev governor-general's office remained remarkably supportive of the Little Russian idea, on which they continued to rely to discredit competing claims on the right bank. In 1898, local and imperial authorities cleared the Kiev chapter of the Imperial Geographic Society to reopen. Its members included Pikhno, Levitskii, and the Storozhenko brothers, as well long-time Hromada activists, including some who had worked with Galician activists to publish editions of Shevchenko's *Kobzar* in Prague.[111] In 1903, the St. Petersburg ministries finally agreed to introduce zemstva in the southwest, a reform for which *Kievlianin* and the southwestern governors-general had long lobbied. Having received the good news, Governor-General Dragomirov and *Kievlianin* contributors encouraged officials to structure the new institutions on a national basis, expanding the franchise of Orthodox East Slavs and limiting that of Polish Catholics.[112] Although the MVD refused to meet this demand—it opted instead to guarantee the reliability of *zemstvo* members by appointing them—Little Russian patriots who had participated in this lobbying effort,

---

108. Vasylenko, "Akademyk," 71–72; see also the correspondence between Hrushevs'kyi and Levitskii in IRNBUV, f. 81, no. 81–82. In this correspondence, it becomes clear that Hrushevs'kyi followed the research of those who remained firmly in the Little Russian camp; in one letter he asks Levitskii to send him a recent article by S. T. Golubev.
109. Dragomirov to Ministry of Internal Affairs, 18 July 1898, TsDIAUK MF-19, op. 1, d. 20, ll. 249–50. The ultimate outcome of this request is unclear.
110. Department of Police to Main Press Directorate, 28 February 1902, ibid., l. 261.
111. Savchenko, *Zaborona*, 118–19.
112. Although Orthodox believers had greatly expanded their landholdings over the previous thirty years, on average their plots remained relatively small. Catholics remained disproportionately represented among the ranks of the wealthiest landlords, a point of great concern for Little Russian activists. In 1897, the vast majority of those who owned more than two hundred desiatins of land in Volynia were Catholic, as were nearly 50 percent of large landowners in Podolia and Kiev provinces. See V. Shul'gin, *Vybornoe zemstvo v Iugo-zapadnom krae* (Kiev, 1909), 36.

including I. M. Reva and A. V. Storozhenko, managed to secure key posts in the new institutions.[113]

::

Over the course of the nineteenth century, the Little Russian idea percolated through the culture, society, and politics of Russia's southwestern borderlands. Having begun as an expression of the historical imagination of a small group of Orthodox gentry, it gradually evolved into a political and social movement that aimed to reclaim the putative heartland of Rus' from the foreign interests that had allegedly exploited local peasants and degraded their culture. As it infiltrated the southwest's educational establishments, periodicals, and voluntary societies, the Little Russian idea offered right-bank residents an opportunity to lead an all-imperial discussion about ethnonational difference and its proper role in imperial governance. Having proven its capacity to serve the de-polonization campaign, it won the support of influential imperial officials, who gradually corroded the imperial estate system in the region. Because it so effectively reconciled the interests of a peripheral locality and the imperial metropole and enlisted in common cause officials and a local intelligentsia eager to claim the southwest for the empire, the Little Russian idea proved remarkably resilient. It survived many vicissitudes—from the Cyrillo-Methodian scandal to the 1863 revolt to the growing hysteria about Ukrainophilism in the late nineteenth century—intact if not unaltered.

Although the Little Russian idea demonstrated remarkable durability in an era of rapid political and social change, it also unleashed forces that the imperial authorities struggled to contain. A clumsy and poorly executed attempt by officials to manage growing rifts within the Little Russian lobby had splintered its proponents into competing camps that interpreted the culture of the southwestern borderlands in dramatically different ways. If many still presented the region as the cradle of East Slavic civilization and the spiritual center of the Russian nation, some southwestern intellectuals co-opted the historical narratives, rhetorical tools, and cultural institutions that they had first encountered in the Little Russian lobby to advance a Ukrainian nation-building process. The struggle to define the national characteristics of the right bank became interwoven with intense ideological conflicts: activists who insisted that only a strong and interventionist state could assure the survival of Little Russian culture clashed with their radical and liberal Ukrainophile opponents.

As the competing camps emerging from the Little Russian lobby struggled for power at the dawn of a new century, this contest would take on a new character. Although Little Russian activists had long claimed to speak for the narod, they aimed primarily to influence officialdom. By the late nineteenth and early twentieth centuries,

---

113. "Zapiska po povodu vvedeniia v deistvie s 1 Maia 1904 g. zakona 2 aprelia 1903 g.," TsDIAUK, f. 442, op. 656, d. 132, ch. 1, ll. 45–51; on *Kievlianin*'s contributions to the debate, see the clippings in TsDIAUK, f. 442, op. 656, d. 132, ch. 2, ll. 9–410b.

however, southwestern intellectuals had begun to court a broad audience, and ordinary people demanded the right to help determine their own destinies. Mass political processes would emerge first in the city of Kiev—the center of culture, politics, and industry in the region—and would soon expand beyond city limits. Peasants, workers, parish clergy, women, and students would play a key role in defining the national characteristics and ideological meaning of southwestern culture. It is their important contributions that we will examine next.

PART TWO

The Urban Crucible

4 Nationalizing Urban Politics

WHILE LITTLE RUSSIAN activists portrayed the southwestern borderlands as the spiritual center of an Orthodox, East Slavic nation, social, political, and economic processes unrelated to the de-polonization campaign were transforming everyday life in the region. The 1860s marked the beginning of several decades of rapid urban and industrial development across the empire, spurred by new state incentives encouraging investments in trade and manufacturing as well as the emancipation of the serfs, which compelled many peasants to leave their communes in search of wage labor.[1] In the southwest, a new capitalist elite coalesced in the regional center of Kiev, acquiring property and cultural capital that the decimated szlachta had abandoned. Meanwhile, tens of thousands of peasants and townspeople struggling to survive in one of the empire's poorest and most densely populated corners descended on the city, finding work in the factories and artisanal workshops springing up on the urban periphery. As a diverse array of newcomers crowded out the bureaucrats, Orthodox clergy, and Little Russian intellectuals who had already gained a foothold in Kiev, new communities—and new conflicts—emerged in the city.

The role of urban politics in shaping national and ideological identifications in nineteenth-century central and western Europe has been well documented. In the first two-thirds of the century, bourgeois liberals seized control of city governments and the urban professions across the continent, creating attractive and orderly urban spaces and founding dense networks of schools, associations, and cultural institutions. Presenting themselves as the architects of a universal modernity built on reason and expertise, they challenged the authority of landed elites and central states while they struggled to both control and acculturate the lower classes.[2] In the last third of the century, representatives of the lower-middle and working classes who resented bourgeois attempts to speak for them mobilized to denounce the liberal order. To

---

1. See Brower, *Russian City*.
2. On the liberal-bourgeois order, see Alan S. Kahan, *Liberalism in Nineteenth-Century Europe* (New York, 2003); Derek Fraser, *Power and Authority in the Victorian City* (New York, 1979); Gordon A. Craig, *The Triumph of Liberalism* (New York, 1988); Berthold Grzywatz, *Stadt, Bürgertum und Staat im 19. Jahrhundert* (Berlin, 2003).

compensate for their limited access to political institutions, they created a mass-oriented and emotionally charged style of politics that defined itself against the staid respectability of bourgeois society. This "politics in a new key" described so elegantly by Carl Schorske gave rise to radical nationalist and antiliberal movements in many European cities, beginning the transition from the era of notable politics to the age of mass mobilization.³

Emphasizing the constraints that the autocratic regime placed on political organization and expression, the literature on Russian urban politics tends to focus on the troubled relationship between individual segments of the urban population and the imperial state. Numerous studies have examined how radical intellectuals and labor organizations courted followers and formulated protest.⁴ While scholars have demonstrated that late imperial Russian cities gave rise to a small but influential middle class that managed to create a vibrant civic life for itself, the autocracy's efforts to manage the fledgling public sphere emerging in Russian cities frustrated and alienated educated urbanites.⁵ Works that examine the experience of the men who ran Russia's semidemocratic municipal governments come to a similar conclusion: although they testify to the existence of a public-spirited urban elite, they also chronicle its growing disenchantment with the paternalism and intrusive behavior of the imperial state.⁶

This chapter, which examines the internal political ecology of Kiev between the 1860s and early 1900s, unearths rather different patterns of political mobilization. It focuses on the intense conflicts that emerged within society itself as Kiev residents debated how best to govern the city and struggled to define the proper place of the southwestern borderlands in the empire. In its political and associational activities, the city's new capitalist elite challenged the nationalizing vision associated with the Little Russian idea. Capitalist Kiev's beau monde—which consisted of Poles, Russians, Little Russians, foreigners, and an especially large number of Jews—prided itself on its cosmopolitanism, welcoming all men who had proven their business acumen. At the same time, it showed limited interest in the welfare of the city's working classes. In response, an emergent class of populist politicians, some of whom can be traced directly to the Little Russian lobby, formulated a harsh critique of the capitalist city fathers' apparent self-interest. Building on the narrative of national struggle that Little Russian activists had developed, they blamed the suffering of the narod

---

3. Schorske, *Fin-de-Siècle Vienna*, 116–80.
4. Reginald E. Zelnik, *Labor and Society in Tsarist Russia* (Stanford, 1971); Robert Eugene Johnson, *Peasant and Proletarian* (New Brunswick, NJ, 1979); Laura Engelstein, *Moscow, 1905* (Stanford, 1982); Gerald D. Surh, *1905 in St. Petersburg* (Stanford, 1989).
5. Laura Engelstein, *The Keys to Happiness* (Ithaca, 1992); Adele Lindenmeyr, *Poverty Is Not a Vice* (Princeton, 1996); Balzer, *Russia's Missing Middle Class*; Lutz Häfner, *Gesellschaft als lokale Veranstaltung* (Cologne, 2004); Bradley, *Voluntary Associations*.
6. Robert W. Thurston, *Liberal City, Conservative State* (New York, 1987); V. A. Nardova, *Samoderzhavie i gorodskie dumy v Rossii v kontse XIX–nachale XX veka* (St. Petersburg, 1994); Guido Hausmann, ed., *Gesellschaft als lokale Veranstaltung* (Göttingen, 2002); L. F. Pisar'kova, *Gorodskie reformy v Rossii i moskovskaia duma* (Moscow, 2010).

on the very diversity of the capitalist elite; in urban economic and political life, they charged, non-East Slavs—and especially Jews—had discovered a new venue in which they could oppress and exploit the children of Rus'. The struggle of the city's working classes to achieve economic stability and social justice, these politicians insisted, was part and parcel of the battle to emancipate the borderlands' East Slavic majority from foreign domination.

The patterns of political mobilization that emerged in Kiev are reminiscent of those in central and western European cities. Kiev's capitalist newcomers, like European liberals, welcomed men of many ethnonational and scoioeconomic backgrounds into the urban beau monde, so long as they demonstrated adequate cultivation and wealth. In spite of the limitations that the autocracy placed on participatory politics, populist demagogues managed to pioneer a new style of mass-oriented politics that challenged the authority of Kiev's city fathers and their cosmopolitan yet elitist worldview. Although Russia was neither a rule-of-law state nor a democracy, members of each of these camps managed to set political agendas and to mobilize parties and organizations to advance their programs—activities classically viewed as key functions of civil society.[7]

However, the behavior of the men who participated in the debates about the future of Kiev also deviated from that of their European counterparts in striking ways. If technocrats and professionals dominated European urban politics, self-made nouveaux riches played the key role in Kiev's urban affairs. Though Kiev's city fathers were substantially wealthier than Europe's bourgeois liberals, their status was less secure. Like all residents of the Russian empire, they remained subjects rather than citizens, lacking inalienable civil rights; indeed, many were members of minority groups that had been subjected to official discrimination and to harsh critiques by the Little Russian lobby.

As a result, Kiev's urban elites failed to develop the universalizing vision and self-confidence of their European counterparts. They expressed more interest in protecting the resources that they had accumulated than in using them to cultivate the masses; rather than attempting to stake off social space free of state intervention, they actively sought out official patronage. Kiev's demagogues, for their part, anticipated the rise of mass politics, but they could not dream of achieving the electoral victories that antiliberal politicians elsewhere in Europe were beginning to enjoy. Absolved of the need to forge broad-based coalitions and to stake out pragmatic positions to win elections, they articulated radical views designed to generate maximal attention—and to frighten the urban public and the local authorities about the putative risks that Kiev's non-Orthodox elites posed to the welfare of the city at large. Rather than heralding the dawn of a more cohesive and harmonious society, the political mobilization of city residents produced the most extreme exclusionary politics that the southwest had seen yet.

---

7. For a study that considers how participatory politics could shape a hierarchical and incompletely democratic society, consult Margaret Lavinia Anderson, *Practicing Democracy* (Princeton, 2000).

Portrait of a Capitalist City

Kiev's sugar industry grew rapidly in the last third of the nineteenth century, spurred by advances in refining technology and rising demand from Europe and North America. Early investors in the industry, who held the capital necessary to consolidate large plots of land and build huge factories, expanded their stature and their fortunes. The Branicki and Potocki families—the wealthiest Polish landlords who had remained loyal to the state in 1863—used their connections to evade de-polonizing measures, buying up the property of ruined szlachta clans. The Balashevs and Bobrinskiis—some of the few large Orthodox landlords in the region, both absentees who resided in St. Petersburg—made large investments in the industry.[8] The Brodskiis remained the most prominent sugar industrialists in the southwest; Lazar (1848–1904) and Lev (1852–1923), the sons of the family patriarch, Israel, would eventually come to control thirteen refineries, which produced a quarter of the sugar in the Russian empire; the Gintsburgs, too, remained key players in the industry.[9]

Prior to the mid-nineteenth century, lesser gentry and upwardly mobile merchants did not possess the capital necessary to compete with the great magnates in the sugar business. By the 1860s, however, they had raised venture capital and created joint stock companies, which allowed them to enter the industry. Little Russian nobles from the left bank such as the Tereshchenkos, Kharitonenkos, and Khanenkos began to buy up land on the right bank and to acquire sugar refineries around Kiev.[10] The Iakhnenko and Simirenko brothers, who had been born serfs, invested the profits they had earned as small-time merchants in the sugar business, becoming self-made millionaires by the 1860s.[11] Despite the restrictions introduced on Jewish landholding in the aftermath of 1863, dozens of Jewish merchants managed to acquire control of refineries and plantations, many through long-term lease arrangements. By 1872, Jews operated one-quarter of the southwest's sugar refineries and controlled six hundred thousand desiatins of rural land, much of it planted with sugar beets.[12]

The expansion of the sugar industry created an insatiable need for professionals—especially in Kiev, where most of the sugar companies were headquartered. Because the regular salaries of engineers, accountants, and managers employed in the industry were regularly supplemented by bonuses based on company earnings, even middle-management and technical positions could prove quite lucrative. Professional positions in the sugar industry were particularly appealing to the well-educated sons of szlachta families who had lost their land in the de-polonization campaign.

---

8. On the southwestern sugar industry, see K. G. Voblyi, *Narysy z istorii rosiis'ko-ukrains'koi tsukroburia-kovoi promyslovosty* (Kiev, 1931), vol. 3, vyp. 1; *Proizvodstvo sakhara na zavodakh Grafov Bobrinskikh Kievskoi gubernii* (Kiev, 1896).
9. Brodsky, *Smoke Signals*, 4–5; Khiterer, "Jewish Life," 78.
10. See the coverage of these families in Kovalinskii, *Metsenaty*.
11. A. P. Ogloblin, *Ocherki istorii ukrainskoi fabriki* (Kiev, 1925), 148–67.
12. A. M. Dondukov-Korsakov, "Zapiska o bolee vazhnykh voprosakh po upravleniiu Iugo-Zapadnym kraem," RGIA, f. 932, op. 1, d. 160, l. 500b.

One account estimates that more than half of the directors of sugar factories in Kiev province were Polish Catholics, and anecdotal evidence suggests that Poles also constituted a large percentage of the industry's engineers and accountants.[13] By the late nineteenth century, this new Polish professional class had created a bustling middle-class neighborhood along the Vasil'kov road, which stretched south of the Kiev city center, and had constructed a new Catholic cathedral in the district.[14]

Educated Jews from the Pale also sought out employment at sugar factories. When the writer Sholem Aleichem arrived in Kiev from his native shtetl, he relied on local Jewish notables to help him find employment in his new hometown; he ultimately obtained a coveted position as an inspector at the Brodskiis' refineries.[15] Although Jewish professionals and managers found work at enterprises operated by merchants from all walks of life, positions in Jewish-owned companies seem to have been particularly valued by newcomers, since the authorities, in the interest of encouraging entrepreneurial activity, authorized Jewish merchants of the first guild to procure permanent residence permits for all their employees. This was, of course, a great prize at a time when opportunities for Jews to settle in Kiev legally remained extremely restricted. As Jewish merchants joined the ranks of the city's wealthiest residents, skilled workers and professionals of Jewish origins secured residence rights, assimilated into the urban middle class, and amassed the means to send their sons to university, where many received training as doctors, lawyers, and accountants. By the early twentieth century, Kiev's free professionals were approximately one-fifth Jewish.[16]

The development of the sugar industry spurred the growth of other sectors of the local economy as well. As mentioned in chapter 2, it necessitated the construction of new rail lines—many built rapidly and with substandard materials by a colorful and diverse cast of capitalists who enjoyed government guarantees on their investments. Just as quickly as railway lines appeared, banks and mutual aid associations cropped up to serve sugar and railroad industrialists desperate for credit. By the 1870s, Kiev boasted one of Russia's densest network of banks, which held a substantial portion of the empire's total deposits.[17] The development of finance and capital in Kiev in turn spurred the creation of the city Stock Committee, which became a powerful lobbying organization representing the interests of the city's largest industrialists. It would also go on to found one of the empire's liveliest commodities exchanges, where, by the

---

13. Walewski, "Cukrownictwo," 2:182. The Kiev Agricultural Society, a group dominated by the large Polish landowners who had survived the de-polonization campaign, helped members of the szlachta who had lost their land and livelihoods to find employment in the sugar industry. See Zygmunt Chojecki, *Kijowskie Towarzystwo Rolnicze* (Kiev, 1911).
14. Leszek Podhorodecki, *Dzieje Kijowa* (Warsaw, 1982), 194.
15. Marie Waife-Goldberg, *My Father, Sholom Aleichem* (New York, 1968), 77, 83.
16. Viktoriia Khiterer, *Dokumenty sobrannye evreiskoi istoriko-arkheograficheskoi komissiei* (Kiev, 1999), 144. Although an 1887 law mandated that Jews not comprise more than 10 percent of the student body at St. Vladimir's, it was erratically enforced. By the 1890s, about one-quarter of the institution's students were Jewish. See Nathans, *Beyond the Pale*, 257–307. Figure from 271.
17. D. I. Pikhno, *Kommercheskie operatsii Gosudarstvennogo Banka* (Kiev, 1876), 88–89; O. K. Kasymenko et al., *Istoriia Kyeva* (Kiev, 1960), 408–9.

early 1880s, most of the region's sugar would be bought and sold as futures.[18] Whereas merchants in the Great Russian interior continued to rely on personal connections to identify business partners and on trade fairs to sell their goods, those operating in the dynamic environment created in the southwest by the rapid growth of the sugar industry enthusiastically embraced modern capitalism. Renowned for their willingness to rely on credit, seek out venture capital, and use modern marketing techniques to sell their goods, the southwestern mercantile elite transformed Kiev into Russia's capitalist Wild West.[19]

Kiev's economic dynamism made it an attractive destination for ambitious entrepreneurs in many fields besides the sugar industry. One merchant family that relocated from central Russia managed to amass assets of over 4.5 million rubles in a single generation; a Swiss subject who was forced to convalesce in the city after breaking his leg on a business trip ultimately decided not to leave, founding a candy enterprise, a jam factory, and a clan that would remain active in the city's economy and politics through the October Revolution.[20] Again many Jews achieved a visible role among the city's mercantile elite. Within a decade of their arrival in the 1860s, the Kogen brothers, Crimean Karaites, were operating the city's two largest tobacco factories and a retail store at the very heart of its main street, Khreshchatik.[21] D. S. Margolin, who founded a small steamboat shipping business, soon came to dominate the river trade on the Dnieper and to enjoy a sizable share of shipping on the Danube as well. He enhanced his wealth by making wise investments in railroad companies and sugar factories and would serve as Kiev's local representative to the Department of Trade and Manufacturing.[22] By the midseventies, more than 86 percent of the city's most elite merchants (those of the first guild) were Jewish.[23] By the late nineteenth century, Jews had acquired 35 percent of the factories and one-sixth of all commercial establishments in Kiev province, including 27 sugar factories, 15 tobacco factories, 22 candle factories, 23 brick factories, 564 viticulture establishments, 148 breweries, and 15,000 shops.[24]

---

18. *Dvadtsatipiatiletie Kievskoi Birzhi, 1869–1894 g.* (Kiev, 1895), xxvii; Voblyi, *Narysy,* 125–30.
19. On the dynamic commercial environment on the empire's southwestern periphery, see Alfred J. Rieber, *Merchants and Entrepreneurs in Imperial Russia* (Chapel Hill, NC, 1982), 106–8; Rainer Lindner, *Unternehmer und Stadt in der Ukraine, 1860–1914* (Konstanz, 2006); Hamm, *Kiev,* 18–54. The vibrant southwestern economy provides a stark contrast to the dire state of Russian capital and noble agriculture described in Peter Gatrell, *The Tsarist Economy, 1850–1917* (London, 1986), 188–230.
20. Kovalinskii, *Metsenaty,* 193; Starozhil [S. V. Iaron], *Kiev v vos'midesiatykh godakh* (Kiev, 1910), 184.
21. Kovalinskii, *Metsenaty,* 399–401.
22. G. B. Sliozberg, *Dela minuvshikh dnei* (Paris, 1933), 1:284; Michael Vetukhiv, "Arnold Davydovych Margolin, 1877–1956," *Annals of the Ukrainian Academy of Arts and Sciences in the U.S.* 7, no. 1–2 (1959): 1671.
23. "Vedomost' o chisle vydannykh, kupecheskikh promyslovykh i prikazchikh bilety," 1881, DAK, f. 163, op. 39, d. 211, l. 56. Ironically, it was partially Kiev's exclusion from the Pale of Settlement that encouraged its Jewish merchants to attain first-guild status, which offered them special settlement privileges. In Odessa, which was located within the Pale and where Jewish merchants could settle permanently regardless of their guild status, a mere half of first-guild merchants were Jewish. Consult Sliozberg, *Dela,* 2:75; Nicholas V. Iljine, ed., *Odessa Memories* (Seattle, 2003), 77.
24. Data culled from G. Ia. Krasnyi-Admoni, *Materialy dlia istorii antievreiskikh pogromov v Rossii* (Petrograd, 1923), 2:xx; *Recueil de matériaux sur la situation économique des israélites de Russie d'après l'ênquete de*

Nationalizing Urban Politics

View of the Podol quarter and the Dnieper River port. Source: *Vidy Kieva* (Kiev, 1917). Courtesy of Slavonic Library, National Library of Finland.

Kiev's rapid capitalist takeoff and its new commercial elite transformed the physical landscape of the city. Industrialists and merchants tore down old wood buildings and constructed handsome stone manors in the aristocratic neighborhoods of Lipki and Old Kiev, located on high bluffs overlooking the Dnieper River. They built a modern port in the low-lying commercial district of Podol, theaters, churches and synagogues, a luxurious merchant hall that hosted concerts and plays when it was not occupied with business meetings, and the Chateau des fleurs, a swank private club at which Polish, Jewish, and Orthodox elites joined bureaucrats for hands of whist and strong drinks. Luxurious shops selling imported fabric, teas, and candies sprang up on Khreshchatik, often advertising their goods in several languages.[25]

But if capitalist development transformed Kiev into a modern metropolis, it initiated a crisis in the city's rural hinterlands. The sugar boom and the acquisition of

---

la *Jewish Colonization Association* (Paris, 1906), vol. 2. N. Kh. Bunge's great nephew left behind a colorful memoir of Kiev's economic life, stressing the leading role that Jewish entrepreneurs played in it. See "Detstvo," 1887, in Nikolai Nikolaevich Flige Collection, BA, box 1, folder 1.

25. Starozhil, *Kiev*, 92; K. Fomenko, "Kiev vtoroi poloviny XIX veka," *KEV* 17 (1909): 393–94.

The busy commercial thoroughfare of Khreshchatik. Source: *Vidy Kieva* (Kiev, 1917). Courtesy of Slavonic Library, National Library of Finland.

massive tracts of land by industrialists and joint stock companies led to rapid increases in the cost of land. This placed the local peasantry in a precarious position. Over the last third of the nineteenth century, the rising value of immovable property encouraged peasants to sell their land to industrialists, leading to rapid contractions in the average allotment size. Unable to sustain their families on their tiny plots, many peasants became wage laborers serving the very sugar barons to whom they had given over control of their land.[26]

Although some peasants remained in their native villages, laboring in the fields that had been bought up by sugar conglomerates or in the rural refineries they operated, tens of thousands migrated to Kiev in search of better economic opportunities. Unskilled and semiskilled laborers found work in the city's sugar refineries and in the flour mills; breweries; tobacco stores; and printing, boatbuilding, and mechanical shops that were proliferating rapidly on the urban periphery. Many others joined the

---

26. Robert Edelman, *Proletarian Peasants* (Ithaca, 1987), 37–69.

ranks of petty traders or artisans or found work with the Southwestern Railroad.[27] Working-class Jews from shtetls across the southwest—primarily Yiddish speakers— also poured into the city. Many found work in factories, constituting about 10 percent of the industrial workforce, which by the 1890s would approach fifty thousand.[28] Even more became small-time traders, middlemen, or artisans; local guilds of tailors, furriers, and candy makers were all more than 50 percent Jewish.[29] Indeed, between 1870 and 1889, Kiev's Jewish population grew more than twice as fast as its overall population, quickly surpassing the number of Poles—previously the city's largest non-East Slavic minority.[30] At the turn of the century, Kiev was about 13 percent Jewish; by 1917 that proportion would near 20 percent.[31]

Working-class newcomers to the city congregated in inexpensive districts on its periphery. Peasant migrants favored cheap apartments in Lybed' on the city's south side and Plossk and Luk'ianovka to the west of the city center; they also built shanty towns on the low-lying left bank of the Dnieper. Jews had fewer choices about where they could settle. Those who did not belong to the first-guild merchantry were obligated to obtain residence permits that authorized them to live only in Lybed' and Plossk. (Taxes on kosher meat funded notorious midnight police roundups of Jews who lacked residence permits or had illegally settled in closed neighborhoods.)[32] Many Jewish migrants also settled in the suburbs of Demievka and Solomenka, which, unlike Kiev, were included in the Pale of Settlement. (See map 4.1.) Kiev's peripheral districts, which were densely populated and plagued by frequent floods, were among the empire's most hazardous corners. Raw sewage flowed through unpaved roads, people lived in shacks alongside animals, cholera epidemics were frequent, and criminal gangs terrorized local residents.[33]

Power, Politics, and the Urban Elite

Although the elite that coalesced in Kiev following the 1863 revolt was diverse in composition, it was also exceptionally close-knit. In a booming capitalist metropolis, displaying ethnic particularism and prejudice was both distasteful and imprudent—an impediment to maximizing one's profits and elevating one's social status. In order to join the elite ranks of the first and second guilds, merchants were obligated not only to amass impressive fortunes but also to present to the authorities attestations from their peers about their character and reliability—a practice that encouraged elites to trust

---

27. On the rapid growth of southwestern industry, see M. Iavors'kyi, *Ukraina v epokhu kapitalizmu* (Kiev, 1925); "Kratkaia zapiska," DAK, f. 226, op. 1, d. 12, ll. 46–510b.
28. *Pamiatnaia knizhka Kievskoi gubernii na 1896 god* (Kiev, 1896), 93.
29. See *Zapiska Senatora A. Polovtsova* (St. Petersburg, 1882), 38–39; *Recueil de matériaux*, 1:240, 349.
30. Wasław Ciechowski, *Kijów i jego pamiątki* (Kiev, 1901), 53.
31. Khiterer, *Dokumenty*, 143; Hamm, *Kiev*, 129.
32. See Khiterer, "Jewish Life," 77; Meir, *Kiev*.
33. *Trud*, 10 April 1881, 1.

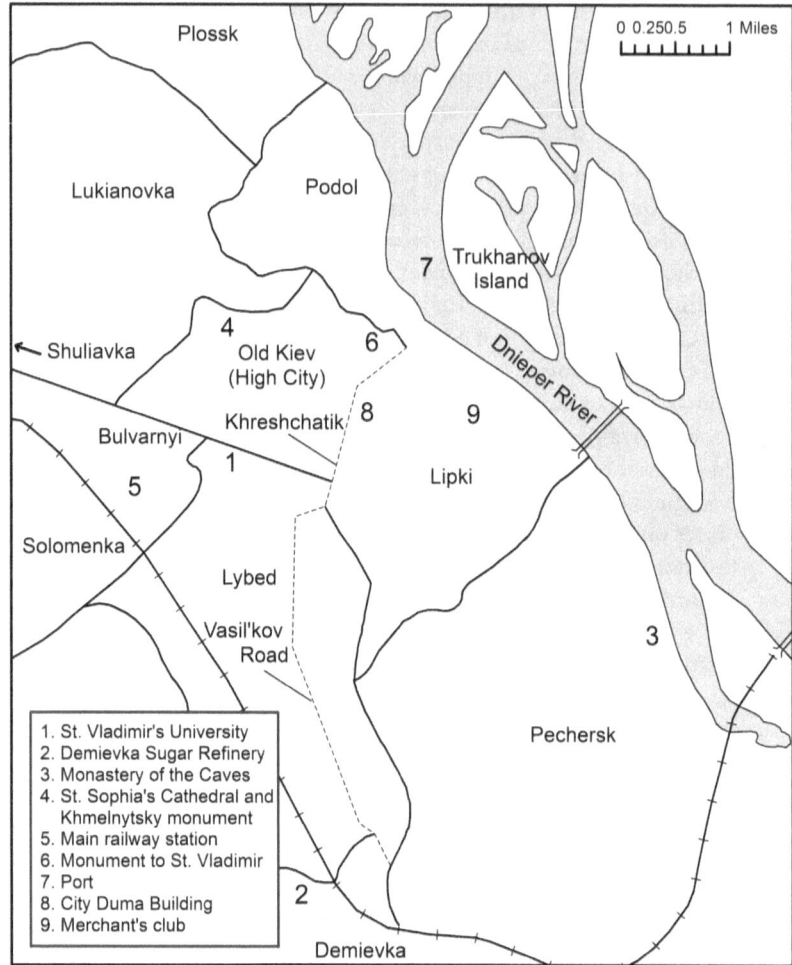

Map 4.1
Kiev, circa 1900. Adapted with permission from Michael F. Hamm, *Kiev* (Princeton, 1993), 26.

and rely on each other.³⁴ Once their place in the urban beau monde had been secured, Kiev's capitalist elites continued to foster a spirit of accommodation. The city's private clubs and its most prestigious voluntary organizations proudly welcomed men from all walks of life into their ranks, provided they had proven their entrepreneurial

---

34. See, for example, "O vydache udostovereniia A. Kuperniku o prinadlezhnosti k kupecheskomu sosloviiu," 1870–1886, DAK, f. 163, op. 7, d. 56; "Delo o vydache udostoverenii remeslennikam-evreiam na pravo zhitel'stva i torgovli v g. Kieve," March 1874, DAK, f. 163, op. 7, d. 365.

acumen and amassed adequate fortunes.[35] And although imperial law mandated that the chair of the Kiev Stock Exchange be an Orthodox believer, that organization, too, made explicit its desire to accommodate the needs of all its members: it scheduled important meetings to avoid Jewish holidays and the Sabbath and welcomed Jewish notables to its board of chairmen, which after the 1880s was never less than half Jewish.[36]

Kiev's mercantile elites made no secret of their ambitions to complement the vast fortunes they had built with social and political influence. The city's wealthiest families gave generously to religious institutions, hospitals, museums, and schools. Although their charitable activities reflected some sense of responsibility to the broader community, contemporaries also saw self-interest as a motivation for their generosity. The Brodskiis—who, as one long-time resident noted, supported virtually every "charitable [and] educational establishment in Kiev"—expected to play a leading role in the organizations they funded, which ranged from synagogues to a bacteriological institute to scholarship programs for needy St. Vladimir's students.[37] Philanthropy could also become a competitive sport: the Tereshchenkos, whose fortune and influence by the 1880s had begun to rival the Brodskiis', clearly struggled to outdo the Brodskiis in their charitable giving. In the 1880s and early '90s alone, the family funded an orphanage, a free hospital for unskilled workers, several schools, and a night shelter; they also organized a commission to build a museum that would open their private art collection to the public.[38]

By the 1890s, Kiev industrialists began to create private municipal utility networks, which offered them a new opportunity to endow their adoptive hometown with a modern, European face while enhancing their political influence. The Brodskiis founded a joint stock company that built the city waterworks and shared ownership of the municipal sewer company with the Tereschenkos. D. S. Margolin, who owned many shares in the local gas and electric utilities, enjoyed sole proprietorship of the company that launched the Russian empire's first electric tramway in 1894.[39] Across Europe, private utility services were widely despised for their corruption and monopolistic practices; this was even more true in the Russian empire, where most companies were operated by foreign capitalists, especially Frenchmen and Belgians.[40]

---

35. Starozhil, *Kiev*, 92.
36. Rieber, *Merchants*, 106. The data about the composition of the Stock Committee leadership are culled from *Dvadtsatipiatiletie; Otchet Kievskogo Birzhevogo Komiteta za 1899 god* (Kiev, 1900).
37. The quote is from Starozhil, *Kiev*, 177. For discussion of the charitable giving of Kiev's Jewish plutocrats, the expectations connected to their gifts, and the resentment that these expectations provoked from the Jewish community at large, see Meir, *Kiev*, 232–37, 261–310.
38. Kovalinskii, *Metsenaty*, 259–60; Oleksandr Donik, *Rodyna Tereshchenkiv v istorii dobrochynnosti* (Kiev, 2004).
39. P. T. Tron'ko, ed., *Istoriia gorodov i sel Ukrainskoi SSR: Kiev* (Kiev, 1979), 157–58; Khiterer, "Jewish Life," 84; P. Golubiatnikov, *Spravka o khode dela po rasshireniiu Kievskoi kanalizatsii v chetyrekhletie s 1902 po 1906 god* (Kiev, 1906), 255–62.
40. On private utilities companies in Russia and popular reaction to them, see John P. McKay, *Pioneers for Profit* (Chicago, 1970), 100–102; D. I. Bagalei and D. P. Miller, *Istoriia goroda Khar'kova za 250 let ego sushchestvovaniia* (Kharkov, 1912), 2:393–98.

The Kiev city duma building on Khreshchatik. Source: *Vidy Kieva* (Kiev, 1917). Courtesy of Slavonic Library, National Library of Finland.

As we shall see, the fact that these companies were operated by homegrown capitalists in Kiev would have a critical impact on local politics.

The 1870 reforms that permitted the largest cities of European Russia to govern themselves created yet another venue in which Kiev's industrialists consolidated their influence and their fortunes. The reform created an elected city council, or duma, which enjoyed the power to oversee public health, education, trade, and commerce. However, the appointed city administration and the imperial authorities enjoyed the right to overturn any of the duma's decisions.[41] The new municipal statute intentionally vested disproportionate power in the hands of the city's wealthiest residents: just under 6,000 of Kiev's 70,500 inhabitants qualified to vote in the city's first municipal elections, held in 1871, by paying substantial property taxes or a large flat tax; the eligible pool of voters was then divided into three curiae vested with unequal electoral powers, again determined by wealth. The first curia (with 121 voters),

---

41. On the new municipal governments and the challenges they faced operating in an autocratic context, see Nardova, *Samoderzhavie*, 19–26.

the second (with 549), and the third (with 5,078) each were empowered to elect 24 representatives to the city duma.[42]

Though the 1870 municipal self-governance statute limited the franchise to the well-off, it offered expansive participatory rights to Jewish and Polish elites. Indeed, the non-Orthodox were slightly overrepresented among the city's most powerful voters: in the 1875 elections, Poles and Jews constituted about 30 percent of the eligible voters of the first two curiae, although the two groups together represented only about one-fifth of the total urban population at that time.[43] (The third curia, by contrast, which was dominated by middling merchants and professionals, was almost exclusively Orthodox.)[44] As might be expected, Kiev's entrepreneurial elite overwhelmingly elected their own; merchants—including members of the Tereshchenko, Brodskii, and Gintsburg families—claimed nearly half of the body's seats in the 1870s and '80s.[45] Of the duma delegates elected in 1879, sixty-two were Orthodox or Protestant, five Catholic, and five Jewish.[46]

The bourgeois liberals who dominated politics in the cities of western and central Europe thought of themselves as representatives of and advocates for the urban community at large. City councils from London to Vienna worked to enlighten the working classes, improve public health and infrastructure, keep commodity prices low through free trade, and municipalize private utility companies in order to regulate their operations and rates.[47] Kiev's city fathers, by contrast, unabashedly used their engagement in urban politics to promote their personal interests. Duma delegates

42. "Statisticheskie svedeniia ob uchrezhdeniiakh Gorodskogo Obshchestvennogo Upravleniia po Gorodskomu Polozheniiu," 16 June 1870, DAK, f. 163, op. 8, d. 1, l. 1. The population estimate is cited in Hamm, *Kiev,* 25. Although Russian law placed serious constraints on the autonomy of city dumas, neither their elitist structures nor the excessive administrative oversight to which they were subjected was uniquely Russian. Although France established universal manhood suffrage in municipal elections in 1848, large cities were not permitted to elect their mayors until 1884. Even after this reform, mayors who had fallen afoul of the authorities could be removed temporarily by appointed prefects or dismissed permanently by presidential decree. Paris and Lyon, which were governed directly by appointed prefects for most of the nineteenth century, enjoyed even less autonomy. William B. Cohen, *Urban Government and the Rise of the French City* (New York, 1998), 24–26; Vivian A. Schmidt, *Democratizing France* (New York, 1990), 58–60. Likewise, the Habsburg emperor was empowered to refuse to install mayors elected by city residents—a prerogative famously exercised twice by Franz Joseph upon the election of Karl Lueger. In the central European context, Kiev's franchise was not unusually narrow. At the close of the nineteenth century, only 6 percent of Viennese residents and 6 percent of Prague residents qualified for the municipal franchise—a proportion less than that entitled to vote in Kiev's first elections. See Boyer, *Political Radicalism,* 509n192; Cathleen M. Giustino, *Tearing Down Prague's Jewish Town* (Boulder, 2003), 4.
43. Statistics based on "Vedomost' o chisle izbiratelei za 1875–79 g.," DAK, f. 163, op. 39, d. 211, l. 51.
44. All 123 Jews who qualified to vote in 1875 were engaged in trade. Most enfranchised Catholics qualified to vote on the basis of the land taxes that they paid. Ibid., l. 51.
45. See "Vedomost' o sostave Gorodskoi duma s 1871 po 1875 god," DAK, f. 163, op. 39, d. 211, l. 99; "Vedomost' o sostave Gorodskoi dumy s 1875 po 1879 god," ibid., l. 97.
46. *Zapiska Senatora A. Polovtsova,* 168.
47. For varied approaches to the public-minded universalism of bourgeois society, see Michael J. Turner, *Reform and Respectability* (Manchester, UK, 1995); Cohen, *Urban Government;* Schorske, *Fin-de-Siècle Vienna,* 24–115; Craig, *Triumph,* 95–180.

devoted considerable sums to beautifying and improving the infrastructure of the city's best districts, where its capitalist elite lived and worked, but they showed less interest in projects that would serve larger segments of the urban population.[48] Indeed, the single largest public works project that the duma undertook between 1870 and 1907 was the construction of a permanent meeting place for itself on Khreshchatik, which cost half a million rubles; between 1875 and 1879, by contrast, the municipal government spent only twenty-seven thousand rubles on popular education initiatives across the city.[49] At times, the self-interest of duma deputies was even more glaring: some passed legislation that lowered their own property taxes and thwarted the construction projects of their business competitors; others embezzled city funds for personal use.[50]

The determination of Kiev's new capitalist elites to monopolize the city's resources for themselves deepened the gulf between the privileged and the struggling working classes. Whereas four thousand Kiev homeowners, primarily in the city center, benefited from connecting to the Brodskiis' water company, thousands of residents died every year from waterborne illnesses in the urban periphery, where the duma made few investments in public health initiatives. Margolin's tram system transported well-heeled riders from the top of Khreshchatik to the bustling mercantile quarter of Podol but failed to serve the districts frequented by working-class residents. The city fathers regularly hosted fireworks shows and light displays to celebrate holidays and welcome special guests to the city, while the unpaved and crime-ridden streets of outlying districts languished in darkness.[51]

Though they were eager to use the city's resources to benefit themselves and their neighbors, Kiev's duma delegates expressed less enthusiasm for urban affairs when they were asked to manage mundane—but vital—aspects of everyday life, such as snow removal and sanitation.[52] Chronic absenteeism plagued the Kiev duma, forcing one out of every five meetings to be canceled for lack of a quorum.[53] And it was the body's most prominent and successful capitalist elites who were most likely to be missing when the duma met to discuss less than scintillating matters. In 1878, for example, Isaak Brodskii (Israel's brother); N. G. Khriakov, the president of the Kiev Stock Exchange; and Moisei Vainshtein, a sugar industrialist—all first-guild merchants elected

---

48. Starozhil, *Kiev,* 80–81; V. G. Sarbei et al., eds., *Istoriia Kieva* (Kiev, 1983), 2:205.
49. "Obozrenie deiatel'nosti Kievskogo gorodskogo obshchestvennogo upravleniia s 1875 po 1879 god," *Kievlianin,* 14 November 1878, 1.
50. For examples of self-interested legislation, see minutes from the 16 November 1889 meeting, DAK, f. 163, op. 8, d. 3, ll. 136–39; gubernatorial circular, 7 March 1873, TsDIAUK, f. 442, op. 106, d. 123, ll. 27–28. On corruption, Kiev Provincial Administration to Kiev City Administration, 16 June 1880, DAK, f. 163, op. 39, d. 196, l. 1; "Doklad. Gubernskoe pravlenie," 26 June 1880, ibid., l. 2.
51. Tron'ko, *Istoriia gorodov i sel,* 157–58; S. M. Boguslavskii, *Sputnik po g. Kievu* (Kiev, 1909), 10; Ciechowski, *Kijów i jego pamiątki,* 66.
52. These issues were at the top of the docket for the 11 February 1893 meeting: see DAK, f. 163, op. 8, d. 8, l. 69.
53. *Zapiska Senatora A. Polovtsova,* 459; see also P. Golubiatnikov, *Sovety Kievlianam, izbirateliam v gorodskuiu dumu* (Kiev, 1906), 9.

The terminus of Kiev's first electric tram line, operated by D. S. Margolin. The line ferried passengers from the top of Khreshchatik to the Podol district. Source: *Vidy Kieva* (Kiev, 1917). Courtesy of Slavonic Library, National Library of Finland.

by the first curia—attended three, five, and zero duma meetings, respectively, far less than the average of 8.1 for all delegates.[54]

As Kiev's capitalist elites used their involvement in formal urban politics to enhance their wealth and power, they also looked to imperial officials for patronage and protection, forging especially close ties with the Ministry of Finance. This relationship was based on long-standing personal and business connections: all four of the men who presided over the ministry's aggressive push to modernize and industrialize Russia between 1881 and 1903 had worked or invested in southwestern ventures. A. A. Abaza, a Kharkov landowner who served as minister of finance from 1880 to 1881, had invested heavily in rail lines on the empire's southwestern periphery operated by S. S. Poliakov.[55] Abaza's successor, N. Kh. Bunge, was a third-generation resident of Kiev who, prior to his appointment to the ministry in May 1881, had served as rector of St. Vladimir's, managed the Kiev branch of the State Bank, and helped found the city's

---

54. Information culled from "Spisok glasnikh i chislo zasedanii, na kotorykh oni prisutstvovali v techenii 1878 g.," DAK, f. 163, op. 39, d. 211, ll. 18–19.
55. *Entsiklopedicheskii slovar'* (St. Petersburg, 1894), s.v. "Abaza," 1:10; Anan'ich et al., *Iz arkhiva*, 1:196; B. N. Chicherin, *Vospominaniia* (Moscow, 1934), 88–89; 99.

Mutual Credit Society.[56] The next two ministers, I. A. Vyshnegradskii and S. Iu. Witte, had both worked as administrators at the Southwestern Railroad after its acquisition by the Polish-Jewish entrepreneur I. S. Bliokh.[57]

Making the most of their friendly relationship with the Ministry of Finance, which sought to emulate the southwest's capitalist takeoff across the empire, Kiev capitalists aggressively lobbied it to implement policies that would benefit them.[58] The Kiev Stock Committee demanded the continued expansion of rail lines, relaxations in the regulations that governed the banking industry, and the implementation of protectionist tariffs that would shield Russian business interests from foreign competition. By the 1880s, the ministry had instituted new laws that met all these demands.[59]

But Kiev's industrial elite continued to press for more concessions. In April 1887, the southwest's major sugar producers gathered in Lev Brodskii's apartment, where they concluded a formal agreement to set production levels for sugar and to export quantities exceeding this limit overseas.[60] By 1893, over 90 percent of the empire's sugar refineries had joined the Kiev-run cartel.[61] In 1895, Witte, by now minister of finance, officially recognized the cartel, now led by F. A. Tereshchenko and several members of the Brodskii family; at least four of its remaining seven chairmen were Jews.[62] The creation of the cartel led to a rapid increase in the cost of sugar—and in the profits of the sugar barons—stimulating another building boom. Over the course of the 1890s, industrialists built nearly one thousand new brick homes; the Jewish owner of a construction firm that made millions off this building boom invested part of his profits in the so-called Kiev skyscraper, which, at twelve stories, became the tallest building in the Russian empire.[63]

Although the southwestern governor-general's office had been a reliable supporter of the Little Russian idea, it also recognized the contributions that local leaders of

56. Ikonnikov, *Biograficheskii slovar'*, s.v. "Bunge, Nikolai Khristianovich," 74–84; George E. Snow, "The Years 1881–1894 in Russia," *Transactions of the American Philosophical Society*, no. 71, pt. 6 (1981): 6.
57. As minister, Vyshnegradskii often promoted Bliokh's personal interests. Indeed, he went so far as to attempt to funnel a bribe through Baron Gintsburg to secure a large loan with advantageous terms for Bliokh from the Rothschild bank; the plan was foiled when Gintsburg refused to pay the bribe. See Anan'ich, *Bankirskie doma*, 43. On the scandal that resulted from the incident, see Anan'ich et al., *Iz arkhiva S.Iu. Vitte*, 1:283–86. For more on Witte's vision of a cosmopolitan and technocratic modernity, see Francis W. Wcislo, *Tales of Imperial Russia* (New York, 2011), especially 90–137.
58. On the policies of the ministry and the views of its leaders in the eighties and nineties, see Rieber, *Merchants*, 107; Wcislo, *Tales*, 138–88.
59. On lobbying and its results, see *Dvadtsatipiatiletie*, 3–4, 16; V. Kirshbaum, *Obzor deiatel'nosti Ministerstva finansov v tsarstvovanie Imperatora Aleksandra III* (St. Petersburg, 1902); B. V. Anan'ich, "Economic Policy of the Tsarist Government and Entrepreneurship in Russia at the End of the 19th–Beginning of the 20th Century" (occasional paper no. 46, Kennan Institute for Advanced Russian Studies, 1978), 7–9; Rieber, *Merchants*, 108.
60. On the formation of the sugar cartel, see Beauvois, *La bataille*, 262; *Dvadtsatipiatiletie*, 13.
61. *Entsiklopedicheskii slovar'* (St. Petersburg, 1900), s.v. "Svelosakharnaia normirovka," 29: 26–30.
62. Sliozberg, *Dela*, 2:230; *Dvadtsatipiatiletie*, 56. Even foreign commentators were shocked by the government's recognition of the cartel, which they viewed as state sponsorship of predatory capitalism. See, for example, *Appletons' Annual Cyclopaedia and Register of Important Events of the Year: 1901* (New York, 1902), 595; G. H. Perris, *Russia in Revolution* (London, 1905), 155–57.
63. Boguslavskii, *Sputnik*, 8–9; Khiterer, "Jewish Life": 83. The building was destroyed in the civil war.

industry had made to the urban economy and richly rewarded them. As a symbol of respect for the city's Jewish elites, officials arranged for kosher dining options at the lavish banquets they hosted to celebrate the accomplishments of Kiev's entrepreneurs; and after years of lobbying from industrialists, the governor-general's office granted Jews "with whom the administration is acquainted to its satisfaction" to settle outside the Plossk and Lybed' districts.[64] Overjoyed by this news, Abraham Brodskii, Israel's brother and Lev and Lazar's uncle, built a home in the very city center, across from the city duma; the Kogen brothers, along with five dozen other merchants, acquired properties in the aristocratic Lipki and Old Kiev districts.[65]

In their political and cultural activities, Kiev's city fathers had propagated a cosmopolitan but elitist worldview that provided a sharp contrast to the organic nationalist and populist orientation of the Little Russian idea. Ultimately, some also intervened directly in the political debates gripping the southwest. In 1880, the Brodskii family and the lawyer L. A. Kupernik (1845–1905) founded a new daily newspaper, *Zaria* (*The Dawn*).[66] The paper vehemently opposed the de-polonization campaign and the laws of the early eighties that placed new limitations on where Jews could work, study, and live. *Zaria* contributors expressed astonishment that an empire beset by poverty and struggling to compete with its European rivals would prevent whole segments of its most productive and well-educated residents from participating fully in civic and political life solely on the basis of their ethnoconfessional identity. "We should not be squeamish about the cultured strata, no matter what nationality [*national'nost'*] they belong to," one contributor wrote.[67] Echoing the arguments that had already been formulated by A. F. Kistkiakovskii, who became a member of its editorial board after breaking with the Little Russian lobby, the publication insisted that only an equal rights regime protected by a rule-of-law state could ensure the well-being of all the region's residents.[68] Hounded by censors, *Zaria* closed in 1886.[69] Shortly thereafter,

---

64. Meir, *Kiev*, 40, 46.
65. Kovalinskii, *Metsenaty*, 214, 399–401; Report of Governor-General to Kiev City Head, 25 June 1879, DAK, f. 163, op. 7, d. 743, l. 1; Starozhil, *Kiev*, 41. Indeed, when the princess Demidova-San Donato returned to Kiev after a long sojourn in Italy, she rented her home from Moisei Zaitsev, a Jewish merchant who had recently joined the ranks of the sugar barons. Starozhil, *Kiev*, 111.
66. Born in Vil'na, L. A. Kupernik migrated to Kiev as a boy with his father, A .A., a lawyer, businessman, and close associate of the Brodskiis. Although it was no secret in educated society that Kupernik served as the paper's editor, the operators of *Zaria* registered the lawyer P. A. Andreevskii as its editor to circumvent laws that limited Jewish ownership of press organs. See *Iz arkhiva S.Iu. Vitte*, 1:297; Sliozberg, *Dela*, 3:113; Starozhil, *Kiev*, 53. On Brodskii's patronage of the publication, see O. Kozyrev, "'Staraia gromada' i evreiskaia intelligentsiia 80-kh godov XIX veka," in *Evreiskoe naselenie Iuga Ukrainy* (Kharkov, 1998), 64–65; Kistiakivs'kyi, *Shchodennyk*, 2:360.
67. Quote from *Zaria*, 7 February 1881, 1. See also "Poliaki, kak prepodavateli," *Zaria*, 21 February 1881, 2.
68. *Zaria* expressed sympathy for the plight of local peasants and insisted that Little Russians should enjoy the opportunity to speak their native language and preserve their cultural traditions. However, the paper insisted that legal equality—rather than the nationalization of governance—was the best means of protecting the narod. For example, 15 February 1881, 2; "Poezdka v g. Kanev na mogilu T.G. Shevchenka," *Zaria*, 26 February 1881, 1.
69. One memoirist of Kiev in the 1880s recalls that the editors of *Zaria* were charged with "slander and defamation" several times a year. See Starozhil, *Kiev*, 94. For examples of the Interior Ministry's

however, S. Iu. Witte, then director of the Southwestern Railroad and a former contributor to *Zaria*, intervened with the Petersburg authorities to launch the daily *Kievskoe slovo (Kiev Word)*; the paper, which remained closely associated with the city's mercantile elite, would remain a reliably liberal alternative to *Kievlianin* through the 1905 revolution.[70]

The Ministry of Finance joined elites such as the Brodskiis in protesting the discriminatory legal regime that faced the southwest's non-East Slavic minorities. Bunge insisted that legislation aimed at limiting the influence of Poles and Jews was economically counterproductive and served only to embitter groups who might otherwise be loyal imperial subjects.[71] Witte, for his part, presented the "gradual abolition of the disabilities" faced by Jews as the only possible solution to the Jewish problem.[72] Viewing anti-Jewish prejudice as an obstacle that stood in the way of Russia's mission to industrialize, he praised railroad entrepreneurs such as Poliakov and Bliokh for their "intelligence and wiliness," and he defended Israel Brodskii from rumors that he had acquired his wealth by forging banknotes during the Crimean War.[73]

Kiev's multiethnic elites had succeeded in crafting a coherent challenge to the Little Russian idea. Rejecting the relevance of ethnic and religious distinctions in business and governmental affairs, they insisted that cultivated and respectable men from any background could help to develop the empire's economic and intellectual potential. However, blatant self-interest and disregard for the welfare of the urban community as a whole coexisted with their cosmopolitanism; indeed, materials produced by the Kiev Stock Committee spoke of the southwest as a conglomeration of resources to be mined and its inhabitants as a source of inexpensive labor.[74] From its inception, the brand of liberalism championed by Kiev's city fathers was tainted by its association with bad governance and cupidity.

Critiquing the Capitalist Order

From its earliest days, Kiev's city duma served as fodder for satirists who mocked its dysfunction and for muckrakers who expressed outrage at its corrupt practices.[75] By the late seventies and early eighties, underground socialist and anarchist movements

---

condemnations of the newspaper's political stance, see "Glavnoe upravlenie po delam pechati Gospodinu Kievskomu Otdel'nomu Tsenzoru po inostrannoi tsenzury," 18 March 1881, TsDIAUK, f. 294, op. 1, d. 15, l. 9; "MVD Otdel'nomu tsenzoru," 25 September 1882, ibid., l. 102.

70. The paper was edited by St. Vladimir's political economist A. Ia. Antonovich (no relation to V. B. Antonovich), a close associate of Witte who later became deputy minister of finance. Witte promoted the newspaper by distributing it for free in the region's railroad stations. Starozhil, *Kiev*, 56–58.
71. See Sliozberg, *Dela*, 2:73; Rogger, *Jewish Policies*, 58–62; Snow, "The Years 1881–1894."
72. *The Memoirs of Count Witte* (New York, 1921), 376.
73. *Iz arkhiva S.Iu. Vitte*, 1:109, 173–74.
74. *Dvadtsatipiatiletie*, 143.
75. Starozhil, *Kiev*, 72–81; S. T. Eremeev, *Kiev i ego gorodovoe polozhenie* (Kiev, 1874) 34–35. See also the satirical series *Kievskii iumoristicheskii kalendar'*, which frequently skewered the city duma.

had also begun to express their dissatisfaction with the urban status quo. Although these groups were unified by their calls for social and political change, they engaged in fierce debates with each other about their aims and tactics. Some sought to topple the status quo by terror; others worked to enlist workers in secret unions promoting "economic revolution."[76] They also differed in their attitudes toward the national question. Many groups united Poles, Jews, and East Slavs from a variety of social stations and argued that all working people must join together to defeat the capitalist system and the regime that supported it.[77] Others, however, treated capitalist exploitation as a by-product of Jewish involvement in local trade and industry, urging their followers to establish a new political order "without masters, without the Yids."[78]

Southwestern authorities relentlessly struggled to disband and prosecute radical groups.[79] Yet at the same time, they permitted proponents of the Little Russian idea to develop a coherent critique of capitalism in the public sphere. D. I. Pikhno, the editor of *Kievlianin*, published several academic monographs in the 1880s and '90s that denounced the concessions the authorities had granted to bankers, railroad entrepreneurs, and industrialists, which he complained unjustly placed the interests of a handful of capitalists over the needs of the masses.[80] Pikhno expressed particular outrage at the Ministry of Finance's cozy relationship with industrial interests. The ministry's implementation of protectionist tariffs and its recognition of the sugar cartel, he charged, greatly enriched producers, who nevertheless failed to raise the wages or improve the working conditions of their employees.[81] Pikhno did not oppose the development of industry and capital altogether. Rather, he believed that the state should promote the rational development of agrobusiness and industry on the basis of "Christian morals," which would ensure the empire's economic growth while protecting the welfare of the Orthodox narod.[82]

In the pages of *Kievlianin*, Pikhno translated his economic theories into layman's terms, presenting himself as a defender of the East Slavic masses who worked as

---

76. Military Prosecutor of the Kiev Military-District Court to Governor-General Drentel'n, 24 June 1883, TsDIAUK, f. 442, op. 832, d. 361, l.20b; "Ezhenedel'nye zapiski ob osobykh proisshestviiakh," 6 May 1879, TsDIAUK, f. 442, op. 829, d. 29, l. 38ob.
77. Gerard Żeberek, *Początki ruchu socjaldemokratycznego w Kijowie w latach 1889–1903* (Cracow, 1981); Jan Euzebiusz Chmielewski, *Pierwsze lata korporacji studentów polaków w Kijowie* (Warsaw, 1939); I. N. Moshinskii (Iuz. Konarskii), *Na putiakh k I-mu s"ezdu R.S.-D.R.P.* (Moscow, 1928).
78. Quote from A. Kozyrev, "Antievreiskie narodnicheskie proklamatsii nachala 80-kh godov XIX veka v Ukraine," in *Evreiskoe naselenie Iuga Ukrainy*, 133. See also Erich Haberer, "Cosmopolitanism, Antisemitism, and Populism," in *Pogroms*, ed. John D. Klier and Shlomo Lambroza (New York, 1992), 98–134; John Doyle Klier, *Russians, Jews, and the Pogroms of 1881–1882* (New York, 2011), 155–73.
79. See, for example, the cases discussed in TsDIAUK, f. 442, op. 832, d. 361.
80. D. I. Pikhno, *O svobode mezhdunarodnoi torgovli i protektsionizme* (Kiev, 1889); Pikhno, *Kommercheskie operatsii*; D. I. Pikhno, *Po povodu polemiki o deshevom khlebe* (Kiev, 1897).
81. A. B. Mukhin, "Ekonomicheskie i upravlencheskie vozzreniia D.I. Pikhno"(PhD diss., St. Petersburg State University, 2003), 20–22. Indeed, in the mid-1880s, Pikhno's critique of Witte's policies as chief of the Southwestern Railroad brought him into direct conflict with the future minister of finance. Starozhil, *Kiev*, 66–67; Theodore H. Von Laue, *Sergei Witte and the Industrialization of Russia* (New York, 1963), 50–53.
82. See Hans-Jürgen Seraphim, *Neuere russische Wert- und Kapitalzinstheorien* (Berlin, 1925), 38–47.

small-time traders, factory workers, and agricultural laborers. Having long been critical of the labor practices of the sugar industry, Pikhno and the Hromada member I. M. Reva also bemoaned the creation of the cartel, which had increased the price of necessary commodities for all consumers.[83] The paper's critiques of the conduct of Kiev's capitalist elite offered it new opportunities to intertwine social and economic concerns with national ideas. Overlooking the role that Orthodox merchants had played in the creation of the cartel and the accumulation of capital (not to mention the suffering of the city's large Jewish working class), Pikhno and other Little Russian activists portrayed the local capitalist economy as the domain of Poles and especially Jews. Connecting the capitalist excess so obvious in the southwest to the diversity of its entrepreneurial elites, at times they went so far as to allege that non-East Slavs in the sugar industry had intentionally limited the upward mobility of the millions of East Slavic peasants they employed.[84]

The trope of the non-Orthodox capitalist as self-interested—even exploitative— ultimately became a fixture of *Kievlianin* and other Little Russian organs. Commentators complained that Orthodox merchants were dependent on high-interest loans from Jewish bankers, that impoverished peasants were forced to sell their grain to greedy middlemen and to rent their land to Jewish-owned joint stock companies, and that the Jews among Kiev's capitalist city fathers promoted their own narrow interests over those of the city as a whole.[85] If Jews had been demonized in earlier Little Russian discourse as agents and enablers of the szlachta, they now emerged as enemies of the southwest's simple folk in their own right—in the words of *Kievlianin*, a "kulak nation that is strong by virtue of its unity, solidarity, [and] single faith... and has mastered the art of exploiting all non-Jews for more than ten decades."[86]

The *Kievlianin* circle denounced as inadequate the laws of the 1880s that further limited Jewish economic and political rights, pointing to cases in which Jews had allegedly managed to circumvent them.[87] It dismissed Jewish commercial elites' calls for an equal rights state as a cynical effort to consolidate their political and economic power and denounced Orthodox liberals such as Kistiakovskii as beholden to Jewish interests.[88] But although the critics of the southwest's vibrant capitalist economy were resolute antiliberals, they were statist modernizers rather than reactionaries. Again

---

83. "Sakharnoe proizvodstvo i normirovka," *Kievlianin*, 21 January 1894, 1; "Zasedanie sakharozavodchikov," *Kievlianin*, 11 January 1894, 3; I. Reva, *Sakharnaia normirovka* (Kiev, 1897).
84. "Zametka nanimaiushchimsia na sakharnye zavody," *Drug naroda*, 1 March 1876, 67. See also "Sakharnoe proizvodstvo i normirovka," 1; "Zasedanie sakharozavodchikov," 3. These critiques built on Chubinskii's research on the southwestern economy, which blamed Jewish "speculators" for the rising cost of sugar. Voblyi, *Narysy*, 159–60.
85. *Kievlianin*, 9 January 1875, 1; "Kto vinovat?" *Kievlianin*, 8 March 1875, 1; "Nado vyslushat' i druguiu storonu," 5 May 1882, 1; *Trud*, 11 March 1881, 2–3; *Kievlianin*, 18 February 1883, 2.
86. "Evrei i trudiashchaiasia massa v nashem krae," *Kievlianin*, 20 March 1881, 1. A similar shift can be seen around the same time in the works of the Kiev Commission, which began to portray Jews less as lackeys of the szlachta than as villains in their own right. See, for example, A. Voronin, *Zapiska o vladel'cheskikh gorodakh i mestechkakh Iugozapadnogo kraia* (Kiev, 1869); *Arkhiv Iugozapadnoi Rossii* 5, no. 1 (Kiev, 1869).
87. "Obkhod novago zakona o evreiiakh," *Kievlianin*, 5 May 1882, 1.
88. "Dostoinyi syn dostoinogo ottsa," *Kievlianin*, 16 February 1883, 2; Kistiakivs'kyi, *Shchodennyk*, 2:360.

and again, they called on the authorities to enhance the self-governance rights of local communities and to expand peasants' access to land and credit. These reforms, they argued, must be directed from above and implemented on a national basis, promoting the culture, traditions, and well-being of the Orthodox East Slavs and refusing to give comfort to Poles and Jews.[89]

When the urban masses themselves voiced discontent with the capitalist system—and employed violence against their putative exploiters—Little Russian organs tended to encourage them, presenting their actions as justified and even laudable forms of popular resistance. In the month following the March 1881 assassination of Alexander II, rumors swirled across southern Russia that the act had been committed by Jewish revolutionaries and that the new tsar, Alexander III, had ordered his subjects to seek revenge on the Jews. By April, isolated instances of anti-Jewish violence had begun to break out in the region. *Trud*, the Hromada paper, praised the bloodshed, characterizing it as a heroic act of self-defense by "the poor mass of the working people and village inhabitants."[90]

By April, the working-class neighborhoods of Kiev had grown more restive; residents frequently gathered in the streets to chant slogans against and harass Jews.[91] On 25 April, large-scale violence erupted in the working-class (and heavily Jewish) suburb of Demievka and eventually spread across the urban outskirts. According to an eyewitness, "common mobs" (*cherni*) broke into wine stores chanting slogans against "Yids and landlords." As they grew drunk, they attacked synagogues, Jewish traders at markets, and even Cossack forces who attempted to arrest them.[92] Governor-General A. R. Drentel'n soon appeared at the scene, but the crowd was unmoved by his pleas to halt their rampage. Exclaiming, "the Jews control all trade, buy up all the bread for nothing and sell it for whatever price they want," and "the Jews killed the tsar," the crowd hurled rocks at Drentel'n's carriage, injuring the city police chief, who sat beside the governor-general.[93]

On the twenty-sixth and twenty-seventh, violence engulfed the entire city, reaching even central areas around St. Vladimir's and the Monastery of the Caves in the riverside neighborhood of Pechersk. Workers at a sugar factory on the south side of the city worked their way down the Vasil'kov road, attacking Jewish enterprises, setting fires and looting along the way.[94] The Brodskiis hid in the home of a business associate as other Jewish merchants fled the city—a wise decision, given that the crowds

---

89. "Zhdat' ili iskazhat'?" *Kievlianin*, 8 April 1871, 1–2; *Kievlianin*, 19 January 1871, 2; "Kredit i sel'skoe khoziastvo," *Kievlianin*, 24 February 1883, 1.
90. Quote from *Trud*, 22 April 1881, 1. See also "Gorodskoi i mestnyi otdel," *Trud*, 20 April 1881, 2. The most comprehensive account of the 1881 violence is Klier, *Russians*.
91. Krasnyi-Admoni, *Materialy dlia istorii antievreiskikh pogromov*, 396; V. P. Rybyns'kyi, "Protyevreis'kyi rukh r. 1881-ho na Ukraini," *Zbirnyk prats' evreis'koi istorychno-arkheohrafichnoi komisii* 2 (1929): 142.
92. Khiterer, *Dokumenty*, 190–91. See also Krasnyi-Admoni, *Materialy*, 404; "Pogrom evreev," *Trud*, 27 April 1881, 3.
93. Rybyns'kyi, "Protyevreis'kyi rukh," 142–43; Krasnyi-Admoni, *Materialy*, 397.
94. "Kievskie ulichnye bezporiadki," *Trud*, 29 April 1881, 1–2; "Dokladnaia zapiska Pristava Pecherskogo uchastka g. Kieva," 28 April 1881, DAK, f. 237, op. 3, d. 46b, l. 6.

attacked one of the Kogens' tobacco shops and properties owned by the Brodskiis.[95] By the twenty-eighth, troops finally quelled the violence, forcing pogromists who escaped arrest to move on to other cities and towns in the region, where sporadic anti-Jewish violence continued until June.[96] During the violence, rioters had destroyed one hundred Jewish homes and businesses, killed several people, and raped more than twenty women.[97] Prominent merchants and working-class Jews alike suffered from the violence: eighteen merchants reported losses exceeding twenty thousand rubles, and hundreds of petty traders, artisans, and workers suffered damage to their homes and businesses.[98]

Zaria and Kistiakovskii blamed the "judeophobic" attitudes of Little Russian activists for having incited the violence and repeated their earlier calls for political reforms that would enfranchise all Russian subjects.[99] Little Russian organs, by contrast, insisted that the carnage was justified, if not heroic. *Trud* blamed the Jews themselves for the bloodshed, alleging that their "predatory instincts" had left the children of Rus' with no other option than to protect themselves with force.[100] *Kievlianin* warned its readers not to be moved by Jewish efforts to use the pogrom as a pretext to win support for their "liberal slogans." "The expansion of Jewish rights," it reiterated, "can lead only to the expansion of arenas for exploitation."[101] Melding anticapitalist sentiment with the Little Russian trope of national struggle against internal enemies, activists had usurped the social platform of the left while connecting Jews and self-avowed liberals to economic exploitation and municipal mismanagement.[102] Capitalizing on social tensions in a rapidly growing city, Little Russian activists insisted that the true liberation of the simple folk could take place only through illiberal means—that is, through state intervention from above and popular violence from below.

---

95. Brodsky, *Smoke Signals*, 11; Kistiakivs'kyi, *Shchodennyk*, 2:345; "Kievskie ulichnye bezporiadki," 1–2.
96. Khiterer, *Dokumenty*, 191; Kistiakivs'kyi, *Shchodennyk*, 2: 357.
97. Khiterer, *Dokumenty*, 188.
98. Krasnyi-Admoni, *Materialy*, 533.
99. *Zaria*, 22 April 1881, 1; "Miloserdiiu druzei chelovechestva!" *Zaria*, 30 April 1881; Kistiakivs'kyi, *Shchodennyk*, 2:345. Kistiakovskii agreed with *Trud* and *Kievlianin* contributors that many southwestern Jews were "exploiters and nationalists." However, he condemned the use of violence against them, as well as efforts to present them as the primary oppressors of the people. "Do Yids exploit the narod?" he asked in an 1881 diary entry. "Well, who doesn't exploit and oppress the narod … ?" Kistiakivs'kyi, *Shchodennyk*, 2:345, also 360.
100. "Stolichnye organy pechati uzhe vyskazali mneniia po povodu fakta, vdrug rezko postavivshago na pervyi plan zlobu kraia nashego. Zastupaias' za evreev, 'Zaria' privodit' vse eti meniia in extenso." *Trud*, 27 April 1881, 1.
101. Quote from *Kievlianin*, 26 April 1881, 1.
102. Some scholars have argued that nationalism has enjoyed too central a position in the historiography of east central Europe, claiming that cultural and social concerns often played a more important role in shaping political identities. See, for example, James E. Bjork, *Neither German nor Pole* (Ann Arbor, 2008), 244–53. By contrast, I argue here that Kiev's populist politicians ingeniously merged the national and the social.

National Struggle in Urban Politics

By the early 1880s, broader segments of educated society—including some who were not themselves East Slavs—had begun to echo the claims of the Little Russian lobby that the city's multiethnic capitalist elite posed an imminent threat to the national interests and economic well-being of its Orthodox majority. In his 1883 State of the City address, city head Gustav-Adol'f Eisman, a Lutheran whose father had immigrated to Kiev from Saxony, complained at length that Jewish influence in local industry and trade was threatening to stamp out the city's "authentic" culture and traditions. Within ten to fifteen years, he predicted, "the native population of the city, under the exploitative yoke of the Jewish *kagal*, will leave.... [T]he historical life of Kiev will be finished... the name Kiev will be resigned to the state archive, and the city will be named "New Berdichev."[103] Announcing his intention to continue "the unending battle against the Yids," he implored Orthodox duma delegates and city residents devoted to preserving the "native" features of the city to join him in this task.[104]

Eisman's speech coincided with the emergence of new patterns of political participation among urban elites, which would have important consequences. Although voters of the first curia (which, as we have seen, was dominated by Kiev's most prominent industrialists and boasted large numbers of Polish and especially Jewish voters) had been much more likely to exercise the franchise than their second- and third-curia counterparts in the first few duma elections, in 1879 the number of third-curia voters who showed up at the polls doubled, while the number of first-curia voters declined.[105] (This shift in voter behavior, along with Eisman's anti-Jewish campaign, might explain why, for the first time in 1883, Kiev voters failed to elect a single Jewish delegate to the city duma.)[106] Change was afoot within the duma as well. Orthodox merchants and professionals of the second and third curiae had begun to take advantage of the chronic absenteeism of the elite merchants who served in the body, playing an increasingly visible role in floor debates and committees.[107]

The Orthodox duma delegates of the second and third curiae who gained prominence in the duma in the 1880s and early '90s aligned themselves with the narod and sought to undermine the influence of their putative oppressors. E. I. Afanas'ev (1837–97), a church elder and a physician, complained about the dire sanitary conditions on the urban periphery.[108] He also proposed electoral reforms that would have

---

103. *Zapiska Senatora A. Polovtsova*, 54. Berdichev was a heavily Jewish district city in Kiev province.
104. Quote from *Zaria*, 2 March 1883, 1. See also *Rech'*, *proiznesennaia gorodskim golovoi v zasedanii dumy 28 fevralia 1883 goda* (Kiev, 1883), 31.
105. A full 40 percent of third-curia voters participated in the city duma elections of 1879, in contrast to a mere 17 percent of the overall electorate. *Zapiska Senatora A. Polovtsova*, 118, 162.
106. On 1883 elections, see "Khronika," *Zaria*, 10 March 1883, 2; Kistiakivs'kyi, *Shchodennyk*, 2:397.
107. As a group, Orthodox merchants of the third curia were the most likely to appear at duma meetings, attending an average of 11.13 sessions in 1878, compared with an average of 8.1 for delegates as a whole. Information culled from "Spisok glasnikh i chislo zasedanii, na kotorykh oni prisutstvovali v techenii 1878 g.," DAK, f. 163, op. 39, d. 211, ll. 18–19.
108. "Gorodskie i mestnye izvestiia," *Trud*, 16 March 1881, 1–2.

further reduced the electoral representation of the city's heavily Jewish neighborhoods.[109] Alongside A. I. Konisskii (1836–1900)—a Hromada member, *Kievskaia starina* contributor, and one of Shevchenko's closest associates—he promoted legislation that aimed to level the competition between Jewish and Gentile merchants, restricting the hours that the former could work on Sundays.[110]

A cohort of like-minded Orthodox duma delegates soon coalesced around Afanas'ev. The accountant A. L. Tsytovich, who expressed outrage that large segments of the city still lacked sewer service, became known for his efforts to improve public services in both the city center and its outlying peripheries.[111] The railroad engineer N. P. Dobrynin, who published pamphlets denouncing state guarantees of the private railroad companies, frequently spoke out about the need to improve sanitation and public health in Kiev and to root out its corrupt officials.[112] I. A. Sikorskii, the Little Russian activist and racial anthropologist whom we encountered in chapter 3, served as a hospital inspector and a leader of a group that aimed to reduce childhood mortality; on the duma floor, he expressed concern about the dire public health conditions in the city's outlying neighborhoods.[113]

These delegates mastered the art of the "special opinion"—a formal objection to legislation passed by the duma that was recorded in its official protocol—which they used to rally coalitions within the duma and to demonstrate their opposition to the "plutocrats" before the urban public. Over the 1880s and '90s, the new deputies of the second and third curiae authored dozens of special opinions in which they denounced the city fathers' corruption and self-interest as well as their disregard for the ordinary people who lived on the urban periphery.[114] By the midnineties, observers described these delegates as constituting an organized opposition party—a novel concept in a society in which political parties remained illegal and in an institution where personal allegiances and financial interests, not ideology, had played the key role in determining voting behavior.[115]

---

109. "Zasedanie dumy 31 ianvaria," *Kievlianin*, 2 February 1883, 2; "Zasedanie dumy 10 fev.," *Kievlianin*, 14 February 1883, 2. The legislation was ultimately defeated.
110. *Zaria*, 26 February 1881, 2. Note the role of civic activists here in promoting antiliberal ideas. For discussion of another context in which the success of Jews prompted private individuals and associations to agitate for anti-Jewish measures, see Nathans, *Beyond the Pale*, 83–122, 377–380.
111. "Zasedanie dumy," *Kievskoe slovo*, 11 August 1891, 3.
112. "K voprosu o narodnykh uchilishchakh," *Kievskoe slovo*, 29 September 1891, 3; Garol'd, *Nashi Glasnye* (Kiev, 1906), 47. For his critique of railroad policy, see N. P. Dobrynin, *Russkie zheleznye dorogi i ikh slabye storony* (Kiev, 1886).
113. "Perechen' predmetov soveshchaniia v ocherednom sobranii KG Dumy 20 Maia 1898 goda," DAK, f. 163, op. 8, d. 58, l. 10b.
114. For the year 1889 alone, see "Osoboe mnenie," 1889, DAK, f. 163, op. 8. d. 55, l. 524; "Osoboe mnenie," ibid., l. 522; A. L. Tsytovich to City Duma, 20 August 1889, DAK, f. 163, op. 8. d. 55, l. 795.
115. See *Kievskoe slovo*, 10 February 1894, 3. A similar spirit of renewal permeated the lower curiae in other cities, including Moscow and Kharkov, in the 1880s and '90s, but there is no evidence that anti-Semitism played an important role in those contexts. On Moscow, see Chicherin, *Vospominaniia*, 184; on Kharkov, see Bagalei and Miller, *Istoriia*, 299.

Meanwhile, growing numbers of Kiev's economic elites joined populist politicians to challenge the beau monde's cosmopolitan traditions. In an 1890 letter to the governor-general, N. I. Chokolov, the elected elder of Kiev's merchants, complained that the Jews' "clannishness [*kagal'nost'*]" offered them unfair advantages in the capitalist marketplace. Reporting that the merchants' elite first guild was composed of 6 Gentiles and 183 Jews, he claimed that the role of Orthodox believers in trade and industry would only continue to decline if the authorities did not limit Jewish access to the first guild and expand the educational opportunities and credit available to Orthodox merchants.[116] The historian Daniel Beauvois has uncovered evidence that Polish magnates, who had been targets of state-sponsored discrimination only years before, lobbied the imperial authorities to further limit Jewish economic opportunities and that some even expelled Jews residing on land that they owned.[117]

Kiev's populist politicians and the elites who endorsed their program adapted the ideas of the Little Russian lobby—a group to which some of these figures can be directly traced—to the urban context. Insisting that the social, economic, and national interests of Kiev's Orthodox masses were intimately connected, they called on the imperial authorities to implement policies designed to benefit the children of Rus' and to restrict allegedly harmful groups' access to resources. Influenced in part by local political culture, Kiev's antiliberal populist politics also reflected pan-European trends. From Paris to Berlin to Vienna, political entrepreneurs channeling the frustrations of the lower-middle and working classes created organized movements that pressed for social reform and political democratization even as they denounced capitalist conglomerates and liberal ideas as expressions of Jewish interests.[118] The limited autonomy of Russian municipalities and their narrow franchise did not prevent the rise of a mass-oriented opposition to the capitalist order in Kiev's urban public sphere.

Accommodation and Exclusion

As the business practices and worldview of Kiev's mercantile elites generated more controversy, the multiethnic city fathers continued to rely on charitable giving, official patronage, and political activism to consolidate their power. In exchange for Witte's recognition of the sugar cartel, local industrialists provided the seed funds for the minister of finance's local pet project, the Kiev Polytechnical Institute. The

---

116. "Dokladnaia zapiska," 18 December 1890, TsDIAUK, f. 442, op. 561, d. 157, ll. 2–4.
117. Beauvois, *La Bataille*, 297, 238, 316–18. One of Lazar Brodskii's close associates recalls that the entrepreneur organized meetings to encourage Polish magnates to halt anti-Jewish agitation. Sliozberg, *Dela*, 1:282.
118. See Philip G. Nord, *Paris Shopkeepers and the Politics of Resentment* (Princeton, 1986); Boyer, *Political Radicalism*, 40–121; Schorske, *Fin-de-Siècle Vienna*, 116–80; Shulamit Volkov, "The Social and Political Function of Late 19th Century Anti-Semitism," in *Hostages of Modernization*, ed. Herbert A. Strauss (New York, 1993), 1:62–79; P. G. J. Pulzer, *The Rise of Political Anti-semitism in Germany and Austria* (Cambridge, MA, 1988), 83–97.

institute, intended to train a new generation of engineers and technocrats capable of sustaining the southwest's economic boom, opened its doors in 1898.[119] The Brodskiis, who provided the largest donation to that project, were particularly active in supporting organizations that promoted intercultural understanding and the equal rights agenda. Continuing their efforts to seek out alliances with liberal Ukrainophiles, the family became one of the major benefactors of the Kiev Literacy Society. Run by I. V. Luchitskii and V. P. Naumenko in these years, the group organized plays and popular readings that raised awareness of the common struggles of the Ukrainian and Jewish people and constructed a "people's house" in the heavily Jewish district of Lybed'.[120] Ukrainophile liberals as well as the Brodskiis, Gintsburgs, L. A. Kupernik, and D. S. Margolin also rallied around the Kiev Literary-Artistic Society, a group that combined its cultural uplift activities with calls for liberal political reforms.[121]

However, Kiev industrialists continued to aggressively promote their own economic interests. The Kiev Stock Committee moved to close its exchange floor to all but the most prominent merchants, insisting that the organization should be "a gathering place where major wholesale deals are brokered and the questions and needs of various industries are discussed" rather than "a market where petty trade is conducted."[122] During the global credit crisis of 1900–1903, industrialists accepted bailouts from Witte's Ministry of Finance even as they laid off thousands of workers.[123] Meanwhile, life remained grim in Kiev's peripheral districts, where access to safe water and basic medical care was scarce.[124] Governor-General Dragomirov himself admitted that the overall population of the southwest had seen few benefits from the immense wealth that the region had created.[125]

As the fortunes of Kiev's privileged few and its toiling masses continued to diverge, socialists grew more aggressive in their efforts to appeal to city dwellers. Activists representing the Social Democratic (SD) and Socialist Revolutionary (SR) Parties staged several demonstrations at St. Vladimir's and began to plaster political posters on street corners under the cover of night. By 1902, the SDs had established two daily newspapers, *Iskra* and *Sotsial-demokraticheskii listok*. Whereas underground groups of

---

119. Kovalinskii, *Metsenaty*, 219. As finance minister, Witte was frequently accused of corruption and influence peddling. See Wcislo, *Tales*, 146–47.
120. "Otkrytie narodnogo doma kievskogo Obshchestva Gramotnosti," *KS* 79, no. 12 (1902): 176–77. On the Kiev Literacy Society as a venue of interethnic cooperation, see Natan M. Meir, "Jews, Ukrainians, and Russians in Kiev," *Slavic Review* 65, no. 3 (Fall 2006): 475–501.
121. *Spisok chlenov pravleniia, pochetnykh chlenov, deistvitel'nykh, sovrevnovatelei i chlenov posetitelei Kievskogo literaturno-artisticheskogo obshchestva* (Kiev, 1904).
122. *Otchet Kievskogo Birzhevogo Komiteta za 1903* (Kiev, 1903), quote from 31; see also 37.
123. On the downturn, see O. Parasun'ko, *Massovaia politicheskaia zabastovka v Kieve v 1903 g.* (Kiev, 1953), 25–32; on bailouts, Anan'ich, *Bankirskie doma*, 92–93; Von Laue, *Sergei Witte*, 213–16.
124. For the perspective of one resident of Demievka, the working-class suburb recently annexed by Kiev city, see *Kievskaia gazeta*, 13 January 1902, 6.
125. *Trudy sozvannogo po rasporiazheniiu nachal'nika kraia soveshchaniia vrachebnykh inspektorov Kievskoi, Podol'skoi i Volynskoi gubernii sostoiavshagosia v g. Kieve 5–12 oktiabria 1900 goda po voprosu o luchshei postanovke vrachebno-sanitarnogo dela v iugo-zapadnom krae* (Kiev, 1901), unpaginated introduction.

the 1870s and '80s had been deeply divided on the Jewish question, the increasingly pronounced national chauvinism and statism of the Little Russian lobby and the duma's demagogues had by now pushed most radicals toward a consensus that all working people must stand together to defeat autocratic and capitalist oppression.[126]

Meanwhile, radical intellectuals deepened their contacts with industrial workers. M. B. Ratner (1871–1917), an SD organizer and a lawyer who had prosecuted *pogromshchiki*, established an underground labor union that united workers from all industries and backgrounds.[127] Under the tutelage of intellectuals such as Ratner, Kiev workers began to file formal complaints with local factory inspectors about the abusive and exploitative behavior of their employers.[128] Several industries even organized strikes, although they tended to be short-lived, limited to a particular shop, and focused on purely economic concerns.[129]

However, socialist organizers faced stiff competition from Little Russian activists and antiliberal, populist politicians, who continued to attribute the injustices of class society and the failures of municipal government to Jewish involvement in local industry and politics. As the 1902 municipal duma elections approached, an organized party demanding a "new duma" hosted large meetings of electors in the peripheral neighborhoods of Lybed', Plossk, Podol, and Luk'ianovka.[130] New Duma activists scored an overwhelming victory in the elections, winning seats for dozens of lesser merchants and professionals who had never before served in city government. P. V. Golubiatnikov, a military engineer and New Duma Party leader, denounced the massive subsidies the city offered to the millionaire operators of the private utility companies and continued to press for the creation of a public, citywide sewer system.[131] A. I. Liubinskii, an employee of the Kiev governor's office, castigated city officials for their frequent violations of proper parliamentary procedure and the municipal code.[132] F. N. Iasnogurskii, a mid-ranking bureaucrat and Luk'ianovka resident, portrayed himself as a champion of the city's most defenseless populations—a reputation he consolidated in his work on behalf of animal rights.[133] S. M. Bogdanov, an agronomist who

---

126. See "Delo o studentcheskikh volneniiakh v gor. Kieve v ianvare 1900 g." TsDIAUK, f. 274, op. 1, d. 519. t. II, ch. 1. 1900; "Materialy o revoliutsionnom dvizhenii studenchestva g. Kieve v 1900–1901 g.g.," DAK, f. 342, op. 1, d. 1; V. Levitskii [V. Tsederbaum], *Za chetvert' veka* (Moscow, 1926), 1: 142–45.
127. Moshinskii, *Na putiakh*, 102, 110–11.
128. Letter of P. A. Berezovskii, 18 December 1897, TsDIAUK, f. 574, op. 1, d. 94, l. 64; letter of L. M. Karavan, 24 November 1897, ibid., l. 58; letter of M. A. Silaev, 24 October 1897, ibid., l. 49.
129. Between 1899 and 1900, workers at a yeast factory, bakers, and railroad workers all walked off the job. See Civil Governor Trepov to Governor-General Dragomirov, 2 April 1899, TsDIAUK, f. 442, op. 849, d. 455, ll. 1–10b.; Parasun'ko, *Massovaia politicheskaia zabastovka*, 48.
130. "Predvybornaia agitatsiia," *Kievskaia gazeta*, 11 January 1902, 3; "V Dume," *Kievskaia gazeta*, 12 January 1902, 3; "Predvybornaia agitatsiia," *Kievskaia gazeta*, 12 January 1902, 3; "V Dume," *Kievskaia gazeta*, 12 January 1902, 3.
131. Golubiatnikov, *Spravka*; Garol'd, *Nashi glasnye*, 9.
132. "Zasedanie dumy," *Kievlianin*, 30 October 1904, 4.
133. Iasnogurskii penned a novel about the perils of cruelty toward animals and donated the proceeds from its sale to the Russian Society for the Protection of Animals: see his *Liudi—zveri i zveri—liudi* (Kiev, 1905).

would serve as a member of the appointive zemstva implemented in the right bank in 1903, wrote frequently in *Kievlianin* about the need to expand peasant land allotments. The longtime Little Russian activists, Kiev Commission, and Hromada members N. V. Storozhenko and O. I. Levitskii also won seats in the 1902 elections. Cooperating with incumbent populists such as Dobrynin and Sikorskii, these delegates formed a powerful opposition party that pressed vigorously for a city government more accountable to the people.[134]

This new force in the duma viewed anything that benefited the city's Jewish elite— or even its Jewish population as a whole—as a danger to the Orthodox narod. Kiev's antiliberal populist delegates vehemently denounced fellow deputies for permitting the Society for the Struggle against Tuberculosis and Consumption—whose board of directors met in Lazar Brodskii's apartment—to open a hospital in Kiev. A special opinion penned by Dobrynin claimed that "the millionaire L. I. Brodskii" would use the facility to draw more Jews to Kiev and insisted that any new hospital facility must be used exclusively to benefit the city's Christian population.[135] Likewise, Iasnogurskii led a group in opposition to the duma's plan to open a school for Jewish girls. The delegate insisted that the duma was obligated to serve only the "native population—and in no way people from other cities, who comprise other communities...who have nothing in common with us and who feel hostile toward Christians." Iasnogurskii echoed Dobrynin's claim that public institutions serving Jews would only encourage more of them to migrate to the city, where they would take jobs, houses, and business from Orthodox East Slavs. Iasnogurskii closed his complaint by reiterating the duma's need to "worry about the interests of the Christian population, for the murmur of Jews is audible at every step, and we, the representatives of the city, by means of our strength and capability must silence this murmur and...protect our *confrères* [*sobrati*] from catastrophes."[136]

The New Duma delegates who denounced the accommodationist ethos that had long prevailed among the urban elite as a danger to the city at large failed to mention that an 1892 counterreform had banned Jews from participating in city dumas altogether.[137] But had they been confronted with this inconvenient fact, commentators critical of Jewish influence likely would have dismissed it as an unimportant detail, for they had begun to attribute traits once associated with the plutocrats—cupidity,

---

134. See, for example, "Osoboe mnenie," 13 March 1903, DAK f. 163, op. 8., d. 94, l. 47; undated "Osoboe mnenie," ibid., l. 79; "Osoboe mnenie," 29 September 1903, ibid., l. 639; "Osoboe mnenie Golubiatnikova," 16 October 1903, ibid., l. 692; "Osoboe mnenie," 12 November 1903, ibid., l. 787.
135. "Raz"iasnenie Glasnogo Dumy N. Dobrynina na raz"iasnenie Gorodskogo Golovi V. Protsenko," 12 June 1903, DAK, f. 163, op. 8, d. 94, l. 467 ob.
136. "Osoboe mnenie," 27 January 1903, DAK, f. 163, op. 8, d. 94, l. 75.
137. The 1892 municipal code also forbade proprietors of taverns and many of the small-scale taxpayers of the second and third curiae from participating in city duma elections. N. P. Eroshkin, *Ocherki istorii gosudarstvennykh uchrezhdenii dorevoliutsionnoi Rossii* (Moscow, 1960), 304–5; V. D. Kalinin, *Iz istorii gorodskogo samoupravleniia v Rossii* (Moscow, 1994), 44–47. Baron Gintsburg attempted but failed to convince the imperial authorities to stop the promulgation of the new law. See Sliozberg, *Dela*, 2:73.

self-interest, and disdain for the children of Rus'—to the Jewish population at large. *Kievlianin* claimed that Jewish artisans had formed fictitious guilds to obtain permanent residence rights for their co-confessionalists and that administrators at the Polytechnical Institute, which remained closely associated with the Brodskiis because of their role in its founding, had admitted Jews in excess of the official quota—both offenses that would disadvantage Gentiles who wished to enter the artisanal trades or pursue a higher education.[138] On the fiftieth anniversary of the second Polish revolt, several authors with roots in the southwest published tracts that highlighted the alleged role that Jews of all social stations had played in the Polish patriotic movement and the insurrection itself.[139] And growing numbers of commentators embraced the trope of racial struggle that permeated Sikorskii's academic work. A tract serialized in *Kievlianin* in 1898 spoke of Jews as a whole as a "lower race" that harbored "fanatical tribal hatred" toward the Orthodox masses and the imperial state.[140]

By the last years of the nineteenth century, parties that combined anti-Semitic and radical nationalist rhetoric with socially emancipatory campaigns had severely undermined the authority of notables in cities across Europe. They had become noisy irritants in many European cities and had seized control of Vienna's municipal government, embarking on campaigns to improve the public health infrastructure, municipalize its utility companies, and reduce the influence of Jews in universities and municipal government.[141] Yet rule-of-law regimes and antiliberal politicians' pragmatic desire to appeal to the greatest possible number of urban dwellers limited the appeal of the most radical and racialized expressions of anti-Semitism. When Vienna's most committed anti-Semitic politician, Georg Ritter von Schönerer, broke into the offices of a liberal paper and threatened its editorial staff, he was imprisoned and stripped of his right to hold office.[142] The historians Carl Schorske and John Boyer agree that Karl Lueger, the founder of the Christian Social Party and Vienna's mayor between 1897 and 1910, instrumentalized and manipulated rather than internalized anti-Semitic prejudice; indeed, in Boyer's words, it was the politician's ability to transcend "desperate, artisan-based antisemitism" and to connect it to broader concerns that allowed his movement to succeed in the first place.[143] Similarly, National Socialist activists in the Bohemian lands, who had denounced Jewish and German capitalists as oppressors of Czech-speaking workers, embraced Jews who professed their allegiance to the Czech national cause—and welcomed Jews into their party organizations.[144]

---

138. "Eshche o tainykh remeslennykh upravakh," *Kievlianin*, 24 August 1901, 3; "Rezul'taty priema v politekhnicheskii institute," *Kievlianin*, 26 August 1901, 3.
139. Dm. Tutkevich, Privislinets and A. N. Druzhinin, *Rossiia i ee zapadnaia okraina* (Kiev, 1903); A. A. Sidorov, *Pol'skoe vozstanie 1863 goda* (St. Petersburg, 1903).
140. The entire piece is reprinted as N. K. Rennenkampf, *Pol'skii i evreiskii voprosy* (Kiev, 1898); 77, 74.
141. John W. Boyer, *Culture and Political Crisis in Vienna* (Chicago, 1995).
142. Boyer, *Political Radicalism*, 221.
143. The quote is from ibid., 3; see also Schorske, *Fin-de-Siècle Vienna*, 138–46.
144. T. Mills Kelly, *Without Remorse* (Boulder, 2006), 62.

By contrast, Kiev's demagogues had no such invitation to moderation. Unless political reforms dramatically expanded the franchise—or political crisis discredited the cosmopolitan views of the city's capitalist elite among high society—antiliberal populists could nourish no hope of governing. At the same time, both local and imperial authorities, who were intently focused on the threats posed to the regime by socialists, anarchists, and other left-wing radicals, paid little attention to the destabilizing potential of the extreme—and often racialized—anti-Semitic rhetoric articulated within the city duma itself. Permitted to indulge in ever more radical rhetoric as the imperial authorities addressed other dangers that seemed more pressing, Little Russian activists and demagogic politicians would only grow more influential in the years to come.

The Rise of Mass Politics

In the last years of the nineteenth century, discontent with the tsarist regime and the capitalist order swept the Russian empire. Progressive nobles and zemstvo activists made contact with socialists, urban intellectuals, dissidents in exile, and national minority groups. Although these evolving discussions produced fierce debates about the future of the Russian government and the empire's people, many within imperial society were reaching a consensus that it was time for the tsar's subjects to liberate themselves from the autocratic state.[145]

Emboldened by the winds of change, many among the empire's working classes joined those calling for reform. But in Kiev, ongoing discussions about the urban crisis had laid out two dramatically different road maps to popular liberation. One, which Little Russian activists first formulated and urban populists further embellished, demanded state intervention to promote the welfare of East Slavs and to protect them from supposedly exploitative foreign populations. Another, devised by socialists, critiqued the injustices of capitalist society while urging all proletarians to fight side by side in pursuit of political change. As ordinary Kiev residents mobilized, which path to freedom would they choose?

In the first years of the twentieth century, it appeared that socialists were gaining the upper hand. Between 1900 and 1902, Kiev workers staged two dozen strikes. Unlike labor actions of the past, many of these strikes united representatives of various industries and social stations; some even issued broader demands for political and economic reform.[146] In another sign of the politicization of society at large, students and left-wing intellectuals began to appear at worker protests, taking to the streets

---

145. Shmuel Galai, *The Liberation Movement in Russia, 1900–1905* (Cambridge, UK, 1973).
146. See F. Iastrebov, *1905 rik u Kyevi* (Kharkov, 1930), 21; Parasun'ko, *Massovaia politicheskaia zabastovka*, 48.

with red flags that proclaimed, "Down with Autocracy," and "An eight-hour working day!"[147]

Gradually, discussions about the need for fundamental changes in the empire's political system transcended shop floors and SD cells, infiltrating the streets of working-class districts. In February 1903, as police arrived in Demievka to arrest drunken revelers celebrating the last days before Lent, the crowd grew unruly and began to chant political slogans. The revelers fought back and denounced "the Autocratic structure," which, they complained, "is controlled by a handful of people who have seized power, decide the fate of all Russia, rob the population, and to top it all off, debase [our] human dignity at every step."[148]

However, committed socialists frequently complained that many proletarians remained indifferent or even hostile toward their movement. In 1901, Kiev workers opposed to socialism interrupted May Day demonstrations.[149] And in some cases, workers used the language and tactics of the labor movement to promote the interests of their own ethnoconfessional group rather than those of the working classes as a whole. When lathe operators at one of the city's biggest mechanical factories walked off the job to protest the dismissal of nearly 10 percent of the workforce in the spring of 1902, they demanded that in the case of further layoffs, the 104 "foreign subjects" employed by the factory should be let go before Orthodox Russian subjects.[150]

Indeed, the events surrounding Kiev's 1903 general strike provide the clearest confirmation that the antiliberal vision of liberation sketched out by Little Russian activists and populist politicians had begun to exercise influence within the labor movement. In the spring of 1903, A. G. Shlikhter (1868–1940), a statistician for the Southwest Railroad who would soon declare his loyalty to the Bolsheviks, began meeting with SD activists and journalists to organize a general strike.[151] But as workers spread word to their comrades of the impending labor action, rumors of an imminent pogrom also swept across factory floors and city streets.[152] Strike organizers expressed concern about these reports, but they continued their organizational

---

147. *Iskra*, 5 June 1901, cited in F. E. Los', I. P. Oleinik, and V .I. Sheludchenko, eds., *Revoliutsiia 1905–1907 gg. na Ukraine* (Kiev, 1955), 1:11; *Iskra*, 15 February 1902, cited in ibid., 1:31.
148. *Kievskii sotsial-demokraticheskii listok*, 22 February 1903, 1.
149. *Iskra*, 5 June 1901, cited in Los', Oleinik, and Sheludchenko, *Revoliutsiia*, 1:11.
150. See Report of Kiev Senior Factory Inspector, 30 April 1902, TsDIAUK, f. 574, op. 1, d. 552, ll. 3–5.
151. V. Vakar [B. Pravdin], *Nakanune 1905 g. v Kieve* (Kiev, 1925), 123. Shlikhter was the son of a skilled worker from Poltava province. A populist in the 1880s who had become a socialist in the 1890s, he arrived in Kiev in 1902 after years living in Switzerland and in exile in the Russian interior. See Anthony Heywood, "Socialists, Liberals, and the Union of Unions in Kyiv during the 1905 Revolution," in *The Russian Revolution of 1905*, ed. Jonathan D. Smele and Anthony Heywood (New York, 2005), 180.
152. Ultimately Kiev remained peaceful in the spring of 1903, and the expected pogrom broke out only in the Bessarabian city of Kishinev. On the rumors of impending anti-Jewish violence, see TsDIAUK, f. 317, op. 1, d. 2207.

efforts, distributing pamphlets that denounced anti-Semitic violence as a tool used by the industrial bourgeoisie to divide the working classes.[153]

On 22 July 1903, more than five thousand machine builders, railroad workers, and printers declared a strike in Kiev. As workers gathered that morning to hear the speeches of strike committee members, police and Cossack units panicked and charged the crowd, killing fifteen workers and injuring two hundred.[154] Outrage over the violence encouraged more workers to join the strike. By the twenty-fifth, large-scale walkouts on the railroad had crippled the transit system; tram drivers, bakers, artisans, tobacco workers, sailors, construction workers, steamboat captains, and employees of flour mills and furniture factories all refused to show up to work.[155] With an estimated twelve to fifteen thousand workers on strike within city limits, the labor action spread along the thoroughfares that led out of the city, reaching nearby towns like Vasil'kov.[156]

Throughout the action, SD activists highlighted the common plight shared by all workers, regardless of their industry, creed, or ethnicity. "Our strength is in unity! All for one and one for all!" read one of the pamphlets that activists distributed.[157] Yet the massive nature of the strike made it difficult for its organizers to control, and participants soon broke into distinct groups pursuing varied goals. Some workers paid visits to prominent merchants and industrialists to voice their demands.[158] At the mills, typesetting plants, tobacco factories, and the municipal electrical station, striking workers attacked comrades who remained on the job.[159] Huge crowds of workers milling around city streets and bazaars admitted that they had no idea why they had walked off work or what they hoped to achieve.[160] Other strikers used the work stoppage as a vacation day, heading for the Dnieper's beaches.[161]

As both the local authorities and labor organizers lost control of the city's public spaces, the strike degenerated into mass violence. One organizer later recalled that many local workers rejected the notion that proletarians could stand in common cause, insisting that Jews, no less than the tsarist authorities, were responsible for the

---

153. "Donosenie kievskogo gubernatora ministru vnutrennykh del o politicheskoi demonstratsii v Kieve," 8 May 1903, cited in Los', Oleinik, and Sheludchenko, *Revoliutsiia*, 1:96; "K russkomu obshchestvu," 17 April 1903, TsDIAUK, f. 296, op. 1, d. 3, l. 13.
154. Los', Oleinik, and Sheludchenko, *Revoliutsiia*, 1:357.
155. V. Vakar [B. Pravdin], *Revoliutsionnye dni v Kieve* (Geneva, 1903), 11–39.
156. See "Kopii telegrafnykh donesenii v Otdel promyshlennosti Ministerstva Finansov o khode iiul'skoi zabastovki v Kieve v 1903," July 1903, TsDIAUK, f. 575, op. 1, d. 370; Senior Factory Inspector V. I. Deisha to Civil Governor, 25 July 1903, TsDIAUK, f. 574, op. 1, d. 681, l. 19.
157. Social Democratic pamphlet, 21 July 1903, TsDIAUK, f. 574, op. 1, d. 681, l. 63.
158. Memorandum of the Chief of the Podol Police District of Kiev, 23 July 1903, ibid., l. 22.
159. Vakar, *Nakanune 1905 g.*, 139–41; Molchanov to V. I. Deisha, 26 July 1903, TsDIAUK, f. 574, op. 1, d. 681, l. 30; telegraph of Regional Factory Inspector to St. Petersburg, 26 July 1903, TsDIAUK, f. 575, op. 1, d. 370, l. 2.
160. *Iskra*, 1 September 1903, cited in Los', Oleinik, and Sheludchenko, *Revoliutsiia*, 1:358–59.
161. Memorandum of the Chief of the Podol Police District of Kiev, 23 July 1903, TsDIAUK, f. 574, op. 1, d. 681, l. 220b.

misery of the working classes.[162] On 25 and 26 July, angry crowds gathered in Podol, where they attacked Jewish businesses, including the Brodskiis' steam mill and several taverns. Panicked strike organizers ordered the protesters to return to their appointed strike centers to await directives from organizers, insisting that the anti-Jewish violence expressed workers' "symbolic offense" against "rich capitalists" rather than deep-seated religious or ethnic hatred.[163] However, the violence raged on in Podol, ending only when police and Cossacks cornered the crowd, shooting and beating those who refused to disband.[164]

With the original aims of the strike forgotten in the melee, the resolve of even the most determined strikers soon broke. By the twenty-eighth, tram drivers and employees at fourteen other establishments returned to work without having received the concessions they had demanded. Over the course of the next week, Kiev's factory inspector negotiated with industrialists, eliciting concessions ranging from pay raises to shorter work days. By 1 August, all the city's workers had returned to the job.[165]

::

In the four decades following the 1863 revolt, Kiev residents from all walks of life had shown that they were capable of organizing and mobilizing themselves politically. But the participation of broader segments of the urban population in the ongoing debate about how best to govern the rapidly growing city had also intensified conflicts and even instigated violence. The 1903 general strike confirmed that Kiev had entered the era of mass politics—and that its working classes were ready to take to the streets to improve the conditions in which they worked and lived. It remained unclear, however, which vision of popular liberation the city's proletarians would embrace. Would they follow the model laid out by socialist activists, who called on all workers to unite in recognition of their common class interests? Or the ideas promoted by Little Russian activists and populist politicians, who insisted that the economic and social conflicts in the southwest were created by irresolvable national (or even racial) conflicts that could be rectified only by illiberal measures that limited the influence of the groups that supposedly had oppressed the children of Rus'? Ultimately, this question would not be resolved in the editorial offices of *Kievlianin*, the chancery of the governor-general, or the lecture halls of St. Vladimir's. Rather, in the years to come, it would be decided by the masses themselves in neighborhood meetings, city streets, and ballot boxes.

---

162. Vakar, *Revoliutsionnye dni*, 35. Vakar agreed that Kiev's Jewish capitalists exploited the working class but noted that many Gentiles did as well.
163. Ibid., 59.
164. *Iskra*, 1 September 1903, in Los', Oleinik, and Sheludchenko, *Revoliutsiia*, 1:359.
165. Los', Oleinik, and Sheludchenko, *Revoliutsiia*, 1:360; telegraph of Regional Factory Inspectorate to Ministry of Finance, 28 July 1903, TsDIAUK, f. 575, op. 1, d. 370, l. 5; Factory Inspector to Senior Factory Inspector, 20 September 1903, TsDIAUK, f. 574, op. 1, d. 68, l. 74.

5   Concepts of Liberation

IN THE FIRST years of the twentieth century, contacts between Russia's progressive nobles, zemstvo activists, socialists, and urban liberals continued to deepen. As diverse groups of imperial subjects joined together to demand political reform and the creation of a rule-of-law state that would offer all citizens equal rights, observers came to speak of them as constituting a unitary Liberation Movement.[1] By 1905, liberationist activism had evolved into a full-fledged revolution that saw protesters of all social stations and ethnoconfessional backgrounds take to the empire's streets demanding fundamental political reforms. In October of that year, liberationists achieved a remarkable victory, wresting substantial concessions, including guarantees of basic civil rights, from the autocracy.

The 1905 revolution is typically seen as a momentous yet discrete event in Russian history—the culmination of political alliances and patterns of mobilization that began to emerge around the turn of the twentieth century.[2] This chapter, which follows Kiev city politics through the tumultuous 1905 period, shows how the ongoing struggle for control of the city and its political institutions informed local political repertoires and cultures during the revolution. Ukrainophiles, non-Orthodox mercantile elites, and socialist activists—all of whom had articulated clear demands for political reform by the 1890s—unified under the Liberation Movement, joining the struggle for equal rights. Little Russian activists and the duma's antiliberal populists led the local opposition to the movement, insisting that the creation of an equal rights regime would only reward and embolden the putative exploiters of the Rus' people. Denouncing the liberationist platform as an attack on "truly Russian" values founded on local folk culture and Orthodox traditions, they insisted that popular liberation could occur only under the auspices of a strong state that prioritized the welfare of the East Slavs.

As the two camps peddled divergent road maps to popular liberation and competed to win the loyalties of the urban masses, the Jewish question became the issue that activists on both sides used to rally their troops. Liberationists seized on the

---

1. See Galai, *Liberation Movement*.
2. The classic overview is Ascher, *Revolution*.

discriminatory legal regimes that mandated where Jews could live and study as symbols of the political disenfranchisement that all tsarist subjects faced. The antiliberationist forces, by contrast, blamed the southwest's cosmopolitan capitalist elite and its Jewish population for the suffering of its Orthodox majority; highlighting the centrality of the Jewish question in liberationist rhetoric, they presented the movement as a whole as a reflection of narrow Jewish national and economic interests.[3]

Over the course of 1905, both liberationists and their antiliberal opponents acquired a mass political following, convincing students, artisans, and workers to join their cause; the revolutionary upheaval produced new communities that unified diverse segments of the urban population behind well-defined ideological agendas. But the political activization of society also polarized the city and radicalized both political camps. By the second half of 1905, moderate liberationist leaders would struggle to retain control of their movement as radical activists advocated armed resistance against the state. Many opponents of the Liberation Movement, for their part, saw violence as a legitimate means of countering the unprecedented threats that they claimed the revolution had posed to the children of Rus' and their traditions. In October 1905—at the precise moment that imperial society celebrated the concessions it had won from the autocracy—Kiev would descend into a maelstrom of violence that would see neighbors and coworkers attack one another. Although the events of 1905 demonstrated the organizational capacity of local society, then, they also revealed its self-destructive potential.

Liberationist Forces Assemble

By 1904, the critics of the imperial regime were growing more restive. Cells of SRs and SDs continued to proliferate rapidly in factories and on the campuses of St. Vladimir's and the Polytechnical Institute; socialist activists had also grown more brazen in their outreach efforts, publishing regular broadsheets and pamphlets that depicted military forces, bureaucrats, and priests as murderers of struggling workers.[4] Zionist and Bundist groups, which promised to resolve the economic and the national struggles of Jews, had made headway in neighborhoods with large Jewish populations.[5] The Revolutionary Ukrainian Party (RUP)—the Ukrainian nationalist and socialist party founded by V. B. Antonovich's son Dmytro—remained active in the countryside, and its members smuggled illegal literature from Austrian Galicia and called for a revolution to seize power from "landlords, the rich, bureaucrats, the government, the tsar."[6]

---

3. Shulamit Volkov describes a similar phenomenon in late imperial Germany in her exploration of anti-Semitism as a "cultural code." See Shulamit Volkov, *Germans, Jews, and Antisemites* (New York, 2005). Note that the prospect of granting Jews full civil rights also prompted an organized anti-Jewish campaign in Bavaria in 1849–50: see James F. Harris, *The People Speak!* (Ann Arbor, 1994).
4. See, for example, undated leaflet, TsDIAUK, f. 274, op. 1, d. 888, l. 24.
5. See Meir, *Kiev*, 264–67; "Agenturnye svedeniia o deiatel'nosti kievskoi organizatsii 'Poalei Tsion,'" TsDIAUK, f. 275, op. 2, d. 13.
6. Quote from a handwritten brochure, c. 1904, preserved in TsDIAUK, f. 275, op. 2, d. 12, l. 8.

Hrushevs'kyi capitalized on the growing interest in the Ukrainian cause on the part of some segments of educated society in the imperial capitals. After liberal scholars in the Imperial Academy of Sciences called on the authorities to remove all special restrictions on the Ukrainian language and to authorize a Ukrainian translation of the Bible, he printed an essay in a collection published by that group that laid the foundations for a Ukrainian national historiography. Written in the Galician-Ukrainian vernacular, it traced the roots of a Ukrainian nation identified by its language and folk traditions to Kievan Rus', railing against Russian attempts to claim Ukraine and its history as part of a unified East Slavic culture.[7]

Kiev intellectuals worked doggedly to unify these disparate groups and causes behind a single liberationist banner. The Literary-Artistic Society—which, as we saw in chapter 4, had become a gathering place for liberal industrialists as well as Ukrainophiles soon after its founding in 1900—had by 1904 evolved into a major center of liberationist activity. Luchitskii and Naumenko remained among the group's most active members, and Lev Brodskii was one of its most generous benefactors; now it also claimed Ukrainian radicals, Socialist Revolutionaries, and Social Democrats among its members.[8] Housed in a handsome building with two large auditoriums, the group regularly hosted public forums that attracted up to five hundred spectators at a time—a fact that greatly concerned the local authorities.[9] By late 1904, it had demanded equal rights for all tsarist subjects and the revocation of the Ems edict.[10]

By late 1904, Kiev liberationists had joined activists across the empire in organizing a series of banquets that aimed to rally broad segments of society behind the calls for reform. (These events were self-consciously modeled on the Parisian revolutionary banquets of 1847–48.) Luchitskii and Prince E. N. Trubetskoi (1863–1920), an alumnus of the early liberationist discussion groups of the nineties who had recently moved to Kiev to teach law at St. Vladimir's, organized Kiev's banquet, which was held in November 1904.[11] Hosted by the Literary-Artistic Society, the event was attended by nearly four hundred invited guests, ranging from liberal industrialists to SRs, Bolsheviks, and Zionists; an additional two hundred spectators, among them students and workers, observed the event.[12] Police agents who had infiltrated the event claimed that the speakers—who included Luchitskii, Trubetskoi, and L.A. Kupernik (a lawyer who had prosecuted the alleged perpetrators of pogroms in several trials across the Pale, a longtime friend of the Brodskiis, and a contributor to their short-lived liberal

---

7. On the academy's views, see Cadiot, "Russia Learns to Write," 135–67. On Hrushevs'kyi's essay and its significance, see Plokhy, *Unmaking Imperial Russia*, 95–116; Shchegolev, *Ukrainskoe dvizhenie*, 138–40.

8. *Otchet Kievskogo literaturno-artisticheskogo obshchestva za 1903 god* (Kiev, 1904); *Spisok chlenov*.

9. See Civil Governor P. S. Savvich to Chief of the Kiev Province Gendarme Division, 25 September 1903, GARF, f. 102, 3-oe deloproizvodstvo, 1903, d. 26, ch. 23, l. A, l. 49; MVD to Civil Governor Savvich, 26 January 1904, ibid., l. 100.

10. Shchegolev, *Ukrainskoe dvizhenie*, 141.

11. On Trubetskoi's background and views, see E. N. Trubetskoi, *Iz proshlogo* (Newtonville, MA, 1976).

12. Civil Governor Savvich to Governor-General N. V. Kleigel's, 24 November 1904, TsDIAUK, f. 442, op. 854, d. 423, l. 1, 11.

Concepts of Liberation

paper of the 1880s)—had discussed the problems of contemporary "social life" with a "clearly revolutionary" tone.¹³ One Polytechnical Institute professor urged the assembled crowd to throw off the "yoke of autocracy"; another demanded the immediate implementation of a free and fair universal, secret, equal, and direct electoral system.¹⁴ The Bolshevik activist A. G. Shlikhter trumpeted the growing revolutionary consciousness of the industrial proletariat, while M. B. Ratner, the lawyer who helped workers organize unions, delivered a speech denouncing legal discrimination and popular violence directed at Jews.¹⁵ In the aftermath of the banquet, liberal activists and representatives of illegal parties continued to meet on a regular basis.¹⁶

From the beginning of the rapprochement between liberals, Ukrainophile activists, and the radical left, opponents of the struggle for equal rights challenged the notion that the liberationists spoke for the needs of the urban masses. Instead, they portrayed the Liberation Movement as a cynical play by Jewish industrialists to consolidate their own power. B. M. Iuzefovich—M. V. Iuzefovich's youngest son, who had begun to write extensively on Russian nationalism in organs such as *Kievlianin* in the 1890s—expressed outrage that Jews, who supposedly had tormented the "tillers of the Russian land" for centuries, now demanded the same rights as the "native Russian people."¹⁷ Demagogues in the city duma continued to blame the difficult plight of the masses on the corrupt and monopolistic practices of the city fathers (and in particular, the Jews among them). These politicians accused the Brodskiis of hypocrisy, asking how they could subsidize groups that popularized liberationist rhetoric while treating the city as their own personal domain. Duma delegates criticized the terms of the July 1904 municipalization of the sewer company, which had seen Kiev pay millions of rubles to the Brodskiis and their coinvestors to acquire the utility; delegates also revealed that municipal funds had been used to maintain private properties owned by the Brodskiis.¹⁸ Highlighting other junctures at which the duma had failed to protect citizens from the allegedly deceptive business practices of Jewish merchants, the delegate A. L. Tsytovich accused Jewish entrepreneurs and the duma itself of being complicit in the

---

13. Memorandum to Director of Department of Police, 27 November 1904, TsDIAUK, f. 274, op. 1, d. 888, l. 1470b; Chief of Kiev Okhrana Division to Governor-General Kleigel's, 21 November 1904, TsDIAUK, f. 442, op. 854, d. 423, l. 10b.
14. Chief of Kiev Okhrana Division to Governor-General Kleigel's, 21 November 1904, TsDIAUK, f. 442, op. 854, d. 423, l. 20b; Untitled and undated memorandum in GARF, f. 102, OO, 1905, d. 3, ch. 37, l. 7.
15. Chief of Kiev Okhrana Division to Governor-General Kleigel's, 21 November 1904, TsDIAUK, f. 442, op. 854, d. 423, ll. 2–30b; "Prazdnovanie 40-letie sudebnykh ustavov v Kieve," *Kievskie otkliki*, 22 November 1904, 2–3.
16. Chief of the Kiev Okhrana Division to Governor-General Kleigel's, 21 November 1904, TsDIAUK, f. 442, op. 854, d. 423, l. 30b.
17. B. M. Iuzefovich, "K evreiskomu voprosu," *Russkii vestnik* 286, no. 1 (1903): 382.
18. Conforming to the pattern we have seen, duma delegates bitterly derided the Brodskiis' role in these companies even as they virtually ignored that of Gentile industrialists such as the Tereshchenkos. See "Zasedanie dumy," *Kievlianin*, 14 July 1904, 3; Golubiatnikov, *Spravka*, 255–62. It was revealed on the duma floor in the fall of 1904 that the city had been paying to maintain a staircase on property owned by the Brodskiis, using the rationale that it was located adjacent to a theater and that theatergoers occasionally used it to approach the building. See "Zasedanie dumy," *Kievlianin*, 20 October 1904, 2.

fleecing of the masses.[19] When the city head and the chairs of the commissions that had been accused of "wasting millions" endeavored to defend themselves and explain their actions, antiliberal populists created a ruckus on the duma floor, engineering an attempt to oust the former and discredit the latter.[20]

Meanwhile, city residents opposed to the campaign for equal rights assumed a growing role in local political life. St. Vladimir's students organized a "party of order" to compete with the liberationist student groups already operating at the institution, which they claimed represented the interests of small "Judeo-Armenian cliques."[21] Professionals and intellectuals who decried "cosmopolitanism, atheism, and anarchism" organized a Kiev chapter of the Russian Gathering, a club that conservative nobles in St. Petersburg had founded several years earlier. More socially variegated (and socially minded) than the St. Petersburg division, the Kiev chapter, led by Iuzefovich, unified veteran Little Russian activists, antiliberal duma delegates, and political neophytes attracted by the group's pledge to defend "Orthodoxy, tsarist Autocracy, and the Russian nationality [*narodnost'*]" from internal enemies and to minimize what they saw as the baleful influence of Jews in the southwest.[22] The Kiev chapter, which soon claimed nearly a thousand members, became one of the group's largest local affiliates; in 1904, it founded the Kiev Russian Circle, a spin-off group aimed at the working class that organized fifteen neighborhood discussion groups and two railroad worker divisions.[23]

Winter and Spring 1905: Social and Political Activation

On 9 January 1905, troops attacked a peaceful workers' demonstration in St. Petersburg led by the populist priest Father Gapon, inciting massive protests across the empire. The event galvanized Kiev liberationists, setting off a series of strikes by bakers and typesetters, sugar factory employees, and railroad workers. While continuing to demand improvements in their working and economic conditions, striking workers also voiced political demands, including freedom of association.[24] Shlikhter, who

---

19. "Zasedanie dumy," *Kievlianin*, 9 October 1904, 2.
20. "Zaiavlenie 10 glasnykh," *Kievskie otkliki*, 4 November 1904, 3; "Zasedanie dumy," *Kievlianin*, 30 October 1904, 3.
21. Report on Meeting of Council of Professors of the Polytechnical Institute, 16 February 1904, TsDIAUK, f. 274, op. 1, d. 888, l. 34.
22. The quotes are from *Prazdnik russkogo samosoznaniia* (Kharkov, 1903), 1, 50. The literary historian Cesare G. De Michelis argues, on the basis of a painstaking linguistic analysis of the *Protocols of the Elders of Zion*, that the text was produced in 1902–3 by Russian Gathering activists who hailed from the southwestern periphery of the empire. See his *The Non-Existent Manuscript*, trans. Richard Newhouse (Lincoln, NE, 2004), 73–109. On the Russian Gathering and its aims more broadly, see Iu. I. Kir'ianov, *Russkoe sobranie, 1900–1917* (Moscow, 2003); Rawson, *Rightists*, 46–55.
23. I. V. Omel'ianchuk, *Chernosotennoe dvizhenie na territorii Ukrainy* (Kiev, 2000), 16–26.
24. Report of Factory Inspectorate, 29 January 1905, TsDIAUK, f. 574, op. 1, d. 905, ll. 3–30b; Iastrebov, *1905 rik*, 28.

emerged as a leader of the railroad strike, encouraged workers not to yield until they had achieved equality for all people *"regardless of race, nationality, and confession!"*[25]

Many residents from different walks of life declared their solidarity with the striking workers. Students at St. Vladimir's and the Polytechnical Institute organized huge meetings on campus; liberationist professors permitted students to take up collections for revolutionary causes in their lectures.[26] By mid-February, the Polytechnical Institute's Council of Professors joined with students in calling for "the replacement of bureaucratic absolutism by a parliamentary regime."[27] Alarmed at the growing radicalism of the institute in particular, the authorities closed the institution to avert further disturbances. But the cancellation of classes only encouraged liberationist students to roam the city streets, fraternize with workers, and organize demonstrations in support of the strikers.[28]

Liberationists continued to demand that the position of the empire's national minorities be improved. Ukrainophile activists appeared at political meetings, in which they delivered speeches in Ukrainian and called on the authorities to introduce Ukrainian instruction into the region's schools.[29] But liberationists were even more energized by the Jewish question. Liberal papers and striking workers now included demands for Jewish equal rights at the very top of their political agendas.[30] At a March 1905 meeting jointly organized by the Literary-Artistic Society, SDs, and SRs and attended by more than three hundred, liberal orators insisted on the need for a constitutional regime that would guarantee equal rights, while radicals called for a revolution. After the meeting, the energized attendees poured into the streets, where they were met by police. Claiming that meeting attendees had sung revolutionary songs, chanted antigovernment slogans, and attacked a police officer in front of the society's building, police cornered the crowd and arrested many of the group's leaders, whom they charged with "inciting the intelligentsia against the Higher Authorities and against the government."[31]

Political demands voiced by liberationists resounded with increasing frequency in Kiev's streets and public spaces. At a February performance of a Maksim Gorkii play at a city theater owned by the Brodskiis, voices from the crowd—which included

---

25. "Tsarizm nakanune Vsenarodnogo vozstaniia," GARF, f. 102, OO, 1905, d. 5, ch. 3, l. A, l. 30b. For more on the railroad strike, see TsDIAUK, f. 274, op. 1, d. 1179.
26. Civil Governor P. S. Savvich to Governor-General Kleigel's, 17 March 1905, TsDIAUK, f. 442, op. 855, d. 74, l. 3.
27. "Zhurnal zasedaniia soveta Kievskogo Politekhnicheskogo Instituta IMPERATORA ALEKSANDRA II ot 12 fev 1905 goda," DAK, f. 18, op. 1, d. 557, ll. 28, 30.
28. Director of the Kiev Province Gendarme Direction to the Department of Police, 2 February 1905, GARF, f. 102, OO, 1905, d. 3, ch. 37, l. 1.
29. "Vecher v pamiat' Shevchenka v Kieve," *KS* 89, no. 4 (1905): 71. See also Shchegolev, *Ukrainskoe dvizhenie*, 156–57.
30. For example, "Pered reformoi," *Kievskie novosti*, 6 April 1905, 1–2; Kiev Factory Inspector to Senior Kiev Factory Inspector, 28 March 1905, TsDIAUK, f. 574, op. 1, d. 905, l. 92.
31. The incident is described in DAKO, f. 2, op. 65, d. 159; the quote is from Chief of Okhrana Division to Civil Governor Savvich, 2 March 1905, l. 4ao0b.

M. B. Ratner and L. A. Kupernik that night—called out "long live freedom," and "down with Autocracy" as soon as the lights dimmed.[32] Two weeks later, a swarm of 1,300 students interrupted a concert in progress, taking to the stage to read political poetry and encourage spectators to arm themselves against the government.[33] Practically every night, brochures with slogans such as "Down with Autocracy. Death to the tsar, a murderer," appeared on city lampposts and buildings.[34]

Faced with similar demands for change across the empire, the imperial authorities announced political concessions. In February 1905, Minister of the Interior A. G. Bulygin announced his intention to convene an imperial parliament (Duma) in the near future. Responding to the prominence of national concerns in the activities of the liberationists, as early as December 1904 Tsar Nicholas II had pledged to expand local autonomy and to review the laws pertaining to the empire's minority groups. In February, the Committee of Ministers took a small step toward following through on the tsar's promise, authorizing the publication of the Ukrainian-language gospels after extensive lobbying from the Academy of Sciences.[35]

These concessions, however, did not appease liberationists, who only intensified their efforts to unite local society and to press for fundamental political reforms. Kiev professors, lawyers, teachers, and journalists joined national unions that represented their professional interests and pressed for equal civil rights for all tsarist subjects.[36] In July 1905, a delegation of liberationist activists from Kiev went to Finland to attend the conference of the Union of Unions, which denounced the "nontransparent" and "bureaucratic" features of the imperial Duma described in Bulygin's rescript.[37] Luchitskii attended two sessions of the Congress of Zemstvo and City Activists, which met in the summer of 1905 to call for legal equality for all citizens, universal elementary education, expanded local autonomy, freedom of conscience and religion, and four-tailed (universal, equal, secret, and direct) suffrage.[38] Ukrainian radicals in attendance at the conference voiced more sweeping demands, calling for autonomy to be granted to non-Russian-speaking areas of the empire.[39]

---

32. Civil Governor Savvich to Department of Police, 9 February 1905, GARF, f. 102, OO, 1905, d. 1350, ch. 15, ll. 9–90b.
33. Civil Governor Savvich to Governor-General Kleigel's, 1 March 1905, TsDIAUK, f. 442, op. 855, d. 77, l. 1.
34. Civil Governor Savvich to Department of Police, 17 February 1905, GARF, f. 102, OO, 1905, d. 5, ch. 3, l. 750b; Civil Governor Savvich to Department of Police, 1 March 1905, ibid., l. 91.
35. Cadiot, "Russia," 146–48.
36. Spisok lits, voshedshikh v sostav Kievskoi gruppy 'Soiuz Professorov,'" GARF, f. 102, OO, 1905, d. 999, ch. 4, l. 3. "V obshchestve pedagogov," *Kievskie novosti*, 30 March 1905, 4; "Rezoliutsiia, priniatye obshchim sobraniem kievskikh," *Pravo* 14 (1905): 1101–4; Governor-General Kleigel's to Civil Governor Savvich, 21 May 1905, DAKO, f. 2, op. 65, d. 159, l. 51.
37. Moscow City Police Chief to Department of Police, 12 July 1905, GARF, f. 102, OO, 1905, d. 1000, ch. 1, ll. 169–1700b.
38. "Spisok," GARF, f. 102, OO, 1905, d. 1000, ch. 1, l. 1050b; "K russkomu narodu ot s"ezda zemskikh deiatelei i gorodskikh predstavitelei v Moskve 6 iiulia 1905 goda," ibid., l. 125.
39. "K russkomu narodu," ibid., l. 124; "Zaiavlenie ukrainskoi demokraticheskoi partii s"ezdu zemskikh i gorodskikh deiatelei v Moskve 6-go iiulia 1905 goda," GARF, f. 102, OO, 1906, I-otd., d. 25, ch. 57, ll. 48–52.

Although the Liberation Movement made rapid gains in the spring of 1905, diverse voices emanating from Kiev continued to insist that non-East Slavs, especially Jews, were to blame for the problems of urban life and the suffering of the working masses. In May 1905, the former governor-general of Kiev, M. I. Dragomirov, published a furious denunciation of "the Yids'" alleged domination of the southwest region's finance, industry, and government in the middlebrow *Razvedchik (Scout)*. Echoing the complaints of Little Russian activists and city duma delegates, he insisted that calls for Jewish civic equality merely masked a Jewish conspiracy to "achieve more rights than native [*prirozhdennye*] Russians."[40] Others portrayed Jews as a dangerous source of foreign, revolutionary ideas that threatened the welfare of the Rus' people. In April, self-professed "conservative" doctors gathered in Kiev to draw up a manifesto to the authorities that denounced the Jewish doctors with whom they had served in the Russo-Japanese War, identifying by name colleagues whose political activities rendered them unfit for public service as well as those who had allegedly professed their support for revolutionary terrorism.[41] Pamphlets blaming Jews for the difficult plight of the toiling masses circulated at workers' demonstrations, urging Orthodox proletarians to turn against their Jewish coworkers.[42] Persistent threats of pogroms hung over labor actions, forcing socialist organizers, much to their chagrin, to cancel their original plans to call a general strike on May Day.[43]

The Jewish Question, the Narod, and Liberation

Over the summer of 1905, the mood across the southwest grew more restive. Peasants and employees of rural sugar refineries organized strikes as well as violent attacks against landlords, long-term leaseholders, and plant managers.[44] Meanwhile, Kiev's outlying neighborhoods emerged as new centers of conflict, as radical Jewish youth, disenchanted by the slow pace of change, vented their frustration. In early July, revolutionary youth interrupted a service at a Demievka synagogue, unfurling political banners and giving speeches. When worshippers chided the protesters, the youth attacked them with sticks and revolvers. As the panicked congregants jumped out of

---

40. M. I. Dragomirov, "Ravnopravnost' zhidov," *Razvedchik* 741 (1905): 415–16.
41. "Unhappy Conservative" to Governor-General N. V. Kleigel's, c. spring 1905, GARF, f. 102, OO, 1905, d. 1200, ll. 11–12; see also "Conservative Doctors of Kiev" to Ministry of Internal Affairs, April 1905, ibid., l. 2. Benjamin Nathans has identified similar mechanisms of exclusion at play in St. Petersburg, where non-Jewish lawyers mobilized to denounce the threats that Jews supposedly posed to the profession's ethics and cohesion. See Nathans, *Beyond the Pale*, 340–66.
42. L. M. Ivanov, A. M. Pankratova, and A. L. Sidorov, eds., *Revoliutsiia 1905–1907 g.g. v natsional'nykh raionakh Rossii* (Moscow, 1955), 64.
43. Chief of the Kiev Okhrana Division to Department of Police, 26 April 1905, GARF, f. 102, 1905, OO, d. 80, ch. 20, l. 128; Chief of the Kiev Okhrana Division to Department of Police, 10 May 1905, ibid., l. 1500b. For the reaction of one disappointed socialist activist, see perlustrated letter from Kiev to "Sharro" in Geneva, 12 May 1905, GARF, f. 102, OO, 1905, d. 5, ch. 3, l. 150.
44. See Edelman, *Proletarian Peasants*, 92–132; Los', Oleinik, and Sheludchenko, *Revoliutsiia*, 136–46, 334–66.

the synagogue's windows to escape the melee, violence poured into the street. Youth wielding red flags fired shots as others struggled to tackle and restrain them.[45]

Liberationists working within Kiev's institutions of higher learning and the Literary-Artistic Society worked to capitalize on the frustration of local residents. After the ministries extended autonomy to educational establishments in late August, St. Vladimir's and the Polytechnical Institute hosted massive, open-air political rallies of students, workers, and educated professionals who demanded immediate reforms to "the existing political and social structure."[46] By September, the Literary-Artistic Society was welcoming nonmembers to its meetings, at which socialist activists delivered speeches and distributed illegal literature.[47] Sensing that he was rapidly losing control of the city, Governor-General N. V. Kleigel's outlawed all "demonstrations and gatherings of people in streets, squares, boulevards, and in other public places."[48]

As much as liberationist organizers cheered the participation of growing numbers of residents in the movement, however, they also expressed concerns about its radicalization. A meeting of "progressive-democratic" intellectuals, attended by Luchitskii and Trubetskoi among others, proclaimed its support for continued democratic and constitutional reforms. But attendees expressed concern that the "mixed composition of the population" could hinder efforts to unite "the different ethnic groups [*narodnosti*] of Kiev, even under the future democratic order."[49] Likewise, even as the Council of Professors at the Polytechnical Institute denounced the Jewish quota system and voted to admit students "without distinction for nationality, faith, or sex," some of its members expressed concerns about the radical ideas circulating on the campus and declared mass political meetings on institute grounds "undesirable."[50]

The radicalization of the Liberation Movement in mid-1905 provoked anxiety among liberals across the empire. But it posed a special dilemma for Kiev's most prominent Jewish elites. Having long challenged the antiliberal ideology and nationalizing vision of Little Russian activists and their supporters, they now found themselves accused by growing numbers of city residents of promoting their private interests under the guise of liberationist rhetoric. The anger of those who believed these charges endangered the urban order, threatening to unleash mass violence and pogroms. At the same time, many working-class Jews denounced the moderate

---

45. Civil Governor Savvich to Governor-General Kleigel's, 6 July 1905, TsDIAUK, f. 442, op. 855, d. 234, ll. 1–10b.
46. Quote from "Rezoliutsiia obshchestudencheskoi skhodki sostoiavsheisia 1 sentiabria 1905 g. v Aktovom zale Kievskogo universiteta," TsDIAUK, f. 274, op. 1, d. 1179, l. 43. See also Chief of the Kiev Provincial Gendarme Direction to Department of Police, 10 September 1905, GARF, f. 102, OO, 1905, d. 3, ch. 37, l. 13; "Protokoly zasedanii Soveta za 1905 god," DAK, f. 18, op. 1, d. 557, l. 990b.
47. Untitled report, 17 September 1905, TsDIAUK, f. 274, op. 1, d. 1179, l. 57; "Protokol," DAKO, f. 2, op. 65, d. 159, ll. 63–64.
48. *Kievskie gubernskie vedomosti*, 17 September 1905, 1.
49. "K Kievskom vyboram v Gosudarstvennuiu Dumu," *Kievlianin*, 5 October 1905, 2.
50. Quotes from minutes of meeting of 24 September 1905, DAK, f. 18, op. 1, d. 557, l. 1120b; "Protokoly" ibid., l. 1270b. For more on the divisions between liberationist professors at the institute and radicals, see Heywood, "Socialists," in Smele and Heywood, *Russian Revolution*, 177–95.

leadership that their elite co-confessionalists had provided, turning instead to armed resistance against the tsarist regime. Families such as the Margolins, Brodskiis, and Kuperniks now struggled to maintain their leading role in the Liberation Movement and to guide it in a moderate direction even as they fended off allegations that they were controlling it.[51] In the summer of 1905, D. S. Margolin toured the southwest's synagogues, urging worshippers to disavow violence and "illegal disturbances." The imperial Duma, he promised, would satisfactorily resolve Russia's troubling "Jewish question"; agitation for equal rights in the streets, he insisted, would only alienate the government and Christian population and turn them against the Jews. However, the crowds greeted Margolin's pleas with anger, interrupting his speeches with whistles and Yiddish-language calls for revolution.[52]

Just as supporters of the equal rights campaign had feared, their opponents continued to point to the involvement of prominent Jewish industrialists in the Liberation Movement as evidence that the unfolding revolution promoted their own narrow interests. In the last months of 1905, Kiev city duma delegates F. N. Iasnogurskii and N. P. Dobrynin observed that liberationist deputies had recently voted to provide a new round of corporate tax breaks and blocked construction of a new mill.[53] Noting that the latter measure would benefit the Brodskiis, who owned the city's largest milling enterprise, Iasnogurskii again took the opportunity to claim that the liberationists' rhetorical devotion to improving the plight of the masses masked their own selfish pursuits. "There is nothing more upsetting than the fact that the duma will not permit the construction of a new mill for the benefit of the capitalist Brodskii. This will slow the development of industry," he exclaimed. "Why is flour expensive in Kiev? Because the mill is in the hands of the millionaire Brodskii.... It's fine that the population drinks water that is dangerous for their health. No, we can't do anything about it."[54]

These aggressive attacks on the capitalist city fathers not only demonized the Jews among them but also seized the mantle of popular liberation from the Liberation Movement. The duma's antiliberal populists presented themselves as the true defenders of the simple folk; when the city head, incensed by Iasnogurskii's insubordination, declared the meeting closed, delegates dramatically protested his conduct as a violation of the people's will.[55] Many of the New Duma delegates who railed against Kiev's multiethnic elite also endeavored to demonstrate their commitment to protecting local culture. In the summer of 1905, the consistently antiliberal delegates O. I. Levitskii and N. V. Storozhenko joined with liberationist delegates such as Luchitskii to support the construction of a monument to Taras Shevchenko in Kiev. As the project

---

51. On the struggle between Jewish plutocrats and the masses for control of communal organizations and local politics, see Meir, *Kiev*, 261–310.
52. Civil Governor Savvich to Minister of Internal Affairs Bulygin, 12 August 1905, GARF, f. 102, OO, 1905, d. 1350, ch. 15, l. 380ob.
53. On tax breaks, see the duma protocol for 15–22 September 1905, DAK, f. 163, op. 8, d. 11, l. 865; "V dume," *Kievskie otkliki*, 4 October 1905, 3.
54. "Duma," *Kievskie otkliki*, 5 October 1905, 3.
55. Ibid.

progressed over the next half decade, the self-professed foes of the Liberation Movement would remain intimately involved in the project, which they hailed as a beacon of hope for the Little Russian simple folk who supposedly had suffered under foreign domination for so long.[56]

By the fall of 1905, *Kievlianin*, too, had joined the chorus of those who insisted that the Liberation Movement promoted the narrow interests of an allegedly unified Jewish nation rather than the welfare of the urban masses. In its coverage of rallies at educational establishments in support of equal rights, it caustically remarked, "Kiev Jews have a lovely synagogue and several houses of prayer for meetings. Why don't they move their gatherings to discuss their own questions and affairs there, rather than occupying auditoriums and disturbing students and professors?"[57] But while *Kievlianin*, like the populist deputies of the duma, often associated the liberationist platform with capitalist excess and self-interest, it also highlighted the movement's connections to cosmopolitan socialism and revolutionary terrorism—two other modes of politics that it attempted to portray as distinctly Jewish and fundamentally unbefitting the children of Rus'.[58] After the sudden death of L. A. Kupernik in late September, thousands of demonstrators gathered in central Kiev to celebrate his role as a proponent of Russia's "social self-recognition," and a "defender of and advocate for the weak."[59] *Kievlianin*, however, chose to focus on the chaos and violence that supposedly unfolded at these sites of collective mourning. It claimed that at a meeting of five thousand at St. Vladimir's—whose attendees the paper characterized as "almost exclusively Jews"—angry crowds had broken windows and even groped a woman; when police confronted demonstrators shouting antigovernment slogans at Kupernik's grave, shots rang out, wounding a police officer and killing a young woman.[60] Even those ignorant of or impervious to the claims of Jewish exploitation being made on the duma floor might have read in the city papers about the putative involvement of Jews in these outbursts of violence or heard these allegations discussed and repeated by their neighbors.

Over the fall of 1905, ordinary city residents expressed their opposition to the Liberation Movement with greater frequency and intensity. Antiliberal students demanded that educational establishments be purged of "social democrats and crowds standing around" so that regular instruction could resume.[61] Reaching out to other

---

56. "K sooruzheniiu pamiatnika T. G. Shevchenku v Kieve," *KS* 89, no. 6 (1905): 258–60; "Znevaha pam'iaty Shevchenka," *Rada*, 7 December 1906, 1. The project was initiated by liberal zemstvo activists in Poltava province, who then enlisted the Kiev duma as a partner. See Governor-General F. F. Trepov to P. A. Stolypin, 19 June 1911, TsDIAUK, f. 442, op. 662, d. 501, l. 32.
57. "Sborishche v universitete," *Kievlianin*, 9 October 1905, 3.
58. See, for example, D. I. Pikhno, *V osade* (Kiev, 1905), 3–7; *Kievlianin*, 9 October 1905, 2.
59. M. Voloshin, "Pamiati L. A. Kupernika," *Kievskie otkliki*, 1 October 1905, 3; "Pokhorony L. A. Kupernika," *Kievskie otkliki*, 2 October 1905, 3.
60. *Kievlianin*, 1 October 1905, 3.
61. Chief of the Kiev Provincial Gendarme Direction to Department of Police, 15 September 1905, GARF, f. 102, OO, 1905, d. 3, ch. 37, l. 18.

local residents, they eventually organized a boycott of the Polytechnical Institute, known as a hotbed of rebellion and closely associated with the Brodskiis because of their generous patronage of the institution. Kiev residents who participated in the boycott refused to step foot on the campus or to have commercial or social dealings with its affiliates.[62]

Documents preserved in the local archives testify to the rapid proliferation in the summer and fall of 1905 of citizens' groups that presented the struggle for popular liberation as a battle against foreign interlopers intent on destroying local culture and mores. In a letter to Kiev's civil governor, one such group, which called itself the Union of Patriots, lamented that the native traditions of the southwest had been displaced by "the shadow of Yiddom" (*zhidovskaia ten'*) and the foreign ideologies of socialism, capitalism, and liberalism. It faulted "flippant" local officials for failing to protect the interests of the Orthodox East Slavs and claimed that Count Witte—the longtime defender of Kiev's elites, now chair of the Council of Ministers—actively promoted Jewish interests, spearheading the campaign "to give the damned Jews [civil] rights." The participation of Jews in the upcoming imperial Duma elections, it warned, would permit them to seize control of the southwest, extinguishing the spirit of "Old Russia" in the birthplace of Orthodoxy and the Russian state.[63]

A political pamphlet published by the Kiev-Pechersk Monastery in August also warned of the dangers of expanding the political rights of Jews:

> Clever and cunning, [they] know how to creep into the souls of others, how to get the simple and good people to trust them, and how to hide their intentions behind seemingly good words. They've made a lot of noise in our cities, at various meetings, have caused more than a few problems in newspapers, have penetrated, unfortunately, into the benighted village, and into factories.... They seduce the most vulnerable with promises... they promise everyone some kind of freedom; in a word, heaven on earth.... What do they care for the Orthodox Russian people?... Holy Russia is not the native motherland for them. It's not *Holy* Russia, but simply a foreign country, where they've lived well until now.

"We are children of our country, and they are only guests," the pamphlet continued. "[W]e built and constructed our native Rus' with our blood and the blood of our ancestors; we should protect her from everything that is contrary to the Russian spirit, remain loyal to our native antiquity."[64] As the civic society of the southwest mobilized, these visions of illiberal liberation—which insisted that the children of Rus' could flourish only once the Jews who had allegedly oppressed and dominated them had been contained—assumed an ever more prominent role in local political culture.

---

62. Clipping from *Russkie vedomosti*, 20 September 1905, in GARF, f. 102, OO, 1905, d. 3, ch. 37, l. 64.
63. V. Gorbunov and D. Titov to Governor-General Kleigel's, 3 August 1905, TsDIAUK, f. 442, op. 855, d. 71, ll. 28–32.
64. "Golos iz obiteli prepodobnogo Sergiia po sluchaiu manifesta 6 avgusta," DAKO, f. 2, op. 41, d. 222b, ll. 350b–36.

Kiev's October Days

As tension between liberationists and their opponents grew, workers in Moscow and St. Petersburg declared a general strike. On 11 October, Kiev's railroad workers walked off the job to declare their solidarity with their comrades in the capitals. Over the next several days, workers in other industries and students joined the strike.[65] On the thirteenth, up to ten thousand gathered on the St. Vladimir's campus, where representatives from the SDs, SRs, and Bund gave speeches and read congratulatory telegrams from the St. Petersburg liberationists.[66] The most memorable orator that day, however, was Shlikhter, who denounced government officials and called on protesters to take the struggle for liberation to the streets. Meeting attendees soon scattered, organizing themselves into brigades to disrupt work at industrial enterprises and educational establishments, armed groups to repulse the police and military units they expected to meet in confrontations, and ambulance units to tend to the inevitable wounded.[67]

On the morning of the fourteenth, police formed cordons around St. Vladimir's, but crowds of students, railroad workers, and radical young Jews nevertheless managed to break through, divide into their units, and disrupt schools and industries still functioning.[68] Tram workers, typesetters, store clerks, mechanical workers, and telegraphists, who refused to accept communiqués not connected with the Liberation Movement, joined the strike.[69] Bands of residents roamed the streets, breaking windows, throwing stones at Cossacks, and collecting donations for those who had been wounded in confrontations with the police.[70] That evening, Governor-General Kleigel's declared martial law and arrested dozens of liberationists. Over the next several days, however, larger and larger crowds continued to pour into the streets, overwhelming police and army units.[71]

Journalists covering the scenes that unfolded in the first days of the strike were struck by residents' unanimous disgust with the political order and their desire to create a more democratic society.[72] Yet Kievans continued to debate the root cause of the people's suffering and the best way to rectify it. Liberationists blamed the tsarist authorities for the suffering of workers, national minorities, and peasants, while strong contingents within the city blamed capitalists, the officials seen as their allies, and

---

65. "O proiskhodivshikh v Kieve i Kievskoi gubernii bezporiadkakh s 18–23 oktiabria 1905," 29 October 1905, TsDIAUK, f. 274, op. 1, d. 1179, ll. 88–88ob.
66. Vice Governor Rafal'skii to Governor-General V. A. Sukhomlinov, 2 November 1905, TsDIAUK, f. 442, op. 855, d. 391, ch. 3, l. 259.
67. Ibid; also "O proiskhodivshikh v Kieve," 29 October 1905, TsDIAUK, f. 274, op. 1, d. 1179, ll. 88ob–89.
68. More than half of those arrested that morning were Jews. Vice Governor Rafal'skii to Governor-General Sukhomlinov, 5 November 1905, TsDIAUK, f. 442, op. 855, d. 391, ch. 3, ll. 260–260ob.
69. See *Kievskie otkliki*, 23 October 1905; TsDIAUK, f. 442, op. 855, d. 391, ch. 1, ll. 259–630b.
70. Rafal'skii to Sukhomlinov, 2 November 1905, TsDIAUK, f. 442, op. 855, d. 391, ch. 3, ll. 261–62; E. F. Turau, *K istorii Kievskogo pogroma* (Kiev, 1906), 16.
71. Rafal'skii to Sukhomlinov, 22 October 1905, TsDIAUK, f. 442, op. 855, d. 391, ch. 1, ll. 253–54ob; "O proiskhodivshikh v Kieve," 29 October 1905, TsDIAUK, f. 274, op. 1, d. 1179, l. 89ob.
72. "Poslednie dni v Kieve," *Kievskie otkliki*, October 23, 1905, 2.

revolutionaries for popular suffering; many continued to portray the liberal and radical wings of the Liberation Movement as expressions of Jewish interests. In response to rumors that Jews were planning to attack the city prison—where Ratner, who had been arrested on the fourteenth, was being held—agitators in markets and on city streets attempted to incite pogroms.[73] A group calling itself the Kiev Fraternal Patriotic Circle of Workers claimed that the general strike had been organized by interests inimical to the children of Rus', imploring workers to defend "Christian and patriotic" values."[74] And as strikers used violence to force those still working to leave their posts, organized bands of antiliberationist workers attacked their comrades on picket lines and in demonstrations.[75]

Outraged by Kleigel's's inability to put down the disorders, the tsar relieved the governor-general of his duties on the evening of 17 October. His replacement, V. A. Sukhomlinov (1848–1926) the commander of the city garrison, was vacationing in France at the time of his appointment; although he rushed to return to Russia, he would not arrive in Kiev for several weeks.[76] That same evening, news arrived from St. Petersburg that the tsar had issued a manifesto granting his subjects basic civil freedoms. Early on the morning of the eighteenth, as news of the October Manifesto spread around the city, residents poured into the streets.

When D. S. Margolin and Lev Brodskii arrived for a meeting of the board of directors of the first commercial school that morning, they were greeted by students clutching copies of the manifesto. In honor of the historic occasion, the men hired a boat to take the students on a Dnieper River cruise; the jubilant pupils declared themselves "young republicans" and hoisted a red flag on the boat's mast as they sang, danced, and gave speeches.[77] Meanwhile, liberationist workers, intellectuals, and professionals began convening in the city center, waving red flags, singing revolutionary hymns, and tearing *Kievlianin* out of newsstands. By midmorning, the liberationists set off for St. Vladimir's, where they found an expectant crowd of nearly ten thousand in front of the university's gates.[78] Antiliberationist workers convened at the workshop of the Southwestern Railroad and staged a counterprotest.[79]

While many who attended the public gatherings on the eighteenth expressed jubilation, depositions later collected by police also emphasize the role that violent

---

73. Vice Governor Rafal'skii to Governor-General Sukhomlinov, 22 October 1905, TsDIAUK, f. 442, op. 855, d. 391, ch. 1, l. 254 ob; Rafal'skii to Sukhomlinov, 2 November 1905, TsDIAUK, f. 442, op. 855, d. 391, ch. 3, l. 263.
74. *Kievlianin*, 4 November 1905, 4.
75. On violence employed by strikers, see TsDIAUK, f. 442, op. 855, d. 391, ch. 3, l. 261; *Die Judenpogrome in Russland* (Cologne, 1910), 2:355. On violence employed by antiliberationists, see Rafal'skii to Sukhomlinov, 2 November 1905, TsDIAUK, f. 442, op. 855, d. 391, ch. 3, l. 261.
76. V. Sukhomlinov, *Vospominaniia* (Berlin, 1924), 119–22.
77. "Eshche o progulke na parakhode," *Kievlianin*, 30 October 1905, 3; Chief of the Kiev Province Gendarme Direction to Commander of Gendarmes, 28 October 1905, GARF, f. 102, OO, 1905, d. 1350, ch. 15, l. 163.
78. "O proiskhodivshikh v Kieve," 29 October 1905, TsDIAUK, f. 274, op. 1, d. 1179, ll. 91–91ob.
79. Turau, *K istorii*, 19–20.

rhetoric and acts played in the demonstrations. Although we must read these sources with skepticism, for we do not know under what circumstances they were solicited or for what purpose they were used, they offer interesting insights into how witnesses framed and interpreted the dramatic events of that day. Bystanders described how a crowd attacked the city prison, chanting, "We don't need the tsar, we don't need the army, a militia should be formed to fight the government." After several hours, the mob managed to free Ratner and others who had been arrested in the preceding days.[80] Protesters who remained at St. Vladimir's desecrated a monument to Nicholas I across from the university and tore tsarist insignias off university buildings. Liberationists marching through city streets destroyed Russian flags and harassed bystanders who refused to doff their hats to the protesters.[81]

By noon, emotional liberationist forces and their opponents began to reassemble in front of the city duma building, the most prominent symbol of the shortcomings of the local status quo. While orators delivered speeches in the square outside the building, some protesters pushed their way inside, where they declared a "people's meeting." Some 1,500 people ultimately entered the duma, where they ripped imperial insignia off the proscenium of its main hall, destroyed portraits of four tsars, broke chairs, smashed windows, and ransacked offices.[82] Shlikhter must have entered the building during the melee, for he soon appeared on the balcony. Observers claimed to have heard him denounce the October Manifesto as inadequate and urge observers to arm themselves against the government.[83] Next, Ratner appeared on the balcony, demanding amnesty for those who had been arrested in the October disturbances; witnesses claimed that the student orator who followed him decried the tsar's manifesto as worth less than "dirty pieces of toilet paper."[84]

According to the Orthodox residents of Kiev who gave depositions, the mood of the crowd in front of the duma building had begun to shift by the afternoon as the jubilation of the morning ultimately gave way to disgust at the conduct of the protesters. Negative emotions pervade eyewitness accounts of that afternoon, as do claims that the most disturbing acts of all were perpetrated by Jews. Bystanders insisted that it was Jews who had desecrated tsarist insignia on buildings around St. Vladimir's, attacked the monument to Nicholas I, and delivered the most incendiary speeches in front of the duma; a city employee insisted that no less than three-quarters of the

---

80. Quote from "Kopiia pokazaniia meshchanina Antona Iosifova Shafranskogo ot 31 okt. 1905," TsDIAUK, f. 274, op. 1, d. 1057, l. 70b. See also "Obvinitel'nyi akt," *Kievskaia mysl'*, 7 December 1907, 4.
81. "Kopiia pokazaniia potomstvennogo dvorianina Evgeniia KORNILOVICHA ot 29 oktiabria s.g.," TsDIAUK, f. 274, op. 1, d. 1057, l. 3.
82. "Kopiia pokazaniia krest'ianina Vladimira Zinkevicha ot 28 oktiabria," ibid., ll. 1–10b; "Kopiia pokazaniia krest'ianina Nikity Ivanova Mazura," 2 November 1905, ibid., l. 9; "Kopiia pokazaniia krest'ianina Alekseia Ziabkina, 2 November 1905, ibid., l. 13; Chief of Kiev Province Gendarme Division to Commander of Gendarmes, 28 October 1905, GARF, f. 102, OO, 1905, 1350, ch. 15, l. 1610b.
83. "Kopiia pokazaniia Zinkevicha," TsDIAUK, f. 274, op. 1, d. 1057, l. 2. "Kopiia pokazaniia krest'ianina Anastasiia Mazurkevicha ot 31 oktiabria," ibid., l. 80b.
84. "Kopiia pokazaniia KORNILOVICHA," ibid., l. 4.

Concepts of Liberation

Demonstration in front of the Kiev city duma, 18 October 1905. Courtesy of TsDKFFAU.

throng that had ransacked the building consisted of Jews.[85] Some claimed to have seen Shlikhter desecrate tsarist portraits and symbols on the duma balcony, while others heard Ratner call for Nicholas II to be hanged, adding, "We gave you God, we'll give you a Tsar."[86]

85. "Kopiia pokazaniia Shafranskogo," TsDIAUK, f. 274, op. 1, d. 1057, l. 7; "Kopiia pokazaniia Zinkevicha," ibid., ll. 1–10b; "Kopiia pokazaniia Pristav Dvortsogo uchastka g. Kieva Ivana Mashira ot 5-go Noiabria," ibid., l. 14; "Kopiia pokazaniia Ziabkina," ibid., l. 12.
86. "Kopiia pokazaniia dvorianina Appoloniia Goriacheva ot 4 noiabria," TsDIAUK, f. 274, op. 1, d. 1057, l. 16; Civil Governor Savvich to Governor-General Sukhomlinov, 27 January 1906, TsDIAUK, f. 442, op. 635, d. 2, ll. 18–18ob.

Protesters on the balcony of the Kiev city duma, 18 October 1905. Courtesy of TsDKFFAU.

A. G. Shlikhter addresses the crowds assembled outside the Kiev city duma, 18 October 1905. Courtesy of TsDKFFAU.

Again, it is impossible to ascertain the veracity of these claims: they could be completely fabricated, generalizations based on the known presence of prominent Jewish activists such as Shlikhter at the duma that day, or examples of circular logic that assumed any offense to the tsar or the Orthodox faith was the work of Jews. What is most important, however, is that many who stood in the city's busiest square that day repeated these allegations. As more and more residents continued to converge on the city duma—including antiliberationist workers from the railway workshop—rumors spread that Jews had taken advantage of the chaos to insult the Orthodox East Slavs in other parts of the city as well. Some claimed that Jewish demonstrators had smoked during a celebratory reading of the Evangelists; others that they had torn a cross off a priest.[87]

As the crowd in front of the duma grew more restive, cavalry squadrons arrived, opening fire on the square.[88] Bystanders and protesters fled the scene; at this point, one witness claimed that he heard "at practically every step discussions and exclamations that Jews want to take power into their own hands, that they openly defamed the Russian tsar, and that the entire Russian people should 'beat the Jews.'"[89] Residents returned to their neighborhoods and workplaces to discuss the events of the day. A group of floor polishers gathered in front of a hotel "loudly blaming the Jews for the disorders [*smuty*]" and proclaiming, "We need to teach the Yids a lesson." A meeting of workers in the mercantile Podol district resolved to "'smash' and to place under arrest on the instructions of His Majesty the Emperor...both Jews and those Russians who instigated the recent disorders." Groups of "night watchmen, small traders, and apprentices" wandered through the city shouting, "What's that? The Yids tore up portraits of the Tsar-Batiushka? Beat them!"[90] By nightfall on the eighteenth, residents of the impoverished, peripheral neighborhood of Plossk were beating Jews and robbing stores, crying, "There's your freedom, there's your constitution and revolution, there's your crown and portrait of our Tsar." Overnight, crowds of pogromshchiki from other outlying (and heavily Jewish) districts returned to the center to ransack Jewish stores on Khreshchatik.[91] The very worker organizations and neighborhood networks to which liberationists had appealed now organized anti-Jewish violence.[92]

On the morning of the nineteenth, antiliberationist workers and intellectuals organized a "patriotic" demonstration that attracted several thousand participants.

---

87. Rafal'skii to Sukhomlinov, 2 November 1905, TsDIAUK, f. 442, op. 855, d. 391, ch. 3, l. 267.
88. "Kopiia pokazaniia KORNILOVICHA," TsDIAUK, f. 274, op. 1, d. 1057, ll. 40b–5.
89. "Kopiia pokazaniia Zinkevicha," ibid., l. 2.
90. Turau, *K istorii*, 27–28. Contemporary sources noted that railroad and telegraph workers, artisans, and unskilled workers were particularly involved in the early stages of the pogrom. See A. Linden, "Gesellschaftliche Erscheinungen in den Oktoberpogromen," in *Die Judenpogrome*, 1:331, 346; *Evreiskaia entsiklopediia* (St. Petersburg, 1913), s.v. "Pogromy v Rossii," 12:619.
91. Turau, *K istorii*, 28; Rafal'skii to Sukhomlinov, 2 November 1905, TsDIAUK, f. 442, op. 855, d. 391, ch. 3, l. 267.
92. Charters Wynn and Gerald Surh have noted that similar patterns of mobilization evolved into anti-Jewish violence in the rapidly growing southern industrial city of Ekaterinoslav. On this point, consult Charters Wynn, *Workers, Strikes, and Pogroms* (Princeton, 1992); Gerald Surh, "Ekaterinoslav City in 1905," *International Labor and Working-Class History* 64 (2003): 139–66.

Demonstrators carrying portraits of the tsar and singing patriotic hymns visited the sites that had been desecrated by liberationist protesters, including the duma building and the statue of Nicholas I. Ultimately, they gathered in front of the *Kievlianin* headquarters to cheer Pikhno.[93] At the end of the demonstration, the participants joined the continuing pogrom, attacking Jewish homes and businesses in the central city as they sang "God Save the Tsar."[94] Similar scenes were unfolding all over town. Near a Plossk market, day laborers pulled Jews out of carriages and beat them, explaining their actions as revenge against the "Yids" who "insulted the crown, who shoot and throw bombs at soldiers and Orthodox Christians."[95] Other pogromists attacked liberal newspapers and individuals known to sympathize with the Liberation Movement.[96] Terrified shop owners began displaying portraits of the tsar and Russian flags in the hope that it would spare their establishments from looters.[97]

Peripheral neighborhoods with sizable Jewish and working-class populations were ravaged by violence on the nineteenth and twentieth. Claiming that Jews had attacked monks at a nearby monastery, a crowd of one hundred—including soldiers—smashed Jewish booths at a bazaar on the city's southwestern periphery.[98] In Luk'ianovka, rumors that Jews were systematically murdering Russians—perhaps based on documented observations of Jews shooting out of windows at pogromshchiki—incited further bloodshed.[99] In a stunning deviation from the 1881 pogrom, aristocratic enclaves in Lipki and central Kiev became the other major center of the violence. As word spread that Margolin and Brodskii had celebrated with liberationist pupils on the eighteenth, angry Kiev residents headed to the city's best districts to ransack the manors of "Jewish millionaires."[100] Pogromists attacked the homes of members of the Brodskii and Gintsburg family, as well as the central Kiev apartment of D. S. Margolin's son, Arnol'd (1877–1956), a liberationist lawyer.[101]

---

93. "Uchastniki patrioticheskoi manifestatsii," *Kievskie otkliki*, 25 October 1905, 4; Report of Police Chief Tsikhotskii to Civil Governor Savvich, 26 October 1905, TsDIAUK, f. 442, op. 855, d. 391, ch. 2, ll. 121–22; "O proiskhodivshikh v Kieve," 29 October 1905, TsDIAUK, f. 274, op. 1, d. 1179, l. 970b.

94. Tsikhotskii to Savvich, 26 October 1905, TsDIAUK, f. 442, op. 855, d. 391, ch. 2, l. 1230b.

95. "Zaiavlenie Deistvitel'nogo Statskogo Sovetnika Platona Modestovicha Bakar Ego Prevoskhoditel'stvu, Gospodinu Ispravliaiushchemu dolzhnost' Kievskogo Gubernatora," 21 October 1905, TsDIAUK, f. 442, op. 855, d. 391, ch. 1, l. 311, l. 3120b.

96. "O proiskhodivshikh v Kieve," 29 October 1905, TsDIAUK, f. 274, op. 1, d. 1179, l. 970b.

97. Rafal'skii to Sukhomlinov, 2 November 1905, TsDIAUK, f. 442, op. 855, d. 391, ch. 3, l. 2670b, l. 268.

98. Vice Governor Tsikhotskii to Civil Governor Savvich, 20 October 1905, TsDIAUK, f. 442, op. 855, d. 391, ch. 2, ll. 179–830b; Pikhno, *V osade*, 50.

99. Vice Governor Rafal'skii to Governor-General Sukhomlinov, 21 October 1905, TsDIAUK, f. 442, op. 855, d. 391, ch. 1, l. 183.

100. Chief of the Kiev Provincial Gendarme Division to Commander of Gendarmes, 28 October 1905, GARF, f. 102, OO, 1905, d. 1350, ch. 15, l. 163. Four angry (Gentile) teachers at the school later wrote a letter to *Kievlianin*, blaming Brodskii and Margolin for the chaotic events of that day. See the letter to the editor printed in *Kievlianin*, 29 October 1905, 4.

101. D. S. Margolin to Governor-General Sukhomlinov, 20 October 1905, TsDIAUK, f. 442, op. 855, d. 391, ch. 1, l. 179; also Rafal'skii to Sukhomlinov, 21 October 1905, ibid., l. 178. "Kievskii okruzhnyi sud: Delo Grigoriia Brodskogo," *Pravo* 48 (30 November 1907): 2658–60.

As early as the eighteenth, Luchitskii and the Polytechnical Institute's liberationist professors attempted to stop the violence. Rebuffed by the commander of the Kiev garrison—who was standing in for Sukhomlinov until the new governor-general arrived—they turned to Witte for help.[102] The next day Witte demanded that the local authorities halt the "pogrom against innocent people in Kiev."[103] The garrison commander finally ordered Kiev citizens and security forces to halt the violence, but large segments of both ignored his order.[104] Violence continued until the twenty-first, when antiliberationist railroad workers pulled Jews off trains and beat them, killing nine and injuring dozens. Gradually, however, drunks and criminals grew more prominent in crowds that had once been dominated by workers; with many of the prime looting targets already destroyed, pogromists scattered by train to smaller district cities, where they continued their rampage.[105]

On the twenty-first, Lev Brodskii met with head of the city police, whom he begged to halt the mayhem.[106] By the twenty-second, the very police and gendarme divisions that had allowed the pogrom to continue unabated for three days were fanning out across the city looking for Brodskii's billiard cues, which had been stolen during the chaos.[107] Kiev's deadliest outburst of violence yet had finally come to an end. Pogromists had destroyed 1,800 homes and businesses, killed twenty-seven, injured three hundred, and incurred 10.5 million rubles' worth of damage; the Kiev pogrom was the costliest outbreak of street violence in the entire empire in 1905.[108] In the words of a reporter covering the devastated city, "Not a single (Jewish) store, warehouse, or office remained untouched."[109]

---

102. Telegraph from unknown Kiev bureaucrat to S. Iu. Witte, 18 October 1905, GARF, f. 102, OO, 1905, d. 1350, ch. 15, l. 139; *Die Judenpogrome*, 2:360, 362.

103. E. F. Turau to N.V. Molchanovskii, 28 November 1905, TsDIAUK, f. 442, op. 855, d. 531, l. 3.

104. "Ob"iavlenie zhiteliam g. Kieva," 19 October 1905, TsDIAUK, f. 442, op. 855, d. 391, ch. 1, l. 92; telegraphs in TsDIAUK, f. 442, op. 855, d. 391, ch. 1, ll. 96–111. Compare the apathetic attitude of Kiev officials toward the violence—and the lack of a strong authority to prevent it in the absence of Sukhomlinov—with the situation in Kharkov, where the authorities made clear that pogroms would not be tolerated: Michael F. Hamm, "Jews and Revolution in Kharkiv," in Smele and Heywood, *Russian Revolution*, 156–76.

105. Chief of the Kiev Province Gendarme Direction to Commander of Gendarmes, 28 October 1905, GARF, f. 102, OO, 1905, d. 1350, ch. 15, l. 1640b; Civil Governor Savvich to Governor-General Sukhomlinov, 8 December 1905, TsDIAUK, f. 442, op. 855, d. 391, ch. 4, ll. 183–830b; Chief of the Southwest Railroad to Governor-General's Chancery, 2 December 1905, TsDIAUK, f. 442, op. 855, d. 391, ch. 4, l. 127.

106. Telegraph of Director of the Political Division Rachkovskii to Civil Governor Savvich, 21 October 1905, TsDIAUK, f. 442, op. 855, d. 391, ch. 1, l. 151. On the changing demographic of the pogromshchiki over the course of the violence, "Spisok: Lits prinimavshikh glavnoe uchastie v antievreiskikh bezporiadkakh, prisshedshikh v g. Kieve 18, 19, i 20-go oktiabria 1905 goda," TsDIAUK, f. 442, op. 855, d. 391, ch. 3, ll. 100–102; Rafal'skii to Sukhomlinov, 2 November 1905, TsDIAUK, f. 442, op. 855, d. 391, ch. 3, l. 267.

107. Governor-General's Chancery to Judicial Investigator of the Kiev First District, 22 October 1905, TsDIAUK, f. 442, op. 855, d. 391, ch. 1, ll. 168–69.

108. These figures are from *Die Judenpogrome*, 1:209. Another source cites 60 dead and 369 wounded. See *American Jewish Year Book 5667* (Philadelphia, 1906), 50–51. More were killed and wounded in Odessa's October pogrom, but the monetary value of the damage there was substantially less than in Kiev.

109. "Khronika Oktiabr'skikh dnei," *Prilozhenie k "Pravu"* (November 1905): 145.

From Ideological Divides to Party Organizations

In the aftermath of the pogrom, Little Russian activists and antiliberal duma deputies continued to capitalize on the divides that had coalesced in 1905, working them into their well-developed narratives of popular suffering and resistance. In the pages of *Kievlianin*, Pikhno described the violence as the revenge of a people whose "national sensibility" had been insulted by foreign populations that had treated them as slaves.[110] Iuzefovich and other Kiev residents who shared their opinions with *Kievlianin* expressed outrage that the liberationists who now mourned Jewish suffering in the pogrom expressed little concern for the Orthodox simple folk whom Jews had allegedly exploited for centuries.[111]

Antiliberal populists in the city duma presented the pogrom as a justifiable act of national resistance by "truly Russian people" against Jewish capitalists and revolutionaries. In the aftermath of the pogrom, a familiar cast of deputies associated with the New Duma Party and Little Russian lobby (Golubiatnikov, Levitskii, N. V. Storozhenko, Dobrynin, and Iasnogurskii) expanded what had begun as a coalition of antiliberal merchants and professionals from the peripheral neighborhoods of Luk'ianovka, Lybed', and Plossk into a parliamentary majority. This coalition passed resolutions insisting that "rich Jews" rather than city taxpayers should pay to repair the damage incurred in the pogrom and urging the children of Rus' to continue their struggle against their putative oppressors.[112] The creation of this bloc prompted Luchitskii, Trubetskoi, and several other delegates who had allied themselves with the Liberation Movement to resign from the body. However, their resignation only gave the "truly Russian" forces in the duma more power. In November, deputies issued a manifesto promising that "ancient Kiev," "the mother of Russian cities," would redeem all "Holy Rus'" from the threats posed by its enemies and would reclaim for the Orthodox East Slavs the "rights" that they deserved in their native land.[113]

As 1905 drew to a close, the opponents of the Liberation Movement continued their efforts to court new supporters and build political coalitions—a tasks only rendered more urgent by impending elections to the imperial Duma, to be held in early 1906. At Iuzefovich's urging, the Russian Gathering drew up a manifesto that hailed the convocation of the Duma as an opportunity for the masses to attain true popular representation; the platform also insisted that the new institution should work to realize a

---

110. Editorial of 19 October 1905, reprinted in Pikhno, *V osade*, 48–49.
111. B. M. Iuzefovich's letter to *Echo de Paris*, dated 28 October 1905, in his *Politicheskie pis'ma* (Kiev, 1908), ch. II, vyp. 1, 18–19; "Ochevidets Mikhail Khanenko," *Kievlianin*, 27 October 1905, 3.
112. The quote is from "Zasedanie dumy," *Kievlianin*, 29 October 1905, 4. For further examples of the duma's treatment of the pogrom as a liberating force and the Jews themselves as the guilty party, see "Opredelenie Goroskoi Dumy," 20 October 1905, DAK, f. 163, op. 8, d. 11, l. 1046; l. 1050; "Pis'mo glasnym kievskoi gorodskoi dumy," *Kievlianin*, 4 November 1905, 3; "Opredelenie gorodskoi dumy," DAK, f. 163, op. 8, d. 11, l. 1075; "Orgiia dumskoi sotnii," *Kievskie novosti*, 8 November 1905, 3.
113. The quote is from "Zaiavlienie kievskikh glasnykh," *Kievlianin*, 30 November 1905, 2. On the resignations, see "Vne partii," *Kievskie novosti*, 17 November 1905, 3; *Kievlianin*, 16 November 1905, 3.

"Russia for Russians" and to halt the "Jews' attempts at world domination."[114] Iuzefovich and other Russian Gathering members played a key role in incorporating other antiliberationist parties, including the Russian Brotherhood and a local branch of the all-imperial Monarchist Party. These parties, which appealed primarily to Orthodox merchants, retired military officers, and civil servants, expressed support for the October reforms and the new parliamentary system but insisted that they must not serve as license for non-Slavs to dominate Russia or to supplant the religious and cultural traditions of the children of Rus'.[115]

Other antiliberationist parties catered to lesser merchants, artisans, and even peasants and workers, pressing for the expansion of credit, land banks, and agricultural and practical education, which they argued would both uplift ordinary people and protect their culture from threatening alien forces. By November, one such group, the Party of Legal Order, which was organized by Kiev duma deputy A. I. Liubinskii, had unified seven hundred "truly Russian" residents opposed to both "revolutionary and reactionary parties."[116] The workers' circles organized by the Russian Gathering remained active, organizing strikebreaking actions and political meetings in outlying districts that called on workers "to fulfill their duty in relation to the faith, fatherland, Tsar, and law" in a "Christian and patriotic" spirit.[117] The Union of Russian People (SRN), a group dominated by merchants, nobles, and bureaucrats and known for its archreactionary views in other locales, attracted strong support from Kiev's populist politicians, including Storozhenko, Iasnogurskii, and Golubiatnikov. With their help, it established a healthy proletarian following as well, creating a network of voluntary associations aimed at the working class and founding at least one formal union, the Union of Russian Workers, which pressed for social reforms but also railed against liberationists and Jews.[118]

Deeply influenced by the populist concerns of Little Russian activists and antiliberal duma deputies, Kiev's antiliberationist parties evolved in a different direction than many other groups in the Russian empire that rejected both liberalism and revolutionary upheaval. Elsewhere in the empire, right-wing groups tended to represent the interests of landed nobles who agitated for a return to the pre-1905 status quo; even organizations that attained a more variegated, urban following, such as the SRN, formally rejected the legitimacy of the imperial Duma and party politics, rightly pointing

---

114. Quotes from brochure in GARF, f. 102, OO, 1906, II-otdelenie, d. 186, l. 140b; l. 150b.
115. See "Ustav 'russkogo bratstva,'" 1906, TsDIAUK, f. 442, op. 636, d. 647, ch. I, l. 79; *Ustav Kievskoi Russkoi Monarkhicheskoi Partii* (Kiev, 1906).
116. "Sobranie chlenov partiia pravogo poriadka," *Kievlianin*, 22 November 1905, 2; N. D. Noskov and I. I. Ivaniukov, *Okhranitel'nye i reaktsionnye partii v Rossii* (St. Petersburg, 1906), 8. On the party's local membership and activities, see "Ustav kievskoi partii Pravovogo poriadka," 1906, TsDIAUK, f. 442, op. 636, d. 647, ch. I, ll. 59–65. By the fall of 1905, the term "truly Russian" had become a common catchphrase that signified opposition to the revolution and devotion to the throne and Orthodox Church.
117. *Kievlianin*, 4 November 1905, 4.
118. Rawson, *Russian Rightists*, 101, 250–5n35.

out that they contradicted the foundations of the autocratic system.[119] Kiev antiliberals shared with the Russian right an opposition to the revolution and equal rights, a belief in the fundamental territorial integrity of the empire, and a devotion to the Orthodox Church. But unlike many on the right, they also welcomed the arrival of mass politics and professed progressive views on social issues. Even as Kiev's antiliberationist forces attempted to conflate the revolutionaries calling for social change with the city's capitalist elite, smearing both as the representatives of Jewish interests, they usurped the social platform of the political left, touting their reformist agenda and its benefits for the working classes.[120]

Kiev's "truly Russian" parties had used the turmoil of 1905 to their advantage, peddling to broad segments of the urban population a political program to claim Russia for the Orthodox East Slavs. But Kiev's Russian nationalists themselves often struggled to define the features that identified the Russian people. Some political parties embraced the ethnonational, even racial, understanding of belonging promoted by earlier generations of Little Russian activists. The Kiev chapter of the Monarchist Party, for example, viewed women as valued members of the national collective, welcoming them into the ranks of the party despite the fact that they remained deprived of the franchise; however, it explicitly banned Jews (even those who had converted to Orthodoxy) from its ranks, casting them as irredeemable enemies of the Rus' people.[121] Other antiliberationist parties, by contrast, defined "Russianness" as a purely ideological position, characterized by opposition to cosmopolitanism, socialism, and capitalism and devotion to the tsar, Orthodox Church, and interests of the narod. There is no evidence that any of Kiev's party organizations banned Poles (who just a generation earlier had been portrayed as the most incorrigible enemies of the Orthodox masses) from their ranks; indeed, there are some indications that substantial numbers of the city's Polish population sympathized with the antiliberationist forces.[122] The debate about how to define "true Russians" would intensify in the years to come and would ultimately create great controversy within the movement.

Unwilling to allow the antiliberationist forces to monopolize mass political mobilization, liberationists, too, created formal party structures and continued their efforts to influence urban public opinion. In November 1905, local activists founded a Kiev division of the all-imperial Kadet Party, whose platform called for a constitutional democracy protected by an equal rights regime that guaranteed "personal

---

119. See, for example, V. A. Gringmut, "Est' li v Rossii partii?," in *Sobranie statei* (Moscow, 1908), 1:11–15; also "Organizatsiia monarkhicheskoi partii," in ibid., 3:156–61.
120. On the unusual profile of the right in the southwest, see Rawson, *Russian Rightists*, 99–103; Omel'ianchuk, *Chernosotennoe dvizhenie*; Mikhail Loukianov, "Conservatives and 'Renewed Russia,'" *Slavic Review* 61, no. 4 (2002): 770.
121. *Ustav Kievskoi Russkoi Monarkhicheskoi Partii*, 2.
122. Polish nationalist activists bitterly complained of the "indifference" of local Poles to the liberationist cause. See "Listovki Korporatsii studentov poliakov Kievskogo universiteta i politekhniki," September 1905, TsDIAUK, f. 838, op. 5, d. 175; Civil Governor Savvich to Governor-General Kleigel's, 4 October 1905, GARF, f. 102, OO, 1905, d. 3, ch. 37, l. 31.

and property rights for Poles, Jews, and all other separate groups of the population."[123] Defending the accommodationist attitudes that had long prevailed among the urban beau monde, the party leadership also embodied the city's diversity. It united liberal Ukrainophiles such as V. P. Naumenko, Luchitskii, and B. A. Kistiakovskii (who had recently returned to Kiev from years living in Germany); Jewish elites, including D. S. Margolin, his son Arnol'd, and the crown rabbi of Kiev, S. A. Lur'e; and Orthodox landed nobles and commercial elites, such as Trubetskoi and G. E. Afanas'ev, the head of the Kiev branch of the state bank.[124] Luchitskii was chosen to represent the Kadet Party—and Kiev's liberationist movement at large—at the November all-imperial Congress of City and Zemstvo Activists, which demanded "full citizenship rights" for Jews and self-governance privileges for other national minorities.[125]

The radical wing of the liberation movement, too, continued to expand its party organization and to struggle for political power. In late October, Polytechnical Institute professors, Union of Unions activists, and Bolshevik and Menshevik worker-intellectuals from the city's largest industrial plants formed a soviet in Kiev. Intended to coordinate the actions of unions in preparation for a new general strike, the soviet urged proletarians to maintain their solidarity, describing anti-Jewish sentiment as a tool that reactionaries used to divide and dominate the working classes.[126] Although the soviet did not, as its leaders had hoped, unite the entire city's workforce, it achieved considerable influence in the Shuliavka neighborhood on Kiev's western periphery—home to many large factories and the Polytechnical Institute. There workers declared the neighborhood a "republic" and worked with soviet leaders to press for further social reforms and political concessions.[127]

Courting the Masses

The new parties and organizations that had emerged to defend the Liberation Movement in November emboldened the movement's supporters, who had been deeply disheartened by October's pogrom. On 18 November, after days of SD incitement of troops, the lower ranks of a pontoon battalion housed in Pechersk left their posts. The mutineers headed to the Luk'ianovka district, where they fraternized with workers at the Southwestern Railroad's machine-building plant.[128] Together, the workers and soldiers staged a spontaneous demonstration, which attracted nearly two thousand

123. I. D. B., *Sbornik programm politicheskikh partii* (Moscow, 1906), 96.
124. "Iz zhizni politicheskikh partii v Kieve," *Kievskii vestnik*, 8 January 1906, 5.
125. "Rezoliutsii, priniatye chastnym soveshchaniem zemskikh i gorodskikh deiatelei 6–13 noiabria sego goda," TsDIAUK, f. 442, op. 855, d. 537, ll. 22–23.
126. V. Manilov, *Kievskii sovet rabochikh deputatov v 1905 g.* (Kiev, 1926), 5–7, 11.
127. F. Alekseev, *Spohady pro 1905 rik u Kyevi* (Kiev, 1930), 28.
128. Chief of the Kiev Garrison Gendarme Command to Chief of the Kiev Province Gendarme Direction, 19 November 1905, TsDIAUK, f. 274, op. 1, d. 1179, l. 109; Chief of the Boulevard Police District to Chief of the Kiev Provincial Gendarme Direction, 19 November 1905, ibid., l. 116.

participants, including other laborers and soldiers who had walked off the job.[129] After their impromptu rally, the protesters wandered around the city, smashing shop windows and waving red flags until they were dispersed by nonmutinying regiments, which killed more than a dozen and wounded hundreds.[130] Over the next several days, steamboat and railroad workers declared three-day sympathy strikes.[131]

The new round of unrest, however, only galvanized Kiev residents who opposed liberationists' calls for equal rights. Workers roamed the streets of Shuliavka, the stronghold of the Kiev soviet, attacking both Jews and liberationists; fettered as much by worker resistance as by official repression, the soviet disbanded in December 1905, and its leaders who were not arrested fled Kiev.[132] Protesters camped outside the homes of liberationist professors, whom they harassed and threatened; Orthodox merchants denounced their elected elder for expressing his willingness to help Jewish merchants recoup the losses they had suffered in the pogrom and for cooperating with an imperial investigation that sought to elucidate the cause of the violence.[133]

Shop floors, city streets, and private clubs hosted impromptu political meetings where residents opposed to both capitalist exploitation and what many branded the "Jewish revolution" discussed politics and recorded their ideological professions. In November 1905 alone, residents of a single street—field doctors, working-class Poles, elders of the merchant estate, St. Vladimir's employees, and city homeowners—gathered to draw up manifestos declaring their opposition to the Liberation Movement and their dedication to "truly Russian" values.[134] Local residents sent hundreds of missives to *Kievlianin* to express the profound emotions that the revolution had summoned up. One correspondent drew graphic cartoons demonstrating how Jewish interests supposedly had "ravaged" the purity of Rus' traditions: one depicted Jewish vampires sucking the blood of the heroes of East Slavic civilization—Ol'ga, Vladimir, Cyril and Methodius, and the tsars and tsarinas of imperial Russia—until nothing was left but skeletons. Another showed "Jews: bankers, merchants, and factory owners" clutching bags full of "Russian capital" and ravaging a naked mother Russia.[135] Others

---

129. Colonel Kovalevskii to Chief of the Kiev Province Gendarme Direction, 20 November 1905, TsDIAUK, f. 274, op. 1, d. 1179, ll. 120–21.

130. Chief of the Boulevard Police District to Chief of the Kiev Provincial Gendarme Direction, 19 November 1905, ibid., l. 116–1160b.

131. Civil Governor Savvich to Governor-General Sukhomlinov, 1 December 1905, TsDIAUK, f. 442, op. 855, d. 391, ch. 4, l. 125–125ob.

132. On worker violence: Manilov, *Kievskii sovet*, 32–33; Civil Governor Savvich to Governor-General Sukhomlinov, 31 December 1905, TsDIAUK, f. 442, op. 855, d. 391, ch. 5, l. 163. On the end of the Soviet: Manilov, *Kievskii sovet*, 52–55; telegram of Kiev Civil Governor to Director of Department of Police, 26 December 1905, TsDIAUK, f. 442, op. 855, d. 391, ch. 5, l. 193.

133. On protests outside the home of liberationist professors, see minutes of 8 November 1905 meeting of the Council of Professors of the Polytechnical Institute, DAK, f. 18, op. 1, d. 557, ll. 154–154ob. On conflict among the merchants, *Kievlianin*, 25 November 1905, 4; *Kievlianin*, 1 December 1905, 4.

134. See, for example, *Kievlianin*, 25 November 1905, 4; *Kievlianin*, 26 November 1905, 4; *Kievlianin*, 27 November 1905, 3; "Iz pisem v redaktsiiu," *Kievlianin*, 8 November 1905, 2.

135. Contained in TsDIAUK, f. 296, op. 1, d. 2, ll. 367–367ob.

expressed pride rather than fear, crediting Pikhno and his paper for bravely defending the children of Rus' from the "cowardly species that follows the bund"; a woman portrayed *Kievlianin* as a school of civic values, arguing that its coverage had helped her understand what it meant to be a "truly Russian citizen [*grazhdanka*]."[136] Although some scholars have sought to portray 1905 as a passing complication in interethnic relations,[137] many of those who came to identify with the Russian cause over the course of the year had a different perspective on the matter, insisting that they were witnessing the dawn of a new era in which the Orthodox narod and its defenders had engaged inimical foreign forces in a struggle that would prove decisive.

Imperial officials expressed mixed opinions about the growing influence of "truly Russian" mass politics in the southwest. Some celebrated the potential of antiliberationists to help the state roll back the revolution. MVD functionaries authorized selected members of the SRN to carry concealed weapons, treating its armed members as a loyalist paramilitary force.[138] Tsar Nicholas II welcomed SRN members to court on several occasions. In spite of laws that barred those in state service from joining political parties, high-ranking officials, including Kiev Civil Governor P. S. Savvich, actively participated in "truly Russian" organizations.[139]

Other officials expressed concern about the destabilizing potential of Russian nationalist politics. As commentators continued to point out, mass political activity—even that which claimed to defend the state—contradicted the very foundations of the autocratic system.[140] The violent rhetoric and acts that accompanied the emergence of the Russian cause in the southwest also became cause for concern. As early as the spring of 1905, Minister of the Interior A. G. Bulygin had warned that "the calculated incitement of certain segments of society against others" could "call forth in the ignorant masses serious ferment and result in havoc."[141] The October pogrom had not only fulfilled Bulygin's prophecy but also laid bare the ineffectiveness of command and control structures. In early November, Minister of the Interior P. N. Durnovo informed Sukhomlinov that an independent investigation of the October events would be undertaken by Senator E. F. Turau.[142] Turau's report, released later that month, portrayed the violent outburst as a direct result of Jews' revolutionary activities. But it also condemned the actions of local officials in no uncertain terms,

---

136. Ol'ga Chubina to D. I. Pikhno, 20 December 1905, TsDIAUK, f. 296, op. 1, d. 27, l. 149. There are dozens of letters in this file that express similar sentiments.
137. For example, Meir, "Jews, Ukrainians, and Russians," 475–501; Victoria Khiterer, "Arnold Davidovich Margolin," *Revolutionary Russia* 18, no. 2 (December 2005): 145–67.
138. Internal memorandum of Ministry of Internal Affairs, 28 February 1906, GARF, f. 102, OO, 1905, op. 316, d. 999, ch. 39, ll. 5–50b.
139. "Spisok Chlenov Russkogo sobraniia s prilozheniem istoricheskogo ocherka sobraniia," GARF, f. 102, OO, 1906, II-otdelenie, d. 186, l. 83. Numerous state employees belonged to the Kiev division of the Russian Brotherhood as well: see "Russkoe Bratstvo v gor. Kieve," GARF, f. 102, OO, 1906, II-otdelenie, d. 430.
140. For example, see the anonymous letter to *Kievlianin*, 3 January 1906, 3.
141. Quote from circular of A. G. Bulygin to governors, 14 April 1905, GARF, f. 102, OO, 1905, d. 2144, l. 11.
142. Telegraph from P. N. Durnovo to Sukhomlinov, 4 November 1905, TsDIAUK, f. 442, op. 855, d. 391, ch. 3, l. 20.

noting that army and police forces stood by in some cases and actively encouraged the pogrom in others.[143] In the aftermath of the report, the officials whom the report criticized—including the vice governor, the city police chief, and the commander of a local army corps—were forced to resign from their posts.[144]

Taking his cues from his St. Petersburg superiors, Sukhomlinov made clear his intention to reassert his control over both the liberationists and their rivals once he arrived in Kiev.[145] He summoned the editors of all the city's newspapers to his office and demanded that they adopt a more moderate tone on the Jewish question; by December, he had outlawed public meetings and the possession of weapons by private citizens.[146] These actions, however, did not stop the flood of complaints and denunciations by "truly Russian" activists inundating his office, many of which rebuked the authorities in the harshest terms for their negligence in responding to alleged threats. A letter to Sukhomlinov replete with grammatical mistakes and misspellings warned the governor-general that "the YIDS and their rented Rusian [sic] studentz [sic]" were planning a "big revolt" for New Year's and claimed that Count Witte—the longtime patron of Kiev's multiethnic elite—planned to install a Jew as the "president" of Russia. Condemning the tsar and his ministers for failing to protect the narod from its supposed enemies, the writer begged Sukhomlinov to intervene.[147] Another correspondent to the governor-general claimed that local officials had granted Jews special rights to free association and permitted them to consolidate power over the entire southwestern region, "from the bureaucracy to the last little stall along the high road." These special privileges that officials had supposedly granted to Jews, he argued, only rendered the obstacles that Orthodox believers faced in their social, economic, and political lives more "insurmountable."[148] As Sukhomlinov had begun to discover, mass political processes would prove difficult to restrain once they had been activated.

::

Over the course of 1905, the struggle for control of Kiev and its future moved into the city's streets. The rise of an all-imperial campaign for popular liberation—and the concomitant breakdown of official authority—offered city residents from all walks of life an opportunity to define the meaning of liberation for themselves. The year 1905 saw the culmination of the social and ideological mobilization processes initiated by

---

143. Turau, *K istorii*.
144. See the correspondence between the Ministry of Internal Affairs and the governor-general's office contained in TsDIAUK, f. 442, op. 855, d. 533.
145. "Sukhomlinov ob"iavliaet zhiteliam g. Kieva," 27 October 1905, TsDIAUK, f. 442, op. 855, d. 391, ch. 2, l. 132.
146. Memorandum of Governor-General Sukhomlinov, 5 November 1905, in TsDIAUK, f. 442, op. 855, d. 391, ch. 3, ll. 21–22ob; "Ob"iavlenie zhiteliam g. Kieva," 13 December 1905, TsDIAUK, f. 442, op. 855, d. 391, ch. 4, l. 290.
147. Anonymous letter, 5 December 1905, TsDIAUK, f. 442, op. 855, d. 391, ch. 4, ll. 144–45 ob.
148. N. M. Poriadinskii to Governor-General Sukhomlinov, 5 November 1905, TsDIAUK, f. 442, op. 855, d. 391, ch. 3, l. 250b.

the debates between Kiev's capitalist city fathers and their populist critics, as urban residents gathered to create organizations, stage demonstrations, compose petitions, and talk about politics. But this flurry of civic activity also produced distinctly uncivil ideas and even violence.

In the winter of 1905–6, Kiev residents excitedly prepared for the elections to the imperial Duma, which would be elected by the broadest franchise in Russia's history and would offer many city residents the opportunity to participate in a formal political process for the first time in their lives. As we shall see, however, the continued democratization of politics would only deepen the crisis in the southwest, intensifying the conflict between liberationists struggling to create a state governed by the rule of law and their opponents, who remained determined to liberate the children of Rus' from their putative oppressors.

PART THREE

Forging a Russian Nation

6 Electoral Politics and Regional Governance

THE POLITICAL SYSTEM that emerged from 1905 permitted the ideological conflicts that had polarized Kiev residents during the revolutionary upheaval to harden into sharp partisan divides. Liberationists and their "truly Russian" opponents continued to debate each other on university campuses, on shop floors, and in city streets, but they also enjoyed a new venue in which to compete: multiparty electoral campaigns in which many peasants and workers could vote. This chapter follows Kiev's warring political camps through three hotly contested elections in 1906–7—two to the new imperial Duma and one to the Kiev city duma.

Kiev's liberationist forces focused on mobilizing a multiethnic coalition in defense of equal rights. Liberationist activities reflected the long-standing cosmopolitanism of Kiev's capitalist elite—no accident, since many industrialists played a leading role in the movement—but they also laid bare the city fathers' elitist biases. The antiliberationist bloc, by contrast, ran on a platform of exclusion, questioning the ability of Poles and especially Jews to live peacefully with the Orthodox East Slavs. At the same time, it relentlessly touted its populist credentials, highlighting its devotion to improving the plight of workers and peasants and to protecting and promoting the Little Russian culture of the borderlands. By 1906, the "truly Russian" coalition had forged a strong, cross-class political coalition in the city of Kiev; soon thereafter it began to look beyond city limits, organizing meetings and voluntary associations to popularize its views in the countryside. In 1907, it won its first electoral victories outside Kiev city.

In a few short years, Kiev's "truly Russian" bloc had achieved remarkable successes. A small but committed group of urban activists, primarily professionals and intellectuals, had begun to assemble a mass-appeal coalition that counted peasants, workers, and nobles, urbanites and rural dwellers among its members. "Truly Russian" leaders proved remarkably adept at navigating Russia's new mass political system, effectively using the press, modern technology, and political spectacle to unify and mobilize voters. But as the antiliberationist movement acquired influence in the southwest, it also grew more radical: some of its members praised violence as a redemptive force, insisted that Poles and Jews be completely marginalized from imperial society, and even criticized the local and imperial authorities for their alleged failures to protect the Orthodox East Slavs from their enemies. The radicalization of the movement concerned some of its leaders, who insisted that the bloc should steer a more moderate course in order to consolidate the broadest popular following. It also created a dilemma for imperial officials. Was the southwest's "truly Russian" coalition a reliable partner of a state struggling to roll back the revolution? Or did the immoderate views and violent rhetoric of many of its members in fact undermine tsarist authority?

The First Attempts at Party Organization

Although antigovernment sentiment remained widespread in early 1906, the power of the radical left was compromised by mass arrests and the Social Democrats' decision to boycott the elections to the imperial Duma.[1] The Kadets moved to the left to fill the void, forging an alliance with the SRs, and quickly established themselves as the leading voice in local liberationist politics. The former hosted several large meetings in Kiev at which party activists called for land to be expropriated from nobles and redistributed to peasants.[2] However, the party remained most closely identified with the campaign for equal rights: the effort to abolish the discriminatory legal regime faced by Jews remained a top priority—and an effective voter mobilization technique. Kiev crown rabbi Lur'e and his fellow Kadet A. D. Margolin (the son of the steamboat industrialist and the liberal lawyer whose apartment had been ransacked in the October pogrom) organized large meetings of voters in Kiev's peripheral neighborhoods and in provincial synagogues at which orators denounced legal discrimination against the Jews. Speakers also encouraged Kiev's Jewish voters—who constituted more than half of the electorate in some urban districts—to support the Kadets, which they characterized as the one "organized and active party pursuing a radical solution to the Jewish question."[3]

Although the status of Jews in Russian society remained a chief concern of local liberationists, by early 1906, the status of the empire's other ethnic minorities had begun to garner more attention. Over the course of 1905, Hrushevs'kyi had published articles in the European press that presented the struggle for Ukrainian autonomy as an inseparable component of the broader Liberation Movement. Arguing that the Ukrainian people had been victimized as much by Russia's "bureaucratic and centralizing" policies as by the szlachta, he complained that the imperial authorities treated every "manifestation of Ukrainian national consciousness" in the Russian empire as a

---

1. Telegram of Governor P. S. Savvich to Ministry of Internal Affairs, 3 January 1906, GARF, f. 102, OO, 1906, I-oe otdelenie, d. 20, ch. 58, l. 13; Chief of the Kiev Okhrana Division, 16 January 1906, GARF, f. 102, OO, 1906, I-oe otdelenie, d. 25, ch. 57, ll. 5–8.
2. "U Kyivi," *HD*, 31 December 1905, 4; "U Kyevi," *HD*, 9 January 1906, 3.
3. The quote is from "Sobranie izbiratelei evreev v lybedskom uchastke," *Kievskie otgoloski zhizni*, 17 March 1906, 3. For more on the operations and platforms of these groups, see "Evrei vsekh partii, soediniaites' dlia dostizheniia grazhdanskikh prav!" DAKO f. 2, op. 41, d. 222b, l. 2300b; "Sredi evreev," *KV*, 20 January 1906, 4; *Khronika evreiskoi zhizni*, 21 February 1906, 27.

"criminal phenomenon."[4] By the winter of 1905–6, many of the right bank's more radical Ukrainian nationalists, who had kept their distance from the all-imperial campaign for equal rights earlier in the year, had begun to press liberationists to pursue a satisfactory resolution to the "Ukrainian question" as well. Hrynchenko, Chykalenko, and other left-wing elements of local hromada organizations joined with Hrushevs'kyi and RUP activists to form the Ukrainian Democratic-Radical Party (UDRP), which called for a federalist, parliamentary order that would offer self-governance rights to the Ukrainian people.[5] The Spilka, an illegal party that merged socialist and Ukrainian nationalist ideas, was also gaining traction in the countryside of both the left and right banks.[6]

Ukrainian activists used the breakdown of imperial control over the press that accompanied the upheaval of 1905–6 to their benefit. By early 1906, the authorities had stopped enforcing the Ems decree, which offered Chykalenko the opportunity to launch *Hromads'ka dumka (Social Thought)*, the right bank's first Ukrainian-language daily. The paper expressed special interest in raising the status of the Ukrainian language, arguing that peasants should enjoy the right to use their native tongue—rather than the "Moscow dialect" spoken by the "pans" of the imperial bureaucracy—in school and in administrative offices.[7] In its writings on history and politics, the paper popularized Hrushevs'kyi's vision of a distinct Ukrainian nation that could be traced to Kievan Rus' and lamented this nation's suffering under both Polish and Russian rule. Although it celebrated the accomplishments of the Liberation Movement thus far, the paper insisted that the Ukrainian people would never truly be liberated until they secured further cultural and political autonomy.[8]

A new law promulgated in March 1906 forbade officials from refusing to register associations or political groups unless it could be proven that they promoted internecine conflict or threatened "social order or state security."[9] This measure, too, benefited Ukrainian nationalist activists, who now founded their own clubs and cultural associations. They convened the Ukrainian Club in Kiev, which organized plays and lectures in the Ukrainian language as well as dances and excursions that showcased the right-bank's unique culture.[10] Hrynchenko and M. V. Lysenko, a long-time Hromada member, established a Kiev chapter of the Ukrainian cultural club Prosvita, which soon would have affiliates on both the right and left banks. It published books,

---

4. M. Grushevskii, "Ukrainskii vopros," in *Osvobozhdenie Rossii i ukrainskii vopros* (St. Petersburg, 1907), 17, 21. Indeed, in this article, the historian also described the disbanding of the Cyril and Methodius Society as a "pogrom"—a clear effort to liken Ukrainian national concerns to the plight of the Jews.
5. "S"ezd ukrainskoi radikal'no-demokraticheskoi partii," *Kievlainin*, 6 December 1905, 1–2.
6. See "Ukrainskaia revoliutsionnaia organizatsiia Spilka," GARF, f. 124, op. 44, d. 246.
7. The quote is from "Iakoi nam treba shkoli," *HD*, 5 January 1906, 2; see also *HD*, 4 January 1906, 1.
8. For example, "Opovidannia z ukrains'koi starovyny," *HD*, 7 March 1906, 2; and a compilation of essays serialized in *Hromad'ska dumka* in the spring of 1906: B. Hrynchenko, *Iak zhyv ukrains'kyi narod* (Kiev, 1906).
9. "Spravka," RGIA, f. 1284, op. 187, d. 260, l. 4.
10. "Ustav Kievskogo Ukrainskogo Obshchestvennogo Sobraniia/Statut Kyivskoho Ukrains'koho Klubu," TsDIAUK, f. 275, op, 1, d. 2700, l. 14.

established a library and bookstore, and distributed stipends to needy students, all in an effort to promote "the development of Ukrainian culture and...the education of the Ukrainian nation in its native tongue."[11]

The southwest's Polish patriots benefited from less stringent censorship and the new laws on voluntary associations as well. Having taken a relatively quiescent stance in 1905, when the all-imperial campaign for equal rights and the intense debate about the Jewish question had all but subsumed other aspects of the liberationist agenda, patriotic Poles now mobilized to defend their national interests. In January 1906 a Volynian landowner launched the southwest's first Polish-language daily, *Dziennik Kijowski (Kiev Daily)*. Sharply critical of the antiliberationist forces, which it denounced as reactionary, the paper embraced the campaign for equal rights, which its contributors insisted would benefit Poles and all other residents of the empire.[12] Meanwhile, activists organized a diverse array of organizations that catered to Polish-speaking Catholics. These groups ranged from mutual aid associations and cultural clubs to Oświata organizations (Polish national unions that grew out of underground patriotic groups).[13] By the winter of 1906, at least one party of Polish landlords and a Polish division of the Kadet Party had become active in the southwest.[14]

The all-imperial leader of the Kadet Party, P. N. Miliukov, expressed alarm about the intensifying efforts of nationalist activists to shape the liberationist agenda, insisting that the interests of individual national groups should remain subordinate to the broader struggle to attain equal rights for all. But Kiev Kadets, who both defended and embodied the cosmopolitan mind-set of the city's multiethnic elite, allied with Ukrainian and Polish parties. Soon after its formation, the party of Polish landlords announced its support for the Kadets; though it never officially endorsed the party, *Dziennik Kijowski* echoed the Kadets' key demands.[15] UDRP activists and *Hromads'ka dumka* contributors also extended support to the Kadets in the Duma campaign.[16] As one *Hromads'ka dumka* columnist explained, the Kadet Party "looks out for the welfare of all people...no matter who they are: whether landlord or priest, whether peasant or Jew, whether Pole or Ukrainian, because all people have the right to live on the earth, because everyone needs bread, because everyone hurts the same when you beat them, because everyone suffers equally when wrong triumphs over right."[17]

---

11. "Ustav obshchestva Tovarystvo Prosvita v Kyivi," 20 May 1906, DAKO, f. 2, op. 42, d. 220, l. 70b.
12. *DK*, 22 February 1906, 2. On the paper's founding and its political orientation, see Tadeusz Zienkiewicz, *Polskie życie literackie w Kijowie w latach 1905–1918* (Olsztyn, Pol., 1990), 24–26.
13. Zienkiewicz, *Polskie życie literackie*, 97–100; see also Chojecki, *Społeczeństwo*, 20–22. The Kiev division of Oświata was led by the director of a local sugar factory.
14. "Obshchee sobranie partii 'Narodnoi svobody,'" *Svoboda i Pravo*, 3 February 1906, 3; "Sobraniia poliakov," *NV*, 4 January 1906, 3.
15. "Obshchee sobranie," 3; *DK*, 22 February 1906, 2; "Społeczeństwo polskie na kresach i socjalizm," *DK*, 21 February 1906, 1.
16. *HD*, 14 March 1906, 1. For more on Ukrainian activists and the political alliances they formed, see Chykalenko, *Spohady*, 285–98.
17. "Koho treba oberati do dumy?" *HD*, 13 April 1906, 1.

By February of 1906, the Kadets had consolidated a reliable support base of Jewish, Ukrainian, and Polish intellectuals as well as mercantile elites, educated professionals, and residents of the city's wealthy central districts.[18] Some party activists expressed concern, however, that the Kadets had been less effective in presenting their ideas to the masses. They urged their comrades to organize agitational activities on factory floors, in teahouses and bars, and in the urban periphery's blighted neighborhoods. Most Kadet loyalists bristled at these suggestions, however. Some insisted that mass agitation was crass and undignified, while others expressed doubt that their antiliberationist rivals could ever attract the support of the city's working masses.[19]

Meanwhile, Kiev's "truly Russian" parties had also begun to mobilize in advance of the elections. In the pages of *Kievlianin* and in public meetings organized by Pikhno in the winter of 1905–6 (at least one of which drew hundreds of attendees), activists met to craft political platforms and strategies.[20] Extreme anti-Semitism and opposition to the equal rights campaigns—both trademarks of the Russian right that emerged from the 1905 revolution—motivated many of those who participated in these debates. Noting the strong support that the Kadets had garnered from local minority groups, activists denounced the Liberation Movement as a conspiracy by foreign interests to dominate the Orthodox masses through both terrorist violence and a liberal order that would offer full and equal citizenship rights to all imperial subjects.[21] *Kievlianin* echoed these claims. Referring to the Kadets as "the Polish-Jewish Constitutional-Democratic Union," the paper complained that "it is hard to tell the difference between the local KD meeting and a synagogue" and alleged that "foreigners" were using the new democratic institutions to override the interests of "true Russian" people.[22] The ethnographer Ia. G. Demchenko (one of the original funders of *Kievskaia starina* and a long-time *Kievlianin* contributor) insisted that the events of 1905 had been an effort by Jewish mercantile elites—and their longtime supporter, Count Witte—to "destroy the economic and political 'equilibrium' for their own use and to subjugate the Russian people."[23]

At the same time, however, Kiev's antiliberationist parties continued to distance themselves from the reactionary programs of Russia's other right-wing parties, embracing democratizing ideas and progressive social reforms more commonly

---

18. "Zasedaniia 'Partii narodnoi svobody,'" *NV*, 17 February 1906, 3; "Iz zhizni politicheskikh partii," *KV*, 30 January 1906, 3.
19. For coverage of these conflicts, see "Uchastkovye sobraniia k-d partii," *KV*, 21 January 1906, 3; "Tsentral'nyi komitet k-d partii," *KV*, 19 January 1906, 3; "Obshchee sobranie," 3; "Iz zhizni partii," *Svoboda i Pravo*, 15 February 1906, 4; letter to the editor in *KV*, 8 January 1906, 5.
20. On one such meeting that attracted hundreds in late 1905, see *Kievlianin*, 2 January 1906, 4.
21. "Sobranie chlenov partiia pravogo poriadka," *Kievlianin*, 22 November 1905, 2; "Partiia pravovogo poriadka," *Kievlianin*, 29 November 1905, 2.
22. "Pol'sko-evreiskii konstitutsionno-demokraticheskii soiuz," *Kievlianin*, 31 January 1906, 2; "Komu zhelatel'na teper Gosudarstvennaia Duma," *Kievlianin*, 19 January 1906, 1; "Inostrantsy izbirateli," *Kievlianin*, 23 January 1906, 3.
23. Ia. Demchenko, "Chto takoe reaktsiia?" *Kievlianin*, 4 February 1906, 2–3.

associated with the left.[24] The Russian Gathering, Party of Legal Order, and local chapters of the SRN all decried the capitalist order and called for enhanced local self-governance, comprehensive land reform, and improved access to education and credit for Orthodox peasants; the Kiev SRN even demanded a minimum wage and a nine-hour workday.[25] Echoing Little Russian activists' long-standing calls to nationalize the economy and the politics of the southwest, these parties insisted that strong state intervention would be necessary to reduce destructive external influences and to liberate the simple folk from their putative exploiters. Pikhno joined members of the Russian Gathering and SRN to call for the abolition of the Pale of Settlement, complaining that the heavy concentration of Jews on the empire's western borderlands unjustly victimized the Orthodox peasants who lived in the region; the SRN went so far as to call for the liquidation of all Jewish property and assets within five years.[26]

By late January, Kiev's antiliberationist parties had reached a formal agreement to cooperate in the Duma campaign, unifying the varied forces that had emerged to contest the local capitalist system, liberal and radical ideas, and urban traditions of interethnic accommodation.[27] Many of the men who played a prominent role in the coalition had long been involved in the Little Russian lobby (D. I. Pikhno, B. M. Iuzefovich, I. M. Reva, O. I. Levitskii, N. V. Storozhenko, A. V. Storozhenko, and I. A. Sikorskii). Other leaders of the antiliberationist bloc included Orthodox clerics who had written on the southwest's struggle to protect its religious traditions from foreign incursions (S. T. Golubev and F. I. Titov) and city duma delegates (Dobrynin, Iasnogurskii, and the aforementioned Levitskii, Storozhenko, and Sikorskii).[28] A new generation of leaders who had come of age amid the revolutionary upheavals of the 1905 period also lent their talents to the struggle against the lib-

---

24. Both moderate rightist parties such as the Octobrists and gentry organizations appear to have remained weak in the southwest, eclipsed by more radical, mass-appeal parties that combined elements of the political right and left. On the unique political climate in Kiev, see Rawson, *Russian Rightists*, 98–103; N. G. Koroleva, "Pravye partii v bor'be s revoliutsiei, 1905–1907 g.g.," *Istoricheskie zapiski* 118 (1990): 134.

25. See Russian Gathering brochure, GARF, f. 102, OO, 1906, II-otdelenie, d. 186, l. 140b; "Partiia pravogo poriadka v Kieve," *Kievlianin*, 14 November 1905, 1; "Ustav kievskoi partii Pravovogo poriadka," 1906, TsDIAUK, f. 442, op. 636, d. 647, ch. I, ll. 59–65; Koroleva, "Pravye partii," 128, 134. Indeed, Iuzefovich described the "truly Russian" movement as an opposition movement at its core: see Loukianov, "Conservatives," 770.

26. On Pikhno, see A. E. Kaufman, *Druz'ia i vragi evreev i D. I. Pikhno* (Kiev, 1907), 10–11; on the Russian Gathering, D. V. Tutkevich, *Chto takoe evrei?* (Kiev, 1906), 70–72; on the SRN, see the pamphlet in TsDIAUK, f. 296, op. 1, d. 2, l. 180b.

27. "K istorii obrazovaniia 'pravykh' partii," *KV*, 31 January 1906, 5; "Torgovo-promyshlennaia partiia," *KV*, 19 January 1906, 3; "Gorodskie dela," *KV*, 28 January 1906, 3.

28. The southwestern clergy was deeply divided over political matters. Some priests expressed liberationist and Ukrainian nationalist views and joined liberal and radical parties: see, for example, Sviash. Grigorii Grushevskii, "O propovedyvanii slova Bozhii na malorossiiskom iazyke," *KEV* 9 (1906): 294–96; F. Pospelovskii, "Otvet o. protoieroeiu Nikandru Kolpikovu na stat'iu ego," *KEV* 11 (1906): 338–46. By contrast, Titov and Golubev, who continued to raise alarms that alien forces were supposedly threatening the native Orthodox heritage of the region, became prominent antiliberationist activists. See F. Titov, "Novogodnie pozhelaniia russkomu narodu," *KEV* 1 (1906): 1–3; V. I. Ul'ianovs'kyi, *Dvichi profesor* (Kiev, 2007). For more on the political views of the clergy, see Vulpius, *Nationalisierung der Religion*, 213–352.

erationists. V. V. Shul'gin (1878–1976), the son of V. Ia. Shul'gin and the stepson of Pikhno, and A. I. Savenko (1874–1922), a native of Poltava province—both recent graduates of St. Vladimir's law faculty and regular contributors to *Kievlainin*—would become among the most prominent ideologists of the "truly Russian" movement.[29] F. Ia. Postnyi (1869–1915), a Poltava peasant who had worked as a petty trader and a lackey for the Brodskiis, was a rising star in the SRN, establishing his reputation as a fiery orator who understood the needs and concerns of the city's working classes.[30]

The antiliberationist bloc made a point of establishing contact with the working classes—a task at which the liberationists had faltered. Emphasizing the importance of reaching the thousands of eligible voters who did not yet identify with a party, antiliberationist duma delegates organized mass political meetings that drew hundreds of participants at a time. At these meetings, orators continued to portray Jews, liberationists, and minority rights activists as enemies of the narod, but they also highlighted the progressive agenda of the "truly Russian" parties and hailed the democratization of politics since 1905.[31] Activists hosted frequent meetings at the People's House in the outlying district of Luk'ianovka, agitated on shop floors and in enterprises, and enlisted antiliberationist priests in the effort to convince parishioners that an equal rights regime would only force "Russians and Orthodox believers... to yield the dominant position in their own state to non-Russians and the non-Orthodox [*inovertsy*]."[32]

In contrast to Kiev, where partisan politics had become highly polarized, in rural areas of the southwest, political identities tended to be less well defined. Right-bank peasants staged well-organized strikes against landowners and factory proprietors, but in spite of their labor activism, many remained politically unaffiliated.[33] Some landlords, both Orthodox and Catholic, joined conservative organizations such as the United Gentry in response to these threats; however, such groups remained relatively weak in the southwest. Large numbers of Orthodox landlords, who had received land through state service during the de-polonization campaign, lived away from their estates and had little involvement in local cultural and political life; substantial numbers of Catholic gentry, alarmed by the stance of the "truly Russian" bloc on equal rights for minorities, defied their class interests, joining liberationist groups or Polish nationalist parties instead.[34]

---

29. On Shul'gin, see D. O. Zaslavskii, *Rytsar' chernoi sotni* (Leningrad, 1925); "Avtobiografiia Vasiliia Vital'evicha Shul'gina," 1932–33, HA, Mariia Vrangel' Collection, box 19, folder 37. On Savenko's background, consult *Nash Kandidat Anatolii Ivanovich Savenko* (Kiev, 1912), 5–6.
30. On Postnyi, see Stepanov and Ivanov, *Chernaia sotnia*, 409.
31. "Sobranie izbiratelei po Starokievskomu uchastku," *Kievlianin*, 17 January 1906, 3; "Predvybornoe sobranie," *NV,* 14 February 1906, 3; "Sobranie izbiratelei po Luk'ianovskomu uchastku," *Kievlianin,* 18 January 1906, 3; "Predvybornaia kampaniia," *KV,* 31 January 1906, 4.
32. The quote is from N. Kolpikov, "Uchastie dukhovenstva v vyborakh v Gosudarstvennuiu Dumu, *KEV* 3 (1906): 79. On agitation on shop floors and in outlying neighborhoods, see "Predvybornaia kampaniia," *KV,* 31 January 1906, 4; "Iz zhizni politicheskikh partii," *KV,* 21 January 1906, 3.
33. On rural protest, despite the weakness of party structures, see Edelman, *Proletarian Peasants,* 92–168.
34. On the problem of absentees, see V. Shul'gin, *Vybornoe zemstvo v Iugo-zapadnom krae* (Kiev, 1909), 34. On Polish nobles and their political behavior, consult "Sobraniia poliakov," *NV,* 4 January 1906, 3.

Although they had recused themselves from the electoral campaign, SDs agitated among workers in Kiev province, which boasted many sugar refineries and was the most industrialized corner of the southwest region outside Kiev. Activists helped peasants and workers to organize strike committees, insisting all the while that the working classes should direct their anger at their poverty and political disenfranchisement toward the capitalist system and tsarist state rather than the Jews. Meanwhile, the Spilka canvassed villages across the southwest, urging peasants to join the liberationist forces.[35] However, it is also clear that antiliberationist forces had begun to penetrate peasant communities. Letters preserved in the archive of *Kievlianin*—many in the shaky hand of the semiliterate and signed by dozens of local residents—repeated the claims being made in Kiev's public political forums: that liberationists were acting on the orders of Jewish elites who wished to expand their domination over the Orthodox narod and that imperial officials had unjustly had permitted "alien" groups to participate in local civic and political life.[36] One particularly memorable missive from a self-described "Russian girl" expressed in graphic detail her desire to strangle Tsar Nicholas II, who she complained had proven himself incapable of resolving the "Yid question" and unprepared to fully endorse a system of "national politics" that could liberate the children of Rus' from their purported enemies.[37]

Electing the First Duma

The elections to the state Duma—a multistage procedure that stretched over several weeks—began in March 1906. Rural areas selected electors in separate meetings of landowners and peasant communes, and these electors then traveled to regional centers to cast their final ballots. Urban residents who owned property or passed tax thresholds chose electors through neighborhood police districts, and workers in the city's largest industrial establishments voted in their workplaces.[38] Thirty-six thousand of Kiev's residents qualified to vote for the first Duma, by far the broadest franchise ever seen in the city. Although the Old Kiev district, which encompassed the ritzy enclave of Lipki and the central commercial district around Khreshchatik, still enjoyed about twice the voting power of neighborhoods on the urban outskirts, the number of voters in peripheral districts far surpassed that of the center.[39]

---

35. Edelman, *Proletarian Peasants*, 133–70; memorandum of Chief of the Kiev Okhrana Division, 28 June 1906, GARF, f. 102, OO, 1906, I-otd. D. 25, ch. 57, l. 105.
36. Hundreds of letters from ordinary people to Pikhno—most of which laud his leadership of the "truly Russian" movement—have been preserved in TsDIAUK, f. 296, op. 1, d. 2; TsDIAUK, f. 296, op. 1, d. 3; and TsDIAUK, f. 296, op. 1, d. 27. It is not clear how many of these letters were actually printed. For a discussion of antiliberationist activism in the countryside, see "'Zubatovshchyna' v derzhavnii dumi," *HD*, 22 April 1906, 1.
37. "Russian girl" to *Kievlianin*, 14 February, 21 June, and 5 August 1906, TsDIAUK, f. 296, op. 1, d. 2, ll. 12–17.
38. "U kyivi," *HD*, 17 March 1906, 2; "Sistema vyboriv," *HD*, 16 March 1906, 3. On the mechanics of the elections, see Terence Emmons, *The Formation of Political Parties and the First National Elections in Russia* (Cambridge, MA, 1983), 237–93.
39. "K vyboram v gosudarstvennuiu dumu," *NV*, 16 February 1906, 4.

As the elections approached, some officials worked to observe the letter of the new electoral law. The Ministry of Internal Affairs reminded local officials that Jews and other minority groups could not be excluded from voting lists and must be extended the same rights as other Russian subjects.[40] Others used their powers to thwart liberationist activism. Censors and police officials closed Kadet papers and printing shops, alleging that the party promoted "exceptionally revolutionary" ideas. Luchitskii and Naumenko were both prosecuted for their "seditious" writings, which deprived them of the right to vote.[41] Still other officials openly promoted "truly Russian" parties. Civil Governor P. S. Savvich, whose office oversaw the electoral process in Kiev province, bitterly complained that the St. Petersburg authorities had taken inadequate measures to limit the electoral power of Polish landowners in the southwest's rural districts and Jews in its cities. In Kiev, he permitted antiliberationist city duma deputies to stack the neighborhood election boards that would supervise the voting with prominent "truly Russian" activists.[42]

In the initial round of elections in Kiev, liberationist parties made a strong showing. All but one of the electors chosen by Kiev's three wealthiest districts belonged to the Kadets or to the more radical parties that stood to the left of it; 80 percent of the electors chosen by residents of less well-heeled neighborhoods such as Plossk, Podol, and Lybed' belonged to the liberationist bloc. Leading liberal, radical, and Ukrainian activists—E. N. Trubetskoi, G. E. Afanas'ev, E. Kh. Chykalenko, B. A. Kistiakovskii, and several Polytechnical Institute professors who had played key roles in the Liberation Movement—all won seats as electors. A full one-quarter of the electors chosen by Kiev residents were Jewish or Polish, and all of these belonged to the Kadets or the radical parties on its left. The "truly Russian" coalition performed better in Luk'ianovka, whose People's House had become the epicenter of antiliberationist organizing efforts, winning about one-third of that neighborhood's electors. It performed best of all in Pechersk, a neighborhood with strong Orthodox traditions as a result of its proximity to the Kiev Cave Monastery; there, more than half of those elected belonged to antiliberationist parties. However, with the exception of N. V. Storozhenko, whom Lybed' voters chose as an elector, none of the more prominent antiliberationist leaders managed to win a position—perhaps an indication that the bloc had alienated some city residents.[43]

---

40. "Svod glavneishikh ukazanii, prepodannykh Ministrom VD po primeneniiu VYSOCHAISHE utverzhdennogo 6 avg. 1905 goda Polozheniia o vyborakh v GD," DAKO, f. 2, op. 41, d. 222v, l. 7.
41. On the closure and persecution of liberationist organs, see Kiev Temporary Committee on Press Affairs to Main Direction on Press Affairs, 31 January 1906, TsDIAUK, f. 295, op. 1, d. 6, ll. 1–10b. On the challenge it presented to the Kadet Party, "Zahal'ni zbory partii 'Narodn'oi Svobody,'" HD, 9 March 1906, 3. On the exclusion of Naumenko and Luchitskii from the voting rolls, "Ne zatverzheno dvokh vybornykh k-d partii," HD, 29 March 1906, 3.
42. Kiev Civil Governor to MVD, 26 January 1906, DAKO, f. 2, op. 41, d. 222v, l. 163; "K vyboram v gosudarstvennuiu dumu," KV, 9 January 1906, 4; "Izbiratel'nye komissii," KV, 5 January 1906, 3.
43. Data culled from "Svedeniia o vyborshchikakh po gor. Kievu, izbrannykh dlia uchastiia v vyborakh v GD," DAKO, f. 2, op. 41, d. 222e, ll. 440–54.

Political identities in the southwest's rural areas and district cities remained less coherent. Few Orthodox landowners exercised the franchise; Polish gentry appear to have voted as a bloc in many locales, supporting the Kadets in some areas and Polish nationalist parties in others. Nearly 60 percent of the electors selected by landowners had no party affiliation. Voters in district cities, in most of which the non-Orthodox constituted a majority, selected electors representing the Kadets, Polish autonomist parties, and Zionist groups. Peasant electoral meetings were lively and well attended, dominated by calls for land expropriation and further political and economic reforms. Yet few peasant voters seem to have connected these demands with the platforms of particular parties: most peasant gatherings chose respected members of their local communities to represent them, and nearly 70 percent of the electors chosen by peasant assemblies had no party affiliation.[44]

When the electors chosen by Kiev province's rural communities and district cities traveled to Kiev to cast their final votes, the city's polarized ideological forces besieged them. Antiliberationist activists and priests begged rural electors to vote for "truly Russian people" who would resist the attempts of interlopers to subjugate the Orthodox peasantry, rather than "Jews or professors."[45] For their part, the Kadets organized a large public meeting at which speakers rebutted their opponents' claims that an equal rights regime would endanger the welfare of ordinary Orthodox people. "That's ridiculous," exclaimed one speaker. "One hundred thirty million Russian people cannot be enslaved by five million Jews. In general, we need to make laws so that no one can live off another! After attaining equal rights, Jews will love their Motherland no less than other Russians."[46]

When the final votes were tallied, the Kadets easily won Kiev city's seat, sending the political newcomer Baron F. R. Shteingel', a thirty-five-year-old industrialist, to the imperial Duma.[47] Liberationists also performed well in Kiev province, which elected ten Kadets (two Jewish doctors from cities, one Polish noble, two Orthodox nobles who professed liberal Ukrainophile views, and five peasants), two Trudoviks (a labor party with close ties to the SRs), one peasant with no party affiliation, one Polish autonomist, and one SD worker. Podolia was one of only three provinces in the entire empire to elect an exclusively peasant delegation—the result of a decision by Orthodox peasant electors to vote as a bloc in order to defeat a coalition that had been forged by Polish landowners and Jewish townspeople. Nearly all of these peasant delegates were illiterate or had only a home education; they were divided roughly evenly between Trudoviks and those with no party affiliation. In Volynia, Orthodox landowners allied with their Polish counterparts in an effort to defeat a coalition of

---

44. On rural elections, see Edelman, *Proletarian Peasants*, 165; DAKO, f. 2, op. 41, d. 222g.; V. V. Shul'gin, *The Years* (New York, 1984), 7–27. The statistics are culled from Emmons, *Formation*, 262–63, 250–51.
45. "K vyboram po Kievskomu uzedu," *Narod*, 8 April 1906, 4; "Sel'iane-vybortsi, chorna sotnia, chentsi ta uriad," *HD*, 21 April 1906, 1–2.
46. "Predvybornoe sobranie vyborshchikov po kievskomu uezdu," *Narod*, 7 April 1906, 3.
47. "K vyboram v gosudarstvennuiu dumu," *Narod*, 10 April 1906, 3.

urban Jewish voters—a union that Orthodox peasants ultimately joined. That province elected three Orthodox nobles with no party affiliation, three Polish nobles who belonged to autonomist parties (including the publisher of *Dziennik Kijowski* and members of the Poniatowski and Potocki families, among the greatest Polish magnates of the southwest), three peasants with no party affiliation, and a peasant and an Orthodox priest who described themselves as moderates.[48]

Continued support for the Liberation Movement and widespread dissatisfaction with the tsarist order had permitted the parties most critical of the autocratic order to triumph in the southwest—a result consistent with electoral outcomes elsewhere in the empire. Overjoyed at this success, a Jewish Kadet activist hailed the election as a turning point in the struggle for equal rights, proclaiming that it portended well "for all of Russia and especially for Jews."[49] Others were more cautious, noting that "truly Russian" activists would not abandon their efforts to use class and national resentments for their own ends.[50] Indeed, before the southwest's Duma delegates had even taken their seats, antiliberationist activists convened public meetings in Kiev at which they claimed that it was only Polish and Jewish support that had permitted the Kadets to triumph.[51] In the months following their defeat in the elections to the first Duma, Kiev's antiliberationist activists would redouble their efforts to enlist the urban population in their cause—and would expand their lobbying efforts across the southwest.

Ukrainian Nation or Russian Citadel?

The southwest's Duma deputies departed for St. Petersburg with high hopes. Nonparty peasant delegates, Kadets, and Trudoviks joined together to demand land expropriation, the abolition of the death penalty, enhanced self-governance rights, and the end to legal discrimination on the basis of religion, nationality, and sex. Kadet leaders remained particularly outspoken on the issue of Jewish rights, and Shteingel' delivered an eloquent speech on the floor of the Duma denouncing anti-Jewish violence.[52] The mood in the southwest remained unsettled, however. Peasants continued their attacks on landlords and industrialists, and in April a new wave of strikes paralyzed industries in the region's cities. Rumors of pogroms again accompanied labor unrest.[53]

---

48. Data on delegates culled from *Chleny 1-oi Gosudarstvennoi dumy* (Moscow, 1906); *Gosudarstvennaia duma. Pervogo prizyva* (Moscow, 1906). The information about alliances is from Emmons, *Formation*, 333–34. Emmons contrasts the behavior of Podolia and Volynia peasants, who mobilized against their non-Orthodox neighbors even as many supported left-wing parties, to that of voters in the northwestern provinces, where some peasant electors forged alliances with urban Jews. Ibid., 335–40.
49. "K vyboram v gosudarstvennuiu dumu," *Narod*, 10 April 1906, 3.
50. "Khristianstvo i evreiskii vopros," *Narod*, 7 April 1906, 1.
51. "Izbiratel'naia kampaniia v Kieve," *Kievskaia zaria*, 26 March 1906, 3.
52. *Stenograficheskii otchet. Gosudarstvennaia duma. Sessiia I* (St. Petersburg, 1906), 1836–37.
53. *Otgoloski zhizni*, 17 May 1906, 2; "Chutky pro pohrom," *HD*, 9 May 1906, 3.

Meanwhile, new divides within the liberationist bloc were beginning to emerge. Within weeks of the Duma's convocation, Hrushevs'kyi distanced himself from the Kadets, angered that the party had cooperated with Polish patriots yet refused to endorse Ukrainian nationalists' calls for a federal arrangement between Ukraine and Russia.[54] Ukrainian Duma delegates hailing from the Dnieper's left bank formed the Ukrainian Parliamentary Club, which demanded autonomy for Ukraine but begrudged Polish nationalists the same right.[55] *Hromads'ka dumka* and Ukrainian cultural organizations complained bitterly that socialists and Kadets had not offered adequate support to Ukrainian national aspirations.[56] By summer, Prosvita had called for an autonomous Ukraine "from the Carpathians to the Don."[57]

Shteingel' supported the cultural aspirations of Ukrainian activists, remarking that he spoke Ukrainian and had hosted plays in both "Muscovite and Ukrainian" on his Volynia estate.[58] Nevertheless, he expressed concern about the activities of the Ukrainian Parliamentary Club—which he referred to as the "Ukrainian Party"—and dismissed the idea of Ukrainian autonomy as "impractical," stating, "the popular masses are poorly prepared for [autonomy] politically, and lack awareness [*vtratili svidomist'*] of their nationality."[59] *Hromads'ka dumka* reacted to this statement angrily, noting, "Ukrainians aren't a party. Ukrainians are a people, Ukrainians are a nation.... The Ukrainian movement isn't a partisan, but rather, a national movement."[60]

Such claims outraged "truly Russian" activists, who now counted Ukrainian nationalists among the servants of dangerous foreign interests. Ia. G. Demchenko, the columnist who had railed against the "Jewish revolution" in *Kievlianin,* claimed that those who promoted Ukrainian autonomy and the Galician-Ukrainian dialect in the Russian empire were guided by "Jewish, Polish and mongrel elements" who hoped to see the demise of the "Russian people" (*Russkii narod*).[61] In the pages of *Kievlianin,* Savenko alleged that Luchitskii had met with Ukrainian nationalist activists in Galicia to plot an Austrian invasion of the Russian empire. (The historian, who had been

---

54. See M. Grushevskii, "Nashi trebovaniia," in *Osvobozhdenie Rossii i ukrainskii vopros,* 86–92; "Konets getto!" in ibid., 146–48; "Za ukrainskuiu kost'," in ibid., 278–91.
55. On the group's activities and demands, see "Zbory ukrains'koho parlaments'koho klubu," *HD,* 24 May 1906, 2–3; "Zbory parlaments'koi hrupy avtonomistiv," *HD,* 28 May 1906, 1; "Zbory ukrainskoi parlaments'koi hrupy," *HD,* 6 June 1906, 1; "Natsional'ni hrupy v Derzhavnii Dumi," *HD,* 10 June 1906, 1.
56. "Rossiis'ka sotsial'na demokratiia i natsional'ne pytannia," *HD,* 2 June 1906, 1; "Ukraintsi, rossiiane i poliaki," *HD,* 2 June 1906, 1–2.
57. "'Prosvita' u Kyivi," *HD,* 10 June 1906, 1. In spite of these demands, local police and gendarmes reported that the founders of Prosvita were politically reliable. See Gendarme Head to Civil Governor Veretennikov, 3 October 1906, DAKO, f. 2, op. 42, d. 220, l. 10; Bul'var Police Chief to Civil Governor Veretennikov, 28 September 1906, ibid., l. 80b.
58. "F. R. Shteingel'," *HD,* 17 April 1906, 2. Born in St. Petersburg in 1870, Shteingel' spent his childhood in Kiev before pursuing his university education in Warsaw. See *Chleny,* 29–30.
59. "Rozmova z F.R. Shteingelem," *HD,* 13 April 1906, 3.
60. "Partiia chy partii?" *HD,* 18 April 1906, 1.
61. The quote is from Ia. Demchenko, *Pravda ob ukrainofil'stve* (Kiev, 1906), 35–36.

in Kiev the whole time, sued for slander.)⁶² T. D. Florinskii, the philologist who had blocked the Galician activists from attending the 1899 Archeological Congress and a stalwart supporter of the antiliberationist coalition, expressed offense at Ukrainian nationalists' efforts to claim Shevchenko as a Ukrainian national hero and devoted separatist.⁶³

Yet "truly Russian" commentators' hostility toward Ukrainian national separatism should not be read as disdain for the peculiarities of the southwest and its culture. Quite the contrary: many antiliberationist activists remained devoted Little Russian patriots, who regarded local folk culture as the most authentic expression of the "truly Russian" values they championed. In the same 1906 tract in which he attacked the Ukrainian national cause, Demchenko praised authors such as Shevchenko, Kulish, and Kostomarov for capturing the "national characteristics" of the Little Russian simple folk and raising awareness of the dignity and value of their "everyday [*bytovaia*] and spiritual life." He professed his love for the Ukrainian language—the tongue in which the toiling masses had expressed their desires for centuries—and he even advocated Ukrainian instruction in local schools.⁶⁴ Like earlier proponents of the Little Russian idea, however, he interpreted local peculiarities as a force that had always promoted the unity of the Orthodox East Slavs, and he condemned the Ukrainian nationalists who now sought to align Little Russian culture with a revolutionary agenda. "The true and conscious Ukrainophile," he wrote, "doesn't rehash [the preachings] of the Jews Marx and Lassalle."⁶⁵

Florinskii expressed a similarly positive view of Little Russian culture, hailing Shevchenko as a "purely national Little Russian poet" who had drawn attention to the dignity of "the Ukraine dear to his heart, its past and present, its simple village folk who suffered under the yoke of serfdom."⁶⁶ Outraged that Ukrainian nationalists were now attempting to claim Shevchenko for their own cause, Florinskii insisted (on the basis of copious citations from *Kievskaia starina*) that the poet had never dreamed of autonomy but had rather sought to renew the empire and the Orthodox Church with a vital, democratic spirit. Shevchenko's denunciations of the autocratic state, Florinskii argued, did not reflect his opposition to "the political unification of the Little and Great Russians" but rather his opposition to bureaucratic intransigence and unnecessary centralization.⁶⁷

Others in the "truly Russian" camp focused on the suffering of the Little Russian masses more than the glories of their culture. Here too, though, ideas raised by the Little Russian lobby in the nineteenth century resurfaced. A pamphlet by a member

---

62. See the undated press clipping in "Materialy sudebnogo dela po isku Luchitskogo I. V. k zhurnalistu Savenko A. I. za rasprostranenie klevety o nem, kak izmennike Rossii v pol'zu Avstrii," IR NBUV, f. 66, l. 20b.
63. T. D. Florinskii, *Slavianofil'stvo T.G. Shevchenka* (Kiev, 1906).
64. Demchenko, *Pravda*, 7–15; the quote is from 7.
65. Ibid., 35–36.
66. Florinskii, *Slavianofil'stvo*, 2.
67. Ibid., 25–26.

of the Russian Brotherhood (and inspired by its discussions on the Jewish question in early 1906) depicted Jews as a group as incorrigible enemies of the southwestern peasantry. Urging local residents to emulate the actions of Khmelnytsky—who, according to the author, had struggled to ensure that "not one Jew was left on the Cossack lands"—the tract presented the destruction of Jewish civilization as a necessary first step to reclaim "Russia for the Russians."[68] A pamphlet circulating in the fall of 1906 lamented the suffering of the "Little Russian" people under Poles and Jews—whom it deemed "most nefarious enemies." But it also insisted that the national struggle already under way in the empire's western borderlands promised to liberate all "Russians" from the "aliens" who sought to turn them into "economic, political, and moral slaves."[69]

"Truly Russian" Mobilization

Casting themselves as the defenders of the interests of the narod on the imperial periphery, Kiev's antiliberationist activists continued to highlight their commitment to resolving the problems that plagued the outskirts of their city. No sooner had the imperial Duma elections concluded than activists began preparing to elect a new city duma in the spring of 1906. Determined to build on the momentum that they had created during the all-imperial campaign, Kiev's "truly Russian" parties redoubled their efforts to overcome voter apathy and to transform local residents into loyal partisans.[70] Activists organized neighborhood town halls and traveled door-to-door. As they met face-to-face with the city's voters, they encouraged residents to defend "Russian and city interests" from the city's multiethnic capitalist elite and its privileged liberationists.[71] In huge gatherings in Kiev's outlying neighborhoods they denounced the inequities of the capitalist system and demanded new schools, the elimination of protectionist tariffs, and the expansion of cheap credit to struggling (Gentile) merchants.[72]

The first round of city duma elections saw historic turnouts, especially in outlying neighborhoods.[73] As voters whittled down candidates in multiple runoffs that

---

68. Tutkevich, *Chto takoe evrei?*, 72, 192. For a similar argument that appeared in a short-lived newspaper edited by Iuzefovich, see "Predosterezhenie malorossam," *Samoderzhavie*, 19 March 1906, 2.
69. *Dlia kogo Rossiia?* (Kiev, 1906), 10.
70. For discussions about the need to reach undecided voters, see I. A. Sikorskii, *Izbiratel'naia programma obshchegorodskikh soveshchanii Novodumskoi partii po vyboram v Kievskuiu Gorodskuiu Dumu* (Kiev, 1906); I. A. Sikorskii, *Partii i "bezpartiinye" v dele vyborov* (Kiev, 1906); P. Golubiatnikov, *Sovety Kievlianam, izbirateliam v gorodskuiu dumu* (Kiev, 1906).
71. Quote from "Vybory hlasnykh z Podil'skoho uch.," *HD*, 29 April 1906, 3; "Mestnaia khronika," *Otgoloski zhizni*, 19 May 1906, 2.
72. "K vyboram v gorodskuiu dumu," *KZ*, 10 April 1906, 3; "K vyboram k gorodskuiu dumu," *Narod*, 10 April 1906, 3.
73. "Vybory hlasnykh z Starokyivs'koho uchastku," *HD*, 28 April 1906, 3; "Vybory u horods'ku dumu," *HD*, 27 April 1906, 3. "Vybory hlasnykh z Luk'ianivs'koho," *HD*, 26 April 1906, 3; "Vybory z Plos'koho uch.," *HD*, 1 May 1906, 3.

stretched over several weeks, antiliberationist activists experimented with a new tactic: encouraging the urban residents who did not meet the economic threshold to vote in the city duma elections to participate in public rallies on city streets. Iuzefovich, who had recently claimed leadership of the local Monarchist Party, began staging daily protests in front of the city duma, at which he invited workers to give their testimony about how they had been exploited by Jews; Dobrynin and Liubinskii attended these gatherings as well, imploring Kiev residents to reclaim their city for the Orthodox East Slavs.[74] At least one of these demonstrations ended in a parade that marched through the city.[75] When the final votes were tallied, the antiliberationist bloc had scored an overwhelming victory, sweeping every neighborhood except the elite Old Kiev district and delivering the "truly Russian" forces their first electoral triumph.[76]

Emboldened by their victory, "truly Russian" organizers continued their efforts to expand their influence and support base over the summer of 1906. In public meetings, activists argued that Jews had no right to live in the southwest and vowed to reform the region on a "national and Russian basis."[77] Iasnogurskii hosted huge SRN rallies on his Luk'ianovka property that attracted residents of the urban periphery as well as Kiev's working-class suburbs.[78] Political activists infiltrated shop floors, and antiliberationist workers' organizations met regularly to draw up petitions and craft strategies.[79] Immediately after the new city duma convened, it invited workers to testify about their struggles, and it introduced legislation that limited the length of the workday in city enterprises.[80]

By June 1906, Kiev-based foes of the Liberation Movement had begun to establish contacts with like-minded intellectuals beyond city limits. Iuzefovich initiated meetings with monks from Volynia's Pochaev Monastery in an effort to create an umbrella political organization that could oversee antiliberationist activities across the southwest.[81] The clergy of Pochaev—a onetime Greek Catholic stronghold that had been claimed by the Orthodox Church in the 1830s—had long viewed themselves as guardians of Orthodox values on the empire's frontier, and they gave Iuzefovich a warm reception.[82] Iliodor (1880–1952), a monk of Cossack descent who had once been an associate of the liberationist priest Father Gapon, by 1906 had come to see the southwest's Polish and Jewish minorities—not the imperial state—as the chief

---

74. "Zbory monarkhystiv," *HD*, 7 May 1906, 3. "V sobranii 'monarkhicheskikh partii,'" *KZ*, 16 May 1906, 3.
75. "Chorna sotnia abo-zh "istynno-russkie" liude," *HD*, 17 May 1906, 1.
76. *KZ*, 19 May 1906, 3.
77. "Sredi liudei 'prava i poriadka,'" *KZ*, 27 June 1906, 3.
78. "Shtab-kvartira chornoi sotni" *HD*, 10 June 1906, 3.
79. "U Kyivi," *HD*, 15 June 1906, 3; "U 'monarkhistov,'" *KZ*, 27 June 1906, 3.
80. "Pervye shagi kievskoi gorodskoi dumy," *KG*, 18 September 1906, 3.
81. "U 'monarkhistov,'" *KZ*, 27 June 1906, 3.
82. On the history of the monastery, see G. Ia. Kryzhanovskii, *Pochaevskaia uspenskaia lavra* (Pochaev, 1897).

impediment to the liberation of the masses.[83] A fellow monk of Cossack parentage, Vitalii (1873–1960), also welcomed Iuzefovich's overtures. A worker in the monastery's printing plant, which supplied much of the right bank's religious literature, he began to produce antiliberationist political tracts; he soon established a local chapter of the SRN and hundreds of "truly Russian" unions in provincial locales and founded a charitable fund to benefit needy peasants. In his work as publicist and organizer, he lobbied for land redistribution in a "Christian manner" that would benefit the Orthodox simple folk and combat the influence of revolutionaries, who he alleged were seeking to destroy the children of Rus'.[84] Antonii Khrapovitskii (1863–1936), the bishop of Volynia and Podolia in these years, welcomed these activities and would later himself become an important member of the antiliberationist coalition.[85]

As the foes of the Liberation Movement expanded their outreach efforts across the southwest, their attempts to influence the imperial authorities grew bolder. Since early 1906, denunciations from Kiev had poured in to police and gendarmes. Correspondents claimed that G. E. Afanas'ev, the director of the Kiev branch of the State Bank and a well-known Kadet activist, offered preferential treatment to Jews seeking credit; that D. S. Margolin had secured land and residence permits for Jews by bribing the local authorities; and that Governor-General Sukhomlinov had failed to act decisively against both violent radicals and capitalist exploitation because he was "scared of perturbing the Jews."[86] By summer, antiliberationist activists repeatedly petitioned the authorities to take drastic measures to protect the children of Rus' from their supposed class and national enemies and to further limit Jewish participation in the economy, politics, and culture of the southwest.[87] Scolding Petersburg bureaucrats for being "poorly acquainted with the mood of the mass of the Russian population of the borderland [okrainnye] provinces," Iuzefovich warned that if the authorities did not submit to their demands, the people themselves would seek vengeance through violence.[88]

---

83. Iliodor boasted in his memoir that he "hated" Jews "with every fiber of my soul." *The Mad Monk of Russia Iliodor* (New York, 1918), 41.
84. Quote from Archbishop Vitaly, "Chto ia pomniu o sebe," in *Motivy moei zhizni* (Jordanville NY, 1955), 180; see also N. D. Talberg, "The Life's Journey of Archbishop Vitaly," *Pravoslavnaya Rus' (Orthodox Russia)*, 3 (1959): 4; Rawson, *Russian Rightists*, 191. By 1906, nearly 700 local divisions of the SRN were active in Volynia and Podolia. Rawson, *Russian Rightists*, 93.
85. Simon Dixon, "The 'Mad Monk' Iliodor in Tsaritsyn," *SEER* 88, no. 1–2 (2010): 381.
86. Memorandum of Director of Department of Police, February 1906, GARF, f. 102, OO, 1906, II-otdelenie, d. 770, ll. 5–50b; Memorandum of the Chief of the Kiev Province Gendarme Direction, 26 April 1906, ibid., ll. 17–18.
87. For example, "Iz Protokola Obshchago Sobraniia Kievskoi Russkoi Monarkhicheskoi Partii," 23 June 1906, GARF, f. 102, OO, 1906, II-otdelenie, d. 770, l. 12. For an indication that Kiev activists' petitions had reached Stolypin, see memorandum of Stolypin, 20 August 1906, RGIA, f. 1276, op. 2, d. 174, ll. 2–4.
88. The quote is from Iuzefovich to Stolypin, 23 June 1906, in GARF, f. 102, OO, 1906, II-otdelenie, d. 770, l. 11. Earlier that month, "truly Russian" activists had overtly threatened to initiate a pogrom if the authorities did not heed their demands: see Monarchist Party to Governor-General Sukhomlinov, 6 June 1906, GARF, f. 102, OO, 1906, II-otdel., d. 550, l. 1510b.

Officials struggled to formulate a coherent response to these developments. P. A. Stolypin (1862–1911), appointed minister of internal affairs in the spring of 1906 and chairman of the Council of Ministers in July, launched an aggressive campaign to end the unrest across the empire, summarily executing suspected revolutionaries and empowering local officials to take drastic action to halt the revolution. It was in this context that Stolypin appointed A. P. Veretennikov the new civil governor of Kiev province. An SRN member and an unabashed anti-Semite, Veretennikov regarded the "truly Russian" forces as partners in the struggle to subdue the revolution and openly used his office to promote their agenda.[89] As eager as he was to use "truly Russian" activists to intimidate and overwhelm liberationists, however, Stolypin also feared that the former might perpetrate further pogroms.[90]

Governor-General Sukhomlinov, for his part, continued to express deep misgivings about the southwest's antiliberationist forces. Although he personally opposed extending equal rights to Jews, he emphasized his commitment to protecting the welfare and physical safety of all subjects under his jurisdiction, "be they Russian, Polish, Little Russian, or Jewish."[91] Sukhomlinov systematically undermined Veretennikov's efforts to reduce Jewish influence in Kiev, confiscated antiliberationist newspapers and pamphlets that sought to incite violence, and supported the prosecution of Iuzefovich and the SRN leader Postnyi on charges that they had undermined state authority and encouraged pogroms.[92]

Reform, Liberation, and Nationalism in Urban and Regional Politics

In July 1906, Tsar Nicholas II, who had been deeply ambivalent about Russia's parliamentary experiment from the start, dismissed the Duma and called for new elections to be held in January 1907. The dissolution of the Duma further radicalized Russian politics, prompting Kadets, Trudoviks, and other liberationist deputies to flee to Finland, where they composed a manifesto calling on tsarist subjects to resist the autocracy. Back in Kiev, these developments placed further strain on the delicate ties that held the liberationist coalition together. Concerned that the Kadets' cooperation with the SRs and other radical parties that endorsed violence against the regime had compromised the former's moral credibility, the moderate Trubetskoi publicly renounced his ties with the party.[93] Meanwhile, the tensions within the multiethnic coalition that the Kadets had built were growing more pronounced. Zionist parties and the Bund attained a stronger following, vying with the Kadets for the loyalty of Kiev's Jewish

---

89. On Veretennikov's views, see William C. Fuller, *The Foe Within* (Ithaca, 2006), 45–46.
90. On Stolypin's views, consult Abraham Ascher, *P. A. Stolypin* (Stanford, 2001), 164–72.
91. "Beseda s gen-leitenentom V. A. Sukhomlinovym," *KG*, 14 September 1906, 3.
92. Sukhomlinov, *Vospominaniia*, 125; "Konfiskatsiia chornosotennoho listka," *HD*, 1 April 1906, 3; "Sprava Iuzefovicha," 17 June 1906, *HD*, 3; "Telegram S-Peterburgskogo Telegrafnogo Agenstva," 14 September 1906, GARF, f. 124, op. 44, d. 974, l. 1.
93. "Pechat'," *KG*, 29 October 1906, 3.

voters.⁹⁴ The rise of Roman Dmowski's National Democratic (ND) Party, which joined with liberationists to call for Polish autonomy but shared the antiliberationist forces' antipathy toward Jews, weakened the Kadets as well. In October 1906, a general meeting of Polish voters in Kiev resolved to withhold support from the Kadets; several months later, *Dziennik Kijowski*, which had by now drifted closer to the NDs, abandoned the liberationist campaign for equal rights, complaining that the "union with the Jews" had offered very little to Polish voters.⁹⁵

Differences had emerged within the Ukrainian camp as well. Although growing numbers of Kiev's Ukrainian activists embraced Hrushevs'kyi's vision of a Ukrainian nation, many felt threatened by the charisma of the historian, who was an increasingly frequent visitor to Kiev.⁹⁶ Others, disappointed by the Kadets' cautious stance on the nationality question, grew more radical. *Hromads'ka dumka* became a gathering place for Spilka organizers, leading the local authorities to close the paper in the fall of 1906.⁹⁷ Chykalenko soon launched a new paper, *Rada (Counsel)*, to replace the repressed organ. Boasting an even more radical editorial board than its predecessor—including Symon Petliura, an RUP activist from the left bank; Ivan Franko; and a handful of Galician anarchists—the paper bitterly complained that Russia's "constitutional experiment" had done nothing for "us Ukrainians" and denounced Poles as a group hostile to the Ukrainian people and culture.⁹⁸

The "truly Russian" parties took advantage of the growing divisions within the liberationist bloc, continuing their efforts to create connections between once disparate class, occupational, and local communities. They created voluntary associations and relief funds that supported proletarians wounded in the battle against the foreign forces allegedly responsible for the social inequities in the urban and imperial

---

94. On political developments in the region, see "Kiev i guberniia," GARF, f. 102, OO, 1906, II-otdelenie, d. 725, ch. 32. Although Zionists and Bundists had made considerable organizational advances, they remained weaker in the southwest than in the northwest: see "Agenturnye svedeniia o deiatel'nosti kievskoi organizatsii evreiskoi burzh. nats. partii 'Poalei Tsion,'" TsDIAUK, f. 275, op. 2, d. 13; Zimmerman, *Poles*. On the continuing efforts of Jewish elites to unite their co-confessionalists behind the liberationist banner, see letter from Kiev Province Jewish Nonparty Committee to Civil Governor P. G. Kurlov, January 1907, DAKO, f. 2, op. 42, d. 300g, l. 68.

95. On the meeting of Poles, see "Soveshchanie izbiratelei-poliakov," *KG*, 1 November 1906, 3. On *Dziennik*'s rapprochement with the NDs and its political stances, see Bohdan Olizar, "Liga narodowa," in *Pamiętnik Kijowski*, 3:168; "Nasze błędy przy wyborach," *DK*, 1 March 1907, 4 (the source of the quote); and "Siły i środki polskie," *DK*, 31 March 1907, 1; *DK*, 13 April 1907, 1. On growing anti-Semitism within the Polish patriotic movement in the Duma period, see Robert Blobaum, ed. *Antisemitism and Its Opponents in Modern Poland* (Ithaca, 2005); Theodore Weeks, *From Assimilation to Antisemitism* (DeKalb, 2006); Pascal Trees, *Wahlen im Weichselland* (Stuttgart, 2007), especially 103–381.

96. Prominent activists bitterly complained of Hrushevs'kyi's "Galicianization" of the Ukrainian dialect spoken by the narod of the Dnieper region. Plokhy, *Unmaking Imperial Russia*, 64.

97. Kiev Prosecutor to Ministry of Justice, 25 July 1907, GARF, f. 124. 1906, op. 44, d. 246, l. 80b; Kiev Prosecutor to Ministry of Justice, 13 October 1906, ibid., ll. 3–4.

98. Quotes from Hr. S'ohobochnii, "Use po staromu," *Rada*, 4 October 1906, 1; "Z'izd ukrains'koi narodnoi partii (U.N.P.)," *Rada*, 16 May 1907, 2. On the paper's contributors, see Evhen Chykalenko, *Shchodennyk* (Kiev, 2004), 1:6.

periphery.[99] Activists formed the Circle of Russian Women, which declared its opposition to "Jewish and Jewish-oriented [*evreistvuiushchii*]" interests; a nobleman and peasant together convened a youth league, the Double-Headed Eagle, which provided scholarships, mutual aid, and a political education to Orthodox East Slavs of all social stations and both sexes—and explicitly excluded the non-Orthodox from its ranks.[100] In September 1906, Iuzefovich launched the penny paper *Zakon i Pravda (Law and Truth)*, which invited workers to submit songs, articles, and poems describing their struggles and praised the spontaneous violence they unleashed against strikebreakers and Jews as heroic acts of national self-defense.[101]

By September of 1906, the antiliberationist coalition in Kiev had amassed ten thousand active supporters, according to one liberal organ (which had little reason to exaggerate the power of its rivals); one historian estimates that the Union of Russian Workers alone claimed three thousand members.[102] In recognition of Kiev activists' impressive successes in political mobilization, the all-imperial council of the SRN granted the city the honor of hosting its national congress in October 1906. Speakers at the congress, who included Iuzefovich, Pikhno, and prominent church officials, used the occasion to repeat their calls to local residents of all social stations to cast off the foreign "yoke" that they had carried for centuries.[103]

However, the SRN conference also revealed cleavages in the expanding "truly Russian" coalition. The all-imperial organization of the group remained dominated by reactionaries who demanded that the reforms of 1905 be rolled back and unfailingly supported the autocratic state. By contrast, right-bank chapters of the group had demanded a broader electoral franchise and social reforms and chided the MVD and the Holy Synod for their "'lenient and unclear' policies toward *inorodtsy* and the non-Orthodox in general." All-imperial leaders of the SRN made their displeasure at the radicalism of their southwestern colleagues clear, and after the conference, rumors of an imminent schism within the organization circulated in local papers.[104]

Unfazed by this criticism, southwestern activists forged ahead with a new campaign to expand their influence in rural communities and district cities. In the fall of

---

99. "Partiia pravovo poriadka," *KG*, 31 October 1906, 3; "K predvybornoi agitatsii," *KG*, 2 November 1906, 2; "Sobranie chlenov 'kassy zhertv dolga,'" *Kievlianin*, 23 October 1906, 3; "Strakhovanie monarkhistov ot revoliutsionerov," *Zakon i Pravda*, 11 October 1906, 3; "Zibrannia robitnikiv," *Rada*, 25 September 1906, 3.
100. *Kievlianin*, 21 September 1906, 3; "Ustav kievskogo patrioticheskogo obshchestva molodezhi pod imenem 'Dvuglavnyi orel,'" 28 October 1906, TsDIAUK, f. 442, op. 636, d. 647, ch. I, l. 6590b.
101. "Svoboda, ravenstvo," *Zakon i Pravda*, 29 September 1906, 1; "Sedletskii pogrom," *Zakon i Pravda*, 23 September 1906, 2–3; see also *Zakon i Pravda*, 25 January 1907, 1.
102. "Kandidaty v chleny GD ot pravykh partii," *KG*, 18 September 1906, 3; Omel'ianchuk, *Chernosotennoe dvizhenie*, 63.
103. See *Tretii Vserossiiskii s"ezd russkikh liudei v Kieve* (Kiev, 1906). The quote is from "Privetstvennoe slovo preosviashchennogo Platona, episkopa Chigirinskogo, Oblastnomu S"ezdu russkikh liudei v Kieve," *KEV* 47 (1906): 1067–70.
104. The quote is from "Tretii z'izd monarkhystiv," *Rada*, 6 October 1906, 3. See also "Raskol sredi 'russkikh' liudei," *KG*, 1 November 1906, 3. For the elliptical response of one all-imperial SRN leader to this conflict, see Gringmut, "Itogi Kievskogo S"EZDA" in *Sobranie statei*, 4:226–28.

1906, Pikhno, Savenko, and I. M. Reva, the longtime Little Russian activist who remained a contributor to *Kievlianin* and a leading figure in the Kiev zemtsvo, organized a political meeting of the southwest's Orthodox landowners. The meeting aimed to combat the political apathy that this group had demonstrated in the first Duma campaign and to convince landowners that the struggle to end agrarian unrest was part and parcel of the movement to create a "Russia first and foremost for Russians."[105] Although scant information on this first meeting has survived, it seems to have brought a powerful new force into the antiliberationist struggle: the region's most powerful Orthodox landlords, many of whom were absentees who had previously played little role in local politics. One such noble, P. N. Balashev, a scion of one of the empire's wealthiest noble families with close ties to the court and the St. Petersburg bureaucratic elite, was elected the conference's president; he would soon become a major figure in the Russian nationalist cause.[106]

After the conference, a small handful of dedicated "truly Russian" activists fanned out across the southwest's rural districts in an effort to educate Orthodox landowners about the importance of voting and to encourage them to support the Russian cause. V. V. Shul'gin, who had acquired a modest estate in Volynia, had calculated that if the region's small landowners (overwhelmingly Orthodox East Slavs) voted as a bloc, they could overwhelm the region's largest (and predominantly Polish Catholic) landlords. In the wake of the conference organized by his stepfather and his compatriots, he returned home to Volynia, where he visited his Orthodox neighbors and sent telegraphs encouraging his friends and associates to vote in the upcoming elections. He also reached out to priests, who in turn encouraged their peasant parishioners to vote the "truly Russian" ticket.[107] Pikhno and Dobrynin, who had also acquired land in Volynia during the de-polonization campaigns, would later join Shul'gin in his efforts to mobilize rural voters.

Meanwhile, the monks of Pochaev launched an orchestrated effort to enlist southwestern peasants in the campaign to defeat the revolution and to establish the primacy of the East Slavs within the empire. They blessed the thousands of pilgrims who traveled to the monastery every year, asking that they "return home and chase from their villages these rats and base freaks [*gady i podlye urody*]"—that is, "Yids and democrats."[108] The monastery's press churned out political pamphlets that circulated as far away as Poltava.[109] One such tract, entitled, "What is better: Russian slavery or the Yids' freedom?," followed the example of Kiev activists in marrying economic concerns, a defense of local traditions, and Russian nationalist rhetoric with

---

105. Quote from "Soiuz 'russkogo naroda,'" *Novoe vremia*, 12 October 1906, GARF, f. 102, OO, 1905, op. 316, d. 999, ch. 39, t. 1, l. 209.
106. Shul'gin, *Years*, 3–4.
107. Ibid., 8–11 21.
108. "Pochaivs'ki chentsi i 'soiuz russkoho naroda,'" *Rada*, 7 October 1906, 2. Although this article is in Ukrainian, this quote, along with several others from the monks, is in Russian.
109. Poltava Governor to Department of Police, 18 January 1907, GARF, f. 102, OO, 1905, op. 316, d. 999. ch. 39, t. 2, ll. 37–38.

an antiliberationist political agenda. The author implored his readers not to be fooled by liberationist slogans; those who claimed to be fighting for equal rights, he argued, were in fact conspiring to install a Jewish president and to sell peasant land to Jews. Lamenting the centuries of suffering that the "Russians" of the southwestern borderlands and their "Ruthenian" brothers across the Austrian border had endured at the hands of foreign interests, the pamphlet urged the authorities to take more aggressive measures to defend the children of Rus' by improving their access to credit, education, and land and by limiting the influence of Jews and other minorities. Again invoking the image of Khmelnytsky, the author insisted that if officials proved unwilling to follow through with these demands, the narod was prepared to liberate itself through force.[110]

Although it is difficult to gauge how peasants and proletarians received these efforts, there are strong indications that at least some segments of the southwest's working classes had come to see the "truly Russian" movement as the force best equipped to protect their economic interests and the culture of their native region. Letters from residents of rural communities poured in to *Kievlianin*, thanking Pikhno for leading the struggle against alleged exploiters, defending local interests, and unifying the children of Rus'.[111] A *Rada* correspondent reported with concern that he had encountered peasants in Volynia who clearly associated the cause of popular liberation with antiliberationist ideas. He described having met Ukrainian-speaking protesters who had refused to work for a Polish landlord until he agreed to increase their wages; despite having organized a labor action, he noted, they sported SRN insignia and chanted slogans against strikes and revolutionaries, which they denounced as contrary to the traditions of the Orthodox East Slavs.[112]

Perhaps the most striking marriage of local patriotism, populist sentiment, and antiliberationist ideologies appeared in one of the many popular journals published by the SRN. A certain A. L-v from Kiev wrote to the paper to report that he had recently visited Shevchenko's grave to "bow before the ashes" of the "Great Little Russian poet." There, much to his consternation, he saw that a Jewish visitor had signed the visitors' book at the site and claimed the poet as a hero of the Liberation Movement:

> You see that even here, in this sacred little corner, a mangy Yid reeking of onion [*parkhatyi tsibulizovannyi zhid*] had tried to sow and propagate anarchy and revolution. The Yid, who signed his name Abrum [sic] Slutskii, scandalously referred in this book to the late Shevchenko as some kind of revolutionary, and ended his comments with words about Yid equality—"proletarians of all countries, unite." ... Scabby Yids everywhere and on every piece of Russian land are trying to insult the Russian Government and every Russian subject.... It's no wonder that the people, angered by the activities of these enemies of our Native land and humanity, are organizing pogroms against them.... This Yid and all his friends forget that the late

---

110. *Chto luchshe: Russkaia nevolia ili zhidovskaia svoboda?* (Pochaev, 1906). This pamphlet was also being circulated in Kiev by early 1907: see *Rada*, 5 January 1907, 3.
111. See, for example, the letter from a "Russian" in Cherkassy, 17 August 1906, TsDIAUK, f. 296, op. 1, d. 2, ll. 23–25; "Golos malorossiiskogo kazaka o sovremennykh sobytiiakh," ibid., l. 28; the letter of a "plebeian" from the Pochaev area, ibid., ll. 374–75.
112. "Lyst z Volyni," *Rada*, 9 November 1906, 3.

Shevchenko in all his poems expressed only suspicion toward Yids, calling them despicable, mangy, vile Yids.[113]

A. L-v, at least, had come to associate the antiliberal ideas of the "truly Russian" parties rather than the vision of their liberal, radical, or Ukrainian nationalist rivals with the struggle to defend the Orthodox peasants of the imperial periphery and their culture.

Elections to the Second Duma

With the Duma elections approaching, the liberationist parties struggled to keep up with the organizational advances of their "truly Russian" opponents. Spilka and Bund activists intensified their lobbying efforts, the former focusing on rural locales and the latter on the Jewish population of district cities. Kiev Kadets, too, formed a regional commission to monitor public opinion and to distribute literature in urban and rural locales.[114] All the while, they continued to support the equal rights agenda and contested the efforts of the antiliberationist forces to portray Jews as the national enemies of the children of Rus' and pogroms as the justified revenge of the long-oppressed masses. In pamphlets and public meetings, liberationist activists argued that peasants, Jews, and other minority groups all suffered equally from the autocratic order and that only guarantees of equal rights could ensure the welfare of all Russian subjects.[115]

Meanwhile, the "truly Russian" forces continued to lobby Kiev's peripheral neighborhoods, blaming social evils on the "enemies of the Tsar, the Fatherland, and our Orthodox Faith." They highlighted their support for an electoral franchise that would offer more power to Orthodox believers and showcased their programs to improve workplace safety and public health.[116] In his *Kievlianin* columns and at large public gatherings in Kiev, Savenko insisted that the class and social differences that divided local Orthodox believers were negligible compared with the immense gulf that separated the children of Rus' from "internal enemies" who for centuries had invoked "cosmopolitan" ideas to justify their exploitation of the masses. Only after the latter had been permanently defeated, he insisted, could the entire East Slavic nation be liberated from the heavy burden it had long carried and its interests aligned with those of the

---

113. *Veche*, 7 September 1906, 4. In response, an incensed *Rada* columnist vehemently objected that Shevchenko had never defamed "others' nations or his own." See Hr. S'ohobochnii, "Chornosotenna brekhnia," *Rada*, 15 September 1906, 1.

114. See the intercepted letters and political reports contained in "Kiev i guberniia," GARF, f. 102, OO, 1906, II-otdelenie, d. 725, ch. 32; "Perepiska s Departamentom politsii o vyborakh v II-uiu Gosudarstvennuiu Dumu," TsDIAUK, f. 274, op. 1, d. 1350.

115. For example, "Pis'ma krest'ianina no. 12. 'O chernoi sotne i evreiiakh,'" 26 January 1907, TsDIAUK, f. 442, op. 857, d. 72, ll. 2–3ob; "Predvybornoe sobranie," *KM*, 22 January 1907, 3.

116. Quote from "Pravoslavnye Russkie Liudi!," TsDIAUK, f. 442, op. 856, d. 817, l. 1. See also "Obshchee sobranie partii pravogo poriadka," *Kievlianin*, 11 January 1907, 3; "Rech', proiznesennaia 7 ianvaria N. I. Chokolovym v Luk'ianovskom Narodnom Dome," *Zakon i Pravda*, 17 January 1907, 2–3; "Narodnyi Dim—na posluhakh pravykh partii," *Rada*, 11 January 1907, 3.

imperial state.[117] Party activists also resorted to dirty tricks to gain the political upper hand: neighborhood electoral committees—which Governor Veretennikov ensured were stacked with antiliberationist activists—made special (and illegal) demands of Jewish merchants who wished to vote, thereby depriving many of their franchise.[118]

"Truly Russian" organizers struggled to reach every segment of the southwest's population. Reva organized an umbrella meeting of "Russian" electors, attended by several hundred from across the southwestern borderlands. The invited speakers at the conference, who included Iuzefovich, Savenko, Reva, Shul'gin, and Kiev city duma deputies, highlighted the historical and contemporary threats that Jews and Poles allegedly posed to the children of Rus' and urged "electors of all circles and classes" to defend the unity, culture, and historical values of the Orthodox East Slavs.[119] Attendees agreed that it would be crucial to enlist peasants and residents of district towns in the electoral campaign, and they organized district electoral committees to mobilize voters and to distribute lists that identified candidates who had pledged to defend Russian traditions. Platon, the bishop of Chigirin (1866–1934), volunteered to enlist Orthodox priests in the Russian cause—as both voters and political propagandists.[120]

In the aftermath of the conference, Reva launched "The Bulletin of the Russian Elector," a series of agitational pamphlets with a circulation of ten thousand that sought to explain the platform of the antiliberationist coalition to the voters of the southwest and to acquaint electors with voting procedures and their rights.[121] Highlighting the "truly Russian" parties' commitment to devolving power to local communities, enhancing peasants' access to affordable land and credit, and restoring social harmony, it encouraged Orthodox believers from all walks of life to join in common cause.[122] Lest this positive encouragement prove unsuccessful, it also resorted to scare tactics. Political apathy or divisions among the children of Rus', it warned, would permit Poles and Jews—who outnumbered East Slavic voters two to one in some rural areas and district cities—to triumph in the elections and reduce the "native" inhabitants of the right bank to mere "ethnographic material."[123]

---

117. A. I. Savenko, "Zametki," *Kievlianin*, 21 November, 1906, 4; "Obshchee sobranie partii pravogo poriadka," *Kievlianin*, 11 January 1907, 3.
118. "V spravi vyboriv," *Rada*, 21 November 1906, 3; "Iudofobstvuiushchaia komissiia," *KM*, 31 December 1906, 3; "Lybedskaia izbiratel'naia komissiia," *KM*, 28 January 1907, 3.
119. Quote from "Oblasnyi z'izd 'russkykh' vybortsiv pivdenno-zakhidnoho kraiu," *Rada*, 22 November 1906, 3; see also "Oblastnoi s"ezd Russkikh izbiratelei v Kieve," *Kievlianin*, 21 November, 1906, 3.
120. *Oblastnoi s"ezd russkikh izbiratelei Iugo-Zapadnogo kraia v Kieve. 19–21 noiabria 1906 goda* (Kiev, 1906). Although the "truly Russian" forces struggled to engage priests in their cause, priests remained exceptionally divided on political and national questions. On the variety of opinions, see GARF, f. 102, OO, 1905, op. 316, d. 999, ch. 39, t. 2; also, Vulpius, *Nationalisierung der Religion*.
121. "Sered pravykh," *Rada*, 17 December 1906, 3.
122. For example, *LRI*, 11 December 1906, 1; *LRI*, 20 December 1906, 2–3.
123. The quote is from *LRI*, 17 January 1907, contained in DAKO, f. 2, op. 41, d. 222g, l. 25. See also "Evrei v vybory v Gosudarstvennuiu dumu," *LRI*, 1 January 1907, 3–4.

Elections to the second Duma began in mid-January 1907. Turnout was high among Kiev's twenty-seven thousand eligible voters, averaging 70 percent citywide.[124] Though preliminary meetings progressed uneventfully in most of the wealthy neighborhoods, polling places in the peripheral neighborhoods (where voting rates neared 80%) witnessed intense conflicts. In Lybed', large crowds implored voters not to support "Yids," adding, "We Russians should vote only for Russians...." In Luk'ianovka, the SRN organized a "security brigade" to maintain order at the electoral meeting, which arrested a passerby who implored the assembled voters not to elect "hooligans." In Plossk, protesters gathered outside the meeting, chanting, "Beat the Jews."[125]

The results of the first round of elections in Kiev were mixed. Liberal and radical parties again swept the city's wealthiest districts, which failed to select any electors to the right of the Kadets; six of the fourteen electors chosen in the Old Kiev police district were Jewish or Polish, and five of these six were classified by police informants as social democrats or radicals. Liberationist parties performed well in the confessionally mixed peripheral neighborhood of Lybed', where voters selected exclusively Kadets and radicals as electors, one-third of whom were not Orthodox. But the antiliberationist forces scored impressive victories in other districts. Pechersk elected seven self-professed monarchists, all Orthodox. The Boulevard district, which surrounded St. Vladimir's University, had selected five Kadet electors in the 1906 elections; now it elected five "true Russians" and one Kadet. In Luk'ianovka, where antiliberationist popular agitation had been most intense, all twelve electors were Orthodox men who identified as "true Russians." Antiliberationist parties also swept two ethnically mixed neighborhoods where the liberationists had performed well in 1906—the mercantile district of Podol and the working-class neighborhood of Plossk.[126] The antiliberationist electors selected by Kiev voters came from all walks of life: peasants, workers, artisans, clergy, merchants, and urban professionals were all represented.[127]

Initial electoral results were more mixed in district cities and rural locales across the southwest. Orthodox landowners in Kiev and Volynia turned out en masse to support "truly Russian" candidates, although this organizational triumph was tempered by Polish landowners' decision to form an autonomous bloc that supported neither the rightist coalition nor the Kadets. District cities, in which Jews represented the majority of voters, tended to choose Kadet or radical electors. The voting behaviors of peasants and rural priests varied widely. Many peasant communes continued to elect trusted community members who did not identify with any party, but a sharp partisan

---

124. "Vybory v Kieve," *KM*, 30 January 1907, 3. Across the empire, 55.7 percent of eligible urban electors participated in the elections. See Aleksei Smirnov, *Kak proshli vybory vo 2-iu Gosudarstvennuiu dumu* (St. Petersburg, 1907), 201. The figure of twenty-seven thousand comes from I. G. Tel'man, *Odin den' Kyeva* (Kharkov, 1937), 10.
125. "Vybory v Kieve," 3.
126. Data culled from the information provided in "Svedeniia o litsakh izbrannykh v vyborshchiki po gorodu Kievu dlia vybora Chlenov Gosudarstvennoi Dumy," DAKO, f. 2, op. 42, d. 300e, ll. 246–550b; "Do vyboriv po Ukrainy," *Rada*, 1 February 1907, 3; "Vybory v Kieve," *KM*, 1 February 1907, 3.
127. "K vyboram," *Kievlianin*, 19 January 1907, 2–3.

struggle emerged in Kiev province, where some peasant gatherings chose dedicated SD activists or Trudoviks and others chose SRN members or affiliates of other "truly Russian" parties. The parish clergy was similarly split: while some supported radical left-wing parties, others favored the antiliberationist coalition.[128]

In early February, electors gathered in the southwest's largest cities to cast their final votes. Antiliberationist parties in Kiev nominated as their candidate Platon of Chigirin, the son of a priest and a committed "truly Russian" activist who had taught in village schools and at the Kiev Theological Academy.[129] Liberationists backed the Kadet Luchitskii. The antiliberationist bloc maintained its electoral discipline, and Platon won a narrow victory over Luchitskii, becoming the first Orthodox bishop elected to the Duma.[130] Kiev gained the distinction of being the only large city in the Russian empire to elect a right-wing deputy—a testament to activists' success in connecting the "truly Russian" cause with progressive social ideas, Little Russian patriotism, and a long-standing narrative of struggle that juxtaposed the interests of the Orthodox children of Rus' with those of the borderlands' non-Orthodox minorities.[131]

Barely pausing to celebrate their victory, Kiev-based activists continued their efforts to influence electors beyond Kiev city. Postnyi and throngs of SRN activists greeted provincial electors when they arrived to vote at the Kiev city duma and later rushed into the hall where elections were taking place, forcing police to drag them out of the building.[132] In Volynia, the Pochaev monks accompanied peasant-electors to the district city of Zhitomir, where the final elections were being held, and paid for their housing there; Shul'gin (himself an elector) lobbied his fellow Volynians to vote a straight "truly Russian" ticket.[133]

Ultimately, "truly Russian" activists' mobilization attempts proved unsuccessful in Kiev and Podolia provinces, where peasants overwhelmingly supported leftist parties. Kiev province voters sent to the Duma five SDs (two peasants, one unskilled worker, one skilled worker, and one teacher) and ten peasant-Trudoviks. Podolia's voters chose one priest and eleven peasants (all Trudoviks), and one Polish doctor

---

128. On results across the southwest, see DAKO, f. 2, op. 42, d. 300a, d. 300v, 300d; "Kievskaia guberniia," GARF, f. 102, OO, 1906, II-otdelenie, d. 828, ch. 8, ll. 2–12; "Poliaki na vyborakh," *Zakon i Pravda*, 8 February 1907, 3; "Chornostenni kandidaty do Dumy vid 'soiuza russkykh liudei,'" *Rada*, 6 February 1907, 3.
129. "Do vyboriv po Ukraini," *Rada*, 3 February 1907, 4. See the biographical information on Platon contained in DAKO, f. 2, op. 42, d. 300e, ll. 71–73.
130. "Vybir posla vid Kyiva," *Rada*, 7 February 1907, 3; "Akt," DAKO, f. 2, op. 42, d. 300e, l. 98.
131. Smirnov, *Kak proshli*, 251. Only in the much smaller city of Kishinev did antiliberationist parties win a higher proportion of urban voters than in Kiev. Many of Kishinev's antiliberationist activists, like their Kiev counterparts, had been involved in zemstvo activism in the early twentieth century; their movement, too, operated largely around a newspaper, P. A. Krushevan's *Bessarabets*. See Rawson, *Russian Rightists*, 96–98. Although no study has explicitly examined the interactions between Kiev and Kishinev activists, Cesare De Michelis notes that right-bank and Bessarabian activists were active in the Russian Gathering from its earliest days. He also remarks that Demchenko published a portion of the *Protocols of the Elders of Zion* in 1906, three years after it first appeared in one of Krushevan's papers. See De Michelis, *Non-Existent Manuscript*, 14.
132. "Vybory v Gosudarstvennuiu dumu," *KM*, 23 January 1907, 3.
133. Shul'gin, *Years*, 20–27.

from the city of Uman' who described himself as a moderate.¹³⁴ Volynia's voters, by contrast, clearly connected the task of popular liberation with the antiliberal yet socially emancipatory program laid out by Kiev activists. That province's electors selected eight peasants, three landowners (including Shul'gin), and one priest—all of whom aligned themselves with the antiliberationist bloc—and one farmer who subscribed to moderate views.¹³⁵

Although "truly Russian" ideologues expressed disappointment at their failings in Kiev and Podolia provinces, they were encouraged by their successes in Volynia and especially Kiev city. Activists exclaimed that while other Russian cities remained in the throes of the Liberation Movement, "ancient Kiev" had intervened to save Orthodoxy, the children of Rus', and the imperial state from dangerous threats.¹³⁶ When city duma delegates, priests, and political activists gathered in Kiev in mid-February 1907 to give the "true Russians" who had been elected to the imperial Duma a warm send-off to St. Petersburg, they expressed their hope that the mass movement developing in the southwest marked the beginning of a new era that would realign the interests of ordinary people, the Orthodox Church, and the tsarist state.¹³⁷

The Second Duma in Action

Much to the chagrin of officials, it soon became clear that the second Duma as a whole was even more radical than its predecessor; socialist, labor, and non-Russian nationalist parties had in fact increased their representation in the body. Soon after its convocation, left-wing delegates pressed for radical land reforms, enhancements in the Duma's powers, and guarantees of equal civil rights for all imperial subjects.¹³⁸ Within a few months of their election, no fewer than three of Kiev province's peasant delegates were arrested for returning to their native province, delivering antigovernment speeches, and distributing illegal materials on behalf of the SD Party.¹³⁹ The Ukrainian Parliamentary Club transcended its left-bank support base, winning the loyalty of several peasant delegates from the right bank.¹⁴⁰ Launching a new Ukrainian-language

---

134. Information culled from M. M. Boiovich, *Chleny Gosudarstvennoi Dumy. Portrety i biografii. 2-oi sozyv* (Moscow, 1907), 123–37, 246–58; DAKO, f. 2, op. 42, d. 300e.
135. Boiovich, *Chleny*, 40–52.
136. Quote from "Provody chlena Gosudarstvennoi Dumy ot Kieva, preosviashchennogo Platona, episkopa Chigirinskogo," KEV 7 (1907): 157. See also "Vybory deputata ot g. Kieva v Gosudarstvennuiu dumu," KEV 6 (1907): 126.
137. Sviashch. D. Sliusarev, "K izbraniiu episkopa Platona v Gosudarstvennuiu Dumu," KEV 8 (1907): 177–80; "Provody chlena Gosudarstvennoi Dumy ot Kieva, preosviashchennogo Platona, episkopa Chigirinskogo," KEV 7 (1907): 156–68.
138. See V. D. Nabokov and A. I. Kaminka, *Vtoraia gosudarstvennaia duma* (St. Petersburg, 1907); V. Ger'e, *Vtoraia gosudarstvennaia duma* (Moscow, 1907).
139. See "Rasprostranenii Chlenami GD protivopravitel'stvennykh proklamatsii," 1907, DAKO, f. 2, op. 223, d. 81; "Perepiska s Departamentom politsii o vyborakh v II-uiu Gosudarstvennuiu Dumu," TsDIAUK, f. 274, op. 1, d. 1350.
140. For a list of those associated with the club, see RS, 12 April 1907, 1.

newspaper, club members pressed for land and education reform, economic development, and cultural autonomy in the Ukrainian lands; portraying the "Moscow government" and the "truly Russian" parties as representatives of Great Russian and landed interests, the club vehemently denounced the imperial state for its indifference to the needs of the periphery.[141]

However, "truly Russian" politicians continued to present their program as the true path to popular liberation. On the floor of the Duma, Platon expressed solidarity with the St. Petersburg SRN members who had assassinated a Jewish Kadet deputy, supported efforts to extend benefits to unemployed workers, and decried alleged incidents in which liberationist activists had employed violence against their political foes.[142] Shul'gin, who demonstrated a canny understanding of the role of political spectacle and grassroots mobilization in Russia's new mass political system, became an even more eloquent spokesman for the "truly Russian" program of illiberal emancipation. In his most notorious display on the Duma floor, he accused the body's entire leftist delegation of concealing terrorist bombs in their pockets and protested loudly as he was subsequently ejected from the chamber.[143] If flamboyant theatrics such as these garnered significant media attention, Shul'gin's contributions as a behind-the-scenes political operative were perhaps even more significant. He frequently returned to the southwest to meet with local activists, published regular columns in *Kievlianin*, which remained the southwest's most influential daily, and quietly cultivated support among St. Petersburg's elite bureaucratic circles. (The appointment of his stepfather, Pikhno, to the State Council in 1907 only enhanced his access to the empire's most influential officials and power brokers.)

Back in the southwest, "truly Russian" activists continued to peddle their nationalizing ideas, progressive social agenda, and antiliberal ideologies among ordinary inhabitants of the region's cities and communes. In the spring of 1907, Kiev activists opened artisanal cooperatives for antiliberationist workers and a bureau that matched employers who opposed the Liberation Movement with mechanical, metal, and stone workers who shared their political views.[144] In May, Iasnogurskii opened a teahouse and reading room on his Luk'ianovka property where workers could socialize, debate, and learn about the newest party initiatives.[145] The Pochaev monks traveled the Volynian countryside, opening new divisions of the SRN.[146] In the spring and summer of 1907, Postnyi launched two separate penny papers, *Veche stol'nogo goroda Kieva*

---

141. Quote from "Ukrains'ka trudova hromada," *RS*, 15 April 1907, 4. See also "Pro narodniu osvitu na Ukraini," *RS*, 29 April 1907, 2; "Chy potriben nam "Soiuz russkogo naroda?" *RS*, 6 May 1907, 1–2; "130 tysiach pomishchykiv," *RS*, 20 May 1907, 3.
142. *Gosudarstvennaia duma: Stenograficheskie otchety. 1907 g.* (St. Petersburg, 1907), 1:604–5, 1275, 1374–75, 1924–25.
143. Nabokov and Kaminka, *Vtoraia gosudarstvennaia duma*, 100–1.
144. "Sered kyivs'kykh soiuznykiv," *Rada*, 28 April 1907, 3; *Zakon i Pravda*, 7 March 1907, 1.
145. See "Chainaia kievskogo otdela 'SRN,'" *KM*, 13 May 1907, 3; *Zakon i Pravda*, 13 May 1907, 1.
146. Governor of Volynia to Department of Police, 9 July 1907, GARF, f. 102, OO, 1905, op. 316, d. 999, ch. 39, t. 2, l. 518.

(Popular Assembly of the Capital City of Kiev) and *Kievskaia dubinka (Kiev Truncheon),* which invited peasants and proletarians to share poems, songs, and political essays with fellow readers. Both papers bemoaned the suffering of the narod and the poverty and underdevelopment of the southwest and called for reforms that would enhance the economic and political power of ordinary Orthodox residents. They too placed the local culture and traditions of the southwest at the very center of the effort to realign the interests of the empire with those of the East Slavs, expressing their desire to recapture the egalitarian spirit and traditions of local autonomy that they argued had been forged in Rus'.[147]

But as "truly Russian" activists expanded their influence in the southwest, the most radical members of the lobby only grew more critical of the state. In his 1907 tract "Jewish Equality or Russian Slavery?" Demchenko complained that virtually all modern Russian statesmen—from Alexander II to Witte and now even Stolypin—had proven too eager to accommodate Jewish interests. Citing authorities as diverse as Theodore Mommsen, Ernest Renan, Peter the Great, and Taras Shevchenko, Demchenko insisted that the dangerous influence of Jews threatened to extinguish the historical and cultural traditions that had been forged in Rus' and protected over the centuries by the "native population" of the borderlands.[148] In essays and open letters that he composed to the authorities, Iuzefovich too complained that both local officials and the St. Petersburg authorities had consistently failed to recognize the sacrifices that the "southern Russian people" had made to defend the integrity of the state and the Orthodox Church over the centuries. Instead, he complained, officials had permitted the East Slavs to be "sold" to their "enemies."[149] He interpreted Stolypin's directives ordering local authorities to do everything in their power to prevent pogroms as evidence that the prime minister served the "Yid press" and Jewish revolutionaries.[150] He denounced the de-polonization polices that the authorities had adopted in "Kievan Rus'" after 1863 as half-hearted, complaining (as his father had in the aftermath of the revolt) that Polish landowners should have been completely expropriated and excluded from civic life.[151]

Expressing growing impatience with the imperial authorities' hesitance to implement the nationalizing reforms that they insisted were necessary to promote the welfare of the simple folk, the southwest's "truly Russian" activists relied on the threat of

---

147. "Obshchestvennaia rol' evreev," *Veche stol'nogo goroda Kieva,* 31 May 1907, 4; "Na odnom iz sobranii Soiuza Russkogo Naroda Predsedatel' KOSRN F.Ia. Postnym skazana sleduiushchaia rech'," ibid., 2–3; "Russkoe natsional'noe dvizhenie," Ibid., 3; "Kliatva chernosotentsev," *Kievskaia Dubinka,* 23 August 1907, 2–3.
148. Iakov Grigor'evich Demchenko, *Evreiskoe ravnopravie ili Russkoe poraboshchenie?* (Kiev, 1907).
149. Quotes from M. M. [B. M. Iuzefovich], *O tom, kak poliaki 40 let ne dremali, podrezyvaia kryl'ia i kogti u nenavistnoi dlia nikh Rossii i kak oni ograbili russkikh pomeshchikov, poselivshikhsia v Kievskoi Rusi posle 1863 goda* (Kiev, 1907), 14, 16.
150. "Otkrytoe pis'mo PA Stolypinu," *Zakon i Pravda,* 15 April 1907, 1. For a similar opinion, see Demchenko, *Evreiskoe ravnopravie,* 83–84.
151. M. M., *O tom.*

popular violence to enhance their power. One of Iuzefovich's open letters to Stolypin warned the minister, "the one thousand year old warrior cannot stand by and wait while the forces who are supposed to be protecting him watch idly as dogs tear him to pieces: he must sooner or later rise in his self-defense."[152] Postnyi's penny papers—which accused Stolypin of permitting Jewish revolutionaries to terrorize the Rus' people and printed cartoons that showed Jewish vampires sucking the blood of peasants and workers—urged vigilantes to punish prominent liberationist activists with death.[153] Contributors to *Kievskaia dubinka* insisted that the weapon named in the publication's title was not merely an implement of violence; the truncheon was also a tool of national regeneration and enlightenment, a means of awakening "Russians from their sleep."[154]

Some of the most prominent leaders of the "truly Russian" lobby expressed concern that violent fantasies such as these threatened to derail their efforts to expand popular support for the movement. In response to demands from some antiliberationist activists that party leaders pledge not to cooperate with "aliens" in any way, Shul'gin argued that membership in the Russian nation should be defined by an ideological rather than a racial litmus test: any individual who opposed the struggle for equal rights and declared his devotion to the Orthodox narod, he insisted, was a loyal proponent of the Russian cause.[155] Pikhno, who earlier had presented Jews and Poles as sworn enemies of the East Slavic simple folk, now backpedaled, urging all sides in the fractious political debates consuming the southwest to avoid physical confrontations and incendiary rhetoric.[156] But these pleas for moderation and pragmatism invited angry retorts from others in the "truly Russian" camp that non-East Slavs would never be able to abandon their "national intolerance [*neterpimost'*]" and their desire to dominate and exploit Orthodox believers.[157]

::

By 1907, southwestern activists claimed to promote the best interests of a supposedly organic and spiritually unified East Slavic nation engaged in a violent struggle for survival against incorrigible enemies. Although Shul'gin and Pikhno attempted to steer activists on a more moderate and inclusive course, the most radical voices in the "truly Russian" movement had set it on a different trajectory from that of the other European antiliberal popular emancipation movements it had once resembled. Prague's National Socialists and Vienna's Christian Democrats moved to the center as they transcended their original urban support base and evolved into major political

---

152. "Otkrytoe pis'mo PA Stolypinu," 1.
153. *Veche stol'nogo goroda Kieva*, 31 May 1907, 1, 8.
154. *Kievskaia dubinka*, 23 August 1907, 1.
155. *Oblastnoi s"ezd russkikh izbiratelei*, 12–16; "Oblasnyi z'izd," 3.
156. *Kievlianin*, 24 September 1906, 2; *Kievlianin*, 27 November 1906, 1.
157. Quote from *Oblastnoi s"ezd russkikh izbiratelei*, 12. For more on these disputes, see "Raskol sredi 'russkikh' liudei," 3; "Oblastnoi s"ezd," 3.

parties; by contrast, Kiev's "truly Russian" coalition only grew more extreme as it attracted new followers. Now the most radical segments of the antiliberationist movement in Russia's southwest resembled a rising force in French politics—the Action Française, generally considered Europe's first integral nationalist movement. Run by provincial patriots hailing from France's peripheries, that movement called for the establishment of a strong state capable of protecting the authentic French traditions that peasants supposedly carried from the existential threats posed by Jews, socialists, capitalists, and foreigners. A royalist movement that championed the Catholic Church, the Action Française also promoted a progressive social agenda informed by syndicalist ideas.[158]

By 1907, imperial officials clearly recognized the threats that the southwest's "truly Russian" forces posed to state stability. In a dispatch to the MVD, Governor-General Sukhomlinov complained of activists' tendency to address the "higher governmental powers" in a "highly insulting" tone and warned that their "exceptional intolerance toward non-Orthodox minorities [inorodtsy] and fanaticism" threatened to "incite one part of the population against the other."[159] After repeated appeals from Sukhomlinov, Stolypin finally agreed to dismiss Veretennikov and expressed his intentions to rein in Iliodor and the Pochaev monks.[160]

Yet Stolypin and his MVD continued to assist southwestern activists at important junctures, overruling Sukhomlinov's decision to outlaw Reva's gatherings of Russian electors and directing local officials to carefully monitor the electoral behavior of "alien"—that is, Polish and Jewish—populations in the southwest.[161] Faced with ongoing threats from liberationists and non-Russian nationalists across the empire, Stolypin also recognized the potential of the southwest's "truly Russian" activists to serve as a party of order. In the years to come, Kiev-based activists would establish even closer ties to Stolypin and the MVD, which would allow them to expand their influence beyond the right bank. However, their arrival on the all-imperial political stage would only intensify the internal political disputes that they had been unable to resolve—and provoke protests from conservative defenders of the regime who insisted that their activities undermined the stability of the state.

---

158. See Eugen Weber, *Action Française* (Stanford, 1962); Ernst Nolte, *The Three Faces of Fascism*, trans. Leila Vennewitz (London, 1965); Paul Mazgaj, *The Action Française and Revolutionary Syndicalism* (Chapel Hill, NC, 1979). Hans Rogger famously argued that the lack of horizontal ties in Russian society thwarted the emergence of integral nationalist movements on the political right. This work, which argues that southwestern activists had indeed created a robust and vibrant civic society, takes a different view. See Rogger, *Jewish Policies*, 212–32.
159. Governor-General Sukhomlinov to Chairman of the Council of Ministers P. A. Stolypin, 14 July 1907, GARF, f. 102, OO, 1905, op. 316, d. 999, ch. 39, t. 2, l. 528.
160. Sukhomlinov, *Vospominaniia*, 125–27; Chairman of the Council of Ministers Stolypin to Holy Synod, 28 July 1907, GARF, f. 102, OO, 1905, op. 316, d. 999, ch. 39, t. 2, l. 561.
161. See "O sozyve v Kieve oblastnogo vnepartiinogo s"ezda russkikh liudei," 1906–7, TsDIAUK, f. 442, op. 636, d. 545; "Raspredelenie kart po kategoriiam," DAKO, f. 2, op. 42, d. 300g, l. 51; "Materialy podgotov. uezdnykh s"ezdov po vyboram v zemskie uchrezhdenii," TsDIAUK, f. 442, op. 637, d. 545, ll. 56–57.

7
Nationalizing the Empire

IN JUNE 1907, Prime Minister P. A. Stolypin dissolved the second Duma on the pretext that its Social Democratic deputies had participated in illegal agitation. Shortly thereafter, he announced alterations to electoral laws, which would be implemented in time for the fall 1907 election of a third imperial Duma. The new laws reduced the electoral power of urban residents and peasants and enhanced that of the largest property owners, who in most locales strongly supported rightist parties.[1]

The so-called Stolypin coup is usually seen as a conservative measure intended to reduce the power of liberationist parties, roll back the social and political reforms of 1905, and produce a Duma that could work productively with the tsar.[2] In the southwest, however, the new electoral system produced a rather different outcome. The region's "truly Russian" partisans argued that it was not mass politics that posed the greatest threat to the imperial system in the western borderlands but rather the continued enfranchisement of the minority groups whom they considered adversaries of the tsar and children of Rus'. Ultimately they convinced Stolypin and the MVD to organize selected electoral contests in the region on a national basis, expanding the electoral power of Orthodox East Slavs and restricting that of Poles and Jews. Rather than restoring the old order in the southwest, then, the Stolypin coup initiated a new experiment in national governance, promoting the putative collective interests of the borderlands' Orthodox East Slavs.

The nationalization of electoral curiae greatly benefited the southwest's "true Russians." With the influence of their political rivals limited, they rapidly enhanced their profile in the right bank, where they now claimed the support of many Orthodox believers, from landowners to urban professionals to peasants and workers. As their local influence grew, they also worked to adapt the concerns and beliefs that had first emerged from the Little Russian lobby and from Kiev urban politics for an empire-wide audience. Southwestern activists—who now frequently referred to themselves

---

1. For details on the new law, see Samuel N. Harper, *The New Electoral Law for the Russian Duma* (Chicago, 1908).
2. Leopold H. Haimson, ed., *The Politics of Rural Russia* (Bloomington, IN, 1979), 94–218; Geoffrey A. Hosking, *The Russian Constitutional Experiment* (New York, 1973), 14–55.

simply as "Russian nationalists"—became a force to contend with in the imperial Duma; meanwhile, they forged relationships with high-ranking officials and joined forces with more traditional right-wing politicians in St. Petersburg to create a formal Russian Nationalist Party, whose influence reached across the empire. This chapter charts the rapid ascent of the southwest's Russian nationalists between 1907 and 1911, showing how they engaged educated society across the empire in a discussion about the characteristics, needs, and prospects of the Russian nation. It also considers the unintended costs of their accomplishments, examining how they unwittingly undermined the stability of the empire.

Preparing for Elections

After the dismissal of the Duma, the southwest's "truly Russian" forces sprang into action to prepare for the upcoming elections. As before, activists convened a Committee of Russian Electors that aimed to unify Orthodox East Slavs from different walks of life against their purported adversaries. Now, however, southwestern intellectuals coupled their efforts to mobilize the masses with more aggressive attempts to convince the authorities to introduce ethnonational status as a consideration in electoral law. Volynia's "truly Russian" electoral committee, which united N. P. Dobrynin, D. I. Pikhno, V. V. Shul'gin, Antonii Khrapovitskii, and local landowners and SRN members, wrote to Stolypin to express its concern that the new electoral laws would strengthen the "alien element" in the region by enhancing the voting power of the wealthiest Polish magnates, who had consistently supported liberationist or Polish nationalist parties. The group added that while the more restrictive franchise in cities and rural communities would reduce the electoral power of liberals and radicals, it would also prevent large segments of the Orthodox population—workers, peasants, artisans—from voting. Imploring Stolypin to prioritize the promotion of "Russian interests" in the southwest, the Volynian committee proposed that the franchise be divided into separate curiae of "Russians and rightists" and "Poles, Jews, and Leftists"; only broadening the voting rights of the first group and restricting those of the latter, they argued, could adequately protect the children of Rus' from the threats supposedly posed by "aliens" and revolutionaries.[3] "Truly Russian" electoral committees in Podolia and Kiev provinces (the latter committee was organized by I. M. Reva) voiced similar demands.[4]

Having long argued that the culture, faith, and language of the East Slavs should enjoy a dominant position in the borderlands, southwestern activists now lobbied for the literal nationalization of the empire's political infrastructure, urging the authorities to make ethnonational identity rather than estate status or property ownership

---

3. Telegram of Volynia Committee of Russian Electors to P. A. Stolypin, summer 1907, TsDIAUK, f. 442, op. 658, d. 95, ch. 6, ll. 61–62.
4. "Kopiia zhurnala zasedaniia predvybornogo komiteta ot russkikh zemlevladel'tsev," 30 June 1907, ibid., l. 17; letter of Kiev Justice of the Peace to V. S. Sukhomlinov, 7 August 1907, ibid., l. 35.

the chief determinant of the rights and responsibilities of corporate groups. Reminiscent of the most radical nationalizing policies promoted by Little Russian activists after the 1863 revolts, these proposals saw the complete marginalization of Poles and Jews as the only reliable means of protecting the well-being of the Orthodox majority.

Although some local officials were determined to reduce the influence of Poles and Jews by any means possible, others warned that the demands of "true Russians" threatened to destabilize the multiethnic empire. The governor of Podolia, who had been present at the planning meeting of self-identified "Russian" electors, informed the MVD that he heartily endorsed the group's recommendations.[5] Governor-General Sukhomlinov, by contrast, was more skeptical. Although he considered promoting the "Russian element" in the southwest a laudable cause, he insisted that this goal could not be treated as a guiding principle of imperial governance.[6] The governor of Volynia agreed with Sukhomlinov, supporting the expansion of the franchise for Orthodox East Slavs in principle. However, he pointed out that this innovation would alienate local landowners, most of whom would see their political power reduced simply because they were classified as Polish Catholics; indeed, he noted that several Polish magnates had already filed protests with his office against the suggested reforms.[7]

Dobrynin, Pikhno, Antonii, and local SRN activists expressed dismay at the mixed responses of local officials to their suggestions. In the words of Dobrynin, bureaucratic resistance to the national curia system threatened the "Russian population [of the region] with full defeat in the elections."[8] In Postnyi's *Veche*, Iasnogurskii expressed outrage that officials had permitted non-East Slavs to "make a mockery of the innocent Russian people."[9]

As discussions between southwestern activists, local officials, and St. Petersburg continued, the MVD proposed a compromise. Officials drew up forecasts that predicted the outcome of electoral contests in every corner of the southwest region.[10] In most local districts, these studies indicated, curial manipulations were not necessary to ensure the defeat of liberationist parties; in these areas elections proceeded under the all-imperial statute, although officials did outlaw preelectoral meetings of Poles.[11] In a handful of districts where "truly Russian" parties were weaker, officials did divide voters into new national curiae. Although the MVD seems not to have expanded the franchise for Orthodox East Slavs in these cases, it did identify local Polish and

---

5. Letter of Podolia Governor Eiler to Minister of Internal Affairs, 9 July 1907, ibid., l. 19.
6. Sukhomlinov to Ministry of Internal Affairs, 9 September 1907, ibid., ll. 120–21.
7. Memorandum of Volynia Governor Shtankel'berg to MVD, 9 August 1907, ibid., ll. 93–112; Shtankel'berg to Sukhomlinov, 4 September 1907, ibid., ll. 91–92ob.
8. Sukhomlinov to Ministry of Internal Affairs, 9 September 1907, ll. 115–17. The quote is from 115.
9. F. N. Iasnogurskii, "Deianiia antikhrista," *Veche stol'nogo goroda Kieva*, 12 August 1907, 2–3.
10. See, for example, the findings of a report based on local data contained in TsDIAUK, f. 442, op. 637, d. 545, ll. 48–61; "Izbirateli v uezdnykh s"ezdakh zemlevladel'tsev," TsDIAUK, f. 442, op, 658, d. 95, ch. 6, l. 9.
11. "O s"ezde predstavitelei poliakov-zemlevladel'tsev 'Litvy i Rusi,'" TsDIAUK, f. 442, op. 857, d. 430.

Jewish residents and reduced their collective electoral power.[12] Although it took pains to avoid unnecessarily alienating non-Orthodox voters, the MVD had taken its first steps toward nationalizing governance in the southwest.

The partial nationalization of the electoral process unified and mobilized rather than demoralized the groups disadvantaged by the new curial system. Across the southwest, Polish landlords turned up en masse at electoral meetings, where they supported the Polish nationalist NDs and expressed outrage at officials' efforts to manipulate the franchise. One Polish landlord who owned an estate outside Zhitomir but resided in Paris reportedly traveled to his home district simply to vote, beginning his return journey to France immediately after he had cast his ballot. But priests, the Pochaev monks, and Kiev-based antiliberationist activists also mobilized, canvassing district towns, cities, and villages across the southwest to explain how their "national party" would improve the plight of ordinary Orthodox believers.[13] Ultimately a strong turnout by "truly Russian" voters—coupled with the nationalization of curiae in key districts—altered the profile of the electors selected by right-bank residents. In Podolia, for example, 35 percent of the electors who chose the delegates to the second Duma had been Polish or Jewish. In the third Duma elections, that proportion dropped to 22 percent.[14]

The meetings at which electors chose the southwest's representatives to the third Duma yielded huge victories for the "truly Russian" parties. Polish nobles and professionals lost their seats to the region's largest Orthodox landowners: F. N. Bezak and A. A. Bobrinskii in Kiev province, and P. N. Balashev, D. N. Chikhachev, and A. S. Gizhitskii in Podolia. These men had all served in the military or bureaucracy in St. Petersburg before settling on their family estates in the late nineties or early 1900s, and many played respected roles in the community, serving as marshals of the nobility, justices of the peace, or zemstvo delegates. Bobrinskii, the leader of the United Nobility during the 1905 revolution and a St. Petersburg city duma and zemstvo delegate, had played an active role in conservative politics in the imperial capital; the other landlords, by contrast, had previously expressed little interest in party politics.[15]

With their wealth, education, and access to elite bureaucratic circles, the southwest's Orthodox nobles would play an important role in the consolidation of an interest group that local officials now described as "Orthodox Russian nationalists."[16] But this group, which comprised one-fifth of the southwest's forty-one Duma deputies,

---

12. Telegram of Kryzhanovskii to Sukhomlinov, 3 September 1907, TsDIAK, f. 442, op. 658, d. 95, ch. 6, l. 113.
13. For descriptions of local elections, see the untitled 1907 report contained in TsDIAUK, f. 442, op. 637, d. 545, ll. 590b–61.
14. "Spravka o raspredelenii vyborshchikov v GD po Natsional'nostiam. Podol'skoi gub.," ibid., l. 16.
15. On Bobrinskii, the United Nobility, and the "Gentry Reaction," see Roberta Thompson Manning, *The Crisis of the Old Order in Russia* (Princeton, 1982), 131–372.
16. Unidentified telegram to Sukhomlinov, 15 October 1907, TsDIAUK, f. 442, op. 658, d. 95, ch. 6, l. 127ob.

was not the only one represented by the "truly Russian" movement.[17] Kiev-based Little Russian activists and urban professionals continued to serve as the movement's leading organizers and ideologists—and as prominent members of the southwest's Duma delegation. V. V. Shul'gin was reelected in Volynia; S. M. Bogdanov, a St. Vladimir's agronomist, zemstvo activist, Kiev city duma member, and *Kievlianin* columnist, won a seat in a rural district of Kiev province. In Kiev city, which now was allotted two delegates, voters of the first curia elected the longtime Kiev city head, a Russian Gathering member; after several runoffs, I. V. Luchitskii narrowly defeated A. I. Savenko in the second.[18] "Truly Russian" professionals from other southwestern cities also won seats in the new Duma, including teachers from Cherkassy and Zhitomir—both officers of their local SRN organizations—and the city head of Lutsk.[19]

Although southwestern peasants continued to elect peers who had achieved the respect of the local community—village scribes and elders, successful farmers, parish priests—they too now gave their vote almost exclusively to self-professed rightists or nationalists. In a striking deviation from the previous elections, when liberationist parties captured the peasant vote in Kiev and Podolia, eight of the ten peasants elected by the voters of those provinces identified as "true Russians"; several boasted of their involvement in local SRN organizations in their official biographies. The southwest's rural electors chose eleven priests to represent them (more than the nine nobles that represented the region). Eight of these delegates identified as "rightists" and one belonged to the Octobrists; several were SRN activists. With thirty-six of the southwest's forty-one Duma representatives aligning themselves with the "truly Russian" parties to the right of the Octobrists—men from all walks of life and social groups—the region had become a major center of the antiliberationist movement.[20]

The Third Duma and Nationalism

Thanks to Stolypin's new electoral statute, the composition of the third Duma was radically different from that of its predecessors. In contrast to the second Duma, in which liberationist parties won more than 60 percent of its seats, parties that opposed equal rights, political amnesty, and the repartition of land now claimed a strong majority. Stolypin aspired to unite these parties behind the Octobrists—now the single largest faction in the Duma—to form a center-right alliance. The Duma majority, he

---

17. Here I differ with Robert Edelman's view of southwestern nationalism, which he characterizes as a reflection of the interests of the local gentry. See Edelman, *Gentry Politics*.
18. Kiev Governor P. N. Ignatiev to Sukhomlinov, 20 October 1907, TsDIAUK, f. 442, op. 658, d. 95, ch. 6, l. 131.
19. Data culled from *3-ii sozyv Gosudarstvennoi Dumy* (St. Petersburg, 1910).
20. Ibid. Only Bessarabia, the province in which Kishinev was located, produced better results for the antiliberationist coalition: seven of its eight deputies (several of whom had been educated in Kiev) belonged to right-wing parties. "Truly Russian" parties performed well in the northwestern borderlands as well, but there their influence was checked by relatively strong Kadet, Trudovik, and Polish Nationalist Party organizations.

hoped, would cooperate with the government and with conservative landowners in the parliament's upper house, the State Council, to produce moderate agrarian, budgetary, and political reforms, to end the revolution, and to strengthen state authority.[21]

By early 1908, the southwest's "truly Russian" Duma delegates routinely described themselves as constituting an organized "Russian nationalist" party. This party remained an ardent foe of the Liberation Movement; it joined with rightist parties to introduce legislation that provided aid to the victims of the revolution and called on loyal Russian subjects to rally behind the tsar.[22] But remaining true to its origins in Kiev's antiliberal populist politics, it continued to endorse a socially emancipatory program. In the first session of the Duma, southwestern deputies joined leftist politicians to demand land repartition, new popular and agricultural education programs, and the expansion of elective zemstva to Siberia and the southwest.[23] Some even called for the introduction of a Ukrainian-language curriculum in local schools, which they argued would better integrate the southwest's peasants into imperial intellectual life.[24]

However, Russian nationalists took pains to distinguish themselves from their "cosmopolitan" rivals on the left, connecting their program for popular emancipation with their ongoing efforts to assure the preeminence of the Orthodox East Slavs. The same southwestern delegates who had supported radical land reforms later clarified that land redistribution should benefit only "native [*korennye*] inhabitants" of the southwest, not "alien" "profiteers and speculators."[25] In a speech on the Duma floor, M. S. Andreichuk, a peasant deputy from Volynia, called on his fellow representatives to increase funding for popular education. Programs to educate and uplift the masses, he argued, were particularly important in the right bank; they would equip his "illiterate, benighted, and hungry" peasant constituents with the confidence and tools that they needed to reclaim their native region from "Jewish hands."[26]

While the southwest's Duma delegates urged St. Petersburg officials to align imperial policies with the putative interests of the East Slavic masses, activists back in Kiev founded a new organization to coordinate lobbying and popular mobilization efforts. In the spring of 1908, Savenko, assisted by I. M. Reva, T. D. Florinskii, and several

---

21. See Hosking, *Constitutional Experiment*, 56–181; Alexandra Shecket Korros, *A Reluctant Parliament* (Lanham, MD, 2002), 107–56.
22. *Prilozheniia k stenograficheskim otchetam Gosudarstvennoi dumy, 1907–1908 g.g.*, vol. 1 (St. Petersburg, 1908), 162–67; letter of A. A. Bobrinskii to editors of *Kievlianin*, 14 November 1907, TsDIAUK, f. 296, op. 1, d. 2, ll. 130–40.
23. See *Prilozheniia k stenograficheskim otchetam*, 1:870–73, 219–28; *Prilozheniia k stenograficheskim otchetam, Gosudarstvennoi dumy, 1907–1988 g.g*, vol. 2 (St. Petersburg, 1908), 484–502; *Gosudarstvennaia duma. Tretii sozyv. Stenograficheskie otchety. Sessiia pervaia*, pt. 3 (St. Petersburg, 1908), 3127–31.
24. "O iazyke prepodavaniia v nachal'nykh shkolakh mestnostei s malorusskim naseleniem," RGIA, f. 1276, op. 4, d. 701, ll. 28–30ob. Several "truly Russian" delegates who boasted of their membership in the SRN in their biographical materials joined with members of the Ukrainian Parliamentary Club and liberationist parties to support this measure. As we shall see, however, their support for this measure would become controversial among self-professed Russian nationalists.
25. *Prilozheniia, 1907–1908*, 1:137–38.
26. *Gosudarstvennaia duma. Tretii sozyv*, pt. 2, 551–52.

other local priests and intellectuals, convened the Kiev Club of Russian Nationalists. Within a year and a half of its founding, the club had amassed nearly six hundred members from all walks of life.[27] It counted among its most active members the urban intellectuals who had presented Little Russian patriotism and antiliberationist ideas as the basis for a Russian national identity—Shul'gin, Pikhno, the Storozhenko brothers, Demchenko, Golubiatnikov, Sikorskii, Iasnogurskii, Bogdanov, and Golubev. However, its membership rolls also included SRN activists of modest means, such as Postnyi, and a healthy contingent of female members and workers. It is interesting to note that dozens of non-Slavic names appear on the list of the club's members; more than a few Lutherans of German descent played an active role in the club, as did some of Polish descent who renounced the Polish nationalist cause and converted to Orthodoxy.[28]

Club members railed against what they saw as the systematic and centuries-long exploitation of the Russian population by Poles and Jews—a pattern, they argued, that had only grown more pervasive after 1905, when powerful minority groups used their newfound political rights to trample the interests of the children of Rus'. On the floor of the club, Sikorskii characterized the ongoing struggle for control of the borderlands as a racial war between the "Aryan" East Slavs on the one hand and Poles and Jews on the other.[29] Although he avoided overtly racist language, Savenko insisted that the southwest's non-Orthodox minorities were incapable of playing a positive role in the empire's social, political, and economic life. "The Poles' and Jews' love for Russia is more than questionable," he claimed. "[T]hey don't want freedom and rights for the Russian people, rather, they want to dominate [Russians], to enslave them."[30]

The Kiev Club promoted a dual mission: to "awaken in the Russian people national sensibility and to deepen their national consciousness" and to assure the "dominance of the Russian people in the state order."[31] The group sponsored archeological excavations of monuments from the Kievan Rus' period and public lectures that celebrated the Orthodox Church, the achievements of East Slavic culture, and the folk traditions of the narod. It opened a public reading room containing materials that its members considered edifying and inspirational.[32] It also joined with southwestern Duma deputies to agitate for the nationalization of the empire's economic and political systems, calling for land reforms and for expanded educational opportunities

---

27. *Sbornik kluba russkikh natsionalistov*, vol. 3 (Kiev, 1911), 13.
28. *Sbornik kluba russkikh natsionalistov*, vol. 2 (Kiev, 1910), 121–40. As Robert Edelman notes, employees of the Southwestern Railroad comprised nearly one-fifth of the club's members. Although Edelman argues that the minister of communications and local railroad officials strongly encouraged their employees to join the club, we have seen that Kiev railroad workers had a long tradition of supporting the "truly Russian" cause, dating back to 1905. See Edelman, *Gentry Politics*, 89.
29. *Sbornik kluba*, 3:18. This speech was later expanded into I.A. Sikorskii, *O psikhologicheskikh osnovakh natsionalizma* (Kiev, 1910).
30. *Nash Kandidat*, 11.
31. The quote is from *Sbornik kluba*, 1:5.
32. On archeology, *Sbornik kluba*, 1:50–51; on lectures, 11, 37, 47; on reading room, 9.

and political rights for Orthodox East Slavs.³³ Bemoaning the inclusion of Kholm, an area with a large number of Ukrainian-speaking Orthodox believers, in the Kingdom of Poland, it agitated for the region—which had been part of the original Rus' domains—be "reunified" with the southwestern borderlands.³⁴

Resurrecting the arguments that Little Russian activists had made in the mid-nineteenth century, club leaders insisted that their efforts to nationalize politics, economics, and culture would not only benefit the southwest but unify and revitalize all the East Slavs and the empire they had created. Savenko and Sikorskii presented the nationalist and populist ideas that had taken root in the southwest as healthy alternatives to the "soulless bureaucratism" that for too long had guided the decision makers of St. Petersburg. Prioritizing the well-being of the "Russians" who stretched from the Black Sea to Siberia, they insisted, would strengthen the capacity of the state and help Russia achieve its historical destiny.³⁵ Resentful of liberal commentators' efforts to portray Russian nationalism as politically retrograde, they also insisted that they were committed modernizers who dreamed of seeing Russia catch and overtake its geopolitical rivals. As Sikorskii put it, "In highly cultured states, for example, in England and Germany, everyone is a nationalist."³⁶

The Kiev Club rapidly expanded its influence, establishing local chapters across the borderlands. (The largest of these, the Podolia Club of Russian Nationalists, claimed two hundred members by 1909 and published its own newspaper.)³⁷ Although the Kiev Club was the most prominent group carrying the national banner, other local "truly Russian" organizations lobbied the authorities as well. In 1908, representatives of the Russian Gathering, Russian Brotherhood, Monarchist Party, Union of Russian Workers, and SRN conducted a study of the Southwestern Railroad company, which revealed that nearly one-third of the railroad's workers and nearly half of its executives were "aliens," and that more than 90 percent of the company's recent contracts had been rewarded to businesses owned by non-East Slavs. In an open letter to Stolypin, members of these groups complained that the strong representation of non-Russians in a strategically sensitive industry imperiled "our native southwest region," as well as "Russian national interests."³⁸ Meanwhile, local SRN divisions demanded that Stolypin diminish the political and economic influence of non-Russian notables,

---

33. On economic opportunity and land reforms, see *Sbornik kluba*, 1:18, 2:8; on education, 1:19, 2:9; on political rights, 1:55–61. Note the similarity of this pressure group to the Pan-German League, which at the turn of the twentieth century sought to align the German empire with the interests of ethnic Germans. See Chickering, *We Men*.
34. *Sbornik kluba*, 3:30–33. On the "Kholm Question," see Weeks, *Nation*, 172–92.
35. The quote is Savenko's: A. Savenko, *Duma i pravitel'stvo* (Kiev, 1909), 3. See also *Sbornik kluba*, 2:35; 3:20.
36. *Sbornik kluba*, 3:20. For one depiction of Russian nationalism as "reactionary," see Paul Miliukov, *"Constitutional Government for Russia"* (New York, 1908), 19.
37. *Sbornik kluba*, 2:61.
38. Quote from Iuzefovich to Stolypin, 20 March 1908, RGIA, f. 1276, op. 4, d. 844, ll. 58–59ob; see also "Zapiska ob inorodcheskom sostave Upravleniia Iugo-Zapadnykh zheleznykh dorog," TsDIAUK, f. 442, op. 638, d. 1, ch. 1, ll. 61–62.

increase land allotments, and lower taxes on the peasantry.[39] They denounced priests who refused to assist their political activities, as well as clerics they considered inadequately devoted to protecting and promoting the children of Rus'.[40]

Conservatives and extreme rightists expressed serious concerns about the rising power of the southwest's Russian nationalists and their socially emancipatory ideas. The central leadership of the SRN criticized Postnyi on several occasions for his progressive stance on social issues and sharp criticism of the tsar; in December 1908, the party expelled Postnyi from its ranks and cut off relations with its Kiev city chapter.[41] The conservative publisher A. A. Suvorin criticized Shul'gin's denunciations of Jewish influence, insisting that the "Jewish problem" described in *Kievlianin,* though a considerable annoyance to Orthodox residents of the Pale, was far from a pressing threat to the empire at large.[42]

Local officials, too, struggled to determine their proper relationship with southwestern nationalists, expressing sympathy for the "truly Russian" cause even as they highlighted its potential to undermine imperial authority and the autocratic system. A. F. Girs, assistant police chief and later civil governor of Kiev, supported the nationalist agenda but also lamented that its supporters rendered pogroms and mass violence a constant threat.[43] For precisely this reason, local court officials continued to prosecute Postnyi and other activists for inciting hatred in their newspapers and political pamphlets.[44]

By contrast, S. E. Kryzhanovskii, the assistant minister at Stolypin's Ministry of Internal Affairs, expressed unwavering support for the nationalist agenda, which he saw as an effective means of reconciling the democratizing processes ushered in by 1905 with a strong autocratic state. (Not coincidentally, Kryzhanovskii was the son of the Little Russian activist E. M. Kryzhanovskii, a Kiev Theological Academy professor who wrote extensively about the Orthodox struggle against the Uniate rite and conducted ethnographic studies of right-bank peasants.)[45] After the completion of

---

39. Iasnogurskii and Postnyi to Stolypin, 11 December 1908, TsDIAUK, f. 442, op. 638, d. 1, ch. 1, ll. 63–640b; "Dokladnaia zapiska Kievskogo Soiuza Russkogo Naroda o neobkhodimosti ustraneniia pravitel'stvom prichin, vyzyvaiushchikh bezporiadki sredi naseleniia Iugo-Zapadnogo Kraia Rossii," RGIA, f. 1276, op. 4, d. 844, ll. 68–730b.
40. For examples of complaints about local priests, see "Ob uchastii dukhovenstva Kievskoi eparkhii v otdelakh chernosotennogo 'Soiuza russkogo naroda,'" TsDIAUK, f. 127, op. 797, d. 260.
41. "Protokol Zasedaniia Chlenov Soveta Kievskogo Soiuza Russkogo Naroda, 10 Noiabria 1908g.," RGIA, f. 1276, op. 4, d. 844, ll. 660b–670b.
42. V. V. Shul'gin, "Po povodu odnoi stat'i," HA, Vasilii Maklakov Collection, box 22, folder, 24, 19–20. On the conflict between Kiev activists and rightists elsewhere in the empire, see Mikhail Loukianov, "Conservatives and 'Renewed Russia,' 1907–14," *Slavic Review* 61, no. 4 (2002): 770, 776.
43. "Evreiskii vopros," BA, A. F. Girs Papers, box 1, folder 4, 3–10. Girs came from a family of Swedish descent that had converted to Orthodoxy and enjoyed an illustrious career in the imperial government.
44. For example, "Delo o Krest. Fedor Iakovleve Postnom, obvin. Po 6 p. 1 ch. 129 st. Ugol. Ulozh.," 8 December 1909, TsDIAUK, f. 318, op. 1, d. 2097.
45. On the elder Kryzhanovskii and his career, see L. S. M., "Zamechatel'nye urozhentsy," 248–49; Theodore R. Weeks, "Between Rome and Tsargrad," in *Of Religion and Empire,* ed. Robert P. Geraci and Michael Khodarkovsky (Ithaca, 2001), 81–83.

an MVD review that advocated the expansion of elective zemstva to the southwest, Kryzhanovskii fils concurred with "truly Russian" activists that the organs of self-governance should be organized on a national basis in order to diminish the power of the Polish landed classes.[46]

Stolypin—though himself a man of the borderlands, having grown up and served in official capacities in the northwest—was more cautious. In dispatches to the Holy Synod, for example, he deemed the democratizing aims and violent rhetoric of Iliodor of Pochaev "completely unacceptable" and demanded that he cease and desist his political activities.[47] The prime minister, who had recently proposed a rather liberal reform measure on the Jewish question that would grant amnesty to Jews residing outside the Pale, also differed with nationalist activists on the issue of minority rights within the empire. Although he had expressed his desire to see a "truly Russian" Duma and had authorized the first measures that nationalized electoral politics, he was not yet prepared to meet southwestern activists' demands that Jews and other "alien" groups be marginalized from the empire's political, social, and economic life.[48]

Non-Russian Nationalism and Its Critics

While Russian nationalists expanded their influence in the southwest, non-Russians continued to benefit from the more liberal laws on press, language, and association introduced in the 1905 period. In 1907 and 1908, the southwestern authorities registered dozens of organizations that catered to minority groups. Many of these groups, such as the Kiev Polish Society for Lovers of Art, the Circle of Polish Writers, and the Society for the Aid of Poor Jews in Kiev (founded by Lev Brodskii), eschewed ideological aims but rested on the assumption that Poles and Jews shared common cultural and social interests. Other groups legally registered with the local authorities—such as Jewish voter mobilization leagues, Zionist cultural groups, Polish political parties, and Oświata organizations (Polish cultural leagues closely associated with the ND Party)—openly participated in political activities.[49]

Ukrainian nationalists continued their agitation as well. Hrushevs'kyi, who now vehemently denounced the constitutionalism of all-Russian liberals as a form of repressive "centralism," announced his intention to settle permanently in Kiev—and his desire to turn that city into the capital of an independent Ukrainian state.[50] In May 1907, Hrushevs'kyi convened the Ukrainian Scientific Society in Kiev, which the historian hoped might "familiarize society with all aspects of the past and present life of Ukraine"

---

46. *Gosudarstvennaia duma. 1908 g. Sessiia Pervaia, chast' II,* 2800.
47. Chairman of the Council of Ministers Stolypin to Holy Synod, 28 July 1907, GARF, f. 102, OO, 1905, op. 316, d. 999. ch. 39, t. 2, l. 561.
48. Ascher, *P.A. Stolypin,* 166–72, 256.
49. On the sheer variety of groups registered, consult TsDIAUK, f. 442, op. 636, d. 647, ch. I.
50. Mikhail Grushevskii, *Edinstvo ili raspadenie Rossii?* (St. Petersburg, 1907), 13. On the historian's growing presence in Kiev, see Plokhy, *Unmaking,* 64.

and serve as the foundation of a future Ukrainian Academy of Sciences.[51] Radicals such as Chykalenko and Ia. M. Shul'gin (the Dragomanovite nephew of V. Ia. Shul'gin), as well as liberals like Naumenko, were among the group's founding members. But in a sign of Hrushevs'kyi's growing influence, some intellectuals who had once been closely connected with the Little Russian cultural project also joined the group: O. I. Levitskii, who had been a prominent member of the "truly Russian" coalition in 1905, now distanced himself from Russian nationalism and joined the Scientific Society instead.[52]

In 1910, the Ukrainian Scientific Society claimed only about one-sixth the membership of the Kiev Club of Russian Nationalists.[53] Nevertheless, the society posed a clear challenge to Russian nationalists' efforts to claim the southwest and its people as integral parts of a nation descended from Rus'—and to the integrity of the empire. As the last members of the generation that had helped define the Little Russian idea passed away—P. I. Zhitetskii and V.B. Antonovich both died in 1908—Hrushevs'kyi and his collaborators canonized them as heroes of the struggle for Ukrainian national independence, overlooking the junctures at which they had collaborated with imperial officials or insisted that they were advancing a program of East Slavic unity. Meanwhile, Scientific Society members expunged the Little Russian idea from Ukrainian history altogether, treating figures such as V. Ia. Shul'gin and M. V. Iuzefovich as Great Russian chauvinists and pawns of the imperial state on the rare occasions in which they were even mentioned.[54]

For their part, officials were no less divided about the proper role of non-Russian cultural associations and political parties in imperial society than they were in their attitudes toward Russian nationalists. Local officials complained frequently that the post-1905 statutes on associations were far too permissive, imploring the MVD to permit provincial governors to outlaw those groups whose activities they saw as a threat to the regime. They expressed particular alarm about Oświata organizations, which in the words of Volynia's governor, promoted "narrow national goals directed at the polonization of the region."[55] Claiming that it encouraged "enmity between Poles and

---

51. "Pershi zbory Ukrains'koho Naukovoho Tovaristva u Kyivi," *Rada*, 1 May 1907, 2. See also Mik. Hrushevs'kyi, "Ukrains'ke Naukove Tovarystvo v Kyivi i ioho naukove vydavnytstvo," *Zapysky Ukrains'koho Naukovoho Tovarystva v Kyivi* 1 (1908): 3–15.
52. For membership data, see "Khronika Ukrains'koho Naukovoho Tovarystva v Kyivi," *ZUNTvK* 1 (1908): 150–59. Levitskii was elected vice president of the independent Ukrainian Academy of Sciences after the 1917 revolution, leaving Hrushevs'kyi the awkward task of explaining how a one-time antiliberationist and Russian nationalist had reinvented himself as a socialist and a Ukrainian patriot. The historian blamed the psychological stress that had resulted from Levitskii's lifelong experience with tsarist repression as the reason for his supposedly erratic political behavior during the 1905 period. See M. Hrushevs'kyi, "Orest Levits'kyi," *Ukraina* 1–2 (1924): 88–96.
53. "Khronika," *ZUNTvK* 7 (1910): 113.
54. For example, Mik. Hrushevs'kyi, "Volodymyr Antonovych, osnovni idei ioho tvorchosty i diial'nosty," *ZUNTvK* 3 (1908): 5–14; V. Peretts, "Pavlo Zhytets'kyi," *ZUNTvK* 2 (1908): 3–38; Iv. Steshenko, "Ukrains'ki shestydesiatnyky," ibid., 39–83.
55. Volynia Governor's presentation to Ministry of Internal Affairs, 31 October, 1907, TsDIAUK, f. 442, op. 636, d. 647, ch. II, l. 620b. See also Kiev Vice Governor to Ministry of Internal Affairs, 31 October 1907, ibid., ll. 56–57.

Russians," Sukhomlinov closed the Kiev province chapter of the group. MVD officials apparently were less convinced of the threat posed by the Kiev Oświata circle; determining that Sukhomlinov's closure of the group had been inappropriate, they reopened it. Months later, however, the imperial Senate overturned the MVD's decision, closing the chapter once more, although it permitted more than fifty other Polish political and cultural organizations to remain active in the southwest.[56]

Policies toward the southwest's Ukrainian nationalist organizations were particularly contradictory. Although "truly Russian" deputies had joined with leftists to call for the introduction of Ukrainian-language instruction in local schools, both local and St. Petersburg officials adamantly opposed this campaign. They insisted that the "Little Russian" tongue was an unsophisticated peasant dialect of Russian; when officials learned that some left-bank zemstvo schools and right-bank parish schools had unilaterally added the Ukrainian language to their curriculum, they insisted that they cease and desist immediately.[57] Nevertheless, in spite of Hrushevs'kyi's open discussion of his plans to build a Ukrainian nation and his efforts to reach out to the masses, officials made no attempt to restrain the historian's activities. Indeed, given the historical centrality of Little Russian culture in the long-running effort to mobilize and unify the children of Rus' against their purported national and ideological enemies, many officials seemed unable to distinguish between salutary and subversive uses of local culture—even when Ukrainian nationalist organizations were promoting this culture. While the Shevchenko Scientific Society openly discussed the need to create national cults of personality, officials permitted the joint efforts of the Poltava zemstvo and Kiev city duma to erect a monument to Shevchenko to continue. (Recall that the project had garnered support from both Ukrainian nationalists and "truly Russian" delegates in the Kiev duma in 1905.) In fact, in 1906, the Committee of Ministers authorized the organizers of the project to collect funds for the project across the empire.[58]

"Truly Russian" activists expressed outrage at officials' hesitance to interfere with the activities of non-Russian nationalist groups. Kiev-based journalists and southwestern Duma delegates asked how government officials could allow Jews and Poles—whom they portrayed not only as age-old exploiters of the Little Russian peasants but also as the organizers of the 1905 revolution—to enjoy any political or associational rights at all.[59] Russian nationalists railed against Ukrainian nationalist activities as well. Kiev Club members denounced Hrushevs'kyi and his followers as pawns of

---

56. Undated report on conditions in the southwest contained in TsDIAUK, f. 442, op. 637, d. 545, ll. 48–61. Quote on l. 56.
57. Memorandum of Director of People's Schools under the Kiev School District, 27 November 1908, TsDIAUK, f. 707, op. 229, d. 122, ll. 127–280b; "Osobyi zhurnal soveta ministrov," 14 May 1908, RGIA, f. 1276, op. 4, d. 701, ll. 26–260b.
58. On national cults of personality, see, for example, an issue of the Shevchenko Scientific Society's publication devoted to Gogol: *ZUNTvK5* (1908). On the approval of the Shevchenko statue, see "Spravka," TsDIAUK, f. 442, op. 662, d. 501, ll. 43–450b.
59. See, for example, D. V. Gotovtsev, *Otkrytoe pis'mo grafu Sergeiu Iul'evichu Vitte* (Kiev, 1908); letter of S. N. Bogdanovich to *Kievlianin*, TsDIAUK, f. 296, op. 1, d. 2, ll. 262–67.

Polish, Jewish, and Austrian interests who intended to destroy Russian civilization by corrupting its spiritual center; what Hrushevs'kyi deemed the "Ukrainian language," they claimed, was his own artificial invention, a tool designed to isolate "southern Russians" from their Great Russian brothers.[60] Despite the fact that some "truly Russian" Duma delegates had demanded the introduction of Ukrainian-language instruction in schools, the club protested the proposal, which it complained would only offer comfort to the East Slavs' enemies.[61]

Yet Russian nationalists' vehement opposition to the Ukrainian national cause should not be mistaken for Great Russian chauvinism or hostility toward the peculiarities of local culture. In 1909, the club established a fund to erect a monument in Kiev to Gogol, whom activists lionized for his devotion to preserving "Little Russian antiquity and Little Russian national customs" as well as the "national and cultural unity of the two branches of the Russian people."[62] The very resolution that Kiev Club members drew up to warn against the dangers of introducing Ukrainian-language curricula in schools proudly highlighted the role that "Little Russia" had played in creating East Slavic culture and the Russian empire: it had given "northern Russia" Church Slavonic, served as the primary supplier of the enlightened clerics who served Peter the Great, and produced talented artists such as Gogol and Kostomarov who captured the authentic Slavic traditions of the local narod.[63] It was precisely because Kiev Club activists identified Little Russia as the birthplace and citadel of East Slavic civilization that they reacted with such fury at the efforts of rival national movements to claim the right bank.

Like their nineteenth-century predecessors, early twentieth-century Russian nationalists presented the Orthodox residents of the southwest as the creators of a national renewal campaign that was poised to unify and strengthen all the children of Rus'. Savenko boasted that "western Russia" had dutifully protected the cultural heritage and faith of the East Slavs even as the inhabitants of central Russia had been deceived and manipulated by foreign interests, revolutionaries, and liberals.[64] In a letter to *Kievlianin*, S. N. Bogdanovich, a "truly Russian" priest who represented the rural voters of Kiev province in the Duma, expressed his hopes that the local narod, which had battled against Tatars, Poles, Lithuanians, and Jews for centuries, would once again channel the "national-popular [*narodnaia*] force of the Cossacks" to deliver

---

60. *Sbornik kluba*, 2:13. Iuzefovich made similar statements in the local press, for which Hrushevs'kyi sued him for slander. Although Iuzefovich was initially convicted, the court's decision was ultimately overturned on appeal. "Prigovor," TsDIAUK, f. 318, op. 1, d. 1758, l. 19; "Apellatsionnaia zhaloba," ibid., ll. 2–20b.
61. "Rezoliutsiia Kluba russkikh natsionalistov," 12 May 1908, RGIA, f. 1276, op. 4, d. 701, ll. 22–250b.
62. Kiev Vice Governor to City Head, 19 March 1909, DAK, f. 163, op. 54, d. 17, l. 5; "Protokol obshchago sobraniia chlenov Kluba Russkikh Natsionalistov ot 14 noiabria 1908 goda," ibid., l. 7. For Savenko's reflections on Gogol as a hero of Little Russia and all the children of Rus', see A. Savenko, "Zametki," *Kievlianin*, 16 November 1908, 1–3.
63. See "Rezoliutsiia Kluba russkikh natsionalistov," ll. 22–24.
64. A. Savenko, "Zametki," *Kievlianin*, 16 November 1908, 1–2. For a similar formulation by Shul'gin on the Kiev Club floor, see *Sbornik kluba*, 2:20.

Cover of a Kiev Club of Russian Nationalists publication. Note that the cover features two prominent monuments to the city's Rus' heritage: the statue of St. Vladimir erected in the 1850s and the statue of Bohdan Khmelnytsky erected in 1888. Source: *Sbornik klub russkikh natsionalistov*, vol. 1 (Kiev, 1908). Courtesy of Slavonic Library, National Library of Finland.

Russia from the dangerous enemies who now threatened it.[65] Continuing to insist that Austrian Galicia comprised an integral part of the Rus' nation, Russian nationalists maintained their efforts to enlist the support of peasants and intellectuals beyond the border. Systematizing earlier outreach efforts, Kiev Club affiliates founded the Carpatho-Rus' Society, which offered moral and material assistance to Galicia's East Slavs and paid for them to visit the southwest, where they could become acquainted with Orthodox holy sites and informed about the "importance of Kiev for the Russian nation."[66]

Nationalizing the Empire, Building a Party

In the spring of 1909, D. I. Pikhno, who continued to hold a seat in the State Council, introduced a bill that would reorganize the upcoming elections to that body on a national basis. Pikhno pointed out that because only those who owned more than two hundred desiatins of land—a demographic still dominated by Polish-speaking Catholics in Volynia and Podolia—were eligible to vote, all the members elected to the body from those provinces in recent memory had been Poles. (Pikhno and the other Orthodox representatives in the State Council from the southwest had received their seats through official appointments.) Pikhno's proposal suggested that Polish electors be placed in a separate national curia whose share of the electorate could not exceed their overall representation in each province (which was less than 10%). Polish gentry and liberals bitterly protested this proposal, denouncing it as illegal and an appalling expression of prejudice; Pikhno's suggestion alarmed many conservatives as well, who noted that it contradicted the basic premises of the estate system.[67] The Kiev Club of Russian Nationalists, by contrast, rallied behind Pikhno's proposition, beseeching the imperial authorities to "correct the political mistakes" that had prevented the East Slavic inhabitants of "western Rus'" from attaining the power in local society and politics that they deserved.[68]

Indeed, Kiev Club members soon called for even more drastic measures to nationalize the region's governing institutions. In a 1909 pamphlet Shul'gin expressed outrage that the Orthodox East Slavic inhabitants of the southwest continued to be deprived of the self-governance rights that inhabitants of other locales had long enjoyed.[69] Although he greeted the appointive zemstva introduced in 1903 as a positive step toward

---

65. Undated letter of S. N. Bogdanovich to *Kievlianin*, TsDIAUK, f. 296, op. 1, d. 2, l. 264.
66. *Sbornik kluba*, 1:16–17; quote from 1:20. Over the years to come, Russian nationalists' interest in the East Slavs of Austrian Galicia would continue to grow as diplomatic relations between the Russian and Habsburg empires deteriorated. On Russian irredentist projects, see Wendland, *Die Russophilen*, 467–539; A. Iu. Bakhturina, *Politika Rossiiskoi Imperii v Vostochnoi Galitsii v gody Pervoi mirovoi voiny* (Moscow, 2000), 34–56.
67. "K voprosu ob izmenenii zakona o vybore chlenov Gosudarstvennogo Soveta v Severo-Zapadnom krae," *Okrainy Rossii*, 11 April 1909, 209–211; Korros, *Reluctant Parliament*, 142–47.
68. *Sbornik kluba*, 1:55.
69. Shul'gin, *Vybornoe zemstvo*, 10–12.

devolving power to localities, he complained that the plutocratic structure of those organs had slowed the consolidation of a strong and self-sufficient Orthodox society in the region; many East Slavic landowners, he complained, remained apathetic or absent, and peasants were impoverished and benighted.[70] Shul'gin echoed Duma delegates' calls to expand the elective zemstva of European Russia to the southwest, with special provisions that would enhance the representation of Orthodox peasants and clergy while limiting the participation of Poles. Smaller minority groups that lived peacefully beside the East Slavs, such as the Czech settlers who had migrated to Volynia in recent years, he argued, should be assigned to the Polish curia so as to further minimize the influence of "unreliable" Polish voters. He did, however, propose a mechanism by which ethnic Poles who had proven themselves loyal to the Russian cause could be assigned to the Russian curia and vested with full voting rights.[71] Kiev Club members greeted this proposal enthusiastically, and in one of the group's meetings, an SRN activist demanded that nationalized curia be introduced into city duma elections as well.[72]

As we have seen, gentry conservatives and radical reactionaries had already expressed concern about southwestern activists' socially emancipatory agenda. With the launch of their campaign to nationalize the empire's governance processes, however, Russian nationalists tirelessly worked to win over these constituencies and to give the nationalist cause an all-imperial presence. Kiev Club members organized a series of meetings in St. Petersburg, at which they highlighted the promise of the movement they spearheaded to destroy revolutionary cosmopolitanism and to unite the empire behind the tsar—agendas that appealed to more conventional rightist groups. Southwestern activists made contact with M. O. Menshikov, a contributor to the reactionary *Novoe vremia*, who began to cooperate with them to craft political strategies.[73] A handful of large landlords in the State Council and conservative Duma delegates from the western borderlands also embraced the nationalist cause, founding a newspaper and a club that purported to represent the concerns of Russians on the empire's western frontier.[74]

Meanwhile, southwestern activists made new inroads in their ongoing effort to influence imperial officials. Having campaigned against Sukhomlinov for years, "truly Russian" activists rejoiced when the governor-general was reassigned to St. Petersburg and replaced by F. F. Trepov, who proved more receptive to their ideas.[75] Meanwhile, they drew closer to Stolypin, who previously had been cautious in his dealings with

---

70. Ibid., 12–20, 25–26, 34.
71. Ibid., 40–43, 47–64.
72. *Sbornik kluba*, 3:97–100; on SRN support, see 2:25. Kiev Club members also argued for the necessity of reducing the influence of Poles in urban affairs and for severe restrictions on the activities of limited corporations and joint-stock companies, which, they complained, often represented Jewish interests.
73. *Zapadno-russkii s"ezd. 4–6 oktiabria 1909 goda* (Kiev, 1911), 3; Edelman, *Gentry Politics*, 74–100.
74. Korros, *Reluctant Parliament*, 112–13. The paper was *Okrainy Rossii*; the club was the Russian Borderlands Society. See *Obzor deiatel'nosti Russkogo okrainnogo obshchestva za 1910* (St. Petersburg, 1911).
75. A. A. Sidorov, "V Kieve (1904–1909)," *Golos minuvshego* 4–6 (1918): 224–27.

Russian nationalists. In the wake of a ministerial crisis in the spring of 1909 and growing rifts within the Octobrist Party, which Stolypin had regarded as the foundation of his center-right government, the prime minister found himself weakened and in need of new allies. After an audience with a united delegation of rightist and nationalist activists, he signaled his support for the Pikhno bill and other nationalizing measures, including the separation of Kholm from the Kingdom of Poland and its addition to the southwestern borderlands. He also promised to introduce a bill in the fall of 1909 that would create nationalized zemstva elected by franchises twice as broad as those in central Russia and place limits on the participation of non-East Slavs in these organs.[76] In light of this victory, rumors swept the empire that Pikhno would soon be invited to head a ministry or even to replace Stolypin.[77]

Emboldened by these successes, southwestern activists, extreme rightists, and moderate conservatives in St. Petersburg organized a conference of "national-patriotic organizations of western Rus'" to lobby for the nationalization of the empire's political institutions. Participants agreed that Kiev should host the conference, remarking, "in our troubled times Kiev first raised the Russian standard, which it continues to hold high."[78] Organized by Pikhno, Savenko, Liubinskii, SRN members, local clergy, and southwestern Duma delegates, the conference convened in October 1909, welcoming more than two hundred city and zemstvo activists who represented more than thirty "national-Russian parties." Nearly half of the attendees hailed from the southwestern borderlands, but the organizers welcomed large delegations from Austrian Galicia, the northwestern borderlands, and central Russia as well. The backgrounds and social status of the attendees were no less diverse than those of the organizers: priests, large landowners, urban intellectuals, and peasants were all in attendance.[79] Vowing that "western Rus'" would lead the struggle against "liberal-cosmopolitan" ideas, conference attendees expressed their strong enthusiasm for nationalized *zemstva* and the separation of Kholm. They also bemoaned the suffering of Galician peasants under Poles and Jews and Austrian imperial rule.[80]

In spite of the efforts of the organizers to present a united front, however, conference attendees fiercely debated how to reconcile the national principles of governance that they were promoting with the empire's supranational structures.[81] Some participants complained that even if Stolypin managed to nationalize electoral structures

---

76. On these cooperative ventures, see Edelman, *Gentry Politics*, 83–86; Hosking, *Constitutional Experiment*, 74–149; *Natsionalisty v 3-ei Gosudarstvennoi Dume* (St. Petersburg, 1912), 98. It is interesting to note that Hrushevs'kyi, a Kholm native, also supported the separation of his native province. See Plokhy, *Unmaking*, 66.
77. Korros, *Reluctant Parliament*, 135.
78. *Zapadno-russkii s"ezd*, 3.
79. Ibid., 5–6; on the profile of those in attendance, see E. S., *Istoricheskoe znachenie Kievskogo "Zapadno Russkogo S"ezda" 4, 5, i 6 oktiabria 1909 g.* (Kiev, 1909), 5.
80. The quote is from *Zapadno-russkii s"ezd*, 6. On the conference's program, see ibid., 61–63.
81. For more on this dilemma, see Mikhail Loukianov, "'Russia for Russians' or 'Russia for Russian Subjects?' Conservatives and the Nationality Question on the Eve of World War I," *Russian Studies in History* 46, no. 4 (2008): 77–92.

in the northwest, Polish influence there was so great that Poles would still win many seats in elections. To prevent this possibility, they argued, non-East Slavs must be banned altogether from voting in local elections or from serving on zemstvo boards. Others, such as Shul'gin and Savenko, insisted that this solution was too extreme. Although they understood Russianness as an expression of the culture and traditions of the Orthodox East Slavs, they maintained that membership in the Russian nation should be open to those of other backgrounds who recognized the primacy of the Rus' people. Punishing Poles who had renounced national separatism and were willing to cede the preeminent role in imperial governance to the East Slavs, they argued, would only alienate the former.[82]

Ultimately, the more moderate vision of Shul'gin and Savenko prevailed: the conference endorsed the implementation of zemstva only in the six western provinces in which nationalized curiae could guarantee "truly Russian" victories. Participants agreed that the implementation of elective zemstva in provinces where outcomes would be less certain should be delayed until officials could guarantee that their introduction would serve the interests of the Russian population. While this compromise endeavored to avoid alienating Catholics of Polish heritage who could potentially join the nationalist cause, conference attendees did not extend the same courtesy to Jews. The resolution they drew up insisted that Jews must be banned not only from the electorate but also from the ranks of professionals (doctors, teachers, accountants, judges, etc.) employed by the zemstva.[83]

Shortly after the conference, "truly Russian" forces from across the empire convened again in St. Petersburg, where they announced the creation of a formal, all-imperial political party, the All-Russian National Union. Uniting southwestern activists from all walks of life, Menshikov and other extreme rightists, and right Octobrists, the party embraced the agenda that Kiev activists had been promoting for years. Its platform relied heavily on the notion that foreign interests had systematically exploited the East Slavs and degraded their faith and culture. It lobbied for aggressive measures to enhance the political and economic power of Orthodox believers; the abolition of the Pale of Settlement, which, activists argued, subjected residents of the western borderlands to constant abuse by Jews; the political "reunification" of the East Slavs of the Habsburg empire with their Russian brothers; and official recognition of the primacy of the Russian language and Orthodox Church across the empire. The party's platform also reflected the progressive social agenda that had long guided the southwest's "true Russians." It called for a constitutional monarchy, an imperial Duma with enhanced powers elected by a broader franchise, the expansion of local self-governance, universal elementary education, and the creation of new social safety nets to protect the most vulnerable members of society. Taken together, party activists

---

82. *Zapadno-russkii s"ezd*, 41–43, 63. For further elaboration of Shul'gin's views, see Shul'gin, *Vybornoe zemstvo*.
83. *Zapadno-russkii s"ezd*, 48–49; "Zapadno-russkii s"ezd v Kieve," *Okrainy rossii*, 2–19 September 1909, 521–22.

Members of the Nationalist Party in the Third Duma. Note the social diversity of the delegates and the divergent localities from which they hail. Pictured from top to bottom, from left to right, are E. K. Akimov, a peasant from Penza province; S. N. Alekseev, a teacher and journalist from Warsaw; V. G. Amosenok, a peasant from Vitebsk province; Prince I. V. Variatinskii, a noble from Kursk province; Count V. A. Bobrinskii, a noble from Tula province; F. N. Bezak, a noble and retired colonel from Kiev province; N. S. Balalaev, a priest from Orenburg province; G. A. Andriichuk, a peasant from Podoliia province; and I. M. Atanazevich, a priest from Kiev province. Source: *3-ii sozyv Gosudarstvennoi Dumy. Portrety. Biografii. Avtografii* (St. Petersburg, 1910), plate 11. Courtesy of Slavonic Library, National Library of Finland.

argued, these measures would reclaim "Russia for Russians," definitively realigning the imperial state with its Orthodox East Slavic population.[84]

Southwestern activists had transformed a regional crusade built on the Little Russian idea into an all-imperial political party; transcending their original support base of urban intellectuals, they had created a socially variegated movement that claimed peasants, workers, nobles, and priests among its members.[85] Celebrating their accomplishments, Kiev Club activists claimed that the victory of the "Russian people" over the "alien world" was near.[86] Savenko predicted that the new National Union would reinvigorate even "cosmopolitan Petersburg" with a healthy national spirit and would create a permanent nationalist majority in the Duma.[87]

However, the very diversity of All-Russian National Union undermined its coherence from the beginning. The club that the party established in St. Petersburg hosted stormy meetings, at which members who decried political parties as divisive and unnecessary wrangled with those such as Savenko, who aimed to create a mass-appeal movement.[88] And although the Nationalist Party had attained all-imperial influence, Orthodox activists from the western borderlands continued to dominate its ranks; more than half of the Duma's nationalist delegation self-identified as Little Russians or Belarusians.[89] The future potential of the movement would depend on its leaders' ability to reconcile their interest in mass political mobilization with their efforts to defend an autocratic empire—and their success in translating the concerns that had emerged from the empire's western frontier to an audience beyond the borderlands.

The Western Zemstvo Campaign

By late 1909 and early 1910, the All-Russian National Union had established a close working relationship with Stolypin. The prime minister cooperated with nationalist Duma deputies to pass a bill that limited Finnish autonomy and protected the rights of East Slavs in the Grand Duchy and another that separated Kholm province from the Kingdom of Poland.[90] Indeed, Stolypin's relations with the Nationalist Party were now so cordial that St. Petersburg buzzed with rumors that he had issued a secret circular ordering bureaucrats to support the Nationalist Party.[91]

---

84. "Proekt platformy, ob"ediniaiushchei russkikh narodnykh natsionalistov" (1911 pamphlet with no further publication information), 1–4; "Russkaia natsional'naia fraktsiia," *Rossiia*, 27 October 1909, 1; "Otkrytie Vserossiiskogo natsional'nogo kluba," *Kievlianin*, 3 December 1909, 2–3; for further details on the party's formation and platform, consult Kotsiubinskii, *Russkii natsionalizm*, 30–75, 149–427.
85. The point that nationalists transformed regional interests into an all-imperial political platform is made strongly in Edelman, *Gentry Politics*, 100.
86. *Sbornik kluba*, 2:5.
87. Quote from *Kievlianin*, 5 December 1909, 1. See also A. Savenko, "Zametki," *Kievlianin*, 5 January 1910, 2.
88. For an analysis of these tensions, see Edelman, *Gentry Politics*, 96–99.
89. *Natsionalisty*, 141.
90. Edelman, *Gentry Politics*, 102–13.
91. See clippings from *Birzhevye vedomosti* and *Novaia Rus'* contained in RGIA, f. 1284, op. 187, d. 260, ll. 138–39.

Nationalist Duma delegates garnered attention for their ongoing efforts to reduce Jewish involvement in the empire's political, cultural, and economic life.[92] But the western zemstvo campaign remained the primary concern of the party. Shortly after the October 1909 conference in Kiev, Stolypin endorsed the proposal backed by its delegates, which called for the expansion of elective zemstva to six (of nine) western provinces where East Slavic majorities could be guaranteed by dividing Russian and Polish voters into separate curiae. The bill dramatically expanded the franchise for those the government classified as Russians—identified primarily by their Orthodox faith, although this criterion would later become controversial—setting the economic threshold that qualified voters in the borderlands at one-tenth the level that prevailed in central Russia. The legislation also encouraged the active participation of Orthodox priests in elections and zemstvo governance, set quotas on the number of non-Russians who could be employed by zemstva, and reorganized city duma elections in the borderlands on a national basis.[93]

Despite Stolypin's enthusiastic support for these nationalizing measures, the Council of Ministers expressed concern about the prime minister's bill. Ministers objected that the national quotas went too far in placing the needs of Orthodox East Slavs over those of the "non-Orthodox [*inoslavnyi*] local population." They also expressed concerns that the expansive involvement of priests in elections might violate canon law.[94] Opposition to Stolypin's bill continued to build as it entered the Duma committee on local self-governance in early 1910. Octobrists worried that the franchise offered to "Russian" voters was too broad. Insisting that economic status was the best predictor of voters' political reliability, they demanded that it should continue to serve as the primary criterion used to determine individuals' eligibility to participate in elections. In response to these critiques, the Nationalist Party was forced to compromise. To placate the Octobrists, party leaders agreed to divide the Russian curia of voters into separate subcuriae with varying electoral powers based on their property ownership; they did manage, however, to retain language in the bill that would bar the non-Orthodox from serving as teachers in zemstvo schools.[95]

Although the Kiev Club of Russian Nationalists worked closely with the Nationalist Party to secure passage of a western zemstvo bill, the group insisted that the curiae must be defined solely by national principles, and it favored the broadest possible franchise for East Slavs.[96] Club pamphlets bitterly decried the Octobrists for defending the narrow class interests of the landed elite, lamenting that the bill that had passed through the Duma committee would fail to halt the age-old exploitation of

---

92. For example, "Summary of Proceedings in the Duma and Council of Empire for the Fortnight Ending April 21, 1910," in *British Documents on Foreign Affairs*, pt. 1, series A, vol. 6 (Lanham, MD, 1983), 26.
93. "Izlozhenie dela," 19 November 1909, RGIA, f. 1276, op. 5, d. 73, ll. 2–35.
94. See the MVD's memorandum on the 8 December 1909 meeting of the Council of Ministers, ibid., ll. 168, 172, 178.
95. Ibid., ll. 167–86.
96. *Sbornik kluba*, 3:57–66. Local meetings of "truly Russian" activists also protested the revisions to the original bill. See ibid., 3:108–10.

the "Russian Orthodox popular masses."⁹⁷ Savenko denounced the hostility of St. Petersburg officials and the elites of central Russia to the original zemstvo bill as further proof of these groups' historic neglect of the needs of the "western Russian masses." "They've never cared to which nationality and religion the 'narod,' the 'khlopy,' belong," he lamented. The determination of Octobrists and officials to place the interests of "several hundred Polish landlords above millions of Russian peasants," he complained, would reverse all the gains that the children of Rus' had made over the nineteenth century, confirming the status of "western Rus'" as a "Polish region."⁹⁸

In May 1910, debate on the western zemstvo bill opened on the floor of the Duma. S. M. Bogdanov, a Nationalist Party leader from Kiev province, invoked the legacy of V. Ia. Shul'gin, arguing that nationalized elective zemstva would realize the late scholar's dream to see the "slaves" of the borderlands liberated from their putative oppressors.⁹⁹ A peasant representing Volynia, M. S. Andreichuk, predicted that the western zemstva would radically improve the quality of life of southwestern peasants and would guarantee their victory in what he described as an ongoing war to reclaim their native land from foreign occupiers.¹⁰⁰

Others, however, continued to voice anxieties about the reorganization of imperial political institutions on a national basis. Some conservative deputies complained that the low economic qualifications for voting in the western borderlands would permit small landholders and peasants to overwhelm landed interests. Moderates feared that far from mitigating the threat that nationalists alleged Poles posed to the empire, the national curia system would destabilize the empire, creating new animosities between the borderlands' inhabitants. Liberals and radicals pointed out that the legislation would create new and arbitrary legal categories that would privilege some and limit the political rights of others. Polish deputies criticized the bill as a shameless attack on the empire's Poles, who had made important contributions to the borderlands' economic vitality and cultural life.¹⁰¹

But when opponents of the zemstvo bill aired their concerns on the Duma floor, the supporters of the legislation pointed to their protests as proof that wealthy (and overwhelmingly non-Russian) interests were engaged in a conspiracy to trample the interests of the Orthodox East Slavs. In response to the charge that the legislation encouraged national hatred, its supporters rebutted that Poles, who had allegedly exploited Little Russians and their Ruthenian brothers across the Austrian border for centuries, were themselves to blame for the popular animosity directed at them.¹⁰²

---

97. Ibid., 3:113, 121; quote from "Byt'-li Zapadnaia Rus' Pol'shei ili Rus'iu?" (Kiev Club pamphlet, 1910), 2.
98. Quotes from A. Savenko editorial, *Kievlianin*, 13 May 1910, 1–2; Savenko editorial, *Kievlianin*, 20 May 1910, 2.
99. *Gosudarstvennaia duma. Tretii sozyv. Stenograficheskie otchety. 1910 g. Sessiia tret'ia*, pt. 4. (St. Petersburg, 1910), 792.
100. Ibid., 825–30.
101. For elaboration on these objections, see E. S., *Istoricheskoe znachenie*; "Prozorlivtsy iz 'Dziennik'a Kijowsk'ago [sic],'" *Kievlianin*, 1 November 1909, 2.
102. *Gosudarstvennaia duma. Tretii sozyv*, pt. 4, 762–67.

When a Social Democrat representing the city of Tiflis alerted his fellow deputies that Witte had condemned the legislation as an unjust attack on the political rights of national minorities, Nationalist delegates shouted back, "COUNT Witte." Thus they dismissed the opposition of a statesman with close ties to the borderlands' multiethnic capitalist elite as a reflection of his own economic privilege.[103]

As the debate intensified, Stolypin took to the floor of the Duma, where he delivered a speech in defense of the bill that could have been written by the Club of Russian Nationalists. Describing "western Rus'" as an age-old battleground between the "Russian-Slavic" people on the one hand and Jewish and "Polish-Latin" civilization on the other, he faulted the bureaucrats who had preceded him for their failure to protect the interests of the former. Between the Polish partitions and 1830, he complained, imperial policies had only consolidated the power of the region's non-East Slavs; the imperial estate system had sanctioned the szlachta's enslavement of Orthodox peasants, and the authorities' affirmation of Magdeburg law had allowed Poles and Jews to seize political power in cities. Stolypin praised Nicholas I for implementing new policies to promote "Orthodoxy and Russian elements" in the region, but he complained that since 1905, government officials again had come to serve the interests of "aliens." (Indeed, in his speech, Stolypin quoted a Ukrainian-language proverb lamenting the plight of the narod under foreign "lords.") Now, he argued, the passage of a bill that established zemstva with national curiae and a broad franchise would signal that the government was once again committed to protecting "the rights of the economically weak Russian majority."[104] On 29 May 1910, a large Duma majority passed the bill, which established nationalized zemstva in six western provinces and set the economic thresholds that qualified "Russians" to vote at half the level required in other provinces.

Expansion and Radicalization

The passage of the western zemstvo bill marked the apex of the power of the nationalist lobby and the southwestern activists who had helped create it. By the summer of 1910, defections from the rightist parties to the Nationalists had made the party the second-largest faction in the State Duma; though Octobrists maintained their numerical advantage, informed observers perceived the Nationalists, who continued to work closely with Stolypin, as the premier political force in Russia.[105] Emboldened by its success, the party intensified its outreach efforts. It established twenty local bureaus from Irkutsk to Minsk and printed one hundred thousand copies of a publication that highlighted its accomplishments in the third Duma. It distributed agitational material aimed at the masses to zemstvo activists, priests, and peasant communes.[106]

---

103. Ibid., 752–59.
104. Ibid., 774–775, 778–786.
105. *British Documents*, 52–56, 73.
106. *Obzor deiatel'nosti Vserossiiskogo natsional'nogo soiuza za 1912–1913 g.* (St. Petersburg, 1914), 14–16.

Back in the southwest, nationalist organizations continued to expand their support base. The Kiev Club of Russian Nationalists, which now claimed over 700 members in its flagship Kiev organization and 250 in its Podolia affiliate, opened new local chapters in Minsk and Vilnius.[107] That same year, Savenko, V. Ia. Demchenko (1875–1933— an engineer and the son of the longtime Little Russian activist Ia. G. Demchenko), the Storozhenko brothers, S. T. Golubev, nationalist landowners, and SRN activists convened a Kiev chapter of the Galician-Russian Society, which pledged to assist "Galician Rus'" in her struggle for national self-definition (*samobytnost'*).[108] In 1910, the Russian National Student Union convened in Kiev. It eventually published a collection of articles penned by its members that surveyed the historical suffering of Russians at the hands of "foreign" interlopers and called on the state to create a "national nucleus," a coherent "cultural-historical unity" that could bind its vast domains into an "organic whole."[109] Nationalist activists also continued their struggle to expand their support among the working classes.[110] The Double-Headed Eagle, the youth group founded in 1906 that sought to encourage cross-class relationships, was reenergized under the leadership of V. S. Golubev (1891–1914), the son of S. T. Golubev. The group now launched a newspaper (*Dvuglavyi orel*) aimed at a popular audience, which frequently bemoaned the difficult plight of urban workers and peasants and presented the nationalization of the local economy as the only solution to their problems.[111]

But in a socially stratified society that continued to be ruled by an estate system, was it really possible to reconcile the interests of urban intellectuals, the landed gentry, and the masses? The most ambitious attempt to create an intellectual framework capable of accomplishing this goal was made by T. V. Lokot' (1869–1942), an agronomist trained at St. Vladimir's and a member of the Kiev Club of Russian Nationalists. Born into a left-bank peasant family of Cossack descent, Lokot' had served as a deputy in the Chernigov zemstvo and as one of that province's representatives to the first Duma. A strong proponent of land reform, he had aligned himself with the leftist parties in the Duma that advocated land repartition and had even signed the Vyborg manifesto, which denounced the government's dismissal of that body.[112] By 1910, however, he had come to see the nationalizing ideas promoted by southwestern activists as the best means of protecting all the children of Rus'—including the most vulnerable members of society.

Lokot' viewed the national and political conflict that had gripped the southwest for centuries as a result of economic conflict between East Slavic peasants and Poles

---

107. Edelman, *Gentry Politics*, 113; *Sbornik kluba*, 3:59.
108. *Otchet o deiatel'nosti Kievskogo Otdeleniia Galitsko-Russkogo Obshchestva* (Kiev, 1915), 19; on membership, see 13, 21. This group was a spin-off of a St. Petersburg organization founded by Bobrinskii.
109. *Sbornik Kievskogo otdela Vserossiiskogo natsional'nogo studencheskogo soiuza* (Kiev, 1912). This quote is from Rod. Kutepov, "Lichnost' i narod," 123–24.
110. For example, A. Volynets, "Novaia polonizatorskaia zateia," *Kievlianin*, 25 January 1910, 1–2; I. Reva, "Krupnyi shag v dele melkogo kredita," *Kievlianin*, 5 May 1910, 1–2.
111. For example, *Dvuglavyi orel*, 16 January 1911, 1–2.
112. On Lokot''s background, see *Gosudarstvennaia duma pervago prizyva* (Moscow, 1906), 93.

and Jews, who he claimed had consistently placed their own narrow interests over the welfare of the population of the borderlands as a whole. Like many nationalist activists, he viewed the 1905 revolution as an intensification of this ongoing conflict. Although Polish magnates and "rich Kiev Jews, the Brodskiis, the Gintsburgs, and others" had embraced liberal slogans and universalist rhetoric, in fact, he argued, the political agenda they advanced aimed only to consolidate their power and wealth.[113] In published essays as well as in *Kiev*, the daily newspaper he founded in early 1910, Lokot' called for the creation of a progressive, national regime to liberate the East Slavs from the heavy yoke that they continued to carry. The "National Democracy" he envisioned would strip Jews and Poles of their influence and vest more property, power, and capital in the hands of the "*native* mass of the population."[114]

Lokot' had no patience for Ukrainian separatism, which, he argued, could benefit only Jews and other "aliens" attempting to divide and conquer the East Slavs.[115] But he, like many of his colleagues in the Kiev Club, remained an ardent Little Russian patriot. Lokot' characterized Little Russian culture as a "deeply positive phenomenon," a powerful weapon against "cosmopolitanism...Jewish nationalism...[and] Polish nationalism." Identifiying Shevchenko, Kulish, Kostomarov, and Dragomanov as the founders of the "progressive-democratic *national* movement," he portrayed the "Little Russian struggling and middling popular masses" as the group that would see this movement to fruition.[116] Lokot' insisted that instilling "tribal-national self-awareness" (*plemennoe natsional'noe samosoznanie*) in the "Little Russian nationality" did not at all detract from the laudable effort to develop "national-state consciousness" (*soznanie natsional'no-gosudarvennoe*); on the contrary, the power of the state and the unity of the East Slavs could best be enhanced by embracing the authentic Orthodox values and strong national spirit that had been preserved by the Little Russian narod.[117] The nationalist agenda of the Little Russian people, explained another *Kiev* contributor, would create a just order that would serve all the children of Rus', one "built on the foundation of the popular will, the native masses, and not on [the principle of] 'equal rights' for Jews."[118]

Although it is difficult to gauge how the largely illiterate workers and peasants of the southwest received the overtures of nationalist intellectuals, it is clear that antiliberal nationalist organizations had become an important part of the fabric of local communities. Despite the fact that the prominence of the SRN had begun to fade on the all-imperial stage, the organization was omnipresent in right-bank towns and villages. Indeed, it assumed key social welfare functions, establishing schools; providing aid

---

113. Quote from T. V. Lokot', *Opravdanie natsionalizma* (Kiev, 1910), 63–64.
114. Quote from "K chitateliam," *Kiev*, 12 January 1910, 2. See also T. V. Lokot', *Natsionalizm i evrei* (Kiev, 1910); *Lado* (St. Petersburg, 1911).
115. Lokot', *Opravdanie*, 14–15.
116. Quotes from ibid., 12; Lokot', *Natsionalizm*, 10.
117. Lokot', *Opravdanie*, 12; "Ukrainskii vopros," 2–4.
118. *Kiev*, 20 February 1910, 5. This article is a laudatory review of *Osnova*'s role in anti-Jewish agitation in the 1860s.

to the needy, sick, and hungry; and even forming voluntary citizens' brigades to police localities.[119] Furthermore, many ordinary residents of the southwest repeated the claims of intellectuals and activists that nationalizing measures were necessary to improve the welfare of the narod. Peasants and workers continued to write to *Kievlianin* expressing their desire to see Polish and Jewish influence eliminated from the region so that the Orthodox East Slavs could claim the wealth, jobs, and resources that non-Russians allegedly enjoyed.[120] Both city residents and rural dwellers informed SRN leaders and imperial officials of Jews whom they had found residing illegally in their local communities, presenting their denunciations as acts of patriotic devotion.[121]

"Alien" Organizations and the Struggle for Local Culture

As the influence of Russian nationalists in local and imperial politics crested, Stolypin's MVD began to reconsider the liberal association laws that had emerged from the 1905 period, arguing that it needed more authority to limit and police the activities of social and political groups that catered to "alien [*inorodcheskii*] elements." A 1909 decision by the Ruling Senate confirmed that the ministry could take more aggressive actions to ban groups that united "alien elements on the basis of their exclusive national interests."[122] In the wake of the ruling, the MVD launched a detailed study of the activities of Polish, Muslim, Finnish, Estonian, and other minority groups across the empire and asked local officials to report on the influence of these organizations in the areas under their control.[123]

The feedback that St. Petersburg received from southwestern officials was alarming. Bureaucrats in Podolia and Volynia noted that even after recent efforts to nationalize governance structures, Polish cultural and political organizations continued to play a powerful role in local society.[124] Governor-General Trepov reported to Stolypin that Polish and Jewish associations that had been established under the liberal 1906 statutes exerted "dangerous foreign influences" that threatened to undermine the foundations of local government. Until the dominance of the "native" population had been guaranteed, he argued, Polish and Jewish political and cultural organizations should be banned altogether.[125]

---

119. See descriptions of local initiatives in the letters that Kiev province SRN members sent to the paper *Russkaia znamia*: RGIA, f. 786, op. 1, d. 1192, ll. 4–5, 10, 12.
120. For example, D. I. Kuznetsov to *Kievlianin*, TsDIAUK, f. 296, op. 1, d. 2, ll. 418–24; A. Krivoshin to *Kievlianin*, ibid., l. 376; letter of "Modest Russian Worker" to *Kievlianin*, TsDIAUK, f. 296, op. 1, d. 27, l. 599.
121. E. I. Kovalenko to Kiev division of SRN, RGIA, f. 786, op. 1, d. 1192, l. 12; telegram of Kiev SRN to Council of Ministers, 5 April 1910, TsDIAUK, f. 296, op. 1, d. 2, l. 336.
122. Memorandum of Department of General Affairs, 17 October 1909, RGIA, f. 1284, op. 187, d. 260, l. 15.
123. Memorandum of Ministry of Internal Affairs Department on Local Economics, 8 November 1909, TsDIAUK, f. 442, op. 637, d. 545, l. 27.
124. For example, "Protokol," TsDIAUK, f. 442, op. 637, d. 545, l. 220b; Chief of the Volynia Province Gendarme Division to Volynia Governor, 6 November 1909, ibid., ll. 18–20.
125. Kiev Governor-General to Ministry of Internal Affairs, 1 September 1909, RGIA, f. 1284, op. 187, d. 260, ll. 7–100b. The quote is from l. 9.

In late 1909, S. N. Shchegolev, a doctor by training, a member of the Kiev Club of Russian Nationalists, and an employee of the Kiev civil governor's office, penned a letter to Trepov's office advocating the implementation of an even more restrictive statute on associations. Arguing that groups as seemingly innocuous as the Polish Ladies' Circle and Circle of Polish Writers and Journalists promoted dangerous forms of "national chauvinism," he agreed with Trepov that they should be banned.[126] But in contrast to the governor-general, who made no mention of Ukrainian organizations in his memorandum to Stolypin, Shchegolev added Ukrainian cultural organizations to the list of groups that threatened state security.[127] In a follow-up letter to the civil governor, he argued that the "Ukrainian movement"—whether or not it was associated with overtly separatist ideas—propagated Western democratic ideals, papist tendencies, and hatred toward Great Russian culture. Each of these tendencies, he complained, threatened to estrange the southwestern borderlands from the Great Russian heartland.[128] The southwest's Russian nationalists had frequently accused Hrushevs'kyi and his followers of perverting salutary Little Russian patriotism to serve foreign interests. Yet they had never attacked the peculiarities of local culture as dangerous in their own right—or agitated for the closure of the numerous local organizations in which Hrushevs'kyi now played a role. Distancing himself from the Little Russian culture that many "truly Russian" activists championed, Shchegolev now presented the very discussion of the southwest's special features as subversive.

Having reviewed the reports he received from localities, Stolypin became convinced that organizations representing the cultural and political interests of the empire's minority groups threatened to undermine the stability of the state and to derail his nationalizing program. In January 1910, Stolypin distributed a circular to governors-general ordering them to close all "alien" organizations that pursued "narrowly nationalist" goals. The directive classified "Ukrainians" as one of the minority groups targeted by the new measures.[129] Leaked to the press, Stolypin's secret circular provoked outrage among liberals. They complained that in discriminating against large groups of subjects on the basis of ethnonational categories ascribed by the state, the new directive dismantled in one fell swoop the reforms of the 1905 period. They also mocked Stolypin for including Ukrainians among the empire's "alien" groups, noting that this categorization contradicted the very foundations of the Russian nationalist project, which considered Little and Great Russians branches of a unitary East Slavic nation.[130]

---

126. "O pol'skikh i malorusskikh prosvetitel'nykh obshchestvakh," 26 December 1909, TsDIAUK, f. 442, op. 639, d. 797, l. 20b.
127. Ibid., ll. 30b-4.
128. Shchegolev to Kiev Civil Governor, 1 April 1910, ibid., ll. 21–27.
129. Circular of Stolypin to Governors-General, 20 January 1910, RGIA, f. 1284, op. 187, d. 260, l. 23.
130. Unidentified *Rech'* clipping, 10 February 1910, RGIA, f. 1284, op. 187, d. 260, ll. 137–370b; "Ukraintsy-inorodtsy," *Rech'*, 11 February 1910, ibid., l. 141; "Novyi tsirkuliar," *Russkoe slovo*, 10 February 1910, ibid., l. 133; Serhii Efremov, "Zhyttia na Ukraini r. 1910-ho," *Rada*, 1 January 1911, 5.

The targeting of Ukrainian organizations also disturbed many who sympathized with the Russian nationalist cause. The governor of Podolia, who had strongly backed the earliest efforts to nationalize elections in his province, complained that the authorities had no right to interfere in the operations of groups such as the Ukrainian club Prosvita, which in his opinion pursued primarily "cultural-educational goals."[131] Contributors to T. G. Lokot''s *Kiev* also found Stolypin's directive alienating. The struggle to build a Russian nation, they argued, could not be accomplished without Little Russian patriotism—the empire's most vital anticosmopolitan force and an expression of the most authentic East Slavic traditions.[132]

In April 1910, the Kiev province Committee on Social Affairs, which operated under the civil governor's office, met to discuss the controversy over the new guidelines and to review the activities of "alien" groups in the province. Having perused pamphlets distributed by local Prosvita activists, the committee found that the group had propagated dangerous democratic ideas, celebrated revolutionaries, and undermined tsarist authority. It declared the group closed and ordered police to liquidate it.[133] Less than a month later, however, the MVD clarified Stolypin's January circular, noting that only "Ukrainian societies that deny the unity of the Russian people and propagate Ukrainian separatism and independence" should be subject to closure, not "Little Russian societies which have a purely Russian character and do not pursue narrowly nationalistic goals."[134]

The designation of Ukrainians as an "alien" group in Stolypin's original circular indicated that officials had grown more concerned about the activities of nationalist separatists in the southwest. But because the MVD failed to provide clear guidance in its second directive about how to distinguish these subversive groups from those that promoted salutary Little Russian patriotism, local officials and intellectuals continued to debate the proper role of the Little Russian idea in the Russian national movement. Even as the MVD conducted its investigation of non-Russian groups, the ministry permitted the Kiev city duma to move forward with the long-planned project to erect a monument to Shevchenko.[135] Duma delegates voted to build the statue atop one of the hills in the city center, which the Kievan princes had once inhabited; it was to be situated midway between the two other monuments to the city's unique historical heritage: the monument to St. Vladimir towering over the Dnieper and the statue of Bohdan Khmelnytsky that stood in front of St. Sophia's.[136] Although the project had received extensive support from "truly Russian" activists for years, none of its Russian nationalist supporters won seats on the final committee overseeing its

---

131. Podolia Governor to Kiev Governor-General, 4 March 1910, TsDIAUK, f. 442, op. 639, d. 797, l. 15.
132. Gr. S'ogobochnii, "Antisemitizm ili razumnyi natsionalizm?," *Kiev*, 12 January 1910, 9–10; "Eshche o ukrainskom 'separatizme,'" *Kiev*, 13 March 1910, 3–5.
133. "Zhurnal no. 54. Kievskogo Gubernskogo po delam ob obshchestvakh Prisutstviia. Ot 8 aprelia 1910 goda," TsDIAUK, f. 442, op. 639, d. 797, ll. 28–29.
134. Memorandum of Department of General Affairs, May 1910, RGIA, f. 1284, op. 187, d. 260, l. 50.
135. Kiev Governor to Governor-General, 30 June 1911, TsDIAUK, f. 442, op. 662, d. 501, ll. 27–270b.
136. "Istoricheskaia zapiska," ibid., l. 560b.

completion. Now the Poltava zemstvo assumed the leading role in the project, and Luchitskii and Naumenko took the lead in fund-raising efforts.[137]

In the wake of the turnover on the statue committee and the growing controversy about the proper role of Little Russian culture in the struggle to build a Russian nation, some Russian nationalists distanced themselves from the Shevchenko project. Savenko—who continued to express his pride at being a "pure-blooded Little Russian"[138]—published an article in *Kievlianin* in May 1910 criticizing the statue's placement as inappropriate. Noting that Shevchenko had made comments critical of the Orthodox hierarchy and Nicholas I, the journalist expressed his concern that erecting the monument on the grounds where the Kievan princes had lived and prayed would insult the "unified Rus'" and the "Russian national consciousness" that they had created.[139]

Others in the Russian nationalist camp, however, defended Shevchenko and his legacy. In the pages of Lokot''s *Kiev*, Ia. G. Demchenko insisted that the poet had been far from a "revolutionary" or a "separatist"; on the contrary, he had struggled to unify the children of Rus' and infuse them with a national spirit. Indeed, he presented Little Russian patriots as the most convinced and forceful Russian nationalists, pointing out the role that they had played in forging East Slavic civilization and the "Russian patriotic organizations" that had transformed southwestern politics. Demchenko even defended the members of the radical Ukrainian organization Spilka, claiming that the group's apparent "political separatism" did not reflect its members' true views but rather indicated that it had been infiltrated by Jewish provocateurs.[140]

Perhaps in an attempt to quell the disputes about the Shevchenko project, Governor-General Trepov secured funds from the tsar to erect a monument that all proud Russians could support; named the Historical Path, it portrayed the princes, princesses, and Orthodox clerics of Kievan Rus'. Having received the governor-general's promise to expedite the project, the committee tasked with overseeing the statue's completion promised to complete it by August 1911.[141] But the Historical Path failed to end the Shevchenko controversy. By the spring of 1911, Savenko and the president of the Russian Gathering—who had both secured seats on the Historical Path committee—had denounced the Shevchenko project altogether. At their urging, the local authorities overturned the duma's decision on the placement of the statue,

---

137. "Kopiia otnosheniia Poltavskoi Gubernskoi Zemskoi Upravy po Rasporiaditel'nomu otdeleniiu, na imia Kievskogo Gorodskogo Golovy ot 15 ianvaria 1909 g. za no. 1235," ibid., l. 61; "Poltava Zemstvo. Doklad no. 133," ibid., ll. 15–16. On the statue as a Ukrainian nationalist project, see Iurii Oleksiiovych Chepely, "Dyskusii navkolo monumenta Tarasovi Shevchenku v Kyevi naperedodni ioho stolitn'oho iubileiu" (master's thesis, Kyiv-Mohyla Academy, 2009).
138. *Sbornik kluba*, 3:35–36.
139. A. Savenko editorial, *Kievlianin*, 9 May 1910, 3.
140. Ia. Demchenko, "Shevchenko i 'patrioty,'" *Kiev*, 17 June 1910, 3–5, continued in *Kiev*, 24 June 1910, 5–7.
141. See "Ob obrazovanii Komiteta po sooruzheniiu 'Istoricheskogo puti,'" TsDIAUK, f. 1196, op. 1, d. 22.

designating the space for the Historical Path instead. It was on this spot in central Kiev that the monument was erected in 1911.[142]

While some self-professed Russian nationalists distanced themselves from Shevchenko's legacy, Ukrainian activists rushed to claim it for themselves. In February 1911, on the occasion of the fiftieth anniversary of the poet's death, Hrushevs'kyi and his followers organized public celebrations in Kiev and distributed popular literature hailing Shevchenko's legacy on both sides of the Russo-Austrian border.[143] By spring, Chykalenko, Naumenko, and Hrushevs'kyi had all secured positions on the Shevchenko statue committee, which was now working to find an alternate location for the monument.[144] But though some officials had warned that discussion of Little Russian cultural peculiarities could undermine imperial stability and the myth of East Slavic unity, the state was not yet prepared to completely disavow the notion that Little Russian patriotism had a key role to play in the defense of the empire and the creation of a Russian nation. In spite of the growing controversy about the Shevchenko statue, officials did not intervene to halt the project altogether; paradoxically, this permitted Ukrainian nationalists to appropriate Little Russian symbols for their own use under official auspices.

The Western Zemstvo Crisis

While Kiev-based intellectuals and officials struggled to define the proper role of Little Russian culture in imperial cultural and intellectual life, the State Council gathered to consider the western zemstvo bill that had been passed by the Duma. Once again, the scheme to nationalize the political institutions of the western borderlands provoked opposition from many quarters. Council members complained bitterly that the broad franchise provided by the bill diluted the power of the "most cultured segments of the local population."[145] They also discussed the contradictions of the national curia system at great length. Some members pointed out that one of the issues that had bedeviled officials in the 1860s—determining how to identify Poles—remained problematic: was a Pole defined by his native language? By his Catholicism? By his surname? How were Catholics who converted to Orthodoxy to be classified? Children of mixed marriages? Others objected that the national curia system would destabilize the empire, encouraging ethnic and national resentment.[146]

Meanwhile, men intimately acquainted with the southwest's vibrant, multiethnic capitalist culture pioneered new arguments against the legislation. Count

---

142. "Gorodskaia duma," *Kievlianin*, 5 March 1911, 3; F. F. Trepov to A. F. Girs, 7 January 1911, TsDAIUK, f. 442, o. 662, d. 501, l. 7.
143. "K 50 letiiu so dnia smerti T. G. Shevchenko," 26 February 1911, TsDIAUK, f. 275, op, 1, d. 2700, ll. 4–5; M. Lozyns'kyi, "Shevchenkovi dni u L'vovi," *Rada*, 8 March 1911, 1; Kiev Governor to Kiev Temporary Censorship Committee, 29 February 1912, TsDIAUK, f. 295, op. 1, d. 373, l. 1.
144. "Sprava z pam'iatnykom T.G. Shevchenkovi," *Rada*, 15 March 1911, 2.
145. *Stenograficheskii otchet. Gosudarstvennyi sovet. Sessiia VI* (St. Petersburg, 1911), 155–57.
146. Ibid., 1198–1239.

Witte denounced the bill as a revolutionary, antigovernment measure that would irrevocably alter the foundations of imperial governance. Destabilizing the estate system and the ideal of the service state, which rewarded subjects of all backgrounds who had demonstrated their loyalty to the throne, the bill would place the interests of one corporate group defined purely by ethnonational criteria above those of others.[147] B. I. Khanenko, a sugar industrialist elected to the Council by representatives of industry in the southwest, voiced a similar objection to the bill. Although he supported the expansion of elective zemstva to the borderlands, he insisted that their nationalization would undermine rather than strengthen the imperial state, which in his mind should promote the common interests of all subjects rather than favor a certain group. Repeating an argument that had often been made by local commercial elites, he insisted that the only way to protect the welfare of the southwestern narod was to ensure "equal rights for all Russian citizens."[148]

Pikhno remained the bill's strongest advocate in the State Council and served as the chief spokesman for its supporters. Countering his opponents' objections that it unjustly penalized Poles and would breed national enmity, he characterized the legislation as a just measure that would assure both Poles and Orthodox East Slavs representation proportionate to their overall share of the population and promote the social and political interests of the Orthodox majority.[149] Dismissing the bill's detractors as unattuned to the needs of the borderlands, he argued that passage of the bill was absolutely essential to assuring the final defeat of Polish revanchism and ending the alleged exploitation of the masses by foreign interests.[150]

In an address he delivered to the State Council before its final vote on the bill, Stolypin did not deny that the legislation would refashion the very foundations of imperial governance. Echoing the claims that southwestern activists had made for years, he insisted that the introduction of broadly democratic, national zemstva in the southwest would herald the emergence of a new social and political order across the empire. For centuries, he noted, the imperial state had been an "amalgam"—an "aggregation of separate individuals, tribes, and ethnicities [narodnosti] united by a single legal regime, a general administration." Now Stolypin hoped to create a state founded on "national-popular [narodnye] and historical foundations" that "exists at the behest of the people [narodnye zavety], possesses will, has the strength and power of coercion; such a government subordinates the rights of separate individuals, of separate groups, to the rights of the whole."[151]

On 4 March 1911, Kadets and Polish representatives in the State Council joined Octobrists and rightists to defeat the western zemstvo bill. Nationalist leaders expressed disbelief at the Council's decision, which, they complained, confirmed that

---

147. Witte's argument is paraphrased in ibid., 943.
148. Ibid., 1239.
149. "Zemstvo v zapadnykh guberniiakh," *Rech'*, 3 November 1910.
150. *Stenograficheskii otchet. Gosudarstvennyi sovet. Sessiia VI*, 1226–30.
151. Ibid., 1240–41.

"western Rus'" was "Polish property."[152] Members of the Kiev Club of Russian Nationalists held many forces culpable for the bill's failure. Some blamed Polish patriotic conspiracies; others condemned Witte—the longtime defender of Kiev's capitalist elite—for having sold the future of the children of Rus' to foreign interests with no more compunctions than a "stockbroker" on the floor of the Kiev commodities exchange. Still others blamed the conservatives and rightists of the State Council who had voted against the bill, labeling them as "rightist cosmopolitans" who had "hand[ed] Russia over to aliens."[153] The southwestern peasant delegation to the State Duma and groups of villagers from as far away as Vilnius expressed outrage that "Russian bureaucrats [*sanovniki*] trust the Polish nobility more than the local Russian peasantry, which for centuries has proven its loyalty to Russia and the Throne."[154]

Joining forces with Kiev's civil governor, A. F. Girs—who by now had joined the Kiev Club of Russian Nationalists—southwestern nationalists aggressively lobbied Stolypin and the tsar himself to implement the western zemstvo bill through extraparliamentary means.[155] In mid-March, Stolypin dismissed the Duma and State Council and implemented the bill under Article 87 of the Fundamental Laws, which permitted him to promulgate laws during breaks in parliamentary sessions. Informing the Kiev Club of his decision, Stolypin lauded its leadership and promised activists that the "light of the Russian national idea, which is flickering in western Russia, will not be extinguished and will soon illuminate all of Russia."[156] The Russian nationalists who had been despondent just days before now rejoiced. Savenko praised the prime minister for definitively aligning imperial policy with the interests of the Rus' people.[157] *Dvuglavyi orel* celebrated Stolypin's leadership, although it continued to express its anger at the "extreme right," which its contributors claimed had stifled national ideas and forsaken the needs of the masses.[158]

When the Duma returned from its forced break, it met in a stormy twelve-hour session. Shul'gin delivered a speech in which he expressed his thanks to Stolypin and his relief that the state had made a decisive intervention that would ease the plight of the toiling masses on its western periphery.[159] Members of the southwest's peasant delegation created a ruckus, shouting invectives at the Octobrists, whose opposition to the original bill had guaranteed its failure.[160] Octobrists defended their actions,

---

152. A. Savenko editorial, *Kievlianin*, 8 March 1911, 2.
153. *Sbornik kluba*, 3:68–72. Quotes from 3:71–72.
154. *Sbornik kluba*, 3:130–32.
155. "K voprosu o vybornom zemstve," *Kievlianin*, 7 March 1911, 3; letter of Kiev Club to Tsar Nicholas II, 9 March 1911, IRNBUV, f. 167, no. 13.
156. *Sbornik kluba*, 3:127.
157. "Zametki," *Kievlianin*, 17 March 1911, 2.
158. See the opinions in "Obozrenie sobytii i okrainnaia zhizn'," *Okrainy Rossii*, 12 March 1911, 168–70; untitled editorial, *Dvuglavyi orel*, 20 March 1911, 1–2; "K voprosu o primeneii 87 st. Osnovnykh Zakonov," *Dvuglavyi orel*, 10 April 1911, 1–2.
159. *Gosudarstvennaia Duma. Stenograficheskie otchety. 1911 g. Sessiia chetvertaia*, pt. 3 (St. Petersburg, 1911), 758–62.
160. Ibid., 772.

denouncing the invocation of Article 87 as illegal and accusing the Nationalists of engaging in class warfare.[161]

::

Having amassed substantial electoral majorities through mass mobilization as well as franchise manipulation, the southwest's Russian nationalists had created a powerful, cross-class political coalition. By 1911, they had expanded beyond their narrow regional base, achieving a presence in all-imperial associational and political life; working closely with Stolypin, they had nationalized key governance institutions. But the more the southwest's Russian nationalists achieved, the clearer the internal tensions in their program became. Would the party's leaders be able to manage the frustration that some of its working-class members had expressed toward the landed gentry and intelligentsia who continued to dominate imperial politics? What role, if any, should the Little Russian idea, which had been so central in the earliest efforts to imagine national collectives and define national interests, play in efforts to identify the features of a larger Russian nation? And most important of all, could national ideas really strengthen the empire, as activists claimed? Or might they destabilize a state that proved unwilling to dismantle its supranational estate system, no matter how much officials and activists had colluded to undermine it? It was only in the years to come that the answers to these questions would begin to grow clearer.

---

161. Ibid., 793–94. Geoffrey Hosking argues that the growing divides between Nationalists and the moderate right (primarily Octobrists) doomed the post-1905 parliamentary order. See Hosking, *Constitutional Experiment*, 182.

8 The Limits of the Russian Nationalist Vision

IN MARCH 1911, less than a week after Stolypin instituted the western zemstva under Article 87, children playing in Kiev's Luk'ianovka district—the neighborhood where the "truly Russian" movement had secured its earliest mass following in the 1905 period—made a horrifying discovery. In a cave on the property of a brick factory they found the body of a young boy. Clad only in underwear, the corpse displayed multiple shallow wounds; it was surrounded by school notebooks and the boy's torn clothes. Police soon identified him as Andrei Iushchinskii, a resident of a shanty settlement on the sandy left bank of the Dnieper and a pupil of the primary school at St. Sophia's Cathedral.[1]

Although the murder of Andrei Iushchinskii was only one of many violent crimes reported in the Kiev press in the spring of 1911, it would ultimately garner the attention of the entire empire. The most radical of Kiev's nationalist activists, who had expressed outrage at the alleged indifference of conservative politicians and imperial elites toward the welfare of the Orthodox East Slavs in the aftermath of the western zemstvo bill's defeat, took great interest in the crime. Alleging that the murder had been perpetrated by Jews as part of a blood ritual, they eventually brought the case to the attention of Minister of Justice I. G. Shcheglovitov (1861–1918). In spite of substantial evidence countering the claims of these activists (and opposition from other prominent figures in the government), Shcheglovitov pursued the ritual murder angle. The case developed into imperial Russia's most notorious anti-Semitic show trial, mobilizing indignant liberals and militant Russian nationalist organizations on either side.[2]

Placing the Iushchinskii case in its local context, this chapter chronicles how the southwest's Russian nationalists once again successfully set an agenda, mobilized followers, lobbied officials, and shaped imperial policy. But this chapter also explores how the flurry of civic activity surrounding the case simultaneously destabilized the Russian nationalist lobby and the empire that it claimed to defend. Discomfited by the

---

1. Memorandum to Kiev prosecutor, 21 March 1911, TsDIAUK, f. 317, op. 1. d. 5482, t.1, l. 1.
2. For a brief discussion of the government response to the case, see Rogger, *Jewish Policies*, 40–55.

ritual murder allegation and the rapid growth of the most radical fringes of the "truly Russian" movement, the most prominent nationalist leaders would distance themselves from the Iushchinskii case. For their part, the radical intellectuals, peasants, and proletarians who insisted that the Iushchinskii murder was part of a broader Jewish plot to destroy the Orthodox East Slavs and their historical traditions complained that the skeptical nationalist leadership had abandoned the children of Rus' to their enemies. The growing discord within the nationalist lobby—and the ever more radical ideas that some of its members endorsed—also forced both local and imperial officials to reconsider their relationship with the group. Even those who had once relied on the southwest's Russian nationalists to serve as a party of order now acknowledged that the movement posed unprecedented threats to the stability of local society and the tsarist regime.

The Iushchinskii Investigation

Police focused their initial investigation of the Iushchinskii murder on the boy's troubled and impoverished family. They discovered that his mother, who had borne him out of wedlock, routinely neglected him. The fact that she had once lived close to the site where his body was found and that she had waited five days to report his disappearance further incriminated her in the eyes of local investigators. Police also suspected that his stepfather, who had physically abused him, might have been involved in his murder.[3] But within days of the discovery of Iushchinskii's body, police and prosecutors began to receive anonymous letters claiming that the murder, which had taken place during Passover, had been committed by Jews, who had drained Iushchinskii's blood and used it to bake matzo.[4] Protesters convened at Iushchinskii's funeral in late March, crying, "The Yids tortured the young boy Andrei Iushchinskii!" "Russian people!" they continued, "if your children are dear to you, beat the Yids! Beat them until there is not one Yid left in Russia!" As the mourners scattered after the funeral, the protesters circulated literature outlining the history of alleged Jewish blood rituals.[5]

Rumors that Iushchinskii had fallen victim to a blood ritual continued to circulate in April. Letters arrived at government offices complaining that Iushchinskii had been "TORTURED BY THE DAMNED JEWS" and begging the authorities to avenge the murder on behalf of "all truly Russian people."[6] The SRN and the Double-Headed Eagle, which had expressed such indignation at the State Council's failure to pass the western zemstvo bill, played a particularly active role in spreading these rumors.

---

3. Prosecutor's memorandum to Kiev District Court, 27 March 1911, in TsDIAUK, f. 317, op. 1, d. 5482, t.1, ll. 3–5.
4. Ibid., l. 30b.
5. Kiev Governor A. F. Girs to Governor-General F. F. Trepov, 31 March 1911, TsDIAUK, f. 442, op. 641, d. 2, ch. 1, ll. 180–180ob.
6. Anonymous letter, 14 April 1911, TsDIAUK, f. 317, op. 1. d. 5482, ch. 1, l. 10.

Activists representing these groups convened regularly at Iushchinskii's grave to condemn the boy's murder and to call for the erection of a chapel in his honor. In mid-April they organized a demonstration that attracted a crowd of one thousand to the Luk'ianovka Cemetery. Incited by the groups' leaders, attendees left the protest and fanned out across Kiev, attacking Jews in city streets and bazaars. Only speedy police intervention prevented the violence from degenerating into a full-fledged pogrom.[7]

In the wake of these protests, the newspaper operated by the Double-Headed Eagle began publishing regular articles that purported to offer proof that Iushchinskii had been killed by Jews. Echoing Sikorskii's claims that the southwest was in the midst of a racial war, the paper insisted that the murder marked the beginning of a new Jewish offensive to destroy once and for all the "weak, helpless, and oppressed" Orthodox masses.[8] Pikhno and Shul'gin, who remained the most prominent proponents of Russian nationalism despite the fact that they had distanced themselves from the more radical and potentially violent undercurrents of the movement, maintained a more measured tone. In editorials in *Kievlianin,* they dismissed the blood ritual rumors as "legends" and expressed full confidence in the ability of the police to solve the case.[9]

By late April, however, proponents of the ritual murder charge had found supporters beyond Kiev. Reactionary Duma deputies and newspapers in the imperial capitals seized on the Iushchinskii case, citing it as evidence of the Jews' alleged desire to destroy Russian civilization—and of the authorities' inability to respond to this threat.[10] Faced with mounting public pressure, Kiev prosecutor G. G. Chaplinskii (himself a member of the Club of Russian Nationalists) finally ordered his subordinates to investigate the blood ritual allegations.[11]

Even as the ritual murder claims gained traction, the most radically anti-Semitic nationalists in the southwest continued to lobby officials to identify those responsible for Iushchinskii's death and to implement more aggressive measures to limit the political and economic power of Jews. In correspondence to the metropolitan of Kiev and Civil Governor A. F. Girs, V. S. Golubev, the president of the Double-Headed Eagle, demanded the expulsion of thousands of Jews from Kiev, insisting that drastic measures were necessary to protect the welfare of the Orthodox masses.[12] Neither Girs nor the metropolitan acted on Golubev's entreaties, but by May, Kiev activists had used their connections to bring the Iushchinskii case to the attention of Minister

---

7. Presentation of G. G. Chaplinskii to Kiev District Court, 16 April 1911, ibid., l. 60b–70b; Vladimir Golubev, "L'Enfant-martyr: Andre Iouchinsky, éleve de l'Ecole religieuse de Sainte Sophie martyrisé par les Juifs," IRNBUV, f. 81, no. 131, ll. 11–12; "Evreiskii vopros," BA, A. F. Girs Papers, box 1, folder 4, 10.

8. Quote from *Dvuglavyi orel,* 8 May 1911, 1. See also "Ritual'nye ubiistva," *Dvuglavyi orel,* 24 April 1911, 1–2; "Dol'she [sic] terpet' nel'zia," *Dvuglavyi orel,* 24 April 1911, 2–4.

9. See the clippings in TsDIAUK, f. 317, op. 1. d. 5482, l. 9.

10. On 9 April the St. Petersburg daily *Zemshchina* alleged that the murder was part of a blood ritual; on the twenty-ninth, thirty-nine members of the Duma signed an interpellation urging the authorities to investigate this possibility. See Chaplinskii to Shcheglovitov, 26 April 1911, TsDIAUK, f. 317, op. 1, d. 5482, l. 15e; *Gosudarstvennaia duma. Tretii sozyv,* pt. 3, 3112–13.

11. Chaplinskii to Kiev District Court, 16 April 1911, TsDIAUK, f. 317, op. 1. d. 5482, ll. 6–8.

12. Chaplinskii to Shcheglovitov, 26 April 1911, ibid., l. 15e.

of Justice Shcheglovitov. Shcheglovitov dispatched his own investigators to Kiev and informed Chaplinskii that he was following the case closely and would expect frequent updates.[13]

In late April, Kiev's most experienced forensic scientist, who had been out of town since the murder and thus had been unable to examine Iushchinskii's body, returned to the city and conducted an autopsy. He concluded that Iushchinskii's skin had been punctured numerous times by knives and other sharp objects and that his death had been caused by a large cut to his neck that caused profuse bleeding. However, he stated that he could not conclude on the basis of his autopsy that the crime had been a ritual murder. In the meantime, the initial leads followed by police had failed to yield a credible suspect: Iushchinskii's stepfather had an alibi, and his mother had held up well under interrogation.[14]

Faced with intensifying pressure from Kiev activists and from Shcheglovitov at the very moment his best leads had turned into dead ends, Chaplinskii soon became more proactive. He invited his Kiev Club comrade I. A. Sikorskii to examine Iushchinskii's body and to compile a psychological profile of the killer. Sikorskii soon concluded that the murder had been a "vendetta of the Sons of Jacob"—an act of Jewish "racial vengeance."[15] Seeking to confirm Sikorskii's findings, Chaplinskii consulted with monks at the Kiev-Pechersk monastery to ascertain whether Jews truly participated in ritual murder. The monks responded that certain sects of Hasidic Jews in the southwest did indeed kill Christian children at Passover to bake matzo from their blood.[16]

Meanwhile, Golubev continued his crusade. He informed local officials that Iushchinskii's mother had received a letter from an anonymous eyewitness claiming to have seen the boy with two Jews shortly before his murder. Noting that the property where the body was found lay adjacent to a large tract of land owned by a Jewish merchant, Golubev even rounded up Jews who resided in the area and brought them to the police for questioning.[17] He penned and circulated a tract among the Kiev intelligentsia that provided a synopsis of the case and a historical overview of alleged Jewish blood rituals. Golubev's pamphlet expressed outrage that the police had suspected the Iushchinskii family, portraying the victim's mother and stepfather as decent Orthodox people tormented by poverty. He praised Shcheglovitov's interest in the case,

---

13. Undated telegram of Shcheglovitov to Chaplinskii, TsDIAUK, f. 317, op. 1, d. 5482, l. 12; "Po obvineniiu v ritual'nom ubiistve," *Dvuglavyi orel,* 8 May 1911, 1. A lawyer involved in the case later insisted that virtually no one in the ministry believed the blood allegation rituals, but that the minister, who owned an estate in Poltava, believed that it was important to maintain the support of southwestern nationalists in the aftermath of the western zemstvo fiasco. See O. O. Gruzenberg, *Yesterday,* trans. Don C. Rawson and Tatiana Tipton (Berkeley, 1981), 38, 104, 109.
14. Presentation of Chaplinskii to Kiev District Court, 16 April 1911, TsDIAUK, f. 317, op. 1, d. 5482, l. 6; report of Chaplinskii to Shcheglovitov, 26 April 1911, ibid., ll. 15a–d.
15. Report of Chaplinskii to Shcheglovitov, 11 May 1911, ibid., l. 260b. This term was coined by the French historian Anatole Leroy-Beaulieu.
16. Ibid., ll. 26–280b.
17. Report of Chaplinskii to Shcheglovitov, 29 May 1911, ibid., ll. 29–300b; report of Chaplinskii to Shcheglovitov, 11 May 1911, l. 28.

but he complained that other government officials and the "Kadet-Jewish-Octobrist majority" in the Duma had failed to protect ordinary people like the Iushchinskiis from "monsters" of the "Jewish race, who hate Christ the Savior."[18]

Kievlianin continued to dismiss these allegations as baseless.[19] Proponents of the blood ritual claim, for their part, skewered the organ as a "Yid paper" and claimed that it was involved in a conspiracy to obfuscate the truth.[20] As tensions between these two camps that had emerged from the Russian nationalist movement intensified, even some convinced of the blood ritual charges expressed concern that the case would polarize urban society and foment communal violence. Civil Governor Girs, the Kiev Club of Russian Nationalists member whose own exam of Iushchinskii's corpse in the morgue convinced him that the boy had been tortured by Jews, sternly warned local SRN and Double-Headed Eagle activists that he would not permit them to incite violence against the city's Jewish population.[21] Continuing to encounter pressure from Shcheglovitov, whose investigators had concluded that the murder had been a ritual killing, Chaplinskii's office was less cautious. It now joined the chorus of those who insisted that "the death of Iushchinskii was certainly committed by people belonging to the Jewish nationality [*narodnost'*] who distinguish themselves through their extraordinary fanaticism." In July, relying on the testimony of an eyewitness who claimed to have seen a Hasidic Jew with Iushchinskii shortly before his death, the Kiev authorities arrested Mendel Beilis, the superintendent of a Jewish-owned brick factory adjacent to the property where the boy's body had been found. Beilis was charged with murder and imprisoned as he awaited trial.[22]

Summer 1911: Radicalization and Conflict

The Iushchinskii case had laid bare the cleavages between radicals in the Russian nationalist camp who propagated the blood ritual allegations (Golubev and Sikorskii) and moderates (Pikhno and Shul'gin) who rejected them. It also deepened the tensions between the urban elites who had transformed the "truly Russian" cause into a mass-oriented movement with all-imperial influence and the proletarian organizations and reactionary forces that had joined the antiliberationist coalition after 1905. Though the former had played a major role in branding Poles and Jews as enemies of the imperial state and the children of Rus', they generally stopped short of advocating violence against these groups—or even endorsing their complete marginalization from society.

---

18. Golubev, "L'Enfant-martyr," ll. 5, 10, 12, 18–20.
19. *Kievlianin*, 28 June 1911, 1.
20. Clipping from *Russkoe znamia*, contained in TsDIAUK, f. 317, op. 1. d. 5482, l. 35.
21. Girs, "Evreiskii vopros," 9–10.
22. Chaplinskii to V. I. Fenenko, 3 August 1911, TsDIAUK, f. 317, op. 1, d. 5482, ll. 59–60. For more on the case and the series of events that led to Beilis's arrest, see *Delo Mendelia Beilisa. Materialy Chrezvychainoi sledstvennoi komissii Vremennogo pravitel'stva o sudebnom protsesse 1913 g.* (St. Petersburg, 1999).

In spite of these divisions, Russian nationalist leaders insisted that the movement must remain focused on its ongoing efforts to reorganize imperial governance on a national basis. The elections to the western zemstva had been scheduled for the summer of 1911, and Tsar Nicholas and Stolypin announced plans to visit Kiev in the late summer to celebrate the opening of the new institutions. Working together, the Kiev Club of Russian Nationalists and the Nationalist Party organized a series of preparatory electoral meetings at which activists drew up platforms and coordinated outreach efforts.[23] The success of southwestern activists in mobilizing voters, along with the new national curia system and widespread Polish boycotts of the elections, delivered overwhelming victories to the nationalist forces. "Truly Russian" parties captured more than 90 percent of the zemstvo seats in Kiev and Podolia and only slightly fewer in Volynia. Prominent Kiev Club activists such as V. Ia. Demchenko, Reva, Bogdanov, A. V. Storozhenko, and Dobrynin won seats in the southwest's new elective zemstva, an outcome that enhanced their influence in local government and offered them a new venue in which to propagate their ideas.[24]

Claiming 1,500 members by the summer of 1911, the Kiev Club of Russian Nationalists remained the southwest's most powerful political lobby, and the organization's members expected to play a leading role in preparing for the visit of the tsar and Stolypin.[25] Working closely with local officials to plan the details of the visit, the club rallied several thousand volunteers to serve on citizens' brigades to supplement the prime minister's security detail. Although the club, whose members included the leaders of local SRN divisions and other "truly Russian" proletarian organizations, had traditionally worked to foster cross-class communication, the relationships between its leaders and the smaller (and less elite) groups with which it cooperated had become more tense and competitive.[26] SRN chapters, nationalist railroad unions, and more than thirty other organizations from across the southwest expressed their desire to be involved in official events to greet Stolypin, and they demanded that Kiev Club leaders include them in the official delegation that would greet the tsar with bread and salt.[27]

Although the two sides ultimately agreed to a compromise that included members from both camps, Savenko bitterly complained in a letter to a fellow Kiev Club

---

23. "Kievskii zemskii s"ezd," *Kievlianin*, 4 April 1911, 2; see also Edelman, *Gentry Politics*, 127–41. Again, Edelman characterizes these efforts as aimed at preserving the political power of the gentry, an interpretation from which mine differs.
24. These data are based on the table in Edelman, *Gentry Politics*, 137. On these figures' involvement in the zemstvo, see "Spisok lits uchastie koikh v soveshchanii zhelatel'no," TsDIAUK, f. 442, op. 665, d. 101b, ch. III, ll. 18–19.
25. Savenko to Chernov, 20 July 1911, IRNBUV, f. 167, no. 99, ll. 1–3.
26. B. M. Iuzefovich, who traditionally had served as a liaison between nationalist activists and the members of the SRN and other proletarian organizations, died in the summer of 1911. His loss may have also contributed to the breakdown of communications between the two camps.
27. F. Postnyi to Chief of Kiev Okhrana, August 1911, TsDIAUK, f. 275, op. 1, d. 2534, l. 2. For lists of participating organizations, see ibid., l. 25; Girs to Chief of Okhrana, 20 August 1911, l. 147.

leader that Nicholas would find himself greeted by bands of "tramps."[28] Meanwhile, the ambitious Golubev, who had achieved local notoriety through his involvement in the Iushchinskii case, appeared intent on supplanting the authority enjoyed by the leaders of the Kiev Club. Under his guidance, the Double-Headed Eagle took to the countryside, hosting "people's readings" at which church officials and club members addressed peasants.[29] When the latest delegation of Galician visitors arrived in Kiev in August 1911, it was Golubev, not Kiev Club activists, who greeted them, accompanied them to Orthodox holy sites, and joined them in singing Russian and Galician "national hymns."[30]

Stolypin arrived in Kiev in late August. He spent most of his first day in town with the leaders of the Kiev Club, with whom he discussed the upcoming elections to the fourth Duma, scheduled for early 1912, the need to improve the economic opportunities available to the East Slavs of the borderlands, and the ongoing struggle against "Ukrainophile propaganda."[31] That evening he accompanied the tsar to a performance at the Kiev opera house. Midway through the performance, Stolypin was shot by D. G. Bogrov, a graduate of St. Vladimir's law school and the son of a prominent Jewish lawyer. Bogrov had been involved in left-wing radical parties and had also served as a double agent for the tsarist secret police.[32]

While doctors treated Stolypin at a nearby hospital, word of the attack spread throughout the anxious city. The Kiev city duma met in extraordinary session to laud Stolypin's accomplishments, to encourage city residents to endow a hospital in his honor, and to launch an investigation into the circumstances that had permitted Bogrov to enter the opera house.[33] The organ of the Double-Headed Eagle ominously warned that after this grievous insult, the Russian people would no longer stand by idly as leftists and Jews violently attacked their traditions and leaders.[34] For their part, local rabbis condemned Bogrov, and the Jewish communities of nearby suburbs and villages sent their best wishes to the prime minister for a speedy recovery. Nevertheless, more than ten thousand Jews fled Kiev, expecting a pogrom. Over the next several days, officials reported several acts of anti-Jewish violence in various corners of the city, but aggressive police intervention forestalled these isolated episodes from developing into a citywide pogrom.[35]

On 6 September, newspapers reported that Stolypin had died from his wounds. The most extreme elements of the Russian nationalist movement responded to the prime minister's death with frenzied denunciations of the Jewish conspiracies that they perceived lurking behind every corner. Nationalist deputies delivered a complaint

---

28. Savenko to Chernov, 20 July 1911, IRNBUV, f. 167, no. 99, ll. 10b–3.
29. Undated note, RGIA, f. 786, op. 1, d. 1192, l. 250b.
30. "Galichane v Kieve," *Dvuglavyi orel*, 21 August 1911, 3.
31. "Priem P. A. Stolypinym deiatelei kluba russkikh natsionalistov," *Kievlianin*, 2 September 1911, 4.
32. "Lichnost' prestupnika," *Kievlianin*, 3 September 1911, 3.
33. "Chrezvychainoe sobranie Kievskoi gorodskoi dumy," *Kievlianin*, 3 September 1911, 3.
34. "Revoliutsiia idet!" *Dvuglavyi orel*, 4 September 1911, 1–2.
35. "K pokusheniiu na P.A. Stolypin," *Kievlianin*, 4 September 1911, 2; Ascher, *Stolypin*, 375.

Delegates of Kiev's "truly Russian" organizations greet the tsar during his 1911 visit to Kiev. Savenko is visible in the foreground, wearing glasses and holding his top hat. Source: *Sbornik klub russkikh natsionalistov*, vol. 4 (Kiev, 1913). Courtesy of Slavonic Library, National Library of Finland.

to the imperial Duma begging it to do more to protect the Orthodox masses from the Jewish people, whom they condemned as "enemies of Russia and its state structure."[36] *Dvuglavyi orel* expressed outrage that the Kiev City duma had not explicitly prevented Jews from contributing to the fund it had established in Stolypin's honor, implying that the duma might secretly be serving Jewish interests.[37] Kiev SRN members denounced acquaintances who they claimed had shown disrespect for Stolypin during his visit, suggesting that they might be involved in conspiracies against the government.[38] A group of peasants from Kiev province condemned their Jewish neighbors as enemies of the Russian state and the children of Rus'.[39]

Meanwhile, new developments in the Iushchinskii case further radicalized the most extreme anti-Semitic elements of the nationalist camp. In the fall of 1911, the lawyer A. D. Margolin, a Kadet activist and the son of the local industrialist, launched an independent investigation of the Iushchinskii murder, along with a journalist employed

---

36. *Gosudarstvennaia duma. Stenograficheskie otchety. 1911 goda. Sessiia piataia*, pt. 1 (St. Petersburg, 1911), 27.
37. "Kievskii lord-mer i evrei," *Dvuglavyi orel*, 25 September 1911, 4.
38. Anonymous denunciation of Kiev SRN members, September 1911, in RGIA, f. 786, op. 1, d. 1192, l. 13.
39. Petition of residents of Iablonovetskii area of Kiev province, ibid., l. 26.

by a liberal Kiev daily. Vera Cheberiak, a professional criminal whose son had been seen playing with Iushchinskii on the day he died, soon became the principal focus of this investigation. Margolin and his associate ultimately set up a meeting with Cheberiak, who informed him that one of her criminal contacts had murdered Iushchinskii.[40] In January 1912, Margolin forwarded the evidence that he had unearthed in his investigation—including a copy of Cheberiak's statement—to the local court. Margolin also challenged the qualifications of the "experts" who had ruled Iushchinskii's killing a case of ritual murder, furnishing a list of professors, psychiatrists, church officials, and theologians from the imperial capitals as well as Europe's major cities who were prepared to testify that Jews did not engage in ritual murder.[41] In the meantime, a senior Kiev police official who was not convinced of Beilis's guilt carried out his own investigation, which also led to Cheberiak's associates. In the spring of 1912, Margolin's collaborator published a full report of these investigations, which condemned the local police and courts for having persecuted an innocent man.[42]

These interventions deeply distressed those certain of Beilis's guilt. SRN activists joined self-professed monarchists and rightists to organize at least one mass meeting that drew participants from Kiev and its outskirts to discuss the latest developments in the case; attendees expressed particular offense at Margolin's involvement in the investigation, which they denounced as a shameless effort by the son of one of Kiev's wealthiest Jewish industrialists to protect a guilty co-confessionalist.[43] Kiev Club officers reported strong sales of pamphlets that laid out the supposed evidence implicating Beilis in the ritual murder of Iushchinskii.[44] Ordinary city dwellers continued to write to local prosecutors and police, sharing their own anecdotes that demonstrated the innate hostility that Jews supposedly harbored toward the Orthodox narod.[45]

As the opponents of Beilis mobilized in Kiev, extreme and mass-oriented "truly Russian" groups continued to proliferate in the right-bank countryside. The Pochaev monks roamed Volynia, helping peasant communities incorporate SRN divisions; they also founded a new penny paper, *Volynskaia zemlia (Volynian Land)*, which called on peasants and workers to rise up against alleged Jewish conspiracies to exploit and abuse them.[46] After a local widow donated a large plot of land to the SRN, the Berdichev area became a new epicenter of "truly Russian activity"; activists established a

---

40. See *Delo prisiazhnogo Poverennogo A.D. Margolina* (St. Petersburg, 1914), 93–98.
41. Margolin and Gruzenberg to Kiev District Court, 31 January 1912, TsDIAUK, f. 317, op. 1, d. 5482, t. 1, ll. 171–73.
42. Report of Chaplinskii to Shcheglovitov, 2 May 1912, ibid., ll. 273–75.
43. "Vypiska iz protokola zasedaniia Predsedatelei ob"edinivshikhsia pravykh Monarkhicheskikh organizatsii g. Kieva," 14 June 1912, TsDIAUK, f. 442, op. 641, d. 2, ch.1, ll. 187–187ob.
44. Kiev Club to Ardashev, 16 May 1913, IRNBUV, f. 167, no. 43, l. 1.
45. For example, anonymous letter, April 1912, TsDIAUK, f. 317, op. 1. d. 5482, t. 1, ll. 250–51.
46. See "Pered Vyborami," clipping from *Rech'*, 3 July 1912, TsDIAUK, f. 442, op. 665, d. 101b, ch. III, l. 46; clipping from *Volynskaia zemlia*, 8 August 1912, ibid., l. 57. For his continued incitement of violence and insubordinate attitude toward his superiors, Iliodor was defrocked in 1912. He emigrated to New York, where he lived until his death in the fifties. Rawson, *Russian Rightists*, 249.

publishing house and a network of trade schools on the property.[47] In Kiev province, at least one rural SRN division successfully staged a strike against Polish landlords and Jewish long-term leaseholders.[48] Kiev-based activists and priests traveled to the city's rural hinterlands and met with villagers, helping them to draw up petitions demanding that officials ban Jewish trading on Sundays and Christian holidays and expropriate land illegally rented by Jews.[49]

In light of the growing regional influence of the SRN, local church leaders encountered new pressure to clarify their relationship to the group. Having commissioned a study revealing that 117 SRN chapters with more than twenty thousand members were active in Kiev province alone, Flavian, the Kiev metropolitan, ultimately decided to cooperate with the organization rather than struggle against it. In late 1911, he distributed a circular to southwestern priests praising the SRN's struggle to develop "Russian national consciousness" and to "resist traitors." The participation of priests in "truly Russian" groups, he stated, was "not only permissible but desirable."[50]

In public, many southwestern officials presented themselves as allies of the Russian nationalist cause. The Kiev civil governor's office promised local SRN activists "full and multifaceted cooperation"; bowing to pressure from the Double-Headed Eagle, Trepov agreed to ban donations from Jews to a project he initiated to create a monument to honor Stolypin.[51] But by 1911–12, at least one official who had once aligned himself with the nationalist movement frequently expressed in secret circulars his concerns about its dangers. Convinced that SRN agitation against "landlords and capitalists" promoted "highly tendentious and dangerous ideas," Civil Governor A. F. Girs directed local police to carefully monitor activists. The reports that he received from localities confirmed his fears, prompting him to warn Trepov of the potential that SRN activists could incite "benighted, ignorant peasant-unionists" to participate in mass violence.[52] Although he had initially supported the prosecution of Beilis, by 1912 Girs had also expressed his concern to his St. Petersburg superiors that it would lead to "nightmarish" results. Noting that the case had polarized public opinion in the southwest, which he feared would lead to political unrest during the upcoming Duma elections, he convinced Shcheglovitov to postpone the beginning of Beilis's trial until after the vote.[53]

---

47. Office of Kiev Province Direction to Girs, 2 August 1911, TsDIAUK, f. 442, op. 861, d. 102, ll. 5–110b; Trepov to Metropolitan Flavian, c. 1911, ibid., l. 155.
48. Memorandum of the Chief of the Kiev Province Gendarme Direction, 6 October 1911, ibid., l. 20.
49. Kazatin chapter of the SRN to A. I. Dubrovin, 29 April 1912, RGIA, f. 786, op. 1, d. 1192, ll. 7–8.
50. Metropolitan Flavian, "Ob uchastii dukhovenstva v Otdelakh Soiuza Russkogo naroda," TsDIAK, f. 127, op. 789, d. 743, ll. 1–2.
51. Gubernatorial circular, 24 February 1912, TsDIAUK, f. 442, op. 861, d. 102, l 65; "V komitete po sboru pozhertvovaniia na pamiatnik P. A. Stolypinu," *Dvuglavyi orel*, 11 September 1911, 4.
52. Quotes from gubernatorial circular, 11 December 1911, TsDIAUK, f. 442, op. 861, d. 102, l. 225; Chancery of Kiev Governor to Trepov, 22 February 1912, ibid., l. 59.
53. Girs to A. N. Kharuzin, 19 April 1912, RGIA, f. 1227, op. 2, d. 203, l. 320b; Minister of Internal Affairs to I. G. Shcheglovitov, 3 May 1912, ibid., l. 33.

The increasing influence of radical "truly Russian" groups aimed at the masses placed the Kiev-based intellectuals at the organizational center of the Russian nationalist movement in a difficult position as well. On the one hand, they endeavored to maintain the unity of their socially variegated movement as the 1912 Duma elections neared. They used sessions of the new western zemstvo to organize platforms and to mobilize "Orthodox and Russian" voters, and they continued to insist that democratizing, nationalizing reforms would benefit the entire "western Russian population."[54] On the other hand, the rhetoric used by activists such as Pikhno and Shul'gin had become substantially more moderate since the Iushchinskii case and Stolypin assassination had threatened to unleash mass violence. Although gatherings of self-identified Russian voters continued to bemoan the oppression and suffering of the simple folk of the borderlands, they avoided the inflammatory language that they had once used to describe the allegedly exploitative practices of Poles and Jews.[55]

However, efforts by officials and urban intellectuals to control the "truly Russian" movement—and to steer it in a moderate direction—further radicalized its most extreme segments. One Kiev province priest composed an angry letter to a reactionary paper reporting that police officials had halted SRN activities in his village. Questioning why officials would interfere with the efforts of local residents to liberate themselves from the "Polish-Yiddish yoke," he implied that the police themselves were complicit in a foreign "cabal" that had aimed to "exploit the people's labor."[56] The more radical voices in the Russian nationalist movement often portrayed its leaders as ineffective if not negligent. *Volynskaia zemlia,* the paper published by the Pochaev monks, claimed that "Yids, Poles, and Russian Kadets" were actively engaged in efforts to infiltrate the Nationalist Party and demanded that its leaders take more aggressive measures to unmask and expel these enemies of "Tsar, Faith, and Fatherland."[57] Nationalist workers' unions joined with Double-Headed Eagle activists and SRN members to denounce the Kiev Club of Russian Nationalists for hosting a ball on the first anniversary of Iushchinskii's death—a misstep that they saw as evidence of the group's indifference to the suffering of the Orthodox narod under Jewish oppression.[58]

Electing the Fourth Duma

Although Kiev Civil Governor Girs had openly expressed his misgivings about the radicalization of the southwest's "truly Russian" activists, he acknowledged that their movement helped to neutralize the continuing threat to state stability posed by liberal

---

54. See the undated press clipping "K vyboram v chetvertuiu Gosudarstvennuiu Dumu," IRNBUV, f. 167, no. 18, l. 23; clippings from 1912 editions of *Kievlianin* in TsDIAUK, f. 442, op. 665, d. 101b, ch. III, l. 34.
55. For example, *Otchet o deiatel'nosti Zapadno-Russkogo Obshchestva za 1912 god* (St. Petersburg, 1913).
56. "S Kievshchiny," *Russkoe znamia,* 2 August 1912, TsDIAUK, f. 442, op. 861, d. 102, l. 119.
57. Clipping from *Volynskaia zemlia,* 7 April 1912, f. 442, op. 665, d. 101b, ch. III, l. 59.
58. President of Kiev Chapter of National Student Union to *Russkoe znamia,* 8 March 1912, RGIA, f. 786, op. 1, d. 1192, l. 18.

and non-Russian nationalist parties. In the lead-up to the 1912 Duma elections, he continued to support the nationalist camp as a party of order, apparently calculating that he could rely on the intellectuals who led the nationalist cause to restrain its more radical elements.[59] Governor-General Trepov and the governors of Podolia and Volynia also extended their support to the nationalist cause, cooperating with Kiev Club activists to mobilize clergy and to organize meetings of Russian nationalist electors.[60]

Indeed, the southwestern governors even intervened with the central authorities on behalf of nationalist activists, requesting further changes to the election statute that would enhance the power of the nationalist forces. The governor of Podolia petitioned the MVD to permit "reliable" electors who qualified for the franchise in multiple districts to vote more than once. His counterpart in Volynia compiled detailed political forecasts, advocating that officials vary the property requirements that determined voter eligibility as well as the structure of the curia system from locality to locality in a manner that would maximize the strength of the "truly Russian" parties.[61] Girs, who reported with concern that Jews comprised more than one-third of voters in Kiev's second curia and over 80 percent of electors in some district towns, proposed the most extreme measures of all. He petitioned the MVD to deny voting rights to Jewish merchants and artisans who did not possess permanent residence rights in Kiev and to purge potentially "unreliable" individuals from the voting rolls.[62] He also reported that he had placed local priests under surveillance to ascertain their political views with the intention of excluding from the voter rolls those who exhibited liberationist sympathies.[63]

MVD officials greeted these suggestions with greater ambivalence than they had under Stolypin's leadership. On the one hand, MVD functionaries now took for granted the notion that national curial divisions were necessary; having introduced national curiae only sparingly in the elections to the third Duma, they now implemented them in most districts of the southwestern borderlands.[64] The Senate responded favorably to Girs's suggestions to further limit the voting rights of Jews, directing the MVD

---

59. Report of Girs to A. A. Makarov, 24 January 1912, RGIA, f. 1227, op. 2, d. 203, ll. 2–5.
60. Trepov to V. V. Shul'gin, 1 February 1912, TsDIAUK, f. 442, op. 665, d. 101b, ch. III, l. 4; Volynia Governor Mel'nikov to Ministry of Internal Affairs, 30 August 1912, ibid., l. 68; Trepov to Vitalii, 23 February 1912, ibid., l. 9; telegram from Girs to MVD, 11 February 1912, RGIA, f. 1227, op. 2, d. 203, l. 17. Note the similarity here to German officials' reliance on the Pan-German league to define and mobilize a German nation—and their concerns that its activities would undermine their power: Chickering, *We Men*.
61. On these schemes, see Mel'nikov to MVD, 30 August 1912, TsDIAUK, f. 442, op. 665, d. 101b, ch. III, ll. 67–72; Girs to MVD, 6 June 1912, RGIA, f. 1227, op. 2, d. 203, l. 38; Podolia Governor A. Ignat'ev to A. A. Makarov, 14 February 1912, TsDIAUK, f. 442, op. 665, d. 101a, ch. II, ll. 7–9; Ignat'ev to Trepov, 3 August 1912, l. 36; Ignat'ev to Trepov, 18 August 1912, ibid., ll. 51–52.
62. Girs to Makarov, 24 January 1912, RGIA, f. 1227, op. 2, d. 203, ll. 40b–5; Girs to A. N. Kharuzin, 25 January 1912, ibid., l. 120b; Girs to Makarov, 4 April 1912, ibid., ll. 21–22ob; Girs to Ministry of Internal Affairs, 6 April 1912, ibid., ll. 23–24ob; Girs to Kharuzin, 16 September 1912, ibid., l. 83.
63. Report of Girs to Makarov, 24 January 1912, ibid., l. 4.
64. MVD Main Direction on Local Economic Matters to Council of Ministers, 31 August 1913, RGIA, f. 1276, op. 5, d. 73, l. 261; Mel'nikov to Trepov, 20 September 1912, TsDIAUK, f. 442, op. 665, d. 101b, ch. III, l. 79.

to enfranchise only those who possessed permanent residence rights in their place of residence.⁶⁵ On the other hand, the new minister of the interior, A. A. Makarov—in general a man less well disposed than his predecessor to the nationalizing program of southwestern activists—expressed alarm at some of the other measures proposed by the governors. The ministry condemned Girs's plan to spy on the clergy, noting that it could "call forth a hostile, exceptionally undesirable mood toward the local administration on the very eve of elections, even on the part of fully reliable priests."⁶⁶ It also forced the governor of Podolia to move the date of some city elections in order to avoid the Jewish Sabbath and refused to stagger preliminary electoral meetings so that candidates not selected as electors in Kiev city would have a chance to hold that honor in rural locales in which they qualified to vote.⁶⁷

As the elections approached, nationalist activists continued their mobilizational efforts and their attempts to maintain the unity of "truly Russian" voters. In July 1912, Reva, Savenko, Demchenko, and other local activists affiliated with the Kiev Club of Russian Nationalists again formed commissions of Russian electors. As in 1907, they managed to reach an agreement with conservative landowners who identified as "rightists" and radical mass-oriented groups to cooperate in the elections in pursuit of a "national-patriotic order" that would protect the interests of Orthodox East Slavs.⁶⁸

The press organ of the Podolia Club of Russian Nationalists hailed this agreement, downplaying rumors of divisions between its signatories. "The center of Russia has begun to be covered by the pallor of national death," it wrote. "[B]ut in the borderlands, on the battlefield, a great spirit is reinvigorating, creating, and emboldening the resilient fighters whom the center of Russia, whom all of Russia, needs so much."⁶⁹ Setting aside his earlier criticism of the urban intellectuals who formed the core of the nationalist movement, Antonii Khrapovitskii also sounded a conciliatory note, writing that rumors of "opposition between 'nationalists' and 'rightists' in Volynia are a JEWISH INVENTION intended to create strife between them and on the basis of this strife to secure victory."⁷⁰ Nevertheless, observers could not help but comment on the obvious tensions within the "truly Russian" forces. Vitalii of Pochaev was conspicuously absent from a preelectoral summit that brought together supporters of the All-Russian National Union.⁷¹ And representatives of the SRN's Kiev railroad bureau complained that the decision to formally revive the "truly Russian" coalition had been made without their input.⁷²

---

65. *British Documents*, 263.
66. Kharuzin to Girs, 5 February 1912, RGIA, f. 1227, op. 2, d. 203, ll. 15–150b.
67. Ignat'ev to Trepov, 24 September 1912, TsDIAUK, f. 442, op. 665, d. 101a, ch. II, l. 67; telegram of Girs to MVD, 29 September 1912, RGIA, f. 1227, op. 2, d. 203, l. 94.
68. "Russkim izbirateliam," September 1912, IRNBUV, f. 167, no. 18.
69. "Ogon' po svoim," clipping from *Podolianin*, 18 August 1912, TsDIAUK, f. 442, op. 665, d. 101a, ch. II, l. 46.
70. "Na volyni," *Kievlianin*, 11 February 1912, 3.
71. "Russkim izbirateliam."
72. Kiev Railroad Division of the SRN to *Russkoe znamia*, 7 July 1912, RGIA, f. 786, op. 1, d. 1192, ll. 14–140b.

Despite the intensifying discord within the Russian nationalist camp, the "truly Russian" coalition swept preliminary elections in both rural and urban Russian curiae across the southwest.[73] Strongly supported by clerics, Orthodox professionals, intellectuals, and landowners, the "truly Russian" parties also received impressive support from below. In contrast to workers outside the southwestern borderlands, who virtually unanimously supported left-wing parties, Volynia's workers strongly supported the coalition, choosing only one leftist elector.[74] The authorities judged only twelve of the more than four hundred electors selected by Volynia's voters as "politically unreliable" (the term government circles used to describe liberals and radicals); along the Austrian border in Dubno district, one of the regions with the broadest franchises for Orthodox East Slavs, all thirty electors chosen by the small landowner curia were members of the SRN.[75] The non-Russian curiae in rural locales, dominated by Poles, overwhelmingly supported liberationist and Polish nationalist parties.[76] Non-Russian curiae in cities, which were overwhelmingly Jewish with a smattering of Polish professionals, tended to support the Kadets.[77]

The election was more bitterly contested in Kiev—which, for reasons that remain unclear, was one of the few locales in the southwest not divided into national curiae. The initial electoral meetings ended in a dead heat between the "truly Russian" coalition and the Kadets. The former announced its intention to run V. Ia. Demchenko for election in the first curia and Savenko in the second. The latter put forth K. P. Grigorevich-Barskii, a lawyer, and S. I. Ivanov, a former Kiev Polytechnic professor and longtime liberationist activist. Both Kadet candidates were outspoken defenders of Beilis: Grigorevich-Barskii served on the defense team of the accused, and Ivanov publicly decried as ridiculous the notion that Jews participated in blood rituals.

The radical fringes of the "truly Russian" party could not resist pointing out that many of the Kadets who continued to press for equal rights rallied around a man accused of murdering a child in cold blood. Activists' eagerness to taint the liberationist platform by connecting it to the blood ritual allegations frustrated the attempts of figures such as Shul'gin and Pikhno to maintain a moderate tone on the Jewish question. At electoral meetings and on city streets, Double-Headed Eagle members distributed incendiary pamphlets that contained graphic photographs of Iushchinskii's corpse. These materials also denounced Grigorovich-Barskii as a "scoundrel lawyer...who is

---

73. "Spisok lits izbrannykh na s"ezdakh zemlevladel'tsev vyborshchikami v Gubernskoe izbiratel'noe sobranie," TsDIAUK, f. 442, op. 665, d. 101b, ch. III, ll. 111–13; Mel'nikov to MVD, 6 October 1912, TsDIAUK, f. 442, op. 665, d. 101a, ch. II, ll. 99–101; Ignat'ev to Trepov, 24 September 1912, ibid., l. 103; telegram of Girs to MVD, 29 September 1912, RGIA, f. 1227, op. 2, d. 203, l. 94.
74. Mel'nikov to MVD, 28 September 1912, TsDIAUK, f. 442, op. 665, d. 101a, ch. II, l. 75.
75. "Spisok lits, izbrannykh v uplolnomochennye ot melkikh sobstvennikov i ot sviashchennosluzhitelei dlia uchastiia v uezdnykh s"ezdakh zemlevladel'tsev, TsDIAUK, f. 442, op. 665, d. 101b, ch. III, ll. 85–95.
76. "Spisok lits izbrannykh na s"ezdakh zemlevladel'tsev vyborshchikami v Gubernskoe izbiratel'noe sobranie," ibid., ll. 111–13. In Volynia, for example, Polish landowners elected four leftists, seven Polish nationalists, and three nonpartisan electors.
77. "Spisok lits izbrannykh po gorodam," ibid., l. 1120b; Mel'nikov to MVD, 6 October 1912, TsDIAUK, f. 442, op. 665, d. 101a, ch. II, ll. 100–101.

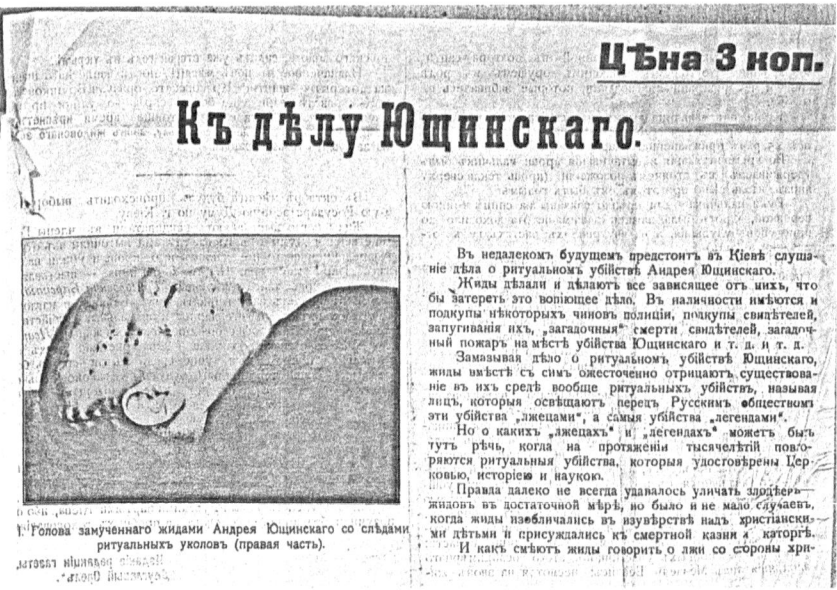

Political pamphlet depicting the corpse of Andrei Iushchinskii and warning of Jewish threats to Orthodox believers. Source: RGIA, f. 1327, op. 2, d. 203, l. 144. Courtesy of RGIA.

defending the Yid Beilis and is trying to con Christians about the legendary nature of ritual murders," criticized Ivanov as a "hanger-on professor who has sold himself to the Yids," and reminded city residents that it was an individual of Jewish descent who had assassinated Stolypin.[78]

At the final electoral meetings in Kiev city, Demchenko won a majority of first curia voters, and Ivanov defeated Savenko by a few hundred votes in the second.[79] Despite its disappointment with its narrow loss of the second curia, the "truly Russian" coalition had much to celebrate elsewhere: indeed, it won every other seat in the southwest's delegation to the Duma. The Nationalist Party fared exceptionally well, claiming 70 percent of the southwest's Duma delegates; southwestern nationalists comprised one-third of the all-Imperial Nationalist Party, which remained the second-largest party in the Duma after the Octobrists. Every delegate elected in Kiev and Podolia provinces—whether noble, professional, former official, priest, or peasant—was a member of the Nationalist Party; and nearly half of these two regions' delegates also served in positions in the newly elected zemstva. All five peasants, three

---

78. The quotes are from the pamphlet "K delu Iushchinskogo," RGIA, f. 1227, op. 2, d. 203, ll. 144–144ob. On the intimidation tactics used by radical "truly Russian" activists, see Girs to Department of Police, 6 October 1912 ibid., ll. 116; "Kopiia raporta Pomoshchnika Kievskogo Politseimeistera Verevkina ot 1 Oktiabria 1912 goda za no. 87 na imia Kievskogo Politseimeistera," ibid., ll. 131–131ob.
79. Girs to MVD, 20 October 1912, ibid., l. 168.

professionals, three priests, and two nobles selected by Volynia's electors belonged to the "truly Russian" coalition as well, though nationalist activists might have perceived a troubling development under way in that province. With the exception of Shul'gin, who was reelected, all of that province's deputies described themselves as rightists rather than nationalists. A testament to the success of the Pochaev monks' aggressive denunciations of the excessive moderation of Kiev's nationalist activists, this shift would bode poorly for Shul'gin and his allies.[80]

Ukrainian Separatism, Russian Nationalism, and the Imperial State

As the urban intellectuals who had built the "truly Russian" movement struggled to maintain their influence over its radical fringes, the proper role of Little Russian culture within the Russian nationalist project remained a subject of controversy.[81] Many prominent southwestern activists continued to portray the Dnieper region as the birthplace not only of a unified East Slavic civilization but also of the Russian national idea. At a speech delivered before the Kiev Club in early 1913, Sikorskii insisted that the East Slavic tribes of Rus' had developed an "ethnic consciousness" as early as the twelfth century, and he argued that the residents of "southern Russia" had faithfully preserved the faith, culture, and language that they had inherited from the Kievan princes.[82] He praised Shevchenko, Kostomarov, and even the activists who had worked to compile a Ukrainian dictionary under *Kievskaia starina* for their efforts to invigorate all of "ethnic Rus'" with a vital national spirit.[83] Railing against Hrushevs'kyi's efforts to define Little Russian traditions as Ukrainian, Sikorskii insisted that the Orthodox inhabitants of Little Russia were in fact "the creators of the *Russian* national idea and the heralds of Russian ethnic unity."[84] A certain A. B. writing in *Kievlianin* concurred: those who presented local traditions as opposed to Russian national unity, he argued, had been led astray by Polish and Jewish conspiracies to divide the children of Rus'. True Little Russian patriots, he insisted, must not allow foreign interests to sow conflict between the "native branches of one people [*narod*], belonging to the same faith, speaking almost the same language"; this would force the "Little Russian national masses" to "abandon their dream to create their own satisfactory national economic life."[85]

But more and more activists now lent their voices to the chorus that decried the very acknowledgment of the peculiarities of local culture as a threat to the unity of the East Slavs and the imperial state. S. N. Shchegolev—who, as we saw in the previous

---

80. Data culled from M. M. Boiovich, ed., *Chleny Gosudarstvennoi Dumy* (Moscow, 1913).
81. For a Polish observer's effort to categorize attitudes on this issue, see Leon Wasilewski, "Inteligencja ukraińska w Rosji," in *Drogi Porozumienia* (Cracow, 2001), 66–70.
82. I. A. Sikorskii, *Russkie i ukraintsy* (Kiev, 1913), 55.
83. Ibid., 35 (source of quote); see also 37, 49, 55.
84. Ibid., 29 (emphasis in original).
85. "Natsionalizatsiia khoziaistvennoi zhizni," *Kievlianin*, 17 February 1912, 2.

chapter, was one of the first Kiev Club members to express this view—published a historical retrospective of the "Ukrainian movement" in 1912. Even more clearly than before, he presented Little Russian particularism as a dangerous force, denouncing Kostomarov, Kulish, and Shevchenko as parties to a foreign conspiracy that sought to "to weaken or cut the ties that united the Little Russian tribe with the Great Russian."[86] A. V. Storozhenko, who had been involved in Little Russian cultural ventures for decades, now found himself an ally of Shchegolev as well. Charging that Polish agitators and "militantly revolutionary Jewry" had invented "Ukrainophile" ideas in the 1830s to serve their own political agendas, he condemned virtually every major nineteenth-century figure who had expressed interest in local culture. Kulish, Kostomarov, Shevchenko, Antonovich, and Chubinskii, he argued, had been led astray by Polish constitutional and federalist ideas; Dragomanov and Hrushevs'kyi, he claimed, served organized Jewish lobbies pressing for equal rights.[87]

Storozhenko was not the only Kiev Club member to reinterpret the legacy of nineteenth-century Little Russian activists through the lens of the stark national competition of the early twentieth century. In 1912, Savenko formulated a more expansive critique of the Shevchenko statue project, for which nearly one hundred thousand rubles had been collected. Having initially objected to the statue's placement on the terrain of the Kievan princes, Savenko now railed against Shevchenko himself, denouncing him as an "uneducated and uncultured" atheist, a "complete nihilist," and a member of the "revolutionary camp." Insisting that any effort to memorialize him would aid the "political propaganda" of forces hostile to Russian civilization, the journalist argued that the statue project should be scrapped altogether.[88] Other Kiev Club members and city residents agreed with Savenko, begging both Kiev Club leaders and local officials to reconsider their support for the project.[89] Antonii, the former elder of the Kiev-Pechersk Monastery, begged Trepov to abandon the statue and donate the funds that he had collected thus far to the Red Cross. Shevchenko had been an "uneducated and barely literate" drunk, he complained.[90] Even worse, the poet had promoted "immoral and deeply criminal" views, fraternizing with "khoklomany" who desired the "separation of Little Russia from Russia."[91] In the eyes of these critics, Shevchenko's ability to give voice to the desires of the toiling masses and his vision of a more equitable social order—projects that Russian nationalists had previously celebrated—undermined the unity of the Rus' people and the stability of the state they had built.

---

86. Shchegolev, *Ukrainskoe dvizhenie*, 5.
87. A. V. Storozhenko, *Proiskhozhdenie i sushchnost' ukrainofil'stva* (Kiev, 1912), quote from 57.
88. *Sbornik kluba*, 3:36–37, 39.
89. S. P. Alekseev to Kiev Club of Russian Nationalists, 28 April 1911, TsDIAUK, f. 442, op. 662, d. 501, l. 40b; undated letter of Kiev residents to Trepov ibid., l. 8.
90. Antonii to Trepov, 13 April 1911, ibid., ll. 110b–12.
91. Ibid., l. 12.

Trepov expressed bewilderment at these complaints. Shortly before Stolypin's death, he forwarded to his St. Petersburg superiors some of the letters that his office had received on the matter and asked them for guidance. Some segments of local society, he noted, saw Shevchenko "as a person who not only did nothing for the fatherland, but who is famous for thoughts of a tendentious character." On the other hand, he noted, "among the educated classes [of Kiev] there are not a few individuals of Little Russian origins who are devoted proponents of the Little Russian movement, which welcomes with uninhibited satisfaction the idea of immortalizing the memory of T. G. Shevchenko by erecting a monument to him and to all those who in one way or another are connected to the past of Ukraine."[92]

Stolypin, however, did not have the opportunity to reply to Trepov, who left the issue unresolved after the prime minister's untimely death. In the meantime, as tension continued to build between the radical fringes of the Russian nationalist movement and more moderate intellectuals, some of the former lent their support to those rallying against the Shevchenko project. A parish priest from Podolia expressed outrage that the authorities would offer moral sanction and financial support to "Ukrainian separatist propaganda."[93] Another correspondent who wrote to Trepov portrayed the project as a Jewish plot, alleging that Shevchenko had "cursed the Christian religion in the spirit of the Yids, as a deception."[94] Reactionary papers seized on this allegation. Ignoring the fact that it had been approved by the local authorities, the St. Petersburg ministries, and the Senate, they claimed that the plan to erect the statue had been crafted by revolutionaries during the chaos of 1905.[95]

Finally, in the summer of 1912, the MVD—which, as we have seen, had vacillated in its attitudes toward cultural activism that highlighted the particularities of southwestern culture—took decisive action. In a dispatch to Trepov, the ministry argued that the Shevchenko project was a "Ukrainophile" plot to spread "separatist ideas" and create a "Mazepist movement." The dispatch ordered Trepov to halt the project on a technicality, noting that Kiev activists had engaged in unauthorized fund-raising efforts; the statute that approved the project permitted the Kiev city duma to collect money only under the auspices of the Poltava zemstvo.[96] Again, though, official opinion on this issue proved far from unanimous. In October 1913, the ruling Senate overturned the MVD's directive, finding that the statue's proponents had secured the proper permissions from the authorities at every stage in the project. Imperial interference in activities that reflected "local interests and needs," it ruled, was illegal.[97]

As St. Petersburg officials struggled to formulate consistent policies to manage Ukrainophile cultural activism in the southwestern borderlands, some also came to

---

92. Trepov to Stolypin, 19 June 1911, ibid., ll. 31–310b.
93. Undated letter of priest of Holy Trinity Church in Volkovnishcha village to Trepov, ibid., l. 34.
94. Anonymous letter from Poltava to Trepov, 22 August 1912, ibid., 470b.
95. "Doky tse bude?" clipping from *Rada*, 23 January 1913, contained in ibid., l. 51.
96. "Spravka," ibid., ll. 43–45ob; MVD to Trepov, 6 July 1912, ibid., 37–370b.
97. "Ukaz ego imperatorskogo velichestva," 8 October 1913, ibid., ll. 40–41.

regard the Russian nationalist project with growing suspicion. Although the MVD had continued to cooperate with right-bank activists to nationalize electoral and governance structures in the southwest, many in the ministry now questioned whether this effort had achieved its aims. Since the introduction of the nationalized zemstva, the MVD had received a constant stream of complaints about the new institutions. Polish notables continued to protest that the nationalized zemstva unfairly infringed on their rights, and conservative gentry objected that they vested excessive power in the hands of peasants and small landowners. As the critics of the western zemstvo bill had predicted, defining the contours of the national curiae also proved problematic. MVD offices had been inundated by letters from voters appealing their national classification or complaining that they had been assigned to the wrong curia.[98]

In 1913, the MVD launched a review of the southwest's national curia system. Concerned that the current statute did not offer enough power to large landholding interests, the ministry's Committee on Local Affairs suggested that the national curia system be retained but that the Russian curia be divided into separate subgroups.[99] The most well-heeled gentry among the nationalist forces, such as the Kiev marshal of the nobility, F. N. Bezak, welcomed this compromise.[100] Other voices, however, denounced it. Polish nobles continued to insist that any system based on national principles was morally despicable.[101] V. Ia. Demchenko and other urban intellectuals informed the MVD that they would not accept any modification to the national curia system, which in their eyes provided the only means of protecting the political and economic interests of the borderlands' East Slavs.[102]

The Beilis Verdict

By mid-1913, the nearly century-long effort of activists to claim the southwest as the center of East Slavic civilization—a project that had benefited from substantial official patronage—had become imperiled. Serious schisms had emerged between Russian nationalist intellectuals who welcomed into their fold those of non-East Slavic origins (as long as they promised to promote the interests of the children of Rus') and more radical activists, who viewed compromise and moderation as signs of weakness. The continuing debate about the proper role of Little Russian culture in the forging of a Russian nation also undermined the coherence of the movement. Substantial segments of the Russian nationalist camp (many themselves onetime Little Russian patriots) had abandoned the Little Russian idea, which had served as the intellectual

---

98. MVD Main Direction on Local Economic Affairs to Council of Ministers, 31 August 1913, RGIA, f. 1276, op. 5, d. 73, ll. 259–60, 272.
99. Ibid., ll. 285–89.
100. "Vechernee zasedanie 27 marta 1913," RGIA, f. 1276, op. 5, d. 73, l. 460.
101. "Zhurnaly komisii po razsmotreniiu zakonoproetka ob izmeneii pravil VYSOCHAISHGO ukaza 14 marta 1911," 26 March 1913, ibid., l. 4570b.
102. "Zhurnal obshchago Prisutstviia Soveta po delam mestnogo khoziastva," 30 March 1913, ibid., ll. 354–560b.

The Limits of the Russian Nationalist Vision

foundation of the "truly Russian" movement that coalesced in the southwest after 1905; for them the very acknowledgment of local peculiarities undermined the integrity of the empire and the unity of the East Slavs. The relationship between officials and nationalist activists was also growing more complicated. Imperial bureaucrats had expressed alarm at the rise of Ukrainian separatism, but they also recognized junctures at which the Russian nationalists who claimed to defend the territorial integrity of the empire had undermined its stability. As each of these parties struggled to make sense (and seize control) of the mass political movement that had taken hold in the southwest, new developments in the Iushchinskii case would only render the local political situation more explosive.

Delayed until after the election of the fourth Duma, the trial of Mendel Beilis finally began in September 1913. Golubev and Sikorskii served as the prosecution's star witnesses. On the stand, they described the alleged instances in which Jews had drained the blood of young boys to bake matzo and insisted that Iushchinskii's injuries were consistent with those that would be sustained in a blood ritual. Professors, Orthodox clergy members, and rabbis from across the empire testified for the defense, denying that Jews engaged in blood rituals; the defense also called the eyewitness who had initially implicated Beilis to the stand, where he disavowed his deposition and claimed that he had been confused and misled by the police to whom he delivered it.[103]

After the death of Pikhno in July 1913, V. V. Shul'gin became the editor of *Kievlianin*—and therefore the most prominent spokesman of the "truly Russian" movement with which that paper had become so closely associated. In a bold move to marginalize the more radical elements of the movement, Shul'gin published an impassioned defense of Beilis shortly after taking control of the paper. Denouncing Jewish blood rituals as a "shameful superstition," Shul'gin condemned Chaplinskii for pursuing a clearly innocent man—and castigated groups such as the SRN and Double-Headed Eagle for exploiting Iushchinskii's murder to promote a radical anti-Semitic agenda that threatened to incite mass violence.[104] Predictably, Shul'gin's editorial provoked outrage from the camps that he criticized. SRN divisions labeled him a crypto-Judeophile and a traitor to the narod. *Dvuglavyi orel* denounced him as a "slave" of Jewish interests—and published an exposé that purported to connect Pikhno to the Brodskiis' industrial interests.[105] A series of crude cartoons that the paper published implied that *Kievlianin*—which had done so much to present Jews as objective enemies of the Orthodox East Slavs—had been bought by Jewish capitalist elites.[106]

---

103. See *Delo Beilisa: Stenograficheskii otchet*, 3 vols. (Kiev, 1913). Interestingly enough, the prosecutors could not find an Orthodox clergyman willing to testify on their behalf; a Catholic priest was the only religious authority who testified for the prosecution.
104. *Kievlianin*, 27 September 1913, 1.
105. "Otkrytoe pis'mo redaktoru 'Kievlianina,'" *Dvuglavyi orel*, 4 October 1913, 3; "Otkrytoe pis'mo redaktoru gazety 'Kievlianin' V. Shul'ginu," *Dvuglavyi orel*, 5 October 1913, 2.
106. *Dvuglavyi orel*, 12 October 1913, 1; 19 October 1913, 1; 20 October 1913, 4.

In response to his critics, Shul'gin explained that he objected to Beilis's prosecution not because he was a friend of the Jews but rather because the blood ritual legend detracted from the "healthy and sensible anti-Semitism" that he had long promoted. Shul'gin insisted that the Jews posed a historically unprecedented threat to the children of Rus'. The struggle between East Slavs and Poles in the western borderlands, he argued, was primarily political; if Polish notables could be convinced to renounce their narrow nationalist interests, they could live peacefully alongside their Orthodox neighbors and prosper in a Russian national state. The conflict with the Jews, by contrast, was a racial struggle: the very existence of a large Jewish population in the western borderlands, he insisted, threatened to destroy Russian traditions. The Jews who dominated the "press, liberal professions, trade, and capital," he complained, had also "Yiddified" Russian culture, encouraging decent Orthodox people to engage in capitalist exploitation and revolutionary violence. It now fell to nationalist activists to encourage the people of Rus' to reclaim their traditions of equality and brotherhood and to reject "Jewish psychology" and "Jewish ethics." Implicating "Yids" in absurd medieval legends, he insisted, could only distract activists from their critical efforts to mobilize a Russian nation strong enough to resist Jewish onslaughts. Furthermore, the obvious weaknesses in the case against Beilis had only emboldened liberals and the defenders of the Jews, supplying them with new opportunities to decry anti-Semitism as a negative force in Russian society.[107]

Meanwhile, the debate between officials who supported the blood ritual allegations and their skeptics also grew more contentious. The St. Petersburg police authorities sent special units to Kiev to protect Beilis's prosecutors; local authorities prosecuted Shul'gin and Margolin for criticizing the conduct of the officials who handled the case.[108] Other officials, however, openly criticized the prosecution of Beilis, predicting that it would yield disastrous results. Alarmed by the continued radicalization of extreme elements of the nationalist camp, the Kiev civil governor and MVD struggled to confiscate incendiary newspapers and pamphlets. They also enhanced local security measures to forestall pogroms.[109] Gendarme units reported that the prosecution of Beilis had turned many segments of the city's residents—even moderates and individuals who previously had demonstrated little interest in politics—against the government.[110] Indeed, intense media scrutiny of the case—and denunciations of the state's

---

107. "Antisemitizm," *Kievlianin*, 15 October 1913, 2.
108. "SPB gradonachal'nik. Okhrannaia komanda," 21 September 1913, TsDIAUK, f. 274, op. 4, d. 311, l. 39; "Delo V. V. Shul'gina," *Kievlianin*, 28 November 1913, 3. Margolin was ultimately disbarred for his role in the case, and Shul'gin was sentenced to three months of arrest. *Delo prisiazhnogo Poverennogo A. D. Margolina*, 27; "Prigovor po delu V. V. Shul'gina," *Kievskaia mysl'*, 5 February 1914, 2.
109. Kiev Governor N. I. Sukovkin to Chief of Provincial Gendarmes Unit, 23 September 1913, TsDIAUK, f. 274, op. 4, d. 311, l. 42; MVD to Sukovkin, 6 October 1913, ibid., l. 119; circular of Sukovkin to local police chiefs, 11 October 1913, ibid., l. 128. In spite of officials' efforts to block the publication of *Dvuglavyi orel* pieces that promoted "ethnic hatred," activists managed to circulate at least ten thousand copies of such materials. Memorandum of Kiev Chief of Gendarmes to Department of Police, 12 October 1913, ibid., l. 130.
110. Internal Memorandum of Gendarme Division, 20 September 1913, ibid., ll. 371–371ob.

handling of it by socialist, liberal, and Ukrainian nationalist activists—had made the case a cause célèbre far beyond the southwest. By late September, universities and educational establishments across the empire declared a strike to protest the prosecution of Beilis.[111]

In late October, a jury consisting exclusively of Orthodox peasants announced its verdict. Although the jurors found that Iushchinskii had likely died as a result of a blood ritual, they concluded that the evidence was not sufficient to convict Beilis of the crime. Beilis's defenders rejoiced that reason and justice had prevailed.[112] The local activists who had promoted the blood ritual charges from the beginning were horrified. The day after the verdict was announced, *Dvuglavyi orel* ran a headline in large print that read, "Understand everywhere and always that Yids are the most dangerous element in Russia."[113] Over the course of the next month, the paper organized a boycott of Jewish businesses and a memorial service for Iushchinskii that drew five thousand to St. Sophia's; it published alarmist articles claiming that Jews were raping Christian woman with impunity.[114] The priests and intellectuals who viewed figures such as Shul'gin as excessively moderate had also begun to talk among themselves, discussing ways to seize control of the banner of the "truly Russian" movement—and to provide stronger leadership to the "simple, good Russian narod" in the final battle against the Jews.[115]

The Beilis verdict created great rancor in the Kiev Club of Russian Nationalists. Some members of the club began a collection for a memorial bell tower to be constructed at the grave of Iushchinskii; others, including Shul'gin, opposed the measure, charging that it would serve as a monument of *"hatred toward Yids"* rather than a memorial to the young boy's memory.[116] In late November, Savenko and Demchenko delivered speeches on the floor of the club and published an editorial in *Kievlianin* urging club members to maintain their solidarity. Yet again these appeals for conciliation were sharply partisan. They railed both against the "extreme rightists" who they claimed wished to return to a pre-1905 order and the radicals, peasants, and workers mobilized by the SRN who sought to express their opinions through mass violence. Both tendencies within the nationalist movement, they argued, were as dangerous as revolutionary and liberationist ideas. Reaffirming their commitment to broad popular representation on national principles, they pledged to lead Russia "forward, not backwards" and to oppose retrograde social forces as well as revolutionary ideologies.[117]

This intervention only further enraged the dissident members of the club. At its next meeting, an angry priest rose to denounce the group's urban intellectuals as

---

111. On strikes and protests across the empire, see RGIA, f. 733, op. 201, d. 473.
112. Gruzenberg, *Yesterday*, 112.
113. *Dvuglavyi orel*, 1 November 1913, 1.
114. *Dvuglavyi orel*, 1 December 1913, 1.
115. A. Tregubov to Flavian, 24 October 1913, RGIA, f. 796, op. 205, d. 739, l. 1.
116. *Dvuglavyi orel*, 10 November 1913, 3; *Kievlianin*, 24 December 1913, 2.
117. "Vynuzhdennoe Raz"iasnenie," *Kievlianin*, 28 November 1913, 3; see also perlustrated letter from A. I. Savenko to K. A. Dvorzhitskii, 30 November 1913, TsDIAUK, f. 274, op. 4, d. 431, l. 36.

poorly attuned to the interests of the toiling masses and unqualified to speak for them. As the discussion that followed devolved into a shouting match, club officers unilaterally closed the meeting, alienating many.[118] The two sides quarreled at the club's next meeting as well. Again, the group's leaders ended its meeting early, and the two camps continued their debates in the pages of *Kievlianin*.[119]

By late December, the conservative landowners and radical intellectuals whose support had expanded the influence of the nationalist movement decisively turned against Shul'gin, Savenko, Demchenko, and their moderate supporters. Antonii Khrapovitskii, Chaplinskii, Bezak, S. T. Golubev, Sikorskii, and A. V. Storozhenko joined together to launch a new daily, *Kiev*, in January 1914. Declaring their intent to stand as a beacon of hope for "truly Russian" people threatened by the "darkness of cosmopolitanism," the paper became an intellectual gathering place for those outraged by Beilis's acquittal. Its editorial board assumed control of the effort to construct a memorial church to Iushchinskii. Its contributors published essays on blood rituals allegedly committed by Jews across the world and denounced Shul'gin as standing "for the Jews and against the cross and the Russian people."[120] (Menshikov, the reactionary St. Petersburg journalist who had worked with southwestern activists to expand the influence of the Nationalist Party in St. Petersburg in the Stolypin years, joined *Kiev* contributors to accuse Shul'gin of betraying the children of Rus' and the legacy of his father and stepfather.)[121]

But while *Kiev* continued to draw attention to the threats that the empire's putative internal enemies posed to the Orthodox narod, its contributors distanced themselves from the populism that had always undergirded the Little Russian idea and the Russian nationalist project that eventually developed out of it. Rather than conceiving of the nation as defined by the people themselves, the paper's contributors called on officials to define the culture and characteristics of a "state nationality" (*natsional'nost' gosudarstvennaia*) from above.[122] Building on the ideas of Shchegolev and Storozhenko, who had argued that any discussion of local peculiarities posed a serious threat to the unity of the Rus' nation, *Kiev* contributors denigrated the "southern Russian culture" that previous generations had lauded as a dangerous creation of foreign agitators. They presented Shevchenko as an agent of the Jews, and Antonovich, the khlopomany, and the *Osnova* circle as Polish provocateurs who hoped to promote Ukrainian identity in order to estrange the southwest from Russia and to lay the groundwork for its reabsorption into Poland.[123]

---

118. "V klube russkikh natsionalistov," *Kievlianin*, 15 December 1913, 6.
119. "V Klube russkikh natsionalistov," *Kievlianin*, 19 December 1913, 4; letter to editor of S. M. Bogdanov, *Kievlianin*, 17 December 1913, 3; *Kievlianin*, 18 December 1913, 3.
120. Quote from "Torzhestvo osviashcheniia redaktsii "Kieva," *Kiev*, 1 January 1914; 4. See also "Mestnaia khronika," and "Za evreev protiv kresta i russkogo naroda," *Kiev*, 3 January 1914, 3–4; "Novye zhesty g. Shul'gina," *Kiev*, 6 February 1914, 4.
121. *Kievlianin*, 24 December 1913, 2.
122. *Kiev*, 8 February 1914, 1.
123. *Kiev*, 27 February 1914, 1; "Chto takoe 'ukrainstvo'?" *Kiev*, 28 February 1914, 2.

Outrage at the Beilis verdict also energized extreme organizations aimed at the working masses. SRN activists charged that Shul'gin, Demchenko, and Savenko were agents of the Kadets working to give Jews equal rights.[124] *Dvuglavyi orel*, which became a daily in January 1914 (previously it had been published only on a weekly basis), described Beilis's prosecutors as national heroes, covered the subsequent disappearances of young boys as possible cases of blood ritual, and ominously predicted that the children of Rus' would soon avenge themselves against the Jews.[125] The paper agitated for the expropriation of Jewish property and condemned the Orthodox believers who maintained friendships or business partnerships with Jews, rebuking one Kiev resident who had recently sold property to the Margolin family for neglecting his duty toward his nation and assisting the "main boss of the Kiev Jewish kabal."[126] The paper continued to publish cartoons that excoriated its adversaries: one particularly memorable image depicted Shul'gin as a monkey who hopped at the command of his Jewish masters.[127]

In contrast to the nobles, intellectuals, and clerics who grouped around *Kiev*, some of the working-class organizations that had denounced the leaders of the nationalist lobby after the Beilis verdict continued to portray Little Russia's cultural heritage as a salutary force, a source of pride and cohesion that had allowed the simple folk to carry on their battle against Jews and Poles for centuries. Certain SRN activists from Kiev province complained to the MVD that "separatist Ukrainophiles" had seized on and distorted the importance of "anticlerical and antigovernment" ideas in Shevchenko's poetry. Nevertheless, they continued to express their admiration for his ability to use "artistic images and the people's language to convey the beauty of the nature of his native Little Russia, her customs, and...the psychological characteristics of her population."[128]

The men who had helped transform what began as an urban movement in Kiev into an all-imperial political party and nationalist movement attempted to reestablish their authority in the wake of these attacks. Shul'gin insisted that he had "never betrayed Rus'," clarifying that his opposition to the Beilis case resulted from his concern that the blood ritual charges had divided Orthodox believers and discredited the government.[129] But the nationalist movement was now in tatters. Kiev Club members hurled abusive invectives at each other at the group's meetings.[130] At a conference of the Nationalist Party in St. Petersburg in February 1914, Savenko and other speakers suffered the embarrassment of delivering their speeches to a

---

124. *Kievlianin*, 28 December 1913, 1.
125. "V obshchestve 'Dvuglavyi orel,'" *Kiev*, 23 January 1914, 3–4; "Ischeznuvshii mal'chik," *Dvuglavyi orel*, 25 February 1914, 2.
126. "Vnimanie g.g. kievskikh domovladel'tsev," *Dvuglavyi orel*, 16 January 1914, 2–3.
127. Cartoon supplement to *Dvuglavyi orel*, 7 January 1914.
128. "Dokladnaia zapiska," 22 January 1914, TsDIAUK, f. 442, op. 864, d. 34, ll. 8–8ob.
129. *Kievlianin*, 24 December 1913, 2–3.
130. *Kiev*, 16 January 1914, 1–2.

Гопъ Шульгинцю, гопъ!

1914 cartoon depicting V. V. Shul'gin as a monkey serving Jewish masters. The caption reads, "Hop, little Shul'gin, hop!" Source: Cartoon supplement to *Dvuglavyi orel*, 7 January 1914. Courtesy of Slavonic Library, National Library of Finland.

half-empty hall.[131] Meanwhile, working-class residents of the southwest who had once supported the nationalist movement were growing increasingly restive, expressing frustration at the slow pace of officials in improving the welfare of the simple folk and limiting the influence of Jews.[132] The acrimonious disputes that now divided the "truly Russian" coalition challenged the central tenet of Russian nationalism—the notion that the children of Rus' shared fundamental common interests.

State and Nation

The growing schisms within the Russian nationalist camp created an opportunity for Hrushevs'kyi. In early 1914, he launched a new periodical under the auspices of the

---

131. "S"ezd natsionalistov," *Kievskaia mysl'*, 3 February 1914, 1. These events corroborate the arguments of those who claim that the Duma party system was breaking down by 1913–14. See Haimson, "The Problem of Social Stability (Part Two)," 3–8; Hosking, *Constitutional Experiment*, 182–243.

132. "Mestnaia khronika"; "Vnimanie g.g. kievskikh domovladel'tsev."

Shevchenko Scientific Society, *Ukraina*, which continued to consolidate a Ukrainian nationalist historiography—and to obscure the importance of the Little Russian idea in shaping local politics by portraying nineteenth-century discussions of local particularities as manifestations of Ukrainian national consciousness. (Indeed, some veterans of the Little Russian movement and even the "truly Russian" movement of the 1905 period, such as O. I. Levitskii, colluded in this effort; in an article in *Literaturno-Naukovyi Vistnyk*, Levitskii described V. B. Antonovich as the leader of the "Ukrainian revival of the second half of the nineteenth century.")[133] The fact that substantial segments of the disintegrating Russian nationalist camp had denigrated the value of local culture enabled Hrushevs'kyi to claim it for his own cause: working with followers on the left and right banks, the historian organized celebrations to mark the centenary of Shevchenko's birth, which would fall in February 1914.[134] Emulating the tactics that the "truly Russian" camp had pioneered in 1905, the historian reached out to the masses, authoring illustrated histories and short political tracts aimed at barely literate readers.[135]

These mobilizational efforts continued with the full knowledge (and in certain cases, the sanction) of the imperial state, which still had not established a consistent policy on the Ukrainian question. Work on the Shevchenko statue project continued: after a display of the prototypes submitted for the project at the Kiev city duma, jury members chose a model by an Italian sculptor that portrayed the poet in the traditional garb of a right-bank peasant. With all the necessary preparations complete, the committee overseeing the project planned to break ground on the anniversary of the poet's birth.[136] As that date approached, Trepov reminded his subordinates to forward local communities' plans for the centenary to his office so that he could review them.[137]

By early 1914, however, all three warring contingents that had emerged from the Russian nationalist camp—conservatives and reactionaries, moderates, and working-class radicals—expressed concern about celebrating the centenary of Shevchenko's birth. The elites who grouped around *Kiev* denounced Shevchenko as a "proponent of separatism, a fanatical enemy of Autocracy, an open blasphemer of the church and Christianity, and a model of depravity."[138] SRN divisions and *Dvuglavyi orel* complained that the project had come under the control of Polish revanchists, Jewish revolutionaries, and "Mazepist separatists," who sought to distort Little Russian culture and to turn it against the imperial state and the children of Rus'.[139] Although Kiev Club

---

133. O Levits'kyi, "Storinka z zhyttia Volodymyra Antonovycha," *Literaturno-naukovyi vistnyk* 4 (1913): 19–26, clipping included in IRNBUV, I.8076, l. 1.
134. "Khronika provintsii," *Kievskaia mysl'*, 6 February 1914, 5.
135. Plokhy, *Unmaking*, 67.
136. "Pamiatnik T.G. Shevchenko," *Kievskaia mysl'*, 4 February 1914, 4; "K stoletiiu so dnia rozhdeniia T.G. Shevchenko," *Kievskaia mysl'*, 5 February 1914, 2.
137. Trepov circular to southwestern governors, 5 February 1914, TsDIAUK, f. 442, op. 662, d. 501, l. 79.
138. *Kiev*, 23 January 1914, 1–2.
139. The quote is from "Dokladnaia zapiska," l. 8. See also "T. G. Shevchenko i 'prisoedinenie' Ukrainy," *Dvuglavyi orel*, 25 February 1914, 2; *Dvuglavyi orel*, 22 February 1914, l. 1.

activists remained divided on the proper role of Little Russian culture within their movement, they agreed to petition officials to halt the project, which they complained had been hijacked by "Ukrainian-Mazepist forces," who wished to create a separate "Ukrainian government" out of the "southern branch of the Russian people."[140]

This uproar finally convinced St. Petersburg officials, who had vacillated about the Shevchenko project for years, that it could not be allowed to go forward. The MVD again used a technicality to delay the impending groundbreaking for the project, informing the committee that construction work could not commence until the ministry received more precise information about the statue's location.[141] Echoing the arguments of *Kiev*, whose editorial board contained several clerics who had broken with more moderate nationalist activists, the Holy Synod ordered church officials to ban services honoring the poet. The "literary activities of Shevchenko clearly reveal negative, antichurch and antigovernment inclinations," argued Synod officials. "[I]n many of his compositions there appear clearly offensive, blasphemous expressions directed against the veneration of the Holy Mother, God's Holy Saints, holy icons, and also against the sovereign government."[142]

The last-minute refusal of the MVD and the Holy Synod to permit the Shevchenko jubilee to progress as planned was the clearest indication yet that their staffs, like southwestern intellectuals, had begun to conflate the peculiarities of local culture with subversive ideas. Their stance on the issue angered many residents of the southwest, who saw the official intervention as heavy-handed. When the statue committee learned that the MVD had ordered it to cease and desist its work on the project, its members refused to comply, continuing their planning efforts.[143] The controversy soon expanded beyond the southwest. Galicia-based dissidents published tracts—which were reprinted as far away as North America—canonizing Shevchenko as a Ukrainian national hero and depicting the "Moscow lords'" refusal to celebrate his contributions as emblematic of the empire's disregard for the Ukrainian people and their culture.[144] Duma deputies from all parties except the rightists and nationalists lodged complaints about the restrictions on the celebrations, which they denounced as a "glaring infringement on the dignity of the people."[145] Radicals, liberals, and moderates all portrayed Shevchenko as a man of the people who had stood up against the injustices of the autocratic state; they printed brochures explaining the poet's significance and organized public celebrations in his honor across the empire.[146] In response

---

140. "K Shechenkovskomu iubileiu. Protest natsionalistov," *Dvuglavyi orel*, 23 February 1914, 2.
141. Sukovkin to Trepov, 5 February 1914, TsDIAUK, f. 442, op. 662, d. 501, l. 75.
142. "Spravka," 19 February 1914, RGIA, f. 796, op. 198, I otd., 2 stol, d. 30, l. 2.
143. "Likvidatsionnoe sobranie gorodskoi iubileinoi komissii," *Kievskaia mysl'*, 6 February 1914, 3.
144. The quote is from Dmytro Dontsov, *Iuvilena zbirka staty [sic] pro Tarasa Hryhorovycha Shevchenka v soti rokovyny ioho narodzhennia* (Winnipeg, 1914), 7.
145. *Kievskaia mysl'*, 13 February 1914, 1.
146. "K chestvovaniiu iubileiia T. G. Shevchenko," *Kievskaia mysl'*, 6 February 1914, 4; "Khronika," *Kievskaia mysl'*, 13 February 1914, 3.

to this outcry, the MVD banned all celebrations of Shevchenko and public gatherings around the anniversary of his birth.[147]

This drastic move did not deter those determined to celebrate the legacy of the poet. City residents and peasants held their own impromptu celebrations.[148] In Kiev, workers declared a strike to protest the government handling of the Shevchenko affair, and hundreds poured into the streets waving red flags as well as blue and gold banners—the hues that Galician activists had designated the national colors of Ukraine. Cossacks and police forces poured onto the streets to break up the demonstrations.[149] The disorders were short-lived, but officials would continue to struggle with the problematic legacy of Shevchenko. By June, Trepov informed the MVD that he opposed erecting a monument to Shevchenko altogether.[150] The Shevchenko project would never be realized under the tsarist regime.

By 1914, officials at all levels of the imperial government had deviated from the traditions of their nineteenth-century predecessors, who had regarded the Little Russian idea, as long as it was properly monitored and directed, as a salutary force capable of claiming the borderlands for the empire. Meanwhile, the government's relationship with some of the factions that had emerged from the Russian nationalist camp had also become strained. Local SRN groups, on which southwestern officials had once relied to protect the existing order, continued their struggle to defend the putative interests of the Rus' nation even when their actions undermined the stability of local society and imperial institutions; in one village in Kiev province, for example, activists denounced a parish priest who had refused to rent church lands to the SRN and later leased them to a Jewish sugar industrialist and lobbied his parishioners not to attend church.[151] By the summer of 1914, Demchenko, Savenko, and Shul'gin expressed growing doubts that they could work with officials to transform the Russian empire into a modern nation-state and began to cooperate more closely with their onetime liberal foes who challenged the authority of the autocracy.[152]

Only the self-professed rightist nobles and intellectuals grouped around the paper *Kiev* maintained a cooperative working relationship with local and imperial officials. Although they continued to invoke the language of nationhood, they had stripped the Russian national project that had emerged from the southwest of its most important distinguishing features. They now perceived the very acknowledgment of the special features of local culture as subversive, railed against the expansion of democratic institutions, and pressed for the centralization of authority. Equating the Russian nation with the tsarist state, their views corresponded more closely with the empire's

---

147. MVD to Trepov, 21 February 1914, TsDIAUK, f. 442, op. 662, d. 501, ll. 82–82ob.
148. *Kievskaia mysl'*, 25 February 1914, 4.
149. "Dlia edinichnoi zabastovki," TsDIAUK, f. 574, op. 1, d. 1831, l. 4; Tregubov to Flavian, 11 March 1914, RGIA, f. 796, op. 205, d. 739, ll. 5–6.
150. Trepov to MVD, 24 June 1914, TsDIAUK, f. 442, op. 662, d. 501, l. 92.
151. Sukovkin to Trepov, 14 January 1914, TsDIAUK, f. 442, op. 864, d. 34, l. 1.
152. On the collapse of the Nationalist Party and the rapprochement between its more moderate members and liberals, see Edelman, *Gentry Politics*, 181–217.

Cossacks and police arrive to disperse Kiev residents celebrating the Shevchenko centenary, February 1914. Courtesy of TsDKFFAU.

conservative elite than with the populist, democratizing, and nationalizing "truly Russian" movement of the southwest to which they had once belonged.[153]

::

The Little Russian idea and the Russian nationalist movement to which it gave rise had initiated an intense, empire-wide dialogue about the prospect of transforming an autocratic empire that possessed no official vocabulary for discussing ethnic and national difference into a nation-state that represented the Rus' people. Through ethnographic and historical research, activists had discovered what they believed were distinct and mutually hostile nations in one of the empire's most diverse corners. Urging both local and St. Petersburg officials to promote the putative collective interests of the Orthodox East Slavs and to reduce the influence of their Polish and Jewish adversaries, right-bank activists insisted that nationalizing the empire would strengthen its foundations and unify its loyal residents. Availing themselves of the space they were granted by a state that relied on their efforts to claim a contested border region for the empire and the Orthodox Church, southwestern nationalists created a vibrant civic society and powerful political movement that united people of many social stations in

153. Edelman, *Gentry Politics*, 185–86.

a common crusade to protect the Rus' people and their traditions. They ultimately expanded their influence beyond the southwest, enlisting imperial officials in their cause and founding a network of associations that commanded influence across the empire.

However, the effort to mobilize a Russian nation in defense of the empire also produced debilitating new conflicts. Internal disputes within the Little Russian lobby evolved into a bitter schism that pitted self-professed Ukrainians against Little Russian patriots and Russian nationalists. Distinct and mutually hostile camps emerged within the "truly Russian" movement as well, struggling for control of the nationalist banner and the right to define the contours of the Russian nation. Nationalist activization divided local communities, as some of the southwest's workers and peasants denounced and even physically attacked their Polish and Jewish neighbors. Clumsy and often belated attempts by imperial officials to address all three of these threats alienated the more moderate nationalists, enhancing the influence of the southwest's most radical voices. If, as generations of activists had argued, the outcome of the struggle for control of the southwest would determine the future of the children of Rus' and the empire they had built, the prospects of both appeared bleak indeed.

By 1914, the Russian nationalist lobby in the empire's southwestern borderlands had disintegrated; falling short of its promise to rejuvenate the East Slavs with a vital national spirit and to reconcile the interests of state and society, it had in fact atomized local residents and turned them against the government. However, the integral nationalist ideas and antiliberal mass politics that southwestern activists had pioneered proved more durable than their movement. The ideological by-products of the Little Russian idea and of southwestern nationalism would remain in the borderlands for decades to come—and they would travel across the globe with the refugees who fled the region as it descended into war and revolution.

Epilogue

WITHIN MONTHS OF the collapse of the Russian nationalist coalition in the southwestern borderlands, Russia plunged into World War I, and Russian troops marched west to engage German and Habsburg forces. In the first weeks of the war, the opposing camps that had emerged from the Russian nationalist lobby were swept, like the rest of Russian society, by patriotic fervor. Despite his criticism of the government in the months before the war, V. V. Shul'gin volunteered for military service and was sent to the Austrian front. There he was joined by the fellow volunteer V. S. Golubev, one of his chief adversaries in the Beilis affair. I. A. Sikorskii hailed the war as the final battle in the racial conflict that had consumed Russia's borderlands for centuries, predicting that it would destroy once and for all the "parasitical" forces "feeding on the Slavic body."[1] The men who fought on the front, however, soon experienced war's sobering realities: Golubev was killed in action on the eastern front in the first weeks of the conflict, and Shul'gin was wounded in 1915.[2]

Russian troops crossed the Austrian border into Galicia in July 1914, seizing Lemberg by September. The invasion of Galicia reinvigorated and reunited the warring camps that had emerged from the southwest's nationalist lobby. Savenko hailed the "reunification" of the Rus' lands, presenting the occupation of Galicia as a new opportunity to revive the nationalist coalition and to unite all the children of Rus' behind the faith and culture of the Kievan princes.[3] Activists from the Kiev Club, some of the radical dissidents who had abandoned it in late 1913, and SRN members all poured into Lemberg, lobbying the Russian occupation forces to marginalize the influence of Poles and Jews and to promote the Orthodox Church, the Russian language, and the putative collective interests of the East Slavs.[4] G. A. Bobrinskii, the cousin of the onetime nationalist activist A. A. Bobrinskii, was named the governor-general of Galicia. Although he considered the occupied territories an integral part of the Russian

---

1. I.A. Sikorskii, *Sovremennaia vsesvetnaia voina 1914 goda* (Kiev, 1914), 10.
2. For SRN condolences sent to S. T. Golubev on the death of this son, see IRNBUV, f. 194, no. 6.
3. A. Savenko, "Ne posramim Zemli russkoi!" IRNBUV, f. 21, no. 1189, l. 1.
4. Mark von Hagen, *War in a European Borderland* (Seattle, 2007), 19–53; Bakhturina, *Politika*, 187–202.

nation, he struggled to contain the influence of southwestern pressure groups in the region—and the anti-Jewish violence that Russian troops perpetrated there.[5]

Other segments of the imperial government, however, used the war as a pretext to promote a radical, nationalizing agenda. The leadership of the Army General Staff demanded the exclusion of Jews from military service—a measure for which members of the Russian nationalist lobby had agitated before the war.[6] Although the War Ministry refused to yield to this demand, the General Staff did succeed in deporting from the borderlands and expropriating the property of more than a million Jewish, Polish, and German civilians, now deemed "unreliable elements" solely by virtue of their ethnonational status.[7] With influential figures in the government now supporting the nationalization of land, property, and capital, "patriotic" violence swept the empire: mobs from Kiev to Kazan' and Moscow attacked foreign subjects, non-Orthodox minorities, and their property.[8] Ministers, politicians, and newspapers claimed to have unearthed treasonous plots by Jews, Germans, and their defenders to deliver Russia into the hands of its enemies. Indeed, Governor-General V. A. Sukhomlinov—now serving as Minister of War—was implicated in one of the most notorious "treason fantasies"; his adversaries cited his long-standing history of associating with and defending non-Orthodox elites during his service in Kiev as evidence of his anti-Russian inclinations.[9]

As Russian nationalist ideas infiltrated growing segments of the bureaucracy and imperial society at large, the proper role of southwestern culture in the Russian national project remained a controversial issue. The Central Powers sponsored and encouraged Ukrainian nationalist activities, which they viewed as an effective means of undermining their Russian adversary.[10] The Russian authorities, for their part, struggled to stamp out Ukrainian nationalism; this effort was particularly intense in Galicia, where the occupying forces arrested Greek Catholic clerics and Ukrainian activists, including Hrushevs'kyi, whom they exiled to central Russia. Resurrecting an argument that many nineteenth-century officials had made, however, some bureaucrats warned that efforts to control the dangerous "Ukrainian-Mazepist" movement should not

---

5. Peter Holquist, "The Role of Personality in the First (1914–1915) Russian Occupation of Galicia and Bukovina," in *Anti-Jewish Violence*, ed. Jonathan Dekel-Chen, David Gaunt, Natan M. Meir, and Israel Bartal (Bloomington, IN, 2011), 52–73.
6. Yohanan Petrovsky-Shtern, "The 'Jewish Policy' of the Late Imperial War Ministry: The Impact of the Russian Right," *Kritika* 3, no. 2 (2002): 249–52.
7. Lohr, *Nationalizing*; Alexander Victor Prusin, *Nationalizing a Borderland* (Tuscaloosa, 2005); Peter Gatrell, *A Whole Empire Walking* (Bloomington, IN, 1999).
8. Lohr, *Nationalizing*, 31–54.
9. Fuller, *The Foe Within*.
10. On Ukrainian nationalist agitation within the Habsburg empire, see Wladimir Kuschnir, *Die Ukraine und ihre Bedeutung im gegenwärtigen Kriege mit Russland* (Vienna, 1914); Michael Hruschewskyj, *Die ukrainische Frage in historischer Entwicklung* (Vienna, 1915); Dmytro Donzow, *Karl XII. Feldzug nach der Ukraine* (Vienna, 1916); M. Trotzkyj, *Die ukrainische national-politische Bewegung* (Vienna, 1917); Viacheslav Budzynovs'kyi, *Iak Moskva nyshchyla Ukrainu* (Vienna, 1917); M. Vozniak, *Ukrains'ka derzhavnist'* (Vienna, 1918).

interfere with the potentially salutary "'Ukrainophile' tendency in southern Russian society," which affirmed the unity of the East Slavs.¹¹ Continued uncertainty about whether discussion of southwestern particularities comprised a vital part of the effort to mobilize a Russian nation or posed a threat to it ultimately benefited Hrushevs'kyi and other proponents of the Ukrainian national cause in the Russian empire; in spite of officials' concerns about his activities, the scholar legally published historical and ethnographic studies of the Ukrainian lands during the war years.¹²

By 1915, devastating Russian military losses on the eastern front led to the collapse of the Russian occupation in Galicia and a rapid retreat. The Central Powers pressed eastward, claiming Galicia, Volynia, and Podolia by year's end. Berlin and Vienna hailed the liberation of the Ukrainian lands, maintaining close contacts with Ukrainian nationalists active in Galicia.¹³ When the Russian army reclaimed much of eastern Galicia after a 1916 offensive, the occupation regime resumed its efforts culturally and politically to "reunite" the children of Rus'.¹⁴ The fate of the lands between the Carpathians and the left bank would be decided only by the outcome of the war. Ironically, however, the successive occupations of the region helped to normalize an idea that both Russian and Ukrainian nationalists had struggled, but largely failed, to popularize before the war—the notion that both banks of the Dnieper and Galicia shared a common culture and history and should be part of the same territorial unit.¹⁵

Although the war had prompted growing segments of Russian officials and military figures to embrace the nationalizing policies that southwestern activists had long promoted, by 1915, relations between prominent right-bank nationalists and the imperial state had again become strained. Outraged by shortages of supplies and ammunition on the eastern front, Shul'gin and Savenko also decried Nicholas II's reliance on his ineffective camarilla. In the summer of 1915, they joined the Progressive Bloc, a political alliance that united members of all parties except the extreme left and the extreme right. The coalition strongly backed the war effort, but it also pressed for "decisive change in the methods of administration" and called on the tsar to create a government that enjoyed "public confidence."¹⁶ In the last years of the old regime, the Progressive Bloc grew more and more critical of the tsar, publicly questioning his ability to win the war and lead the empire. Indeed, it was Shul'gin, along with one of the

---

11. See the discussions in RGIA, f. 733, op. 201, d. 503. The quoted passage, from l. 9, was written by the Guardian of the Kiev School District.
12. The historian published a two-volume survey of the Ukrainian people and their history in the Russian empire in 1914 and 1916. It located the origins of a Ukrainian nation in Rus' and traced its fortunes through the twentieth century, identifying Cossacks, the *Istoriia Rusov*, Kostomarov, Kulish, Antonovich, and *Kievskaia starina* as beacons of the Ukrainian national idea. See M. S. Grushevskii, F. K. Volkov et al., eds., *Ukrainskii narod v ego proshlom i nastoiashchem*, 2 vols. (St. Petersburg, 1914–16).
13. Von Hagen, *War*, 54–71.
14. Ibid., 72–79.
15. Von Hagen makes this point repeatedly.
16. Cited in Rex A. Wade, *The Russian Revolution, 1917* (New York, 2005), 20.

EPILOGUE

founders of the Progressive Bloc, who traveled to a railroad car on the eastern front in February 1917 and finally convinced Nicholas to abdicate the throne.

Ukrainian nationalists hailed the demise of the autocracy. Hrushevs'kyi's supporters in Kiev convened a revolutionary parliament (Rada) that declared itself the legislative body of a Ukrainian nation that stretched across both banks of the Dnieper. (Most of Galicia, which had enjoyed a short-lived period of autonomy as the Western Ukrainian National Republic, was transferred to the independent state of Poland after the war.) The new body elected Hrushevs'kyi as its president, even before he had been released from exile and returned to Kiev. The Rada passed protections for workers, implemented agrarian reforms, and declared Ukrainian autonomy in June 1917.

Setting a moderate course amid the radical ideologies left behind in the wake of the empire's collapse, Hrushevs'kyi worked to create a Ukrainian national state that would protect the rights of its diverse inhabitants. His inner circle reflected the heterogeneity of those who had now embraced the Ukrainian cause: it included O. I. Levitskii, the longtime Little Russian activist; D. V. Antonovych; E. Kh. Chykalenko; A. D. Margolin, the defender of Beilis, who would hire a private tutor to learn Ukrainian as a middle-aged man; and Oleksandr Shul'hyn—V. V. Shul'gin's cousin and the son of Iakov Shul'gin, who had disowned V. Ia. Shul'gin and his Little Russian project in the late nineteenth century and embraced a Ukrainian identity instead. Hrushevs'kyi urged his followers to demonstrate tolerance for their Jewish neighbors and attempted to forge a productive relationship with Russia. (His attitude toward Ukraine's Polish minorities was more ambivalent).[17]

Hrushevs'kyi's nation-building efforts were not uncontested, however. V. V. Shul'gin and Savenko, who applauded the social reforms implemented by the Rada but vehemently opposed its "Ukrainianization" of local society, organized a political party called the Bloc of Russian Voters. Building on southwestern nationalists' earlier experience with voter mobilization and echoing their continued claims to represent the interests of the working classes against non-East Slavic capitalists and plutocrats, the group won the most votes of any party in the free and fair elections that Kiev hosted in 1917.[18] Indeed, a census commissioned by the Ukrainian government in 1917 revealed that 49 percent of Kiev's population self-identified as Russian and 4 percent as Little Russian; only 12 percent of city residents described themselves as Ukrainians.[19]

In November 1917, the Bolsheviks seized control of Russia. In the winter of 1918, they invaded Ukraine, unleashing a brief but bloody Red Terror in occupied Kiev

---

17. On Hrushevs'kyi's views, see Mikhail Grushevskii [Hrushevs'kyi], *Na porozi novoi Ukrainy* (1918; repr., New York, 1992). On Shul'hyn: Oleksandr Shul'hyn, *Polityka* (Kyiv, 1918). On Margolin: Victoria Khiterer, "Arnold Davidovich Margolin," 145–67.
18. Steven L. Guthier, "Ukrainian Cities during the Revolution and the Interwar Era," in *Rethinking Ukrainian History*, ed. Ivan L. Rudnytsky (Edmonton, AB, 1981), 162. Guthier notes that if the votes of large numbers of Ukrainian military forces stationed in Kiev are factored in, Ukrainian nationalist parties slightly outperformed the Bloc of Russian voters. For an example of Shul'gin's continued efforts to mobilize society behind the Little Russian idea, see V. V. Shul'gin, ed., *Malaia Rus'*, 3 vols. (Kiev, 1918).
19. I. S. Bisk, *K voprosu o sotsial'nom sostave naseleniia g. Kieva* (Kiev, 1920), 3.

before they were repulsed by a new German invasion. The March 1918 Treaty of Brest-Litovsk, in which Soviet Russia and Germany agreed to a separate peace, compelled the Bolsheviks to withdraw their troops from Ukrainian territory and designated the German military as a temporary occupying force. After extensive lobbying of the Central Powers, Shul'hyn and other members of the Ukrainian government extracted a promise that the occupying force would support Ukrainian independence and reinstall the Rada government.[20] For now, a foreign state had guaranteed Ukraine's independence. In the years to come, however, multiple parties would continue to compete for the right to determine its future. The contest for Ukraine would soon devolve into a bloody civil war that pitted Bolsheviks, Polish forces, various factions of Ukrainian and Russian nationalists, anarchists, and peasant armies against one another.

Alumni of the old regime's Little Russian lobby found themselves on many sides of this struggle. In the spring of 1918, Hrushevs'kyi's Ukrainian government fell in a coup supported by the German occupation regime. The new right-wing government, headed by P. P. Skoropadsky (1873–1945), a former tsarist military officer and the scion of an elite Cossack family from Poltava, gave new life to the Little Russian idea—and benefited from the support of stalwart Little Russian activists, including V. Ia. Demchenko, the Storozhenkos, Antonii Khrapovitskii, and Vitalii of Pochaev. Although it rejected Hrushevs'kyi's socialist and Ukrainian nationalist politics and worked to retain cultural ties to Russia, the Skoropadsky government celebrated and affirmed the peculiarities of local culture. Skoropadsky declared himself the Hetman of Ukraine and appropriated Cossack imagery, implemented Ukrainian-language instruction in primary schools, and founded the Ukrainian Academy of Sciences in Kiev. He reversed some of the protections that the Hrushevs'kyi government had offered to non-Ukrainian minorities and declared Orthodoxy the official state religion.[21]

After the defeat of the German forces on the western front, Skoropadsky's foreign patrons withdrew from Ukraine, and his government collapsed. After a chaotic power struggle—accompanied by a new Bolshevik assault from the east—Symon Petliura, a left-bank intellectual of Cossack extraction, emerged as the leader of the directorate now ruling the right and left banks. A member of the RUP and contributor to *Kievskaia starina* and *Rada*, Petliura had now become a staunch Ukrainian nationalist and radical populist, resuming Hrushevs'kyi's efforts to promote Ukrainian culture and language and to safeguard Ukrainian independence.[22]

The men who had belonged to the moderate and radical wings of the prerevolutionary Russian nationalist movement reunited to face the dual threat posed by the Bolsheviks and Petliura. The Storozhenko brothers, T. V. Lokot', and Sikorskii sided

---

20. See *Proceedings of the Brest-Litovsk Peace Conference* (Washington, 1918); *Texts of the Russian "Peace"* (Washington, 1918).
21. Iaroslav Lebedynsky, *Skoropadsky et l'édification de l'Etat ukrainien* (1918; repr., Paris, 2010); Von Hagen, *War*, 87–114.
22. On Petliura's youth, see A. Zhuk, ed., *Symon Petliura v molodosti: Zbirka spomyniv* (Lviv, 1936); on his government, O. Lotots'kyi, *Derzhavnyi provid Symony Petliury* (Paris, 1930).

with the White Army, which now unified liberals, priests, and conservative nobles fighting the Bolshevik regime; so too did Shul'gin and Savenko, whose earlier efforts to gauge public opinion in revolutionary politics had gradually evolved into Azbuka, a sophisticated intelligence and propaganda agency serving the Whites. Opposed to the authoritarianism and atheism of the Bolsheviks, White intellectuals were equally determined to defeat the Ukrainian nationalist disciples of Hrushevs'kyi and Petliura, whom they denounced as traitors.[23] The Whites, however, soon faced the same dilemma that had bedeviled prerevolutionary Russian nationalists: how to reconcile the interests and agendas of the conservatives, the moderate nationalists, and the radicals within the movement. Azbuka operatives hoped to see a modern Russian nation-state emerge from the war, drawing up plans to reform local governance and to redistribute land among the peasantry. Conservative nobles, by contrast, expressed alarm at these blueprints for a "broadly democratic" order. Meanwhile, rank-and-file White forces, more concerned with settling old scores than with planning for the future, perpetrated multiple attacks against Jewish communities across the right bank.[24]

Petliura's government struggled to limit the influence of the Whites, arresting over one hundred clerics and intellectuals (many former members of the Kiev Club of Russian Nationalists) even as it continued to wage war against the Bolsheviks.[25] Although Petliura officially disavowed anti-Jewish violence, his forces, who like their White adversaries denounced the Jews as incorrigible enemies of the Orthodox narod, also participated in widespread pogroms.[26] In this unsettled environment, the loyalty of the masses—the ultimate prize for all sides—shifted quickly and frequently. Peasants' demands for land reform, political democratization, and the protection of their interests from "alien" forces might lead them to support anarchists on one day, Bolsheviks the next, Whites the third, and Petliura the fourth.[27]

Over the course of 1919, the Red Army scored key victories over the Whites and Petliura's forces, and by 1920 the Bolsheviks had begun to consolidate their control over right-bank Ukraine. Hrushevs'kyi, Petliura, and many Ukrainian nationalist intellectuals fled to Europe; Margolin, who had served in Petliura's government, left for America. Skoropadsky and his followers settled in Germany, where they founded

---

23. See A. I. Savenko, *Ukraintsy ili Malorossy?* (Rostov-on-Don, 1919); A. Storozhenko, *Trudy podgotovitel'no po natsional'nym delam komissii* (Rostov-on-Don, 1919). On Azbuka and its operations, see Peter Kenez, *Civil War in South Russia, 1918–1919* (Berkeley, 1977), 65–71; Victor Bortnevskii, "White Intelligence and Counter-Intelligence during the Civil War," *The Carl Beck Papers*, no. 108 (1995).
24. For examples of reform plans, see HA, Vrangel' Collection, box 29, folders 2, 14, 15. On conservative skepticism toward the democratizing program of White intellectuals, see ibid., folder 29. On the ideological divisions within White forces, see Christopher Lazarski, *The Lost Opportunity* (Lanham, MD, 2008); Anna Procyk, *Russian Nationalism and Ukraine* (Edmonton, AB, 1995).
25. HA, Vrangel' Collection, box 30, folder 8.
26. The most even-handed overview of Petliura's Jewish policy is Henry Abramson, *A Prayer for the Government* (Cambridge, MA, 1999), 109–40.
27. Savenko complained of the political volatility of the masses: see Savenko, *Ukraintsy ili Malorossy?*, 27. On the struggle for the hearts and minds of the peasantry, see Andrea Graziosi, *The Great Soviet Peasant War* (Cambridge, MA, 1996).

a Ukrainian studies institute. The Whites retreated toward the Black Sea. Sikorskii, A. V. Storozhenko, and Savenko all perished, victims of disease or political terror. The White forces who survived evacuated by ship from Odessa. Shul'gin and T. V. Lokot' fled to Berlin, Demchenko settled in Wiesbaden, and other émigrés congregated in Munich. Antonii Khrapovitskii and Vitalii of Pochaev, who had joined the Whites after the fall of Skoropadsky, settled in Serbia, where they became leaders of the Orthodox Church in exile.[28] Still others fled to Asia or North America.[29] By the early twenties, the symbolic prize of Kiev, which had changed hands a dozen times during the civil war, lay in ruins. The city's powerful mercantile elite, which had insisted that its diverse inhabitants could live peaceably together under an equal rights regime, had fled en masse. Many of the physical marks that they left on the urban landscape had vanished as well: the Brodskiis' and Gintsburgs' manors and the famous Kiev skyscraper had all been reduced to rubble.[30]

Now in control of the left and right banks (though not Galicia or western Volynia, which became part of interwar Poland), the Bolsheviks embarked on a nationalizing experiment of their own—one that aimed to speed "the assimilation of diverse peoples into nationality categories," which Communist Party officials hoped would accelerate the "assimilation of nationally categorized groups into the Soviet state and society."[31] Soviet nationality policy recognized Ukrainians as the titular nationality of the newly formed Ukrainian Soviet Socialist Republic; it also created hundreds of small autonomous regions in Ukraine that offered Polish, Jewish, and other minority communities substantial self-governance rights.[32] Lured by Soviet officials' stated commitment to Ukrainianization, Hrushevs'kyi and other associates who had fled after the collapse of the Ukrainian state returned to Kiev, where they continued their efforts to write the history of the Ukrainian nation.[33]

The Ukrainian nationalist project that emerged in the early Soviet Union was socialist and revolutionary—seemingly the antithesis of the antiliberal Little Russian idea that had flourished under the old regime. Hrushevs'kyi and his followers chronicled

---

28. In the forties, Vitalii emigrated to New York, where he became the first abbot of the Holy Trinity Monastery near Cooperstown. His onetime collaborator at the Pochaev Monastery, Iliodor, who had emigrated to the United States earlier, also resided in New York in these years. When he died, in the early fifties, he was reportedly working as a janitor at the Met Life building.

29. Sikorskii's son, Igor, escaped to the United States in 1919. He settled in coastal Connecticut and founded the Sikorsky Aircraft Corporation, which created the first mass-produced helicopter.

30. On the fate of the city's architecture in the civil war, see Ol'ha Druh and D. V. Malakov, *Osobniaky Kyeva* (Kiev, 2004). Mikhail Bulgakov's *Belaia gvardiia* and *Dni turbinykh* are famous literary depictions of the turmoil of the wartime years in Kiev.

31. Francine Hirsch, *Empire of Nations* (Ithaca, 2005), 146. Terry Martin has argued that these policies also aimed to win the loyalty of Jews and Ukrainians in the Second Polish Republic, whose treatment of its minorities tended to be less generous than that of the Soviets. See Martin, *Affirmative Action*, 8–9.

32. For more on early Soviet nationalities policy, see Yuri Slezkine, "The USSR as a Communal Apartment, or How a Socialist State Promoted Ethnic Particularism," *Slavic Review* 53, no. 2 (1994): 414–52; Martin, *Affirmative Action*, 29–124; Kate Brown, *A Biography of No Place* (Cambridge, MA, 2004), 20–47.

33. See, for example, the journals *Ukraina* and *Letopis Revoliutsii*. More generally, Plokhy, *Unmaking*, 219–380.

the struggle of the Ukrainian peasant masses against tsars, landowners, and even Cossack officers, whom they decried as class enemies of the narod. On state holidays, Soviet officials boarded up the monument to Bohdan Khmelnytsky that still stood in central Kiev; some pressed for the statue's removal.[34] However, Hrushevs'kyi's nationalist project still contained at least one trace of the Little Russian milieu in which he had come of age. A committed anti-Normanist, he insisted that Ukrainians were the direct descendants of the Rus' people and that their culture was the purest manifestation of ancient Slavic traditions.[35]

The experience of the civil war—and the seizure of the right bank by a nationalizing communist state—further radicalized the émigrés who had fled the region. In the 1920s, V. V. Shul'gin repeatedly characterized Bolshevism as a Jewish plot to destroy East Slavic traditions, faulting "northern Russians" for their failure to join their southern brothers in what he saw by now as a racial struggle.[36] He expressed interest in the fascist movements coalescing across Europe, recognizing their potential to challenge Bolshevik power.[37] He was not alone: followers of Skoropadsky as well as onetime members of the Kiev Club of Russian Nationalists who had settled in Germany established contact with military officers and early Nazi activists, scheming to overthrow "Jewish Bolshevism" and to reclaim Russia for the Orthodox East Slavs.[38] Admiringly referring to Stolypin as the "first Russian fascist," émigrés in Manchuria argued that the struggle to mobilize a nation on the Russian empire's southwestern frontier had initiated the campaign—now gaining traction across the globe—to forge a new world order.[39]

In the late twenties, Stalin, who had consolidated his power after the 1924 death of Lenin, embarked on a "cultural revolution" and laid out an ambitious plan to industrialize and collectivize the Soviet Union. Closely controlled by Moscow and driven by substantial coercion, these programs also set ambitious targets that proved virtually impossible to meet. As a result, they led to endemic shortcomings and failures that many officials interpreted as evidence that "wreckers" and "internal enemies" were at work on Soviet soil. In the Ukrainian SSR, fears about anti-Soviet conspiracies,

---

34. Plokhy, *Unmaking*, 316–20; Serhy Yekelchyk, *Stalin's Empire of Memory* (Toronto, 2004), 17.
35. Plokhy, *Unmaking*, 128.
36. The quote is from V. V. Shul'gin, "Po povodu odnoi stat'i," HA, Vasilii Maklakov Papers, box 22, folder 24, 6; on race, 25. For more on Shul'gin's views in these years, see V. V. Shul'gin, *Chto nam v nikh ne nravitsia* (Paris, 1929); O. V. Budnitskii, ed., *Spor o Rossii* (Moscow, 2012), 7–44. Lokot', too, interpreted the revolution as the culmination of a long-running Jewish plot to degrade Russian traditions: see his *"Zavoevaniia revoliutsii" i ideologiia russkogo monarkhizma* (Berlin, 1921).
37. Cited in Robert C. Williams, *Culture in Exile* (Ithaca, 1972), 216–17.
38. For coverage of one 1921 meeting, see "Vpechatleniia na s"ezde," *Dvuglavyi orel*, 1 July 1921, 4–11. For further details, consult Johannes Baur, *Die russische Kolonie in München, 1900–1945* (Wiesbaden, 1998), 102–56; Michael Kellogg, *The Russian Roots of Nazism* (New York, 2005), 109–244.
39. F. T. Goriachkin, *Pervyi Russkii fashist* (Harbin, 1928). For more on the activities of self-professed fascists in Manchuria, see Erwin Oberlander, "The All-Russian Fascist Party," *Journal of Contemporary History* 1, no. 1 (1966): 158–73; John J. Stephan, *The Russian Fascists: Tragedy and Farce in Exile, 1925–1945* (New York, 1978).

coupled with war scares brought about by the deteriorating international situation, became intertwined with concerns that the nationalizing policies of the twenties had escaped from official control. Expressing discomfort with the ardent nationalism of Hrushevs'kyi and his associates, Party historians declared an assault on "bourgeois nationalist" scholars and denounced Hrushevs'kyi; exiled in 1931, the scholar died in the Caucasus in 1934.[40] When newly collectivized farms failed to meet their output targets—or to supply the full amount of grain demanded in subsequent requisition orders—Stalin's inner circle blamed these failings on "Petliurite" conspiracies to destroy the Soviet system. In response to this supposed threat, Stalin increased the requisition levels and sealed off the countryside to prevent peasant flight, creating a massive man-made famine that killed millions in the Ukrainian countryside in 1932–33.[41] Implicating Poles, Germans, and other minority groups in espionage rings and anti-Soviet plots, Party functionaries disbanded the Ukrainian SSR's autonomous minority districts and deported many of their inhabitants.[42] By the mid-1930s, the Soviet police apparatus, or NKVD, had launched a full-fledged program of "national terror" in the borderlands. Continuing through the 1937–38 terror, the violence disproportionately targeted minority groups (particularly Poles).[43]

If the violence that the Soviet state employed against putative internal enemies was unprecedented, the anxieties that drove and justified this violence were not new. Official fears that minority groups in the borderlands and Ukrainian nationalists were engaged in plots to destroy the integrity of the Russian state revived ideas that right-bank activists had promoted in the nineteenth century. The new Ukrainian national policies that emerged in the thirties also echoed older precedents. Although the Stalinist state had launched a deadly assault against supposed nationalist conspiracies, its cultural program aimed to manage and direct rather than decimate Ukrainian culture. Like nineteenth-century Little Russian patriots, Moscow Party bosses and Ukrainian functionaries celebrated the distinctive qualities of Ukrainian culture and history but insisted that they were an integral part of a broader Russian/Soviet civilization. By the late thirties Party historians had rehabilitated the Cossacks, whom they now portrayed as leaders of the people's struggle against feudalism and as the architects of Russian-Ukrainian unity (thus Kiev's Khmelnytsky monument was saved).[44] In 1939, Soviet officials finally saw to fruition the project that had energized so many prerevolutionary Ukrainian nationalists—the erection of a monument to Shevchenko in central Kiev. A throng of two hundred thousand cheered the unveiling of the statue,

---

40. Plokhy, *Unmaking*, 264–77.
41. Martin, *Affirmative Action*, 273–308 (quote from 301); Timothy Snyder, *Bloodlands* (New York, 2010), 21–58.
42. Brown, *Biography*, 84–191.
43. The term is Snyder's: see *Bloodlands*, 89–109; Martin, *Affirmative Action*, 311–43.
44. Yekelchyk, *Stalin's Empire*, 19–23. Like the Little Russian lobby in the nineteenth century, Ukrainian Party bosses played an important role in guiding this shift.

which occupied the exact spot where the monument to Nicholas I desecrated in the disorders of October 1905 had once stood.[45]

Ukrainian nationalists beyond Soviet borders refused to permit Stalin to define their culture and the fate of their people, however. Dmytro Dontsov (1883–1973), the son of a left-bank family of Cossack origins who had participated in illegal Ukrainian nationalist parties under tsarism and had served in the Skoropadsky government, spent the early thirties in Galicia developing an integral nationalist alternative to Stalin's Soviet-Ukrainian project. Distancing himself from the "cosmopolitanism" and "humanitarianism" that he complained had guided Dragomanov and Ukrainian activists of the revolutionary period, Dontsov argued that the survival of the Ukrainian people and their culture demanded violent resistance against Russian and Polish nationalism, Jewish "exploitation," and communism.[46] Although Dontsov's Russophobia and insistence on Ukrainian self-determination provided a sharp contrast to the views of prerevolutionary Russian nationalists, his vision of the nation as an organic and unbreakable unit, his antiliberal politics, and his interest in violence as a tool of transformation betrayed their influence.[47] Dontsov relocated to Germany in 1939, but nationalist paramilitary groups that remained behind in Galicia championed his ideas.[48] Some Ukrainian émigrés, too, celebrated the potential of integral nationalism to advance their aims. Although Skoropadsky and his followers struggled to maintain the independence of their national liberation movement under the Third Reich, they dreamed that the Nazi state would restore an independent Ukraine under the leadership of a Hetman.[49]

By the 1930s, growing numbers of émigrés who denounced communism *and* Ukrainian nationalism rallied behind fascism. Shul'gin, who by now had settled in Yugoslavia, along with other aging alumni of the Kiev Club of Russian Nationalists, joined the National Union of a New Generation, a youth group with chapters from Belgium to Australia to San Francisco.[50] Championing the ideas of Hitler, Mussolini, and Franco,[51] this group aimed to incite a "national revolution" in the Soviet Union that would destroy the alien forces of liberalism and communism and create a strong

---

45. Ibid., 23.
46. Serhii Kvit, *Dmytro Dontsov* (Kiev, 2000), 135. The author of this admiring biography is currently the rector of the Kyiv-Mohyla Academy, which was resurrected after the Soviet collapse.
47. For the reflections of another right-bank activist who embraced socialism in the revolutionary period and integral nationalism in the interwar, see Danylo Shumuk, *Life Sentence* (Edmonton, AB, 1984).
48. For more on Dontsov and his influence, see Frank Golczewski, *Deutsche und Ukrainer, 1914–1939* (Paderborn, Ger., 2010), 512–20, 571–603, 921–1016. Dontsov emigrated to Canada in the late forties and spent the rest of his life there.
49. Ibid., 469–87, 648–56, 667–678, 1030. Skoropadsky was killed in an April 1945 Allied bombing raid on a village outside Munich.
50. On the involvement of Shul'gin and other Kiev Club members in the organization, see "Po soiuzu," *Za Novuiu Rossiiu* (Sophia), January 1936, 4.
51. For positive views of European fascist movements, see "Heil Hitler!" *Za Rossiiu* (Sofia), October 1932, 3; "Sut' ne v Ispanii," *Za Novuiu Rossiiu*, September 1936, 1; "Dostizheniia ital'ianskogo fashizma," *Za Rossiiu*, December 1936, 4.

nation-state serving the interests of East Slavic peasants and workers.⁵² The traces of the Little Russian idea are clear in the National Union's ideology: the group railed against Ukrainian national separatism but also lavished attention on the local culture and needs of the Dnieper region, which it depicted as the spiritual heart of Russian civilization and the logical center of a future national state. The National Union adopted the trident—the insignia of St. Vladimir, which Ukrainian nationalists had also appropriated—as its symbol; it described the Ukrainian famine with horror; and it surveyed the Cossacks' past efforts (and future promise) to liberate the children of Rus'.⁵³ In his boldest attempt to adapt the Little Russian idea to the interwar context, Shul'gin went so far as to claim that the Dnieper region was the birthplace of fascism. In a pamphlet celebrating Hitler's annexation of Austria, he described Khmelnytsky's efforts to "reunify" the Rus' lands and to expel foreign elements from Little Russia as the original *Anschluss,* the first effort to create "Ein Volk! Ein Reich! Ein Führer!"⁵⁴

In the end, neither the residents of the right bank nor its native sons who had fled the region would determine its fate—that privilege would belong to the superpowers that would wage a total war for (and in) the borderlands. But the epic battle that unfolded in mid-twentieth-century Ukraine was not only a contest between Moscow and Berlin; it also became intertwined with a much older—and more local—struggle to determine the future of the right bank and the identity of its inhabitants.⁵⁵ Ukrainian Party apparatchiks claimed the right bank as a distinctive yet fundamental part of a larger Soviet/imperial whole; radical intellectuals and paramilitary units fought to establish a Ukrainian nation based on integral nationalist ideas; and right-wing émigrés proclaimed the Dnieper region the cradle of a Russian nation whose long-standing opposition to socialism, cosmopolitanism, and foreign influence had presaged the fascist new world order. Although they would never admit it, each of these battling camps had repurposed for its own means the ideas and practices that had first emerged from the borderlands in the nineteenth century. The Little Russian idea and the antiliberal, mass-oriented, organic nationalist movement to which it gave rise were creations of the tsarist old regime, but they proved remarkably adaptable to the violent new world that took shape in the twentieth century.

---

52. The quote is from Al. D. Bilimovich, *K voprosu ob ekonomicheskoi programme natsional'noi Rossii* (Belgrade, 1936), 13. On fascism's "liberating" potential, see N. Babkin, "Fashizm i osvobozhdenie Rossii," *Za novoiu Rossiiu,* June 1934, 3.
53. For examples of antipathy to Ukrainian national claims, see "Ukraina i sovetskie 'ukraintsy,'" *Za Rodinu,* 1 April 1939, 2–3; V. Shul'gin, *Ukrainstvuiushchie i my!* (Belgrade, 1939). On concern about the famine and the centrality of the concept of Little Russia to fascist émigré culture, see "Ukraina-Malorossiia-Velikorossiia," *Za Novuiu Rossiiu,* October 1936, 4; "Golod v Rossii," *Za Rossiiu,* January 1933, 1; "Kazachestvo: Istoricheskii ocherk," *Za Rossiiu,* July 1933, 4.
54. V. V. Shul'gin, *Anshluss i my!* (Belgrade, 1938).
55. Accounts that emphasize the role of outside invaders in escalating borderlands violence include Snyder, *Bloodlands;* Brown, *Biography.*

SELECTED BIBLIOGRAPHY

Archival Sources

Bakhmeteff Archive (BA), New York

N. N. Flige Papers
A. F. Girs Papers

Derzhavnyi arkhiv Kyivskoi oblasti (DAKO), Kyiv

Fond 2, Kievskii gubernator

Derzhavnyi arkhiv mista Kyeva (DAK), Kyiv

Fond 17, Kievskaia gorodskaia duma
Fond 18, Kievskii politekhnicheskii institut
Fond 163, Kievskaia gorodskaia uprava
Fond 226, Kievskii birzhevoi komitet
Fond 237, Kievskaia gorodskaia politsiia
Fond 301, Komitet po sooruzheniiu v g. Kieve pamiatnika Bogdanu Khmel'nitskomu

Gosudarstvennyi arkhiv Rossiiskoi Federatsii (GARF), Moscow

Fond 102, Departament Politsii
Fond 124, Ministerstvo Iustitsii

Hoover Archive (HA), Stanford

M. D. Vrangel' Papers
V. A. Maklakov Papers
Vrangel' Family Collection

Instytut rukopysu Natsional'noi biblioteky Ukraini imeni V. I. Vernads'koho (IRNBUV), Kyiv

Fond I, Literature collection
Fond II, History collection
Fond III, Correspondence collection
Fond 8, Kievskii universitet
Fond 21, Iu. A. Iavorskii

Fond 57, N. Kh. Bunge
Fond 66, I. V. Luchitskii
Fond 81, O. I. Levitskii
Fond 129, F. I. Titov
Fond 167, P. N. Ardashev
Fond 172, M. P. Dragomanov
Fond 179, I. A. Stepovich
Fond 194, S. T. Golubev

Rossiiskii gosudarstvennyi istoricheskii arkhiv (RGIA), St. Petersburg

Fond 733, Departament narodnogo prosveshcheniia
Fond 776, Kantseliariia Glavnogo upravleniia po delam pechati
Fond 786, Redaktsiia gazety "Russkaia Znamia"
Fond 796, Kantseliariia Sinoda
Fond 821, Departament dukhovnykh del inostrannykh ispovedanii MVD
Fond 932, A. M. Dondukov-Korsakov
Fond 1088, S. D. Sheremet'ev
Fond 1276, Kantseliariia soveta Ministrov
Fond 1282, Kantseliariia MVD
Fond 1284, Departament Obshchikh del MVD

Tsentral'nyi derzhavnyi istorychnyi arkhiv Ukrainy, m. Kyiv (TsDIAUK), Kyiv

Fond 127, Kievskaia dukhovnaia konsistoriia
Fond 274, Kievskoe gubernskoe zhandarmskoe upravlenie
Fond 275, Kievskoe okhrannoe otdelenie
Fond 289, Kievskaia krepostnaia zhandarmskaia komanda
Fond 293, Kievskii tsenzurnyi komitet
Fond 294, Kantseliariia Kievskogo otdel'nogo tsenzora
Fond 295, Kievskii vremennyi komitet po delam pechati
Fond 296, Gazeta "Kievlianin"
Fond 317, Prokuror Kievskoi sudebnoi palaty
Fond 318, Kievskaia sudebnaia palata
Fond 442, Kantseliariia Kievskogo, Podolskogo i Volynskoi General-Gubernatora
Fond 473, Sledstvennaia komissiia dlia politicheskikh del pri Kievskomu, Podol'skomu i Volynskomu General-Gubernatoru
Fond 574, Starshii fabrichyi inspektor Kievskoi gubernii
Fond 575, Fabrichnyi inspector Kievskogo okruga
Fond 707, Kantseliariia popechitelia Kievskogo uchebnogo okruga
Fond 832, V. B. Antonovich
Fond 838, Kollektsiia listovok
Fond 873, M. V. Iuzefovich
Fond 1196, Kievskii otdel russkogo voenno-istoricheskogo obshchestva
Fond 1235, M. S. Hrushevs'kyi
Fond 1475, G. P. Galagan
KMF-19, 22, Microfilm collections

Published Primary Sources

Newspapers

Den'
Drug naroda
Dvuglavyi orel
Dziennik Kijowski
Hromads'ka dumka
Khronika evreiskoi zhizni
Kiev
Kievlianin (1840–1850)
Kievlianin (1864–1917)
Kievskaia gazeta
Kievskaia mysl'
Kievskaia zaria
Kievskie novosti
Kievskie otgoloski zhizni
Kievskii golos
Kievskii sotsial-demokraticheskii listok
Kievskii telegraf
Kievskii vestnik
Kievskoe slovo
Listok russkogo izbiratelia
Narod
Novyi vek
Okrainy Rossii
Otgoloski zhizni
Rada
Rech'
Ridna sprava
Rus'
Samoderzhavie
Slovo
Svoboda i pravo
Trud
Veche
Veche stol'nogo goroda Kieva
Zakon i Pravda
Za novoiu Rossiiu
Zaria
Za Rossiiu

Journals and Serials

Arkhiv iugozapadnoi Rossii
Hromada
Izvestiia Kievskoi gorodskoi dumy
Izvestiia XI Arkheologicheskogo s"ezda v Kieve
Kievskaia starina
Kievskie eparkhial'nye vedomosti
Kievskie gubernskie vedomosti
Kievskii iumoristicheskii kalendar'
Literaturno-naukovyi vistnyk
Lystok hromady
Meta
Nashe mynule
Osnova
Pravda
Pravo
Pravoslavnaia Podoliia
Ridnii krai
Sion
Svitlo
Trudy Kievskoi dukhovnoi akademii
Ukraina (1914–1915)
Ukraina (1924–1932)
Ukrainets
Ukrainskaia zhizn'
Vestnik Iugo-Zapadnoi i zapadnoi Rossii
Vestnik zapadnoi Rossii
Zapysky Ukrains'koho Naukovoho Tovarystva v Kyivi

Books, Pamphlets, and Memoirs

A. B. *Gorodskoe samoupravlenie v Rossii*. Moscow: Kolokol, 1905.
Aksakov, I. S. *Izsledovanie o torgovle na Ukrainskikh iarmarkakh*. St. Petersburg: Imp. Akad. Nauk, 1858.
Alekseev, F. *Spohady pro 1905 rik u Kyevi*. Kiev: Proletars'koi pravdy, 1930.

Anan'ich, B. V. et al., eds. *Iz arkhiva S. Iu. Vitte: Vospominaniia*. St. Petersburg: Dmitrii Bulanin, 2003.
Antonii, Mitropolit. *Khristos Spasitel' i evreiskaia revoliutsiia*. Berlin: Stiag, 1922.
Antonovich, V. B. *Izsledovanie o gaidamachestve: po aktam 1700–1768 g*. Kiev: I. Zavadskii, 1876.
Bantysh-Kamenskii, D. N. *Istoriia Maloi Rossii*. Moscow: Semen Selivanovskii, 1830.
Bartoszewicz, Joachim. *Na Rusi: Polski stan posiadania, kraj, ludność, ziemia*. Kiev: L. Idzikowski, 1912.
Berlinskii, Maksim. *Kratkoe opisanie Kieva*. St. Petersburg: Departament Narodnogo Prosvescheniia, 1820.
Bernshtein, M. D., ed. *Panteleimon Kulish: Tvory v dvokh tomakh*. Kiev: Naukova dumka, 1994.
Bilimovich, Al. D. *K voprosu ob ekonomicheskoi programme natsional'noi Rossii*. Belgrade: Glavyi Komitet Sodeistviia national'nomu soiuzu, 1936.
Bobrowski, Tadeusz. *Pamiętnik mojego życia*. 2 vols. Warsaw: Państwowy Instytut Wydawniczy, 1979.
Boguslavskii, S. M. *Sputnik po g. Kievu*. Kiev: L. V. Khmeliovskii, 1913.
Boiovich, M. M. *Chleny Gosudarstvennoi Dumy. Portrety i biografii. 2-oi sozyv. 1907–1912 g*. Moscow: I. D. Sytin, 1907.
——, ed. *Chleny Gosudarstvennoi Dumy (Portrety i biografii). Chetvertyi sozyv, 1912–1917 g*. Moscow: I. D. Sytin, 1913.
——. *Chleny Gosudarstvennoi Dumy: Tretii sozyv*. Moscow: I. D. Sytin, 1908.
Budilovich, A. S. *O edinstve russkogo naroda*. St. Petersburg: V. D. Smirnov, 1907.
Budnitskii, O. V., ed., *Spor o Rossii: V. A.Maklakov–V. V. Shul'gin. Perepiska 1919–1939*. Moscow: ROSSPEN, 2012.
Budzynovs'kyi, Viacheslav. *Iak Moskva nyshchyla Ukrainu*. Vienna: Naklad Soiuza vyzvolennia Ukrainy, 1917.
Bulgakov, Prot. Sergii. *Avtobiograficheskie zametki*. Paris: YMCA Press, 1991.
"Byt'-li Zapadnaia Rus' Pol'shei ili Rus'iu?" Kiev Club of Russian Nationalists, 1910.
Chernyshevskii, N. G. *Polnoe sobranie sochinenii*. 10 vols. St. Petersburg: Ts. Kraiza, 1905–6.
Chicherin, B. N. *Vospominaniia. Zemstvo i moskovskaia duma*. Moscow: Sever, 1934.
Chleny 1-oi Gosudarstvennoi dumy. Moscow: Pechat' i Graviura, 1906.
Chto luchshe: Russkaia nevolia ili zhidovskaia svoboda? Pochaev: Tipografiia Pochaevo-Uspenskoi Lavry, 1906.
Chubinskii, P. P. "Ocherk narodnykh iuridicheskikh obychaev i poniatii v Malorossii." *Zapiski Imperatorskogo russkogo geograficheskogo obshchestva, po otdeleniiu etnografii* 2 (1869): 677–715.
——, ed. *Trudy etnografichesko-statisticheskoi ekspeditsii v Zapadno-Russkii krai*. 6 vols. St. Petersburg: Imperatorskoe Russkoe Geograficheskoe obshchestvo, 1872.
Chubinskii, P. P., P. A. Gil'tebrandt, N. I. Kostomarov, S. V. Mishanich, eds. *Pavlo Chubyns'kyi, Pratsi etnohrafichno-statystychnoi ekspeditsii v zakhidno-rus'kyi krai*. Donetsk: Nord-Pres, 2008.
Chykalenko, Evhen. *Shchodennyk*. 2 vols. Kiev: Tempora, 2004.
——. *Spohady (1861–1907)*. Kiev: Tempora, 2003.
Ciechowski, Wasław. *Kijów i jego pamiątki*. Kiev: S. V. Kul'zhenko, 1901.
Delo Beilisa: Stenograficheskii otchet. 3 vols. Kiev: S. P. Iakovleva, 1913.
Delo Mendelia Beilisa. Materialy Cherzvychainoi sledstvennoi komissii Vremenogo pravitel'stva o sudebnom protsesse 1913 g. St. Petersburg: Dmitrii Bulanin, 1999.

Delo prisiazhnogo Poverennogo A. D. Margolina. St. Petersburg: MV Popov, 1914.
Demchenko, Ia. G. *Evreiskoe ravnopravie ili Russkoe poraboshchenie? Izsledovanie tainykh evreiskikh planov i programm, napravlennykh k oslableniiu i razrusheniiu korennago naseleniia ego evreistvu.* Kiev: Kushnerev, 1907.
——. *Pravda ob ukrainofil'stve.* Kiev: I. N. Kushnerev, 1906.
Die Judenpogrome in Russland. 2 vols. Cologne: Jüdischer Verlag, 1910.
Dlia kogo Rossiia, dlia russkikh ili inorodtsev ili est-li Severo-Zapadnyi i Iugo-Zapadnyi krai pol'skii ili litovskii krai, ili eto—russkaia zemlia? Kiev: Tipo-Litografiia Gubernskogo Pravleniia, 1906.
Dnevnik P.A. Valueva. 2 vols. Moscow: Izd-vo Akademii nauk SSSR, 1961.
Dobrynin, N. P. *Russkie zhelezyne dorogi i ikh slabye storony.* Kiev: I. N. Kushnerev, 1886.
Dontsov, Dmytro. *Iuvilena zbirka staty [sic] pro Tarasa Hryhorovycha Shevchenka v soti rokovyny ioho narodzhennia.* Winnipeg: Nakl. Shevchenkivskoho iuvilenoho komitetu, 1914.
——. *Karl XII. Feldzug nach der Ukraine.* Vienna: Gustav Roettig & Sohn, 1916.
Dragomanov, M. P. *Liberalizm i zemstvo v Rossii.* Geneva: H. Georg, 1889.
——. *Arkhiv Mykhaila Drahomanova: Lystuvannia Kyivs'koi staroi hromady z M. Drahomanovym (1870–1895 r.r.).* Warsaw: Ukrains'kyi naukovyi instytut, 1937.
——. *Literaturno-publitsystychni pratsi.* 2 vols. Kiev: Naukova dumka, 1970.
——. *Malorusskie narodnye predanye i razskazy.* Kiev: M.P. Frits, 1876.
——. *M. P. Drahomanov. Vybrane.* Kiev: Lybid', 1991.
——. *Velikorusskii internatsional i pols'ko-ukrainskii vopros.* Kazan: Okruzhnogo shtaba, 1906.
Dragomanov, M. P., and V. B. Antonovich. *Istoricheskie pesni malorusskogo naroda.* 2 vols. Kiev: M. P. Frits, 1874–75.
Dragomirov, M. I. "Ravnopravnost' zhidov." *Razvedchik* 741 (1905): 415–16.
Dubnov, S. M., and G. Ia. Krasnyi-Admoni, eds. *Materialy dlia istorii antievreiskikh pogromov v Rossii.* 2 vols. Petrograd: Kadim, 1919.
Dvadtsatipiatiletie Kievskoi Birzhi, 1869–1894 g. Kiev: S. V. Kulzhenko, 1895.
Efremov, S. *Pradznik ukrainskoi intelligentsii.* Kiev: Korchak-Novitskii, 1903.
E. S. *Istoricheskoe znachenie "Kievskogo Zapadno-Russkogo S"ezda" 4, 5, i 6 oktiabria 1909 g.* Kiev: R.K. Lubkovskii, 1909.
Florinskii, T. D. *Malorusskii iazyk i "Ukrains'ko-Rus'kyi" literaturnyi separatizm.* St. Petersburg: A. S. Suvorin, 1900.
——. *Slavianofil'stvo T.G. Shevchenka.* Kiev: Imperatorskii Universitet St. Vladimira, 1906.
Fomenko, Kl. *Iz pamiatki prikhodskogo sviashchennika o Kieve.* Kiev: N. T. Korchak-Novitskii, 1904.
——. *K tridtsatipiatiletiiu sviashchenstva (1864–1899 g.g.).* Kiev: Petr Barskii, 1899.
Garol'd. *Nashi Glasnye: Otkrytki s momental'nymi snimkami nashikh dumtsev.* Kiev: P. K. Lubkovskii, 1906.
Gawrónski, Fr. Rawita. *Włodzimierz Antonowicz.* Lviv: Jakubowski i Sp., 1912.
——. *Rok 1863 na Rusi.* Lviv, 1909.
General-gubernator ili gubernator? Kiev: I. N. Kushnerev, 1889.
Ger'e, V. *Vtoraia gosudarstvennaia duma.* Moscow: S. P. Iakovlev, 1907.
Gogotskii, S. *Eshche neskol'ko slov ob ukrainofilakh.* Moscow, 1875.
Gol'denveizer, A. A. *Iz Kievskikh vospominanii (1917–1921 gg.).* Berlin: Arkhiv russkoi revoliutsii, 1922.
Golubev, S. T. *Neskol'ko stranits iz noveishei istorii Kievskoi Dukhovnoi Akademii.* Kiev: I. I. Gorbunov, 1907.
Golubiatnikov, P. *Sovety Kievlianam, izbirateliam v gorodskuiu dumu.* Kiev: Petr Barskii, 1906.

———. *Spravka o khode dela po rasshireniiu Kievskoi kanalizatsii v chetyrekhletie s 1902 po 1906 god: Prilozheniia*. Kiev: Tipografiia okruzhnogo shtaba, 1906.
Gorchakova, E. *Kiev*. Moscow: I. D. Sytin, 1896.
Goriachkin, F. T. *Pervyi Russkii fashist: Petr Arkad'evich Stolypin*. Harbin: Merkurii, 1928.
Gosudarstvennaia duma. Pervogo prizyva. Portrety, kratkie biografii i kharakteristiki deputatov. Moscow: Vozrozhdenie, 1906.
Gosudarstvennaia duma: Stenograficheskie otchety. St. Petersburg: Gosudarstvennaia tipografiia, 1906–17.
Gosudarstvennaia duma: Ukazatel' k stenograficheskim otchetam. St. Petersburg: Gosudarstvennaia tipografiia, 1906–17.
Gosudarstvennyi sovet. Stenograficheskii otchet. Sessiia VI. St. Petersburg: Gosudarstvennaia tipografiia, 1911.
Gotovtsev, D. V. *Otkrytoe pis'mo grafu Sergeiu Iul'evichu Vitte*. Kiev: Russkaia pechatnia, 1908.
Gringmut, V. A. *Sobranie statei*. 4 vols. Moscow: Universitetskaia tipografiia, 1908.
Grushevskii, Mikhail [Mykhailo Hrushevs'kyi]. *Dvizhenie politicheskoi i obshchestvennoi ukrainskoi mysli v XIX stoletii*. St. Petersburg: Obshchestvennaia Pol'za, 1907.
———. *Edinstvo ili raspadenie Rossii?* St. Petersburg: Obshchestvennaia Pol'za, 1907.
———. *Na porozi novoi Ukrainy*. New York: Ukrains'ke istorychne tov., 1992.
———. *Osvobozhdenie Rossii i ukrainskii vopros*. St. Petersburg: Obshchestvennaia pol'za, 1907.
Grushevskii, Mikhail, and F. K. Volkov, eds, *Ukrainskii narod v ego proshlom i nastoiashchem*. 2 vols. St. Petersburg: Obshchestvennaia pol'za, 1914–16.
Gruzenberg, O. O. *Yesterday: Memoirs of a Russian-Jewish Lawyer*. Edited by Don C. Rawson. Translated by Don C. Rawson and Tatiana Tipton. Berkeley: University of California Press, 1981.
Halahan, Mykola. *Z moikh spomyniv*. Lviv: Chervona kalyna, 1930.
Harcave, Sidney, ed. *The Memoirs of Count Witte*. Armonk, NY: M.E. Sharpe, 1990.
Hermaize, O. *Narysy z istorii revoliutsiinoho rukhu na Ukraini: Revoliutsiina Ukrain'ska Partiia (RUP)*. Kiev: Knyhospilka, 1926.
Hrynchenko, B. *Iak zhyv ukrains'kyi narod (Korotka istoriia Ukrainy)*. Kiev: T-va Hyrych, 1906.
Hrushevs'ka, Ol'ha. "Z diial'nosty Kulisha v 1850-x rokakh." *Naukovyi Zbirnyk za rik 1924: Vseukrains'ka akademiia nauk. Istorychna sektsiia* 19: 165–175.
Hrushevsky, Mykhailo. *History of Ukraine-Rus'*. 10 vols. Edmonton: Canadian Institute of Ukrainian Studies Press, 1997–2012.
Iasnogurskii, F. N. *Kharakteristika deiatel'nosti Kievskogo Gorodskogo Obshchestvennogo Upravleniia za istekaiushchee chetyrekhletie 1906–1910 gg*. Kiev: I. I. Vrublevskii i T. V. Ozerov, 1910.
———. *Kiev: Byloi, Nastoiashchii i Budushchii: Razskaz ochevidtsa*. Kiev: F. D. Dubovik, 1913.
———. *Liudi—zveri i zveri—liudi*. Kiev: N.A. Girich, 1905.
Iastrebov, F. *1905 rik u Kyevi*. Kharkov: Proletar, 1930.
I. D. B. *Sbornik programm politicheskikh partii*. Moscow: G. Lissner and D. Sobko, 1906.
Istoriia rusov ili Maloi Rossii. Moscow: Universitetskaia tipografiia, 1846.
Iuzefovich, B. M. *Otkrytoe pis'mo B.M. Iuzefovicha k chlenam kievskikh monarkhicheskikh organizatsii ot 29 sentiabria 1908 goda*. Kiev: Russkaia pechat', 1909.
———. *Ottsy i deti XX veka*. Kiev: S. V. Kul'zhenko, 1904.
———. *Politicheskie pis'ma: Materialy dlia istorii russkogo politicheskogo umopomracheniia na rubezhe dvukh stoletii (1898–1908 g.g.)*. Kiev: Russkaia Pechatnia, 1908.
Iuzefovich, M. V. *La question Russo-Polonaise jugée par un petit-russien*. Leipzig: Wolfgang Gerhard, 1863.

SELECTED BIBLIOGRAPHY

———. *Nasha liberal'naia intelligentsiia.* Kiev: G. G. Ivanov, 1882.
———. *Neskol'ko slov ob istoricheskoi zadache Rossii.* Kiev: G. L. Frontskevich, 1895.
———. *17-e aprelia v Kieve.* Kiev: Fedorov i Min., 1863.
———. *Vozmozhen li mir s nami pol'skoi shliakhty?* Vil'na, 1864.
Ivaniukov, I. I., and N. D. Noskov. *Okhranitel'nye i reaktsionnye partii v Rossii.* St. Petersburg: S. M. Propper, 1906.
Ivanov, A. A. *Zabavny-li khokhlomanskie zamysly?* Kiev: Universitetskaia tipografiia, 1882.
Izbirateliam goroda Kieva v Gosudarstvennuiu dumu: Izdanie partii pravovogo poriadka. Kiev: I. I. Chokolov, 1906.
Jablonowski, Aleksander. *Akademia Kijowsko-Mohilanska: Zarys Historyczny na tle Rozwoju Ogolnego Cywilizacyi Zachodniej na Rusi.* Cracow: Druk W.L. Anczysa i Spolki, 1899–1900.
Katkov, M. N. *Imperiia i kramola.* Moscow: FondIV, 2007.
———. *Tysiacha vosem'sot shestdesiat' tretii god. Sobranie statei po pol'skomu voprosu.* Moscow: Universitetskaia tipografiia. 1887.
Kaufman, A. E. *Druz'ia i vragi evreev. D.I. Pikhno.* Kiev: Rabotnik, 1907.
"*Kievlianin.*" Kiev: I. I. Zavadskii, 1880.
Kistiakivs'kyi, O. F. *Shchodennyk (1874–1885).* 2 vols. Kiev: Naukova dumka, 1994.
Kostomarov, N. I. *Bogdan Khmel'nitskii.* Moscow: Charli, 1994.
———. *Istoricheskie proizvedeniia. Avtobiografiia.* Kiev: Izdatel' pri Kievskom gosudarstvennom universitete, 1989.
———. "Istoricheskoe znachenie iuzhno-russkogo narodnogo pesennogo tvorchestva." *Beseda* 4 (1872): 5–68.
———. *Kostomarov's "Books of the Genesis of the Ukrainian People."* New York: Research Program on the USSR, 1954.
———. *Mazepa: Istoricheskaia monografiia.* Moscow: I. N. Kushnerev, 1882.
———. "Nachalo Rusi." *Sovremennik* 79 (1860): 5–32.
———. "862–1862." *Sankt-peterburgskie vedomosti,* 3 January 1862, 1–2.
Kostomarov, N. I., and M. O. Mikeshin, eds., *Kobzar.* Prague: Nakladem knihkupectvi dra Grega a Ferd. Dattla, 1876.
Krasnyi-Admoni, G. Ia. *Materialy dlia istorii antievreiskikh pogromov v Rossii: Vos'midesiatye gody (15 aprelia 1881 g.–29 fevralia 1882 g.).* 2 vols. Petrograd: Gosudarstvennoe izdatel'stvo, 1923.
Kr-l', M. A. *Kak proshli vybory v gosudarstvennuiu dumu.* St. Petersburg: R. S. Vol'pin, 1906.
Kryzhanovskii, G. Ia. *Pochaevskaia uspenskaia lavra.* Pochaev: Tipografiia Pochaevskoi lavry, 1897.
Kulish, P. A. *Istoriia vozsoedineniia Rusi.* 3 vols. St. Petersburg: Obshchestvennaia pol'za, 1874–77.
———. *Zapiski o iuzhnoi Rusi.* Heidelberg: Carl Winter, 1989.
Kuschnir, Wladimir. *Die Ukraine und ihre Bedeutung im gegenwärtigen Kriege mit Russland.* Vienna: Verlag der Ukrainischen Rundschau, 1914.
Lado: Sbornik literaturno-obshchestvennyi posviashchennyi narozhdaiushcheisia russkoi national-demokratii. St. Petersburg, M. G. Kornfel'd, 1911.
Levitskii, O. I. *Chtenii v Istoricheskom Obshchestve Nestora letopistsa.* Kiev: V. I. Zavadskii, 1891.
———. *Opyt izsledovaniia o letopisi samovidtsa.* Kiev: K. N. Milevskii, 1878.
———. *Piatidesiatiletie Kievskoi Kommissii dlia razbora drevnikh aktov, 1843–1893: Istoricheskaia zapiska o eia deiatel'nosti.* Kiev: S. V. Kul'zhenko, 1893.
Levitskii, V. [V. Tsederbaum]. *Za chetvert' veka: Revoliutsionnye vospominaniia, 1892–1917 g.g.* 2 vols. Moscow: Gosudarstvennoe izdatel'stvo, 1926.

Listopad, Ia.G. *Znachenie Kieva v istorii Rossii*. Kiev: K.N. Milevskii, 1889.
Lokot', T. V. *Natsionalizm i evrei*. Kiev: Petr Barskii, 1910.
——. *Opravdanie natsionalizma. Rabstvo russkoi radikal'noi intelligentsii. Natsional-demokratii*. Kiev: Petr Barskii, 1910.
——. *"Zavoevaniia revoliutsii" i ideologiia russkogo monarkhizma*. Berlin: Dvuglavyi orel, 1921.
Lotots'kyi, O. *Derzhavnyi provid Symony Petliury*. Paris, 1930.
L-v, P. *Istoricheskie zametki o Kieve*. Kiev: Kievskaia starina, 1884.
M. M. [B. M. Iuzefovich]. *O tom, kak poliaki 40 let ne dremali, podrezyvaia kryl'ia i kogti u nenavistnoi dlia nikh Rossii i kak oni ograbili russkikh pomeshchikov, poselivshikhsia v Kievskoi Rusi posle 1863 goda*. Kiev: Russkaia Pechatnia, 1907.
Maksimovich, Mikhail. *Ob"iasnitel'nye paragrafy o Kieve*. Kiev: I. and A. Davydenko, 1869.
——. *Otkuda idet russkaia zemlia, po skazaniiu Nestorovoi povesti i po drugim starinnym pisaniiam russkim*. Kiev: Universitetskaia tipografiia, 1837.
——. *Pis'ma o Bogdane Khmel'nitskom k M.P. Pogodinu*. Kiev, 1859.
——. *Vospominanie o Bogdane Khmel'nitskom*. Kiev, 1857.
Malorossiia: Opisanie kraia v istoricheskom, geograficheskom i etnograficheskom otnoshenii. St. Petersburg: Mirskoi Vestnik, 1876.
Margolin, Arnold D. *From a Political Diary: Russia, the Ukraine, and America, 1905–1945*. New York: Columbia University Press, 1946.
——. *Ukraine and the Policy of the Entente*. New York: Ukrainian Academy of Arts and Sciences in the U.S., 1988.
Markevich, N. A. *Istoriia Malorossii*. Moscow: O. I. Khrustalev, 1842–43.
Materialy k istorii russkoi kontr-revoliutsii: Pogromy po offitsial'nym dokumentam. 2 vols. St. Petersburg: Obshchestvennaia pol'za, 1908.
"Mémoire du Baron Alexandre de Gunzburg." Unpublished manuscript, 1939.
Mertens, Oskar. *K voprosu o podvoznykh zheleznykh dorogakh v Rossii*. Riga: N. Kiumell, 1887.
M. G. "Istoriia odnogo pamiatnika." *Golos minuvshego* 7 (1913): 284–85.
Migulin, P. P. *Nasha noveishaia zheleznodorozhnaia politika i zheleznodorozhnye zaimy (1893–1902)*. Kharkov: Pechatnoe Delo, 1903.
Miiakovskii, V. "Kievskaia gromada," *Litopys' revoliutsii* 4 (1924): 127–50.
Miliukov, Paul. *"Constitutional Government for Russia." An Address Delivered before the Civic Forum in Carnegie Hall*. New York: Civic Forum, 1908.
——. *Political Memoirs, 1905–1917*. Edited by Arthur P. Mendel. Ann Arbor: University of Michigan Press, 1967.
Mikeshin, M. O., ed., *Kobzar*. St. Petersburg: P. A. Kulish, 1860.
Mishchenko, F. *G. P. Galagan (Nekrolog)*. Kiev: G. T. Korchak-Novitskii, 1888.
Moshinskii, I. N. (Iuz. Konarskii). *Na putiakh k I-mu s"ezdu R.S.-D.R.P. 90-tye gody v kievskom podpol'e*. Moscow: Vsesoiuznoe obshchestvo politicheskikh katorzhan i ssyl'noposelentsev, 1928.
Nabokov, V. D., and A. I. Kaminka. *Vtoraia gosudarstvennaia duma*. St. Petersburg: Obshchestvennaia pol'za, 1907.
Nash Kandidat Anatolii Ivanovich Savenko. Kiev: S.V. Kul'zhenko, 1912.
Natsionalisty v 3-ei Gosudarstvennoi Dume. St. Petersburg: A. S. Suvorin, 1912.
Naumenko, V. P. *Reshen-li prof. T. D. Florinskim vopros o knizhnoi malorusskoi rechi?* Kiev: N.T. Korchak-Novitskii, 1900.
Nechkina, M. V., ed., *Kolokol: Gazeta A. I. Gertsena i N. P. Ogareva*. 10 vols. Moscow: Izdatel'stvo Akademii Nauk SSSR, 1962.

Nikitenko, Aleksandr. *The Diary of a Russian Censor*. Edited and translated by Helen Saltz Jacobson. Amherst: University of Massachusetts Press, 1975.
Oblastnoi s"ezd russkikh izbiratelei Iugo-Zapadnogo kraia v Kieve. 19–21 noiabria 1906 goda. Kiev: I. N. Kushnerev, 1906.
Obzor deiatel'nosti Ministerstva finansov v tsarstvovanie Imperatora Aleksandra III (1881–1894). St. Petersburg: V. Kirshbaum, 1902.
Obzor deiatel'nosti Russkogo okrainnogo obshchestva za 1910. St. Petersburg: Akademiia Nauk, 1911.
Obzor deiatel'nosti Vserossiiskogo natsional'nogo soiuza za 1912–1913 g. St. Petersburg: Gr. Skachkov, 1914.
Ocherk deiatel'nosti Kievskogo slavianskogo blagotvoritel'nogo obshchestva za 25 let ego sushchestvovaniia, 1869–1894. Kiev: S. V. Kul'zhenko, 1894.
Ocherki, razmyshleniia. Nakanune vybornogo nachala. Kiev: R. K. Lubkovskii, 1905.
Otchet Kievskogo Birzhevogo Komiteta za 1899 god. Kiev: Gubernskaia tipografiia, 1900.
Otchet Kievskogo Birzhevogo Komiteta za 1903 god. Kiev: Imperatorskogo Universiteta Sv. Vladimira, 1903.
Otchet Kievskogo literaturno-artitisticheskogo obshchestva za 1903 god. Kiev: N. T. Korchak-Novitskii, 1904.
Otchet Kievskogo obshchestva vzaimnogo kredita s 2-go Ianvaria 1904 goda po 1-e Ianvaria 1905 goda. Kiev: I. Kryzhanovskii and V. Avdiushenko, 1905.
Otchet Kievskogo obshchestva vzaimnogo kredita za 1901 g. Kiev: I. I. Gorbunov, 1902.
Otchet Kievskogo obshchestva vzaimnogo strakhovaniia sakharozavodchikov za 1907–1908 god. Kiev: Petr Barskii, 1909.
Otchet Kievskogo Sviato-Vladimirskogo bratstva revnitelei pravoslaviia za 1895 g. Kiev: G. T. Korchak-Novitskii, 1896.
Otchet Kievskoi evreiskoi bol'nitsy za 1894 god. Kiev: V. I. Zavadskii, 1895.
Otchet o deiatelnosti Kievskogo otdela Vysochaishe utverzhdennogo Slavianskogo blagotvoritel'nogo komiteta za 1871 god. Kiev: M. P. Frits, 1872.
Otchet o deiatel'nosti Kievskogo Otdeleniia Galitsko-Russkogo Obshchestva. Kiev: Kushnerev, 1915.
Otchet o deiatel'nosti v Kieve Obshchestva Rasprostraneniia Religiozno-Nravstvennogo prosveshcheniia v dukhe Pravoslavnoi tserkvi za 1894 god. Kiev: G. T. Korchak-Novitskii, 1894.
Otchet o deiatel'nosti Zapadno-Russkogo Obshchestva za 1912 god. St. Petersburg: Novoe vremia, 1913.
"Otzyv iz Kieva." *Sovremennaia letopis'* 46 (1862): 3–6.
Pamiati chlena-uchreditelia Istoricheskogo Obshchestva Nestora-letopistsa Vladimira Bonifat'evicha Antonovicha. Kiev: T. G. Meinander, 1909.
Pamiatnaia Knizhka Kievskoi Gubernii. Kiev: Gubernskaia tipografiia, 1915.
Pamiatnaia knizhka Kievskoi gubernii na 1896 god. Kiev: Gubernskaia tipografiia, 1896.
Pamiatniki, izdannye Vremennoiu kommissieiu dlia razbora drevnikh aktov, Vysochaishe uchrezhdennoiu pri Kievskom voennom, Podol'skom i Volynskom General-Gubernatore. 3 vols. Kiev: I. K. Val'ner, 1845–59.
Pamiatnik Imperatoru Nikolaiu I v gorode Kieve. Kiev: S. V. Kul'zhenko, 1899.
Panaev, V. A. *Finansovye i ekonomicheskie voprosy*. St. Petersburg: Tipografiia Vtorogo Otdeleniia Sobstvennoi E. I. V. Kantseliarii, 1878.
Partiia mirnogo progressa: Ee ideal'nye osnovy i zhiznennaia programma. Kiev: I. I. Chokolov, 1905.
Perris, G. H. *Russia in Revolution*. London: Chapman and Hall, 1905.
Pikhno, D. I. *Glavneishie nuzhdy russkogo sel'skogo khoziaistva*. Kiev: Kushnerev, 1902.

———. *Kommercheskie operatsii Gosudarstvennogo Banka*. Kiev: Universitetskaia tipografiia, 1876.
———. *O svobode mezhdunarodnoi torgovli i protektsionizme*. Kiev: I.N. Kushnerev, 1889.
———. *Po povodu polemiki o deshevom khlebe*. Kiev: I. N. Kushnerev, 1897.
———. *Predstavitel'stvo zapadnoi Rusi v Gosudarstvennom sovete*. Kiev: I. N. Kushnerev, 1909.
———. *V osade: Politicheskie stat'i*. Kiev: I. N. Kushnerev, 1905.
Pirogov, N. I. *Sochineniia*. 2 vols. St. Petersburg: M. M. Stasiulevich, 1887.
Pis'mo Kievskogo General-Guberatora N. N. Annenkova k M. V. Iuzefovichu," *Russkii arkhiv* 3 (1883): 203–4.
Popov, R. S. *O malorossii i malorossakh: Chtenie dlia naroda*. Moscow: A. A. Torletskii, 1877.
Pravye partii: Dokumenty i materialy. 2 vols. Moscow: Rosspen, 1998.
Prazdnik russkogo samosoznaniia: Otkrytie Khar'kovskogo Otdela "Russkogo Sobraniia." Kharkov: Tipografiia Gubernskogo pravleniia, 1903.
Prilozheniia k stenograficheskim otchetam Gosudarstvennaia dumy, 1907–1908 g.g. St. Petersburg: Gosudarstvennaia tipografiia, 1906–1914.
Privislinets, Dm. Tutkevich, and A. N. Druzhinin. *Rossiia i ee zapadnaia okraina*. Kiev: Tipografiia Gubernskogo Pravleniia, 1903.
Proceedings of the Brest-Litovsk Peace Conference. Washington: Government Printing Office, 1918.
Proizvodstvo sakhara na zavodakh Grafov Bobrinskikh Kievskoi gubernii. Kiev: S. V. Kul'zhenko, 1896.
Ratner, M. B. *O natsional'noi i territorial'noi avtonomii*. Kiev: Serp, 1906.
Rebinin, F. *Kursko-Khar'kovo-Azovskaia zheleznaia doroga*. Kharkov: S. P. Iakovlev, 1896.
Rech', proiznesennaia gorodskim golovoi v zasedanii dumy 28 fevralia 1883 goda, o deiatel'nosti gorodskogo obshchestvennogo upravleniia v period vremeni s 1879 po 1883 g. Kiev: I. N. Kushnerev, 1883.
Rechi po pogromnym delam. 2 vols. Kiev: D. N. Tiagai, 1909.
Rech' nad grobom kievskogo, podol'skogo i volynskogo general-gubernatora, general-ad"iutanta Aleksandra Pavlovicha Bezaka skazannaia u ego mogily kafedral'nym protoierem Petrom Lebedintsevym. Kiev: I and A Davidenko, 1869.
Rennenkampf, N. K. *Kievskii Politekhnicheskii Institut Imperatora Aleksandra II*. Kiev: Russkaia mysl', 1899.
———. *Pol'skii i evreiskii voprosy (Otkrytye pis'ma B.N. Chicherinu)*. Kiev: Kushnerev, 1898.
Reva, I. M. *Kievskoe sel'skokhoziastvennoe obshchestvo, ego deiateli i ego deiatel'nost'*. Kiev: V. Zavadskii, 1892.
———. *Sakharnaia normirovka*. Kiev: Kushnerev, 1897.
———, ed. *Umanskaia rezna (Zapiski Veroniki Krebs)*. Kiev: SV Kul'zhenko, 1879.
Savchenko, Fedir. *Zaborona ukrainstva 1876 r*. Munich: Wilhelm Fink Verlag, 1970.
Savenko, A. I. *Duma i pravitel'stvo*. Kiev: Kushnerev, 1909.
———. *Ukraintsy ili Malorossy? (Natsional'nost' samoopredelenie naseleniia Iuzhnoi Rossii)*. Rostov-on-Don, 1919.
Sbornik Kievskogo otdela Vserossiikogo natsional'nogo studencheskogo soiuza. Kiev: Petr Barskii, 1912.
Sbornik kluba russkikh natsionalistov. 5 vols. Kiev: I. N. Kushnerev, 1908–13.
Sbornik statei i materialov po istorii iugo-zapadnoi Rossii, izdavaemyi Kommissiei dlia razbora drevnikh aktov, sostiashchei pri Kievskom, Podol'skom i Volynskom General-Gubernator. Kiev: N. T. Korchak-Novitskii, 1911.
Shamurina, Z. *Kiev, kul'turnye sokrovishcha Rossii*. Moscow: Obrazovanie, 1912.
Shcherbina, V. *O kievskoi starine: Dva chteniia*. Kiev: Sotrudnik, 1910.

Shesterin. *O narodnykh vybornykh.* Kiev: E. P. Gorskii, 1905.
Shlikhter, A. G. *Kyiv za zhovtenvikh dniv 1905 roku.* Kharkov, 1926.
Shmakov, A. S. *Evreiskii vopros, na stsene vsemirnoi istorii.* Moscow: V. Rikhter, 1912.
——. *Svoboda i evrei.* Moscow: Moskovskaia gorodskaia tipografiia, 1906.
Shul'gin, V. Ia. "Iugo-zapadnyi krai pod upravleniem D.G. Bibikova." *Drevniaia i novaia rossiia* 6 (1879): 89–131.
Shul'gin, V. V. *Anshluss i my!* Belgrade: N.Z. Rybinskii, 1938.
——. *Chto nam v nikh ne nravitsia: Ob antisemitizme v Rossii.* Paris: Izd-vo Russia minor, 1929.
——. *Days of the Russian Revolution: Memoirs from the Right, 1905–1917.* Translated by Bruce F. Adams. Gulf Breeze, FL: Academic International Press, 1990.
——, ed. *Malaia Rus'.* 3 vols. Kiev: L. I. Raitsis, 1918.
——. *Ukrainstvuiushchie i my!* Belgrade: N. Z. Rybinskii, 1939.
——. *Vybornoe zemstvo v Iugo-zapadnom krae.* Kiev: Kushnerev, 1909.
——. *The Years: Memoirs of a Member of the Russian Duma, 1906–1917.* Translated by Tanya Davis. New York: Hippocrene Books, 1984.
Shul'hyn, Oleksandr. *Polityka.* Kiev: Drukar', 1918.
Sidorov, A. A. *Pol'skoe vozstanie 1863 goda.* St. Petersburg: N. P. Karbasnikov, 1903.
——. "V Kieve (1904–1909)." *Golos minuvshego* 4–6 (1918): 221–30.
Sikorskii, I. A. *Izbiratel'naia programma obshchegorodskikh soveshchanii (Novodumskoi partii) po vyboram v Kievskuiu Gorodskuiu Dumu.* Kiev: Kushnerev, 1906.
——. *O psikhologicheskikh osnovakh natsionalizma.* Kiev: Kushnerev, 1910.
——. *Partii i "bezpartiinye" v dele vyborov.* Kiev: Kushnerev, 1906.
——. *Russkie i ukraintsy.* Kiev: SV Kul'zhenko, 1913.
——. *Sovremennaia vsesvetnaia voina 1914 goda. Prichiny voiny i ustranenie ikh.* Kiev: S. V. Kul'zhenko, 1914.
Sliozberg, G. B. *Dela minuvshikh dnei.* Paris: Pascal, 1933.
Smilians'ka, V. I., ed. *M. I. Kostomarov: Tvory v dvokh tomakh.* Kiev: Dnipro, 1990.
Smirnov, Aleksei. *Kak proshli vybory vo 2-iu gosudarstvennuiu dumu.* St. Petersburg: Obshchestvennaia pol'za, 1907.
Sobolevskii, A. *K voprosu ob istoricheskikh sud'bakh Kieva.* Kiev: Universitetskaia tipografiia, 1885.
Sobranie rechei Gg. Deputatov Gosudarstvennoi Dumy. St. Petersburg: Razum, 1908.
Sobranie Sochinenii M. A. Maksimovicha. Kiev: M.P. Frits, 1876.
Sokhan', P. S., ed., *Kyrylo-Mefodiievs'ke tovarystvo.* 3 vols. Kiev: Naukova dumka, 1990.
Solukha, V. *Kratkaia istoricheskaia zapiska o sostoianii Kievo-Podol'skoi zhenskoi gimnazii.* Kiev: Gubernskaia tipografiia, 1896.
Spasaite Kiev ot razoreniia! Kiev: I. N. Kushnerev, 1910.
Spisok chlenov pravleniia, pochetnykh chlenov, deistvitel'nykh, sorevnovatelei i chlenov posetitelei Kievskogo literaturno-artisticheskogo obshchestva. Kiev: Tipografiia Imperatorskogo Universiteta Sv. Vladimira, 1904.
Stakhovich, Aleksandr. *Kak i kogo vybrat' v Gosudarstvennuiu Dumu. Chto takie partiinye vybory? Kratkii obzor russkikh politicheskikh partii.* Moscow: I. D. Sytin, 1907.
Starozhil [S. V. Iaron]. *Kiev v vos'midesiatykh godakh.* Kiev: Petr Barskii, 1910.
Stepovich, A. G. *25-letie Kollegii Pavla Galagana v Kieve.* Kiev: N. I. Chokolov, 1896.
Storozhenko, A. V. *Proiskhozhdenie i sushchnost' ukrainofil'stva.* Kiev: S. V. Kul'zhenko, 1912.
——, ed. *Slavianskii ezhegodnik: Al'manakh i sbornik statei po slavianovedeniiu.* 5 vols. Kiev: I. and A Davidenko, 1878–82.

———. *Trudy podgotovitel'no po natsional'nym delam komissii. Malorusskii otdel.* Rostov-on-Don, 1919.
Storozhenko, Mykola. *Z moho zhyttia.* Kiev: Lybid', 2005.
Struve, P. B. "Velikaia Rossiia." *Russkaia mysl'* 29, no. 1 (1908): 143–57.
Sukhomlinov, V. *Vospominaniia.* Berlin: Russkoe universal'noe izdatel'stvo, 1924.
Tel'man, I. G. "Komediia 'vyboriv' u dorevoliutsiinomu Kyevi." *Radians'kii Kyiv* 16 (1939): 25–27.
———. *Odin den' Kyeva.* Kharkov: M. V. Frunze, 1937.
Terlets'kyi, O. *Moskvofily i narodovtsi v 1870-ykh rr.* Lviv: NTSh im. Shevchenka, 1902.
Texts of the Russian "Peace." Washington, DC: Government Printing Office, 1918.
Titov, F. I. *Russkii tsarstvuiushchii dom Romanovykh v otnosheniiakh ego k Kievo-Pecherskoi Lavre, 1613–1913 g.g.* Kiev: Tipografiia Kievo-Pecherskoi Uspenskoi Lavry, 1913.
———. *Russkoe dukhovenstvo v Galitsii (iz nabliudenii puteshestvennika).* Kiev: Korchak-Novitskii, 1903.
Tolstoi, I. and N. Kondakov, eds., *Russkie drevnosti v pamiatnikakh iskusstva.* St. Petersburg: Ministerstvo Putei Soobshcheniia, 1891.
3-ii sozyv Gosudarstvennoi Dumy. Portrety. Biografii. Avtografii. St Petersburg: N. Olshanskii, 1910.
Tretii Vserossiiskii s"ezd russkikh liudei v Kieve. Kiev: I. N. Kushnerev, 1906.
Trotzkyj, M. *Die ukrainische national-politische Bewegung.* Vienna: Vorwärts, 1917.
Trubetskoy, Evgenii. *Iz proshlogo. Vospominaniia iz putevykh zametok bezhentsa.* Newtonville, MA: Oriental Research Partners, 1976.
Trudy sozvannogo po rasporiazheniiu nachal'nika kraia soveshchaniia vrachebnykh inspektorov Kievskoi, Podol'skoi i Volynskoi gubernii sostoiavshagosia v g. Kieve 5–12 oktiabria 1900 goda po voprosu o luchshei postanovke vrachebno-sanitarnogo dela v iugo-zapadnom krae. Kiev: Tipo-Litografiia Gubernskogo Pravleniia, 1901.
Trudy tret'iago arkheologicheskogo s"ezda v Rossii byvshogo v Kieve v Avguste 1874 goda. 3 vols. Kiev: Tipografiia imperatorskogo universiteta sv. Vladimira, 1878.
Trufanov, Sergei Mikhailovich. *The Mad Monk of Russia Iliodor.* New York: Century Company, 1918.
Turau, E. F. *K istorii Kievskogo pogroma.* Kiev: Progress, 1906.
Tutkevich, D. V. *Chto takoe Evrei?* Kiev: Tipografiia I.I. Gorbunov, 1906.
Umanskii, A. M. "Pamiati M. O. Mikeshina." *Istoricheskii vestnik* 67 (1897): 624–51.
Ustav Kievskogo Obshchestva Gramotnosti. Kiev: I. I. Chokolov, 1894.
Ustav Kievskoi Russkoi Monarkhicheskoi Partii. Kiev: I. N. Kushnerev, 1906.
Ustav Podol'skogo Ukrainskogo obshchestva "Prosvita." Kiev: n.p., 1906.
Ustawa Towarzystwa pod mianem: "Związek oficjalistów, pracujących w rolnictwie i przemyśle rolnym na Rusi." Kiev: Drukarnia polska, 1906.
Vakar, V. [B. Pravdin]. *Revoliutsionnye dni v Kieve.* Geneva: Tipografiia Partii, 1903.
Vasylenko, Nikolai. "Akademyk Orest Ivanovych Levyts'kyi." *Zapysky Sotsiial'no-ekonomichnoho Viddilu Ukrainskoi Akademii Nauk* 1 (1923): 46–106.
Velychko, Samiilo. *Hryhorij Hrabjanka's The Great War of Bohdan Xmel'nyc'kyj.* Cambridge, MA: Ukrainian Research Institute, 1991.
———. *Litopys.* Kiev: Dnipro, 1991.
Verzilov, A. V. *Pamiati Vladimira Bonifat'evicha Antonovicha.* Chernigov: Tipografiia Gubernskogo Zemstva, 1908.
Vitalii Iakovlevich Shul'gin: Nekrolog i rechi, proiznesennye nad ego grobom. Kiev: I. I. Zavadskii, 1880.
Vitaly, Archbishop. *Motivy moei zhizni.* Jordanville, NY: Holy Trinity Monastery: 1955.

Vodovozov, V. V., ed. *Sbornik programm politicheskikh partii v Rossii.* St. Petersburg: Nasha zhizn', 1906.
Vodvorenie Monopolii elektrichestva v Kieve. Kiev: I. N. Kushnerev, 1899.
Voronin, A. *Zapiska o vladel'cheskikh gorodakh i mestechkakh Iugozapadnogo kraia.* Kiev: E. Ia. Fedorov, 1869.
Vozniak, M. *Ukrains'ka derzhavnist'.* Vienna: Adol'f Gol'tsgavzen, 1918.
Vsepoddanneishie telegrammy i postanovleniia IV Vserossiiskogo S"ezda Ob"edinennogo Russkogo Naroda v Moskve (26 aprelia–1 maia 1907 goda). Moscow: Universitetskaia tipografiia, 1907.
Vsepoddanneishii Otchet Kievskogo, Podol'skogo i Volynskogo General-Gubernatora. Kiev, 1901.
V-tskii, N. "Vnutrennye izvestiia." *Sankt-peterburgskie vedomosti,* 12 November 1872, 1.
Vydumki "Kievlianina" i pol'skikh gazet o malorusskom patriotizme. Kiev: Kievskii telegraf, 1874.
Waife-Goldberg, Marie. *My Father, Sholom Aleichem.* New York: Simon and Schuster, 1968.
Wierzejski, Witold Kazimierz. *Fragmenty z dziejów polskiej młodzieży akademickiej w Kijowie 1834–1920.* Warsaw: Instytut Józefa Piłsudskiego, 1939.
Z. [N. A. Rigel'man]. "Sovremennoe ukrainofil'stvo." *Russkii vestnik* 2 (1875): 838–68.
Zakharchenko, M. M. *Kiev: Teper' i prezhde.* Kiev: S. V. Kul'zhenko, 1888.
Zakrevskii, N. *Letopis' i opisanie goroda Kieva.* Moscow: Universitetskaia tipografiia, 1858.
Zaleskii, V. F. *Chto takoe Soiuz Russkogo Naroda i dlia chego on nuzhen?* Kazan: I. S. Perov, 1907.
Zapadno-russkii s"ezd. 4–6 oktiabria 1909 goda. Kiev: Kushnerev, 1911.
Zapiska Senatora A. Polovtsova o sostoianii obshchestvennogo upravleniia i khoziaistva v gorodakh Kievskoi gubernii. Kiev, 1882.
Zhivogliadov, A. I. *Neskol'ko slov po povodu vospominanii starozhila.* Kiev: S. V. Kul'zhenko, 1910.

Secondary Literature

Abragamson, A. *Kievskii Politekhnicheskii Institut Imperatora Aleksandra II-go. Kratkii ocherk ego vozniknoveniia.* Kiev: I. N. Kushnerev, 1898.
Abramson, Henry. *A Prayer for the Government: Ukrainians and Jews in Revolutionary Times, 1917–1920.* Cambridge: Harvard University Press, 1999.
American Jewish Year Book 5667 (1906–1907). Philadelphia: Jewish Publication Society of America, 1906.
Anan'ich, B. V. *Bankirskie doma v Rossii, 1860–1914 gg.* Leningrad: Nauka, 1991.
———. "Economic Policy of the Tsarist Government and Entrepreneurship in Russia at the End of the 19th–Beginning of the 20th Century." Occasional paper no. 49, Kennan Institute for Advanced Russian Studies, 1978.
Anderson, Benedict. *Imagined Communities: Reflections on the Origin and Spread of Nationalism.* London: Verso, 1983.
Anderson, Margaret Lavinia. *Practicing Democracy: Elections and Political Culture in Imperial Germany.* Princeton: Princeton University Press, 2000.
Andriewsky, Olga. "The Politics of National Identity: The Ukrainian Question in Russia, 1904–12." PhD diss., Harvard University, 1991.
Applegate, Celia. *A Nation of Provincials: The German Idea of Heimat.* Berkeley: University of California Press, 1990.
Appletons' Annual Cyclopaedia and Register of Important Events of the Year: 1901. New York, 1902.
Ascher, Abraham. *P. A. Stolypin: The Search for Stability in Late Imperial Russia.* Stanford: Stanford University Press, 2001.
———. *The Revolution of 1905.* 2 vols. Stanford: Stanford University Press, 1988–92.

Aster, Howard, and Peter J. Potichnyj, eds. *Ukrainian-Jewish Relations in Historical Perspective*. Edmonton: Canadian Institute of Ukrainian Studies, 1988.
Avrekh, A. Ia. *P. A. Stolypin i sud'by reform v Rossii*. Moscow: Izdatel'stvo politicheskoi literatury, 1991.
——. *Stolypin i tret'ia duma*. Moscow: Nauka, 1968.
Avrutin, Eugene. "Racial Categories and the Politics of (Jewish) Difference in Late Imperial Russia." *Kritika* 8, no. 1 (2007): 13–40.
Bagalei, D. I., and D. P. Miller. *Istoriia goroda Khar'kova za 250 let ego sushchestvovaniia (s 1655-go po 1905-i god)*. 2 vols. Kharkov: M. Zil'berberg i synov'ia, 1912.
Bakhturina, A. Iu. *Politika Rossiiskoi Imperii v Vostochnoi Galitsii v gody Pervoi mirovoi voiny*. Moscow: AIRO XX, 2000.
Balzer, Harley D., ed., *Russia's Missing Middle Class: The Professions in Russian History*. Armonk, NY: M.E. Sharpe, 1996.
Bassin, Mark. *Imperial Visions: Nationalist Imagination and Geographical Expansion in the Russian Far East, 1840–1865*. New York: Cambridge University Press, 2004.
Bater, James F. *St. Petersburg: Industrialization and Change*. Montreal: McGill University Press, 1976.
Baur, Johannes. *Die russische Kolonie in München, 1900–1945: Deutsch-russische Beziehungen im 20. Jahrhundert*. Wiesbaden: Harassowitz, 1998.
Baycroft, Timothy, and Mark Hewitson, eds. *What Is a Nation?* New York: Oxford University Press, 2006.
Beauvois, Daniel. *La bataille de la terre en Ukraine, 1863–1914: Les Polonais et les conflits socio-ethniques*. Lille: Presses Universitaires de Lille, 1993.
——. *Le noble, le serf et le révizor: La noblesse polonaise entre le tsarisme et les masses ukrainiennes, 1831–1863*. Paris: Editions des Archives contemporaines, 1985.
——. *Pourvoir russe et noblesse polonaise en Ukraine: 1793–1830*. Paris: CNRS, 2003.
Bilenky, Serhiy. *Romantic Nationalism in Eastern Europe: Russian, Polish, and Ukrainian Political Imaginations*. Stanford: Stanford University Press, 2012.
Bill, Valentine Tschebotarioff. "The Early Days of Russian Railroads." *Russian Review*, 15, no. 1 (1956): 14–28.
Bisk, I. S. *K voprosu o sotsial'nom sostave naseleniia g. Kieva (po dannym perepisi 1917 g.)*. Kiev: Zhizn', 1920.
Bjork, James E. *Neither German nor Pole: Catholicism and National Indifference in a Central European Borderland*. Ann Arbor: University of Michigan Press, 2008.
Bliokh, I. S. *Finansy Rossii XIX stoletiia. Istoriia-statistika*. 3 vols. St. Petersburg: Obshchestvennaia pol'za, 1882.
Blobaum, Robert E., ed. *Antisemitism and Its Opponents in Modern Poland*. Ithaca: Cornell University Press, 2005.
——. *Rewolucja: Russian Poland, 1904–1907*. Ithaca: Cornell University Press, 1995.
Boeck, Brian J. "What's in a Name? Semantic Separation and the Rise of the Ukrainian National Name." *Harvard Ukrainian Studies* 27, nos. 1–4 (2004–5): 33–65.
Bojanowska, Edyta M. *Nikolai Gogol: Between Ukrainian and Russian Nationalism*. Cambridge: Harvard University Press, 2007.
Bortnevskii, Victor. "White Intelligence and Counter-Intelligence during the Civil War," *The Carl Beck Papers*, no. 108 (1995). Pittsburgh: University of Pittsburgh, Russian and East European Studies Program.

Boyer, John W. *Culture and Political Crisis in Vienna: Christian Socialism in Power, 1897–1918.* Chicago: University of Chicago Press, 1995.
——. *Political Radicalism in Late Imperial Vienna: Origins of the Christian Social Movement, 1848–1897.* Chicago: University of Chicago Press, 1981.
Bradley, Joseph. *Muzhik and Muscovite: Urbanization in Late Imperial Russia.* Berkeley: University of California Press, 1985.
——. *Voluntary Associations in Tsarist Russia: Science, Patriotism, and Civil Society.* Cambridge: Harvard University Press, 2009.
British Documents on Foreign Affairs: Reports and Papers from the Foreign Office Confidential Print. Pt. I, ser. A, vol. 6. Lanham, MD: University Publications of America, 1983.
Brodsky, Alexandra Fanny. *Smoke Signals: From Eminence to Exile.* London: Radcliffe Press, 1997.
Brokgauz, F. A. and I. A. Efron, eds. *Entsiklopedicheskii slovar'*. 82 vols. St. Petersburg: Brokgauz-Efron, 1890–1904.
Brower, Daniel R. *The Russian City between Tradition and Modernity, 1850–1900.* Berkeley: University of California Press, 1990.
——. *Turkestan and the Fate of the Russian Empire.* New York: Routledge, 2003.
Brown, Kate. *A Biography of No Place: From Ethnic Borderland to Soviet Heartland.* Cambridge: Harvard University Press, 2004.
Brubaker, Rogers. *Ethnicity without Groups.* Cambridge: Harvard University Press, 2004.
Brumfield, William Craft, Boris V. Anan'ich, and Yuri A. Petrov, eds. *Commerce in Russian Urban Culture, 1861–1914.* Washington, DC: Woodrow Wilson Center Press, 2001.
Brustein, William I. *Roots of Hate: Anti-Semitism in Europe before the Holocaust.* New York: Cambridge University Press, 2003.
Bryant, Chad. *Prague in Black: Nazi Rule and Czech Nationalism.* Cambridge: Harvard University Press, 2007.
Budnitskii, O. V., ed. *Istoriia i kul'tura rossiiskogo i vostochnoevropeiskogo evreistva: Novye istochniki, novye podkhody.* Moscow: Dom evreiskoi knigi, 2004.
Burbank, Jane, and Frederick Cooper, *Empires in World History: Power and the Politics of Difference.* Princeton: Princeton University Press, 2010.
Bushkovitch, Paul. "The Ukraine in Russian Culture, 1790–1860: The Evidence of the Journals." *Jahrbücher für Geschichte Osteuropas* 39, no. 3 (1991): 339–63.
Cadiot, Juliette. *Le laboratoire impérial (Russie-URSS 1860–1940).* Paris: CRNS, 2007.
——. "Russia Learns to Write: Slavistics, Politics, and the Struggle to Redefine Empire in the Early 20th Century." *Kritika* 9, no. 1 (2008): 135–67.
Chepely, Iurii Oleksiiovych. "Dyskusii navkolo monumenta Tarasovi Shevchenku v Kyevi naperedodni ioho stolitn'oho iubileiu." Master's thesis, Kiev-Mohyla Academy, 2009.
Chickering, Roger. *We Men Who Feel Most German: A Cultural Study of the Pan-German League, 1886–1914.* Boston: George Allen and Unwin, 1984.
Chmielewski, Edward. *The Polish Question in the Russian State Duma.* Knoxville: University of Tennessee Press, 1970.
Chmielewski, Jan Euzebiusz. *Pierwsze lata korporacji studentów polaków w Kijowie (R. 1884–1892).* Warsaw: Instytut Józefa Piłsudskiego, 1939.
Chojecki, Zygmunt. *Kijowskie Towarzystwo Rolnicze.* Kiev: Czcionkami Drukarni Polskiej w Kijowie, 1911.
——. *Społeczeństwo polskie na Rusi.* Warsaw: Pamiętnik Kresowy, 1937.

Clowes, Edith W., Samuel D. Kassow, and James L. West, eds. *Between Tsar and People: Educated Society and the Quest for Public Identity in Late Imperial Russia*. Princeton: Princeton University Press, 1991.
Cohen, William B. *Urban Government and the Rise of the French City: Five Municipalities in the Nineteenth Century*. New York: St. Martin's, 1998.
Coleman, Heather J. "Pravoslavnoe dukhovenstvo, istoricheskaia pamiat' i malorossiiskaia identichnost' v Kieve XIX v." In *Istoricheskaia pamiat' i obshchestvo v Rossiiskoi imperii i Sovietskom soiuze (konets XIX–nachalo XX veka)*. St. Petersburg: forthcoming.
Confino, Alon. *The Nation as a Local Metaphor: Württemberg, Imperial Germany, and National Memory, 1871–1918*. Chapel Hill: University of North Carolina Press, 1997.
Craig, Gordon A. *The Triumph of Liberalism: Zürich in the Golden Age, 1830–1869*. New York: Charles Scribner's Sons, 1988.
Crews, Robert D. *For Prophet and Tsar: Islam and Empire in Russia and Central Asia*. Cambridge: Harvard University Press, 2006.
Dahlmann, Dittmar. *Die Provinz Wählt: Russlands Konstitutionell-Demokratische Partei und die Dumawahlen, 1906–1912*. Cologne: Böhlau, 1996.
Danylenko, Andrii. "The Ukrainian Bible and the Valuev Circular of July 18, 1863." *Acta Slavica Japonica* 28 (2010): 1–21.
Dekel-Chen, Jonathan, David Gaunt, Natan M. Meir, and Israel Bartal, eds. *Anti-Jewish Violence: Rethinking the Pogrom in East European History*. Bloomington: Indiana University Press, 2011.
De Michelis, Cesare G. *The Non-Existent Manuscript: A Study of the Protocols of the Sages of Zion*. Translated by Richard Newhouse. Lincoln: University of Nebraska Press, 2004.
Dixon, Simon. "The 'Mad Monk' Iliodor in Tsaritsyn." *Slavonic and East European Review* 88, no. 1–2 (2010): 377–415.
Dmitriev, M. V., B. N. Floria, and S. G. Iakovenko, eds., *Brestkaia uniia 1596 g. i obshchestvenno-politicheskaia bor'ba na Ukraine i v Belorusii v kontse XVI–nachale XVII v.* Moscow: Indrik, 1996.
Dolbilov, Mikhail. "Prevratnosti kirillizatsii: Zapret latinitsy i biurokraticheskaia rusifikatsiia litovtsev v vilenskom general-gubernatorstve v 1864–1882 gg." *Ab Imperio* 2 (2005): 255–96.
———. "Russification and the Bureaucratic Mind in the Russian Empire's Northwestern Region in the 1860s." *Kritika* 5, no. 2 (2004): 245–71.
———. *Russkii krai, chuzhaia vera: Etnokofessional'naia politika imperii v Litve i Belorussii pri Aleksandre II*. Moscow: NLO, 2010.
Dolbilov, Mikhail, and A. Miller, eds. *Zapadnye okrainy rossiiskoi imperii*. Moscow: Novoe literaturnoe obozrenie, 2006.
Donik, Oleksandr. *Rodyna Tereshchenkiv v istorii dobrochynnosti*. Kiev: Instytut Istorii Ukraini, 2004.
Doroshenko, D. *History of the Ukraine*. Translated by Hanna Keller. Edmonton, AB: Institute Press, 1939.
Druh, Ol'ha, and D. V. Malakov, *Osobniaky Kyeva*. Kiev: Kyi, 2004.
Dubnow, S. M. *History of the Jews in Russia and Poland, from the Earliest Times until the Present Day*. Translated by I. Friedlaender. 3 vols. Philadelphia: Jewish Publication Society of America, 1920.
Edelman, Robert. *Gentry Politics on the Eve of the Russian Revolution: The Nationalist Party, 1907–1917*. New Brunswick, NJ: Rutgers University Press, 1980.
———. *Proletarian Peasants. The Revolution of 1905 in Russia's Southwest*. Ithaca: Cornell University Press, 1987.

Eklof, Ben, John Bushnell, and Larissa Zakhraova, eds., *Russia's Great Reforms, 1855–1881*. Bloomington: Indiana University Press, 1994.
Emmons, Terence. *The Formation of Political Parties and the First National Elections in Russia*. Cambridge: Harvard University Press, 1983.
——. *The Russian Landed Gentry and the Peasant Emancipation of 1861*. London: Cambridge University Press, 1968.
Engelstein, Laura. *The Keys to Happiness: Sex and the Search for Modernity in Fin-de-Siècle Russia*. Ithaca: Cornell University Press, 1992.
——. *Moscow, 1905: Working-Class Organization and Political Conflict*. Stanford: Stanford University Press, 1982.
Epstein, Tadeusz. *Edukacja dzieci i młodzieży w polskich rodzinach ziemiańskich na Wołyniu, Podolu i Ukrainie w II połowie XIX wieku*. Warsaw: DiG, 1998.
Eremeev, S. T. *Kiev i ego gorodovoe polozhenie*. Kiev: S. T. Eremeev, 1874.
Ernst, F. *Kontrakty i kontraktovyi budynok u Kyivi*. Kiev: Vseukrains'koi Akademii Nauk, 1924.
Eroshkin, N. P. *Ocherki istorii gosudarstvennykh uchrezhdenii dorevoliutsionnoi Rossii*. Moscow: Gosudarstvennoe uchebno-pedagogicheskoe izdatel'stvo, 1960.
Evreiskaia entsiklopediia. 16 vols. St. Petersburg: Brokgauz-Efron, 1906–13.
Evreiskoe naselenie Iuga Ukrainy. Kharkov: Evreiskii mir, 1998.
Evtuhov, Catherine. *Portrait of a Russian Province: Economy, Society, and Civilization in Nineteenth-Century Nizhnii Novgorod*. Pittsburgh: University of Pittsburgh Press, 2011.
Ford, Caroline. *Creating the Nation in Provincial France: Religion and Political Identity in Brittany*. Princeton: Princeton University Press, 1993.
Fowler, Mayhill Courtney. "Beau Monde: State and Stage on Empire's Edge, Russia and Soviet Ukraine, 1916-1941." PhD diss., Princeton University, 2011.
Frankel, Jonathan. *Prophecy and Politics: Socialism, Nationalism, and the Russian Jews, 1862–1917*. New York: Cambridge University Press, 1981.
Frankel, Jonathan, and Steven J. Zipperstein, eds. *Assimilation and Community: The Jews in Nineteenth-Century Europe*. New York: Cambridge University Press, 1981.
Franklin, Simon, and Jonathon Shepard. *The Emergence of Rus', 750–1200*. London: Longman, 1996.
Fraser, Derek. *Power and Authority in the Victorian City*. New York: St. Martin's, 1979.
Freeze, Gregory L. "The *Soslovie* (Estate) Paradigm and Russian Social History." *American Historical Review* 91, no. 1 (1986): 11–36.
Fuller, William C. *The Foe Within: Fantasies of Treason and the End of Imperial Russia*. Ithaca: Cornell University Press, 2006.
Galai, Shmuel. *The Liberation Movement in Russia, 1900–1905*. Cambridge: Cambridge University Press, 1973.
Gatrell, Peter. *The Tsarist Economy, 1850–1917*. London: B. T. Batsford, 1986.
——. *A Whole Empire Walking: Refugees in Russia during World War I*. Bloomington: Indiana University Press, 1999.
Gellner, Ernest. *Nations and Nationalism*. Ithaca: Cornell University Press, 1983.
Geraci, Robert P. *Window on the East: National and Imperial Identities in Late Tsarist Russia*. Ithaca: Cornell University Press, 2001.
Geraci, Robert P., and Michael Khodarkovsky, eds. *Of Religion and Empire: Missions, Conversion, and Tolerance in Imperial Russia*. Ithaca: Cornell University Press, 2001.
Gerasimov, Ilya, Jan Kusber, and Alexander Semyonov, eds. *Empire Speaks Out: Languages of Rationalization and Self-Description in the Russian Empire*. Boston, Brill, 2009.

Giustino, Cathleen M. *Tearing Down Prague's Jewish Town: Ghetto Clearance and the Legacy of Middle-Class Ethnic Politics around 1900.* Boulder: East European Monographs, 2003.

Glaser, Amelia M. *Jews and Ukrainians in Russia's Literary Borderlands: From the Shtetl Fair to the Petersburg Bookshop.* Chicago: Northwestern University Press, 2012.

Głębocki, Henryk. *Fatalna sprawa: Kwestia polska w rosykskiej myśli politycznej (1856–1866).* Cracow: Arcana, 1997.

Golczewski, Frank. *Deutsche und Ukrainer, 1914–1939.* Paderborn, Ger.: Ferdinand Schöningh Verlag, 2010.

Gorizontov, L. E. *Paradoksy imperskoi politiki: Poliaki v Rossii i russkie v Pol'she.* Moscow: Indrik, 1999.

Gorshkov, Boris B. *Russia's Factory Children: State, Society, and Law, 1800–1917.* Pittsburgh: University of Pittsburg Press, 2009.

Graziosi, Andrea. *The Great Soviet Peasant War: Bolsheviks and Peasants, 1917–33.* Cambridge: Harvard Ukrainian Research Institute, 1996.

Grimsted, Patricia Kennedy. "Archeography in the Service of Imperial Policy: The Foundation of the Kiev Archeographic Commission and the Kiev Central Archive of Early Record Books." *Harvard Ukrainian Studies* 17, nos. 1–2 (1993): 27–44.

Grzywatz, Berthold. *Stadt, Bürgertum und Staat im 19. Jahrhundert: Selbstverwaltung, Partizipation und Repräsentation in Berlin und Preußen 1806 bis 1918.* Berlin: Duncker & Humblot, 2003.

Haberer, Erich. *Jews and Revolution in Nineteenth-Century Russia.* New York: Cambridge University Press, 1995.

Häfner, Lutz. *Gesellschaft als lokale Veranstaltung: die Wolgastädte Kazan' und Saratov, 1870-1914.* Cologne: Böhlau, 2004.

Haimson, Leopold, ed., *The Politics of Rural Russia, 1905–1914.* Bloomington: Indiana University Press, 1979.

———. "The Problem of Political and Social Stability in Urban Russia, 1905–1917 (Part One)." *Slavic Review* 23, no. 4 (1964): 619–42.

———. "The Problem of Political and Social Stability in Urban Russia, 1905–1917 (Part Two)." *Slavic Review* 24, no. 1 (1965): 1–22.

Hamm, Michael F., ed. *The City in Late Imperial Russia.* Bloomington: Indiana University Press, 1986.

———. "Khar'kov's Progressive Duma, 1910–1914: A Study in Russian Municipal Reform." *Slavic Review* 40, no. 1 (1981): 17–36.

———. *Kiev: A Portrait, 1800–1917.* Princeton: Princeton University Press, 1993.

Harper, Samuel N. *The New Electoral Law for the Russian Duma.* Chicago: University of Chicago Press, 1908.

Harris, James F. *The People Speak! Anti-Semitism and Emancipation in Nineteenth-Century Bavaria.* Ann Arbor: University of Michigan Press, 1994.

Hausmann, Guido, ed. *Gesellschaft als lokale Veranstaltung: Selbstverwaltung, Assoziierung und Geselligkeit in den Städten des ausgehenden Zarenreiches.* Göttingen: Vandenhoeck & Ruprecht, 2002.

Haywood, Richard Mowbray. *Russia Enters the Railway Age.* Boulder: East European Monographs, 1998.

Herlihy, Patricia. *Odessa: A History, 1794–1914.* Cambridge: Harvard Ukrainian Research Institute, 1986.

Herzog, Tamar. *Defining Nations: Immigrants and Citizens in Early Modern Spain and Spanish America.* New Haven: Yale University Press, 2003.

SELECTED BIBLIOGRAPHY

Heuman, Susan. *Kistiakovsky: The Struggle for National and Constitutional Rights in the Last Years of Tsarism.* Cambridge: Harvard University Press, 1998.
Hildermeier, Manfred. *Bürgertum und Stadt in Russland, 1760–1870: Rechtliche Lage und Soziale Struktur.* Cologne: Böhlau, 1986.
Hillis, Faith. "Ukrainophile Activism and Imperial Governance in Russia's Southwestern Borderlands." *Kritika* 13, no. 2 (2012): 301–26.
Himka, John-Paul. *Galician Villagers and the Ukrainian National Movement in the Nineteenth Century.* Edmonton: Canadian Institute of Ukrainian Studies, 1988.
Hirsch, Francine. *Empire of Nations: Ethnographic Knowledge and the Making of the Soviet Union.* Ithaca: Cornell University Press, 2005.
Hobsbawm, Eric, and Terence Ranger. *The Invention of Tradition.* New York: Cambridge University Press, 1983.
Hoffmann, David L., and Yanni Kotsonis, eds. *Russian Modernity: Politics, Knowledge, Practices.* New York: Palgrave-Macmillan, 2000.
Holquist, Peter. *Making War, Forging Revolution: Russia's Continuum of Crisis, 1914–1921.* Cambridge: Harvard University Press, 2002.
Horkina, L. P. *Narysy z istorii politychnoi ekonomii v Ukraini.* Kiev: Naukova dumka, 1994.
Hosking, Geoffrey. *Russia and the Russians.* Cambridge: Harvard University Press, 2003.
———. *The Russian Constitutional Experiment: Government and Duma, 1907–1914.* New York: Cambridge University Press, 1973.
Hroch, Miroslav. *Social Preconditions of National Revival in Europe: A Comparative Analysis of the Social Composition of Patriotic Groups among the Smaller European Nations.* Translated by Ben Fowkes. New York: Cambridge University Press, 1985.
Hrytsak, Iaroslav. *Narys istorii Ukrainy: formuvannia modernoi ukrains'koi natsii XIX–XX stolittia.* Kiev: Heneza, 2000.
Hunchak, Taras, ed. *Tysiacha rokiv ukrains'koi suspil'no-politychnoi dumki.* 9 vols. Kiev: Dnipro, 2005.
Hundert, Gershon David. *Jews in Poland-Lithuania in the Eighteenth Century.* Berkeley: University of California Press, 2004.
Iakovenko, N. M. *Ukrains'ka shliakhta z kintsia XIV do seredyny XVII st.* Kiev: Naukova dumka, 1993.
Iavors'kyi, M. *Ukraina v epokhu kapitalizmu: Na shliakhu kapitalistychnoi akumuliatsii.* Kiev: Derzhavne vydavnytstvo Ukraini, 1925.
Ikonnikov, V. S., ed. *Biograficheskii slovar' professorov i prepodavatelei imperatorskogo universiteta Sv. Vladimira (1834–1884).* Kiev: Imperatorskii Universiteta Sv. Vladimira, 1884.
———, ed. *Istoriko-statisticheskie zapiski ob uchenykh i uchebno-vspomogatel'nikh uchrezhdeniiakh Imperatorskogo Universiteta sv. Vladimira (1834–1884).* Kiev: Tipografiia Imperatorskogo universiteta sv. Vladimira, 1884.
———. *Kiev v 1654–1855 gg.: Istoricheskii ocherk.* Kiev: Tipografiia Imperatorskogo Universiteta sv. Vladimira, 1904.
Iljine, Nicholas V., ed. *Odessa Memories.* Seattle: University of Washington Press, 2003.
Iuditskii, A. D. "Evreiskaia burzhuaziia i evreiskie rabochie v tekstil'noi promyshlennosti pervoi poloviny XIX v." *Istoricheskii sbornik* 4 (1935): 107–33.
Ivanov, L. M., A. M. Pankratova, and A. L. Sidorov, eds. *Revoliutsiia 1905–1907 gg. v natsional'nykh raionakh Rossii.* Moscow: Gosudarstvennoe izdatel'stvo politicheskoi literatury, 1955.
Ivshyna, Larysa, ed. *Viiny i Myr, abo Ukraintsi-poliaky: Braty, vorogy, susidy...* Kiev: ATZT, 2004.

Jahn, Hubertus. *Patriotic Culture in Russia during World War I*. Ithaca: Cornell University Press, 1995.

Johnson, Robert Eugene. *Peasant and Proletarian: The Working Class of Moscow in the Late Nineteenth Century*. New Brunswick, NJ: Rutgers University Press, 1979.

Jones, Stephen F. *Socialism in Georgian Colors: The European Road to Social Democracy, 1883–1917*. Cambridge: Harvard University Press, 1995.

Judson, Pieter M. *Guardians of the Nation: Activists on the Language Frontiers of Imperial Austria*. Cambridge: Harvard University Press, 2006.

Kahan, Alan S. *Liberalism in Nineteenth-Century Europe: The Political Culture of Limited Suffrage*. New York: Palgrave, 2003.

Kalinin, V. D. *Iz istorii gorodskogo samoupravleniia v Rossii (XVII–nachala XX vv.)*. Moscow: Institut ekonomiki Rossiiskoi Akademii nauk, 1994.

Kamanin, I. *Poslednie gody Samoupravleniia Kieva po Magdeburgskomu Pravu*. Kiev: Korchak-Novitskii, 1888.

Kamiński, Aleksander. *Prehistoria polskich związków młodzieży*. Warsaw: Państwowe wydawnictwo naukowe, 1959.

Kappeler, Andreas. "The Ambiguities of Russification." *Kritika* 5, no. 4 (2004): 291–97.

——. " 'Great Russians' and 'Little Russians': Russian-Ukrainian Relations and Perceptions in Historical Perspective." *Donald W. Treadgold Papers* 39. Seattle, WA: Henry M. Jackson School of International Studies, University of Washington, 2003

——. *The Russian Empire: A Multi-Ethnic History*. Harlow, UK: Pearson Education, 2001.

Kappeler, Andreas, Zenon E. Kohut, Frank E. Sysyn, and Mark von Hagen, eds. *Culture, Nation, and Identity: The Ukrainian-Russian Encounter (1600–1945)*. Edmonton: Canadian Institute of Ukrainian Studies Press, 2003.

Kas"ianov, H. V. *Ukrains'ka intelligentsiia na rubezhi XIX–XX stolit: Sotsial'no-polytychnii portret*. Kiev: Lybid', 1993.

Kas"ianov, H. V., and Philipp Ther, eds. *A Laboratory of Transnational History: Ukraine and Recent Ukrainian Historiography*. New York: Central European University Press, 2009.

Kasymenko, O. K. *Istoriia Kyeva*. 2 vols. Kiev: Vydavnytstvo Akademii nauk Ukrains'koi RSR, 1960.

Katz, Martin. *Mikhail N. Katkov: A Political Biography, 1818–87*. Paris: Mouton, 1966.

Kellogg, Michael. *The Russian Roots of Nazism: White Émigrés and the Making of National Socialism, 1917–1945*. New York: Cambridge University Press, 2005.

Kelly, T. Mills. *Without Remorse: Czech National Socialism in Late-Habsburg Austria*. Boulder: East European Monographs, 2006.

Kenez, Peter. *Civil War in South Russia, 1918–1919: The Defeat of the Whites*. Berkeley: University of California Press, 1977.

Khiterer, Victoria. "Arnold Davidovich Margolin: Ukrainian-Jewish Jurist, Statesman and Diplomat." *Revolutionary Russia* 18, no. 2 (2005): 145–67.

——, ed. *Dokumenty po evreiskoi istorii XVI–XX vekov v Kievskikh arkhivakh*. Kiev: Institut Iudaiki, 2001.

——, ed. *Dokumenty sobrannye evreiskoi istoriko-arkheograficheskoi komissiei*. Kiev: Institut Iudaiki, 1999.

——. "Jewish Life in Kyiv at the Turn of the Twentieth Century." *Ukraina moderna* 10 (2006): 74–94.

——. "The October 1905 Pogrom in Kiev." *East European Jewish Affairs* 22, no. 2 (1992): 21–37.

Kieniewicz, Stefan. *Powstanie styczniowe*. Warsaw: Państwowe Wydawnictwo Naukowe, 1972.

King, Jeremy. *Budweisers into Czechs and Germans: A Local History of Bohemian Politics, 1848–1948*. Princeton: Princeton University Press, 2005.

Kir'ianov, Iu. I. *Pravye partii v Rossii, 1911–1917*. Moscow: ROSSPEN, 2001.

——. *Russkoe sobranie, 1900–1917*. Moscow, ROSSPEN, 2003.

Klier, John D. *Imperial Russia's Jewish Question, 1855–1881*. New York: Cambridge University Press, 1995.

——. "*Kievlianin* and the Jews: A Decade of Disillusionment, 1864–1873." *Harvard Ukrainian Studies* 5, no. 1 (1981): 83–101.

——. "Krug gintsburgov i politika shtadlanuta v imperatorskoi Rossii." *Vestnik Evreiskogo universiteta v Moskve* 3, no. 10 (1995): 38–55.

——. *Russians, Jews, and the Pogroms of 1881–1882*. New York: Cambridge University Press, 2011.

Klier, John D., and Shlomo Lambroza, eds. *Pogroms: Anti-Jewish Violence in Modern Russian History*. New York: Cambridge University Press, 1992.

Knight, Nathaniel. "Constructing the Science of Nationality: Ethnography in Mid-Nineteenth-Century Russia." PhD diss, Columbia University, 1995.

Kohut, Zenon E. "The Image of Jews in Ukraine's Intellectual Tradition: The Role of 'Istoriia Rusov'." *Harvard Ukrainian Studies* 22 (1998): 343–58.

——. "The Khmelnytsky Uprising, the Image of Jews, and the Shaping of Ukrainian Historical Memory." *Jewish History* 17, no. 2 (2003): 141–63.

——. "Origins of the Unity Paradigm: Ukraine and the Construction of Russian National History (1620–1860)." *Eighteenth-Century Studies* 35, no. 1 (2001): 70–76.

——. *Russian Centralism and Ukrainian Autonomy: Imperial Absorption of the Hetmanate, 1760s–1830s*. Cambridge: Harvard University Press, 1988.

Kollard, Iu. Zh. *Spohady iunats'kykh dniv, 1897–1906: Ukrains'ka students'ka hromada v Kharkovi i Revoliutsiina ukrains'ka partiia (RUP)*. Toronto: Sribna surma, 1972.

Komzolova, A. A. *Politika samoderzhaviia v Severo-Zapadnom krae v epokhu Velikikh reform*. Moscow: Nauka, 2005.

Korbych, Halyna. *Zhurnal "Literaturno-naukovyi visnyk" l'vivs'koho periodu (1898–1906)*. Kiev: Oberehy, 1999.

Koroleva, N. G. "Pravye Partii v bor'be s revoliutsiei, 1905–1907 g.g." *Istoricheskie zapiski* 118 (1990): 102–138.

Korros, Alexandra Shecket. *A Reluctant Parliament: Stolypin, Nationalism, and the Politics of the Russian Imperial State Council, 1906–1911*. Lanham, MD: Rowman and Littlefield, 2002.

Kotsiubinskii, D. A. *Russkii natsionalizm v nachale XX stoletiia: Rozhdenie i gibel' ideologii Vserossiiskogo natsional'nogo soiuza*. Moscow: ROSSPEN, 2001.

Kovacs, Maria M. *Liberal Professions and Illiberal Politics: Hungary from the Habsburgs to the Holocaust*. New York: Oxford University Press, 1994.

Kovalinskii, V. V. *Metsenaty Kieva*. Kiev: Kyi, 1998.

——. *Sem'ia Tereshchenko*. Kiev: Presa Ukraini, 2003.

Kozyrev, A. "Antievreiskie narodnicheskie proklamatsii nachala 80-kh godov XIX veka v Ukraine." *Evreiskoe naselenie Iuga Ukrainy*. Khar'kov: Evreiskii mir, 1998.

Krainii, Kostiantyn. *Istoryky Kyevo-Pechers'koi lavry XIX–pochatku XX stolit'*. Kiev: Pul'sary, 2000.

Król-Mazur, Renata. *Miasto trzech nacji: Studia z dziejów Kamieńca Podolskiego w XVIII wieku*. Cracow: Avalon, 2008.

Kruhlashov, Anatolii. *Drama intelektuala: Politychni idei Mykhaila Drahomanova*. Chernivtsi: Prut, 2000.

Kvit, Serhii. *Dmytro Dontsov: Ideolohichnyi portret*. Kiev: Kyivskyi universytet, 2000.

Landau, Jacob M. *Pan-Turkism: From Irredentism to Cooperation*. Bloomington: Indiana University Press, 1995.

Lazarski, Christopher. *The Lost Opportunity: Attempts at Unification of the Anti-Bolsheviks, 1917–1919*. Lanham, MD: University Press of America, 2008.

Lebedynsky, Iaroslav. *Skoropadsky et l'édification de l'Etat ukrainien (1918)*. Paris: Harmattan, 2010.

Lieven, Dominic. *Empire: The Russian Empire and Its Rivals*. New Haven: Yale University Press, 2002.

Lincoln, W. Bruce. *In the Vanguard of Reform: Russia's Enlightened Bureaucrats, 1825–1861*. DeKalb: Northern Illinois University Press, 1982.

Lindenmeyr, Adele. *Poverty Is Not a Vice: Charity, Society, and the State in Imperial Russia*. Princeton: Princeton University Press, 1996.

Lindner, Rainer. *Unternehmer und Stadt in der Ukraine, 1860–1914: Industrialisierung und soziale Kommunikation im südlichen Zarenreich*. Konstanz: UVK Verlagsgesellschaft mbH, 2006.

Loewe, H.-D. *The Tsars and the Jews: Reform, Reaction, and Anti-Semitism in Imperial Russia, 1772–1917*. New York: Harwood Academic Publishers, 1993.

Lohr, Eric. *Nationalizing the Russian Empire: The Campaign against Enemy Aliens during World War I*. Cambridge: Harvard University Press, 2003.

Los', F. E., I. P. Oleinik, and V.I. Sheludchenko, eds. *Revoliutsiia 1905–1907 gg. na Ukraine*. 2 vols. Kiev: Gosudarstvennoe izdatel'stvo Politicheskoi literatury USSR, 1955.

Loukianov, Mikhail. "Conservatives and 'Renewed Russia,' 1907–1914." *Slavic Review* 61, no. 4 (2002): 762–86.

———. "'Russia for Russians' or 'Russia for Russian Subjects?' Conservatives and the Nationality Question on the Eve of World War I," *Russian Studies in History* 46, no. 4 (2008): 77–92.

Luckyj, George S. N. *Seven Lives: Vignettes of Ukrainian Writers in the Nineteenth Century*. New York: Ukrainian Academy of Arts and Sciences in the U.S., 1999.

———. *Young Ukraine: The Brotherhood of Saints Cyril and Methodius, 1845–1847*. Ottawa: University of Ottawa Press, 1991.

Luckyj, George S. N., and Ralph Lindheim, eds. *Towards an Intellectual History of Ukraine: An Anthology of Ukrainian Thought from 1710 to 1995*. Toronto: University of Toronto Press, 1996.

Łukawski, Zygmunt. *Ludność polska w Rosji, 1863–1914*. Warsaw: Wydawnictwo Polskiej Akademii Nauk, 1978.

Lypyns'kyi, Viacheslav. *Ukraina na perelomi, 1657–1659*. Vienna: Dniprosoiuz, 1920.

Magocsi, Paul Robert. *The Roots of Ukrainian Nationalism: Galicia as Ukraine's Piedmont*. Toronto: University of Toronto Press, 2002.

Maiorova, Olga. *From the Shadow of Empire: Defining the Russian Nation through Cultural Mythology, 1855–1870*. Madison: University of Wisconsin Press, 2010.

Malia, Martin E. *Alexander Herzen and the Birth of Russian Socialism, 1812–1855*. Cambridge: Harvard University Press, 1961.

Manchester, Laurie. *Holy Fathers, Secular Sons: Clergy, Intelligentsia, and the Modern Self in Revolutionary Russia*. DeKalb: Northern Illinois University Press, 2008.

Manilov, V. *Kievskii sovet rabochikh deputatov v 1905 g*. Kiev: Gosudarstvennoe izdatel'stvo, 1926.

Manning, Roberta Thompson. *The Crisis of the Old Order in Russia*. Princeton: Princeton University Press, 1982.

Marakhov, G. I. *Pol'skoe vosstanie 1863 g. na pravoberezhnoi Ukraine.* Kiev: Izdatel'stvo Kievskogo Universiteta, 1967.
———. *Sotsial'no-Politicheskaia bor'ba na Ukraine v 50–60-e gody XIX veka.* Kiev: Vyshcha shkola, 1981.
Martin, Alexander M. *Romantics, Reformers, Reactionaries: Russian Conservative Thought and Politics in the Reign of Alexander I.* DeKalb: Northern Illinois University Press, 1997.
Martin, Terry. *The Affirmative Action Empire: Nations and Nationalism in the Soviet Union, 1923–1939.* Ithaca: Cornell University Press, 2001.
Matsuzato, Kimitaka. *Imperiology: From Empirical Knowledge to Discussing the Russian Empire.* Sapporo, Jap.: Slavic Research Center, 2007.
———. "The Issue of Zemstvos in Right Bank Ukraine, 1864–1906. Russian Anti-Polonism under the Challenges of Modernization." *Jahrbücher für Geschichte Osteuropas* 51, no. 2 (2003).
Mazgaj, Paul. *The Action Française and Revolutionary Syndicalism.* Chapel Hill: University of North Carolina Press, 1979.
McKay, John P. *Pioneers for Profit: Foreign Entrepreneurship and Russian Industrialization, 1885–1913.* Chicago: University of Chicago Press, 1970.
Meir, Natan M. "Jews, Ukrainians, and Russians in Kiev: Intergroup Relations in Late Imperial Associational Life." *Slavic Review* 65, no. 3 (2006): 475–501.
———. *Kiev: Jewish Metropolis: A History, 1859–1914.* Bloomington: Indiana University Press, 2010.
Menzhulin, Vadim. *Drugoi Sikorskii: Neudobnye Stranitsy Istorii Psikhiatrii.* Kiev: Sfera, 2004.
Miller, Alexei. "Natsiia, Narod, Narodnost' in Russia in the Nineteenth Century: Some Introductory Remarks to the History of Concepts." *Jahrbücher für Geschichte Osteuropas* 56, no. 3 (2008): 379–90.
———. *The Romanov Empire and Nationalism: Essays in the Methodology of Historical Research.* New York: Central European University Press, 2008.
———. *The Ukrainian Question: The Russian Empire and Nationalism in the Nineteenth Century.* New York: Central European University Press, 2003.
Mogil'ner, Marina. *Homo imperii: Istoriia fizicheskoi antropologii v Rossii.* Moscow: Novoe literaturnoe obozrenie, 2008.
Moon, David. "The Inventory Reform and Peasant Unrest in Right-Bank Ukraine in 1847–48." *Slavonic and East European Review* 79, no. 4 (2001): 653–97.
Moore, James R. *The Transformation of Urban Liberalism: Party Politics and Urban Governance in Late Nineteenth-Century England.* Aldershot, UK: Ashgate, 2006.
Mukhin, A. B. "Ekonomicheskie i upravlencheskie vozzreniia D. I. Pikhno." PhD diss., St. Petersburg State University, 2003.
Mykhailyn, I. L. *Istoriia Ukrains'koi zhurnalistyky XIX stolittia.* Kiev: Tsentr navchal'noi literatury, 2003.
Nardova, V. A. *Samoderzhavie i gorodskie dumy v Rossii v kontse XIX–nachale XX veka.* St. Petersburg: Nauka, 1994.
Nathans, Benjamin. *Beyond the Pale: The Jewish Encounter with Late Imperial Russia.* Berkeley: University of California Press, 2002.
Nikitin, S. A. *Slavianskie komitety v Rossii v 1858–1876 godakh.* Moscow: Izd-vo Moskovskogo universiteta, 1960.
Nolte, Ernst. *The Three Faces of Fascism: Action Française, Italian Fascism, National Socialism.* Translated by Leila Vennewitz. London: Weidenfeld and Nicolson, 1965.
Nord, Philip G. *Paris Shopkeepers and the Politics of Resentment.* Princeton: Princeton University Press, 1986.

Oberlander, Erwin. "The All-Russian Fascist Party." *Journal of Contemporary History* 1, no. 1 (1966): 158–73.
Ogloblin, A. P. *Narysy z istorii ukrains'koi fabryky: Krypats'ka fabryka.* Kiev: Proletar, 1931.
——. *Ocherki istorii ukrainskoi fabriki: Predkapitalisticheskaia fabrika.* Kiev: Gosudarstvennoe izdatel'stvo Ukrainy, 1925.
Okenfuss, Max J. *The Rise and Fall of Latin Humanism in Early Modern Russia: Pagan Authors, Ukrainians, and the Resiliency of Muscovy.* Leiden: Brill, 1995.
Okinshevych, Lev. *Znachne viis'kove tovarystvo v Ukraini-Het'manshchyni XVII–XVIII st.* Munich: Zahrava, 1948.
Omel'ianchuk, I. V. *Chernosotennoe dvizhenie na territorii Ukrainy (1904–1914 gg.).* Kiev: NIURO, 2000.
Owen, Thomas C. *Dilemmas of Russian Capitalism: Fedor Chizhov and Corporate Enterprise in the Railroad Age.* Cambridge: Harvard University Press, 2005.
Palienko, Maryna. *"Kievskaia starina" u hromads'komu ta naukovomu zhytti Ukrainy (kinets' XIX–pochatok XX st.).* 3 vols. Kiev: Tempora, 2005.
Pamiętnik Kijowski. 3 vols. London: Nakładem Koła Kijowian, 1959.
Panashenko, V. V. *Sotsial'na elita het'manshchyny (druha polovyna XVII–XVIII st.)* Kiev: Instytut istorii Ukraini NAN, 1995.
Papazian, Dennis. "N. I. Kostomarov and the Cyril-Methodian Ideology." *Russian Review* 29, no. 1 (1970): 59–73.
Parasun'ko, O. *Massovaia politicheskaia zabastovka v Kieve v 1903 g.* Kiev: Izdatel'stvo akademii nauk Ukrainskoi SSR, 1953.
Pearson, Thomas S. *Russian Officialdom in Crisis: Autocracy and Local Self-Government, 1861–1900.* New York: Cambridge University Press, 1989.
Petrovsky-Shtern, Yohanan. *The Anti-Imperial Choice: The Making of the Ukrainian Jew.* New Haven: Yale University Press, 2009.
——. "The 'Jewish Policy' of the Late Imperial War Ministry: The Impact of the Russian Right." *Kritika* 3, no. 2 (2002): 217–54.
Pisarkova, L. F. *Gorodskie reformy v Rossii i moskovskaia duma.* Moscow: Institut Rossiiskoi istorii, 2010.
——. *Moskovskaia gorodskaia duma, 1863–1917.* Moscow: Mosgorarkhiv, 1998.
Plokhy, Serhii. *The Cossack Myth: History and Nationhood in the Age of Empires.* New York: Cambridge University Press, 2012.
——. *The Cossacks and Religion in Early Modern Ukraine.* New York: Oxford University Press, 2002.
——. "The Ghosts of Pereiaslav: Russo-Ukrainian Historical Debates in the Post-Soviet Era." *Europe-Asia Studies* 53, no. 3 (2001): 489–505.
——. *The Origins of the Slavic Nations: Premodern Identities in Russia, Ukraine, and Belarus.* New York: Cambridge University Press, 2006.
——. *Unmaking Imperial Russia: Mykhailo Hrushevsky and the Writing of Ukrainian History.* Toronto: University of Toronto Press, 2005.
Podhorodecki, Leszek. *Dzieje Kijowa.* Warsaw: Książka i Wiedza, 1982.
Podraza, Antoni, ed. *Kraków-Kijów: Szkice z Dziejów Stosunków Polsko-Ukraińskich.* Cracow: Wydawnictwo Literackie Kraków, 1969.
Polovynchak, Iuliia. *Hazeta "Kievlianin" i Ukrainstvo: Dosvid natsional'noi samoidentyfikatsii.* Kiev: Natsional'na akademiia nauk, 2008.

SELECTED BIBLIOGRAPHY

Polunov, Alexander. *Russia in the Nineteenth Century: Autocracy, Reform, Social Change, 1814–1914*. Armonk, NY: M.E. Sharpe, 2005.
Porter, Brian. *When Nationalism Began to Hate: Imagining Modern Politics in Nineteenth-Century Poland*. New York: Oxford University Press, 2000.
Potichnyj, Peter J., Marc Raeff, Jaroslaw Pelenski, and Gleb N. Zekulin, eds. *Ukraine and Russia in Their Historical Encounter*. Edmonton: Canadian Institute of Ukrainian Studies, 1992.
Pritsak, Omeljan. "The Pogroms of 1881." *Harvard Ukrainian Studies* 11, nos. 1–2 (1987): 8–43.
Procyk, Anna. *Russian Nationalism and Ukraine: The Nationality Policy of the Volunteer Army during the Civil War*. Edmonton: Canadian Institute of Ukrainian Studies, 1995.
Prusin, Alexander Victor. *Nationalizing a Borderland: War, Ethnicity, and Anti-Jewish Violence in East Galicia, 1914–1920*. Tuscaloosa: University of Alabama Press, 2005.
Prymak, Thomas M. *Mykhailo Hrushevsky: The Politics of National Culture*. Toronto: University of Toronto Press, 1987.
———. *Mykola Kostomarov: A Biography*. Toronto: University of Toronto Press, 1996.
Pulzer, P. G. J. *The Rise of Political Anti-Semitism in Germany and Austria*. Cambridge, MA: Harvard University Press, 1988.
Rawson, Don C. *Russian Rightists and the Revolution of 1905*. New York: Cambridge University Press, 1995.
Recueil de matériaux sur la situation économique des israélites de Russie d'après l'enquete de la Jewish Colonization Association. 2 vols. Paris: Librairies Félix Alcan et Guillaumin Réunies, 1906.
Remy, Johannes. *Higher Education and National Identity: Polish Student Activism in Russia, 1832–1863*. Helsinki: Suomalaisen Kirjallisuuden Seura, 2000.
———. "The Valuev Circular and Censorship of Ukrainian Publications in the Russian Empire (1863–1876): Intention and Practice." *Canadian Slavonic Papers*, 49, nos. 1–2 (2007): 87–110.
Renner, Andreas. "Defining a Russian Nation: Mikhail Katkov and the Invention of National Politics," *Slavonic and East European Review* 81, no. 4 (2003): 659–82.
———. *Russischer Nationalismus und Öffentlichkeit im Zarenreich 1855–1875*. Cologne: Böhlau, 2000.
Reynolds, Michael A. *Shattering Empires: The Clash and Collapse of the Ottoman and Russian Empires, 1908–1918*. New York: Cambridge University Press, 2011.
Riabchouk, Mykola. *Vid Malorosii do Ukrainy: Paradoksy zapizniloho natsiitvorennia*. Kiev: Krytyka, 2000.
Riasanovsky, Nicholas V. *Nicholas I and Official Nationality in Russia, 1825–1855*. Berkeley: University of California Press, 1959.
———. *Russian Identities: A Historical Survey*. New York: Oxford University Press, 2005.
Rieber, Alfred J. *Merchants and Entrepreneurs in Imperial Russia*. Chapel Hill: University of North Carolina Press, 1982.
Rimskii, S. V. *Rossiiskaia tserkov' v epokhu velikikh reform*. Moscow: Obshchestvo liubitelei tserkovnoi istorii, 1999.
Rodichev, Fedor. "The Veteran of Russian Liberalism: Ivan Petrunkevich." *Slavonic and East European Review* 7, no. 20 (1929): 316–26.
Rodkiewicz, Witold. *Russian Nationality Policy in the Western Provinces of the Empire (1863–1905)*. Lublin: Scientific Society of Lublin, 1998.
Rogger, Hans. *Jewish Policies and Right-Wing Politics in Imperial Russia*. Berkeley: University of California Press, 1986.
Roshwald, Aviel. *Ethnic Nationalism and the Fall of Empires: Central Europe, Russia, and the Middle East, 1914–1923*. New York: Routledge, 2002.

Rudnitskaia, E. L., ed. *V razdum'iakh o Rossii (XIX vek)*. Moscow: Arkheograficheskii tsentr, 1996.
Rudnytsky, Ivan L. *Essays in Modern Ukrainian History*. Cambridge: Harvard Ukrainian Research Institute, 1987.
———, ed. *Rethinking Ukrainian History*, Edmonton: Canadian Institute of Ukrainian Studies, 1981.
Russkie pisateli, 1800–1917: Biograficheskii slovar'. Moscow: Bol'shaia rossiiskaia entsiklopediia, 1994.
Rutherford, Andrea. "Vissarion Belinskii and the Ukrainian National Question." *Russian Review* 54, no. 4 (1995): 500–515.
Ryan, Daniel C. "The Tsar's Faith: Conversion, Religious Politics, and Peasant Protest in Imperial Russia's Baltic Periphery, 1845–1870s." PhD diss, UCLA, 2008.
Rybakov, M. O. *Nevidomi ta malovidomi storinki istorii Kyeva*. Kiev: Kyi, 1997.
Rybyns'kyi, V. P. "Protyevreis'kyi rukh r. 1881-ho na Ukraini." *Zbirnyk prats' evreis'koi istorychno-arkheohrafichnoi komisii* 2 (1929): 139–82.
Sahlins, Peter. *Boundaries: The Making of France and Spain in the Pyrenees*. Berkeley: University of California Press, 1989.
Sanborn, Joshua. *Drafting the Russian Nation: Military Conscription, Total War, and Mass Politics, 1905–1925*. DeKalb: Northern Illinois University Press, 2003.
Sanders, Thomas, ed. *Historiography of Imperial Russia: The Profession and Writing of History in a Multi-National State*. Armonk, NY: M.E. Sharpe, 1999.
Sarbei, V. G., I. I. Artemenko, and N. I. Suprunenko, eds. *Istoriia Kieva*. 3 vols. Kiev: Naukova Dumka, 1982-1984.
Saunders, David B. "Historians and Concepts of Nationality in Early Nineteenth-Century Russia." *Slavonic and East European Review* 60, no. 1 (1982): 44–62.
———. "Russia and Ukraine under Alexander II: The Valuev Edict of 1863." *International History Review* 17, no. 1 (1995): 23–50.
Schmidt, Vivian A. *Democratizing France: The Political and Adminstrative History of Decentralization*. New York: Cambridge University Press, 1990.
Schorske, Carl E. *Fin-de-Siècle Vienna: Politics and Culture*. New York: Vintage Books, 1981.
Seraphim, Hans-Jürgen. *Neuere russische Wert- und Kapitalzinstheorien*. Berlin: Walter de Gruyter & Co., 1925.
Sereda, Ostap. "'Whom Shall We Be?' Public Debates over the National Identity of Galician Ruthenians in the 1860s." *Jahrbücher für Geschichte Osteuropas*, 49, no. 2 (2001): 200–212.
Ševčenko, Ihor. *Ukraine between East and West: Essays on Cultural History to the Early Eighteenth Century*. Edmonton: Canadian Institute of Ukrainian Studies Press, 1996.
Shandra, Valentyna. *Kyivs'ke general-gubernatorstvo, 1832–1914*. Kiev: UDNDIASD 1999.
———. *Malorosiis'ke heneral-hubernatorstvo, 1802–1856*. Kiev: Derzh. kom. Arkhiviv Ukrainy, 2001.
Shchegolev, S. N. *Ukrainskoe dvizhenie kak sovremennyi etap iuzhnorusskago separatizma*. Kiev: I. N. Kushnerev, 1912.
Siefert, Marsha, ed. *Extending the Borders of Russian History: Essays in Honor of Alfred J. Rieber*. New York: Central European University Press, 2003.
Skinner, Barbara. "Orthodoxy Triumphant? Reassessing the 1839 'Reunification' of Greek Catholics." Unpublished paper, 2011.
———. *The Western Front of the Eastern Church: Uniate and Orthodox Conflict in 18th-Century Poland, Ukraine, Belarus, and Russia*. DeKalb: Northern Illinois University Press, 2009.

Slezkine, Yuri. "The USSR as a Communal Apartment, or How a Socialist State Promoted Ethnic Particularism." *Slavic Review* 53, no. 2 (1994): 414–52.
Sliosberg, Henri. *Baron Horace-O. de Gunzbourg: Sa vie, son oeuvre*. Paris: Pascal, 1933.
Slocum, John W. "Who, and When, Were the Inorodtsy? The Evolution of the Category of 'Aliens' in Imperial Russia." *Russian Review* 57, no. 2 (1998): 173–90.
Smele, Jonathan D., and Anthony Heywood, eds., *The Russian Revolution of 1905: Centenary Perspectives*. New York: Routledge, 2005.
Smirnov, Viktor. *Rossiia v bronze: Pamiatnik Tysiacheletiiu Rossii i ego geroi*. Novgorod: Russkaia provintsiia, 1993.
Snow, George E. "The Years 1881–1894 in Russia: A Memorandum Found in the Papers of N. Kh. Bunge." *Transactions of the American Philosophical Society* 71, pt. 6 (1981): 1–76.
Snyder, Timothy. *Bloodlands: Europe between Hitler and Stalin*. New York: Basic Books, 2010.
———. *The Reconstruction of Nations: Poland, Ukraine, Lithuania, Belarus, 1569-1999*. New Haven: Yale University Press, 2003.
Staliunas, Darius. *Making Russians: Meaning and Practice of Russification in Lithuania and Belarus after 1863*. New York: Rodopi, 2007.
Stauter-Halsted, Keely. *The Nation in the Village: The Genesis of Peasant National Identity in Austrian Poland, 1848–1914*. Ithaca: Cornell University Press, 2001.
Stepanov, A. D., and A. A. Ivanov, eds., *Chernaia sotnia: Istoricheskaia entsiklopediia*. Moscow: Institut Russkoi tsivilizatsii, 2008.
Stephan, John J. *The Russian Fascists: Tragedy and Farce in Exile, 1925–1945*. New York: Harper and Row, 1978.
Stone, Daniel. *The Polish-Lithuanian State, 1386–1795*. Seattle: University of Washington Press, 2001.
Strauss, Herbert A., ed. *Hostages of Modernization: Studies on Modern Antisemitism, 1870–1933*. 2 vols. New York: Walter de Gruyter, 1993.
Subtelny, Orest. *The Mazepists: Ukrainian Separatism in the Early Eighteenth Century*. Boulder, East European Monographs, 1981.
Suny, Ronald Grigor. *Looking toward Ararat: Armenia in Modern History*. Bloomington: Indiana University Press, 1993.
———. *The Making of the Georgian Nation*. Bloomington: Indiana University Press, 1988.
Suny, Ronald Grigor, and Terry Martin, eds. *A State of Nations*. New York: Oxford University Press, 2001.
Surh, Gerald D. "Ekaterinoslav City in 1905: Workers, Jews and Violence." *International Labor and Working-Class History* 64 (2003): 139–66.
———. *1905 in St. Petersburg: Labor, Society, and Revolution*. Stanford: Stanford University Press, 1989.
Svatikov, S. G. *Rossiia i sibir': K istorii sibirskogo oblastnichestva v XIX v*. Prague: Izd. Obshchestva sibiriakov v CHSR, 1929.
Svitlenko, S. I. *Narodnytstvo v Ukraini 60–80-kh rokiv XIX stolittia*. Dnipropetrovsk: Navchal'na kniha, 1999.
Sysyn, Frank. "The Changing Image of the Hetman: On the 350th Anniversary of the Khmel'nyts'kyi Uprising." *Jahrbücher für Geschichte Osteuropas* 46, no. 4 (1998): 531–45.
———. "The Cossack Chronicles and the Development of Modern Ukrainian Culture and National Identity." *Harvard Ukrainian Studies* 14, no. 3–4 (1990): 593–607.
Tabiś, Jan. *Polacy na uniwersytecie Kijowskim, 1834–1863*. Cracow: Wydawnictwo Literackie, 1974.

Talberg, N. D. "The Life's Journey of Archbishop Vitaly." *Pravoslavnaya Rus' (Orthodox Russia)*, 3 (1959): 4.
Tarasenko, Ol'ha. *Stanovlennia ta rozvytok istorychnoi osvity i nauky u Kyivs'komu Universyteti u 1834–1884 rr.* Kiev: Lohos, 1995.
Thaden, Edward C. *Russification in the Baltic Provinces and Finland, 1855–1914*. Princeton: Princeton University Press, 1981.
Thurston, Robert W. *Liberal City, Conservative State: Moscow and Russia's Urban Crisis, 1906–1914*. New York: Oxford University Press, 1987.
Tkacz, Virlana, and Irena Makaryk, eds. *Modernism in Kyiv: Jubilant Experimentation*. Toronto: University of Toronto Press, 2010.
Tolz, Vera. *Russia: Inventing the Nation*. New York: Bloomsbury, 2001.
———. *Russia's Own Orient: The Politics of Identity and Oriental Studies in the Late Imperial and Soviet Periods*. New York: Oxford University Press, 2011.
Trees, Pascal. *Wahlen im Weichselland: Die Nationaldemokraten in Russisch-Polen und die Dumawahlen, 1905–1922*. Stuttgart: Franz Steiner, 2007.
Tron'ko, P. T. ed. *Istoriia gorodov i sel Ukrainskoi SSR: Kiev*. 6 vols. Kiev: Institut istorii akademii nauk USSR, 1979.
Tuminez, Astrid S. *Russian Nationalism since 1856: Ideology and the Making of Foreign Policy*. New York: Rowman and Littlefield, 2000.
Turner, Michael J. *Reform and Respectability: The Making of a Middle-Class Liberalism in Early Nineteenth-Century Manchester*. Manchester, UK: Carnegie Publishing, 1995.
1905 rik u Kyivi ta na Kyivshchini. Kiev, 1926.
Ułaczyn, Henryk. *Kontrakty kijowskie: Szkic historyczno-obyczajowy, 1798–1898*. St. Petersburg: K. Grendyszyński, 1900.
Ul'ianovs'kyi, V. I. *Dvichi profesor: Stepan Holubev v akademichnomu ta universytets'komu kontekstakh*. Kiev: Feniks, 2007.
Vakar, V. [B. Pravdin]. *Nakanune 1905 g. v Kieve (Iiul'skaia stachka 1903 goda)*. Kiev: Kiev-Pechat', 1925.
Velychenko, Stephen. *National History as Cultural Process: A Survey of the Interpretations of Ukraine's Past in Polish, Russian, and Ukrainian Historical Writing from the Earliest Times to 1914*. Edmonton: Canadian Institute of Ukrainian Studies, 1992.
Venturi, Franco. *The Roots of Revolution: A History of the Populist and Socialist Movements in Nineteenth-Century Russia*. New York: Knopf, 1960.
Vetukhiv, Michael. "Arnold Davydovych Margolin, 1877–1956." *Annals of the Ukrainian Academy of Arts and Sciences in the U.S.* 7, nos. 1–2 (1959).
Voblyi, K. G. *Narysy z istorii rosiis'ko-ukrains'koi tsukroburiakovoi promyslovosty*. 3 vols. Kiev: Vseukrains'ka akademiia nauk, 1931.
Vol'f, Efraim. *K istorii ukrainskogo i evreiskogo natsional'nykh dvizhenii do 1917*. Jerusalem: VERBA Publishers, 2000.
Volkov, Shulamit. *Germans, Jews, and Antisemites: Trials in Emancipation*. New York: Cambridge University Press, 2006.
Volokhov, L. F. *Sakharnaia promyshlennost' Rossii v tsifrakh*. Kiev: R. K. Lubkovskii, 1913.
von Hagen, Mark. "Does Ukraine Have a History?" *Slavic Review* 54, no. 3 (1995): 658–73.
———. *War in a European Borderland: Occupations and Occupation Plans in Galicia and Ukraine, 1914–1918*. Seattle: University of Washington Press, 2007.
Von Laue, Theodore H. *Sergei Witte and the Industrialization of Russia*. New York: Columbia University Press, 1963.

Vulpius, Ricarda. "Iazykovaia politika v Rossiiskoi imperii i ukrainskii perevod Biblii (1860–1906)." *Ab Imperio* 2 (2005): 191–224.

———. *Nationalisierung der Religion: Russifizierungspolitik und ukrainische Nationsbildung, 1860–1920*. Wiesbaden: Harrassowitz, 2005.

Wade, Rex A. *The Russian Revolution, 1917*. New York: Cambridge University Press, 2005.

Walicki, Andrzej. *The Slavophile Controversy: History of a Conservative Utopia in Nineteenth-Century Russian Thought*. Oxford: Clarendon Press, 1975.

Wandycz, Piotr. *The Lands of Partitioned Poland, 1795–1918*. Seattle: University of Washington Press, 1974.

Wcislo, Francis W. *Tales of Imperial Russia: The Life and Times of Sergei Witte, 1849-1915*. New York, Oxford University Press, 2011.

Weber, Eugen. *Action Française: Royalism and Reaction in Twentieth-Century France*. Stanford: Stanford University Press, 1962.

Weeks, Theodore R. *From Assimilation to Antisemitism: The "Jewish Question" in Poland, 1850–1914*. DeKalb: Northern Illinois University Press, 2006.

———. *Nation and State in Late Imperial Russia: Nationalism and Russification on the Western Frontier, 1863–1914*. DeKalb: Northern Illinois University Press, 1996.

Wendland, Anna Veronika. *Die Russophilen in Galizien: Ukrainische Konservative zwischen Österreich und Rußland, 1848–1915*. Vienna: Verlag der Österreichischen Akademie der Wissenschaften, 2001.

Werth, Paul W. *At the Margins of Orthodoxy: Mission, Governance, and Confessional Politics in Russia's Volga-Kama Region, 1827–1905*. Ithaca: Cornell University Press, 2002.

Whittaker, Cynthia H. *The Origins of Modern Russian Education: An Intellectual Biography of Count Sergei Uvarov, 1786–1855*. DeKalb: Northern Illinois University Press, 1984.

Williams, Robert C. *Culture in Exile: Russian Émigrés in Germany, 1881–1941*. Ithaca: Cornell University Press, 1972.

Wirtschafter, Elise Kimerling. *Social Identity in Imperial Russia*. DeKalb: Northern Illinois University Press, 1997.

Wortman, Richard S. *Scenarios of Power: Myth and Ceremony in Russian Monarchy*. 2 vols. Princeton: Princeton University Press, 1995–2000.

Wynn, Charters. *Workers, Strikes and Pogroms: The Donbass-Dniepr Bend in Late Imperial Russia, 1870–1905*. Princeton: Princeton University Press, 1992.

Yekelchyk, Serhy. *Ukraine: Birth of a Modern Nation*. New York: Oxford University Press, 2007.

———. *Ukrainofily: Svit ukrains'kykh patriotiv druhoi polovyny XIX stolittia*. Kiev: K.I.S., 2010.

Zahra, Tara. *Kidnapped Souls: National Indifference and the Battle for Children in the Bohemian Lands, 1900–1948*. Ithaca: Cornell University Press, 2008.

Zaionchkovskii, P. A. *Kirillo-Mefodievskoe obshchestvo, 1846–1847*. Moscow: Izd-vo Moskovskogo Universiteta, 1959.

Zaslavskii, D. O. *Rytsar' chernoi sotni: V. V. Shul'gin*. Leningrad: Byloe, 1925.

Żeberek, Gerard. *Początki ruchu socjaldemokratycznego w Kijowie w latach 1889–1903*. Cracow: Wydawnictwo Literackie, 1981.

Zelnik, Reginald E. *Labor and Society in Tsarist Russia: The Factory Workers of St. Petersburg, 1855–1870*. Stanford: Stanford University Press, 1971.

———. *Law and Disorder on the Narova River: The Kreenholm Strike of 1872*. Berkeley: University of California Press, 1995.

Zhuk, A., ed. *Symon Petliura v molodosti: Zbirka spomyniv*. Lviv: Khortytsia, 1936.

Zienkiewicz, Tadeusz. *Polskie życie literackie w Kijowie w latach 1905–1918*. Olsztyn: Wyższa szkoła pedagogiczna w Olsztynie, 1990.
Zimmerman, Joshua D. *Poles, Jews, and the Politics of Nationality: The Bund and the Polish Socialist Party in Late Tsarist Russia, 1892–1914*. Madison: University of Wisconsin Press, 2004.
Zorin, A. L. "Ideologiia 'Pravoslaviia-samoderzhaviia-narodnosti': Opyt rekonstruktsii," *Novoe literaturnoe obozrenie* 26 (1997): 71–104.
———. *Kormia dvuglavogo orla*. Moscow: NLO, 2001.

INDEX

Page numbers followed by letters *m* and *i* refer to maps and illustrations, respectively.

Abaza, A. A., 131
Abdülhamid II (Ottoman sultan), 8
Action Française, 210
Afanas'ev, E. I., 139–40
Afanas'ev, G. E., 173, 189, 196
Akimov, E. K., 229*i*
Aksakov, Ivan, 44, 61
Aleichem, Sholem, 121
Alekseev, S. N., 229*i*
Alexander I (Emperor of Russia), 3, 32
Alexander II (Emperor of Russia): assassination of, 137; Great Reforms of, 5–6, 51; on Khmelnytsky monument, 82, 85; on minority groups, 69; on Sunday school network, 55; Ukrainian separatism and, 88, 93
Alexander III (Emperor of Russia), 6, 137
All-Russian National Union (Nationalist Party), 14, 228–30; delegates in fourth Duma, 258–59; delegates in third Duma, 229*i*, 231; and western zemstva elections of 1911, 249; and western zemstvo bill, 231–33, 242–43
Amosenok, V. G., 229*i*
Andreichuk, M. S., 216, 232
Andriiashev, A. F., 81
Andriichuk, G. A., 229*i*
Annenkov, N. N., 65–66, 66n37, 69, 70–71, 73
antiliberationist movement, 170–72, 185–86; anti-Semitic views in, 157, 159–61, 172; leaders of, 186–87; mobilization of, 198–99; radicalization of, 181–82; resilience of, 273; southwest as major center of, 215; support base of, 187–88. *See also* "truly Russian" movement
anti-Semitism: antiliberationists and, 157, 159–61, 172; Iushchinskii murder case and, 244–48, 251–52, 257–58, 258*i*, 263–65; labor movement and, 148–49; Little Russian lobby and, 13, 14, 16, 21, 31, 34, 53, 59, 61, 77, 81, 97–99, 100, 110, 136, 138, 139; populist politicians and, 141, 144–46, 153–54; radical liberationists on, 173; revolution of 1905 and, 163, 164–69, 174–76; Russian nationalist movement and, 16, 174–76, 217, 219, 228, 235, 236, 244, 245, 252–53, 257–58, 263–64, 273; Stolypin assassination and, 250–51; "truly Russian" movement and, 185, 186, 194, 195, 199, 200–204, 208–9; World War I and, 275. *See also* pogroms
Antonovich, A. Ia., 134n70
Antonovich, Dmytro (D. V.), 107, 151, 277
Antonovich, Vladimir, 50–51, 221; as Hromada's leader, 100–101; and Imperial Geographic Society, 79; and imperial officials, 56, 74, 110; and international archaeological conference (1899), 107; and Khmelnytsky statue project, 81, 82; and Kiev Slavic Philanthropic Society, 80; and Lemberg University, 105–6; and *Osnova*, 52, 53; after Polish revolt of 1863, 64; on radicalization of Little Russian activists, 109; Russian nationalists' rejection of, 266; at St. Vladimir's University, 76, 102; Ukrainian nationalists' claim on, 269

Atanazevich, I. M., 229*i*
Austria. *See* Galicia; Habsburg empire
autocracy: in borderlands, imperial policies promoting, 31–32, 36–38; demise of, 277; Little Russian idea and, 13, 34–35, 39, 42–47, 55–56, 63–64, 67–68, 72–74, 77, 87, 88, 112, 230, 271; Little Russian idea and potential threats to, 45–46, 48–49, 55, 57, 65–67; nationality concept and, 38; national minorities and struggle against, 6–7; Russian nationalism and challenges to, 5–6, 175
Azbuka (agency), 279

Balalaev, N. S., 229*i*
Balashev, P. N., 200, 214
Balashev family, 120
banking industry, in Kiev, 121, 132
Bantysh-Kamenskii, D. N., 34
Beauvois, Daniel, 141
Beilis, Mendel, 17, 248, 252, 253, 257
Bezak, A. P., 69, 70, 71, 74
Bezak, F. N., 214, 229*i*, 262, 266
Bezborodko, A. A., 30
Bibikov, D. G., 40, 42–43
Bliokh, I. S., 68n50, 132, 134
Bobrinskii, A. A., 214, 274
Bobrinskii, G. A., 274–75
Bobrinskii, V. A., 229*i*
Bobrinskii family, 120
Bogdanov, S. M., 143–44, 215, 217, 232, 249
Bogdanovich, S. N., 223
Bogrov, D. G., 250
Bolsheviks: in civil war, 278–79; invasion of Ukraine, 277; nationalizing experiment of, 280
Boyer, John, 145
Branicki, Vladislav, 68n50
Brest-Litovsk, Treaty of, 278
Brodskii, Abraham, 133
Brodskii, Isaak, 130
Brodskii, Israel, 120, 134
Brodskii, Lazar, 120, 141n117, 144
Brodskii, Lev, 120, 132, 152, 220; during October days of 1905, 163, 168, 169
Brodskii family, 69, 120; charitable activities of, 127, 142; in Kiev city council, 129; and Kiev Literacy Society, 142, 152; and Kiev Polytechnical Institute, 142, 145; and liberationists, 152, 153, 159; newspaper founded by, 133; pogrom of 1881 and, 137–38; water company of, 130
Brotherhood of Taras, 107
Bulygin, A. G., 156, 175
Bundists, 151, 202
Bunge, N. Kh., 131, 134

Carpatho-Rus′ Society, 225
cartel, sugar, 132, 135, 136
Catherine II the Great (Empress of Russia), 3, 30, 31–32
Chaplinskii, G. G., 246, 247, 248, 266
Cheberiak, Vera, 252
Chernyshevskii, N. G., 49, 50, 54, 60
Chikhachev, D. N., 214
Chokolov, N. I., 141
Chubinskii, P. P., 64, 79, 91–92, 93–94
Chykalenko, Evhen, 107, 109, 183, 189, 198, 221, 240, 277
Circle of Russian Women, 199
civil war, 278–79
Commission for the Analysis of Historical Documents. *See* Kiev Commission for the Analysis of Historical Documents
Committee of Young Ukraine, 107
constructivist theories of nationalism, 10
Cossack Hetmanate, 26–29, 28*m*, 44; relations with Russia, 26–27, 29–30
Cossacks: as defenders of Orthodox faith, 25–26, 30, 30n24, 31; after Hetmanate's demise, 30; and Little Russian idea, 12, 13, 21; origins of, 24; and Polish-Lithuanian Commonwealth, 25, 26; Soviet historians on, 282
Cyril and Methodius, 22
Cyril and Methodius Brotherhood, 44–47
Czech nationalism, 145

Demchenko, Ia. G., 185, 192, 208, 217, 234, 239
Demchenko, V. Ia., 234, 265, 267, 271, 278, 280; in Duma elections of 1912, 256, 257, 258; western zemstvo bill and, 249, 262
Den′ (periodical), 61
Dmowski, Roman, 198
Dnieper region: Cossack Hetmanate in, 26–29, 28*m*; diverse population of, 21;

and East Slavic civilization, 35, 38–39, 40, 41, 56; Gogol on, 38–39; "Istoriia Rusov" on, 34, 34n37; and Little Russian idea, 12–13, 21–22, 33–34, 35; Mongol rule in, 22–24; Polish-Lithuanian Commonwealth in, 12, 13, 21, 27, 28*m*, 29; in Russian empire, 30–32; Rus' state in, 22. *See also* left bank of Dnieper; right bank of Dnieper; southwestern borderlands
Dobrynin, N. P., 140, 144, 159, 170, 200, 249; in "truly Russian" movement, 186, 195, 212, 213
Dolgorukov, V. A., 65
Dondukov-Korsakov, A. M., 79–80, 84, 85, 91, 92, 93, 94
Dontsov, Dmytro, 283
Double-Headed Eagle, 199, 234, 253; Iushchinskii murder case and, 245, 246, 248, 257–58, 258*i*, 263, 265, 267
Dragomanov, M. P., 50, 51–52; critique of Little Russian idea, 90–91; ethnographic research by, 78; exile of, 93, 94–95; after Polish revolt of 1863, 64; radical reinterpretation of Little Russia idea, 95, 99; rise in Little Russian lobby, 91–92; Russian nationalists on, 235; and Shul'gin, 77, 78, 90; at St. Vladimir's University, 76; on unity of East Slavs, 87n2, 90; writings of, 101, 104
Dragomirov, M. I., 110, 111, 142, 157
Drentel'n, A. R., 104, 137
Drug naroda (newspaper), 81, 84
Duma, imperial: first, dissolution of, 197–98; first, elections to (1906), 188–91; first, southwestern deputies at, 191–92; fourth, elections to (1912), 254–55; plans for, 6, 156, 170–71; second, dissolution of, 211; second, elections to (Jan 1907), 202–6; second, southwestern deputies at, 206–7; third, delegates at, 215–16, 229*i*, 231; third, elections to (fall 1907), 212–15; third, western zemstvo bill and, 231–33, 242–43
duma, Kiev, 128–31; anti-Semitic rhetoric in, 144, 146; building of, 131*i*; corruption in, 130, 134, 140, 153; elections of 1871 for, 128–29; elections of 1902 for, 143–44; elections of 1906 for, 194–95; during October days of 1905, 164–65, 165*i*, 166*i*; Orthodox delegates in, 139–40; populist politicians in, 153–54, 159, 170
Durnovo, P. N., 175
Dvuglavyi orel (newspaper), 234, 242, 251, 263, 265, 267, 269; cartoon of Shul'gin in, 267, 268*i*
Dziennik Kijowski (newspaper), 184, 191, 198

East Slavic civilization: Dnieper region as spiritual center of, 35, 38–39, 40, 41, 56; Kievan Synopsis on, 27, 29; Little Russian idea and, 12, 14, 53, 223, 259; Slavophiles on, 44; "truly Russian" activists on, 202–3, 208; Ukrainian nationalists on, 152. *See also* Orthodox East Slavs
Eisman, Gustav-Adol'f, 139
elections, imperial Duma: of 1906, 188–91; of 1907 (fall), 212–15; of 1907 (January), 202–6; of 1912, 254–55
elections, Kiev's municipal: of 1871, 128–29; of 1902, 143–44; of 1906, 194–95
electoral curiae, nationalization of, 211, 249; calls for, 225, 227, 228, 231–33; opposition to, 232, 240, 241, 242, 262; western zemstvo bill and, 240–43
emancipation of the serfs, 51, 54, 117
émigrés, 279–80; radicalization of, 281, 283–84
Ems decree, 93, 104, 183; efforts to reverse, 94, 110; impact on Little Russian lobby, 99, 100
equal rights, campaign for. *See* liberationist parties
estate system, 32; Cossack Hetmanate and, 27, 29; in Dnieper region, 21, 32; vs. Little Russian idea, 22, 35, 42; vs. popular sovereignty, 1–2; vs. western zemstvo bill, 241
Europe: antiliberal popular emancipation movements in, 209–10; city councils in, 129; populist politics in, 141, 145; spread of nationalism in, 1; urban politics in, 117–18, 119

famine, Ukrainian (1932–33), 282, 284
fascism, 281, 283–84
Flavian (metropolitan of Kiev), 253

Florinskii, T. D., 107–8, 193, 216
France: nationalist movement in, 210; voting rights in, mid-nineteenth century, 129n42. *See also* French Revolution; Napoleonic wars
Franko, Ivan, 95, 100, 101, 106, 198
French Revolution, and modern nationalism, 1, 38

Galagan, G. P., 41, 47, 51, 52, 74, 80
Galicia, 22; Dragomanov's influence in, 95; Hrushevs'kyi's move to, 106; Kiev-based activists and, 44, 54, 72–73, 80; Little Russian idea and, 41–42, 55; after partition of Commonwealth, 31; radical activists in, 87, 88, 90, 106–8; Russian nationalists' interest in, 225, 227, 234; Ukrainian nationalism in, 72, 87, 88, 107, 283; World War I and, 274–76, 280
Galician-Russian Society, Kiev chapter of, 234
Galician Ukrainian orthography, 55, 62, 104
Gapon, Father, 154, 195
Gintsburgs, 69, 120, 129, 142
Girs, A. F., 219, 242, 246, 248, 253, 254–55
Gizhitskii, A. S., 214
Gogol, Nikolai, 38–39, 223
Golden Horde, 22–24
Golovnin, A. V., 66
Golubev, S. T., 101, 186, 217, 234, 266
Golubev, V. S., 234, 250, 274; Iushchinskii murder case and, 246, 247, 248, 263
Golubiatnikov, P. V., 143, 170, 171, 217
Gorkii, Maksim, 155
Grand Duchy of Lithuania, 24
Great Reforms, 5–6. *See also* emancipation of the serfs
Great Russians: comparison with Little Russians, 53; and Rus' state, theories of, 48
Greek Catholic Church. *See* Uniate (Greek Catholic) Church
Grigorevich-Barskii, K. P., 257–58

Habsburg empire: city councils in, 129n42; harnessing of national ideas in, 8; Ruthenian people in, 41–42; and Ukrainian nationalism, 8, 72, 95, 106. *See also* Galicia
Haidamak revolts, 31, 105
Herzen, A. I., 44, 49, 50, 60
Hetmanate. *See* Cossack Hetmanate

Historical Path (monument), 239–40
Hromada. *See* Kiev Hromada; Odessa Hromada
Hromads'ka dumka (newspaper), 183, 184, 192, 198
Hrushevs'kyi, M. S., 102–3; emigration of, 279; exile under Stalin, 282; fracturing of Russian nationalist movement and, 268–69; government under, 277, 278; growing influence of, 221; and international archaeological conference of 1899, 107; and Kadet Party, 192; vs. Kiev Hromada, 110; move to Galicia, 106; and National Democratic Party, 106; relations with southwestern activists, 111; return to Kiev under Soviet rule, 280–81; vs. Russian nationalists, 237, 259, 260; and Shevchenko's legacy, 240; and Ukrainian national historiography, 152, 183; and Ukrainian separatism, 182–83, 220–21, 222, 277; during World War I, 275, 276
Hrynchenko, Borys, 106, 109, 183

Iakhnenko brothers, 120
Iasnogurskii, F. N., 143; in antiliberationist movement, 170–71, 186, 195; anti-Semitic views of, 144, 159, 213; in Russian nationalist movement, 217; and worker mobilization, 207
Iliodor (monk), 195, 210, 220, 252n46, 280n28
Imperial Academy of Sciences, on Ukrainian language, 152
Imperial Geographic Society, 39, 44; ethnographic expedition to western borderlands, 63, 79; southwestern chapter of, 79–80, 91, 93, 111
inorodtsy (term), 7
intelligentsia, Russian: emergence of, 43–44; and Little Russian idea, 13–14, 44–49; radical critics of late 1850s-early 1860s, 49–56
"Istoriia Rusov," 34, 34n37, 39
Iushchinskii, Andrei, murder of, 244–48, 251–52, 257, 258i; trial following, 263–65
Iuzefovich, Boris (B. M.), 92n18, 108–9, 153, 154, 249n26; in antiliberationist movement, 186, 195, 196, 199, 208; first

INDEX

Duma and, 170–71; penny paper launched by, 199; and Stolypin, 208, 209
Iuzefovich, M. V., 39–40; and ethnographic research, 47; fracturing of Little Russian lobby and, 87, 88, 91–93, 96, 99; and Khmelnytsky project, 81; and *Kievskaia starina*, 101; and Kiev Slavic Philanthropic Society, 80; on Little Russian idea and imperial state, 42, 73–74, 77; and *Osnova*, 52; after Polish revolt of 1863, 65; Ukrainian nationalists on, 221
Iuzefovich, V. M., 49, 50, 52
Ivanov, S. I., 257, 258

Jews: Cossack attacks on, 26; in Duma elections of 1906, 189, 190, 191; in Duma elections of 1907 (fall), 213; in Duma elections of 1907 (January), 204; in Duma elections of 1912, 257; Khmelnytsky monument and, 82, 85; in Kiev, expulsion in 1830s, 37; in Kiev, return after 1863, 69; in Kiev's capitalist elite, 118, 122, 127, 133, 136, 139, 158–59; in Kiev's professional and working classes, 121, 125; in Kiev's urban politics, 129; liberationist parties and, 173, 182; Liberation Movement and, 150–51, 155, 158; Ministry of Finance and, 134; populist politicians on, 119; radical groups and, 135; railroad lines and, 68; on right bank of Dnieper, 31; scientific racism on, 103; in southwestern borderlands, 32; in sugar industry, 68, 120; Ukrainian nationalists and, 277. *See also* anti-Semitism

Kadet Party, 172–73; dissolution of first Duma and, 197–98; in Duma elections of 1906, 182, 189, 190, 191; in Duma elections of 1907, 202, 204; in Duma elections of 1912, 257; and nationalist movements, 184; Polish division of, 184; support base of, 184–85
Katkov, M. N., 5, 6, 66, 71n62, 82n128
Khanenko, B. I., 241
Khanenko family, 120
Kharitonenko family, 120
khlopomany, 51, 52, 56, 64

Khmelnytsky, Bohdan, 26; monument to, 81–85, 83*i*, 86*i*, 224*i*, 238, 281, 282
Khmelnytsky rebellion, 26; Little Russian activists on, 47–48, 61; motivations for, 29
Kholm, 76, 102, 218, 227, 230
Khrapovitskii, Antonii, 196, 212, 213, 256, 260, 266, 278, 280
Khriakov, N. G., 130
Kiev: capitalist development of, 120–25, 123*i*, 124*i*, 127–28, 128*i*, 132; as center of East Slavic civilization, 27; after civil war, 280; districts in, 126*m*; elites in, 118, 119, 122–23, 125–34, 141–42, 158–59, 181; Jewish population of, 37, 69, 118, 121, 122, 125; Little Russian activists in, 13, 14, 39–40, 44–45; Mogila's campaign to revive Orthodox Church in, 25; October days (1905) in, 162–69, 165*i*, 166*i*; Orthodox intelligentsia in, emergence of, 75–78, 85; outlying districts of, 125, 130, 137, 142, 157, 168; pogrom of 1881 in, 137–38; pogrom of 1905 in, 167–69, 175; populist politicians in, 118–19, 139–41, 143–44; private utility companies in, 127–28, 143; professional classes in, 120–21; Russian population of, 277; in Rus' state, 12, 22; Shevchenko centenary celebration in, 271, 272*i*; socialist movements in, 134–35, 142–43; strikes in, 146–49, 154–55, 174; Tatar sacking of, 22; universities in, 37–38; urban planning campaign of 1830s-50s in, 36; urban politics in, 118–19, 128–29; working classes in, 124–25; during World War I, 277. *See also* duma, Kiev
Kiev (newspaper), 235, 238, 266, 267, 271; on Shevchenko statue project, 239, 270
Kievan Synopsis, 27, 29
Kiev Club of Russian Nationalists, 217–18, 221, 222–26, 230; activities of, 237, 255; membership of, 234, 235; publication of, 224*i*; rifts within, 254, 265–66, 267; on Shevchenko statue project, 269–70; western zemstvo bill and, 231, 242, 249
Kiev Commission for the Analysis of Historical Documents, 40–43; Cyrilo-Methodian affair and, 45; emancipation of the serfs and, 51; Hrushevs'kyi and, 103, 106;

Kiev Commission for the Analysis of Historical Documents (*continued*) imperial de-polonization policies and, 63, 74; journal of, 48; and Khmelnytsky statue project, 81; and new Orthodox intelligentsia, 75, 76, 77

Kiev Hromada, 52; in 1890s, 109–10; diverse views within, 72, 100–101; imperial policies and, 55, 63, 65–66; Polish patriots' complaints against, 56; on Ukrainian language, 62

Kievlianin (historical almanac), 40, 77

Kievlianin (newspaper), 79, 100; antiliberationist views in, 160; anti-Semitic views in, 138, 145; censors' reactions to, 84; contributors to, 105; critique of capitalism in, 135–36; on Iushchinskii murder, 248; on Khmelnytsky monument, 84, 85; liberal alternative to, 134; under Pikhno, 97, 98; on pogrom of 1905, 170; rift within Russian nationalist movement and, 265, 266; Russian nationalist views in, 153, 174–75; under Shul'gin, 77–78, 263; and "truly Russian" movement, 192, 201, 207; on Ukrainian nationalism, 259

Kiev Literacy Society, 97, 142
Kiev Literary-Artistic Society, 142, 152, 158
Kiev Polytechnical Institute, 141–42, 145, 155, 158, 169
Kiev Russian Circle, 154
Kievskaia dubinka (penny paper), 208, 209
Kievskaia starina (journal), 101, 102, 103, 104, 110, 111
Kievskii narodnyi kalendar' (almanac), 81
Kievskii telegraf (newspaper), 92, 93
Kievskoe slovo (newspaper), 134
Kiev Slavic Philanthropic Society, 80–81, 102
Kiev Stock Committee, 121–22, 132, 134, 142
Kiev Stock Exchange, 127
Kiev Theological Academy, 38, 101–2, 103
Kingdom of Poland: emancipation of the serfs and, 51n110; Kholm in, 76, 218; railroad development and, 68; Russification measures in, 74; separation of Kholm from, 227, 230

Kishinev: antiliberationist parties in, 205n131, 215n20; pogrom of 1903 in, 147n152

Kistiakovskii, A. F., 76; in Imperial Geographic Society expedition, 79; Jewish sympathies of, 133, 136, 138n99; and Kiev Hromada, 100, 101; and liberal critique of Little Russian idea, 96, 99; and Luchitskii, 97; and *Zaria*, 133

Kistiakovskii, Bogdan (B. A.), 107, 173, 189
Kleigel, N. V., 158, 162, 163
Kochubei, V. P., 30
Kogen brothers, 122, 133
Kolokol (periodical), 49, 60
Konisskii, A. I., 140
Konstantin Nikolaevich (Grand Duke), 84
Kostomarov, N. I., 41, 55, 73; and Cyril and Methodius Brotherhood, 44, 45; exile of, 46–47; fracturing of Little Russian lobby and, 89, 94; vs. Herzen, 60; and imperial state, 63, 66, 79, 90; and *Osnova*, 52, 53; after Polish revolt of 1863, 64; publications of, 53, 78–79, 101; Russian nationalists on, 223, 235; on southern and northern Russians, 53, 79; in St. Petersburg, 47, 54, 63
Kotliarevskii, Ivan, 33–34
Kryzhanovskii, E. M., 219
Kryzhanovskii, S. E., 219–20
Kulish, P. A., 41, 42, 55; critique of fellow Little Russians, 72; and Cyril and Methodius Brotherhood, 44; exile of, 46; and imperial state, 74, 89; and *Osnova*, 52; response to radical critics, 61; Russian nationalists on, 235; in St. Petersburg, 47; on unity of East Slavs, 73, 79
Kupernik, L. A., 133, 142, 152, 156, 159, 160

labor movement, 143, 146–49. *See also* strikes
language(s): and Rus' identity, 22; in southwestern borderlands, 2–3. *See also* Russian language; Ukrainian language
Lebedintsev, A. G., 76
Lebedintsev, F. G., 76, 101, 102, 103
Lebedintsev, P. G., 75
left bank of Dnieper: acquisition by Russian empire, 12–13; under Cossack Hetmanate,

27, 28m; gentry from, relocation to Kiev after 1830, 39–40; and Little Russian idea, origins of, 33–34, 35; and Little Russian idea in 1880s, 95–96; and Little Russian idea in 1890s, 106–7; right bank under Polish-Lithuanian Commonwealth and, 31

Lemberg University, chair of Ukrainian history at, 105–6

Lenin, Vladimir Ilyich, 281

Levitskii, O. I., 89–90, 102; in antiliberationist movement, 170, 186; fracturing of Little Russian lobby and, 92n18; and Hrushevs'kyi, 110–11, 221, 221n52, 269; and imperial state, 105, 111; and international archaeological conference of 1899, 107; and *Kievskaia starina*, 101; in municipal elections of 1902, 144; and Shevchenko statue project, 159; and Ukrainian nationalist movement, 221, 277

liberationist parties, 172–73; in Duma elections of 1906, 182, 189, 191; in Duma elections of 1907, 202, 204–5; growing divisions within, 197–98; Kiev's capitalist elite and, 181; Stolypin coup and, 211. *See also* Kadet Party

Liberation Movement, 150; backlash against, 196–97; debate on root cause of people's suffering, 162–63; Jews and, 150–51, 155, 158; and nationalist movements, 182–84; after October (1905) pogroms, 173–74; opposition to, 150, 153–54, 157, 159–61, 170–72, 174; radicalization of, 157–59; rise in Kiev, 151–57; and Ukrainian separatism, 182–84

Lithuania. *See* Polish-Lithuanian Commonwealth

Little Russian activists: antiliberal vision of popular liberation, 146, 147, 149, 150; and antiliberationist parties, 171–72, 186; anti-Semitic views of, 13, 14, 16, 21, 31, 34, 53, 59, 61, 77, 81, 97–99, 100, 110, 136, 138, 139; critique of capitalism by, 135–36, 138, 139; elitist vs. populist elements in, 85–86; emancipation of the serfs and, 51, 54; ethnographic research by, 78–79, 103; expansion of influence of, 13–15, 59, 74–75, 78–80, 85; fracturing of lobby of, 86, 87–100, 105–10, 112; in Galicia, 44, 54, 72–73; vs. Galician radicals, 87, 90; Galician radicals' influence on, 106–8; generational turnover in 1870s, 91–92; and imperial bureaucrats, 22, 78–80, 85, 88, 89, 104–5; vs. industrial leaders, 69; in Kiev, 13, 14, 39–40, 44–45; vs. Kiev's capitalist elites, 133–34; liberal camp of, 95–97, 99, 101; vs. liberationists, 150, 153–54; Moscow Party bosses and Ukrainian functionaries compared to, 282; newspapers published by, 77–78, 81, 84, 93; outreach efforts of, 49, 81; after pogrom of 1905, 170–71; after Polish revolt of 1830-31, 75; after Polish revolt of 1863, 59, 64–65, 75–78; and populist politicians, 118–19, 141, 146, 159–60; radical camp of, 95, 99, 101; scholarship by, 101–3; vs. socialist organizers, 143; in St. Petersburg, 47; vs. Ukrainophiles, 89; violent rhetoric of, 82, 85

Little Russian idea, 12–13; criticism in early 1860s, 60–63, 86; and de-polonization campaign, 73–74; Dnieper region and origins of, 12–13, 21–22; durable ideological byproducts of, 273; in early 1860s, 60–64; evolution of, 112; as fantasy, 35; imperial state and, 13, 34–35, 39, 42–47, 55–56, 63–64, 67–68, 72–74, 77, 87, 88, 112, 230, 271; in interwar context, 284; liberal reinterpretations of, 95–97, 99; literary and historical efforts in support of, 38–43, 78–79; origins of, 33–34; and pan-Slavic movement, 80; vs. Polish nationalism, 13, 14, 22, 34, 42, 43, 46, 49, 52–53, 55–56, 63, 65; after Polish revolt of 1830-31, 13, 22, 56–57; after Polish revolt of 1863, 59, 72–74; and potential threats to autocracy, 45–46, 48–49, 55, 57, 65–67; radical reinterpretation of, 95, 99; and Russian intellectual life of mid-nineteenth century, 13–14, 44, 47–49, 59–60; and Russian nationalist movement, 109, 217, 223, 235, 237, 238–39, 243, 259, 262–63, 266, 267, 272–73; and Slavophiles, 44, 61–62; and "truly Russian" movement, 181, 193–94, 205, 215; and

Little Russian idea (*continued*)
  Ukrainian nationalism, 16–17, 87, 94, 112, 221, 240, 269, 278; and unity of East Slavs, 12, 14, 53, 223, 259
Little Russian language, 66. *See also* Ukrainian language
Little Russians, 2, 12
Liubinskii, A. I., 143, 171, 195, 227
Lokot', T. V., 234–35, 238, 278, 280
Luchitskii, I. V., 97, 100, 101; Duma elections of 1906 and, 189; Duma elections of 1907 and, 205, 215; and Kadet Party, 173; and Kiev Literacy Society, 97, 142; and Kiev Literary-Artistic Society, 152; liberal views promoted by, 109, 156, 158; pogrom of 1905 and, 169; resignation from Kiev duma, 170; and Shevchenko statue project, 159, 239; and Ukrainian nationalists, 192–93
Lueger, Karl, 145
Lur'e, S. A., 173, 182
Lysenko, M. V., 183

Magdeburg law, 24, 32, 36, 233
Maiorova, Olga, 54
Makarov, A. A., 256
Maksimovich, M. A., 40, 41, 47, 53, 54, 66, 77, 80, 81, 91
Margolin, Arnol'd, 168, 196; emigration of, 279; Iushchinskii murder case and, 251–52, 264; Kadet Party and, 173, 182; Ukrainian autonomy and, 277
Margolin, D. S., 122; and Kiev Literary-Artistic Society, 142; and Liberation Movement, 159; during October days of 1905, 163, 168; tram system of, 127, 130
Mariia Nikolaevna (Grand Duchess), 47
Markevich, N. A., 39, 43
mass politics, in southwestern borderlands, 18, 119, 273; antiliberationist movement and, 172; revolution of 1905 and, 14; rise of, 146–49; "truly Russian" movement and, 175, 181, 211. *See also* populist politicians
Mazepa, Ivan, 29–30
Menshikov, M. O., 226, 228, 266
Mickiewicz, Adam, 45

Mikeshin, M. O., 81–82; Khmelnytsky statue, 82–85, 83*i*, 86*i*
Miliukov, P. N., 184
Ministry of Finance, and Kiev's capitalist elites, 131–32, 134, 135, 142
minority groups: as *inorodtsy*, 7; Kiev governor-general's policies on, 69–72; liberationists on, 182–85; nationalist movements of, 6–7; radical critics vs. Little Russian activists on, 60; after revolution of 1905, 220–21; Soviet terror campaign and, 282; Stolypin's directives on, 236–38; during World War I, 275. *See also* Jews; Poles
Mogila, Petr, 25–26, 101, 110
Mogila Collegium/Academy, 25, 27, 29, 38, 283
Monarchist Party, 171, 172, 195
Mongol rule, 22–24
Muscovy, 12, 24; and Cossack Hetmanate, 26–27, 29

Napoleonic wars: Polish patriots during, 3, 4; and spread of national ideals, 1, 32
narod (term): meanings of, 13n48. *See also* peasants
narodnost' (term), 38
"national amphibianism," 11n46
National Democratic (ND) Party, 106, 198
nationalism: as challenge to Russian empire, 1–2, 3–9; constructivist theories of, 10; empires harnessing, 8; French Revolution and, 1, 38; Napoleonic wars and spread of, 1, 32; as product of protracted agitation, 10–11; role in shaping modern societies, 11. *See also* Polish nationalism; Russian nationalist movement; Ukrainian nationalist movement
Nationalist Party. *See* All-Russian National Union
nationalization of political structures, in southwest: calls for, 69–72, 217–18, 225–30; elections to third Duma and, 212–14; imperial bureaucracy and, 211, 262; opposition to, 240–41, 262; western zemstvo campaign and, 231–33, 240–43
National Socialism, 145

National Union of a New Generation, 283–84

Naumenko, V. P., 96–97, 100; imperial Duma elections of 1906 and, 189; and international archaeological conference of 1899, 107, 108; and Kadet Party, 173; and Kiev Literacy Society, 97, 142; and Kiev Literary-Artistic Society, 152; and *Kievskaia starina*, 101, 104, 111; liberal views promoted by, 109; and Shevchenko statue project, 239, 240; and Ukrainian Scientific Society, 221

ND. *See* National Democratic Party

New Duma Party, 143

Nicholas I (Emperor of Russia): Little Russian idea and, 35, 43, 46; and nationality concept *(narodnost')*, 38; policies after Polish revolt of 1830-31, 4, 35–36, 233

Nicholas II (Emperor of Russia): dissolution of Duma by, 197; nationalist movements and, 7; response to liberationists, 156; and SRN, 175; visit to Kiev, 249, 250, 251*i*; during World War I, 276–77

Normanist theory, 22; rejection of, 40, 54, 106, 281

northwestern borderlands, after Polish revolt of 1863, 14, 58–59

October Manifesto, 163

Octobrist Party, 215, 227, 231, 233, 242

Odessa: Jewish merchants in, 122n23; October (1905) pogrom in, 169n108

Odessa Hromada, 95

Orlov, A. F., 45

Orthodox clerics: and Cossack leaders, 26; in imperial Duma, 215, 229*i*; Iushchinskii murder case and, 263; and Little Russian idea, 12, 13, 21; right-bank activities after 1830, 40; and Russian nationalists, 253, 257; and "truly Russian" activists, 195–96, 200, 203, 214; western zemstvo campaign and, 231

Orthodox East Slavs: Little Russian idea on, 12, 21, 55; "Russians" as shorthand for, 2. *See also* East Slavic civilization

Orthodox faith: adoption by Rus' state, 22; in borderlands, imperial policies promoting, 31–32, 36–38; under Cossack Hetmanate, 27; Cossack leaders as defenders of, 25–26, 30, 30n24; Little Russian idea and, 34; preservation under Mongol rule, 24; preservation under Polish-Lithuanian Commonwealth, 41; Slavophiles on, 44

Orthodox landowners: absentee, 120, 187, 200; in Duma elections, 173, 190–91, 200, 204; vs. Polish landowners, 71–72; in third Duma, 214; "truly Russian" activists and, 200, 204

Osnova (journal), 52–54, 61, 62, 72, 92

Oświata organizations, 220, 221–22

Ottoman empire, harnessing of national ideas in, 8

Pale of Settlement: calls for abolition of, 186; Kiev excluded from, 37, 69, 125

pan-Slavic movement, 80, 80n114

Party of Legal Order, 171, 186

peasants *(narod)*: antiliberationist forces and, 188; capitalist development and, 123–24; under Cossack Hetmanate, 27, 29; Duma delegates, 206, 216, 229*i*, 258; in elections to first Duma (1906), 188, 190; in elections to second Duma (January 1907), 204–5; in elections to third Duma (fall 1907), 215; emancipation of the serfs and, 51, 54, 117; Kiev duma's Orthodox delegates and, 139–40; Little Russian activists and, 50–51, 78–79; in Little Russian idea, 13, 41, 43; migration to Kiev, 124, 125; vs. Polish aristocracy, 51–53; under Polish-Lithuanian Commonwealth, 24, 31, 41; political parties of early 1900s and, 187, 188; populist groups of 1850s-60s and, 49–50; Slavophiles on, 44; "truly Russian" movement and, 201; western zemstvo campaign and, 232

Peter the Great (Emperor of Russia), 29–30

Petliura, Symon, 198, 278, 279

Petrunkevich, I. I., 95–96

Pikhno, D. I., 97–99, 263; anti-Semitic views of, 186; critique of capitalism by, 135–36; in Imperial Geographic Society, 111; Iushchinskii murder and, 246, 248; Little Russian idea and, 99; moderate views

Pikhno, D. I. (*continued*)
 of, 209, 254; on pogrom of 1905, 170; and Reva, 105; and Russian nationalist movement, 217; and Shul'gin, 97, 98; in State Council, 207, 225; in "truly Russian" movement, 186, 199, 200, 201, 212, 213; and western zemstvo bill, 225, 227, 241
Pirogov, N. I., 55
Platon (bishop of Chigirin), 203, 205, 207
Pobedonostsev, K. P., 98
Pochaev monks, 195, 200, 205, 207, 210, 214, 259; newspaper published by, 252, 254
Pogodin, M. P., 44, 48, 53, 54
pogroms: of 1881, 137–38, 168; of 1905, 167–69, 175; of 1918, 279
Poland: after World War I, 277, 280. *See also* Kingdom of Poland; Polish-Lithuanian Commonwealth
Poles: antiliberationist parties and, 172; capitalist development and, 68, 120–21; in Duma elections of 1906, 189, 190; in Duma elections of 1907, 204, 213, 214; in Duma elections of 1912, 257; Kadet Party and, 198; Khmelnytsky monument and, 82, 85; Kiev Hromada on, 100; in Kiev's elite, 136; in Kiev's professional classes, 120–21; in Kiev's urban politics, 129; Little Russian idea on, 13, 14, 16, 21, 31, 34, 52, 59, 73–74, 77, 81, 97–99; Ministry of Finance and, 134; policies discriminating against, in 1860s, 69–70; radical groups and, 135; Russian nationalists on, 16, 217, 228, 234; Russian radicals on, 49, 60; Soviet terror campaign and, 282; in State Council, 225; "truly Russian" parties on, 194, 203, 208; Ukrainian nationalists and, 277; western zemstvo bill and, 232, 240, 241, 242, 262. *See also* Polish nationalism; Polish nobles (*szlachta*)
Poliakov, S. S., 68n50, 131, 134
Polish-Lithuanian Commonwealth, 24; Cossacks and, 25, 26; in Dnieper region, 12, 13, 21, 27, 28m, 29; Khmelnytsky rebellion in, 26; partitions of, 2, 3, 31; peasants under, 24, 31, 41; Rus' lands under, 24–25

Polish nationalism: imperial officials' efforts to respond to, 58; Liberation Movement and, 184; Little Russian idea as counterbalance to, 13, 14, 22, 34, 42, 43, 46, 49, 52–53, 55–56, 63, 65; after revolution of 1905, 220, 221–22; Russian radicals' sympathy for, 49, 60; in southwestern borderlands, origins of, 32–33; in western borderlands, 3–4, 6, 35
Polish nobles (*szlachta*): Antonovich and, 50–51; Cossack attacks on, 26; in Dnieper region, 21, 31; emancipation of the serfs and, 51–52; imperial policies toward, 4, 13, 32; insurrections against Russian state, 4, 13; move to Rus' lands, 24; peasant suffering under, 41; after revolt of 1830-31, 36, 40, 42–43; in southwestern borderlands, 3, 32; in sugar industry, 68; in western borderlands, 3–4, 6, 35
Polish revolt of 1830-31, 35; imperial policies after, 4, 13; Little Russian activists after, 13, 22, 56–57, 75
Polish revolt of 1863, 58; imperial policies after, 4, 14, 57, 59, 68–69; Little Russian activists after, 59, 64–65, 75–78
Poltava, Battle of, 30
popular sovereignty: vs. estate system, 1–2; vs. Russian nationalism, 5–6
populist politicians, Kiev's: antiliberal vision of popular liberation, 146, 147, 149, 150; anti-Semitic views of, 141, 144–46, 153–54; emergence of, 118–19, 139–41, 143–44; vs. liberationists, 150, 153–54, 159; Little Russian activists and, 118–19, 141, 146, 159–60; after pogrom of 1905, 170–71
Postnyi, F. Ia., 187, 197, 205, 217, 219; penny papers launched by, 207–8, 209, 213
Potocki family, 120
Progressive Bloc, 276
Prokopovich, Feofan, 29
Prosvita (club), 183–84, 192, 238

Rada (newspaper), 198, 201
Rada (parliament), 277
radical movements: of 1870s, 87; of 1880s, 95; of 1890s, 106–7; of 1900s, 173

radicals, Russian: criticism of Little Russian activists, 60; sympathy for Polish cause, 49, 60
railroads, southwestern, 68, 121, 125, 132, 134
Ratner, M. B., 143, 156, 163, 164, 165
Red Terror, 277
Repnin, N. G., 34
Reva, I. M., 105, 136, 256; new zemstva and, 112, 249; in "truly Russian" movement, 186, 200, 203, 212, 216
Revolutionary Ukrainian Party (RUP), 107, 151
revolution of 1905, 6; anti-Semitism in aftermath of, 174–76; Kiev's October days, 162–69, 165*i*, 166*i*; Little Russian activists after, 14; minority groups after, 7; period leading up to, 151–61; reverberations in Kiev, 150–51; Russian nationalists on, 235
Rieber, Alfred J., 8
right bank of Dnieper: acquisition by Russian empire, 13, 31–32; in Polish-Lithuanian Commonwealth, 27, 28*m*, 31; Polish nationalist movement in, 32–33; Ukrainian nationalist movement in, 107. *See also* southwestern borderlands
right-wing parties, 171–72. *See also* "truly Russian" movement
Rogger, Hans, 210n158
Rus': imperial government's interest in history of, 32, 36; Kievan Synopsis on, 27, 29; origins of, 22, 40, 48, 54, 106; Orthodox East Slavic people as descendants of, 12, 21
Rus' lands: in eleventh century, 23*m*; under Cossack Hetmanate, 26–29, 28*m*; under Golden Horde, 22–24; under Polish-Lithuanian Commonwealth, 24–25; under Russian rule, 29–35, 33*m*
Russia: histories of, southwestern borderlands in, 39, 40; Kievan Synopsis on, 27
Russian Brotherhood, 171, 194
Russian empire: and Cossacks, 29–30; and Dnieper region, 12–13, 21; ethnic diversity in, discussions of, 4–5; nationalism as challenge to, 1–2, 3–9; Rus' lands under, 29–35, 33*m*; southwestern nationalism and fate of, 15–17
Russian Gathering (club), 154, 170–71, 186

Russian language: imperial policies and, 4; Little Russian activists and, 62, 77–78, 80–81, 98, 108; primacy of, All-Russian National Union on, 228
Russian nationalist movement, southwestern, 2, 9, 14; all-imperial political party of, 228–30; and anti-Semitism, 16, 174–76, 217, 219, 228, 235, 236, 244, 245, 252–53, 257–58, 263–64, 273; and challenges to autocratic system, 5–6, 175; during civil war, 278–79; destabilizing impact of, 16–17, 175, 243; Duma delegates representing, 216, 229*i*, 231; Duma elections of 1912 and, 256–59; emergence of, revolution of 1905 and, 174–76; expansion of, 233–36, 243; and imperial politics, 14–15, 225–27, 230–31, 233, 244; Little Russian idea and, 109, 217, 223, 235, 237, 238–39, 243, 259, 262–63, 266, 267, 272–73; officials' attitudes toward, 219–20, 230, 253, 254–55, 262, 263, 271; radicalization of, 245, 250–54, 259–60, 273; rise of, 212–13, 216–20; and Shevchenko statue project, 260–61, 269–70; tensions within, 243, 245, 248, 254, 256, 262–68, 273; Ukrainian nationalist movement and, common origins of, 16–17; vs. Ukrainian nationalists, 192–93, 221, 222–23, 235, 237, 238, 259–61; and western zemstva elections of 1911, 249; and western zemstvo campaign, 231–33; World War I and, 274–76. *See also* "truly Russian" movement
Russian Nationalist Party, 212
Russian nationality, Uvarov on, 36
Russian National Student Union, 234
Russification: Kiev Hromada and, 56; after Polish revolt of 1863, 4, 59; problems for, 5–6
Ruthenians, 42, 54

Savenko, A. I., 251*i*, 280; during civil war, 279; in Duma elections of 1912, 256, 257; and liberationist movement, 271, 276; moderate views of, 228, 265; and nationalization of political structures, calls for, 227, 232; Nicholas II's visit to Kiev and, 249; on occupation of Galicia, 274;

Savenko, A. I. (*continued*)
  opposition to Ukrainian separatism, 277;
  vs. radical nationalists, 267; in Russian
  nationalist movement, 216, 218, 223, 230,
  234, 242; and Shevchenko statue project,
  239, 260; in "truly Russian" movement,
  187, 192, 200, 202
Savvich, P. S., 175
Scandinavian Vikings, in Rus' history, 22,
  40, 54
Schönerer, Georg Ritter von, 145
Schorske, Carl, 118, 145
scientific racism, 103-4
SD. *See* Social Democratic Party
serfs: emancipation under Alexander II, 51,
  54, 117; in Polish-Lithuanian Commonwealth, 24
Shcheglovitov, I. G., 244, 247, 248, 253
Shchegolev, S. N., 237, 259-60, 266
Shevchenko, T. G., 41; centenary celebration
  in Kiev, 271, 272*i*; imperial policies and,
  55; imprisonment of, 46; influence of, 75,
  82; and Little Russian idea, 41, 44; monument to, 159-60, 222, 238-40, 260-61,
  269-71, 282-83; problematic legacy of,
  271; Russian nationalists on, 235, 266,
  267, 269; in St. Petersburg, 47; Ukrainophile claims on, 94, 193, 240
Shevchenko Scientific Society, 106, 222, 269
Shlikhter, A. G., 147, 153, 154-55; during
  October days of 1905, 162, 165, 166*i*
Shmakov, A. S., 110
Shteingel', F. R., 190, 191, 192
Shul'gin, Iakov (Ia. M.), 77, 95, 101,
  221, 277
Shul'gin, Vitalii Iakovlevich, 76-78, 97, 232;
  fracturing of Little Russian lobby and,
  87, 88, 90, 91, 96; Imperial Geographic
  Society expedition and, 79; and *Kievlianin*,
  77-78; and Kiev Slavic Philanthropic
  Society, 80; and Pikhno, 97, 98; Ukrainian
  nationalists on, 221
Shul'gin, V. V.: and art of political spectacle,
  207; during civil war, 279; denounced
  as Jewish sympathizer, 263, 266, 267,
  268*i*; efforts to mobilize rural voters, 200;
  emigration and radicalization of, 280,
  281, 283-84; in fourth Duma elections,
  259; Iushchinskii murder case and, 246,
  248, 263-64, 265, 267; and liberationist
  movement, 271, 276-77; moderate views
  of, 209, 228, 254; opposition to Ukrainian
  separatism, 277; and Russian nationalist
  movement, 217, 219; in third Duma elections, 212, 215; and "truly Russian" movement, 187, 200, 205, 207; and western
  zemstvo bill, 225-26, 242; during World
  War I, 274, 276-77
Shul'hyn, Oleksandr, 277, 278
Sikorskii, I. A., 103, 140, 144, 280; in antiliberationist movement, 186; during civil
  war, 278; Iushchinskii murder case and,
  247, 248, 263; Little Russian idea and,
  259; in Russian nationalist movement,
  217, 218, 266; scientific racism of, 103,
  145, 246; during World War I, 274
Sikorskii, Igor, 280n29
Simirenko brothers, 120
Sinegub, Vladimir, 52n118
Skoropadsky, P. P., 278, 279, 283
Slavophiles, 44, 80n114; Little Russian idea
  and, 44, 61-62
Slovo (newspaper), 54, 60, 80, 93
Social Democratic (SD) Party, 142-43, 151,
  155; in Duma elections of 1906, 182, 188;
  in first Duma, 190; in Kiev's October
  days, 162; in second Duma, 205, 206, 211;
  strikes organized by, 147, 148, 173, 188
Socialist Revolutionary (SR) Party, 142-43,
  151, 152, 155; and Kadet Party, 182, 197;
  in Kiev's October days, 162
socialists, in Kiev, 134-35, 142-43; and
  labor action, 146-49; before revolution of
  1905, 151; road map to popular liberation,
  146, 149
southwestern borderlands, 2, 31, 33*m*; civic
  society in, 15-17; de-polonization of,
  40, 42-43, 75; diversity in, 2-3, 35; and
  East Slavic civilization, 35, 38-39, 40,
  41, 56; in histories of Russia, 39, 40; Little Russian idea and, 56; nationalizing
  experiment in, 2, 15-16; orthodoxy and
  autocracy in, imperial policies promoting,
  31-32, 36-38

Southwestern Railroad company: Witte and, 132, 134, 135n81; workers at, 163, 173, 217n28, 218
soviet, Kiev, 173, 174
Soviet Union: nationality policy of, 280; under Stalin, 281–82; Ukrainian question in, 9
Sovremennik (periodical), 49, 54, 60, 61
Spilka, 188, 198, 202, 239
SR. *See* Socialist Revolutionary Party
SRN. *See* Union of Russian People
Stalin, 281–82
Staliunas, Darius, 59
Stolypin, P. A., 197; assassination of, 250; and minority policies, 220, 236–38; and Russian nationalists, 230–31, 233, 243; second Duma dissolved by, 211; and southwestern activists, 2, 15, 197, 208, 209, 210, 212, 220, 226–27; and third Duma, 215–16; visit to Kiev, 249, 250, 251i; and western zemstvo bill, 231, 233, 241, 242
Storozhenko, A. P., 74
Storozhenko, A. V., 102, 186, 260, 266, 280; new zemstva and, 112, 249
Storozhenko, N. V., 102, 144, 170; in antiliberationist movement, 171, 186; and imperial Duma elections of 1906, 189; and Shevchenko statue project, 159
Storozhenko brothers: during civil war, 278; in Imperial Geographic Society, 111; and Russian nationalist movement, 217, 234
strikes, in Kiev, 146–49; of 1903, 147–49; of 1905, 154–55, 174
St. Sophia Cathedral, Kiev, 25, 75
St. Vladimir's University, 37–38; first rector of, 40; Gogol and, 39n55; Liberation Movement and, 154, 155, 158; Little Russian activists at, 76, 91, 101–2; during October days of 1905, 163, 164; radical youth in 1890s, 107
sugar industry, 68, 69, 120–21; cartel in, 132, 135, 136
Sukhomlinov, V. A., 163, 169, 175, 176; Polish nationalists and, 222; "truly Russian" activists and, 196, 197, 210, 213, 226; during World War I, 275

Sunday schools, southwestern, 50, 52, 55, 63
Suvorin, A. A., 219
szlachta. *See* Polish nobles

Tatars, invasion of Rus' lands by, 22–24
Tereshchenko, F. A., 132
Tereshchenko family, 120, 127, 129
Titov, F. I., 102, 186
Tolstoi, D. A., 104
Trepov, F. F., 226, 236, 237, 239, 253, 255, 260, 261; Shevchenko statue project and, 269, 271
Trubetskoi, E. N., 152, 158, 170, 173, 189, 197
Trud (newspaper), 100, 137, 138
Trudovik Party, 190, 197
"true Russians," debate on how to define, 172
"truly Russian" movement, 7, 181; anti-Semitism within, 185, 186, 194, 195, 199, 200–204, 208–9; after dissolution of first Duma, 198–99; divisions within, 199–200, 273; Duma delegates from, 207, 216; in Duma elections of 1906, 189; in Duma elections of fall 1907, 212–15; in Duma elections of January 1907, 202–6; leaders of, 187; Little Russian idea and, 181, 193–94, 205, 215; mobilization of, 185–86, 194–97, 207–8; nationalization of electoral curiae and, 211; on non-Russian nationalist groups, 222–25; Orthodox landowners and, 200, 204; after pogrom of 1905, 170–72, 174–76; radicalization of, 208–10; vs. Ukrainian nationalists, 192–93, 222–23. *See also* Russian nationalist movement
Tsytovich, A. L., 140, 153
Turau, E. F., 175

Ukraina (periodical), 269
Ukraine: Bolshevik invasion of, 277; declaration of autonomy, 277; famine in (1932-33), 282, 284; German occupation of, 278
Ukrainian Academy of Sciences, 278
Ukrainian Club, in Kiev, 183
Ukrainian Democratic-Radical Party (UDRP), 183, 184

Ukrainian language: activists' disagreements regarding, 107–8; education in, 278; Galician orthography of, 55, 62, 104; Imperial Academy of Sciences on, 152; imperial policies on, 55, 88, 94, 104, 222; Little Russian activists on, 62; after Polish revolt of 1863, 14; publications in, 80, 152, 156, 183; Russian nationalists on, 223; Slavophiles' concerns about, 61, 62; subversive function of, officials' concerns about, 65, 66–67; "truly Russian" commentators on, 193, 194; Valuev decree on, 66–67
Ukrainian language dictionaries, 101, 104
Ukrainian nationalist movement: in 1890s, 106–7, 108; during civil war, 279; demise of autocracy and, 277; divisions within, 198; first imperial Duma and, 192; fracturing of Little Russian lobby and, 88–89, 94; fracturing of Russian nationalist movement and, 268–69; Galician radicals and, 87, 88; Habsburg policies encouraging, 8, 72, 95, 106; Hrushevs'kyi's interpretation of Rus' culture and, 106, 152; liberationists and, 153, 155, 182–84; literature on, 9–10; Little Russian idea co-opted by, 16–17, 87, 94, 112, 221, 240, 269, 278; officials' attitudes toward, 88, 93, 222, 237–38, 261; origins of, 16; outside of Soviet Union, 279–80, 283; rapprochement among camps of, 108; after revolution of 1905, 220–21; before revolution of 1905, 151–52; on right bank, 107; vs. Russian nationalists, 192–93, 221, 222–23, 235, 237, 238, 259–61; in Soviet Union, 9, 280–81; during World War I, 275–76
Ukrainian Parliamentary Club, 206–7
Ukrainian Scientific Society, 220–21
Ukrainian Soviet Socialist Republic, 280
Uniate (Greek Catholic) Church: creation of, 25; dissolution under Cossack Hetmanate, 27; dissolution under Russian empire, 37; in Polish-Lithuanian Commonwealth, 25, 29
Union of Russian People (SRN), 171, 175, 186, 235–36; central leadership vs. Kiev chapter of, 219; congress of 1906, 199; in Duma elections of 1907, 204, 205, 213; growing regional influence of, 253, 254; Iushchinskii murder case and, 245, 248, 252, 263, 267; journals published by, 201; Nicholas II's visit to Kiev and, 249; on Shevchenko statue project, 269
Union of Russian Workers, 171, 199
Union of Unions, 156
United Gentry, 187
urbanization, 117
urban politics: in Europe, nineteenth-century, 117–18, 119; in Kiev, 118–19, 128–29; in Russia, literature on, 118
Ustrialov, N. G., 39
utility companies, in Kiev, 127–28, 143
Uvarov, S. S., 35–36, 38, 39n55, 46, 48

Vainshtein, Moisei, 130
Valuev, P. A., 4, 63, 64, 68, 69, 70, 71, 80
Valuev decree, 66–67, 73, 100
Varangians, in Rus' history, 22, 40, 54
Variatinskii, I. V., 229i
Vasil'chikov, I. I., 43, 55, 63, 65
Veche stol'nogo goroda Kieva (penny paper), 207, 213
Veretennikov, A. P., 197, 203, 210
Vestnik Iugo-Zapadnoi i Zapadnoi Rossii, 64, 72
violence: antiliberationist movement and, 181; opponents of Liberation Movement and, 151, 160; revolutionary agitation of 1905 and, 157–58, 163, 167–69; strike of 1903 and, 148–49. *See also* pogroms
Vitalii of Pochaev (monk), 196, 256, 278, 280, 280n28
Vladimir (Kievan prince), 22; monument to, 36, 37i, 224i, 238
Volynskaia zemlia (newspaper), 252, 254
voting rights: economic vs. ethnic criteria for, 231, 232; in western Europe, mid-nineteenth century, 129n42. *See also* zemstva
Vyshnegradskii, I. A., 132

western borderlands: Imperial Geographic Society expedition in, 63; nationalist challenge in, 3–4, 6, 35
Westernizers, in Russian intelligentsia, 44

White Army, 279–80
Witte, S. Iu.: antiliberationists on, 161; Kiev pogrom of 1905 and, 169; and Kiev's elites, 141, 142; and Southwestern Railroad, 132, 134; western zemstvo bill and, 233, 241, 242
women: antiliberationist parties and, 172; in Russian nationalist movement, 217
working classes: antiliberationist activists and, 187, 195; in Kiev, 124–25; Russian nationalist movement and, 217, 257; Social Democrats and, 147, 148, 173, 188; "truly Russian" activists and, 199, 201, 207
World War I, 8–9, 274–76
World War II, 284

Young Turks, 8

Zakon i Pravda (penny paper), 199
Zaporozhian Cossacks, 26, 38
Zaria (newspaper), 133–34, 138
zemstva: in central Russia, 68, 70; left-bank, 95–96, 99; nationalized, efforts to create, 225, 227, 228, 231–33; nationalized, opposition to, 262; nationalized, western zemstvo bill and, 240–43; in southwest, calls for, 70–71, 105; in southwest, elections in summer of 1911, 249; in southwest, introduction of, 111–12
Zhitetskii, P. I., 50, 62, 109, 110, 221
Ziber, N. I., 95
Zionists, 151

www.ingramcontent.com/pod-product-compliance
Lightning Source LLC
Chambersburg PA
CBHW030326240426
43673CB00040B/1293